FIFTH EDITION

D0781808

The American President

Robert E. DiClerico

West Virginia University

Prentice Hall, *Upper Saddle River, New Jersey 07458*

Library of Congress Cataloging-in-Publication Data

DiClerico, Robert E.
    The American president : Robert E. DiClerico. —5th ed.
    p.   cm
    Includes bibliographical references and index.
    ISBN 0-13-083575-7
    1. Presidents—United States.   I. Title.
JK516.D52   1999
352.23'0973—dc21   99-12744
                                                 CIP

Editorial Director: Charlyce Jones Owen
Editor in Chief: Nancy Roberts
Senior Acquisitions Editor: Beth Gillett
Editorial Assistant: Brian Prybella
Project Manager: Merrill Peterson
Prepress and Manufacturing Buyer: Ben Smith
Cover Director: Jayne Conte
Marketing Manager: Christopher DeJohn

This book was set in 10/11 Times Roman by Stratford Publishing
Services and was printed and bound by Courier Companies, Inc.
The cover was printed by Phoenix Color Corp.

Printed in the United States of America

10 9 8 7 6 5 4 3 2 1

ISBN 0-13-083575-7

PRENTICE-HALL INTERNATIONAL (UK) LIMITED, *London*
PRENTICE-HALL OF AUSTRALIA PTY. LIMITED, *Sydney*
PRENTICE-HALL CANADA INC., *Toronto*
PRENTICE-HALL HISPANOAMERICANA, S.A., *Mexico*
PRENTICE-HALL OF INDIA PRIVATE LIMITED, *New Delhi*
PRENTICE-HALL OF JAPAN, INC., *Tokyo*
PEARSON EDUCATION ASIA PTE. LTD., *Singapore*
EDITORA PRENTICE-HALL DO BRASIL, LTDA., *Rio de Janeiro*

To my Mother
and in memory of my Father

# Contents

5 THE PRESIDENT AND THE BUREAUCRACY   *171*

6 DECISION MAKING IN THE WHITE HOUSE   *206*

Preface

An examination of the presidency is appropriate at any time, for it is the focal point and energizing force in our national government. During the last thirty years, however, the office has been the subject of considerable controversy and for this reason has proven an even more intriguing topic for study.

Although presidential actions on several fronts contributed to this controversy, it was nurtured primarily by the role of the presidency in the Vietnam War and the Watergate scandals. These two dramatic events in our national life brought with them equally dramatic reassessments of the presidency. It was Senator William Fulbright (D-Ark.) who asserted in 1961 that "the price of survival in a world of aggressive totalitarianism is to give up some of the democratic luxuries of the past . . . through the conferral of greatly increased authority on the President."[1] Yet nine years later, this same senator was warning us that in the conduct of foreign policy the American political system had moved "far along the road to an executive despotism."[2] Similar reversals in position were evident in the scholarly community. One eminent historian, for example, complained in 1965 that congressional involvement in the executive branch was adversely affecting presidential effectiveness.[3] Just eight years later, however, he wrote an influential book titled *The Imperial Presidency* warning that the growth of presidential powers and prerogatives threatened our cherished principle of balanced government.[4]

As the full import of the Watergate scandals became known, more and more people joined the ranks of those calling for the reining in of presidential power. In some instances, the proposals were very drastic indeed. One recommended the creation of a plural executive, while another proposed that Congress be given the power to terminate a president's tenure by a vote of "no confidence."[5] Yet even as various reform proposals were being bandied about, other observers were cautioning against an overreaction to abuses of presidential power. Overreacting, they argued, could lead to restrictions that would deny the office its capacity for creative leadership.

Speaking to this point, an adviser to two presidents noted that "the single largest difficulty with curbing executive authority is that the power to do great harm is also the power to do great good"—a fact not fully appreciated by those who would "carelessly reshape or curb an office that over the long haul has served us well."[6]

Responding to the perceived overextension of presidential power under presidents Johnson and Nixon, Congress grew more assertive; so much so, in fact, that warnings of an imperial presidency gave way to concerns over an increasingly imperial Congress. This development, in conjunction with the continuing decline of political parties, elevated public expectations for the presidency, and seemingly intractable problems at home and abroad, led scholars to characterize the office as "beleaguered," "impotent," "impossible," "no-win," "imperiled," "tethered," and "perilous."[7] But no sooner had these assessments gained currency than the Reagan presidency occasioned yet another round of rethinking. Charismatic, determined, and rhetorically skillful, Reagan appeared to wield the resources of the office more adroitly than his two predecessors. Accordingly, many political observers, whether they agreed with his policies or not, now voiced the belief that his stewardship had reinvigorated the presidency as an instrument of national leadership.[8] Some even warned that the office was once again assuming the "imperial" characteristics we had witnessed in the seventies.[9] Others, however, remained unconvinced of a rejuvenated presidency, insisting that an intrusive Congress continued to weaken presidential power and influence: "Congress has become the King Cong [sic] of Washington's political jungle, dominating an executive branch that can no longer claim the coequal status that the Founding Fathers saw as crucial."[10]

As we approach the beginning of the twenty-first century, debate over the proper role of the president persists. It is hoped that the knowledge and perspectives gained from this text will better equip the reader to evaluate this debate.

 THE CONCERNS OF THIS BOOK

Although this text will address itself to a variety of specific topics, there are six major areas of concern that underlie it:

1. *Presidential selection.* Operating on the assumption that what a president is depends in part upon how we get him (or her), it is imperative to assess the process by which we go about choosing our president. Specifically, we shall be concerned with who can contend for this high office and to what extent the selection process succeeds in attracting, nominating, and retaining the most plausible candidates.

2. *Presidential power.* Although the presidency is alleged to be the most powerful office in our government, rarely have presidents ever thought they had enough power. Upon succeeding to this office, they begin to see more clearly than ever that they are not operating in a vacuum but rather must compete with other power centers in our political system. We shall examine their relationship with these other power centers (Congress, Court, bureaucracy, the public, the press), emphasizing those factors that enhance and constrain the exercise of presidential power over them.

3. *Presidential accountability.* Any examination of presidential power must be accompanied by still another consideration, namely, to what extent is the president held accountable for the exercise of that power? Surely one of the most widespread criticisms currently directed against this institution is the absence of adequate accountability. We shall examine the validity of this criticism along with the desirability and feasibility of proposals that have been put forth to enhance it.

4. *Presidential decision making.* While it may be argued that presidents are elected to perform a variety of functions in the political system, in a fundamental sense we elect them to make decisions. The issues coming over a president's desk will all be important ones, and what he (or she) chooses to decide or not decide can have important implications for the country and possibly the world. Consequently, we shall spend considerable time examining the nature of the decision-making process in the White House. Specifically, we shall be concerned with who participates and with how much impact. Knowing how decisions are made may help us understand some of the great successes and failures in presidential decision making.

5. *Presidential personality.* If the office of the presidency influences the individual who occupies it, it is also equally clear that the personality of the individual helps to shape the office. Accordingly, here we shall first consider how the personalities of various presidents have influenced the tone and style of their presidencies; second, we shall consider whether certain personality types may be more suited to the demands of the office than others; and, finally, we shall consider if it is possible to do a better job of screening the personalities of individuals seeking to be president.

6. *Presidential leadership.* This consideration will of necessity inject itself into the discussion at various points throughout the book, but it will also be treated by itself in a separate chapter because it draws upon and integrates much of the subject matter that precedes it. We tend to view leadership as being synonymous with the presidency, yet experience has shown us that some have led better than others and some have scarcely led at all. In addressing this matter we shall consider the requirements for effective leadership, given the nature of our political institutions and given also the problems we currently face as a nation.

 DIFFICULTIES IN STUDYING THE PRESIDENCY

Writing in 1969, one respected student of the presidency remarked that

> the eminence of the institution . . . is matched only by the extraordinary neglect shown to it by political scientists. Compared to the hordes of researchers who regularly descend on Congress, local communities, and the most remote foreign principalities, there is an extraordinary dearth of students of the Presidency, although scholars ritually swear that the Presidency is where the action is before they go somewhere else to do their research.[11]

Five years later another political scientist began his assessment of the presidency literature by remarking that "it reflects the worst of all possible worlds: it is neither empirically rich nor revealing about how the presidency affects who gets what, when, and how in the United States."[12] During the twenty-five years or so that have intervened since these scholarly concerns were voiced, our knowledge of the presidency has expanded considerably and approaches to investigating it have become more innovative. Yet even as late as 1993, a conference of presidency scholars concluded that "our view of the present status of presidential scholarship is that, although developments are promising, we are still short of a well developed subfield that meets standards of cumulativeness and theoretical consistency."[13] This and other assessments should not be altogether surprising, for the presidency is in many ways the most difficult of our three national institutions to investigate with some degree of empirical rigor.

The proceedings on the floor of the House of Representatives and the Senate are, with rare exception, open to the public. In addition, a daily record is published of the previous day's proceedings on the floor of each house. To be sure, most of the important work done by the Congress takes place in committees and not on the floor, but most of the committees in each house have for some time now opened many of their proceedings to the public. In those cases where proceedings are not open, the scholar still has a variety of potential sources to tap, such as committee members and their staffs, all of whom are far more accessible than the president.

The Supreme Court presents a greater problem. It consists of only nine members in contrast to the 535 in Congress; thus, the potential sources of information are severely limited. And not only will the justices not discuss cases currently before the Court or sensitive issues that might come before it, but they are rarely willing to discuss its inner workings while they are members of the Court. At the same time, however, the Court's proceedings are partially open to public scrutiny, at least to the extent that the public and the press may observe what goes on in the courtroom itself. While it is true that the actual decision-making process takes place in utmost secrecy, nevertheless, each decision of the Court is published in the form of one or more opinions, which are likely to give a fairly accurate reflection of the issues discussed and the positions taken by the judges during their deliberations on a given case.

Unlike the Congress and the Court, the White House opens no part of the decision-making process to the public. Nor is a record published of the daily proceedings in the White House. Beyond this, the central figure in the presidency is not accessible to the scholar. The president may from time to time grant interviews to members of the press, but the newspaper reporter's concerns are not likely to be those of the scholar. And although presidential papers provide a valuable source of information, much of what we need to know about the presidency cannot be gained from reading correspondence and written statements. Many presidents upon leaving office write their memoirs, but those also must be viewed with caution. With the Court or the Congress, praise or blame must be apportioned among the total membership, but the success or failure of any given presidency will be largely determined by an assessment of one person, the president himself. Presidents are acutely aware of this fact. Thus, in attempting to seek a favorable judgment from history, their memoirs are likely to present their own stewardship in the most favorable light possible.

Other sources of information about the presidency include the recollections of individuals who have served under a given president. These also have their drawbacks, however. Some are written by speechwriters who may have participated at only one particular stage in the decision-making process. Others have been written by close aides to the president. Their proximity to the central figure would seem to put them in the best position to evaluate the inner workings of the White House. But it is just this fact that must put us on our guard, for those closest to the president are often likely to be his most ardent admirers, in awe of both the individual and the office he holds. Finally, the number of people close to the president is relatively small indeed, and even they may not all decide to write about their White House experiences. This means that when accounts about the person or events differ, the scholar has few alternative sources to consult in order to resolve such contradictions.

Finally, of course, the number of presidencies available for study is still relatively small—only forty-two from Washington to Clinton. Moreover, the database for our earlier presidents is necessarily less complete than for more recent occupants of the White House.

All of which is not to say that the presidency cannot be studied. Rather, it is to say that it cannot be studied easily. When we examine this institution, we will often be looking through a keyhole rather than an open door.

 NOTES

1. Cited in Theodore Sorensen, *Watchmen in the Night* (Cambridge, Mass.: MIT Press, 1975), p. 71.

2. Address to the American Society of Newspaper Editors, April 16, 1971.

3. Arthur Schlesinger, Jr., *A Thousand Days* (Boston: Houghton Mifflin, 1965), pp. 707–8.

4. Arthur Schlesinger, Jr., *The Imperial Presidency* (Boston: Houghton Mifflin, 1973).

5. James L. Sundquist, "What Happened to Our Checks and Balances?" in Charles Roberts, ed., *Has the President Too Much Power?* (New York: Harper's Magazine Press, 1973), p. 109; Sorensen, *Watchmen in the Night,* p. 81.

6. Sorensen, *Watchmen in the Night,* pp. 75, 82.

7. Aaron Wildavsky, *The Beleaguered Presidency* (New Brunswick, N. J.: Transaction Publishers, 1991); Godfrey Hodgson, *All Things to All Men* (New York: Simon & Schuster, 1980), p. 3; Harold M. Barger, *The Impossible Presidency: Illusions and Realities of Executive Power* (Glenview, Ill.: Scott, Foresman, 1984); Paul Light, *The President's Agenda* (Baltimore: Johns Hopkins University Press, 1983), ch. 9; Thomas Frank, ed., *The Tethered Presidency* (New York: New York University Press, 1981); Bernard Hirschhorn, *The Perilous Presidency* (New York: Richard Rosens Press, 1979).

8. See, for example, *National Journal,* April 6, 1985, pp. 743–47; *National Journal,* September 6, 1989, p. 2148; *Washington Post,* September 1, 1985, p. A10; *Washington Post,* January 12, 1986, p. A4; *Time,* January 6, 1986, p. 73.

9. John Orman, "Reagan's Imperial Presidency" (Prepared for delivery at the annual meeting of the American Political Science Association, New York, N.Y., September 3–6, 1987); Arthur Schlesinger. Jr., "The Imperial Temptation," *New Republic,* March 16, 1987, pp. 17, 18; *Chronicle of Higher Education,* September 17, 1986, pp. 1, 8.

10. Joseph Califano, "Imperial Congress," *New York Times Magazine,* January 23, 1994, p. 40. See also Colin Campbell, *The U.S. Presidency in Crisis* (New York: Oxford University Press, 1998); Arthur Schlesinger, Jr., "So Much for the Imperial Presidency," *New York Times,* August 3, 1998, p. A21; Jim Hoagland, "The Unimperial Presidency," *Washington Post,* April 7, 1994, p. A27; L. Gordon Crovitz and Jeremy A. Rabkin, eds., *The Fettered Presidency* (Washington, D.C.: American Enterprise Institute, 1989); Dick Cheney, "Congressional Overreaching in Foreign Policy" (Prepared for delivery at American Enterprise Institute conference on "Foreign Policy and the Constitution," March 14–15, 1989); *Congressional Quarterly Weekly Report,* January 7, 1989, pp. 3–11.

11. Aaron Wildavsky, ed., *The Presidency* (Boston: Little, Brown, 1969), p. ix.

12. John F. Manley, "The Presidency, Congress, and National Policy-Making," in Cornelius Cotter, ed., *Political Science Annual,* vol. 5 (Indianapolis: Bobbs-Merrill, 1974), p. 228.

13. George C. Edwards III, John H. Kessel, and Bert A. Rockman, *Researching the Presidency: Vital Questions, New Approaches* (Pittsburgh: University of Pittsburgh Press, 1993), p. 6.

 Acknowledgments

Although revising a book is a less formidable task than the initial writing, it still requires the assistance of numerous individuals at various stages of the process. My thanks go first to Beth Gillett for her general support of this project. In addition, thanks go to Bryce Dodson for sharing with me the wisdom he has gained through his many years of service with Prentice Hall. Finally, I owe a very special debt of gratitude to Merrill Peterson, who had immediate responsibility for this revision and guided it through to completion with great efficiency and professionalism.

Colleagues at other institutions read the last edition and provided valuable suggestions on how the next one could be improved. A special debt of gratitude is also owed to my teacher and friend, the late Charles S. Hyneman. Even though he had no direct involvement with this book, he greatly influenced my thinking about the broader context in which the presidency must function.

As any author knows, tracking down factual information can be enormously time-consuming. In my case, this burden was lessened considerably by the Research Division of Congressional Quarterly, Inc. On several occasions, when my own sources proved inadequate, I turned to their staff for assistance and was supplied with answers to my queries within hours after I made them. My thanks also to individuals in various government agencies, whose cooperation belies the conventional wisdom of a vast, unresponsive bureaucracy.

Perhaps the greatest debt of gratitude is owed the editorial staff who, after all, have the most direct and persistent involvement in an undertaking such as this. The copy editor, Jan McDearmon, exhibited an extraordinarily keen eye for detail and, on more occasions than I care to recall, improved upon my own phraseology.

Finally, I would like to express my appreciation to the Political Science Department at West Virginia University for bearing the photocopying and mailing costs associated with this project, and to its chairman, Allan Hammock, for his unfailing support throughout all five editions of this book.

Robert E. DiClerico
West Virginia University

The Selection Process

 PRESIDENTIAL SELECTION:
A HISTORICAL OVERVIEW

Of the many issues commanding the attention of the Founding Fathers, few confounded them as much as how the nation's chief executive should be chosen. James Wilson, one of the most influential Founders, affirmed this point as he defended the newly proposed Constitution at the Pennsylvania ratifying convention: "The Convention, sir, were perplexed with no part of this plan so much as with the mode of choosing the President of the United States."[1] Indeed, the matter was raised as early as the first week (May 29, 1787) of the Constitutional Convention and would not be wholly resolved until September 6—just eleven days prior to final adjournment.

The Virginia Plan, which was the first blueprint for a new government considered by the convention, proposed that the president be chosen by the national legislature. A majority of the delegates were clearly taken by this mode of selection. In fact, they would vote for it on four different occasions during the course of their deliberations. In the final analysis, however, the collateral issue of reeligibility forced them to reject selection by the legislature. Convinced that the president must be free to seek as many additional terms as he wished, the framers concluded that a president reliant upon Congress for reelection would lack the necessary independence from that branch.[2] As they searched about for alternatives, direct election by the people surfaced but failed for reasons both practical and political. Some delegates felt that the vastness of the country would prevent the people from becoming sufficiently acquainted with presidential candidates. Southern states, meanwhile, feared that direct election would inevitably lead to the selection of presidents from northern states, where more people were eligible to vote. Small states, paranoid about their potential loss of power under the new Constitution, rejected direct election because they felt it would always produce winners from large states. A host of other proposals

1

surfaced, including selection of the president by electors, but none commanded enough support. Finally, in the closing weeks, the matter was referred to the Committee of Eleven, which was charged with recommending solutions to all outstanding issues. Drawing upon a proposal earlier made by James Wilson and modified by Gouverneur Morris, the committee recommended that the president be chosen by a group of electors. These electors, in turn, would be chosen in a manner to be determined by each state's legislature. Each elector would be authorized to cast two votes, at least one of which had to be for a presidential candidate outside of the elector's own state. The candidate with a majority of electoral votes would become president, and the runner-up, vice president. In the event that no candidate received a majority of electoral votes, the election would be referred to the U.S. Senate. When the committee's recommendations were laid before the full convention, the Founding Fathers decided to replace the Senate with the House, where, for purposes of choosing the president, each state would have one vote.[3]

This final compromise had something in it for everyone. Those favoring an independent executive were gratified by the fact that a national body of electors would do the choosing rather than the legislative branch. The large states reacted positively, since a state's electoral votes were a function of the number of representatives it had in Congress. The southern states were pleased with the compromise because the convention had already decided that slaves could count as three-fifths of a person for purposes of determining representation in the House. Nor did the small states come away from this compromise empty-handed. They would have at least two electors by virtue of their two U.S. senators, and should the election be forced into the House, their voting power would be equal to that of the large states. Finally, because many convention delegates believed that the diversity of interests within the country would prevent presidential candidates from garnering a majority of electoral votes, the prospect of selection by the House was no doubt especially appealing to those favoring legislative selection all along.

Little did the Founding Fathers realize that the advent of political parties was destined to force changes—constitutional and otherwise—in the mode of selection so painstakingly crafted by them. The constitutional change was precipitated by the circumstances surrounding the election of 1800. Although the Democratic Republicans had nominated Thomas Jefferson for president and Aaron Burr for vice president, the two votes cast by each elector did not allow a separate vote for president and vice president. As fate would have it, Jefferson and Burr tied in the number of electoral votes cast, and the election was forced into the House, where, after much acrimony, Jefferson was chosen. The Twelfth Amendment (1804), designed to prevent these circumstances from recurring, stipulated that electors would vote separately for president and vice president. In addition, should the election be forced into the House, the choice would now be among the top three finishers rather than the top five.

Of even greater importance were the extraconstitutional changes in the selection process. As the democratic spirit gained momentum throughout the country, state legislatures came under increasing pressure to allow the voters in their states to choose the presidential electors. And indeed, by the end of the Civil War all states had succumbed to this pressure. In addition, as parties grew in strength, they began to recruit electors who were bound informally to their party's presidential nominee; hence, the electors no longer exercised the independent judgment contemplated by the Founding Fathers. Although electors are not legally bound in most states today, only a minuscule number have proven to be "faithless," and in no instance have they affected the outcome of a presidential election.[4] In any event, *popular* election of *pledged* electors in essence created a system of popular election of the president—a change that would greatly strengthen the bond between the nation's chief executive and the public.

The Nominating Function

As noted earlier, many delegates to the Constitutional Convention believed that division within the country would make it difficult for a presidential candidate to win an election outright. Thus, the election would nearly always be decided in the House, with the electoral college serving essentially as a nominating body.[5] These assumptions, however, failed to anticipate the development of political parties. Not only did parties nearly always mobilize enough votes to win the election in the electoral college—the election of 1824 being the sole exception following passage of the Twelfth Amendment—but they also assumed the nominating function. As with the electoral college, the nominating process was destined to undergo considerable change.

The congressional caucus was the initial mode of nomination, with the membership of each party in Congress meeting to decide who would be its standard-bearer in the general election. Employed from 1800 to 1824, the caucus gradually fell into disrepute. It drew heavy criticism from such notables as Andrew Jackson, Henry Clay, and John Quincy Adams, all of whom had been passed over for the Republican presidential nomination in 1824. The caucus instead had chosen John Crawford, who promptly went on to lose badly in the general election. A growing number of state and local party leaders also objected to the congressional caucus because it denied them any role whatsoever in determining the nominee. Finally, the limited number of participants in this process was increasingly seen as inappropriate once Jacksonian democracy took hold in the country.[6]

Following a brief transition period during which presidential candidates were nominated by state legislatures and local conventions, political parties instituted a new system—national party conventions. First employed in 1831, these conventions were composed of delegates chosen by each state's political party. The process for selecting these delegates varied. In some states the *appointment* method was used for picking some or all of the delegates, with the governor or the party's state committee having the appointing authority. The most common practice adopted by state parties, however, was the *caucus-convention*. Under this system, party members met in their precincts and selected delegates to a county-level caucus; the county caucus then picked delegates to a district caucus, which in turn chose delegates to the state convention; the state convention then selected delegates to attend the party's national convention.

By the turn of the twentieth century, many had become disillusioned with this method of nominating presidents as well. It was perceived as subject to near total manipulation by the party bosses. Few regulations existed on convention procedures, and even those were honored more in the breach. Strongman tactics were used to prevent some delegates from entering the conventions and to intimidate others once they got there, and many of the delegates chosen by the party bosses proved to be unsavory characters who were more than willing to sell their votes to the highest bidder.[7] This state of affairs gave rise to a reform movement spearheaded by the Progressives, the purpose of which was to involve voters directly in the nominating process. The instrument for achieving this goal was the primary. Administered by the states rather than the parties, this mechanism would allow the voters themselves to elect their state's delegates to the national conventions. By 1916, twenty-six states had adopted a primary of one kind or another.[8] The initial enthusiasm for primaries gradually waned, however, not only because the party bosses opposed them but also because of cost, disappointing turnouts, and the refusal of many presidential contenders to enter them. Thus, by 1935, eight states had abandoned this method of choosing delegates and returned to the caucus-convention and appointment systems. In subsequent years, some states reinstituted the primary and others repealed it, "until by 1968 the number appeared to have stabilized at sixteen states plus the District of Columbia."[9]

The 1968 Democratic nominating contest would prove to be a catalyzing agent for yet another burst of reform. Senator Eugene McCarthy, strongly opposed to President Johnson's Vietnam War policy, decided to challenge Johnson for the Democratic nomination. McCarthy's better-than-expected showings in the early primaries encouraged Senator Robert Kennedy to toss his hat into the ring as well, and their combined popularity led Johnson to conclude that his renomination was by no means a certainty. This belief, combined with a desire to avoid having the war become a political football, precipitated Johnson's withdrawal from the race in March 1968. Nearly one month later Vice President Hubert Humphrey entered the race with Johnson's blessing. A campaign already characterized by the unexpected took yet another dramatic turn on June 1, when Robert Kennedy was assassinated just minutes after his big win in the California primary. Only McCarthy and Humphrey remained to fight it out. Even though the vice president had entered the race late and declined to enter a single primary, when the convention balloting was completed, he had received 1,760 delegate votes and McCarthy only 601. That Humphrey managed to win so handily can be explained by two factors: (1) In 1968 a majority of delegates were chosen not in the primaries but rather by the caucus-convention and appointment methods, and (2) both of these methods were controlled by the party leaders, most of whom had aligned themselves behind Humphrey.

Not surprisingly, many McCarthy and Kennedy supporters came away from the nomination campaign bitter and disillusioned. The Democratic Convention had in the final analysis selected a nominee whose views on Vietnam were not measurably different from those of Lyndon Johnson. On top of this, during the course of the nominating process, McCarthy supporters repeatedly found themselves victimized by arbitrary rules and procedures employed in delegate selection, particularly as they related to the caucus-convention method. The convention voted to create a commission to investigate these charges and recommend changes in the delegate selection process. Known as the McGovern-Fraser Commission, after its two chairmen, Senator George McGovern and Congressman Donald Fraser, it proposed sweeping reforms that were ultimately adopted by the Democratic National Committee. Required to be implemented in the 1972 nominating contest, the major reforms may be broadly characterized as follows: (1) the establishment of uniform and detailed procedures for selecting delegates via the caucus-convention method; (2) a significant reduction in the number of delegates who could be selected through the appointment method and a prohibition against reserving delegate slots for certain elected and party officials; and (3) a requirement that state parties take immediate steps to increase the number of blacks, women, and young people in their state delegations. Taking its cue from the Democrats, the Republican Party also reformed its caucus-convention method and abolished reserved delegate slots for party and elected officials; it declined, however, to go beyond encouraging states to include more blacks, women, and young people as delegates. Although some of these reforms would be modified and others added in subsequent years, one overriding reality would remain: Party leaders no longer exercised the strong control over presidential nominations that they had enjoyed prior to 1972.

Just as Democratic and Republican party reforms served to reduce the influence of party elites, so too did another equally important development—the proliferation of primaries. Although neither the McGovern-Fraser Commission nor any subsequent reform commissions called for more primaries, their number increased steadily through 1980, dropped off some in 1984, and grew again in 1988, 1992, and 1996 (see Table 1-1).

Several factors appear to have influenced the movement toward primaries. First, some states felt that the complexity of the McGovern-Fraser Commission reforms were such that they could be implemented more easily in a primary than in a caucus-convention system. Second, with the growing amount of media attention given to primaries, states saw a chance to enhance their visibility and derive some financial benefit by switching to this mode. Finally, it seems likely that some states, perceiving the broad-based sentiment for expanding participation in the presidential selection process, understandably saw the primary as the most effective means of achieving this end.

In summary, as a consequence of both the rise of political parties and periodic demands for greater participation within those parties, the selection of the president has evolved from a process in which a very small number of individuals did the choosing into one that now involves participants numbering in the many millions. But it must also be noted that during the course of its many twists and turns toward greater democratization, the presidential selection process has not been free of criticism. On the contrary, in his celebrated book *The American Commonwealth,* published in the early part of this century, the British commentator Lord James Bryce felt compelled to include a chapter titled "Why Great Men Are Not Chosen President." More recent commentaries by American scholars have been similarly critical, with one political scientist describing the selection process as "the most ramshackle, the flimsiest method ever used to select the supreme leader of a nation";[10] another asserting that we "possess . . . one of the worst top-leadership recruitment systems in the

TABLE 1-1   Growth in Number of Presidential Primaries

	Democrats	Republicans
Year	Number of Primaries	Number of Primaries
1968	17	16
1972	23	22
1976	29	28
1980	35	34
1984	25	30
1988	34	35
1992	37	39
1996	36	41

Source: Adapted from William Crotty and John S. Jackson, *Presidential Primaries and Nominations* (Washington, D.C.: Congressional Quarterly Press, 1985), p. 63. Figures for 1988 taken from *Congressional Quarterly Weekly Report,* February 27, 1988, p. 532; figures for 1992 taken from *Congressional Quarterly,* Special Report, September 7, 1991, p. 2413; figures for 1996 taken from *Congressional Quarterly Weekly Report,* August 19, 1995, p. 2485.

democratic societies of the world";[11] and yet another claiming that "in our system, there is nothing to prevent a man who is absolutely incapable of being President from becoming President."[12]

The remainder of this chapter is concerned with the central question of whether the presidential selection process provides us with qualified individuals. Our attention, it should be noted, will focus heavily upon the nominating stage, since it structures the choices we ultimately confront on election day. To this extent, it is clearly the most critical part of the selection process. The eminent student of politics E. E. Schattschneider reminded us of this fact when he observed that "the definition of the alternatives is the supreme instrument of power."[13] Nor was his point lost on such noted political practitioners as Boss Tweed, who was fond of telling his compatriots, "I don't care who does the electin', so long as I do the nominatin'."

 WHO CONTENDS? WHO IS NOMINATED?

Because someone may decide that he wants to seek the presidency does not necessarily mean that his candidacy will be taken seriously by party influentials, the press, and the public. A variety of factors operating in the selection process serve to include some and exclude others from serious consideration. To the extent that a candidate is included, his nomination is facilitated, though not guaranteed.

Legal Criteria

The pool of potential contenders is restricted at the very outset by three constitutional requirements. An individual must be at least thirty-five years of age, a requirement that obviously excludes millions from consideration. In addition, the president of the United States must be a natural-born citizen. This means, then, that no current American citizen who was born as a citizen of another country can hold the presidential office. As of 1996, there were a little over six million such individuals in our population.[14] The precise meaning of this particular requirement became a minor issue with respect to the candidacies of Barry Goldwater in 1964 and George Romney in 1968. Goldwater was born in the Arizona Territory before it became a part of the United States, and George Romney was born to American parents in Mexico. Were they in fact natural-born American citizens? The issue still remains unresolved because the Court has never rendered a definitive judgment on this question. Finally, in order to be eligible for the presidency, an individual must have resided in the United States for at least fourteen years.

The intent behind these constitutional provisions seems clear. Both the age and fourteen-year residency requirements were designed to ensure that presidents would be sufficiently knowledgeable and experienced. In actuality, our presidents have been considerably beyond thirty-five years of age. Excluding vice presidents who succeeded to the presidency following a president's death, the average age of incoming presidents has been fifty-five.[15] The insistence on a natural-born citizen was intended to prevent election of a president whose loyalties might be divided between the United States and the country of his birth. While all of these legal requirements make some sense, it may be argued that they unduly restrict the number of presidential possibilities. Furthermore, some might contend that whether or not an individual is qualified is a judgment that should be rendered by the voters and not predetermined by constitutional restrictions.

Informal Criteria

In addition to the constitutional requirements for holding the office of president, there exist informal criteria that serve to include some and exclude others from serious contention. While they are not written down anywhere, they are nevertheless equally important.

Government Experience.   Those individuals with some previous government experience in either an elected or appointive capacity appear to be viewed most favorably for presidential consideration. An examination of contenders in our two major parties from 1868 to 1996 reveals that only eleven lacked previous government experience at the national or state level. As for the major party nominees themselves, only four (Horace Greeley, Winfield Hancock, Wendell Wilkie, and Dwight Eisenhower) during this period were without previous government experience. It should not be surprising that both contenders and nominees have typically served in government; not only is such experience considered by most to be a requisite for the presidency, but government positions are also likely to provide their occupants with some degree of national recognition.

If the experience of public office adds to a candidate's prospects for being viewed as a serious contender, then some government positions clearly provide a better route to the nomination than others. As Table 1-2 indicates, from 1868 to 1956 the governorship provided the best springboard to the presidency, followed by federal appointive office. Note that the House, Senate, and vice presidency yielded relatively few nominees during this period.

A very different picture emerges, however, when we examine the period from 1960 to 1996. If we exclude Johnson and Ford, both of whom succeeded to the presidency, five nominees emerged from the governorship, four from the Senate, and five from the vice presidency (counting Nixon twice). Moreover, all but one of the elected vice presidents came to that office via the Senate.

TABLE 1-2   Career Patterns of Major Party Presidential Nominees, 1868–1956

Last Office Held Prior to Nomination	Percentage of Nominees	Number of Nominees
Governor	40	12
Federal appointive office	20	6
None	13.4	4
House	6.7	2
Senate	6.7	2
Statewide elective office (exclusive of governorship)	3.3	1
Succession to presidency and renomination	10	3

Source: Adapted from Robert Peabody and Eve Lubalin, "The Making of Presidential Candidates," in C. Dunn, ed., *The Future of the American Presidency* (Morristown, N.J.: General Learning Press, 1975), p. 33. Reprinted by permission of Silver Burdett Company.

That the Senate has become a more competitive launching pad vis-à-vis the governorship can be explained by several developments. For much of our history, governors exercised considerable influence over their state party organizations, thereby often enabling them to control their state's delegation to the national nominating conventions. Thus, governors from large states especially could take their presidential candidacies to the national convention with a significant block of delegates already in hand. Reforms in the delegate selection process have largely eroded this advantage, however. Another asset of governors is the analogy often drawn between the presidency and the governorship. Governors, like presidents, are chief executives. They must preside over a bureaucracy and contend with a legislature. This advantage, however, has been offset by the growing importance of foreign policy and defense issues—matters that senators must deal with on a regular basis. Nor do the advantages of the Senate end here. With the advent of television and its primary focus upon national politics, senators have been able to achieve a much higher degree of national visibility. This development is reflected in the frequency with which network public affairs programs invite senators to appear as guests. For example, from 1964 to 1974 senators appeared on *Meet the Press* and *Face the Nation* a total of 288 times, whereas governors appeared only 100 times. Moreover, in 1973 alone, senators frequented these programs 26 times, while governors failed to make even a single appearance.[16] Finally, senators are in a better position to cope with the amount of time now required to run in the president-by-primary process, for they can be absent from their jobs more easily. Not only is the major work of the Senate confined to Tuesday through Thursday, but one absent senator out of one hundred is not likely to be missed. Governors, on the other hand, are on tap at least five days a week. Repeated absences will not only be noticed but may have consequences for governing as well, particularly if a governor hails from a reasonably large state.

Of course, it should be noted that although governors were unsuccessful in gaining the presidential nomination from 1960 to 1972, they have been considerably more successful since then—Carter (1976), Reagan (1980), Dukakis (1988), Clinton (1992). Do these examples undermine to some extent the points made above? Not necessarily. What may have facilitated the candidacies of Carter and Reagan was not service in the governorship per se, but rather the fact that neither man was holding public office at the time he undertook his quest for the presidency. Both, therefore, were in a position to invest inordinately large amounts of time in a nominating process that now requires precisely that. While the Dukakis and Clinton candidacies demonstrate that it is certainly possible to wage a successful nomination campaign as an incumbent governor, the Dukakis candidacy highlights the potentially high price to be paid for doing so. For Clinton the task was decidedly more manageable than for Dukakis, who ran while attempting to govern a state (Massachusetts) with more than twice the population of Arkansas. Criticized for neglecting his duties as governor during his quest for the White House, Dukakis returned to Massachusetts following his general election defeat only to discover that his state was now in financial crisis— a crisis for which he was blamed and which effectively ended his political career. In his final State of the State address, Dukakis acknowledged his neglect: "I lost and in the process Massachusetts took an unfair beating and I feel terrible about it. . . . Trying to do two jobs at the same time was more difficult and gruelling than I had expected."[17]

In the presidential sweepstakes four years later, Governor Mario Cuomo (D-N.Y.) declined to enter, explaining that he simply could not run for president and manage his state's budget crisis at the same time. Governor Douglas Wilder (D-Va.), on the other hand, did enter the race, only to withdraw some four months later because he too concluded that he could not simultaneously run for president and lead his state.[18]

Although the vice presidency, like the Senate, was not an especially fertile recruiting ground for the presidency between 1868 and 1956, it has since given us five presidential nominees. Whether these individuals enjoyed an added advantage by virtue of their vice presidential tenure is unclear, however. Three of the nominees (Humphrey, Mondale, and Bush) were well-established political figures prior to assuming the number-two spot. Humphrey and Mondale had made substantial reputations for themselves in the Senate, and Bush had held several administrative positions and served a brief stint in the House. All three, moreover, had run for the presidency prior to becoming vice president. Thus, it could be argued that it was their prior reputations that made them credible, not their service in an office that has never been highly esteemed by either politicians or the public. These considerations, however, should not necessarily cause us to completely dismiss potential benefits conferred by the vice presidency. Although the vice presidency is still derided from time to time as a meaningless office, presidents Carter, Reagan, and Clinton made conscious efforts to elevate the responsibilities of their vice presidents. Their efforts, in conjunction with the greater media attention now focused on the White House, have given the office more visibility and a higher standing than it enjoyed during most of our history. In addition, service in the vice presidency for eight or even four years provides an opportunity to establish important contacts with individuals and groups throughout the country—contacts that may be of assistance in a future run for the presidency.

Before turning to other factors that serve to include and exclude individuals as presidential timber, one additional matter deserves mention here. Some would argue that we unduly restrict the pool of contenders to the extent that only those with previous government experience are given serious consideration. Accordingly, they have proposed that we cast the net more widely to include individuals from private as well as public life: "In private life, the people who have the jobs most nearly comparable to the U.S. President's are those who head corporations, banks, universities, labor unions, and large civic or public service institutions."[19] Like presidents, they must be able to recruit and organize talent, mediate among conflicting constituencies, oversee a complex organization, and withstand enormous pressures. Although there is considerable merit to this line of argument, there are certain advantages to recruiting nominees from among those individuals who have held elective public office. Voters have an opportunity to evaluate how the candidate has performed in a public capacity, a situation in which he or she is required to face the judgment of the people. Second, not only is the performance of an elected official to a considerable extent a matter of public record, but such a record is likely to be more easily evaluated by and relevant to the concerns of the voter than is the record of a university or corporation president. Finally, an individual who has taken his or her candidacy directly to the people, who has rubbed elbows with them and listened to their problems, may very well develop a feel for and sensitivity to public moods that cannot be so easily gained in a corporation boardroom.

Money.   It is often said that only individuals with a great deal of money can run for and win the presidency. While there is an element of truth in this assertion, it oversimplifies a rather complex issue.

Although it is certainly true that several individuals of considerable wealth (e.g., Harold Stassen, John Kennedy, William Scranton, George Romney, Nelson

Rockefeller, Milton Shapp, John Connally, Lloyd Bentsen, George Bush, Peter du Pont, and Malcolm Forbes, Jr.) have run for the presidency, they have been the exception rather than the rule. Nor is it likely that these individuals were viewed as serious contenders merely because of their great personal wealth. All of them occupied positions of visible success in our society, and it was this fact rather than their money that put them in contention. To be sure, money and, in some cases, the social backgrounds of many of these candidates may have played an important part in helping them to attain these positions of visible success.[20]

If great personal wealth has not been a prerequisite for seeking the presidency, *access* to big money has been for most candidates. Even this statement must be qualified, however, for there have been several dramatic examples of strong nomination campaigns waged largely from small contributions. In 1964, for example, Barry Goldwater raised $5.5 million dollars from some 300,000 contributors. In 1968, Eugene McCarthy raised $11 million, the bulk of which came from 150,000 small contributors. In that same year, George Wallace accumulated $6.7 million, with 85 percent consisting of contributions of $100 or less.[21] It is important to note, however, that each of these candidates represented highly committed constituencies on the left and right of the political spectrum. More moderate candidates appeal to more moderate voters, who are likely to lack the intensity of commitment that would motivate them to give.

Prior to 1976, those with great personal wealth or access to wealth enjoyed certain advantages in the presidential selection process. These advantages were most apparent at the nominating stage, when candidates could not receive any money from their parties or the government but rather had to rely exclusively on their own sources. First, their money conferred a special advantage as a campaign resource simply because money is so easily convertible into other resources. Beyond this, these candidates could more easily meet the crucial "start-up" costs of a campaign, thereby achieving an initial threshold of viability not possible for the candidate lacking access to big money. Moreover, if their campaigns began to falter, a condition that typically leads to faltering contributions as well, they were in a better position to keep their candidacies afloat by drawing upon their own money or that of a few wealthy supporters. But if big money provided an advantage at the starting gate and at certain points around the track, it is far less clear that having it was sufficient to ensure nomination. Had this been the case, then the candidacies of Stassen, Rockefeller, Scranton, Romney, and others should have met with greater success. More important than money were a candidate's image, past record, and issue positions. If, as with John Kennedy, the candidate was judged favorably on these factors and also enjoyed considerable personal wealth, then he was in a very advantageous position indeed. If he lacked personal wealth but was viewed favorably on these other criteria, then his financial support was likely to be forthcoming. Finally, if he was perceived as deficient in past accomplishments, image, and issue stances, no great amount of money was likely to save him.

In 1974, Congress passed a landmark piece of legislation that served to reduce the money advantage in the presidential selection process. Known as the Federal Election Campaign Act, it was enacted in response to numerous fund-raising and influence-buying scandals associated with the 1972 Nixon reelection campaign. Under its provisions, an individual's annual contribution to a presidential candidate cannot exceed $1,000 at the nominating stage; and PACs (political action committees) are limited to contributions no greater than $5,000. The act also stipulated that no person could spend more than $1,000 *on behalf of* a presidential candidate, but the Supreme Court in *Buckley v. Valeo* (1976) declared this provision to be an unconstitutional infringement on the right of free speech.

Perhaps the most significant provision of Federal Election Campaign Act as it bears upon the nominating process is that candidates may now receive partial funding of their campaigns from the government. In order to qualify for such funds, a candidate must first raise $5,000 in each of twenty states in contributions no greater than $250. Once an individual has qualified, the government will then match up to the first $250 of individual private contributions. Presidential candidates are also limited in the total amount of money (inclusive of matching funds) they may spend on their nominating campaigns. Adjusted every four years for inflation, this limit was set at $37 million for 1996. In addition to this overall spending limit, the act imposes limits on how much a candidate may spend in each state. Finally, candidates who opt for matching public funds may spend no more than $50,000 of their own money. On the other hand, should candidates reject matching funds and decide to garner all their money exclusively from private sources, they not only are free to spend as much of their own money as they wish but may also raise and spend as much as they want from private sources. Such private-source contributions, however, are still subject to the $1,000 limit set for individual contributions and $5,000 limit established for PACs. Since 1974, only two presidential candidates have financed their nomination bids exclusively from private sources—John Connally (1980), two-term governor of Texas and treasury secretary in the Nixon administration, and business entrepreneur Malcolm Forbes, Jr. (1996).

This legislation has not been without its critics.[22] Scholars and politicians alike have argued that the $1,000 limit on individual contributions is set too low, as are some of the state spending ceilings and the overall national spending limit. These deficiencies, they contend, have forced candidates to spend much more of their time raising money—1996 presidential candidate Lamar Alexander estimated that he spent 70 percent of his time doing so[23]—and thinking up ingenious ways to circumvent the state and national spending limits.

Although these criticisms have considerable merit, the act has had several salutary effects in relation to the nominating process. First, no longer is it possible for candidates to receive huge sums of money such as the $2.8 million channeled into Richard Nixon's 1972 reelection campaign by W. Clement Stone. Nor, if they opt for public funds, can they any longer infuse their campaigns with huge sums of their own or their family's money, as Nelson Rockefeller did in 1968.[24] Candidates are free, of course, to reject public funding. From 1976 through 1996, however, only four presidential candidates have declined matching public funds, and none of these individuals even came close to winning the nomination.

It might also be argued that the well-connected candidate, who is able to establish a broad network of wealthy fund-raisers, still enjoys a money-raising advantage and can now have contributions matched with federal dollars to boot. While this is true, under the new spending limits, the gaps between those raising more and less money are smaller than they used to be. Also, the opportunity to secure matching public funds increases the likelihood that the less well known and well connected will at least attain a threshold of viability. For example, an extensive study of fund-raising in the 1976, 1980, and 1984 nominating contests concluded that "for all but a few candidates, there was enough early money for a credible run in the first few states."[25] Of course, the candidate who has accumulated more money at the outset can probably hang on for a while if he or she loses those critical early contests, whereas poor showings for the candidate with more limited funds will likely prove fatal. On the other hand, if the latter candidate now has enough money to run a viable campaign in the early contests and does well, his success will generate more financial support.

It is worth reiterating here that money does not necessarily guarantee victory. John Connally's bid for the 1980 presidential nomination is a case in point. Having rejected public financing, he relied instead upon strong ties with the business community to raise his campaign war chest. Although he managed to raise a hefty $12 million, he was ultimately unsuccessful in overcoming public doubts surrounding his character. Consequently, he wisely decided to withdraw from the race after all his effort and money had yielded only one convention delegate in support of his candidacy. The 1984 Democratic nominating contest provides yet another illustration. In only ten of the twenty-nine primaries contested by Democratic candidates in that year did the biggest spender manage to win a plurality of the vote.[26] Moreover, another study, which examined sixty primary contests in both parties during the 1988 nominating process, found that the big spender won only twenty-six.[27]

Finally, and still more recently, we have the case of Malcolm Forbes, Jr., who ran for the presidency in 1996. Declining to accept matching funds, he instead opted to raise money exclusively from private sources, spending $41.7 million dollars, a record $37.5 million of which was his own money.[28] Although personal wealth undoubtedly made it possible for this relative unknown to establish a national profile, the massive sums spent on his media ad blitz were not able to overcome his several liabilities. These included a lack of government experience, considerable skepticism about his flat tax proposal, and a lackluster speaking style. He withdrew from the race five weeks into the primary season, his $41 million expenditure having garnered him only seventy delegate votes, at a cost of roughly $585,000 per delegate.

In short, money counts for a lot, but so do candidate image, past record, and issue positions.

Ideology.   Not only do prior government experience and money serve to include and exclude individuals from consideration for the nomination, but so too do the political beliefs of a candidate. The major goal of any political party is usually to nominate a candidate who can win in November, and such a candidate is likely to be someone whose political beliefs coincide with those of a majority of Americans. Most Americans do not locate themselves on the far left or the far right of the political spectrum, but rather situate themselves somewhere in the broad middle. Consequently, those candidates will be favored whose political beliefs place them in the middle also. This is not to say that the middle of the political spectrum will always remain in one spot. It may move to the left or to the right, depending upon changing moods in the population. Thus, for example, in 1968, Americans tended to move in a conservative direction. Richard Nixon, detecting this movement, moved with them, and that is precisely why he won.[29]

There have, of course, been some startling exceptions to the rule that moderates will be favored for the nomination, but these exceptions also point up the necessity—from the party's point of view—of following this rule. In 1964, the Republicans did nominate a candidate (Barry Goldwater) who was considerably to the right of center, and in 1972 the Democrats awarded their nomination to a candidate (George McGovern) who was considerably left of center. Whereas Goldwater maintained his position on the right throughout his campaign, McGovern moderated his position, but not enough to convince rank-and-file Democrats that he was not a radical. Both candidates not only lost but lost badly, with Goldwater carrying only six states and McGovern only one.

But how then can we explain the success of Ronald Reagan, who in the 1980 presidential election succeeded in carrying all but five of the fifty states? For one thing, though distinctly right of center, his issue positions during the campaign were certainly not as extreme as those of Goldwater in 1964. Unlike Goldwater, for example, he did not come out against social security, farm subsidies, diplomatic relations with the Soviet Union, the ban on nuclear testing in the atmosphere, and the Supreme Court's 1954 school desegregation decision. The fact remains, however, that Reagan was elected even though a majority of Americans perceived him as considerably to right of themselves on the political spectrum. What appears to have been the key to his success was not so much that he had such great appeal, but rather that Jimmy Carter had so little. Having presided over the humiliation of the United States abroad and the deterioration of the economy here at home, Carter was ultimately viewed as lacking the competence necessary to lead. Thus, under the circumstances, the electorate appeared willing to give Reagan the benefit of the doubt, despite his conservative posture.

Background Factors.   In the past, a variety of factors related to background also served to include and exclude individuals from serious consideration for the presidency. These factors include one's race, sex, religion, and geographical location. Candidates were favored who were male, white, Anglo-Saxon, Protestant, and from a large northern state. Many of these factors seem to be receding in importance, however. In recent years, not only have contenders been of the Catholic, Jewish, and Mormon faiths, but we nominated and elected a Catholic (Kennedy) in 1960 and nominated a candidate of Jewish background (Goldwater) in 1964. On the other hand, the nation has so far failed to nominate candidates who were either black or female; nor has any woman ever been among the serious contenders for the presidency. To the extent that race and sex still operate as important exclusionary factors in the nominating process, we severely restrict the pool of potential contenders: As of 1995 there were 13.2 million blacks and 68.2 million women who were thirty-five years of age or older.[30] There are, however, some encouraging signs that race and sex may be decreasing in their importance. Jesse Jackson ran for the presidency in 1984, and again in 1988, finishing a very respectable second in the delegate count. Likewise, 1984 marked the first time in our history that a woman (Geraldine Ferraro) was chosen as a vice presidential nominee. Polling data also provides some grounds for optimism. A Gallup poll taken in 1997 found that 93 percent of white Americans said they would vote for a black as president, and in a 1991 National Opinion Research Center poll, 86 percent said they would vote for a woman.[31] Of course, even if the country is prepared to give serious consideration to blacks and women, they must first occupy those elected offices that serve as the primary recruiting grounds. As of 1999, there were no African Americans in the U.S. Senate and none serving as governor. Women were in a somewhat better position, with three holding the office of governor and nine serving in the U.S. Senate.

The importance of coming from a large state has also declined. As mentioned earlier, the governorship was for many years the primary recruiting ground for the presidency. Governors from large states were especially favored, not only because they could take a significant block of delegate votes to the convention but also because they enjoyed greater visibility than governors from smaller states. In the last twenty-five years, however, the Senate has emerged as an increasingly important recruiting ground, and there a state's size has very little bearing on the ability of its senators to gain public visibility.

 ## CRITICISMS OF THE PRESIDENTIAL NOMINATING PROCESS

Thus far, we have considered those factors that render individuals more or less plausible as presidential candidates. It does not necessarily follow, however, that all plausible candidates will seek the nomination. Nor does it follow that of those who do enter, all will remain in the race, or, for that matter, that the most plausible candidate will be nominated. In fact, many political observers contend that the capacity of our nominating process to attract, retain, and select the most plausible candidates has been seriously compromised by the proliferation of primaries. We now consider these criticisms in greater detail.

The Problem of Length

In 1960, John Kennedy declared for the presidency on January 2 and Lyndon Johnson did not throw his hat into the ring until July 5, shortly before the Democratic National Convention. Since 1972, however, a majority of presidential candidates—excluding incumbent presidents—have formally announced their candidacy at least twelve to eighteen months prior to their national conventions.[32] Some have formally entered the race as much as two to three years before the conventions, with several of these candidates actually campaigning in Iowa and New Hampshire on an informal basis even earlier.[33] Of the twelve Republican candidates who entered the race for the presidency in 1996, eight had formally announced by the end of April 1995.

Of course, the nominating process was configured very differently when Kennedy and Johnson ran for president. At that time a majority of delegates were chosen by the appointment and caucus-convention methods, both of which were firmly controlled by the party leaders. Thus, candidates faced the considerably less demanding task of lining up support within this relatively small group of individuals. Primaries, though usually not completely ignored by candidates, were entered selectively and viewed principally as a means of demonstrating vote-getting ability to the party elites.

The increased significance of early nominating contests, campaign finance reforms, and, most important, the necessity of taking one's candidacy to a host of different primary electorates, have all forced candidates to start running much earlier and harder. Indeed, the critics maintain that the process has now become so taxing that many able candidates are discouraged from even entering the presidential sweepstakes. One political scientist makes the point in the bluntest of terms: "The primary system has made it so that nice guys, including the competent ones, stay out of the whole ordeal. Right from the start, the primary system means that only those who possess near psychopathic ambition will get involved and stay involved."[34] In 1988, especially, this concern was given point as individuals in both parties, presumed to be of presidential timber, declined to enter the race. Among Republicans, these included former senators Howard Baker and Paul Laxalt, governors James Thompson and Thomas Kean, and former governor Lamar Alexander. Those declining to run on the Democratic side included senators Sam Nunn, Edward Kennedy, Dale Bumpers, and Bill Bradley; governors Mario Cuomo and William Clinton; and former governor Charles Robb.[35] The declared Democratic candidates, meanwhile, were disparagingly characterized in various media as the "seven dwarfs."[36]

Of those who declined to enter the 1988 race and were willing to say why, some noted the amount of time they would have to spend away from their families. Others mentioned that a presidential run would prevent them from fulfilling their responsibilities as incumbent officeholders, and one allowed as how he simply was not ready for the presidency.[37]

In 1996 as well, some prominent Republicans mentioned as presidential timber pointed to the process as a discouragement to candidacy. Said Willam Bennett, a member of both the Reagan and Bush administrations, "If you want everything you believe in to be caricatured, made fun of and belittled, then run for President."[38] Likewise, Richard Cheney, a former Republican congressman and secretary of defense in the Bush administration, observed: "The more I thought about it, the more the process you have to subject yourself to weighed heavily on my mind. I concluded I was not prepared to pay the price."[39] And Jack Kemp, a former congressman and member of the Bush cabinet, opined that "my passion for ideas is not matched with a passion for partisan or electoral politics."[40] Although the likelihood of winning was not mentioned as a reason for abstaining, one can be forgiven for doubting that this consideration was wholly absent from their minds.

Even if the current demands of the nominating process do discourage some presumably able candidates from entering, it would be difficult to sustain the charge that it has failed to attract individuals of experience and accomplishment. First, it should be noted that those who stay out of the race are likely to appear more attractive if only because they have escaped the close media scrutiny that is given to declared candidates. This point aside, it is worth looking more closely at the field of candidates in the 1988 race since, more so than in the races of 1992 and 1996, it was subject to particularly harsh criticism. With respect to experience in public office, Democratic candidates in fact compare favorably with the noncandidates in their party. Those from the ranks of Congress (Gore, Simon, Gephardt, Biden, Hart) had served between twelve and sixteen years in that body. Only noncandidate Senator Edward Kennedy served a substantially greater period of time. Meanwhile, the current or former Democratic governors running for president (Dukakis and Babbitt) served longer in that position than any noncandidate governor (Cuomo, Clinton). Moreover, as the noted political commentator David Broder observed, not only were the Democratic candidates experienced but they were also "serious government professionals, esteemed by their colleagues as unusually hard-working and engaged leaders."[41] Among the Democrats, only Jesse Jackson was without any previous government experience.

With the exception of evangelist Pat Robertson, experience in the Republican field was even more pronounced. Jack Kemp had served in Congress for eighteen years. Robert Dole had twenty-seven years of congressional experience, with six as Senate minority leader; he was also a former chairman of the Republican National Committee and a former vice presidential nominee. George Bush had held six different positions in government—congressman, chairman of the Republican National Committee, U.S. ambassador to the United Nations, director of the Central

Intelligence Agency, chief of the U.S. Liaison Office in China, and vice president. Pierre du Pont had been an eight-year governor, and Alexander Haig had served in the executive branch for some ten years, mostly in the White House, followed by a brief stint as secretary of state. Although three of the Republican noncandidates (Baker, Laxalt, Thompson) had served in government longer than Haig and du Pont, none had logged as much time as Kemp, Dole, or Bush.

Not only do individuals of considerable experience and accomplishment continue to seek the presidency, but there are some advantages to a distinctly longer nominating process. First, it tests as never before the candidates' physical and mental stamina, both of which will be required in the presidency. Second, a longer campaign increases the likelihood that candidates will reveal more of themselves and provides both the voters and media with a greater opportunity to scrutinize them. Third, once in office, presidents are invariably called upon to respond to unforeseen events. A nomination race of such length all but guarantees that unexpected events will arise during this period, thereby enabling the public to gauge how the candidates respond to them.

Early Eliminations

Neither the candidates nor the voters are well served if the nominating process forces the elimination of candidates before they have had an adequate opportunity to make their case. Yet this is precisely what happens, largely because the early contests have assumed so much importance in the race for the presidency. In 1980, for example, a Republican field of eight candidates was reduced to two (Reagan and Bush) after only four contests. Those falling by the wayside included such notables as senators Robert Dole and Howard Baker and former treasury secretary John Connally. On the Democratic side in 1984, poor showings in Iowa and New Hampshire eliminated three-fourths of the field, with such heavyweights as senators Fritz Hollings and Alan Cranston and Governor Reubin Askew among them. John Glenn and George McGovern, meanwhile, limped along for only two more weeks before withdrawing. These eliminations, incidentally, were based upon the casting of 62,625 votes in Iowa—11.5 percent of the votes cast in all Democratic caucuses that year—and 101,000 votes in New Hampshire—a mere 0.005 percent of the nearly 18,000,000 who would ultimately vote in all the Democratic primaries.[42] In 1988, Democrats Bruce Babbitt and Paul Simon were declared dead after their poor finishes in Iowa and New Hampshire, as were Jack Kemp, Pierre du Pont, and Alexander Haig on the Republican side. In short, wins in Iowa and New Hampshire (Jimmy Carter, 1976) would appear to place a candidate in a very advantageous position indeed. A win in either state keeps you in the running, while a loss in both effectively eliminates you from the race. This generalization did not hold in 1992, of course, because Iowa was neither seriously contested by the candidates nor closely covered by the media. This departure from the norm was not surprising given that one of the Democratic contenders, Senator Tom Harkin, hailed from that state and thus was virtually assured a victory there. With Iowa out of the spotlight, the opening contests receiving most attention were New Hampshire (February 18) and Georgia (March 3). A win in New Hampshire by former Massachusetts senator Paul Tsongas kept him in the running as did a better-than-expected second-place finish by Bill Clinton. Kerrey, Harkin, and Brown, meanwhile, did poorly in New Hampshire and would fare no better in Georgia some two weeks later. Fatally wounded, Harkin and Kerrey immediately withdrew. Brown, on the other hand, despite having little chance of winning, limped along all the way to the convention, winning a total of two primaries, neither one by a convincing margin. Clinton, on the other hand, managed a decisive win over Tsongas in Georgia, thereby establishing the necessary momentum to sweep most of the Super Tuesday primaries held on March 10—a result that forced Tsongas to suspend his candidacy.

In 1996, Louisiana attempted to steal Iowa's thunder by holding its caucus a week earlier, but to no avail. Except for Senator Phil Graham of Texas, the contest was largely ignored by the other candidates, and by the media as well. As in the past, those candidates who lost in Iowa and New Hampshire (Alexander, Forbes, Graham, Lugar) were, with but one exception, effectively eliminated from the race following these two contests. Alexander stumbled along for two more weeks and then withdrew. Forbes, however, despite losses in Iowa and New Hampshire, soldiered on for three more weeks, winning in Delaware, where he alone campaigned, and Arizona. What enabled Forbes to continue on as he did was money. Money dries up very quickly as soon as candidates look like losers, but Forbes did not face this problem because he was bankrolling his own candidacy to the tune of $37.5 million.

The quantity and quality of media coverage serve to explain why these early contests have assumed so much importance. In the last twenty-five years television has greatly expanded its commitment to news programming, and because nominating contests involve drama and conflict, they have become prime candidates for media attention. Moreover, Iowa (except in 1992) and New Hampshire are especially newsworthy because they are typically the two opening contests and face no competing contests on the same day. In 1980, for example, Iowa and New Hampshire each received 14 percent of all the coverage CBS gave to the caucuses and primaries. The closest any other state came was Illinois, which received 10 percent. Similarly, UPI gave 13 percent of all its coverage to Iowa and 15 percent to New Hampshire. Illinois, Michigan, and Pennsylvania finished a distant second, each with 7 percent.[43] Thus, Iowa and New Hampshire together garnered 28 percent of UPI's total coverage, whereas Illinois, Michigan, and Pennsylvania together received 21 percent. Note also that these latter three states together had more than 700 convention delegates and a total of 5,853,000 votes cast in their contests. Iowa and New Hampshire, on the other hand, had a combined total of only 130 convention delegates, with 259,087 voting in their 1980 contest. In 1984, Iowa and New Hampshire together captured 32 percent of the primary coverage on CBS, ABC, and NBC, and in the 1988 primary season that percentage rose to 34.[44]

If quantity of coverage enhances the importance of these early contests, so too does quality of coverage. More precisely, candidates who win or exceed expectations typically receive far greater media attention than those who fail to get off the mark quickly enough.[45] This approach to coverage is not without consequence, for presidential hopefuls who are not widely known to begin with and who fail to do well early are likely to experience considerable difficulty in gaining the necessary exposure. This fact, in turn, impedes their ability to succeed in subsequent contests, because voters do not support candidates about whom they know little. Thus, they find themselves in a catch-22 predicament: In order to secure coverage, they must do well; but in order to do well, they need coverage.

Aware that the early part of the nominating process is of such crucial importance, more and more states have been moving their primaries and caucuses toward the front end of the process in order to have a greater impact on the outcome. Thus, by 1996 some 70 percent of the delegates to the national conventions were chosen in just the first six weeks of the race, forcing candidates to campaign earlier than ever, and spend more money sooner. Add to this the fact that they had little time to catch their breaths between contests and voters had equally little time to digest the results. Furthermore, suppose a candidate less established and well known than Robert Dole had caught fire early, winning Iowa, New Hampshire, and Arizona. There could well have been a rush to judgment in six weeks, leaving us with a candidate who may have looked much less compelling in April and May.

Parties do, of course, have an interest in seeing the field of contenders narrowed, for a race that drags on indefinitely runs the risk of accentuating internal divisions. At the same time, however, it is reasonable to question whether the field should be narrowed so soon, and if so, should it not be on the basis of results more substantial and representative than those of Iowa and New Hampshire? Iowa, after all, has just under 1 percent of the country's population, and 97 percent of its citizens are white. New Hampshire's population is also overwhelmingly white (98 percent), and low in union membership, and constitutes a mere 0.4 percent of the nation's citizens.

The Problem of Quality Control

Perhaps no feature of the president-by-primary process has disturbed its critics as much as the vastly diminished influence of the party elites. Speaking to this point, one political scientist observes:

> When the state presidential primaries became the mode rather than the exception after 1968, a basic safeguard in the presidential election process was lost. Previously an elite of party leaders performed a screening function. They administered a kind of competence test; they did not always exercise the duty creditably, but they could. More important, they could—and did—ensure that no one was nominated who was not acceptable to the preponderance of the party elite as its leader. . . . Usually, then, the nominee was an insider in the political system, a person who had established some credentials as a politician or an administrator, or both, of national stature and of demonstrated competence.[46]

This view was echoed by no less a figure than James Reston, the dean of American journalists and longtime political columnist for the *New York Times.* In his final regular column preceding retirement in 1987, he told his readers: "So I'm off for a while, and I have some plans for what's left of my vertical years. . . . I'm going to try to bring back the smoke-filled room so that the next presidential candidates will be chosen by people who know something about them."[47]

The Democratic Party had in fact made some effort to accommodate these concerns by creating a new category of delegates to their 1984 national convention. Known as "super delegates," these slots comprised 14 percent (568) of all delegates chosen and were reserved exclusively for party and elected officials. Their super-delegate status entitled them to go to the convention uncommitted to any candidate. Although their number was slightly increased to 15.5 percent (650) for the 1988 convention, 18 percent (772) for 1992, and 20 percent (850) for 1996, they are still too small to have an impact unless the race is close—and even then, only if they are unified.

Having said this, however, it must be noted that the party elites probably exerted greater influence over the 1996 Republican nominating process than they had in any presidential election since 1972. That they did so was largely an artifact of the heavily front-loaded primary process. More specifically, after Iowa and New Hampshire, the contests came so quickly that it would have required extraordinary financial resources to field a campaign organization in all or even most of these states. Fortunately for Dole, as the primary season opened he not only had the endorsement of 37 senators and 125 House members, but, most important, he had also secured the support of 27 Republican governors, all of whom placed the weight of their state party organizations behind Dole's candidacy.[48] Nowhere was that organizational support more decisive than in the crucial South Carolina primary where Dole handily defeated his major competitor, Patrick Buchanan, who lacked the financial and organizational resources to compete effectively in so many states at once.

Whether the party elites have actually provided the quality control function ascribed to them is by no means clear. Parties, after all, seek to win elections. Given this fact, it should come as no surprise that from 1936 through 1968, when party leaders were firmly in control of the nominating process, the conventions on all but one occasion nominated the candidate most preferred by their party rank and file.[49] These data would appear to invite one of two conclusions: Either the rank and file were fully as discerning as their party leaders, or, alternatively, the party leaders were just as unenlightened as the rank and file. Either way, the alleged screening function of the party elites would appear to be of questionable value. Moreover, let us consider the single instance during this period when the views of the party leaders diverged from their fellow voters. Senator Estes Kefauver arrived at the 1952 Democratic Convention after having entered thirteen of seventeen primaries and won twelve of them. He also enjoyed a decisive lead in the polls (Kefauver, 45 percent; Stevenson, 12 percent; Russell, 10 percent; Harriman, 5 percent.)[50] Yet because Stevenson was the clear preference of the party leaders, he was selected and, incidentally, went on to lose in the general election. The rejection of Kefauver, however, does not appear to have been based upon the belief that he was not of presidential timber. Indeed, one longtime chronicler of American elections states that "he seemed most qualified for the leadership denied him."[51] Rather, the party leadership's rejection of Kefauver was motivated primarily by the fact that his Senate crime committee investigations had uncovered connections between organized crime and some big-city Democratic machines. To make matters worse, Kefauver had also fallen out of favor with Truman because he announced his candidacy before the president had made known his own intentions on whether to seek another term.[52] With some justification, the critics argue that the results of the president-by-primary process have not been reassuring. As one skeptic put it, "the old rules—the old bosses—gave us Franklin Roosevelt. The new rules gave us McGovern and Carter and Reagan."[53] George McGovern, nominated over the strong opposition of party leaders, took the Democratic Party to one of its greatest electoral defeats in this century. In 1976, the president-by-primary process brought forth Jimmy Carter, an avowed political outsider of limited experience, whose tenure in office manifested both of these limitations. The case of Reagan, however, is far less clear. Although the wisdom of his policies and administrative style have come in for considerable criticism, he was the first president since Eisenhower to serve two terms, and he left office with a public approval rating higher than any of his predecessors.

Even if the primary process has struck out on two (or even three) occasions, this fact should not necessarily cause us to believe that we were appreciably better off when the party elites controlled the process. For one thing, in the cases of Carter and

Reagan, it is by no means clear that they would have been denied the nomination even under the old system. Carter, after all, came into the convention with 53 percent of the party rank and file supporting his candidacy, and Reagan had led in the polls since 1978 and came into the 1980 Republican Convention with 46 percent of his party's voters lined up behind him.[54] Second, the record of the party elites in choosing nominees has not been unblemished either. Warren Harding proved to be the most inept president in this century. And it could be argued that Herbert Hoover's first four years in office did not justify his renomination for another four. More recently, we have the example of Richard Nixon, who, besides Franklin Roosevelt, was the only individual in this nation's history to be nominated for national office five times— twice for vice president and three times for president. Moreover, in his three bids for the presidency, he had the support of his party's leaders as well as its rank and file. Although subsequent events have demonstrated that such confidence was misplaced, the screening function of the party elites did not prove a very effective safeguard— this, despite the fact that Nixon's previous career in politics ought to have engendered considerable skepticism among those presumed to be most discerning in identifying presidential timber.[55]

PROPOSALS FOR CHANGE

The considerable amount of criticism directed at the presidential selection process has also led to several proposals designed to improve it. Some of these proposals would alter the process rather dramatically, whereas others call for more limited changes.

Before considering these proposals, it should be noted that as of this writing one change has already been made by the Republican Party for the 2000 presidential race. Responding to criticisms that the 1996 primary calendar was too heavily front-loaded, the 1996 Republican National Convention approved a rule which awards bonus delegates to states scheduling their contests later in the spring. Specifically, those waiting until March 15 will have their state delegations increased by 5 percent. The bonus increases to 7.5 percent for states that wait until April 15, and 10 percent for those holding off until May 15 or later. How many states will take the bait remains to be seen. Unclear also is how, if at all, the Democratic Party will address this issue.

Primary/Caucus Clusterings

Some suggestions for improving the nominating process include primary/caucus clusterings of one kind or another. One such plan calls for grouping these contests by region, with one-month intervals between each regional contest. This arrangement would help to conserve candidates' energy and financial resources, enabling them to focus their attention in one area rather than hopping about the country. Furthermore, given the fact that the nominating season would open with a group of contests, the potential influence of any one would be diluted. Consequently, a candidate's prospects would not be boosted or dashed solely on the basis of results as meager as those of Iowa or New Hampshire. And the one-month interlude between contests might well lessen the fallout from the previous round and provide candidates more time to prepare for the next. The major limitation of this proposal, however, is that a candidate could be either advantaged or disadvantaged, depending on which region goes first. For example, had the 1976 primaries begun in the West instead of the East, Jimmy Carter would have been knocked out of the race early. Likewise, had this region begun the race in 1980, Reagan would have eliminated George Bush from the race even sooner.

Others have suggested that the nominating contests be clustered according to the four time zones in the continental United States, thereby mitigating the potential regional bias for or against a given candidate. This proposal also has its drawbacks, however. First, several states span more than one time zone. Second, nearly one-half of the primary states, including a majority of the big ones (New York, New Jersey, Pennsylvania, Ohio, and Florida), are in the eastern time zone. Thus, campaigning for this particular cluster would be a formidable task indeed and disadvantage the candidate of limited visibility and financial resources. In 1988, we had what amounted to a regional primary, with eleven southern states holding their contests on "Super Tuesday." The results were not reassuring. In an effort to reach so many primary electorates, candidates were forced to rely heavily on television and confine their state visits to little more than brief appearances at local airports.

National Primary

Others would favor a change that expands public participation beyond what exists under the current system.[56] Known as the national primary, it would allow the rank and file in each party to vote directly for their nominee in a single nationwide election. The national conventions would then convene primarily for the purpose of drawing up the party's platform. As of 1988, this proposal was favored by 65 percent of the American people.[57]

The national primary has much to recommend it. Since primaries bring out considerably more voters than caucuses—in 1992, for example, 19,000,000 voted in primaries and only 291,000 in caucuses[58]—fifty state primaries would no doubt involve even greater numbers of voters in the nominating process. In addition, a national primary would eliminate one of the major deficiencies in the current nominating process, namely, the disproportionate influence of early contests. Finally, in contrast to the current system, all of a party's voters would have the same choice of candidates. This was not possible in 1988, for example, because several Democratic (Babbitt, Simon, Gephardt) and Republican (Haig, Kemp, du Pont, Robertson) candidates dropped out of the race before some or most of the contests had been held.

If the benefits associated with a national primary are compelling, so are its liabilities. Certainly for those who think the current system is already too demanding and expensive, a national primary would merely make a bad situation worse. In addition, since party and elected officials would have no formal role in this process, the national primary would deal yet another blow to the already diminished role of political parties in our political process. A nationwide primary would also place less well known candidates at a distinct advantage. Under our current arrangement of discrete primaries, presidential aspirants with limited national visibility have an early opportunity to demonstrate their viability as candidates. They would have no such opportunity in a national primary because it is a one-shot affair. Furthermore, we face the problem of what to do in the event that no candidate receives a majority of the vote—a very real possibility given the fact that presidential fields in the out-party have ranged anywhere from five to twelve candidates in the last six elections. This eventuality would presumably necessitate a runoff. Thus, we could be faced with three separate national elections (national primary, runoff, general election), which would not only be a very expensive proposition but also impose a heavy burden on the stamina of candidates and the attention span of the public.

Party Elite Selection

Whereas the aforementioned proposals would reorganize or expand the number of primaries, others would totally eliminate them. Jeane Kirkpatrick, believing that a candidate's peers are best able to assess qualifications for the presidency, calls for abolishing primaries and leaving the nominating decision up to national conventions composed entirely of party and elected officials.[59] Others would place the nomination decision in Congress, thereby returning us to the congressional caucus method used from 1800 to 1824.[60] Such a change would, it is argued, ensure a nominee of high caliber and foster a more cooperative relationship between the president and his or her party in Congress. Former Senator J. William Fulbright would go even further. Disturbed by the lack of cooperation between the president and Congress and convinced that candidates are now elected not on the basis of experience but on their astute use of television and access to money, he advocated turning the entire matter of presidential selection over to Congress.[61]

Quite obviously, none of these proposals is very realistic, for once the opportunity to participate has been extended, the beneficiaries will be little inclined to see it rescinded. Nor would any of these proposals, on balance, be an improvement. Although the Fulbright plan would probably ensure a Washington insider as president and tie him more closely to Congress, its drawbacks are severe. For one thing, removing the population from any direct role whatsoever in presidential selection would greatly weaken the bond that currently exists between the president and the people, thereby adversely affecting his ability to mobilize them behind his policies. We may also question whether capable politicians who reside beyond the confines of Washington would stand much chance of being seriously considered for the presidency under Fulbright's plan. Finally, as the Founding Fathers realized only too well, congressional election of the president would render him overly dependent upon that branch. This defect, which applies as well to nomination by congressional caucus, was vividly revealed during the presidency of James Madison. Earnestly seeking renomination by his party's congressional caucus and recognizing that they strongly supported war with Britain, he acquiesced in the ill-considered War of 1812 despite strong misgivings.[62] Nor do the problems with nomination by congressional caucus end here. Like the Fulbright proposal, it would heavily bias the selection process in favor of individuals residing in the legislative branch. Moreover, if a state's congressional delegation were composed exclusively of representatives from one party, that state would be denied any representation in the congressional caucus of the other party.

A national convention composed exclusively of party and elected officials does not labor under any of these drawbacks. Yet there are still grounds for questioning whether such a system would yield different candidates and, if so, whether they would be any better. Even in the absence of primaries, presidential candidates would continue to campaign around the country in an effort to generate public support for their candidacy. Moreover, if the previous record (1936–1968) of party-elite-controlled conventions is any indication, party leaders would in all likelihood choose the individual who came into the convention as the clear leader in the polls. On the other hand, it might be argued that the absence of primaries would mitigate against the emergence of a clear leader, partly because there would be no opportunity to generate momentum by actually winning and partly because the field would not be narrowed by losing. This being the case, national conventions would have greater discretion in choosing a nominee. But would their choices produce candidates any more qualified than those yielded in the president-by-primary process? As noted earlier in this chapter, some critics argue that the candidates emerging from the old party-controlled process were superior to the likes of McGovern (1972), Carter (1976), and Reagan (1980). This comparison is not entirely fair, however, for the president-by-primary process has not been in existence long enough to provide us with a sufficient number of cases to evaluate. The critics would also assert that McGovern, Carter, and Reagan won over more qualified candidates, notably, Edmund Muskie (1972), Morris Udall (1976), and Howard Baker (1980). In order to make this assertion with any confidence, however, we would have to know how these latter three individuals would have performed had they won. In short, we know what we got, but cannot know what we did not get.

Finally, expensive and demanding though it is, the president-by-primary process subjects the candidates to more intense and protracted scrutiny by the public, media, and the party elites than the pre-1968 system did. To be sure, it does not guarantee that the most qualified candidate will be chosen. No system can. Yet it does a reasonably good job of ensuring that we do not select a very bad candidate. Certainly the president-by-primary process has not yet produced a nominee whose views were as decidedly at variance with a majority of Americans as those of Barry Goldwater (1964). Nor has it yielded a nominee whose overall level of competence was as deficient as Warren Harding's (1920). Nor, finally, has it given us a president whose insensitivity to constitutional and ethical questions approached that of Richard Nixon (1960, 1968, 1972).

☆ NOTES

1. Johnathan Elliot, ed., *The Debates in the Several Conventions on the Adoption of the Federal Constitution,* vol. 2 (Philadelphia: Lippincott, 1861), p. 511.

2. Robert DiClerico, "James Wilson's Presidency," *Presidential Studies Quarterly* 17 (Spring 1987), 306.

3. Martin Diamond, *The Electoral College and the American Idea of Democracy* (Washington, D.C.: American Enterprise Institute, 1977), pp. 3–5; DiClerico, "James Wilson's Presidency," pp. 307–11.

4. Lawrence D. Longley and Alan G. Braun, *The Politics of Electoral College Reform* (New Haven, Conn.: Yale University Press, 1972), pp. 28–32.

5. On this point see Theodore Lowi, *The Personal Presidency* (Ithaca, N.Y.: Cornell University Press, 1985), p. 33.

6. Austin Ranney, *Participation in American Nominations, 1976* (Washington, D.C.: American Enterprise Institute, 1977), pp. 2, 3.

7. William Crotty, *Political Reform and the American Experiment* (New York: Crowell, 1977), pp. 201, 202.

8. Ranney, *Participation in American Nominations, 1976,* p. 4.

9. Ibid.

10. Herman Finer, *The Presidency* (Chicago: University of Chicago Press, 1960), p. 23.

11. James MacGregor Burns, *The Power to Lead* (New York: Simon & Schuster, 1984), p. 43.

12. James Sundquist, "What Happened to Our Checks and Balances?" in Charles Roberts, ed., *Has the President Too Much Power?* (New York: Harper's Magazine Press, 1974), p. 110.

13. E. E. Schattschneider, *The Semi-Sovereign People* (New York: Holt, Rinehart and Winston, 1960), p. 68.

14. U.S. Census Bureau, "The Foreign-Born Population: 1996," *The Current Population Survey Report,* http://www.census.gov/population/www/socdemo/foreign96.html (8/13/97 2:16PM).

15. Laurance Urlang, ed., *CBS News Almanac 1976* (Maplewood, N.J.: Hammond Almanac, 1975), p. 147.

16. Arthur Hadley, *The Invisible Primary* (Englewood Cliffs, N.J.: Prentice Hall, 1976), p. 179.

17. *New York Times,* January 18, 1990, p. Y11. Copyright © 1990 by The New York Times Company. Reprinted by permission.

18. *Congressional Quarterly Weekly Report,* December 21, 1991, p. 3734; *Congressional Quarterly Weekly Report,* January 11, 1992, p. 66.

19. "New Places to Look for Presidents," *Time,* December 15, 1975, p. 19.

20. Kenneth Prewitt and Alan Stone, *The Ruling Elites* (New York: Harper & Row, 1973), pp. 131–58.

21. Herbert Alexander, *Money in Politics* (Washington, D.C.: Public Affairs Press, 1972), pp. 31, 72; David Adamany and George Agree, *Political Money* (Baltimore: Johns Hopkins University Press, 1975), p. 30.

22. See, for example, Michael J. Malbin, "You Get What You Pay for, but Is That What You Want?" in George Grassmuck, ed., *Before Nomination: Our Primary Problems* (Washington, D.C.: American Enterprise Institute, 1985), pp. 72–86; Robert DiClerico and Eric Uslaner, *Few Are Chosen* (New York: McGraw-Hill, 1984), pp. 88–94.

23. *Washington Post,* March 28, 1996, p. A27.

24. Alexander, *Money in Politics,* p. 140; Herbert E. Alexander, *Financing Politics,* 2nd ed. (Washington, D.C.: Congressional Quarterly Press, 1980), p. 51.

25. Michael R. Hawthorne, "Effects of the Federal Election Campaign Act on Presidential Nomination Campaigns" (Paper delivered at the 1985 annual meeting of the American Political Science Association, New Orleans), p. 11.

26. Michael Robinson, "The Power of the Primary Purse: Money in 1984," *Public Opinion* 7 (August/September, 1984), 49.

27. Michael Robinson, Clyde Wilcox, and Paul Marshall, "The Presidency Not for Sale," *Public Opinion* 12 (March/April, 1989), 51.

28. Gerald Pomper, et al., *The Election of 1996* (Chatham, N.J.: Chatham House, 1997), p. 138.

29. Richard Scammon and Ben Wattenberg, *The Real Majority* (New York: Coward, McCann & Geoghegan, 1970), pp. 72–81, 209.

30. U.S. Department of Commerce, *Statistical Abstract of the United States* (Washington, D.C.: U.S. Government Printing Office, 1996), p. 21.

31. *New York Times,* June 15, 1997, p. 4; R. Darcy, S. Welch, and J. Clark, *Women, Elections and Representation,* 2nd ed. (Lincoln: University of Nebraska Press, 1994), p. 176.

32. Harold W. Stanley and Richard G. Niemi, *Vital Statistics on American Politics* (Washington, D.C.: Congressional Quarterly Press, 1988), p. 73.

33. *U.S. News and World Report,* October 1, 1984, p. 18.

34. Cited in Anthony King, "How Not to Select Presidential Candidates: The View from Europe," in Austin Ranney, ed., *The American Electorate of 1980* (Washington, D.C.: American Enterprise Institute, 1981), p. 321. See also *Washington Post,* March 29, 1987, pp. C1, C2; Everett Ladd, "A Better Way to Pick Our Presidents," *Fortune,* May 5, 1980, pp. 133, 134.

35. *Washington Post,* March 29, 1987, pp. C1, C2.

36. *Washington Post,* September 9, 1987, p. A21.

37. *New York Times,* June 22, 1988, p. E26; *New York Times,* February 22, 1987, p. E4; *Washington Post,* March 3, 1987, p. A15; *Washington Post,* August 28, 1987, p. A3; Randall Rothenberg, "Why Bradley Isn't Running," *New York Times Magazine,* August 2, 1987, p. 29ff.

38. Cited in *New York Times,* February 5, 1995, p. E1.

39. Cited in *Congressional Quarterly Weekly Report,* January 4, 1995, p. 175.

40. Cited in *Washington Post,* January 31, 1995, p. A5.

41. *Washington Post,* March 25, 1987, p. A23.

42. *Congressional Quarterly Weekly Report,* June 2, 1984, p. 1317; June 16, 1984, p. 1143; February 15, 1984, p. 462.

43. Michael Robinson and Margaret Sheehan, *Over the Wire and on TV* (New York: Russell Sage Foundation, 1980), p. 76.

44. S. Robert Lichter, Daniel Amundson, and Richard Noyes, *Video Campaign: Network Coverage of the 1988 Primaries* (Washington, D.C.: American Enterprise Institute, 1988), p. 14.

45. On this point, see Thomas E. Patterson, *The Mass Media Election* (New York: Praeger, 1980), pp. 43–53; David Moore, "The Death of Politics in New Hampshire," *Public Opinion* 7 (February/March, 1984), 57; William Adams, "Media Coverage of Campaign '84: A Preliminary Report," *Public Opinion* 7 (April/May, 1984),10–13.

46. James Sundquist, "The Crisis of Competence in Government," in Joseph Pechman, ed., *Setting National Priorities: Agenda for the Eighties* (Washington, D.C.: Brookings Institution, 1980), p. 543. See also Terry Sanford, *A Danger of Democracy* (Boulder, Colo.: Westview Press, 1981); Jeane Kirkpatrick, *Dismantling the Parties* (Washington, D.C.: American Enterprise Institute, 1978); Nelson Polsby, *Consequences of Party Reform* (New York: Oxford University Press, 1983).

47. *New York Times,* August 2, 1987, p. E23. Copyright © 1987 by The New York Times Company. Reprinted by permission.

48. *Washington Post,* March 15, 1996, p. A14.

49. William Ludy, "Polls, Primaries and Presidential Nominations," *Journal of Politics* 35 (November 1973), 837.

50. William Keech and Donald Matthews, *The Party's Choice* (Washington, D.C.: Brookings Institution, 1976), p. 185; George Gallup, *The Gallup Opinion Poll: Public Opinion, 1935–1971,* vol. 2 (New York: Random House, 1972), p. 1075.

51. Theodore White, *America in Search of Itself* (New York: Harper & Row, 1982), p. 75.

52. James W. Davis, *Presidential Primaries: Road to the White House* (New York: Crowell, 1967), p. 176.

53. Robert S. Hirschfield, ed., *Selection/Election: A Forum on the American Presidency* (New York: Aldine, 1982), p. 107.

54. *The Gallup Opinion Index,* December 1980, Report No. 183, pp. 13, 16; Gerald Pomper, with colleagues, *The Election of 1980: Reports and Interpretations* (Chatham, N.J.: Chatham House, 1981), p. 33.

55. See, for example, Theodore White, *Breach of Faith* (New York: Atheneum, 1975), p. 65.

56. See, for example, Michael Nelson, "Two Cheers for the National Primary," in Thomas Cronin, ed., *Rethinking the Presidency* (Boston: Little, Brown, 1982), pp. 55–63; *Congressional Quarterly Weekly Report,* July 8, 1972, pp. 1650–54.

57. *National Journal,* May 21, 1988, p. 1374.

58. *Congressional Quarterly Weekly Report,* July 4, 1992, pp. 69, 70.

59. Jeane Kirkpatrick, et al., *The Presidential Nominating Process: Can It Be Improved?* (Washington, D.C.: American Enterprise Institute, 1980), pp. 16, 17.

60. Although I do not share his view, my coauthor espouses this idea in Robert DiClerico and Eric Uslaner, *Few Are Chosen* (New York: McGraw-Hill, 1984), pp. 193–98.

61. See letter to the editor, *Washington Post,* March 7, 1987, p. A22.

62. James L. Sundquist, *Constitutional Reform and Effective Government* (Washington, D.C.: Brookings Institution, 1986), p. 182.

The President and Foreign Affairs

☆ SOME GENERAL CONSIDERATIONS: THE TWO PRESIDENCIES

For analytical purposes, we can divide the impact of presidential actions into two broad areas, the foreign and the domestic. In the past, it has been argued that presidents enjoyed much greater freedom of action in foreign, as opposed to domestic, affairs. Indeed, in a now-classic article published back in 1966 titled "The Two Presidencies," Aaron Wildavsky found that between 1948 and 1964 a president's foreign policy initatives were supported by Congress approximately 70 percent of the time, in contrast to domestic initiatives, which achieved only 40 percent support.[1] Indeed, Wildavsky was struck by the president's apparent ability "to control defense and foreign policies and so overwhelm those who might wish to thwart him."[2] His concept of "two presidencies" has not gone unchallenged, however. On the contrary, in the last decade, other scholars have put his thesis to the test and come up with results that in varying degrees raise serious questions about the concept of two presidencies. These challenges include the contention that the concept was never valid; that it was valid only during the Eisenhower presidency; or that it was evident only in Republican presidencies.[3] Other scholars, meanwhile, have examined the evidence and, depending on the particular study, found strong or partial support for the two presidencies concept.[4] The rather curious variation in these findings is traceable primarily to the presidential foreign policy initiatives that scholars chose to examine. Some, for example, considered all presidential initiatives, whereas others, seeking to avoid trivial votes, focused only on nonunanimous votes; and still others included only key votes, with further variation occuring in how they defined "key." Each of these approaches carries with it certain advantages and limitations that will not occupy our attention here.[5] Suffice it to say that these studies, when viewed in their totality, suggest the continued viability of the two presidencies concept, although not to the degree stipulated by Wildavsky. We now consider those factors that in the past have given presidents added leverage in foreign affairs.

Information is power, and in foreign affairs the president has more information at his disposal than either Congress or the public. He is constantly being informed of international developments by the Bureau of Intelligence and Research in the State Department, the Defense Intelligence Agency at the Defense Department, and the Central Intelligence Agency. Neither Congress nor the public has any comparable source of information, and consequently, they are largely dependent upon the executive branch and the press for learning about what is happening outside the United States. He is free to define for the public and Congress the nature of important developments in the area of foreign affairs, to the extent that the president has a monopoly on such information. He enjoys no such advantage in the domestic area, however. Many issues such as interest rates, medical costs, crime, and the environment are experienced directly by members of Congress and the American public, thus providing them with an information base independent of the president.

The presidential advantage in foreign affairs has derived not only from his near-monopoly of information but also from the fact that on many issues in foreign affairs people have no preexisting opinions, a condition that no doubt results from a lack of knowledge or interest, or both. Lacking such, they are highly susceptible to having their opinions on a given issue shaped by the president. Moreover, even where public opinion is firm on a foreign policy issue, the president may still prove successful in altering it. For example, Americans for many years held rather hostile attitudes toward the People's Republic of China. When asked in 1968 to rate China on a scale ranging from most favorable to least favorable, only 5 percent of the American people gave it any kind of a favorable rating.[6] In 1973, however, following President Nixon's initiation of "détente" and his trip to China, 49 percent of the population gave China a favorable rating.[7] The public's inclination to bring its opinions into line with the president's foreign policy position reflects its greater willingness to trust the judgment of the president in the area of foreign affairs.

In the past, presidents have also been able to exert greater leverage in foreign, as opposed to domestic, affairs because there are fewer interest groups attempting to exert influence over foreign policy matters. Many of those groups that do enter the foreign policy arena are temporary, arising over a particular issue and then dissipating after the issue has been resolved. Among the most active interest groups in foreign policy are American ethnic associations that seek to influence the government's policy toward their homelands. Cuban Americans, for example, have long sought the continuation of a hard-line policy toward Castro's Cuba. American Jewish organizations have been active in attempting to influence the United States' role in the Arab-Israeli conflict. Similarly, the Greek lobby in this country exerted considerable pressure on Congress in the 1974 dispute between Greece and Turkey over the island of Cyprus. These organizations, however, do not even approach in number the many interest groups seeking to influence our domestic policy. In nearly every area of domestic life there is a formidable number of powerful organizations that represent the interests of various groups within our population, such as the business community, farmers, labor, and consumers. To the extent that a president must compete with many more alternative power centers in domestic affairs, he finds it more difficult to get his way. The Kennedy administration, for example, was repeatedly frustrated in its attempts to gain congressional approval for Medicare because of an alliance of powerful interest groups consisting of the American Medical Association, the U.S.

Chamber of Commerce, the National Association of Manufacturers, and the American Farm Bureau Federation.[8] More recently, as President Clinton attempted a massive overhaul of the health care system, he had to contend with a panoply of interests including those of doctors, hospitals, insurance and pharmaceutical companies, employers, and the elderly.

Furthermore, in his conduct of foreign policy, the president benefits from what may be characterized as the "us against them" syndrome. There is a natural inclination on the part of the population to rally around the president when he is acting against what is perceived as an outside threat to the interests of the United States. As is evident in Table 2-1, approval of the president typically increases after he has faced an international crisis of any kind. Note also that this support increases even after the president's or the government's actions have resulted in a major foreign policy blunder or failure, such as when an American U-2 plane was shot down over the Soviet Union, when President Kennedy ordered the abortive Bay of Pigs invasion of Cuba, and when Jimmy Carter attempted to rescue American hostages in Iran. In domestic affairs, however, the president is not likely to receive this kind of support, for domestic crises usually "divide popular opinion and thereby dilute support for presidents who act decisively."[9]

Finally, and by no means least important, the president's foreign policy advantage derives from his capacity to *initiate*. Our Constitution accords the president greater freedom of action in foreign affairs, bestowing on him the role of commander-in-chief of the armed forces as well as the power to negotiate treaties and extend diplomatic recognition to other governments. The Senate, of course, may decline to ratify a treaty, and a majority of Congress may be able to halt other presidential actions by refusing to appropriate the necessary funds. The problem, however, is that once a president initiates or, if you will, commits the nation to a given course of action, it may be quite difficult for Congress to renege on that commitment without appearing to undermine the credibility of the president and the government as a whole.

Although the president continues to benefit from the "us against them" syndrome as well as from his ability to initiate, his other advantages in the foreign policy area have diminished. Certainly our experience in Vietnam may be viewed as instrumental in leading to this diminution, for not only did the president's presumed superior information fail to save us from this costly nightmare, but it also became apparent that the government was less than candid with the American people regarding our role and goals in the conflict. As a consequence, both Congress and the public are less inclined to defer to the president's judgment on foreign policy matters— witness, for example, the considerable congressional and public concern that was expressed over the Reagan administration's growing involvement in Nicaragua and over Clinton's decision, quickly abandoned, to expand the U.S. military's role in Somalia beyond a purely humanitarian one to a more ambitious mission of seeking to influence political events there.

Add to this skepticism the fact that Congress, with its rapidly growing staff capability, is now in a better position to generate its own information and analyses on foreign policy issues. As noted in one study on this subject, "Congress, in the last five years, has developed a virtual counter-State Department composed of predominantly young, experienced and aggressive experts who are out to make their own marks on the foreign policy map."[10] The ability of Congress to secure information has been further enhanced by technological advances that now enable the media to provide live coverage of international events (for example, the massacre of Chinese citizens

TABLE 2-1   Percentage Approving the Way a President Is Handling His Job
and Percentage Disapproving

Before Event	Event	After Event
June 1950 37 pro/45 anti	U.S. enters Korean War (Truman)	July 1950 46 pro/37 anti
July 1958 52 pro/32 anti	U.S. sends Marines to Lebanon (Eisenhower)	August 1958 58 pro/27 anti
May 1960 62 pro/22 anti	U-2 incident, summit meeting collapse (Eisenhower)	Early June 1960 68 pro/21 anti
March 1961 73 pro/7 anti	Bay of Pigs invasion (Kennedy)	April 1961 74 pro/15 anti
October 1961 61 pro/24 anti	Cuban missile crisis (Kennedy)	December 1961 74 pro/5 anti
March 1970 53 pro/30 anti	Cambodian invasion (Nixon)	May 1970 57 pro/31 anti
March 1972 53 pro/37 anti	Mining of Haiphong harbor (Nixon)	May 1972 61 pro/32 anti
May 1975 40 pro/43 anti	*Mayaguez* incident (Ford)	June 1975 51 pro/33 anti
October 1979 31 pro/56 anti	Seizure of American embassy in Iran (Carter)	November 1979 38 pro/49 anti
March 1980 41 pro/45 anti	Attempted rescue of American hostages (Carter)	April 1980 46 pro/42 anti
October 1983 49 pro/41 anti	Grenada invasion	November 1983 53 pro/37 anti
April 1986 62 pro/29 anti	Libyan bombing	May 1986 68 pro/23 anti
September 1986 61 pro/25 anti	Reykjavík summit	October 1986 63 pro/29 anti
December 1989 71 pro/20 anti	Invasion of Panama	January 1990 80 pro/11 anti
August 1990 60 pro/25 anti	Iraq invades Kuwait	August 1990 74 pro/16 anti
June 1993 39 pro/50 anti	U.S. bombing of Iraq's intelligence headquarters	June 1993 46 pro/47 anti
October 1993 47 pro/44 anti	Navy warships sent to Haiti	October 1993 48 pro/45 anti
December 1998 63 pro/33 anti	U.S./British air attacks against Iraq	December 1998 73 pro/25 anti

Sources: Hazel Gaudet Erskine, ed., "A Revival: Reports from the Polls," *Public Opinion Quarterly* 25 (Spring 1961), 135–37; *Gallup Opinion Index* (Princeton: American Institute of Public Opinion, 1972), p. 3; *Gallup Opinion Index* (Princeton: American Institute of Public Opinion, 1976), p. 12. Figures for 1979–1998 provided by George Gallup Associates, Princeton, New Jersey.

in Tiananmen Square, the Gulf War) in a way not possible twenty years ago. In an unanticipated crisis, however, where a swift response by our government is required, Congress is likely to remain heavily dependant upon the president's definition of the situation.

Presidents may also find their freedom of action restricted to the extent that they must now compete with an increasing number of interest groups in the foreign policy arena.

With growing international interdependence and complexity, foreign policy is no longer a distant enterprise, remote from the lives of citizens. On the contrary, one or another aspect of international relations now affects some segment of the population. To the extent that they are able, those affected will attempt to influence foreign policy in ways that are favorable to them. The linkage between the domestic and foreign policy processes has been most noticeable in foreign economic policy, although ethnic politics has been and promises to remain another important area of policy in which domestic groups become important participants in the formulation of policy. In addition, environment, ecology, transportation, communication and related areas are not merely domestic concerns but overlap with foreign policy to a growing extent.[11]

Farm groups, for example, took a keen interest in supporting the Ford administration's decision to sell wheat to the Soviet Union. At the same time, however, the AFL-CIO and the Longshoreman's Union temporarily prevented this agreement from being implemented by refusing to load the grain until the Soviet Union agreed to allow it to be transported on American rather than Soviet ships. The Ford administration also encountered resistance over its decision to allow the British and French supersonic planes to land at American airports. Several environmental interest groups contended that the Concorde jet would expose various parts of our country to unacceptable air and noise pollution, and consequently they decided to fight the government's decision in the courts. Although they ultimately lost, their efforts did cause a lengthy delay in granting landing rights to the Concorde—a delay that proved more than a little embarrassing to the Ford administration.

Nor did the Reagan administration escape the problems arising from the growing interface of foreign and domestic issues. Despite his repeated commitment to a policy of free trade, the president found himself buffeted by protests from many domestic industries, all claiming to have been hurt by increased foreign competition. Thus, in response to pleas from both the beleaguered automobile industry and the United Auto Workers, the administration in 1981 pressured the Japanese to voluntarily limit its auto exports to the United States for three years. Domestic economic interests also intruded upon another administration foreign policy, namely, improving relations with China. When a trade agreement regulating Chinese textile exports to the United States came up for renewal in 1982, the president bowed to heavy pressures from the domestic textile industry and reduced the quota on Chinese textiles. The Chinese, outraged by this decision, proceeded to retaliate by boycotting all American farm products. Feeling the heat from farmers, members of Congress representing agricultural states then insisted that the Reagan administration restore the original quota. The president finally agreed to restore half of it. This compromise satisfied the Chinese, thereby ending a year-long dispute during which Sino-American relations had become seriously strained.

In the early months of his administration President Clinton was also forced to address relations between the United States and China, and once again domestic economic considerations intruded—so much so, in fact, that he was forced to back down from a campaign pledge. More specifically, throughout his presidential campaign Clinton had criticized the Bush administration for granting China most favored-nation trading status despite repeated human rights violations, the most brutal manifestations of which were starkly revealed in the Tiananmen Square massacre. But when China's trading status came up for renewal in June 1993, the Clinton administration found itself inundated with pleas from some three hundred business groups and companies, all insisting that failure to renew China's most favored-nation trading status could force the Chinese government to restrict American access to its growing market economy, thereby causing U.S. companies to lose out to foreign competition. Having made job creation and economic growth his top priorities, President Clinton discreetly retreated from his more hard-line position and decided to renew most favored status for one year with the stipulation that China would be expected to show improvement in its human rights policies by the following year. This policy, too, would change the following year when the Clinton administration announced that China's status as a trading partner would no longer be linked to its record on human rights.

The intrusion of domestic considerations was also responsible for one of the major defeats of Bill Clinton's presidency—the failure of Congress in 1997 to renew his "fast track" authority on trade issues. This authority allows trade agreements negiotiated by the president to be voted up or down by Congress, thereby avoiding potentially crippling amendments. It had been granted to every president since Gerald Ford, but this time around organized labor and some civil rights groups mounted a fierce campaign to deny Clinton such authority, fearing that such agreements would result in a loss of jobs for American workers. With a majority of his own party declining to support Clinton on this issue, the president, recognizing that he faced certain defeat, requested that the vote on "fast track" be indefinitely postponed.

As other nations continue to become more competitive in basic industries, agriculture, textiles, and technology, we may anticipate that presidential efforts to make foreign policy will be increasingly complicated by the push and pull of domestic economic interests.

THE WAR-MAKING POWER

In no area have the actions of recent presidents evoked greater controversy than by their involvement in war making. Acting in their capacity as commander in chief, Lyndon Johnson committed the United States to a protracted war in Vietnam, and Richard Nixon committed air and ground forces in Cambodia. These actions were responsible for much of the political and social upheaval in our society during the late 1960s and early 1970s, as individuals in and outside of government asked by what authority these two recent presidents justified the commitment of our human and material resources to such undertakings. We must consult history in order to gain a proper perspective on their actions specifically and on the president's war-making power generally.

The Intent of the Founders

The Founding Fathers were not at all ambiguous on the matter of who should possess the war-making power. In their judgment, prudence clearly dictated that this power should be given to the legislative branch. In the words of James Madison, "The Constitution supposes, what the History of all Govts. demonstrates, that the Ex. is the branch of power most interested in war, & most prone to it. It has accordingly with studied care vested the question of war in the Legisl."[12] The Constitutional Convention did qualify this grant of power in one respect, however. The first draft of the Constitution stated that Congress would have the power to "make war." This was later changed to "declare war," in recognition of the fact that swiftness of action would be a necessity in the event of a sudden attack on the United States. Since the president would be better able to act with dispatch under such circumstances, the Founders expected him to repel sudden attacks without having to receive the prior approval of Congress. Although the Constitution accorded the president the power to act as commander in chief of the armed forces, it is clear that the Founders did not intend for this role to confer any authority upon him to wage war. Rather, as Alexander Hamilton noted, "it would amount to nothing more than the supreme command and direction of the military and naval forces, as first general and admiral of the confederacy."[13] In short, the president was to be in charge of the armed forces once committed to battle, but the decision on whether or not to commit them was to rest solely with Congress.

That war making must rest with the Congress was recognized and scrupulously adhered to by our early presidents. When in 1793 George Washington declared that the United States would remain neutral in the war between Britain and France, it was argued by many that his declaration in effect prevented Congress from exercising its right to side with France in the conflict and declare war against Britain. Washington ultimately agreed, stating that "it rests with the wisdom of Congress to correct, improve, or enforce the neutrality."[14] Thereafter, declarations of neutrality rested with the Congress.

From 1798 to 1800, the United States was involved in a limited maritime war with France. When the trouble began, President Adams called Congress into secret session in order to determine what measures would be appropriate on the part of the United States. Although Congress never officially declared war on France, it nevertheless passed legislation authorizing Adams to wage a limited war against France.

Americans encountered further difficulty on the high seas during the administration of Thomas Jefferson, when an American schooner was attacked in the Mediterranean by a cruiser from Tripoli. Although the cruiser was captured and disabled by the American schooner, both the cruiser and its crew were released because the American commander, as Jefferson told Congress, "was unauthorized by the Constitution, without the sanction of Congress, to go beyond the line of defense."[15] Jefferson then asked Congress if it would authorize measures to allow American forces to take offensive action against the ships from Tripoli. Alexander Hamilton, however, thought that in this particular instance Jefferson was being overly sensitive to the right of Congress to declare war. In his judgment, once someone declared war on you, a state of war automatically existed, and thus a congressional declaration of war became unnecessary.

James Monroe did not share Jefferson's view when he became president. In 1817, when Seminole Indians conducted raiding parties into American territory, President Monroe ordered General Andrew Jackson to chase them back into Spanish Florida, and Jackson did so with great relish. Monroe gave this order to send American troops into foreign territory without consulting Congress. This doctrine of "hot pursuit" would, incidentally, be invoked by later presidents to justify certain military actions in Korea and Laos.[16] Andrew Jackson, however, behaved a good deal more cautiously as president than he did as general. During his administration, he ordered an armed American ship to South America to protect American ships there from Argentine raiders. Although he did so without first seeking congressional approval, he immediately went before Congress and asked for the "authority and means" to protect "our fellow citizens fishing and trading in these seas."[17] Both in this case and in future instances, Congress was apparently willing to allow presidents to commit American forces into situations where armed hostilities might result, provided that protection of American lives and property was the justification for doing so—a justification that would be subject to considerable abuse by future presidents.

Presidential War

It was during the presidency of James Polk that the first of several blows was struck against the war-making power of Congress. In an effort to provoke hostilities with Mexico, President Polk instructed General Zachary Taylor to proceed to Corpus Christi, Texas, and station his army there. Since Mexico regarded all of Texas as its own territory, this act constituted an obvious provocation. Mexico, however, showed restraint and declined to engage American forces at this point. In January 1846, Polk decided to goad the Mexicans still further and ordered Taylor's 3,000-man army to move to the Rio Grande. Not unexpectedly, Mexican soldiers attacked the Americans, whose presence they viewed as an invasion of their territory. Polk immediately asked Congress to recognize that a state of war now existed between the United States and Mexico.[18] This event clearly demonstrated that although Congress had the exclusive power to declare war, the president could nevertheless precipitate a set of circumstances that would make war unavoidable, thereby giving Congress little choice in the matter. Several members of Congress challenged the constitutionality of Polk's actions, with Congressman Abraham Lincoln among the president's most vocal critics. Indeed, two years later the House passed a vote of censure against Polk, but the Senate declined to go along with it.

Lincoln's perspective on the war-making power changed substantially once he ascended to the presidency. Without calling Congress into session, Lincoln ordered a naval blockade of the Confederacy. His authority to do so was ultimately challenged in the courts in a series of suits known as the *Prize* cases. It was argued that a naval blockade constituted an act of war under international law, and since Congress had not declared war in this instance, Lincoln had no authority to institute the blockade. The Supreme Court did not agree and instead ruled that an "invasion or insurrection created a state of war as legal fact," and thus the president did not have to wait for a congressional authorization before responding.[19] Lincoln's action has been cited as a precedent for presidential war making, but this claim is in error, for the Court specifically stated that such action could only be constitutional in times of invasion or rebellion. Lincoln never claimed that the right to take the nation into war was a routine power of the president. Rather, he repeatedly maintained that he was justified in exercising this power only because the very survival of the nation was at stake.

At the turn of the century, presidential actions further eroded the war-making power of Congress. In 1900, President William McKinley ordered 5,000 American soldiers to China to help put down the Boxer Rebellion. He alleged that the purpose of our intervention was to protect American lives and property, but in fact his motives were purely political. Although the approval of Congress was never sought by McKinley, Congress did not see fit to raise any objections, despite the fact that China promptly declared war on the United States. This event is significant because it marks the first time that an American president unilaterally committed troops to combat against another sovereign state outside of the Western Hemisphere.

The need to protect lives and property was also used by Theodore Roosevelt and Woodrow Wilson as a pretext for intervening militarily in the political affairs of several Caribbean countries without consulting Congress. Since most of Congress supported such actions, they chose not to dwell on their legality. Lyndon Johnson would resort to the same justification in 1965 when he sent 22,000 American soldiers to the Dominican Republic, although he admitted privately that the real reason for doing so was to avoid a communist takeover of its government.[20] The congressional war-making power suffered further setbacks during the presidency of Franklin Roosevelt. The boldness of his actions, however, may well have been encouraged by a Supreme Court decision in the *Curtiss-Wright* case, which was handed down at the end of his first term. The central issue in the case had no bearing at all upon the war-making power. On the contrary, it was concerned with the right of the president to regulate foreign commerce. After disposing of this immediate issue, however, the Court's majority opinion launched into a general discussion of the role of the president in foreign affairs, arguing that he had the right to exercise certain powers in this area, even though they were not specified in the Constitution. They contended that this *inherent authority* must be accorded the president in foreign affairs because only he had adequate knowledge in this area. Just exactly what these powers were the Court never made clear, but future presidents would draw on this inherent authority as one of their justifications for committing American troops to hostilities. Whether or not they were entitled to do so is open to serious question, since the issue in this Court case did not involve the war-making power and since the point at issue was not whether the president could act without congressional authorization, but rather whether Congress had the right to delegate to the president its own power to regulate foreign commerce.

Prior to our entry into the Second World War, President Roosevelt undertook several actions of doubtful constitutionality, the most dramatic of which was his "shoot at sight" order given to American naval forces convoying military materiel to a beleaguered Great Britain. This order grew out of a prior incident in which the U.S.S. *Greer* had two torpedoes fired at it by a German submarine while cruising in waters off the coast of Iceland. In relaying the news of this incident to Congress and the public, however, Roosevelt failed to note that the *Greer* was not cruising innocently off the coast of Iceland. On the contrary, it had been tailing a German U-boat and reporting its position to a British plane that was dropping depth charges from overhead.[21] Nor did Roosevelt volunteer that no injury had been done to either the ship or its personnel. Finally, he issued his order to attack German vessels without seeking any prior authorization from Congress; indeed, the formal declaration of war by Congress did not come until three months later, following the attack on Pearl Harbor. Thus, as one distinguished historian has noted, "from the date of the *Greer* incident, 4 September 1941, the United States was engaged in a *de facto* naval war with Germany on the Atlantic Ocean."[22] Roosevelt himself acknowledged that he was uncertain about the constitutionality of his order when he informed Congress that his actions "whether strictly legal or not were ventured upon under what appeared to be a popular demand and a public necessity; trusting then as now that Congress would readily ratify them."[23] Once again, Congress raised no objections.

It was under the presidency of Harry Truman that the congressional war-making power was dealt one of its severest blows. Two days after Truman was informed that the North Koreans had invaded South Korea, he ordered American air and naval forces to the area to support the South Koreans. Although he did indeed summon congressional leaders to the White House, it was not to seek their advice and consent but rather to inform them of the decision he had already made. The boldness of Truman's actions takes on greater significance when one considers, first, that Truman gave the order even before South Korea made any request for such assistance and, second, that the United States was not bound by any mutual defense pact to come to the aid of South Korea.[24] In fact, one year prior to the Korean conflict, the secretary of state did not even mention South Korea when discussing those countries in the Pacific that were deemed vital to our national security.[25] Finally, although the United Nations Security Council did pass a resolution recommending that armed force be used to repel the North Korean attack, this resolution came the day *after* Truman issued his order.[26]

Several days after his initial commitment of air and naval forces to the area, Truman made the decision to commit ground forces as well. In a meeting with congressional leaders to inform them of these developments, it was suggested that he ask Congress for a joint resolution giving approval to his actions. Truman replied that he would take this request under advisement, but after consulting with his aides he concluded that no such approval was necessary. Rather, he argued that his role as commander in chief provided him with the necessary authority to commit armed forces into combat.[27] Thus, for the first time in our history, a president of the United States was asserting that his responsibilities as commander in chief provided him with the constitutional authority to take the country into a major war against another sovereign state thousands of miles away from home. Although some members of Congress questioned Truman's authority in this regard, they were overwhelmed by the vast majority who acquiesced. Once again, Congress had willingly surrendered its constitutional authority to the president.

Given the more restrained view that Eisenhower took toward the powers of the presidency, it is not surprising that he sought advance congressional approval for committing American troops into combat. Thus, he asked for and received joint resolutions from Congress authorizing him to employ the armed forces to defend Formosa and the Pescadores and to thwart communist aggression in the Middle East.[28] One aspect of these resolutions, however, demonstrates how low had fallen Congress's concern for its war-making power. Prominent members of both the House and the Senate were, in fact, denying that Eisenhower even needed to seek congressional approval on these matters. Lyndon Johnson, who was Senate majority leader at the time, asserted that "we are not going to take responsibility out of the hands of the constitutional leader and try to arrogate it to ourselves."[29] In a similar vein, the Speaker of the House stated that "if the president had done what is proposed here without consulting with Congress, he would have had no criticism from me."[30] Such statements undoubtedly would have shocked the Founding Fathers.

Two years into his administration, President Kennedy found himself confronted with a grave crisis when he learned that the Soviet Union was in the process of installing missile bases in Cuba. He ordered American naval forces to set up a blockade around the island to prevent Soviet ships from reaching it. As he knew only too well, this action could have resulted in a military confrontation with the Russians on the high seas, one that could ultimately have led to a nuclear war. Yet he gave the order without any prior advice or consent from Congress. Unlike the other examples we have discussed in this chapter, however, here was a situation in which both secrecy and a swift response seemed a necessity. To have consulted Congress might well have denied Kennedy the opportunity to act with both dispatch and surprise. Congress agreed, although many argued that Kennedy had not acted forcefully enough.

We now consider an event in our history—the Vietnam War—that would ultimately force Congress to reassess the desirability of presidential encroachment upon its war-making power. This reconsideration grew not only out of the apparent futility of our policy in Vietnam but also out of the deception with which this policy had been undertaken. It was reported to Congress that in August 1964 two torpedoes were fired at the U.S.S. *Maddox* while it was cruising in the Gulf of Tonkin off the coast of North Vietnam. The secretary of defense stated that this attack was "deliberate and unprovoked."[31] At the request of President Johnson, Congress responded to this event by passing the Tonkin Gulf Resolution, authorizing the president "to take all necessary measures to repel any armed attack against the forces of the United States and to prevent further aggression." Only two members of Congress voted against the resolution. Not until several years later did Congress discover that the circumstances surrounding this incident may have been different from what they were told earlier. For example, Congress learned that the commander of the U.S.S. *Maddox* had sent the following cable back to the Defense Department immediately after the "incident":

> Review of action makes many recorded contacts and torpedoes fired appear doubtful. Freak weather effects and overeager sonarman may have accounted for many reports. No actual visual sitings by *Maddox*. Suggest complete evaluation before any further action.[32]

Yet despite the uncertainty of the situation as evidenced by the content of this cable, President Johnson ordered fifty bombing strikes against North Vietnam. Congress also learned later that the U.S.S. *Maddox* was not lying inoffensively in the waters of the Tonkin Gulf. On the contrary, it was a spy ship "collecting military intelligence and collaborating operationally with South Vietnamese patrol boats shelling the northern coast."[33] Had members of Congress been in possession of all this information when they considered the Gulf of Tonkin Resolution, they might well have withheld their approval of it. Unfortunately, however, at the time the incident allegedly took place, they had no source of information other than the president himself. This event highlights a point made earlier in this chapter—the information advantage the president enjoys in the area of foreign affairs. In this particular case, his monopoly of information allowed him to define the Tonkin Gulf incident as he wished.

Although Johnson did see fit to seek the approval of Congress for his actions, it seems clear that he did so for political rather than constitutional reasons. Four years after Congress passed the Gulf of Tonkin Resolution, he expressed the following view: "We stated then, and we repeat now, we did not think the resolution was necessary to what we did and what we're doing."[34] He based his action partly on precedents set by previous presidents and, more important, on the right of the president to repel a sudden attack. Although the Founding Fathers intended that presidents should be able to respond to a sudden attack, they clearly had in mind an attack upon the United States itself. The Johnson administration, however, was arguing that in this day and age the security of the United States could be threatened by events occurring thousands of miles away from our shores, in this case, Vietnam. In essence then, it appeared that a president could commit American troops to combat anywhere and at any time he thought the security of the United States was threatened. As one student of this subject has noted, "under this theory it is hard to see why any future President would ever see any legal need to go to Congress before leading the nation into war."[35]

Richard Nixon came into the presidency inheriting the Vietnam War from his predecessor, and his attempts to deal with it proved equally controversial. During the course of American troop reductions in Vietnam, he ordered American soldiers into the neighboring country of Cambodia to eliminate enemy sanctuaries there. It was his judgment that these sanctuaries were inhibiting the safe withdrawal of American soldiers. This decision to invade a neutral country with which we were not at war was made in the absence of any consultation with Congress either before or after the order was given. Nixon justified his actions on grounds that as commander in chief he had a responsibility to protect the lives of American men, a responsibility that superseded his obligation to Congress.

> In the modern world, there are times when the Commander in Chief . . . will have to act quickly. I can assure the American people that this President is going to bend over backward to consult the Senate and consult the House whenever he feels it can be done without jeopardizing the lives of American men. But when it is a question of the lives of American men or the attitudes of people in the Senate, I am coming down hard on the side of defending the lives of American men.[36]

This justification had a hollow ring to it, however, not only because the enemy sanctuaries had been in Cambodia for years but also because they had been largely evacuated by the time Nixon ordered the invasion.

Equally controversial was the president's decision to conduct bombing raids on Cambodia from March 1969 to May 1970. These raids, some 3,600 in all, were undertaken without any prior consultation with Congress. Indeed, Congress was not even informed after the fact. To ensure the absolute secrecy of these raids, records of the missions were burned in South Vietnam and radar officers were instructed to feed false statistics into the Pentagon's top-secret computer system. Since the enemy quite obviously knew that such raids were taking place, the inescapable conclusion was that this activity was being kept secret in order to prevent Congress and the public from finding out about it. When Congress finally did learn of the bombings two years later, this information came not from the Nixon administration, but rather from a radar operator who disclosed the operation to Senator William Proxmire.[37]

Equally puzzling was the fact that these bombing raids were accelerated in March 1973, after American forces had been withdrawn from Vietnam. Since the president's justification for these bombings in Cambodia was the protection of American troops, how could their continuance be justified when there were no longer any American soldiers there? In responding to queries by members of Congress on this question, one State Department official finally replied, "The justification is the reelection of President Nixon."[38] Thus, it appeared that if an individual could get himself elected to the presidency, he was free to do as he wished. The justification for presidential war making had finally reached its farthest point.

If President Nixon's actions could be challenged on constitutional grounds, so also could those of many other presidents. Where Nixon differed was not so much in what he did, but rather in the manner in which he did it. Franklin Roosevelt had at least acknowledged that his actions might be unconstitutional and thus asked Congress to approve them after the fact. Truman did not feel any constitutional responsibility to consult with Congress on going into Korea, but he did not keep any of our military actions secret from them. And even though Lyndon Johnson did not feel congressional approval was necessary for taking us into the Vietnam War, he asked for their approval anyway. President Nixon, however, sought the advice and consent of

Congress neither before nor after he committed American troops into hostilities thousands of miles from home. And with respect to the secret bombings in Cambodia, he chose not even to *inform* Congress after the fact.

Congress Reacts: The War Powers Resolution

Although the erosion of the congressional war-making power was a gradual process, it ultimately became complete. The Founding Fathers saw the role of commander in chief as nothing more than the "first general and first admiral" of the armed forces. Yet a succession of later presidents would expand upon this role until it was finally viewed as empowering presidents to lead the United States into major undeclared wars in various places around the world. If such actions were questionable on constitutional grounds, it is clear that presidents could not have undertaken them successfully if Congress had not been a willing accomplice. Indeed, only after our experience in Vietnam did Congress begin to reassess its own role and that of the president with regard to the war-making power. This reassessment led in 1973 to passage of legislation known as the War Powers Resolution. The major provisions of this act are summarized below.

1. The president *in every possible instance shall consult* with Congress before introducing United States Armed Forces into hostilities, or into situations where imminent involvement in hostilities is clearly indicated by the circumstances.
2. Within *forty-eight hours* after (1) introducing troops into hostilities or into a situation where hostilities are imminent, or (2) introducing troops into territory, airspace or waters of a foreign nation equipped for combat, or (3) substantially increasing troops equipped for combat already located in a foreign nation, the president shall *submit a report* to Congress explaining his actions.
3. Within *sixty days* after the report is submitted regarding the introduction of troops *into combat or into a situation where combat is imminent,* the president *shall terminate the use of such armed forces* unless Congress has: (a) declared war, or (b) extended the sixty-day period, or (c) cannot meet because of an armed attack upon the United States.
4. *Notwithstanding anything said* in the above provisions, *at any time* the United States Armed Forces are engaged in hostilities outside the United States *without a declaration of war or specific statutory authorization,* such forces *shall be removed by* the president if the *Congress so directs* by a concurrent resolution.[39] (This provision was ruled unconstitutional by the Supreme Court in 1983.)

Note that the president is not absolutely required to consult Congress before introducing armed forces into combat. Rather, he is to do so "in every *possible* instance." Whether or not it is "possible" will be left up to the president to decide. Furthermore, the term *consult* is not clearly defined in the act. Does it mean that he merely informs Congress, or is he to seek their advice? Of course, even if it is the latter, he is still free to ignore it. And exactly who within Congress is to be consulted should he choose to do so? In short, the War Powers Resolution now gives the president the legal authority to commit troops into hostilities without the prior approval of Congress. The reasons for doing so, however, are not without merit. First of all, Congress realized that under emergency conditions, a president may not have time to gain the approval of Congress. Second, they also recognized that the conditions surrounding the commitment of troops to combat are not likely to provide the necessary climate for careful evaluation. As stated earlier, the public is likely to unite behind the president at such times, and thus their support could possibly stampede Congress into giving its approval also. Congress was also aware that at the time of the initial crisis, they would have to rely almost exclusively upon the president for information. And as they learned from the Gulf of Tonkin incident, a president may not always be completely candid in apprising Congress of the circumstances surrounding a given crisis. Thus, rather than giving their initial approval on the basis of possible misinformation, they concluded that it would be better to let the president go ahead and commit troops on his own. Then, after Congress had had more time and more information with which to assess the situation, it would be able to render a more considered judgment concerning the president's actions.[40] The problems here, however, are whether or not Congress will be able to find alternative sources of information and whether it can do so before we become so deeply involved in hostilities that withdrawal is not possible.

Despite the flexibility provided to the president in the resolution, President Nixon decided to veto it. For one thing, he felt that it infringed upon his constitutional powers as commander in chief. In addition, he reasoned that the resolution could further inflame a conflict situation. On the one hand, the possibility that Congress might terminate hostilities at the end of sixty days would discourage an adversary from negotiating an end to the conflict prior to that time. On the other hand, the very presence of a deadline could itself foster an intensification of hostilities in order to achieve certain objectives before the deadline passed. Finally, Nixon maintained that having to consult Congress on the commitment of troops into a situation of imminent or actual combat would deny the president "a wide range of important peace-keeping tools by eliminating his ability to exercise quiet diplomacy backed by subtle shifts in our military deployments."[41]

The War Powers Resolution in Action

Before considering the circumstances under which the War Powers Resolution has come into play, it is necessary to examine the Supreme Court decision rendered in *Immigration and Naturalization Service v. Chadha* (1983). Although not directly related to the War Powers Resolution, this decision nevertheless had significant implications for one of its most important provisions. The case centered on the *legislative veto*—a power exercised by Congress since 1939. In order to ensure that the executive would implement laws as Congress intended, Congress has on more than two hundred occasions drafted statutes containing a legislative veto provision.[42] This type of veto may take several different forms. In some cases, for example, Congress has provided that an executive action could be vetoed if *either* house of Congress passed a resolution of *disapproval;* in other instances, if *both* houses passed a resolution of disapproval. In still another variation, Congress has drafted laws stipulating that executive action *could* be taken provided one or both houses passed resolutions of *approval.* Finally, in some cases, Congress has even limited the necessary approval or disapproval to a single committee of Congress. Opponents of the legislative veto, including presidents, have long questioned its constitutionality—in part because it allows Congress to legislate without according the president an opportunity to exercise his veto, and partly because it involves Congress in the implementation of laws, which, under our Constitution, is the responsibility of the executive branch.[43]

The Immigration and Nationality Act (1952) is one of the many statutes to which Congress attached a legislative veto provision. More specifically, this act authorized the attorney general to suspend deportation of aliens in cases of "extreme hardship," but it also stipulated that the attorney general's decision could be overturned if either house passed a resolution so ordering. In 1975 the House did in fact pass a resolution overturning the attorney general's decision to grant permanent residency to six aliens, including Jagdish Chadha. Chadha appealed his case all the way to the Supreme Court, arguing that Congress lacked constitutional authority to pass such a resolution. The Court agreed, stating that the resolution passed by the House constituted lawmaking without following the constitutionally mandated process for lawmaking—namely, approval by both houses of Congress and presentation to the president for his signature or veto.[44]

How then is this decision relevant to the War Powers Resolution? Note that Section 4 of the resolution states that, not withstanding any other provision within it, whenever American armed forces are engaged in hostilities outside the United States without a declaration of war or some other congressional authorization, they *shall be removed by the president if Congress so directs by a concurrent resolution.* In short, this provision enabled Congress to terminate hostilities even prior to the sixty-day limit contained in Section 3. But since a concurrent resolution is not sent to the president for his signature or veto, this provision also constituted a legislative veto and thus became null and void following the Supreme Court's ruling in the *Chadha* case.

Turning now to the War Powers Resolution in action, as of this writing presidents have committed troops abroad on more than thirty occasions since 1973. Some of the more notable instances include the following: evacuating some 400 Americans from Cyprus (1974); evacuating several thousand Americans and refugees from Da Nang, Phnom Penh, and Saigon (April 1975); rescuing the crew of the *Mayaguez* (1975); transporting European troops by plane into the country of Zaire (1976); evacuating some 1,400 Americans from Lebanon (1976); attempting to rescue 52 Americans held hostage by Iran (1980); joining a multinational peacekeeping force in Lebanon (1982); maintaining peace in Lebanon after the assassination of the Lebanese president and the massacre of Palestinians (1982); protecting some 1,000 Americans in Grenada and removal of a Cuban-backed revolutionary regime (1983); bombing Libya in retaliation for acts of terrorism (1986); providing military escorts for Kuwaiti oil tankers in the Persian Gulf (1987–1988); landing troops in Panama to protect American citizens and the canal (1989); commiting troops to the Gulf in order to remove Iraqi forces from Kuwait (1990–1991); commiting 30,000 troops to Somalia to protect relief efforts there (1992); bombing Iraq in retaliation for its refusal to comply with UN resolutions (1993); dispatching 300 troops to Macedonia as part of a UN peacekeeping force (1993); bombing Iraq in retaliation for the plot to assassinate former president George Bush (1993); directing retaliatory air strikes against Mohamed Farah Aideed in Somalia (1993); commiting air forces to Bosnia (1993); committing troops to Haiti as a peacekeeping force (1994); committing 8,000 ground troops to Bosnia as part of peacekeeping force (1996); directing Tomahawk missile strikes against Iraq following the killing of Kurds (1996); and committing 44,000 troops to the Gulf following Saddam Hussein's refusal to allow UN weapons inspections (1998); bombing terrorist sites in Afghanistan and Sudan (1998); bombing Iraq, following its refusal to permit full UN weapons inspections (1998).

Reporting.   With respect to the *reporting* provision of the War Powers Resolution, in only three of these incidents were no reports submitted by the president. Moreover, in two of these, a case can be made that the War Powers Resolution was not applicable. The American planes landing European troops in Zaire did so some one hundred miles from the fighting, and the military personnel evacuating Americans in Lebanon were unarmed.[45] On the other hand, the naval task force dispatched to rescue Americans in Cyprus was quite obviously armed, and it entered a situation where hostilities had already begun between the Greeks and Turks. Yet President Nixon submitted no report to Congress on his actions.[46] Although his failure to do so did not provoke any significant outcry from within Congress, Senator Thomas Eagleton characterized the president's behavior as a "glaring and serious omission of the law."[47]

Presidents have been reasonably conscientious about reporting to Congress on the commitment of troops; however, from the congressional perspective, the reports themselves have been less than satisfactory in two respects. First, no president has ever acknowledged the constitutionality of the War Powers Resolution.[48] Rather, in reporting to Congress each has justified his actions on the basis of his constitutional authority as commander in chief, noting also that his decision to inform Congress was out of choice and not pursuant to the War Powers Resolution. Thus, for example, when President Reagan committed troops to Lebanon, his report to Congress stated that "this deployment of the United States Armed Forces to Lebanon is being undertaken pursuant to the President's constitutional authority with respect to the conduct of foreign relations and as commander in chief of the United States Armed Forces." It went on to note that Reagan was informing Congress "in accordance with my desire that Congress be fully informed on this matter."[49] Similarly, when American aircraft downed four Serbian planes over Bosnia in 1994, President Clinton reported to Congress that the United States was participating "in these operations pursuant to my constitutional authority to conduct U.S. foreign relations and as Commander in Chief."[50]

Second, in their reports to Congress, presidents Ford, Carter, Reagan, and Bush did not always specify the circumstances under which they were committing troops (i.e., into actual or imminent hostilities; or into a foreign country equipped for combat; or to substantially increase troops already in a foreign country). The failure to specify circumstances is significant because the sixty-day time limit applies only if hostilities are occuring or are imminent. Not wanting to be subject to the time limit, these presidents declined to specify which one of the three circumstances characterized their commitment of troops.[51]

Consultation.   To the extent that presidential compliance with the *consultation* provision was questioned at all, it was in connection with the *Mayaguez* incident, the attempted rescue of hostages in Iran, the Grenada invasion, the bombing of Libya, and the commitment of American forces to Haiti and Bosnia.

In the course of rescuing the crew of the *Mayaguez,* there was every reason to believe that hostilities would ensue, as in fact they did. American planes bombed airfields and other military targets on the Cambodian mainland; three Cambodian gunboats were sunk; and forty-one American troops were killed. Shortly before he acted, President Ford informed twenty-one members of Congress that he intended to use some kind of force. Seventeen congressional leaders were also briefed after the operation began. Senate Majority Leader Mike Mansfield reflected the view of many congressional members, however, when he observed that "I was notified after the fact about what the administration had already decided to do."[52] But given the public jubilation following the safe return of the crew, Congress had little incentive to press the point. In the case of the hostage rescue, there was once again no prior consultation with Congress. Indeed, only Senate Majority Leader Robert Byrd was informed that some covert action would be taken, and he received this word only the day before the mission commenced. Carter's failure to consult brought only some mild rebuffs, however, as the chairman of the Senate Foreign Relations Committee expressed "regret that the President failed to consult congressional leaders prior to making a final decision" and the chairman of the House Foreign Affairs Committee remarked that "it was stupid on the part of the President not to consult with us."[53]

President Reagan consulted extensively with members of Congress prior to committing troops to Lebanon, but he followed the lead of his predecessors in taking military action against Grenada and Libya. Thus, the night before the invasion of Grenada, in which 18 American soldiers would be killed and another 116 wounded, five congressional leaders were called to the White House and told that the invasion would begin early the next morning. Commenting on the apparent low priority given to the views of the congressional leadership, then-Senator Charles Mathias observed that "congressional leaders were simply called to the Oval Office and told that the troops were under way. That was not consultation. The Prime Minister of Great Britain was advised about the invasion before the Speaker of the House of Representatives or the Majority Leader of the Senate."[54] The leadership fared no better on the Libyan bombing, having been summoned to the White House just three hours prior to the bombing and after American planes were already headed toward their targets.[55] In the aftermath of the Libyan bombing the chairman of the Senate Foreign Relations Committee, Richard Lugar (R-Ind.), called for the creation of a special eighteen-member "leadership committee" with whom the president would consult when considering military action. Other Republicans, however, believing that the president should have greater flexibility in responding to terrorism, introduced legislation exempting all military action against terrorists from coverage under the War Powers Resolution.[56]

In the four incidents described above, the presidents contended that the necessity for absolute secrecy precluded any prior consultation with Congress—a view that, incidentally, was shared by many members of Congress. Moreover, in the case of the hostage rescue, the Carter White House maintained that consultation was not required in any event because the mission was a humanitarian and not a military operation. This claim is certainly open to question, however, for there is evidence to suggest that had the rescue succeeded, the second and third stages of the operation called for taking military action against certain targets in Iran.[57]

With respect to sending American armed forces to Saudi Arabia, the initial commitment of some 150,000 troops was made by President Bush in August 1990, with the president noting that the troops constituted a defensive force. Since Congress was in recess at the time, no consultation took place. On November 16 the president announced, again without any prior consultation with Congress, that he was increasing the number of troops to half a million in order to provide the force with an "adequate offensive option." This significant step was also taken while Congress was in adjournment. Although a bipartisan committee of senior lawmakers had placed themselves at the president's disposal for any consultations during the adjournment, President Bush declined to seek their counsel, but did inform Senate Armed Services Committee Chairman Sam Nunn of his decision.[58] It is also worth noting here that in light of the volatile situation in the Gulf, the adjournment resolution itself empowered the congressional leadership to call Congress back into special session—an option that the leadership declined to exercise.[59]

While Clinton's decision not to consult Congress before his bombing of Iraq in 1993 drew little vocal criticism, rumblings were more apparent in connection with introducing troops into Haiti and Bosnia. Even here, however, there was more bluster than substance. As Clinton denied that he needed congressional authorization to commit forces into Haiti, Congress debated resolutions that would have required prior congressional authorization. All but one was voted down, however, and the other passed with nonbinding language.[60] Likewise, when the president committed air power to Bosnia in 1993, he initially stated that he welcomed congressional authorization but later asserted that ultimate authority to do so rested with him. There were once again attempts in Congress to pass legislation preventing the president from sending more troops to Bosnia, and from placing them under foreign command, but none of these efforts succeeded.[61]

As for Clinton's commitment of some 28,000 troops to the Gulf in February 1998 as a means of forcing Saddam Hussein to readmit UN weapons inspectors, the president declined to ask for congressional approval, asserting that Congress had already consented when it passed the Gulf War resolution in 1991. Members of Congress generally acknowledged this point but suggested that it would be wise politically to seek a resolution of support. Indeed, some members of Congress introduced such a resolution, but it never came to a vote. Initial enthusiasm for it quickly waned in the face of growing public doubt that a military strike against Hussein would achieve much.[62]

Sixty-Day Cutoff.   We come finally to that part of the War Powers Resolution requiring that at *the end of sixty days* the president shall *terminate the use of armed forces in combat or in situations where combat is imminent,* unless Congress has declared war or otherwise authorized their continuation, or else is unable to meet. Of the more than thirty occasions when presidents have committed troops abroad since 1973, this particular provision has become a subject of controversy in only three cases—the commitment of troops to Lebanon for the second time in late September 1982, the use of naval forces to escort Kuwaiti tankers in the Persian Gulf in 1987, and the commitment of troops into the Gulf in 1990.

As noted earlier, when President Reagan reintroduced troops into Lebanon, his report to Congress failed to specify the circumstances under which they were being committed. This omission was deliberate in order to avoid triggering the sixty-day deadline. Moreover, in public statements administration officials also contended that the sixty-day provision was not applicable in this instance because American marines were not in a situation where hostilities were occurring or were imminent. This claim, however, lost its persuasiveness on August 29, 1982, when several marines were killed. Angered by the president's attempt to circumvent the time limit, Senator Mathias introduced a resolution that called for starting the sixty-day clock on August 29. Aware that this resolution had broad support and wishing to avoid a constitutional showdown, the administration began to search for some kind of accommodation with Congress. The compromise finally reached related in part to the length of time American troops could be kept in Lebanon. The president had wanted Congress to pass a resolution allowing the troops to remain indefinitely. Congress rejected this suggestion, but the president pushed for and won congressional acceptance of an eighteen-month extension—a time period viewed as overly generous by several members of Congress. The other part of the compromise related to the signing of the resolution by the president. More specifically, even though Reagan would agree to sign the resolution, he would at the same time deny that he was bound by it. This disavowal was designed to avoid any implication that he regarded the War Powers Resolution as constitutional.[63] And indeed, after the resolution passed Congress and was sent to the president, Reagan signed it stating, "I do not and cannot cede any of the authority vested in me under the Constitution as Commander-in-Chief. . . . Nor should my signing be viewed as any acknowledgement that the president's constitutional authority can be impermissably infringed by statute."[64] Some members of Congress saw the president's disavowal, along with the lengthy extension (eighteen months), as a defeat for the War Powers Resolution. But others felt Reagan's actions were more important than his words, for in signing the resolution he was implicitly acknowledging the validity of the War Powers Resolution. Probably the most accurate assessment of this whole episode came from Secretary of State Shultz, who observed that the compromise was "an effort to put that [constitutional] issue aside for the time being."[65]

Five years later, Reagan and Congress again locked horns over the time-clock provision of the War Powers Resolution. In July 1987 the president decided to dispatch 15,000 troops to the Persian Gulf to provide safe passage to Kuwaiti oil tankers caught in the middle of the Iran-Iraq war. Once more, he refused to state that American forces were being committed into a situation of actual or imminent hostilities. Moreover, he would continue to maintain this fiction despite that fact that during the Navy's stay of many months in the Persian Gulf, it entered into hostilities with Iranian vessels seven different times, each of which was reported to Congress by President Reagan. These confrontations included the seizing of an Iranian landing craft, during which three Iranian sailors were killed and twenty-six captured, and the shelling of two Iranian oil rigs in retaliation for a Silk Worm missile attack on a Kuwaiti tanker. Although Reagan's behavior irritated many in Congress, legislation proposed in the Senate to terminate funds for the Persian Gulf operation failed to pass, as did repeated efforts to trigger the War Powers Resolution. That a Senate majority could not be mustered to support these measures did not signal approval of Reagan's action as much as it did a reluctance to renege on a presidential commitment to Kuwait. Finally, Senate Majority Leader Robert Byrd fashioned a compromise measure that essentially sidestepped the War Powers Resolution. It called for the president to report to Congress on the Persian Gulf operation sixty days after the legislation passed. Thirty days after his report, Congress would then consider whether to continue or terminate the presence of U.S. naval forces in the Persian Gulf. Note that this measure required legislation by Congress in order to terminate and thus would be subject to a presidential veto, whereas the War Powers Resolution automatically triggers termination at the end of sixty or ninety days, unless Congress otherwise authorizes continuance. Although this legislation passed the Senate, the House deferred action, pending a suit filed by 110 House Democrats asking the U.S. district court to order the president to comply with the War Powers Resolution. Both this court and a U.S. court of appeals dismissed the case, however, arguing that it was a nonjusticiable political dispute. Byrd's legislation, meanwhile, languished in the House and never came up for a vote.[66]

Like his predecessors, when President Bush placed the first installment of troops in Saudi Arabia, he asserted that these forces were not in imminent danger, thereby avoiding the triggering of the sixty-day time limit. This proved to be a rather curious assertion given that one month later he informed the Iraqi people that our two nations were "on the brink of war" and also certified that troops stationed in Saudi Arabia qualified for "imminent danger" pay.[67] It was not until the president raised the troop level to nearly 500,000 in order to achieve an "offensive option" that members of Congress decided to act. More specifically, fifty-six members filed suit in federal court asking it to order the president to refrain commencing combat unless he first received the approval of Congress.[68] In the meantime, the UN Security Council passed a resolution authorizing the use of force against Iraq if it did not withdraw from Kuwait by January 15, 1991. Moreover, in testimony before congressional committees both Bush's secretary of state and his secretary of defense asserted that the president needed no authorization from Congress to initiate military action.[69]

Although the suit filed by members of Congress was turned down in federal court on the grounds that it had not been brought by a majority of the congressional membership, nevertheless on January 8, 1991, President Bush did finally ask Congress to authorize the use of force. Congress provided that authorization in a resolution that passed comfortably in the House (250 to 183) but only narrowly in the Senate (52 to 47). Even while Congress was debating the resolution, however, the president continued to assert that he did not think it necessary: "I don't think I need [a resolution from Congress]. . . . I feel I have the full authority to fully implement the United Nation's resolutions."[70] Several months later when speaking at Princeton University he stated: "I feel after studying the question that I had inherent power to commit our forces to battle after the UN resolution."[71] That his role as commander in chief provided him with such authority is, as noted earlier in this chapter, highly dubious on constitutional grounds. Equally dubious was the claim that the UN resolution authorizing force provided him with the authority to act without congressional approval. The very legislation Congress passed committing the United States to the UN Charter stated that any commitment of American forces under the auspices of the United Nations would be subject to the approval of Congress.[72]

The Gulf War constituted the largest military undertaking by the United States since the Vietnam War and passage of the War Powers Resolution. Although the president asserted that he needed no authorization from Congress for such a massive commitment of forces, the fact remains that he did ask for it. That he did so, some might argue, represents a victory for Congress in reasserting its constitutional role in war making. Such a conclusion, however, is not fully warranted. President Bush, after all, committed close to 500,000 troops to Saudi Arabia in the absence of either consultation or authorization from Congress. In doing so, he placed Congress in the position where it had little choice but to authorize the use of force when Bush finally requested it—a point stressed repeatedly by members of Congress as they debated the resolution of approval.[73]

Conclusion.   Although there have been grumblings in the legislature over the degree of presidential compliance with the War Powers Resolution, Congress has thus far shown no inclination to go to the mat over the issue, particularly with respect to the reporting and consultation provisions. To be sure, Congress did assert itself when President Reagan attempted to circumvent the sixty-day time clock in connection with the commitment of troops in Lebanon, but even here the lengthy extension given the president essentially gave him a free hand. And when the same issue reared its head again during the Persian Gulf operation to protect Kuwaiti oil tankers, the Senate chose to pass legislation that, in contrast to the War Powers

Resolution, would have made it more difficult for Congress to terminate hostilities there. Finally, the response by the majority of Congress to the president's commitment of troops to Saudi Arabia in both August and November 1991 can only be characterized as tepid right up until the time they were asked to approve the use of force.

The reluctance of Congress to take a firmer stand vis-à-vis the War Powers Resolution may be explained in part by continuing congressional ambivalence over what its role should be in committing American forces into combat. It is worth recalling here that prior to final passage in 1973, the War Powers Resolution had been defeated by Congress on two previous occasions. Moreover, as has been noted by former Speaker of the House Carl Albert, the required votes to override President Nixon's veto of the resolution were obtained primarily because the resolution was presented for override just four days after the Saturday Night Massacre—one of the most controversial acts of the Nixon presidency.[74] The circumstances surrounding events such as the Libyan bombing and the invasion of Panama, on the one hand, and hostage rescue in Iran, on the other, suggest another reason for congressional ambivalence. If a president takes swift, limited military action and it succeeds (Libyan bombing, Panama invasion), the public approval that follows will likely discourage any vigorous objection from Congress, regardless of any doubts it may have about the legality of such action. And even if such action fails (the hostage rescue) but the public supports the attempt nevertheless, Congress is not likely to call the president to account. All of which is to suggest that presidents will be most vulnerable to congressional rebuke when their action is floundering or failing and lacks public support as well. The commitment of American troops to Somalia in 1993 is instructive in this regard.

With thousands of Somalians dying of hunger as a result of both famine and a breakdown of order within their country, George Bush in December 1992 committed American forces to Somalia as part of an international humanitarian effort. The troops were to assist in the delivery of food to a starving population, but were not to become involved in the country's internal political struggles. Under the Clinton administration, however, and with UN backing, the mission gradually changed as U.S. forces now began bombing a radio station and storage facilities of Mohamed Fara Aideed—a political strongman believed responsible for killing twenty-three Pakistani UN peacekeepers in Somalia. Soon American forces became involved in hunting down Aideed, as administration officials voiced their belief that a new political order must be created within the country. This mission creep alarmed members of Congress, as did the growing number of American soldiers being killed. In a battle with Aideed forces in October 1993, eighteen Army Rangers died and dozens were wounded. This, combined with public revulsion over the spectacle of seeing a naked, dead American soldier dragged through the streets of Mogadishu, created irresistible pressure for Congress to act. On the floor of the Senate, Appropriations Committee Chairman Robert Byrd (D-W.Va.) demanded that the president "Bring them home."[75] Although the Clinton administration was able to beat back an amendment attached to a defense appropriations bill requiring an immediate withdrawal of troops, the president reluctantly agreed to a March 31 deadline and was forced as well to greatly narrow the mission of U.S. forces there.

In this confrontation between the two branches, Congress did not resort to any provision of the War Powers Resolution. Rather, it asserted itself by using the power of the purse, namely, threatening to cut off funds for the Somalia operation unless the president agreed to a withdrawal date.[76]

☆ TREATIES AND EXECUTIVE AGREEMENTS

The Founding Fathers sought to involve both the executive and legislative branches of government in treaty making. They felt that if the president were not involved, he would not enjoy sufficient respect among foreign governments. They also believed that treaties would often have to be negotiated with secrecy and dispatch, and these were conditions that could be better met by the president than by Congress. At the same time, however, the Founding Fathers recognized the possibility that a president might be corrupted by foreign governments, and thus they decided that the Senate should both advise and consent to treaties negotiated by him.[77]

George Washington at first appears to have taken seriously the advising role of the Senate, on one occasion making a personal appearance before it to seek advice on pending negotiations with the southern Indians and on another going so far as to ask the Senate to approve as well as instruct a team of negotiators. When it came time to negotiate the Jay Treaty (1794) with the British, however, his enthusiasm for consultation had waned, for the Senate played no advisory role either prior to or during the negotiations. Although there have been subsequent presidents who sought to involve the Senate by including some of its members on the negotiating team or by inviting them to participate as observers, presidents have just as frequently ignored the Senate until the ratification stage. Not surprisingly, therefore, several presidents have watched with embarrassment as the Senate made significant changes in their draft treaties or, as with the Treaty of Versailles, failed to approve them at all.[78]

If the historic role of the Senate in the ratification process cannot be characterized as one of rubber-stamping the president's treaty drafts, the more assertive posture assumed by Congress in the post-Vietnam era has nevertheless caused the Senate to pursue its treaty responsibilities with added vigor. President Carter, for example, having decided to establish full diplomatic relations with mainland China, agreed to the Peking demand that the United States withdraw its formal recognition of Taiwan. This withdrawal included terminating a 1958 mutual defense pact between the United States and Taiwan. Although a provision in the treaty did provide that either party could terminate the agreement, President Carter undertook to do so without any prior consultation with the Senate. Convinced that Senate consent was required, Senator Barry Goldwater and several others decided to bring suit against the president. A U.S. district court judge ruled that both the president and the Senate must share in the decision to terminate a treaty, but he dismissed the case because the Senate had not formally expressed an opinion on the president's authority in this area.[79] As the case was making its way up to the Supreme Court, the Senate passed a resolution stating that the president lacked the authority to take such action unilaterally. In the final analysis, however, the Supreme Court declined to hear the case, apparently wishing to avoid entangling itself in a dispute between the other two branches.[80] Yet Congress was ultimately able to exact its pound of flesh from the president, for portions of the recognition agreement with China required implementing legislation. In the course of its deliberations on this legislation, Congress inserted a statement that noted that any attempt by China to resolve its dispute with Taiwan by force would be viewed as a "threat to the peace and security of the Western Pacific and of grave concern to the U.S." The Carter administration fought to have this statement removed, since Peking regarded its dispute with Taiwan as a purely internal matter, not subject to interference by any outside party. The president finally acquiesced to the statement, however, when it became apparent that the legislation would not pass otherwise.

The Senate proved to be equally contentious when faced with ratification of the Panama Canal treaties. Not only was its debate one of the longest in the history of treaty ratifications, but during the course of the debate, close to half the Senate membership journeyed to Panama to discuss the treaty provisions with government officials there. Indeed, this unprecedented degree of involvement by the membership caused foreign governments to wonder who was empowered to negotiate treaties— the president or the Senate. By the time the Senate voted to ratify the treaties, it had proposed 192 changes (145 amendments, 26 reservations, 18 understandings, and 3 declarations), some of which were incorporated into the ratification resolution.[81]

Although the Panama Canal treaties were inherently controversial, the task of securing ratification was undoubtedly rendered more difficult by President Carter's failure to consult more fully with the Senate as the negotiations proceeded. In the words of his deputy secretary of state Warren Christopher, "We should have brought the Senate leadership in much sooner."[82] Having learned from this experience, the Carter administration wisely decided to involve the Senate more directly in negotiations with the Soviets on the Second Strategic Arms Limitation Treaty (SALT II). The president's chief negotiator, Paul Warnke, asked the Speaker of the House and the president of the Senate to appoint several "advisers" from Congress to observe the negotiations and consult with the American negotiating team between sessions. In addition, a special twenty-three member Senate SALT Group was created to help make the administration's case for ratification, and the White House consulted with certain key senators as the negotiations progressed. During the course of these consultations, various senators prevailed upon the administration to make seven substantive changes in its negotiating positions. Moreover, as a condition for their support, three key senators insisted that the president publicly commit himself to seeking development of a new weapons system, the MX missile.[83] In the end, of course, the fate of SALT II was determined not on the merits of the treaty itself, but rather by events. More specifically, as the Senate debated the treaty, the Soviet Union embarked upon a full-scale invasion of Afghanistan; recognizing that this action would kill any chance for passage, the president decided to withdraw the treaty from consideration.

Two historic treaties were ratified during the second term of the Clinton presidency. One, which provided for the expansion of NATO to include Poland, Hungary, and the Czech Republic, had widespread support in the Senate and passed easily. The Chemical Weapons Convention, on the other hand, was quite another matter. Prohibiting the production and use of chemical weapons, this controversial treaty had been signed by President Bush and submitted to the Senate for ratification by President Clinton in 1993. Not until 1997, however, did the Senate give its blessing, and as a condition for doing so, Clinton had to make a number of concessions to the Republican-controlled Senate. He agreed to twenty-eight of the thirty-three conditions that Republicans wanted attached to the treaty and also promised to submit for Senate approval changes in two existing treaties—one on antiballistic missiles and the other on conventional forces in Europe—both of which changes the Clinton adminstration had previously argued were technical in nature and thus did not require Senate approval.[84]

Executive Agreements

Agreements with foreign governments have not been arrived at solely through treaties. Indeed, since the time of George Washington, such arrangements have also been made through what have come to be known as *executive agreements*. These are agreements made by the president of the United States with a foreign government. Although they enjoy the same *legal* status as treaties under international law, they do *not* have to be ratified by the Senate. Note, however, that if the appropriation of funds is necessary in order to implement the provisions of a given executive agreement, then Congress must approve such an agreement, as it did in 1993 with both the North American Free Trade Agreement (NAFTA) and the General Agreement on Tariffs and Trade (GATT).

The right of a president to enter into such agreements was never entirely clear. In 1817, for example, James Monroe made an executive agreement with the British that was designed to reduce the number of American and British naval forces on the Great Lakes. He asked Congress whether or not he had the right to make such an agreement, but Congress never provided him with an answer. They simply gave their approval and then one year later formalized the agreement by a treaty. The president's right to make such agreements was firmly established in 1937 by a Supreme Court ruling in the *Belmont* case. This decision, unfortunately, did not do much to resolve the confusion over what matters were appropriate for negotiation by treaty on the one hand and executive agreement on the other.[85]

As Table 2-2 indicates, over the years treaties have gradually been replaced by executive agreements. Most of these agreements have been routine and noncontroversial in nature, dealing with such matters as, for example, food deliveries, customs enforcements, international radio regulations, and the maintenance of lights in the Red Sea. Others, however, have dealt with matters of great moment. Some presidents have viewed the executive agreement as a device for the accomplishment of ends that they knew would be rejected if submitted in the form of a treaty. Thus, in 1844, President Tyler sought the annexation of Texas through a treaty that, though it had the support of a majority of the senators, was rejected because the vote fell short of the two-thirds majority necessary for ratification. Undeterred, he merely recast the treaty as an executive agreement and asked both houses of Congress to implement it by passing a joint resolution—a procedure that requires only a simple majority vote. Congress complied. Franklin Roosevelt provides another dramatic example of a president using an executive agreement to circumvent the treaty process. In desperate need of military assistance in the fight against Hitler, Prime Minister Churchill asked for fifty old American destroyers, in return for which he would give us several naval bases in the Caribbean. At the very least, such a deal required some kind of authorizing legislation from Congress, because two statutes then on the books prohibited such a disposition of our military equipment. Moreover, it can well be argued that a treaty was the appropriate instrument for such an agreement, given the fact that our military assistance to the British would alter our status of neutrality in the conflict. Roosevelt, however, correctly perceived that the isolationist mentality then pervasive throughout the country would prevent Congress from giving any kind of approval to the exchange.[86] Accordingly, he finalized the deal in the form of an executive agreement. More recently, Jimmy Carter, taking a cue from some of his predecessors,

TABLE 2-2   Treaties and Executive Agreements, 1798–1998

Period	Treaties	Executive Agreements
1789–1839	60	27
1839–1889	215	238
1889–1939	524	917
1940–1970	310	5,653
1971–1977	110	2,062
1978–1983	114	1,999
1984–1988	65	1,890
1989–1993	84	1,606
1994–1998	147	1,372

Sources: The President and Congress: Power and Policy by Louis Fisher, p. 45. Copyright © 1972 by The Free Press. Reprinted with permission of The Free Press, a division of Simon & Schuster Inc. Figures for 1971–1998 provided by Department of State, Washington, D.C.

indicated that if the Senate emasculated or rejected the SALT II treaty, he would change it to an executive agreement and ask Congress to implement it by a simple majority vote in both houses.[87]

Not only have some presidents used the executive agreement to make an end run around the treaty process, but in some instances they have not even informed Congress as to the content of these agreements. Although Congress passed a law in 1950 requiring the secretary of state to publish annually all executive agreements entered into during the previous year, the executive branch has in fact withheld those agreements that it considered sensitive to our national security.[88] The impact of such secret agreements was impressed upon Congress when they were told that our commitment to the South Vietnamese grew in part out of executive agreements made between American presidents and the South Vietnamese government.[89] This startling revelation persuaded Congress to set up a special committee in 1969 to investigate the nature of American commitments abroad reached through executive agreements. The investigation turned up several important commitments of which Congress was not previously aware. These commitments included American military support for the Ethiopian army, apparent commitments to the defense of Thailand and the Philippines, and a commitment to defend the Franco regime in Spain against *internal* uprisings.[90] Perhaps most startling of all was the revelation that, as a result of agreements reached between the executive branch and the Laotian government, the United States had been secretly assisting the government of Laos in fighting communist insurgents in that country since 1964. This assistance took the form of the training of Laotian soldiers by American advisers, as well as bombing raids by American planes against communist insurgents in Laos.[91]

Congress Reacts: The Case Act (1972)

The chairman of the House International Relations Committee voiced the growing concern among members of Congress that the legislative branch had been excluded from participating in decisions involving major American commitments: "In recent years Presidents of both parties have resorted increasingly to executive agreements in place of treaties, involving the United States in far-reaching commitments abroad.

This practice has abridged Congress's foreign affairs power under the Constitution."[92] In an attempt to achieve some control in this area, Congress passed the Case Act, which was signed into law by the president in 1972. The provisions of this act require that the president transmit all executive agreements to Congress within sixty days after they have been negotiated. It states further that Congress must be informed of all executive agreements in effect at the time this act was passed. However, only the House International Relations Committee and the Senate Foreign Relations Committee need to be informed of secret executive agreements. Several members of Congress did not think this act went far enough. Senator Sam Ervin, for example, thought Congress should also have the power to reject any agreement that it found unacceptable and introduced a bill to that effect. His bill did not receive much support, however, because President Nixon made it clear that he would veto any bill containing such a provision.

Whether or not the Case Act has accomplished its purpose is open to serious question. The major weakness of the act was its failure to define what it was in fact attempting to control, namely, executive agreements. The consequence of this omission is that the executive branch has informed Congress only of those accords that fall under its own definition of executive agreements. Thus, in 1975, Congressman Les Aspin of Wisconsin estimated that since the Case Act was passed, the executive branch had entered into between four hundred and six hundred accords with foreign governments, none of which had been reported to Congress.[93] The most dramatic recent example of such an accord was President Nixon's letter to President Thieu of South Vietnam in which he stated that the United States would "respond with full force should the settlement (the Paris Peace Agreement) be violated by North Vietnam."[94] Senator Clifford Case, author of the Case Act, contended that this secret commitment by President Nixon constituted an international agreement that should have been transmitted to Congress.[95] Nixon's failure to do so proved extremely embarrassing to the United States, for Congress ultimately refused to provide the South Vietnamese government with additional assistance after North Vietnam's renewed invasion of the South in 1975.

In the past, several proposals have been introduced in Congress that are designed to correct the most fundamental weaknesses of the Case Act. These proposals not only seek to clarify what constitutes an executive agreement but also provide that Congress may, if it wishes, reject such agreements within sixty days after they have been concluded. Any legislation along these lines, however, is likely to face stiff opposition from the president. Presidents have argued with some justification that they cannot be effective negotiators if they are denied the right to make firm commitments with foreign governments. They also point out that delicate compromises might well come undone while waiting for Congress to approve or reject such agreements.[96]

★ THE CIA AND FOREIGN POLICY

Only in the last twenty years has it become generally known how important the Central Intelligence Agency (CIA) is as an arm of presidential foreign policy. Revelations have shown, for example, that much of the United States involvement in the secret war in Laos was coordinated by the Central Intelligence Agency.[97] The CIA also engaged in assassination attempts against heads of foreign governments, with Fidel Castro among those targeted for elimination. In Chile, the CIA sought to destabilize the Marxist government of President Salvador Allende by supporting various groups within the country who were opposed to him.[98] Whether or not any or all of these activities constitute legitimate goals of American foreign policy has been the subject of considerable debate both in and outside of government. Legitimate or not, however, these activities are of such magnitude and gravity that Congress has concluded they ought to be informed of them. That they have lacked such knowledge in the past is due both to their own laxity and to the nature of the activities themselves.

The Central Intelligence Agency was created under a provision of the National Security Act of 1947. While this act did not foresee that the CIA would perform any activity other than intelligence gathering, the vague wording of the legislation was used by the CIA as a justification for expanding its role to include military and political interventions in other countries.[99] Congress also saw fit to pass legislation in 1949 exempting the CIA from disclosing to Congress information that is normally required of all other agencies. Specifically, the CIA was not required to divulge information regarding the organization of the agency, its functions, or the number of people it employed. Furthermore its budget was not made public, nor was it made available to most of Congress. Rather, its annual budget requests were to be concealed in the budget requests of other agencies. Finally, the agency was also exempted from statutory limits on spending. Following the recomendation of a special commission, President Clinton did decide to reveal the overall 1998 budget figure for all intelligence organizations in the government but not the amount earmarked for any specific organization.[100]

All this is not to say that Congress completely surrendered its control over the activities and budget of the CIA. In theory, two subcommittees in the Senate and two in the House were charged with overseeing the activities of the agency. In reality, these four subcommittees did not prove very effective in monitoring the activities of the CIA. In part, this ineffectiveness resulted because information on many CIA operations was relayed only to the subcommittee chairmen, who were usually highly sympathetic to the agency and did not inform the rest of their subcommittee membership of the more controversial activities undertaken by the CIA.[101] In addition, these subcommittees had very few staff workers attached to them, and consequently systematic oversight of the agency was not possible.[102]

In response to revelations regarding the CIA's secret political and military activities, Congress passed the Hughes-Ryan Amendment in 1974.

> This legislation stated that no money could be spent by or on behalf of the Central Intelligence Agency for operations in foreign countries, other than activities intended *solely for obtaining necessary intelligence,* unless and until the president finds that each such operation is important to the *national security* of the United States and *reports, in a timely fashion,* a description and scope of such operation to the appropriate committees of Congress. (Emphases added.)[103]

The amendment also provided that two more committees, the House International Relations Committee and Senate Foreign Relations Committee, now be informed of CIA activities. In the judgment of many, this legislation was not adequate because of the stipulation that the president must inform Congress *in a timely fashion* of those CIA activities that go beyond foreign intelligence gathering. This phrase was never clearly defined, and the president and the CIA interpreted it to mean that Congress need not be informed of these activities until after they had already taken place.[104]

In the years 1975 to 1977, the CIA was subjected to intense scrutiny by both the executive and legislative branches. In 1975, President Ford created a special commission to inquire into the agency's activities. Based upon its recommendations, he issued an executive order in February 1976 prohibiting the CIA from engaging in further assassination plots. In addition, he established the Intelligence Oversight Board, composed of civilians who were charged with monitoring the activities of the CIA. Shortly after assuming office, President Carter ordered his own review of U.S. intelligence operations and subsequently made several sweeping changes through a series of executive orders. First, in order to ensure greater coordination and accountability, he gave the director of the CIA responsibility for all U.S. intelligence operations (Defense Intelligence Agency; National Security Agency; the intelligence divisions of the Army, Navy, and Air Force; the FBI's counterintelligence unit; and the Department of Energy's research and development unit). The CIA director was charged with preparing the budgets of the entire intelligence community and given the authority to assign tasks to all intelligence units except those housed in the Department of Defense. The latter would remain under the authority of the secretary of defense. Carter also ordered other changes designed to increase oversight of the intelligence community. The attorney general was given the authority to veto covert CIA activities directed against American citizens living at home or abroad. This was designed to check the use of such clandestine practices as electronic surveillance and the opening of mail. Carter decided to retain the Intelligence Oversight Board created by President Ford, but established as well a Special Coordination Committee within the National Security Council. Chaired by the president's adviser for national security affairs, this committee has responsibility for assessing the CIA's operations and its methods of gathering information. Finally, Carter reaffirmed the right of the Senate and House intelligence committees to be supplied with any information they might request from the CIA. Nothing was said, however, about informing the appropriate congressional committees of covert CIA operations in advance of their occurrence.

Efforts to make the CIA more accountable came from Congress as well as the White House. Both the House and the Senate conducted separate inquiries into the agency's activities and concluded that Congress must make a more concerted effort to monitor intelligence operations. Accordingly, a new Select Committee on Intelligence was established in both the Senate and the House. Moreover, in order to minimize the possibility that the membership might be co-opted by the agency, service was limited to eight years on the Senate committee and six years on the House committee. Both committees were empowered to demand information from the various intelligence agencies, compel testimony, review budgets, and receive reports. In addition, the Senate committee was given a staff of fifty people, and the House committee a staff of twenty-two. This represented a substantially greater commitment of resources than Congress was willing to make in the past.

In the aftermath of this initial burst of reform, debate persisted on what should be the proper role of Congress in overseeing CIA activities. Some members of Congress continued to maintain that the nebulous wording of the Hughes-Ryan Amendment should be replaced by new legislation that would unequivocally require the agency to give Congress prior notice of covert undertakings. Others, however, were beginning to feel that the agency had been unduly shackled by Congress and that it was time to rethink some of these restrictions. This latter view was fed in part by world developments. With terrorism on the rise, a major foreign policy setback in the Middle East (i.e. the toppling of the Shah of Iran), and Soviet probings in Africa and the Caribbean, the U.S. position in the world seemed increasingly precarious. In addition, the president and the CIA were complaining that the secrecy of covert actions was greatly jeopardized by the necessity of having to inform eight different congressional committees—some fifty members of Congress—of such activities. Indeed, CIA Director Stansfield Turner testified that he had canceled several highly sensitive covert operations rather than report them to the eight committees and thereby run the risk of a leak.[105]

In an effort to accommodate concerns voiced on both sides of this issue, Congress passed the Accountability for Intelligence Activities Act. Signed into law by President Carter in October 1980, this act (1) terminated the Hughes-Ryan Amendment; (2) reduced to two the number of committees that must be informed of covert actions—the House and Senate inelligence committees; (3) required that these committees be kept "fully and currently informed of all U.S. intelligence activities"; (4) stipulated that these committees cannot veto an intelligence operation reported to it; (5) provided that if the president concludes that the vital interests of the country are at stake, he may restrict prior notice to the chairperson and ranking minority members of the Senate and House intelligence committees, the Speaker and minority leaders of the House, and the Senate majority and minority leaders; (6) stipulated that if the president, for extraordinary reasons, is not able to give prior notice even to these eight individuals, he must report to the appropriate committees in "timely fashion," stating what the operation was and why he was not able to give prior notice; and (7) required the president to report in "timely fashion" any significant illegal intelligence activity or failure, as well as any corrective measures taken or contemplated by him.[106]

A careful reading of these provisions reveals that the president is accorded considerable freedom of action in the area of covert operations. He continues to be the final arbiter of when it is possible to give Congress advance notification, and, even when he does so, the two oversight committees cannot veto the operation reported to them. That Congress approved these provisions is understandable, however. First, there may in fact be occasions when the press of events will not permit the president to give advance notice; second, any legislation that had provided a congressional veto of covert operations would almost certainly have been vetoed by President Carter as an unconstitutional interference with his role as commander in chief. But Congress did not come away from this new act empty-handed, for it is clearly stated that the president would normally be required to provide Congress with advance notification of any covert operations contemplated by the CIA. This represented a significant change from previous legislation, which merely obligated the president to report covert undertakings in a "timely fashion." Or so it seemed.

In reality, this act has not always operated as Congress had intended. During the Reagan administration there were frequent complaints that CIA Director William Casey was less than forthcoming in providing information to Congress on covert operations. As one member of the House Intelligence Committee wryly observed, "If you were talking to Casey, and your coat caught on fire, he wouldn't tell you about it unless you asked."[107] Early in 1984, for example, the CIA embarked upon a covert operation involving the mining of Nicaraguan ports as a means of exerting further pressure on that country's Marxist regime. Casey informed the House Intelligence Committee, but his references to the operation before that committee were so oblique as to be meaningless. In fact, not until it was reported in the press some two months later did the Senate Intelligence Committee learn of the mission. Angered by this lack of candor, the committee chairman, Barry Goldwater, wrote Casey expressing his displeasure. The letter, which Goldwater released to the press, minced no words: "All this past weekend, I've been trying to figure out how I can most easily tell you my feelings about the discovery of the president having approved mining some of the harbors of Central America. It gets down to one little simple phrase: I am pissed off."[108] Having been summoned before the Senate Intelligence Committee and chastised for his behavior, Casey pledged that henceforth he would inform the committee of covert operations no later than forty-eight hours after their occurrence.[109] Meanwhile, revelations about the mining operation, combined with general skepticism over growing U.S. military involvement in Nicaragua, prompted Congress to pass legislation cutting off all military aid to the anticommunist Nicaraguan rebels.

The strains between the Reagan administration and Congress over covert operations did not end with the mining of Nicaraguan ports. In what proved to be the most controversial policy decision of his presidency, Reagan in January 1986 issued a secret executive order authorizing the CIA to sell American arms to the Iranian government. Allegedly, the purpose of this policy was to improve relations with moderate factions there, but in reality the arms were to be traded for the release of Americans held hostage in Lebanon. More important, in his executive order the president instructed the CIA director to withhold notification of this covert operation from Congress. In fact, not until some ten months later were the congressional intelligence committees briefed on the arms sales, and then only because reports had already surfaced in the press. Although the Accountability for Intelligence Activities Act allows the president to withhold "prior notice" for extraordinary reasons, he must report to the appropriate congressional committees in a "timely fashion," stating what the covert action was and why he was not able to give prior notice. Members of Congress understandably argued that in delaying notification for a full ten months, the president was violating the "timely fashion" reporting requirement. Reagan, on the other hand, exploiting the ambiguity of this phrase, maintained that it was up to him to determine what constituted timely notice.[110] In retrospect, of course, the president would have been better served had he provided advance notice to the intelligence committee, for they would surely have raised the same strenuous objections ultimately voiced by most members of Congress and the American public. This input may in turn have forced the administration to reconsider the wisdom of such an undertaking, thereby avoiding what is generally regarded as the major foreign policy blunder of the Reagan presidency.

In view of Reagan's excessive delay in reporting to congressional intelligence committees, some legislators sought to amend the Accountability for Intelligence Activities Act so as to reduce the president's discretion in deciding when to notify Congress of covert actions. This legislation, which came up for formal consideration after George Bush became president, stipulated that the president could not under any circumstances delay notification beyond forty-eight hours. Bush, while pledging to give prior notice most of the time, argued that the president must have the option of witholding notification until after a covert action has commenced and, in some instances, for even longer than forty-eight hours. Accordingly, he threatened to veto legislation containing any time limit. Under compromise legislation finally worked out and passed in 1991, the president continues to have the option of delaying notification in "extraordinary circumstances," but he must nevertheless inform Congress "in a timely fashion." Although the reporting language accompanying the amending legislation states that Congress interprets a "timely fashion" to mean a few days, it seems unlikely that presidents will feel bound by this.[111] Indeed, President Bill

Clinton's nominee for CIA director, when asked by senators if he would commit to notifying Congress of covert actions within forty-eight hours, declined to do so.[112]

The amending legislation more effectively addressed other questionable practices associated with the covert actions surrounding Iran-contra. Henceforth presidents would be required to authorize in writing all covert operations before they commence, not after, and must identify all U.S. government agencies and any third parties that are participating in the operation.

☆ FOREIGN AID AND TRADE

Foreign aid and trade have long been instruments by which presidents have sought to influence the direction of policy and events in other nations. How presidents make use of these instruments is ultimately determined by Congress, since the Constitution grants to the legislative branch exclusive authority to appropriate money and regulate commerce. Given its determination to play a more active role in other areas of foreign affairs, it should come as no surprise that Congress has become more assertive with respect to aid and trade as well.

Although presidential requests for foreign aid have never been very popular with Congress, both presidents Nixon and Ford found Capitol Hill less receptive than ever. From 1950 to 1968, Congress cut presidential foreign aid requests by 19 percent,[113] whereas from 1969 through 1974, such requests were cut back by an average of 28 percent.[114] Most notable among these cutbacks were the restrictions on military and economic aid to Turkey and Vietnam. To the chagrin of President Ford and Secretary of State Henry Kissinger, Congress declined to grant additional military aid requests to Turkey and temporarily suspended current military aid following Turkey's 1974 invasion of Cyprus. Similarly, over the strong objections of Ford and Kissinger, Congress reduced the 1974 aid request for Vietnam from $1.45 billion to $700 million. Nor did Congress act on President Ford's request in 1975 for an additional $522 million in aid for Vietnam. In 1976, Ford once again protested that Congress was denying him the ability to influence the course of events, this time in Angola. Convinced that the United States must act to stop Soviet inroads in Africa, the president began giving covert aid to the anti-Marxist guerrilla factions fighting in the Angolan civil war. Having been briefed about Angola and our activities there, Congress became alarmed that the United States might be drawn into another conflict reminiscent of Vietnam. To prevent this, it enacted the Clark Amendment, which prohibited the president from giving any further aid to Angola unless Congress passed a joint resolution authorizing him to do so.

In the area of trade, Congress not only denied trade concessions to members of the international oil cartel (OPEC) but also refused to go along with the 1972 Nixon-Brezhnev agreement in which the Soviet Union was to be accorded most favored-nation status in its trade relations with the United States. The refusal to do so resulted from the Soviet Union's unwillingness to permit greater freedom to Soviet Jews. Both of these congressional actions were taken despite strong warnings from President Ford that our relations with oil-producing countries and the Soviet Union would be seriously damaged.

Jimmy Carter came into the presidency pledging to double the foreign aid budget before he left office. Unfortunately, his performance fell far short of his promise. In 1978 he asked for $7.6 billion, and Congress gave him $6.7 billion. In his final budget request for fiscal 1981, he called for $7.6 billion in foreign aid and Congress appropriated $7 billion. Thus, far from doubling foreign aid, Carter's final request failed even to keep up with the rate of inflation. Yet, although Carter was decidedly unsuccessful in achieving the funding level he once promised, he did win some victories in specific areas. Even these, however, did not come easily nor, in some instances, without compromise.

In 1977, Carter narrowly averted a major setback to the foreign aid program. The House voted overwhelmingly to reduce U.S. contributions to international lending agencies (World Bank, Asian Development Fund, International Development Association) if the agencies lent any portion of their U.S. contributions to Vietnam, Cambodia, Cuba, and several countries in Africa and South America. Because the United States is the major contributor to these agencies and because these agencies cannot accept contributions with strings attached, passage of this legislation could have had a disastrous effect upon the World Bank and other such agencies. The House ultimately backed off from this legislation, but it was able to extract a promise from President Carter in return, namely, that U.S. representatives to these international lending agencies would be instructed to vote against aid to the countries singled out by the House. Both the House and Senate did approve a provision in the Foreign Assistance Act (1977) that would prohibit the United States from giving any *direct* aid to Cuba, Vietnam, Laos, Mozambique, Cambodia, and Angola.

Carter's difficulties with Congress were also evident in the area of military foreign aid. Like his predecessor, Carter implored Congress to lift the arms embargo against Turkey imposed after Turkey used American arms in its 1974 invasion of Cyprus. (In retaliation for the embargo, the Turkish government closed U.S. intelligence and military installations located in its country.) Although past congressional opposition to lifting the embargo was undoubtedly influenced by the powerful Greek lobby, two other considerations loomed large as well. First, the law mandated a suspension of U.S. arms to any country that used them for aggressive purposes; second, the arms embargo constituted the only significant leverage the United States could exert to pressure Turkey into resolving its differences with Cyprus. The Carter administration, however, was now arguing that the strategy of exerting pressure through the embargo had clearly not worked. Moreover, the administration also expressed the fear that a continuance of our present policy could precipitate Turkey's withdrawal from NATO and encourage it to come to terms with the Soviet Union. In the summer of 1978, the issue once again came to a vote in Congress, but this time Congress voted to lift the embargo. No doubt, this change of heart resulted not only from the president's extraordinary lobbying effort but also from the increased strain in U.S.-Soviet relations. However, the president's victory was a very narrow one indeed, for in the House the vote to repeal carried by a margin of only three votes.

Carter also had to contend with Capitol Hill on the *sale* of arms to foreign countries; in 1976, Congress had passed legislation giving itself a veto over presidential decisions in this area. It took several months, for example, to gain approval to sell an air defense system to Iran, our strongest ally in the Middle East at that time. And as a condition for Senate approval of his arms package to Egypt, Saudi Arabia, and Israel, Carter reversed himself and agreed to an increase in the number of F-15s going to Israel. He faced an even tougher fight in 1980 with his decision to sell 38 tons of nuclear fuel to India. As with arms sales, Congress had legislated its involvement in this decision, for the Nuclear Non-Proliferation Act (1978) provided that it could veto the president's decision if *both* houses passed a resolution of disapproval.

By a vote of 298 to 98, the House registered its vigorous disapproval of the president's decision, but after what one senator described as "some of the heaviest lobbying I have ever seen," the Senate gave its approval to the shipment by the narrow vote of 48 to 46.[115]

As Carter moved into his final year in office, there were some fifty-six restrictions that Congress had imposed concerning the dispersal of foreign aid, most having been passed in the aftermath of Vietnam.[116] Some of these were outright prohibitions, and others made presidential action contingent upon congressional approval. Chafing under certain of these restrictions, the president attached to his final 1981 foreign aid request a letter in which he appealed to Congress to give him greater flexibility: "Developments over the past year, and in particular in recent months, have underscored perhaps more than ever before the importance of affording the president the ability to employ, promptly and effectively, foreign assistance to meet unforeseen foreign policy and security emergencies."[117] Toward this end, he first asked Congress to increase from $10 million to $50 million the amount of arms, equipment, and services he could send to foreign countries in the event of an unforeseen emergency. Second, he requested authority to waive laws that then banned aid to certain countries. Several amendments to the Arms Export Control Act (1968), for example, prohibit aid to foreign governments for all kinds of reasons, including the fact that they are communist controlled, or violating human rights, or building nuclear weapons. Pakistan was accused of the last violation, and thus the president was unable to provide it with military aid, even after neighboring Afghanistan had been invaded by the Soviet Union. Third, in an effort to expedite the sale of arms to important allies, Carter called upon Congress to relinquish its right to veto commercial and government arms sales to NATO countries, Japan, Australia, and New Zealand. Fourth, he asked the legislative branch to surrender its veto over Defense Department contracts involving the design and construction of military facilities in foreign countries. Finally, he requested that Congress rescind a 1976 amendment to the Arms Export Control Act that prevents selling the expertise of U.S. military advisers and trainers to perform services that are in any way combat-related. The president argued that this current regulation would, for example, force the United States to withdraw advisers from an ally under attack.

Members of Congress had imposed most of these restrictions when Vietnam was fresh in their minds and détente appeared to be thriving. As they now considered Carter's requests, however, the world was considerably different. Our most steadfast ally (the Shah of Iran) in the Middle East had been toppled from power; the Soviets had invaded Afghanistan; and the deteriorating situation in Poland made a Soviet invasion of that country a possibility as well. In view of these developments, Congress acquiesced to much of what the president had recommended. It increased the emergency military aid limit to $50 million and allowed the president to waive laws banning aid to certain countries. Congress did stipulate that such action must be "vital" to our national interest and that the president must consult with Congress before taking such action. Congress also exempted from congressional veto commercial arms sales to our allies and, though declining to relinquish completely its veto over the construction of military facilities in other countries, exempted projects not in excess of $200 million. Finally, restrictions on the use of American advisers in combat-related activities abroad were loosened but not eliminated.[118]

Like his predecessor, President Reagan continued to press for a freer hand in dispensing foreign assistance. Thus, in his foreign aid request for fiscal 1982, he asked Congress to repeal legislation (the Clark Amendment) that prohibited the president from providing aid of any kind to anti-Marxist guerrillas fighting in Angola. While he claimed that his administration had no immediate plans to assist these groups, he was nevertheless seeking repeal of this restriction as a matter of principle. As Secretary of State Haig put it, the amendment constituted "a blatant restriction on executive authority." The president also called upon Congress to lift its ban on military assistance to Pakistan in light of the Soviet Union's invasion of neighboring Afghanistan. With respect to assisting countries in our own hemisphere, he requested that Congress refrain from cutting off aid to El Salvador and lift its ban on aid to Argentina and Chile. All three of these countries fell into congressional disfavor following repeated human rights violations by their governments. Finally, Reagan also repeated Jimmy Carter's request that Congress relinquish its authority to veto government-sponsored arms sales to our NATO allies.

In responding to Reagan administration requests, Congress for the most part continued to move in the direction of providing the president more discretion over foreign aid. Thus, although it took a while, in 1985 legislators finally decided to repeal the Clark Amendment banning U.S. aid to Angolan rebel forces. Congress also agreed to exempt Pakistan from the law that prohibited assistance to countries engaged in nuclear enrichment technology, and it approved a $3.2 billion aid program to that country. As for the president's aid requests to Latin America, Congress agreed to resume aid to Argentina and Chile, provided Reagan certified that these countries were making significant progress in the area of human rights. A similar condition was attached to aid for El Salvador in 1982 but would ultimately be dropped by Congress in 1985. On aiding Nicaraguan contras, however, Congress proved more contentious. Skeptical of growing U.S. involvement in Nicaragua and unconvinced that the contra rebels were succeeding militarily, legislators in 1984 terminated all aid to the contra cause. When Congress resumed funding to the rebels in 1985, it stipulated that the funds must be used exclusively for humanitarian purposes and barred the CIA from any role in distributing the money. Only after intense pressure from the White House was Congress persuaded to renew military aid the following year.[119]

Apart from one very notable exception, Reagan otherwise enjoyed considerable success in the area of arms sales. These successes, however, nearly always entailed considerable struggle and a heavy investment of presidential resources. Thus, in 1981 he narrowly averted a congressional veto of his controversial decision to sell AWAC airplanes to Saudi Arabia, and in 1986 he just barely escaped being defeated on a second proposed arms sale to the Saudis. In its foreign aid bill for 1986, Congress also sought to bar the sale of advanced weapons to Jordan unless King Hussein publicly recognized and agreed to negotiate with the state of Israel. Finding this condition wholly unacceptable, the White House responded with a threat to veto the entire foreign aid bill. Congress finally agreed to a compromise whereby it stated its opposition to such a sale but allowed the president to go ahead if he certified that Jordan was committed to recognizing and negotiating with Israel. Only in his arms-for-hostages sale to Iran did the president suffer a major defeat. Since the sale was undertaken covertly, Congress quite obviously had no opportunity to stop it before the fact. But once revealed, both congressional and public reaction was swift and highly critical, thereby forcing the president to abandon the policy.[120]

Pleas by presidents Carter and Reagan for greater flexibility in using foreign aid and trade as an instrument of American foreign policy, while not leading to a reduction in congressional involvement, nevertheless saw Congress provide greater opportunities for the president to waive the various restrictions it was imposing. These loopholes typically stated that a given congressional restriction could be waived if the president "determined" or "certified" that it was "essential" or "vital" to the national interest.[121] As president, George Bush fought hard for the inclusion of these waivers, on one occasion vetoing an otherwise desirable piece of legislation because Congress included stiff sanctions—without the option of a presidential waiver—against countries and companies trafficking in chemical and biological weapons. The following year Congress agreed to recast the bill, this time allowing the president to waive the sanctions if he "determines and certifies that such a waiver is essential to the national security interests of the United States."[122] Similar waivers were included in congressional legislation banning aid to Jordan, which had provided assistance to Iraq during the Gulf War, and prohibiting arms sales to terrorist states.

President Clinton saw Congress impose still more trade sanctions, but not without the accompanying waiver option. Seeking to punish companies in Cuba that profit from property once owned by Americans, the Helms-Burton Act passed in 1996 allowed Americans to sue such companies in our courts, and also denied U.S. visas to company executives that profit from this property. The Iran-Libya Sanctions Act of 1996, meanwhile, imposed sanctions on foreign companies whose exports contributed to the petroleum reserves or military presence of these countries. Both laws so enraged our allies, many of whom trade with Cuba, Iran, and Libya, that President Clinton repeatedly waived the sanctions, opting instead to work out a face-saving accomodation.[123] In other areas where Congress had previously mandated sanctions, Clinton was disposed to issue waivers as well. Thus, Mexico was certified as cooperating in antidrug efforts despite considerable evidence to the contrary, and sanctions were waived against China and Russia, even though the former provided Pakistan and Iran with nuclear weapons–related equipment, and the latter was assisting Iran in missile development. In order that arms and aid could be sent to Bosnia in 1996, Clinton also certified to Congress that Bosnia had ceased its military and intelligence cooperation with Iran—this, despite the fact that Iranian-controlled training camps were being established in the Muslim areas of Bosnia.[124]

If Clinton appeared to be fudging on the facts in these cases, he was certainly not the first president to do so.[125] He was the first to acknowledge it, however, doing so in a White House meeting where he thought no reporters were present: "What always happens if you have automatic sanctions legislation is it puts enormous pressure on whoever is in the executive branch to fudge an evaluation of the facts of what is going on. And that's not what you want. What you want is to leave the President some flexibility, including the ability to impose sanctions, some flexibility with a range of appropriate actions."[126]

 ## SWING OF THE PENDULUM

For most of this century, the president has enjoyed almost total preeminence in foreign affairs. Time and again American soldiers were committed to combat, agreements with foreign governments were made, and covert military and political actions were undertaken, all without any prior approval from Congress. In some cases, Congress was not even informed of such activities after the fact. Congressional willingness to let the pendulum swing so far in the direction of presidential discretion was due to several factors: (1) a recognition on the part of Congress that the president had superior information in the area of foreign affairs; (2) a desire to provide the president with the necessary flexibility in dealing not only with the Nazi threat of the 1940s but also with the threat of communist aggression during the Cold War period of the 1950s and early 1960s; and (3) the development of a congressional state of mind that simply became accustomed to presidential dominance—in other words, the more initiatives the president undertook, the more appropriate it seemed for him to do so. What Congress failed to appreciate, however, was that the discretion it was willing to accord presidents under certain circumstances would ultimately be seen by presidents as their *right* under any circumstances. It failed, in short, to recognize that presidential discretion feeds upon itself.

Only with our involvement in Southeast Asia did Congress come to see the consequences of its permissiveness. One president took us into Vietnam claiming that he needed no congressional authorization for his actions. His successor extended the war into Cambodia and asserted that it was wholly within his power to do so. But the issue here was not simply the arrogance with which they claimed their authority, but also their judgment. Although Congress had in the past usually acceded to the president's superior expertise in foreign policy, Vietnam proved to be a case where his judgment was lacking. Neither Congress nor the public was ultimately convinced that our security was so threatened by events in Southeast Asia that we were required to make such a vast commitment of human and material resources.

The question was not whether Congress had the power to rein in the president in foreign affairs, but rather whether it had the will to do so. With Vietnam, however, came the catalyst that was to motivate Congress to reassert itself in a variety of areas related to foreign policy. As noted earlier, Congress in 1972 passed legislation to increase its role in executive agreements. In 1973 it passed, and the president reluctantly signed, a bill that prohibited the use of any funds to finance further combat activity in Indochina after August of that year. As a result of this action, President Nixon was forced to halt the bombings in Cambodia. Not long thereafter, Congress also passed the War Powers Resolution over a presidential veto. In the mid-1970s, Congress turned its attention to the CIA and established two new committees charged with overseeing the agency's activities. Throughout the 1970s, Congress enacted numerous statutes designed to restrict the president's power to disperse foreign aid.

That Congress was able to reassert itself in the aftermath of Vietnam was due not only to its own determination but also to a weakened adversary. Engulfed in the scandals of his presidency, Richard Nixon was in no position to challenge or change the will of Congress. His successor also operated from a diminished power base, partly because he was an unelected president and partly because he succeeded to an office diminished in stature by the scandals of Watergate. Although Jimmy Carter did not labor under the disadvantages of Nixon and Ford, his own liabilities prevented any significant reduction in the momentum developed by Congress. Congress quickly saw that he, an avowed outsider of limited political experience, did not fully grasp the nature of his own power or that of others in Washington.

Following years of deference to the president in foreign affairs, the willingness of Congress to play a more active role in this area represents a healthy development. At the same time, however, we would do well to bear in mind that although excessive deference to the president in this area has had distinct drawbacks, so too may excessive involvement on the part of Congress. Foreign policy, after all, requires the direction of one hand—a reality appreciated only too well by our Founding Fathers. With a membership totaling 535 individuals, Congress is ill suited to developing a coherent and integrated approach to foreign policy matters. Nor is this problem of size mitigated to any significant extent by organization, for fourteen of the seventeen standing committees in the Senate and seventeen of the twenty standing committees in the House have at least some jurisdiction over matters related to foreign affairs. Given such a wide dispersal of responsibility, coordination of policy understandably becomes extremely difficult. Finally, to a far greater extent than the president, Congress is susceptible to the pleadings of special interests, and this too inhibits its ability to take a holistic view of foreign policy matters. These limitations are not meant to indicate that Congress should keep hands off, but rather to suggest that congressional involvement should be directed toward more vigorous oversight of foreign policy rather than toward attempts to determine the details of it.

As the 1970s came to an end, there was in fact growing concern that the pendulum had swung too far in the direction of congressional activism—that responsible involvement was giving way to irresponsible meddling. Perhaps the most blatant manifestation of this behavior was the willingness of legislators to negotiate with foreign governments on their own. Thus, as the Senate considered the Panama Canal treaties in 1978, there was a steady parade of senators to Panama, where they negotiated certain treaty provisions with officials of that country. In 1979, President Carter dispatched an emissary to Nicaragua for the purpose of persuading the head of its government, General Anastasio Somoza, to resign. To the astonishment of the emissary, sitting in on the meeting was Congressman John Murphy, chairman of the House Committee on Merchant Marine and Fisheries and longtime ally of Somoza. During that same year, Senator Jesse Helms sent two of his staff members to London to participate in negotiations under way to end the fighting between whites and blacks in Zimbabwe-Rhodesia. In 1980, Congressman George Hansen, having designated himself a one-man negotiating team, traveled to Iran and attempted to negotiate the release of Americans held hostage there.[127] Intrusions of this sort have understandably been a cause for concern both at home and abroad. A Soviet official reflected the view held in many foreign capitals when he observed that it was "still not clear who exactly in the U.S. can speak in international relations on behalf of the United States." Even former Senator William Fulbright, who had spearheaded the move toward greater congressional involvement in foreign policy, voiced his displeasure with the behavior of his compatriots: "I confess to increasingly serious misgivings about the ability of Congress to play a constructive role in our foreign relations . . . those of us who prodded what seemed to be a hopelessly immobile herd of cattle [Congress] a decade ago, now stand back in awe in face of the stampede."[128]

As we moved into the 1980s, however, there were indications that legislators were becoming somewhat more sensitive to charges of congressional meddling. This chapter earlier noted that Congress passed legislation in 1980 designed to give the president and the CIA greater flexibility with respect to covert operations abroad. Likewise, in response to pleas by presidents Carter and Reagan, legislators appeared willing to lift or modify some of the restrictions imposed in the areas of foreign aid and trade. As the Bush administration learned, however, Congress's retreat was far from complete. Indeed, when President Bush signed legislation in 1990 authorizing funding for the State Department, he felt compelled to state in writing that he would not be bound by a number of restrictions that Congress had written into the bill. These included requiring the secretary of state to notify Congress of certain diplomatic contacts; denial of funds for the U.S. Delegation to the Conference on Security and Cooperation in Europe unless a member of Congress was included in the delegation; denial of funds for talks with any member of the Palestinian Liberation Organization who had engaged in terrorism against the United States; and prohibiting the establishment of a Soviet consulate in New York unless they allowed an American consulate in Kiev. While noting that he did not in every instance disagree with these restrictions on policy grounds, he insisted that congressional attempts to dictate on these subjects constituted an impermissible limitation on his constitutional authority to conduct foreign relations.[129]

Bill Clinton had his frustrations as well, finding his clout on the world stage diminished when Congress refused to grant him "fast track" authority in trade negotiations, held our UN dues obligations hostage to antiabortion legislation, and delayed the appropriation of funds for the International Monetary Fund.

It hardly seems likely that Congress will return to the more passive foreign policy role it played from the 1930s through most of the 1960s. The growing interface of foreign and domestic issues provides Congress with the incentive to become more involved, and its increased staff resources give it the capacity to do so. In addition, now that the high-stakes confrontation between the United States and what was once the Soviet Union appears ended, the need for a unified front within the government may be seen as less compelling by members of Congress, over half of whose members in the House have been elected since the fall of the Berlin Wall. This reality was not lost on President Clinton, who observed wistfully, "I envy Kennedy having an enemy."[130] Finally, of course, whatever inclination exists within Congress to give the president more leeway will only be further discouraged by presidents' foreign policy mishaps, particularly if, as with Iran-contra, they involve presidential attempts to mislead or circumvent the will of Congress.

✮ NOTES

1. Aaron Wildavsky, "The Two Presidencies," in Aaron Wildavsky, ed., *The Presidency* (Boston: Little, Brown, 1969), p. 231.

2. Aaron Wildavsky, "The Two Presidencies," *Trans-Action* 4 (December, 1966), 7.

3. See Steven Shull, ed., *The Two Presidencies* (Chicago: Nelson-Hall, 1991), chaps. 3, 6, 9, and 10.

4. See Ibid., chaps. 4, 5, 8, 11, and 12.

5. For further discussion on these points see Jon R. Bond and Richard Fleisher, *The President in the Legislative Arena* (Chicago: University of Chicago Press, 1990), chap. 3.; George Edwards III, *At the Margins: Presidential Leadership of Congress* (New Haven: Yale University Press, 1989), chap. 2.

6. *The Gallup Opinion Index,* February 1968, p. 24.

7. *The Gallup Opinion Index,* June 1973, p. 15.

8. Arnold Rose, *The Power Structure* (New York: Oxford University Press, 1967), p. 401.

9. Erwin Hargrove, *The Power of the Modern Presidency* (New York: Knopf, 1974), p. 111.

10. Cited in Cecil Crabb and Pat Holt, *Invitation to Struggle: Congress, the President and Foreign Policy* (Washington, D.C.: Congressional Quarterly, 1980), p. 192.

11. Ronald Terchek, "Foreign and Domestic Policy Linkages: Constraints and Challenges to the Foreign Policy Process," in Don Piper and Ronald Terchek, eds., *Interaction: Foreign Policy and Public Policy* (Washington, D.C.: American Enterprise Institute, 1983), p. 57.

12. Cited in Arthur Schlesinger, Jr., *The Imperial Presidency* (Boston: Houghton Mifflin, 1973), p. 5. Copyright © 1973 by Arthur Schlesinger, Jr. Reprinted by permission of Houghton Mifflin Company.

13. Jacob Cooke, ed., *The Federalist* (New York: World, 1961), p. 465.

14. Cited in Schesinger, *Imperial Presidency,* p. 20.

15. Ibid., p. 22.

16. Louis Fisher, "War Powers: A Need for Legislative Reassertion," in Rexford Tugwell, ed., *The Presidency Reappraised* (New York: Praeger, 1974), pp. 64, 65.

17. Cited in Schlesinger, *Imperial Presidency*, p. 28.

18. Thomas Bailey, *The Pugnacious Presidents: White House Warriors on Parade* (New York: Free Press, 1980), pp. 148–52.

19. Ibid., p. 64.

20. Ibid., p. 178.

21. Robert Dallek, *Franklin D. Roosevelt and American Foreign Policy, 1932–1945* (New York: Oxford University Press, 1979), p. 287.

22. Cited in Merlo Pusey, *The Way We Go to War* (Boston: Houghton Mifflin, 1969), p. 3.

23. Cited in Schlesinger, *Imperial Presidency*, p. 112.

24. Emmet John Hughes, *The Living Presidency* (New York: Coward, McCann & Geoghegan, 1973), p. 244. Copyright © 1973 by Emmet John Hughes. Reprinted by permission of Coward, McCann & Geoghegan.

25. Ibid.

26. Louis Fisher, *President and Congress* (New York: Macmillan, 1972), p. 195.

27. Schlesinger, *Imperial Presidency*, p. 132. For a more recent and excellent discussion of presidential war making from Truman onward, see Gordon Silverstein, *Imbalance of Powers: Constitutional Interpretation and the Making of American Foreign Policy* (New York: Oxford University Press, 1997).

28. Ibid., pp. 160, 161.

29. Ibid., p. 160.

30. Ibid., pp. 160, 161.

31. Hughes, *Living Presidency*, p. 236.

32. Cited in Charles Hardin, *Presidential Power and Accountability* (Chicago: University of Chicago Press, 1974), p. 103.

33. Hughes, *Living Presidency*, p. 237.

34. Cited in Schlesinger, *Imperial Presidency*, p. 180.

35. Ibid., p. 184.

36. Cited in Ibid., p. 189.

37. William Shawcross, "Through History with Henry A. Kissinger," *Harper's,* November 1980, pp. 90–92.

38. Cited in Schlesinger, *Imperial Presidency*, p. 198.

39. Adapted from the appendix to C. W. Tarr, Jr., "The War Powers Resolution and the Problem of Information" (Prepared for delivery at the annual meeting of the American Political Science Association, Chicago, Ill., August 29–September 2, 1974).

40. Ibid., p. 8.

41. Cited in Pat Holt, *The War Powers Resolution: The Role of Congress in U.S. Armed Intervention* (Washington, D.C.: American Enterprise Institute, 1978), p. 8

42. John R. Bolton, *The Legislative Veto* (Washington, D.C.: American Enterprise Institute, 1977), p. 9. See also *Congressional Quarterly Weekly Report,* August 9, 1986, p. 1822.

43. Bolton, *The Legislative Veto,* pp. 1, 2, 31–39.

44. *National Journal,* July 2, 1983, p. 1380.

45. Thomas Franck and Edward Weisband, *Foreign Policy by Congress* (New York: Oxford University Press, 1979), p. 72; Holt, *The War Powers Resolution,* p. 20.

46. Robert Bresler, "War Powers: The Illusory Reform," *Inquiry,* June 26, 1978, p. 14.

47. Cited in Holt, *The War Powers Resolution,* p. 12.

48. *Congressional Quarterly Weekly Report,* August 28, 1982, p. 2157.

49. Ibid.

50. Cited in Louis Fisher, *Presidential War Power* (Lawrence: University Press of Kansas, 1995), pp. 159–60.

51. Ibid., pp. 2157, 2158. See also Michael Glennon, "The War Powers Resolution Ten Years Later—More Politics than Law," *American Journal of International Law* 78 (July 1984), 571, 572.

52. Cited in *Congressional Quarterly Weekly Report,* April 26, 1980, p. 1068.

53. Cited in *National Journal,* May 3, 1980, p. 740.

54. Cited in Jacob Javits, "War Powers Reconsidered," *Foreign Affairs* 64 (Fall 1985), 137; *Congressional Quarterly Weekly Report,* October 29, 1983, p. 2221.

55. *Congressional Quarterly Weekly Report,* May 10, 1986, p. 1021.

56. Ibid.

57. *Washington Post,* August 24, 1980, p. C7.

58. James Nathan,"Salvaging the War Powers Resolution," *Presidential Studies Quarterly* 23 (Spring 1993), 236.

59. Michael J. Glennon, "The Gulf War and the Constitution," *Foreign Affairs* 70 (Spring 1991), 97.

60. Fisher, *Presidential War Power,* pp. 154–57.

61. Ibid., pp. 158–60.

62. *Congressional Quarterly Weekly Report,* February 7, 1998, p. 326; *Congressional Quarterly Weekly Report,* February 21, 1998, p. 448.

63. *National Journal,* May 19, 1984, pp. 992, 993; *Congressional Quarterly Weekly Report,* October 1, 1983, pp. 2016, 2017.

64. Cited in *National Journal,* May 19, 1984, p. 990.

65. Cited in *Congressional Quarterly Weekly Report,* September 24, 1983, p. 1965.

66. *Congressional Quarterly Weekly Report,* October 24, 1987, pp. 2595–98; *National Journal,* June 25, 1988, p. 1690.

67. Glennon, "The Gulf War and the Constitution," 100.

68. Ibid., 92.

69. Nathan, "Salvaging the War Powers Resolution," 237.

70. *Congressional Quarterly Weekly Report,* January 12, 1991, p. 71.

71. Nathan, "Salvaging the War Powers Resolution," 238.

72. Glennon, "The Gulf War and the Constitution," 100, 101; Nathan, "Salvaging the War Powers Resolution," 238.

73. Jean Edward Smith, *George Bush's War* (New York: Henry Holt, 1992), p. 254; *Congressional Quarterly Weekly Report,* January 12, 1991, p. 65.

74. William Livingston, Lawrence Dodd, and Richard Schott, eds., *The Presidency and Congress* (Austin: Lyndon B. Johnson School of Public Affairs, 1979), pp. 391, 392.

75. Cited in *New York Times,* September 26, 1993, p. A11.

76. *Congressional Quarterly Weekly Report,* October 23, 1993, p. 2898.

77. Cooke, *The Federalist,* pp. 505–7.

78. Franck and Weisband, *Foreign Policy by Congress,* pp. 135–41.

79. *Washington Post,* June 7, 1979, p. A1.

80. *Washington Post,* December 14, 1979, p. A1.

81. Crabb and Holt, *Invitation to Struggle,* pp. 75, 80.

82. Cited in Franck and Weisband, *Foreign Policy by Congress,* p. 281.

83. Ibid., p. 290.

84. *Washington Post,* April 18, 1997, p. A10; *Washington Post,* April 25, 1997, p. A19.

85. Schlesinger, *Imperial Presidency,* p. 104.

86. Richard Pious, *The American Presidency* (New York: Basic Books, 1979), p. 54.

87. James Burns, "Jimmy Carter's Strategy for 1980," *Atlantic,* March 1979, p. 42.

88. *Congressional Quarterly Weekly Report,* August 2, 1975, p. 1713.

89. Schlesinger, *Imperial Presidency,* p. 201.

90. *Congressional Quarterly Weekly Report,* January 1, 1971, p. 24.

91. Ibid., p. 23.

92. Cited in *Congressional Quarterly Weekly Report,* August 2, 1975, p. 1712.

93. *New York Times,* April 17, 1975, p. E2.

94. Cited in *Congressional Quarterly Weekly Report,* August 2, 1975, p. 1714.

95. Ibid.

96. Ibid., p. 1716.

97. Edward Kolodziej, "Congress and Foreign Policy: The Nixon Years," in Harvey Mansfield, ed., *Congress Against the President* (New York: Academy of Political Science, 1975), p. 177.

98. Victor Marchetti and John Marks, *The CIA and the Cult of Intelligence* (New York: Knopf, 1974), pp. 18, 19.

99. Harry Ransom,"Congress and the Intelligence Agencies," in Mansfield, *Congress Against the President,* p. 158.

100. *Washington Post,* March 12, 1996, p. A11; *Washington Post,* April 24, 1996, p. A19.

101. *New York Times,* February 1, 1967, p. E1.

102. Ransom, "Congress and the Intelligence Agencies," p. 160.

103. *New York Times,* July 20, 1975, p. E3. Copyright © 1975 by The New York Times Company. Reprinted by permission.

104. Ibid.

105. Tad Szulc, "Putting Back the Bite in the C.I.A.," *New York Times Magazine,* April 6, 1980, p. 62.

106. *Congressional Quarterly Weekly Report,* September 27, 1980, p. 2875.

107. Cited in *Congressional Quarterly Weekly Report,* January 19, 1985, p. 120.

108. Cited in *Congressional Quarterly Weekly Report,* April 14, 1984, p. 833.

109. *New York Times,* November 16, 1986, p. 6.

110. *Washington Post,* December 22, 1986, p. A26.

111. *Washington Post,* February 6, 1987, p. A10; *Congressional Quarterly Weekly Report,* October 28, 1989, pp. 2884, 2885; *Congressional Quarterly Weekly Report,* November 4, 1989, p. 2969; *Congressional Quarterly Weekly Report,* July 27, 1991, p. 2097.

112. *New York Times,* February 4, 1993, p. A15.

113. *Congressional Quarterly Almanac* (Washington, D.C.: Congressional Quarterly, 1968), p. 605.

114. Kolodziej, "Congress and Foreign Policy," p. 175.

115. Cited in *Congressional Quarterly Weekly Report,* September 27, 1980, p. 2871.

116. *National Journal,* July 15, 1978, pp. 1120, 1121.

117. Cited in *Congressional Quarterly Weekly Report,* April 26, 1980, p. 1136.

118. *Congressional Quarterly Weekly Report,* April 26, 1980, pp. 1136, 1137; *Congressional Quarterly Weekly Report,* November 29, 1980, pp. 3450, 3451.

119. *Congressional Quarterly Weekly Report,* August 3, 1985, p. 1546, *Congressional Quarterly Weekly Report,* April 26, 1980, pp. 1136, 1137; *Congressional Quarterly Weekly Report,* November 29, 1980, pp. 3450, 3451; *Congressional Quarterly Weekly Report,* August 3, 1985, p. 1544; *National Journal,* December 20, 1986, p. 3062.

120. *Congressional Quarterly Weekly Report,* December 5, 1981, p. 2412; *Congressional Quarterly Weekly Report,* July 27, 1985, pp. 1476, 1477.

121. *Congressional Quarterly Weekly Report,* December 5, 1992, pp. 3753–57. For a useful discussion of these restrictions and waivers, see Barbara Hinckley, *Less Than Meets the Eye: Foreign Policy Making and the Myth of the Assertive Congress* (Chicago: University of Chicago Press, 1994), chap. 6.

122. Ibid., p. 3754.

123. *New York Times,* May 19, 1998, p. A6.

124. *New York Times,* April 28, 1998, p. A6; *Washington Post,* May 11, 1996, pp. A1, A24; *U.S. News and World Report,* September 9, 1996, p. 16.

125. I. M. Destler and Ivo H. Daalder, "Yes, A Fudge Factor," *Washington Post,* May 19, 1998, p. A21.

126. Cited in *New York Times,* April 28, 1998, pp. A1, A6.

127. William Rogers, "Who's in Charge of Foreign Policy?" *New York Times Magazine,* September 9, 1979, p. 50; Crabb and Holt, *Invitation to Struggle,* p. 200.

128. Cited in Crabb and Holt, *Invitation to Struggle,* pp. 204, 206.

129. *Washington Post,* February 17, 1990, p. A23.

130. Cited in Richard Reeves, *Running in Place: How Bill Clinton Disappointed America* (Kansas City: Andrews & McMeel, 1996), p. 94.

The President and Congress

Much of what a president wishes to accomplish must be done in partnership with the legislative branch. Establishing and maintaining this partnership is, as presidents have inevitably discovered, one of the great frustrations of the office. One adviser to three presidents speaks to this point: "I suspect that there may be nothing about the White House less generally understood than the ease with which a Congress can drive a president quite out of his mind and up the wall."[1] Theodore Roosevelt gave vent to his frustrations on one occasion when he remarked, "Oh, if I could only be President and Congress too for just ten minutes." Even Gerald Ford, who was a long-time member of the congressional establishment, was not in the presidency very long before he acknowledged some frustration with his former home.

> The only thing that is disappointing—I guess any president has this. The president thinks he has the right answers. The facts of history are that he doesn't always—but he thinks he does. And he would like to implement, he'd like to execute—to get things done. But under our system, Congress has a very definite partnership. Right now we are going through an extraordinary trauma in the relationship between Congress and the president. I understand that. I've been on the other end of it. But if there was one part which I would really like to change, it would be the speed with which you could make decisions and carry them out.[2]

In this chapter we shall examine this critically important relationship between the executive and legislative branches, noting those factors that make for antagonism as well as those that can serve to mitigate it. We shall also consider how and why the relationship between these two branches has changed over the years.

**THE PRESIDENT AND CONGRESS:
A STRAINED RELATIONSHIP**

Shortly after he took over the reins of the presidency, Gerald Ford spoke before a joint session of Congress and stated that he wanted their relationship to be "a marriage, not a honeymoon." Although such words expressed an admirable sentiment, a man of his longtime Washington experience surely knew that he was asking for the impossible. There exist a variety of factors that make it inevitable that the relationship between the president and Congress will be a less-than-harmonious one. These factors are rooted in the very structure of our political system and as such are ever-present. To be sure, other factors can help to reduce this antagonism, but it is just that—reduction rather than elimination.

Separation of Powers

Under our constitutional system, the executive and legislative branches were created as two organically distinct components of the government. Each has a strong sense of its own responsibilities and importance in the scheme of things; each has powers that, if exercised, can frustrate the will of the other. Consequently, it is not surprising that an institutional rivalry develops between the two branches. In order to impress upon Congress that it was he who was running the government, Franklin Roosevelt would on occasion ask his aides for "something I can veto."[3] Richard Nixon exhibited this same sense of institutional rivalry between the two branches when he remarked, "The moment that a President is looking over his shoulder down to Capitol Hill before he makes a decision, he will then be a weak President."[4]

The old adage "What one sees depends upon where one stands" is applicable here. The separation of powers principle locates the president and Congress at different points in our political system. They each have different responsibilities and face different pressures, and consequently they may not always view matters from the same perspective. As a congressman from Illinois, Abraham Lincoln was horrified by President James Polk's misuse of power when he took the United States into war against Mexico. Yet, as president, Lincoln was not at all reluctant to take actions that far exceeded his constitutional powers. Similarly, in 1950, Congressman Richard Nixon voted in favor of a House resolution designed to prevent presidents from making executive agreements with heads of state. President Nixon, however, not only made frequent use of executive agreements but also announced that he would veto pending legislation that sought to restrict this power. Likewise, when President Truman invoked executive privilege and thus refused to hand over certain information requested by a congressional committee, Congressman Nixon objected strenuously, arguing that Truman's actions simply "cannot stand from a constitutional standpoint."[5] As president, however, Richard Nixon defended and extended the use of executive privilege to a greater degree than any other American president.

Structure of Congress

The very structure of Congress ensures that the president will not have an easy time getting what he wants. First of all, Congress is divided into two different bodies, thus requiring the president to gain the support of two separate and distinct groups of legislators. Power is dispersed still further as a consequence of the committee system, which consists of fourteen standing committees in the Senate and twenty in the House. Since virtually all important legislation must be referred to committees for study, they occupy a highly strategic position in the legislative process. A given committee may even decline to consider a piece of presidential legislation, which means that the bill will most likely die a quiet death there, or a chairperson and his or her committee may decide to report the bill out of committee with a favorable recommendation, but not before they have made substantial changes in it.

Most congressional committees are divided into subcommittees whose operations used to be firmly controlled by those who chaired their parent committees. In 1973, however, the Democratic caucus in the House implemented a significant set of reforms known as the "subcommittee bill of rights." These reforms authorized subcommittees to choose their own chairpersons, formulate their own rules and procedures, and maintain their own staffs; they also required that chairpersons of full committees respect the jurisdictions of their subcommittees. These changes served to reduce the power of committee chairpersons, but they also vastly increased the number of power centers, since there are some eighty-six subcommittees in the House. That Jimmy Carter experienced considerable difficulty in forging a consensus behind his energy legislation is explainable, at least in part, by the fact that thirty committees and subcommittees had jurisdiction over some portion of it.

Finally, the rules and procedures of Congress serve to diffuse power still further. In the Senate, especially, the rules permit a minority of one or more senators to frustrate the passage of legislation through filibuster—the use of which has grown steadily since 1967. Indeed, in the 102nd (1991–1992) Congress alone, there were thirty-five filibusters, more than occurred in the entire nineteenth century. And during just a two-month period in 1994, there were twenty Republican filibusters against legislation supported by President Clinton. Although this legislative tactic may ultimately be stopped by the rest of the membership, extraordinary majorities (three-fifths) are usually required to do so.[6]

In summary, the point to be made here is simply this: To the extent that the president must deal with a large number of independent power centers within Congress, the task of gaining acceptance for his legislative proposals is rendered all the more difficult.

Different Constituencies

Another traditional source of conflict between the president and Congress stems from the fact that each is chosen by a different constituency. The president is elected by the entire nation and thus he is likely to view problems and policies in terms of their national implications. On the other hand, because members of Congress are elected from districts or states, they see themselves as representing primarily the interests of these smaller geographical entities rather than the nation as a whole.[7] Understandably, therefore, they bring a more local perspective to the evaluation of problems and policies. The clash of these different perspectives was dramatically revealed in Jimmy Carter's heated confrontation with Capitol Hill concerning federal water projects. Convinced that these costly projects were a luxury that the nation could no longer afford to fund, he decided to eliminate thirty of them from the federal budget. Members of Congress, however, were just as strongly convinced that these projects were a necessity their states and districts could ill afford to lose. Out of this clash of perspectives came a compromise settlement in which the president gave the most ground—the number of projects stated for elimination was reduced from thirty to nine.

We can also see the impact of constituency on those individuals who have moved from Congress to the presidency. Lyndon Johnson, as president, felt he could take a more visible and assertive position in favor of civil rights than he could as a senator representing only the conservative and southern state of Texas. Similarly, it seems unlikely that President Ford would have proposed even his limited amnesty program for Vietnam draft evaders had he continued to represent only his conservative congressional district in Michigan.

Erosion of Support

Although the ability of the president to get his way with Congress fluctuates a good deal throughout his tenure in office, he appears to enjoy greater success earlier as opposed to later in his term. Lyndon Johnson was acutely aware of this fact.

> We'll have nine, eh, maybe even eighteen months before the Hill turns around on us. We have that much time to get it all through. . . . You can have anything you want for a time. . . . No, they'll be glad to be aboard and to have their photograph taken with you and be part of all that victory. They'll come along and they'll give you almost everything you want for a while and then they'll turn on you. They always do. They'll lay [sic] in waiting, waiting for you to make a slip and you will. They'll give you almost everything and then they'll make you pay for it.[8]

Presidents come into office on a wave of goodwill, which has often been characterized as the "honeymoon period." There is a natural inclination on the part of those in and outside of Congress to unite around and cooperate with the newly elected leader of the nation. This reservoir of goodwill does not last long, however. A president must inevitably expend his political capital in attempting to accomplish his goals. Nearly every major decision he makes will irritate some, even while pleasing others. Over the course of his presidency, such dissatisfactions are likely to accumulate, thus making it increasingly difficult for him to work his will on Congress. As one long-time congressman has noted, "the rule here is to forgive—and remember."[9] This erosion of support is made still worse for a president who is ineligible to run again, for as he moves through his final term of office, he is likely to become increasingly less persuasive with those who realize his days are numbered.[10]

Given the fact that a president's support in Congress erodes over time, presidents would be well advised to introduce their most important legislation during their first year in office. Moreover, as Paul Light has demonstrated, they should do so as early in their first year as possible. Based upon an examination of presidencies from Kennedy through Carter, Light found that Congress passed 72 percent of the domestic legislation introduced between January and March of the first year. For legislation introduced between April and June, the success rate drops rather significantly to 39 percent; from July to September the rate drops again to 25 percent, where it remains stable through December.[11] Moving quickly in the first year is more easily said than done, however. Not only are presidents still in the learning stage, but a considerable period of time may be required to find legislative solutions to complex problems.

LESSENING OR WORSENING THE ANTAGONISM: INTERVENING FACTORS

Up to this point, I have discussed certain *ever-present* factors that serve to frustrate the development of a harmonious relationship between the president and Congress. We now consider another set of factors that may or may not be present. To the degree that they are, the president's relationship with Congress is made easier. To the extent that they are absent, his dealings with Congress are likely to be even more difficult.

Nature of the Times

Not surprisingly, Congress is much more disposed toward cooperating with the president during times of crisis. Under such conditions decisive leadership is required, and Congress recognizes that a single person can provide it more effectively than a legislative body composed of 535 individuals. Franklin Roosevelt was accorded considerable freedom of action and strong support by Congress in fighting the Great Depression as well as in waging war against Germany and Japan. Similarly, when Lyndon Johnson succeeded to the presidency upon the death of President Kennedy, he initially received extraordinary support for his legislative programs. Although his success was undoubtedly enhanced by his own persuasive skills and his thorough understanding of congressional politics, he also benefited from a desire on the part of Congress and the public to unite around their new president at this critical time.

Later in his administration Johnson would seize upon another domestic crisis—the assassination of Martin Luther King, Jr.—in order to work his will on Congress. In 1966 he had proposed a bill to Congress known as the Fair Housing Act, the purpose of which was to prevent discriminatory practices in housing. It was defeated. Johnson reintroduced the bill in 1967 and early 1968, but Congress failed to pass it both times. Immediately following the assassination of Dr. King on April 4, 1968, Johnson realized that the mood of Congress would now be more hospitable to his housing bill. Accordingly, he introduced the bill once again, and this time it passed both houses of Congress. The Fair Housing Act was signed into law by the president on April 10, 1968, just six days after the King assassination.

Public Prestige

Presidents who are fortunate enough to enjoy considerable support from the population are likely to encounter less resistance from Congress. Although the absence of such support does not by any means render presidents powerless to act, their freedom of action is nevertheless likely to be restricted.

> The weaker his apparent popular support, the more his cause in Congress may depend on negatives at his disposal like the veto. . . . He may not be left helpless, but his options are reduced, his opportunities diminished, his freedom of maneuver checked in the degree that Washington conceives him unimpressive to the public.[12]

This is not to say that the congressional mood will respond to any sudden and temporary decline or increase in the president's public prestige. Rather, Congress is more likely to react to the long-run trends in a president's popularity. Throughout most of

Truman's second term in office, for example, his public approval rating declined steadily from around 80 percent to as low as 23 percent. Lyndon Johnson's public approval rating went from 71 percent in 1965 all the way down to 36 percent in 1968.[13] Richard Nixon suffered a similar fate as the Watergate scandals gradually unraveled before the American public. His approval rating was at 51 percent in January 1973, but fell all the way to 24 percent by August 1974.[14]

For each of these presidents, the persistent erosion of public support was accompanied by a general decline in his ability to get the legislation he wanted from Congress. While it would be incorrect to presume that these declines in legislative success were due exclusively to decreasing popular support, they surely played a role.[15]

The blow of decreasing public support may, however, be cushioned to some extent by other factors. Lyndon Johnson, for example, was quite adept at exercising leadership over the legislature. He also benefited from the fact that his party controlled both houses of Congress. Had both of these factors been absent, his declining success with Congress would most likely have accelerated. Eisenhower, on the other hand, did not have Republican majorities in control of Congress for most of the time he was in office, and he was not especially effective as a legislative leader. At the same time, however, his public approval rating never dropped below 49 percent during his eight years as president.[16] If his success rate with Congress was not outstanding, neither was it disastrous; but it might have been had he not enjoyed such widespread public support. Lyndon Johnson, who was then the powerful Senate majority leader, was keenly aware of Eisenhower's popularity in Texas. Accordingly, during his frequent radio broadcasts to his Texas constituents, Senator Johnson never passed up an opportunity to remind them of how many times he had supported President Eisenhower on several important issues.[17] Four presidencies later, another Texan (Congressman Kent Hance) would, like Johnson, feel compelled to take account of another Republican president's popularity: "Reagan won 72 percent of the vote in my district and he's a lot more popular there now than he was on Election Day. It's mighty tough to go against a popular President in a district like mine."[18]

Legislative Leadership Style

If the president wishes favorable consideration of his legislative proposals, then he must be willing to involve himself in the legislative process. He must make a special effort to cultivate the good will of members of Congress; he must make them aware of his legislative priorities—that is, what he cares about most; and he must be willing to press his advantages in seeking to persuade them. By virtue of their interest, temperament, and political astuteness, some presidents have proven more adept at this task than others.

Among our earlier presidents, Jefferson was by far the most assertive in seeking congressional support, and he did so in a manner unmatched by those who preceded or came after him. While Congress was in session, he held White House dinners for legislators on an almost nightly basis. To ensure an intimate atmosphere, no more than twelve were invited at any one time, but almost all were invited more than once while Congress was in session. Invitations were written personally by Jefferson and were often accompanied by an additional note. A round dinner table was used for the occasion, "thus avoiding a place of precedence for the president, and putting him among his peers, at the same time that it prevented separate, private conversations."[19] In an effort to encourage frank and open conversation, Jefferson did not permit any servants to be present but instead had a dumbwaiter installed from which he personally served the dinner. The good food and wine, the informal atmosphere, and free and easy conversation all helped to make such dinners the talk of Washington. Their importance should not be underestimated in explaining why Jefferson enjoyed such extraordinary support among members of his party in Congress.

Jefferson had the luxury of occupying the presidency at a time when fewer demands were made upon it and when Congress was considerably smaller than it is today. Although twentieth-century presidents lack the time to cultivate Congress in the manner to which Jefferson was accustomed, they do attempt to establish a working relationship in other ways. Harry Truman was the first president to officially designate certain members of his staff as legislative liaisons. Eisenhower went further by establishing within his staff an Office of Congressional Relations, which has been continued under subsequent presidents.

Eisenhower himself, however, did not assume a very assertive role in his dealings with Congress, for his conception of the presidency and his personal style were not suited to such a role. Beyond making his views known to Congress, he did not think it appropriate for the presidency to intrude itself into the legislative process. In addition, he made it quite clear that he found distasteful the role of a president as a partisan politician, prodding and cajoling the members of Congress: "I think it is quite apparent that I am not very much of a partisan. The times are too serious, I think, to indulge in partisanship to the extreme."[20]

This refusal to politick with Congress was clearly demonstrated in Eisenhower's response to the death of Senator Robert Taft, the Republican majority leader in the Senate. The top contender to succeed Taft was Senator William Knowland of California, a Republican who had strongly opposed Eisenhower's presidential candidacy. Since support by the majority leader is of considerable importance to the success of the president's legislative program, it was expected that Eisenhower would fight to prevent the selection of Senator Knowland. Thus, it came as quite a surprise when the president announced to his cabinet that "this Administration has absolutely no personal choice for new Majority Leader. *We* are not going to get into *their* business."[21] Knowland ultimately was selected, and he did indeed prove to be unsympathetic to many of Eisenhower's programs. The president's reluctance to involve himself in partisan politics is not altogether surprising, for he had very little training for it. As he himself noted, he had been isolated "from boyhood from nearly all politics."[22]

John Kennedy took a more activist view of the presidency and was committed to the belief that this posture included presidential involvement in partisan politics: "Legislative leadership is not possible without party leadership. . . . No President can escape politics."[23] He retained the Office of Congressional Liaison, but unlike Eisenhower, who kept it out of politics, he staffed it with a group of strong Democratic partisans headed by Larry O'Brien. He was not in the presidency very long before he vigorously asserted his office into congressional affairs. Sensing that his liberal legislative programs were destined to be killed by the powerful and conservative House Rules Committee, he pressured the Democratic House leadership to push for an expansion of the House Rules Committee so more liberals could be placed on it. After a long legislative battle, the plan was ultimately approved by a slim margin of eight votes.

Kennedy was equally willing to bestow presidential favors upon members of Congress as payment for past or future support. There were limits to his assertiveness, however. When push came to shove, he was reluctant to use high-pressure tactics. According to Senator Everett Dirksen, Kennedy prefered to persuade by rely-ing "entirely on the intrinsic merits of the request."[24] This assessment is confirmed by Kennedy's chief legislative liaison, who recalls that the president would make his case in a rational fashion, hoping that a given member of Congress would see the issue as he did, but that he "rarely asked a member for his vote on a specific piece of legislation."[25] His reluctance to do so is perhaps explained by the fact that his rela-tionship with members of Congress was correct rather than friendly. In the words of a former aide, "Kennedy's Congressional relations were marked by a formality and stiffness, which I believe stemmed from the fact that he never really felt comfortable as a member of the legislature, nor did he personally identify with it. He was unwill-ing to pay the dues, so to speak, and felt something of an aloofness, if not disdain, for the legislative body."[26]

Among recent presidents none exercised presidential leadership over Congress with greater skill, energy, and success than did Lyndon Johnson. Twenty-three years of experience in Congress—eight of which were spent as Senate majority leader—undoubtedly provided him with an invaluable opportunity to gain a thorough under-standing of the process and its people. And he was determined to make every use of this advantage. Unlike his predecessor, moreover, Johnson was genuinely fascinated by the legislative process, and consequently his involvement with it was undertaken with great relish. Furthermore, he had an abiding respect for the abilities of its mem-bership, frequently reminding his advisers that "not all the patriotism and wisdom reside in the Executive branch. They [Congress] will change our bills and often as not, they will improve them."[27] Acutely aware of Congress's importance in the poli-cymaking process, Johnson went to extraordinary lengths to cultivate its support. His instructions to staff aides conveyed his determination to do so: "The most important people you will talk to are senators and congressmen. You treat them as if they were President. Answer their calls immediately. Give them respect. . . . They are your most important clients."[28]

To an unprecedented degree, Johnson also sought to involve Congress in the formulation of legislation. He put representatives and senators on task forces that were charged with identifying problem areas in need of legislative solutions. When it actually came time to begin drafting a piece of legislation, Johnson dispatched his aides to Capitol Hill, where they met secretly with those representatives and senators who had a special interest in the legislation. The purpose of these meetings was to incorporate their suggestions into specific provisions of the bill. Finally, on the eve of formally introducing the bill before Congress, Johnson would hold a White House dinner meeting with congressional leaders to consider last-minute suggestions for changing the bill and to plan legislative strategy once the bill was before Congress.

Johnson's meticulous efforts to include Congress in the process of formulating legislation greatly enhanced the possibility that his programs would be favorably received by the legislative branch.[29] When additional pressure was needed, however, Johnson was not at all reluctant to intervene personally. Whereas Kennedy tried to convince primarily on the merits of the case, Johnson went further—he begged, flat-tered, and twisted arms when necessary. On one occasion he even went so far as to contact a senator's mistress to see if she could persuade the senator to vote in favor of closing off a filibuster that was being waged against the 1964 civil rights bill.[30] Such high-pressure tactics ultimately produced considerable resentment and resistance among members of Congress, but not before Johnson had produced one of the most remarkable legislative records of any president in our history.

In several respects, Richard Nixon provided a marked contrast to his predecessor. Whereas Johnson was genuinely fascinated by the legislative process, Nixon found it singularly uninteresting. And whereas Johnson felt an abiding respect for the institution, his successor regarded Congress as a nuisance. One explanation for these attitudes may be that Nixon's own experience in Congress was not an altogether happy one. In the House he functioned as a loner, and as a senator never gained entry into the Senate's inner club of influentials.[31]

Although Nixon did appoint a highly respected political pro by the name of Bryce Harlow to head his legislative liaison office in the White House, Harlow's efforts to develop a working relationship with Congress were largely nullified by Nixon's two closest advisers, H. R. Haldeman and John Ehrlichman. Having never had any Washington experience themselves, these two Nixon aides failed to appreciate the delicate nature of the relationship between the president and Congress. Indeed, the legislative branch was viewed by them as an "awkward and obnoxious obstacle, a hostile foreign power."[32] Accordingly, members of Congress experienced great difficulty in gaining access to the president. Phone calls to the White House by longtime supporters went unanswered, and appointments with the president were hard to come by. And, apparently, not even the Republican leadership in Congress was consulted on legislative matters as evidenced in a complaint voiced by the Republican minority leader of the Senate: "They never invite me for the take-offs but they damned well want me there for the crash landings."[33] Although Nixon was not at all reluctant to assert himself in his relations with Congress, his actions usually took the form of negative as opposed to positive action. Unlike Johnson, he did not enjoy face-to-face bargaining with legislators; nor did he make a strenuous effort to gain their support, especially on domestic matters.

> Nixon did not seem to want anything from Congress. To be sure, he initiated domestic programs and proclaimed priorities, but he seemed to lose interest in them quickly. In fact, Congress found itself upbraiding him for not really trying to get what he said he wanted, which many members wanted more than he did. Trying to oppose Nixon on domestic programs was, as some congressmen put it, "like pushing on a string." There was no resistance.[34]

Rather, his assertiveness took the form of frequent condemnations of Congress as irresponsible, frequent use of the veto, and refusal to spend money that had been duly authorized and appropriated by Congress. Needless to say, presidential action of this sort served only to further aggravate an already strained relationship.

Jimmy Carter and his top aides came into the White House believing that Congress would present no greater problem to them than the Georgia legislature. To say the least, this view proved to be unfounded, for Carter's overall success rate with Congress fell considerably short of his two Democratic predecessors. This track record can no doubt be partially explained by the fact that he confronted a legislature significantly different from the one faced by Kennedy and Johnson. Power within Congress was now more fragmented, party discipline was on the decline, and the influence of special-interest groups on the membership was more pronounced than ever. Even after one acknowledges all of this, however, the fact remains that much of Carter's difficulty with Congress was a function of his own limitations.

Having arrived in Washington as an "outsider," he had few personal contacts in Congress and little understanding of how it operates. To make matters worse, the president appointed an equally inexperienced aide to head the White House Office of Congressional Liaison. This combined lack of experience in congressional relations was manifest in several areas. For one thing, the Carter White House showed little sensitivity to the care and feeding of Congress. Legislators were not given advance notice when the president appointed someone from their districts; presidential visits to congressional districts were made without notifying the representative from that district; phone calls to the White House went unanswered; invitations to White House functions were rare, as were presidential birthday greetings.[35] This apparent lack of concern for the congressional ego stood in marked contrast to what one member of Congress described as the more solicitous approach taken by Lyndon Johnson: "Nobody but Lyndon Johnson would have helicoptered in to help me celebrate an anniversary in office—but he did. Nobody but Johnson would have remembered to write birthday greetings, to send pictures, to send invitations, in short, to do anything possible to help the most junior member of Congress feel recognized, wanted, cared for, and cared about."[36]

The ineptness of the Carter White House was also apparent on substantive legislation that, in some instances, was drafted without any prior consultation with key members of Congress. Carter's 1977 proposals on energy and water projects fell victim to this oversight. Moreover, once legislation was formally introduced in Congress, the White House often neglected to follow up on it. Thus, legislation designed to realize one of Carter's major campaign promises—creation of a Consumer Protection Agency—failed for this reason. Exasperated at the defeat, the president's special assistant for consumer affairs complained to him that "your people don't know how to get a bill through Congress. They don't know the basic tools of how to operate there, of using the power we have there as a party."[37]

In addition to inadequate consultation and follow-up, the president's legislative program suffered from an excess of proposals. In a relatively short span of time, Carter sent to the Hill legislation dealing with such matters as energy, election and welfare reform, government reorganization, the Panama Canal treaties, Social Security, and agriculture. In so doing, he failed to provide Congress with any indication of what should take priority. As one congressman noted, "With almost no exceptions every issue that has come down from the White House or agency has been viewed as *the* big issue."[38] Moreover, by thrusting all of this legislation upon Congress—most of which was highly controversial—the president was forced to deal with opposition from many different quarters all at once.

Finally, Carter also failed to make adequate use of some important tools of persuasion. For example, rather than keeping hold of the patronage lever, he initially gave his department heads the responsibility for filling appointive positions in government. In many instances, members of Congress suggested individuals for positions in the government, only to have them ignored by department heads. Needless to say, this kind of treatment did not serve to build up a store of congressional goodwill toward the administration. Carter's apparent insensitivity to the importance of such presidential carrots as patronage and projects stemmed from an aversion to the LBJ style of wheeling and dealing. In the words of the House majority leader, "He does not like to indulge in quid pro quo. . . . I think he came to the office thinking there was something a bit corrupt about the political give-and-take of Washington."[39]

In Carter's defense, it ought to be noted that as he moved further into his term, there was some improvement in his legislative leadership style. He and his staff made a greater effort to consult with key members of Congress before introducing legislation, and follow-up was pursued more systematically. Carter refrained from placing too much on the congressional table at one time, and, although not comfortable in doing so, he evinced a greater willingness to engage in horse trading. But he paid a price for this learning experience, for presidents typically enjoy their greatest legislative success early in their term when their support in and outside Congress is at its peak.

That Reagan's relationship with Congress began more auspiciously than Carter's was not a matter of luck but rather the consequence of shrewd political instincts and a winning personal style. Whereas Carter came to Washington announcing that he would, if necessary, take his case over the heads of Congress to the American people, Reagan sought to project a spirit of cooperation from the very start. Toward this end, he journeyed to Capitol Hill after his election and met with key leaders of Congress—a gesture he would repeat only a few days following his inauguration. Similarly, whereas Carter installed a man of little political experience as head of the White House Office of Congressional Liaison, Reagan chose someone (Max Friedersdorf, who had to resign his position after one year because of health reasons and was replaced by his top assistant, Kenneth Duberstein) actively involved in congressional politics for over twenty years. Keenly aware of the need to consult with the membership and massage their egos, Friedersdorf was instrumental in helping Reagan to establish a working relationship with Congress. Reflecting the general consensus on Capitol Hill, one Senate veteran characterized the White House liaison operation as "the best we've seen in recent years, since LBJ's guys operated up here."[40]

Lyndon Johnson once remarked to an aide, "Doesn't matter what kind of majority you come in with. You've got just one year when they [Congress] treat you right, and before they start worrying about themselves."[41] To a far greater extent than the Carter administration, Reagan and his aides grasped the strategic importance of a president's first several months in office—the period during which his political leverage is likely to be greatest. Accordingly, before February was out Reagan had placed before Congress what he wanted most, spending reductions and tax cuts. To ensure that congressional and public attention would remain focused on his economic package, he avoided overloading the legislative agenda with other proposals; when issues such as El Salvador and the sale of planes to Saudi Arabia surfaced as distractions, he promptly placed them on the back burner. Carter, on the other hand, did not present his crucial energy legislation to Congress until three months after taking office. To make matters worse, this legislation was preceded and followed by the introduction of numerous other Carter proposals, some of which were highly controversial. The results of inundating Congress with so much legislation were twofold: The president failed to convey any sense of what his priorities were, and he had to contend with opposition from many different quarters simultaneously, across a broad range of issues.

Reagan's smooth start with Congress was a function not only of his astute political instincts but also of his personal style. Whereas courting legislators was regarded as a chore by the more introverted Carter, Reagan genuinely enjoyed the personal interaction. Within his first three months in office, he had already met with most members of Congress, either individually or in groups. Moreover, when additional persuasion was required to secure support for his legislation, he showed no reluctance to engage in personal lobbying. For example, in seeking support for his important tax-cut legislation, dozens of legislators were invited to the White House to meet personally with the president. In addition, some fifteen undecided legislators (twelve of these ultimately voted for the tax bill) were brought to Camp David for a cookout and tax talk by Reagan. And five days before the critical vote in the House, Reagan ventured up to Capitol Hill and delivered a final rallying speech to the House Republican Caucus.[42] His direct involvement in key congressional votes prompted Republican Whip Trent Lott to observe, "I've got the best whip organization because Ronald Reagan is in it."[43]

Although Reagan exhibited considerable skill in congressional relations, he was not able to escape the fate that befalls every president, namely, an overall decline in his legislative success rate, with just a slight increase in his final year (1981, 82 percent; 1982, 72 percent; 1983, 67 percent; 1984, 65 percent; 1985, 59 percent; 1986, 56 percent; 1987, 43 percent; 1988, 47 percent).[44] At the same time, however, it seems likely that Reagan's highly astute legislative liaison staff, combined with his own talents as a legislative leader, not only helped to cushion this decline but also contributed significantly to the passage of landmark legislation—the largest tax cut in history, the greatest peacetime buildup in defense, unprecedented cuts in domestic spending, and a comprehensive revision of the tax code.

George Bush, however, was not as fortunate as the fellow Republican who preceded him. On the contrary, by the time he left office his average legislative success rate over four years was the lowest (51.9 percent) of any first-term president in forty years.[45] While his legislative leadership style may not, as we shall see shortly, have been primarily responsible, it surely played a part. His problem was not lack of knowlege about how the political game is played with Congress. On the contrary, as a one-time congressman and vice president, he was no stranger to the ways of Congress, and his legislative aides in the White House were seasoned professionals as well. Furthermore, in contrast to Nixon and Carter, President Bush interacted freely and easily with legislators and was attentive to the presidential gestures that constitute part of the care and feeding of Congress. What he failed to project from the start, however, was a sense of what he stood for and really cared about in the area of domestic policy. Presidents who fail to convey what policy issues they really care about are likely to find that members of Congress will care less as well and be more inclined to pursue their own agendas.

Unlike Jimmy Carter, Bill Clinton brought to the presidency a gregarious and ingratiating personality—one thoroughly comfortable interacting with members of Congress and more than ready to engage in the bargaining and horse-trading so essential to the legislative process. Moreover, he had signaled early on his commitment to cultivating a workable relationship with Congress, having visited the Hill during the general election campaign, several times again before his inauguration, and on a number of occasions once in office.

On the other hand, Clinton also came to the presidency with some major political liabilities. He was elected with only 43 percent of the vote—the fourth-lowest winning percentage in American history; ran behind House winners in all but five congressional districts; and began his presidency with 14 percent fewer House Democrats and 11 percent fewer Senate Democrats than his Democratic predecessor, Jimmy Carter. To these must be added other limiting factors that pertain to Clinton the man. For one thing, his leadership appeared to lack the requisite constancy and decisiveness. Evidence of this came early in his presidency when, in the face of strong opposition from several powerful legislators, he abandoned his position on admitting gays into the military. This was followed by reversals on other issues, including tax cuts, deficit reductions (second budget), relations with China, our role in Bosnia, and the plight of Haitian refugees. Twists and turns such as these prompted congressman David Obey (D-Wis.) to observe that "most of us learned some time ago that if you don't like the president's position on a particular issue, you simply need to wait a few weeks."[46] Particularly for more moderate congressional Democrats, who saw in Clinton a political soulmate, some of his policy decisions brought disillusionment. He had, after all, campaigned as a "New" Democrat, not a traditional liberal; and yet he now supported admission of gays into the military, comprehensive national health insurance, family medical leave, and the nominations of Lani Guinier (for assistant attorney general, civil rights) and Joselyn Elders (for surgeon general), whose views on social issues were deemed out of the mainstream. In short, as Clinton moved further into his first term many in Washington began to wonder, as did a Clinton operative, "Where is the hallowed ground? Where does he stand? What does he stand for?[47]

Clinton was also disadvantaged by the lack of any previous Washington experience—a limitation he freely acknowledged: "I never dealt with Congress before last year. I'm still learning."[48] Although, in contrast to Carter, he had the good sense to appoint as his legislative liaison someone (Howard Paster) who had logged a great many hours on the Hill, Paster's role was seriously hampered by yet another Clinton weakness—an undisciplined approach to managing his staff. Because staff positions were left vaguely defined, several White House aides were free to dabble in congressional relations, thereby undermining the credibility and effectiveness of Paster, who resigned at the end of the first year.[49] Furthermore, the lack of discipline within the White House generally—as evidenced by delayed decisions, a high staff turnover rate, inadequate background checks on Clinton appointees, the clumsy handling of personnel matters in the White House Travel Office, to name a few—fed the impression that Clinton might not be up to the challenge of governing; and this impression, in turn, reduced his credibility with Congress.

The 1994 midterm election was a particularly stinging verdict on the first two years of Clinton's stewardship, as it gave Republicans control of Congress for the first time since 1953. And yet this setback was not without benefit. The Republicans' ideological fervor and reluctance to compromise enabled Clinton to more sharply define his presidency. Thus, a president who had not vetoed any bills during his first two years, exercised fourteen vetoes in the second two years, including vetoes that brought a temporary shutdown of the government. In crossing swords with Republicans, Clinton positioned himself more toward the center of the political spectrum even as the Republican Congress veered farther to the right. This strategic move, along with a growing economy, and personnel changes that brought a more tightly managed White House, combined to convince Americans that Clinton deserved another term. Thus, a president who early in office seemed rather inept in dealing with Congress, proved quite agile in learning from his mistakes and in adapting to a changed strategic environment. As of this writing the president's second term has brought with it a historic agreement with Congress to balance the budget, but the storm clouds of personal scandal could well limit his ability to do much else.

Party Control

If a president's legislative leadership style counts for something in getting his way with Congress, the evidence strongly suggests that having his party in control of Congress counts for very much more.[50] Indeed, it may prove a greater advantage to presidents than any other single factor. Thus, although Lyndon Johnson's persuasive skills were considerable, his extraordinary legislative record in 1964 and 1965 was facilitated primarily by the fact that his party enjoyed such substantial majorities in the House (239 to 140) and the Senate (69 to 32) during this time. Conversely, not only did Richard Nixon's leadership style create antagonism between himself and Congress, but the president was further disadvantaged because his party did not control either house of Congress during the entire time he was in office. Bush was disadvantaged to an even greater extent, for not only did the opposition party control Congress, but Bush took office with fewer members of his own party in Congress than any newly elected president in this century.[51] Clinton, whose party did control both Houses during his first two years in office, provides perhaps the most dramatic testimony to the costs that can come with losing it, as he did following the 1994 midterm election. For both 1993 and 1994, Clinton's average legislative success rate with Congress was 86 percent. Although this figure overstates his success, as we shall see shortly, nevertheless in 1995 it dropped all the way down to 36 percent, the lowest ever recorded for a president since Congressional Quarterly developed its legislative success index. To be sure, Clinton improved to an average of 54 percent in 1996 and 1997, but this was still well below the success levels he achieved in his first two years. In 1998, moreover, he dropped down to 51 percent.[52]

Of course, it should be emphasized that although presidents prefer to have their party in control of Congress, this advantage is by itself no guarantee that they will get all they want from it. From 1962 to 1968, for example, the Democrats controlled both the House and the Senate. The average support among Senate Democrats for Johnson's legislative programs over this period was 59 percent; among House Democrats it was 72 percent. And from the period 1977 to 1980, support for Jimmy Carter's legislative programs averaged 66 percent among Senate Democrats and 62 percent among Democratic members in the House. For the first two years of the Clinton presidency, when the Democrats controlled Congress, the president's legislative support averaged 76 percent among House Democrats and 87 percent among Democrats in the Senate. These figures hide much, however. Health care, the most important legislative initiative of the Clinton presidency, failed even to reach the floor of either chamber in 1994. He did manage to achieve a substantial deficit reduction package in his first year but only after he agreed to abandon the centerpiece of his tax proposal—the BTU tax—and made a host of other compromises. Even then, the bill cleared the House by only one vote, with eleven Democratic subcommittee chairpersons voting against the president. In the Senate, meanwhile, it passed only after Vice President Albert Gore cast the tie-breaking vote. The president also won a hard-fought victory on NAFTA, but over half of the House Democrats abandoned him, and he faced the spectacle of vocal opposition in the House from two leaders within his own party—Majority Leader Richard Gephardt (D-Mo.) and Majority Whip John Bonior (D-Mich.). Nor was this the last time that Congressman Gephardt would fail to support the president on legislation of critical importance. He declined to side with Clinton on renewing normal trade status with China, and as the Democratic minority leader in 1997, refused to give Clinton "fast track" authority on trade issues, and voted against the balanced budget agreement worked out between the president and the Republican-controlled Congress.

Nor should the president count on the full support of his party when it is in the minority in Congress. As already noted, Republicans lacked majorities in both houses while Richard Nixon was in office. During this time House Republicans supported Nixon's stand on legislation 63 percent of the time, and Senate Republicans 62 percent of the time.[53] More recently, the average support for George Bush was 61 percent among House Republicans and 73 percent among Republicans in the Senate.[54] Ronald Reagan faced a situation somewhat different from that of Nixon and Bush. From 1981 to 1988, Republicans were a minority in the House but did manage to maintain a majority in the Senate through 1986. During Reagan's eight years in office House Republican support averaged 64 percent, while Senate Republican support averaged 73 percent.[55]

It should be apparent from the discussion in the previous section that a president's leadership style can help to explain his failure to gain the full support of legislators in his party. But other factors may intrude here as well. Members of Congress may be philosophically opposed to the president's position on a given issue, or they may be under strong pressure from their constituencies to vote against one of his programs. As Lyndon Johnson aptly observed, "It is day dreaming to assume that any experienced congressman would ignore his basic instincts or his constituents' deepest concerns in quaking fear of the White House." Finally, failure to support their party's president is undoubtedly encouraged by the fact that they pay little penalty for withholding such support. They are not likely to suffer any sanctions within Congress, nor, more important, is their reelection likely to be seriously jeopardized. Members of Congress are not easily defeated. In fact, an examination of the twenty-one elections from 1950 through 1990 reveals that the reelection rate of House incumbents exceeded 90 percent on seventeen occasions and never dropped below 86.6 percent. For senators, the reelection rate was lower but still an impressive 78 percent.[56] To be sure, a disloyal member of Congress may suffer the displeasure of the president, but even this is likely to be only temporary, for the president will almost certainly have to enlist his or her support on some future occasion.

If presidents have never been able to count on the wholehearted support of their party in Congress, it must also be emphasized that this problem has become even more acute in recent years.[57] Lamenting this fact, former House Speaker O'Neill commented that "when Sam Rayburn [for many years Speaker of the House] was around here, he could call up one person, the leader of a state delegation, and that one man could deliver the entire delegation. Today you can't do that. The nature of the institution is not the same. . . . You don't have the discipline out there." Former Senate Majority Leader Robert Byrd has expressed a similar view: "Going back to my earliest years in the Senate, I think there was more of an allegiance to party, more of an establishment-minded feeling. There was more cohesiveness on the part of the parties than there has been in recent years. The emergence of the 'individual' has been a kind of phenomenon."[58]

This decline in party loyalty may be explained by changes that have occurred both in and outside of Congress. For one thing, the population is no longer as strongly attached to political parties as it was in the fifties and early sixties. Fewer individuals now identify with a political party, and even among those who do, the weak identifiers outnumber the strong.[59] It should not be surprising, therefore, that this attitude is also reflected among their elected representatives.

Second, accompanying the decline in the population's attachment to party—indeed perhaps because of it—we have witnessed an ever-growing number of highly organized and well-financed special-interest groups. These groups, moreover, are focusing their attention on Congress to a greater extent than ever before. Political action committees (PACs), for example, gave $35 million to House and Senate candidates from 1977 to 1978, but had increased this sum to $106 million from 1985 to 1986; and for the 1994 election cycle alone, PACs spent a total of $387 million on congressional races.[60] Clearly, to the extent that the president's plea for loyalty must compete with those of well-organized special-interest groups, his task of forging a consensus within his own party is rendered more difficult.

Third, the influence of these groups has been enhanced further by certain changes in the rules and procedures of Congress. Votes taken on the floor of the House are now recorded, whereas prior to 1970 they were not. In addition, although bills used to be marked up in committees behind closed doors, now this process is open to the public in both the House and the Senate. These changes, to be sure, provide a greater opportunity to see what Congress is doing, but they also make it more difficult for members to escape the watchful eye of special-interest groups.

Fourth, the fragmentation of our society into a variety of single- and multiple-interest groups has manifested itself within Congress as well. Indeed, there are now some 120 different informal caucuses in Congress organized to protect and further the interests of blacks, women, Hispanics, blue-collar workers, textiles, tourism, mushrooms, steel, solar energy, gasohol, suburbia, rural America, and the Northeast, to name but a few.[61]

Fifth, the leadership of both parties in Congress no longer wields the power it once did. This is due partly to the fact that an important element of the leadership, committee chairpersons, have less power. Until the early 1970s, the chairs of congressional committees were determined solely on the basis of seniority, and thus chairpersons could wield a heavy hand with little fear of retribution. Although seniority continues to be an important factor in determining chairpersons, members of the majority party in the House now vote on who will occupy these positions, and they are not required to consider seniority in their decision. In the Senate any given chair can be put to a vote if one-fifth of the majority party so requests. Needless to say, these new selection procedures compel committee chairpersons to be more accommodating toward the rest of the members of their party. The leadership also appears less inclined to wield even the power it does have, because the post-Watergate breed of representative is not so easily intimidated by pressure tactics. As an administrative assistant to former House Speaker O'Neill observed, "Now members are young, bright, highly educated, independent. . . . It makes it infinitely harder for the leadership."[62] Jim Wright, at one time Speaker of the House, echoed this assessment, "Being Speaker gives you nothing more than a license to persuade. These Democrats, they elect a leader to advise them, and then they ignore his advice."[63]

Finally, in seeking to account for the diminished significance of party within Congress, it is important to note that with burgeoning staffs, abundant campaign funds, and the availability of public relations firms, incumbents no longer have to rely upon the party organization in their bids for reelection.

☆ THE ASCENDANCY OF THE PRESIDENT AS LEGISLATOR

Although in this day and age we readily accept as a given the role of the president as an initiator of legislation, his ascendancy in this area represents one of the most profound changes in the relationship between the president and Congress. Accordingly, we shall now consider this development in some detail.

In drawing up the Constitution, the Founding Fathers provided that the president "shall from time to time give Congress Information on the State of the Union, and recommend to their Consideration such Measures as he shall judge necessary and expedient." Notwithstanding this provision, however, the primary function of the executive was to execute the legislation that was proposed and passed by Congress. Even the veto power was intended as a mechanism to be used by the president chiefly against legislation that threatened the constitutional powers of his office.[64] Although such presidents as Jefferson, Jackson, and Lincoln did inject themselves into the legislative process, these initiatives were clearly the exception rather than the rule. Indeed, the predominant view was one voiced by Congressman Abraham Lincoln: "Were I President, I should desire the legislation of the country to rest with Congress, uninfluenced in its origin or progress, and undisturbed by the veto unless in very special and clear cases."[65] Although, as president, Lincoln did not see fit to follow his own advice, his successors did. Indeed, for the three decades following the Civil War Congress exercised a virtual monopoly over the legislative agenda, prompting one observer of the time to comment:

> The president's wishes conveyed in a message have not necessarily any more effect on Congress than an article in a prominent party newspaper, and in fact the suggestions which he makes, year after year, are usually neglected even when his party has a majority in both Houses. . . .[66]

Congressional domination in this area slowly began to change during Theodore Roosevelt's first term. Believing that the president should be an active force in the political system, he submitted a great number of legislative proposals to Congress. He trod gingerly, however, on one occasion warning a frustrated adviser of the "extreme unwisdom of irritating Congress by fixing the details of a bill concerning which they are very sensitive."[67] Woodrow Wilson went one step further than Roosevelt. He not only submitted legislative proposals for consideration but also went so far as to make personal appearances before Congress to speak on behalf of his legislation.

The growth in the role of the president as a legislative initiator continued to a greater or lesser degree under subsequent presidents and came to full fruition under President Truman, who established the presidential practice of submitting an entire, integrated legislative program at the beginning of each session of Congress. That Congress had come to accept this executive initiative was reflected in its reaction to Eisenhower's failure to submit promptly a legislative program to Congress after he became president. Holding to a strict view of the president's responsibilities under the Constitution, Eisenhower was extremely reluctant to intrude into the legislative process. He changed his mind, however, when the Republican leadership in Congress complained about having no legislative agenda on which to act. The point was made clearly by one Republican committee chairman in his remarks to an administration spokesman: "Don't expect us to start from scratch on what you people want. That's not the way we do things here—you draft the bills and we work them over."[68] Such an admission by a member of Congress would undoubtedly have stunned the Founding Fathers.

The ascendancy of the president in the legislative area should not be construed to mean that Congress no longer performs an important legislative function. On the contrary, it still makes valuable contributions, which take the form of criticizing and amending presidential proposals. As one student of Congress has observed, however, the fact remains that a president now defines "the bulk of the legislative agenda for Congress with his various annual and specific messages. Thus, even before specific actions are taken, the president, in effect, decides what is and is not most important for Congress to consider."[69]

Several factors are responsible for this change. In the first place, much of the twentieth century has been marked by periods of domestic and international crisis. The presidency has been more suited to exercising the necessary leadership at such times, for unlike Congress, it speaks with one voice. Equally important was the fact that during these times of war and economic crisis, the presidency was usually occupied by individuals whose conception of the office embodied vigorous leadership. Accordingly, they took the initiative in proposing legislative solutions to many of the nation's pressing problems. Finally, presidential dominance of the legislative agenda has been enhanced by the complexity of the problems we face as an advanced industrialized nation. Information and expertise are required in order to formulate legislative solutions to these problems. In the past, however, Congress has found itself deficient in both, primarily because it has not been adequately staffed. Congress was not unaware of the problem. Indeed, as far back as 1946, the Joint Committee on the Organization of Congress pointed out that "the shocking lack of adequate congressional fact-finding services and skilled staffs sometimes reaches such ridiculous proportions as to make Congress dependent upon 'hand-outs' from Government departments and private groups or newspaper stories for its basic fund of information on which to base legislative decisions."[70] Even as late as 1965, the support staff of Congress consisted of only 5,386 in the House and 3,218 in the Senate.[71] This rather modest staff component had to compete with an executive branch whose analysts and experts numbered in the hundreds of thousands.

The limited ability of Congress to generate information was further compounded by lack of analytic capability that computer technology provides. More specifically, in the early 1970s it had less than a half dozen computers, which was equivalent to the computer capacity of the First National Bank of Kodoka, South Dakota.[72] On the other hand, the executive branch had several thousand computers, manned by more than 50,000 individuals, at a cost in excess of $2.7 billion a year.[73] Because of the vastly superior information base that computers gave to the executive branch, Congress was frequently forced to rely upon it for facts and figures. For example, when the House Ways and Means Committee was considering the financial impact of various proposals for welfare reform, it was compelled to turn to the Department of Health, Education and Welfare and its computers for the needed information. As former senator and vice president Walter Mondale points out, however, such assistance from the executive branch was not always forthcoming: "I recall hearings on legislation dealing with multi-billion dollar education programs where we asked the Executive branch for computer assistance. We received either no help at all or information that was often useless. But the congressional backers of Administration positions received full and very valuable support as well as computer assistance."[74] To the extent that Congress had to rely upon the information and expertise of the executive branch, it was hampered in its ability to make an independent evaluation of presidential programs, let alone present alternatives to them.

In discussing the dominant role of the president in initiating legislation, special mention must be given to the federal budget, which is the most important piece of legislation submitted to Congress. Presidential ascendancy over the budgetary process had its genesis in the Budget and Accounting Act, which was passed by Congress and signed into law by President Harding in 1921. This act gave to the president the responsibility for submitting an executive budget to Congress every January. Prior to this act, each department and agency in the executive branch submitted its own budget estimates directly to Congress, a procedure that created considerable confusion and inefficiency.

Although Congress has been free to make any changes it wishes in the president's budget, its handling of this important piece of legislation has in the past been ineffective. In the first place, no group in Congress ever examined the budget in toto. Rather, each congressional committee would deal only with that portion of the budget that came directly under its jurisdiction. For example, those committees charged with recommending the authorization and appropriation of money related to agriculture would concern themselves only with those parts of the budget related to agriculture. Consequently, no committee knew how its own budgetary recommendations affected the total budget expenditure. Second, Congress had put itself in a position of reacting to the president's budget rather than generating its own budget as an alternative to it. This state of affairs was hardly surprising, given the piecemeal fashion in which Congress approached the budget. Equally important, however, was the fact that Congress lacked the staff capability possessed by the president on budgetary matters. In drawing up his budget, the president is assisted by an arm of the executive branch known as the Office of Management and Budget (OMB), which has a staff of over six hundred. Populated by budget analysts and possessing a formidable computer capacity, the OMB provided the president with an analytic capability that Congress simply could not match. Thus, in conducting its own analysis of the budget, Congress often was compelled to rely on the OMB for needed facts and figures.

Congressional Reassertion

Beginning in the early 1970s, Congress took several steps designed to increase its capacity for policy initiation and analysis. Under the Legislative Reorganization Act of 1970, congressional committees were allowed to contract out for the assistance of groups with special expertise—for example, the National Academy of Sciences and the National Academy of Engineering. In addition, the act provided for the expansion of committee staffs, with an emphasis upon hiring individuals trained in policy analysis. In conjunction with enhancing the size of committee staffs, the personal staffs of legislators were increased as well. Thus, by 1993 the combined committee and personal staffs had reached 9,405 in the House and 7,409 in the Senate. To these figures, however, must also be added the various congressional support agencies, whose total staff component by 1993 numbered 17,840.[75] As a means of enhancing the retrieval and analytical capacities of this vastly increased staff—and of the legislators themselves—Congress decided to invest considerable sums of money in computers. By 1985, some 7,500 computer units had been installed in Congress, with total legislative branch spending on computers for that year reaching $75 million.[76]

In 1972, Congress also passed the Technology Assessment Act, which created the Office of Technology Assessment (OTA), whose purpose was to provide the legislative branch with its own independent source of expertise in analyzing complex policy questions. As Senator Edward Kennedy points out, Congress had lacked such a capability in the past:

> Over the past two decades the Executive branch's capability in science and technology has grown immensely, while the ability of Congress to evaluate such programs has stumbled along at a snail's pace. Thus, in recent years we have witnessed great controversies

over the technical facts involved in programs such as the SST, the space shuttle, the use of chemical pesticides, and food and drug additives, the impact on human health of air pollution and waste disposal, not to mention the enormous number of questions regarding the current energy crisis. In such cases, Congress has not had a reliable source of technical expertise on which it could draw to provide an independent technical appraisal of the various alternatives under consideration.[77]

In recent years, the OTA has conducted studies on a variety of policy questions, including climate change, the implications of environmental regulations for American industrial trade and competitiveness, information security and privacy, the human genome project, and the proliferation of weapons of mass destruction. But the office was not without its critics who, although acknowledging the high quality of OTA reports, argued that they came too late to assist legisators in delibertations on matters of technology. Accordingly, when Republicans gained control of Congress in 1995, they voted to shut down the office as a cost-saving measure.[78]

Of greatest potential significance in helping Congress to gain greater control over the policymaking process was the Budget Control and Impoundment Act.[79] Passed by Congress in 1974, this act was designed to correct the rather haphazard manner in which the legislature had previously approached the budget. Specifically, it established a budget committee in each house of Congress. These two committees are charged with making revenue estimates and recommending spending limits for each of the twenty-one major categories in the federal budget. This process must be completed by April 15 of each year. Each house then acts upon the recommendations of its budget committee. If the houses pass budget resolutions that differ in their spending limits, a compromise is worked out in a conference committee. Once this first budget resolution has been adopted, the appropriate congressional committees in the House and Senate proceed to allocate funds for specific items within each of the budget's major categories. By September 15, Congress must approve a second budget resolution, which may retain or change the overall spending limits established in the first resolution. Finally, in a process known as "reconciliation," congressional committees whose spending recommendations exceed the overall spending limits are ordered to reconcile them with the mandated levels contained in the second budget resolution. These reconciliations are then grouped together and brought to the floors of the House and Senate by the chairpersons of their respective budget committees.

Also provided for in the Budget Control and Impoundment Act was the establishment of a Congressional Budget Office (CBO). Now staffed by more than 200 employees, over half of whom are budget and program analysts, this office was created to provide congressional committees with the analytic capability for better evaluating the president's budget recommendations and proposing alternatives to them. It is, in short, the legislature's counterpart to the Office of Management and Budget.

Having now been in effect for nearly twenty-five years, the Budget Control and Impoundment Act has received mixed reviews. Conservatives complain that it has not led to restrained spending, and liberals maintain that it has not enabled Congress to take a more systematic approach to setting national priorities.[80] Others complain that the reconciliation period discussed above occurs so close to the new fiscal year (two weeks) that committees do not have enough time to bring their spending recommendations into line with the spending limits mandated in the second budget resolution.[81] Congress has also been sloppy about complying with certain provisions of the act. On numerous occasions, for example, it has missed the dates for setting both the first and second budget resolutions and has thereby been forced to fund government agencies on the basis of continuing resolutions.[82] Finally, and most directly relevant to our discussion, this act does not necessarily guarantee that legislators will take a more independent approach to the president's budget. To demonstrate that this is so, we need only look at Congress's adoption of President Reagan's 1982 budget request.

The president's 1982 budget was noteworthy not only for the size of its spending reductions—some $36 billion in over 250 federal programs—but also for the manner in which it was passed. Although the president had won essentially the budget reductions he requested in the Republican-controlled Senate, he faced a greater challenge in the House, where Democrats were in a majority. In the final analysis, however, southern Democrats in the House would provide the president with the necessary margin of victory on key budget-related votes. Reagan strategists first won House approval to apply the reconciliation process to the first budget resolution rather than the second. Technically, reconciliation requires only that committees bring their spending recommendations into line with spending ceilings mandated in the budget resolution, leaving the committees to decide where the cuts should be made. However, the administration-sponsored budget resolution specified in many instances precisely what programs were to be cut, thereby reducing committee discretion.[83] This budget resolution was adopted by the House, and immediately thereafter some fourteen committees proceeded to make the necessary cuts. The cuts were then brought to the House in a reconciliation bill presented by the Democratic chairman of the House Budget Committee.

The Reagan administration meanwhile had won another key vote, allowing the reconciliation bill to be voted on by the House as a total package rather than having each spending cut considered separately. This tactic was designed to prevent the bill from being debated, voted on, and possibly picked apart piece by piece. The reconciliation bill itself, however, was not acceptable to the Reagan administration. Even though it produced a greater overall spending reduction than Reagan had requested, several of the cuts came from programs other than those targeted by the administration. With time running out (the reconciliation process must be completed in less than three weeks), and at the urging of Reagan strategists, House conservatives literally overnight put together a substitute reconciliation bill embracing the president's proposed cuts. When presented on the floor of the House the next day, the bill's appearance reflected the haste with which it had been put together. As described by a member of the House Budget Committee staff, it contained "duplications, errors, an indecipherable jumble of multiple page numbers, handwritten scrawls and extraneous material, including an unfortunate bureaucrat's phone number."[84] But shrewd White House lobbying, an ever-burgeoning deficit, and sympathy for a president recuperating from an attempted assassination all combined to give Reagan one of the greatest legislative wins of his presidency. The victory was not without its critics, however. Indeed, from in and outside Congress came charges that the president had run roughshod over the congressional budgetary process and that House members could not possibly have weighed the implications of a bill they passed in such haste.

Even if the above illustration suggests that the Budget Control and Impoundment Act has not always worked precisely as it was supposed to, this fact should not cause us to underestimate its potential significance. Indeed, President Carter's chief domestic policy adviser observed that "it's one of the most important government reforms in decades. But it increases the power of Congress vis-à-vis the Executive. They've set up a competing power system which makes it more difficult for the president to have his way."[85] Its significance is echoed by a scholar of the budgetary process who asserts that "next to the Budget and Accounting Act of 1921, it was the most important budget legislation in the history of the country."[86] Admittedly, Congress did not evince much independence in its approach to Reagan's 1982 budget request. But this outcome was the consequence of personal choice made by members of Congress and not the result of shortcomings inherent in the Budget Control and Impoundment Act. Unquestionably, the analytical capacity provided by computers and the Congressional Budget Office has vastly increased Congress's ability to make its own independent assessments on matters related to revenue, deficits, and spending. In examining Clinton's first budget submission, for example, the CBO found $61.4 billion dollars of unsupported deficit reduction, a finding that helped conservative Democrats force the president to make more spending cuts in his budget. In 1994, the CBO weighed in again, this time dealing a severe blow to Clinton's health care plan by announcing that it was nearly impossible to implement as he proposed it.[87] One former congressional aide, commenting on such a display of budgetary independence by Congress, observed that "in the old days, the idea that a Democratic Congress would not only not accept the figures of a Democratic White House, but not even accept help from a Democratic White House in analyzing the figures is incredible to any of us who watched Congress accept administration figures."[88]

Up to this point, we have been considering the Budget Control and Impoundment Act as it relates to the formulation of the budget. Another portion of this act, however, was designed to ensure that the budget would be implemented as passed by Congress. Why would this be a problem? Rarely, if ever, does Congress pass a budget giving the president exactly the amount of money in exactly the program areas he requests. Under our Constitution, however, the president is responsible for executing all legislation, including the budget. During the course of implementing the budget, presidents have been known to reallocate funds for purposes that Congress was not willing to support when he submitted it. Although presidents have relied upon several spending practices to accomplish these reallocations,[89] the one that has excited most concern in Congress is *impoundment*. Before discussing how legislators attempted to curb this practice, it is first necessary to examine how presidents have made use of it.

Impoundment is a practice by which the president temporarily or permanently withholds the spending of funds that have been appropriated by Congress. The practice dates all the way back to Thomas Jefferson, who at one time refused to spend money appropriated for gunboats on the Mississippi River. Several justifications have been given for the impoundment power. For one thing, circumstances may arise that render the spending of money unnecessary or inappropriate. Thus, in Jefferson's case, he impounded money for gunboats because the purchase of the Louisiana Territory rendered them unnecessary. Congress agreed. Similarly, at the end of the Second World War, Congress appropriated a substantial sum of money to build veterans' hospitals. Truman temporarily impounded the money, believing that it would be better to wait until the veterans returned home and settled down, thus enabling the government to better determine where the hospitals should be located. In some instances, Congress itself provides the president with statutory authority to impound funds. Such was the case with the 1964 Civil Rights Act, which allows the president to withhold funds from federally financed programs in which discrimination is being practiced. Similarly, when President Truman impounded funds that had been appropriated by Congress to expand the size of the Air Force, he was simply exercising an option specifically provided to him in the bill.[90] Congress has been especially willing to provide the president with broad spending discretion on appropriations related to national defense because of his constitutional role as commander in chief. Finally, presidents have justified impoundment on the grounds that it is necessary to stop inflation. Lyndon Johnson invoked this justification when he temporarily withheld funds totaling $5 billion in order to dampen the fires of inflation resulting from the Vietnam War.

Richard Nixon's use of the impoundment power differed from his predecessor's in two important respects. First, he impounded $18 billion, which far exceeded the amount impounded by any president in our history.[91] Furthermore, he sought to completely eliminate programs to which he was opposed by withholding all of the funds appropriated for them. In most cases previous presidents had withheld funds only temporarily, or else had cut back on the funds appropriated for a given program. In those few cases where they withheld all funds from a program, they did so because the legislation was written in such a way as to provide them with this option. Finally, it should be noted that President Nixon undertook these impoundments in spite of an advisory opinion from his attorney general that questioned the constitutionality of such actions: "With respect to the suggestion that the president has a *constitutional* power to decline to spend appropriated funds, we must conclude that the existence of such a broad power is supported neither by reason nor precedent."[92]

When the Founding Fathers were dispersing power among the three branches of government, they gave the power over the purse strings to that branch that most directly represented the people, namely, the legislature. As James Madison remarked, they did so because "this power over the purse may in fact be regarded as the most effectual weapon with which any Constitution can arm the immediate representatives of the people for obtaining a redress of every grievance and for carrying into effect every salutary measure." Richard Nixon's use of the impoundment power represented a fundamental assault against this most potent of legislative powers. And the power was wielded with unusual arrogance, as when John Ehrlichman put Congress on notice that "the Administration will not spend money it considers wasteful even if Congress appropriates the funds over a presidential veto."[93] This was not an idle threat. In 1972 Congress overwhelmingly passed a $5 billion water pollution bill, and it was promptly vetoed by the president. Within twenty-four hours Congress overrode his veto by an overwhelming margin. Indeed, the president received only twelve Senate votes and twenty-three House votes in favor of sustaining his veto. Yet in spite of this action, the president announced that he would impound $3 billion out of the $5 billion that had been appropriated in the bill. Reaction to the Nixon impoundments finally came from both the courts and Congress. Members of Congress as well as private citizens brought suit against the executive branch in order to compel the release of the impounded funds. In most of the cases the courts ruled that the president's impoundments violated the expressed will of Congress and ordered their release.

Congress also sought to restrict the use of the impoundment power by passing the Budget Control and Impoundment Act of 1974. Title X of this legislation stipulates, first, that the president must inform Congress in writing of any intentions to defer or permanently terminate the expenditure of funds for any program. Second, in those cases where the president makes known his intention to *defer* the spending of funds, he can be compelled to spend them if either house passes a resolution ordering him to do so. (This provision became inoperative in 1983 when the Supreme Court ruled the legislative veto unconstitutional.) Third, the president cannot *terminate* the funds for a program unless Congress passes a bill of rescission—within forty-five days after the president makes known his intention—permitting him to do so. Since this legislation has been in effect, a clear pattern has emerged in how Congress reacts to presidential impoundment requests. Most requests for deferrals have been approved because they have been viewed as routine efforts to bring about greater efficiency in spending. On the other hand, most rescission proposals have been rejected on the grounds that they constituted an attempt to alter congressional intent. From 1974 through March of 1992 presidents had, incidentally, submitted some 947 rescission requests totaling $63.5 billion dollars.[94]

The determination of Congress to retain the restrictions imposed on the presidential impoundment power was made abundantly clear on two separate occasions during the Reagan presidency. First, in the fall of 1981 President Reagan called for a second round of cuts in the fiscal 1982 budget. Convinced that their colleagues lacked the stomach for these additional cuts, the Republican leadership in Congress suggested that the president be given the authority to impound up to 10 percent of the funds for any item in the 1982 budget appropriations, excepting entitlement programs. President Reagan embraced the idea enthusiastically. Most of the congressional membership, however, reacted coolly to the suggestion, despite the fact that it would have lifted the budget-cutting burden from their own shoulders and placed it squarely on those of the president. Sensing that their proposal had little support, the Republican leadership quickly discarded it.

In 1986 the impoundment issue provoked a more spirited confrontation between the president and Congress. To fully understand the nature of this dispute, it is first necessary to recall the Supreme Court's 1983 decision in the *Chadah* case. As pointed out in the previous chapter, the Court's ruling declared the "legislative veto" resolution unconstitutional because the president was denied the opportunity to veto it. This decision had the effect of voiding numerous statutes, including that portion of the Budget Control and Impoundment Act that allows either house to pass a resolution forcing the president to spend funds he wants to defer. Thus, if Congress wanted to overrule presidential deferrals, it now had to pass legislation and send it to the president for his signature or veto. In the case of a presidential veto, Congress would then have to muster a two-thirds majority in each house to override. In short, presidential deferrals that once could be nullified merely by a simple majority vote in either house now required extraordinary majorities in both houses. Not unmindful of his newfound advantage and believing that the *Chadha* ruling in no way limited the deferral authority granted him in the Budget Control and Impoundment Act, President Reagan in February 1986 decided to defer some $5.4 billion earmarked for low-income housing. Because he had opposed the appropriation of these funds in the first place, legislators saw his impoundment as a deliberate attempt to substitute his own policy preferences for theirs.[95] Four Democratic congressmen—joined by the National League of Cities, the U.S. Conference of Mayors, and others—immediately brought suit against the president in federal court. There they argued that the president's authority to impound for policy reasons should be invalidated on the grounds that Congress would not have granted him this authority in the absence of a legislative veto. The U.S. District Court judge agreed, whereupon the Reagan administration took its case to the Court of Appeals. A three-judge panel unanimously upheld the lower court ruling and ordered the president to release the $5.4 billion. The panel found that the deferral power and legislative veto were inseparable; that is, when the legislative veto was voided by the Court, the president's authority to defer funds for policy reasons became invalid as well.[96] With two defeats in the lower courts, the Reagan administration decided not to appeal to the Supreme Court.

Budget Enforcement Act (1990)

As the decade of the 1980s was drawing to a close, concern over the nation's fiscal health took on a new sense of urgency. By the time George Bush took office the national debt had grown to nearly $3 trillion; and the budget deficit, although projected to be $100 billion in the 1990 budget left by Reagan, actually went as high as $218.5 billion. Placing most of the blame for this on an undisciplined Congress, Bush called upon legislators to propose a balanced budget amendment to the Constitution; give him the line item veto; require a congressional vote on presidential rescission proposals—a change from the current procedure whereby Congress can kill such requests by taking no action at all (see pp. 89–90); change its budget resolution from a concurrent resolution (see p. 86), which does not require his signature or veto, to a joint resolution, which does. Last, Bush asked Congress to join him in discussions on cutting the budget deficit. After much wrangling, Congress passed and Bush signed the Budget Enforcement Act of 1990. Under provisions of this act, entitlement programs must be funded on a pay-as-you-go basis. Second, spending caps are imposed in the remaining general budget categories—defense, international, and domestic. Third, if either the pay-as-you-go or the spending-cap provisions are violated, the president is then authorized to sequester funds in the amount that exceeds the pay-as-you go or spending-cap provisions. By providing the president with this sequester authority, Congress appeared to be giving him some ability to do what the Budget Control and Impoundment Act sought to prevent, namely, the impoundment of funds without congressional approval.[97]

 ## TOOLS AND TACTICS OF PRESIDENTIAL PERSUASION

Although the president now sets the legislative agenda of Congress, it does not necessarily follow that his agenda will receive ready congressional approval. Indeed, sufficient support for passing a presidential proposal is rarely present initially. Some members of Congress may be indifferent to it; others may have philosophical objections to it; and still others may be under pressure from constituents or special-interest groups to vote against it. Accordingly, if a president wants favorable action on his legislative programs, he usually has to work for it. We shall now consider the specific tools and tactics employed by a president in seeking to persuade members of Congress to see things his way. It is important to note here that these tools and tactics are not reserved exclusively for those occasions when the president needs the support of a legislator on a given bill. They are also used in order to build up a reservoir of goodwill that the president hopes to be able to tap when the specific need arises.

Status Conferral

Presidents are not unaware that the office they occupy enjoys extraordinary status in our political system. They also recognize that members of Congress, like most politicians, are individuals with considerable egos. Accordingly, shrewd presidents will often attempt to persuade by using the status of their office to flatter the egos of representatives and senators. This tactic may take a variety of forms, such as an invitation to a legislator to have his or her picture taken with the president, a personal letter written by the president asking for a legislator's support, an invitation to dine with the president in the family quarters of the White House, or a phone call from the president. In all of these examples, the president is conferring some of his own status upon the individual he is seeking to persuade or to thank. And as a Congressman Silvio Conto (R-Ma.) notes in the following passage, this kind of personal treatment is not without its effects.

> You know, I was sitting in my office and the phone rang telling me it was the president calling. I damn near collapsed right on the spot. Sure enough, it was the president. He said, "Silvio, this is Lyndon Johnson, and I just wanted to thank you on behalf of this nation for your vote. You stood up and you were counted at the right time. I am mighty grateful to you." It's the only time since I have been in Congress that a president called me. I will never forget it.[98]

President Clinton even went so far as to call Congressman James Jeffords (R-Vt.), who was traveling in Damascus, Syria, to thank him for his vote in support of the family leave bill. Jeffords's reaction was no less restrained than Conti's: "It was unbelievable. No one would believe that the president would call me in Damascus. No matter how long we've been around the Hill, there's nothing more exciting than a call from the President."[99]

This tactic of status conferral was frequently used by President Kennedy to secure the goodwill of Harry Byrd, the powerful and conservative senator from Virginia. Indeed, on Byrd's birthday, the president even went so far as to arrive by helicopter on the front lawn of the senator's Virginia estate. He got out and wished him a happy birthday. Senate Minority Leader Everett Dirksen received similar kinds of attention from Kennedy, one of the favorites being special rides in the presidential helicopter.

Legislative Assistance

A president also uses his considerable influence and power to assist members of Congress with their own pet legislation. Such a favor is rendered with the understanding—sometimes implicit and sometimes explicit—that the legislator will reciprocate by supporting some current or future legislative proposal of the president's. Legislative assistance may take several forms. The president may agree to sign a given bill even though he may not be strongly supportive of it. Kennedy, for example, was once approached by one of his legislative aides and advised to sign a particular bill in order to maintain the continued support of a given member of Congress. After reading the bill, Kennedy turned to his aide and remarked, "Chuck, I just want you to be sure you understand that this bill is a goddamn boondoggle." As the aide nodded his agreement, the president went ahead and signed it anyway.[100]

Presidential assistance may also take the form of helping a member of Congress to get his or her own legislation passed by Congress. Any legislator recognizes that it is a great asset to have the prestige and resources of the White House thrown behind a bill. Finally, presidents may decide to alter their own legislative proposals in order to accommodate the wishes of a representative or senator. President Kennedy made use of this tactic in his dealings with Senator Robert Kerr of Oklahoma, who was regarded by many as the most powerful man in the Senate. The Kennedy administration initially intended to push for legislation that would create a publicly owned communications satellite corporation. Senator Kerr, however, felt very strongly that the corporation should be under private ownership. Kennedy recognized that passage of many of his own legislative proposals depended upon having the future support of the powerful senator from Oklahoma. Consequently, in spite of his reservations about a privately owned satellite corporation, the president introduced a bill that accommodated the wishes of Senator Kerr. The full resources of the administration were used to get it through Congress.[101] After a difficult fight, the legislation was finally passed and signed into law by the president. This tactic paid off, for shortly thereafter President Kennedy introduced to Congress one of the most important pieces of legislation of his entire administration, namely, the trade expansion bill. There on the floor of the Senate leading the successful fight for its adoption was Senator Kerr of Oklahoma.[102]

Programs, Projects, and Patronage

In their efforts to persuade members of Congress, presidents are armed with several inducements, such as economic assistance, military projects, federal contracts, post offices, courthouses, dams, and jobs, all of which may be channeled into a congressional district in return for its representative's support. Although civil service laws have reduced the number of federal jobs that can be handed out by a president, he still has effective control over approximately 6,700 of them. Among these are 3,500 positions in the executive branch, 140 ambassadors, 523 federal judges, 93 U.S. attorneys, 94 U.S. marshals, and approximately 2,100 part-time positions on various commissions and boards.[103]

In his attempt to win the favor of conservative Democrats, President Kennedy saw to it that southern states were made the beneficiaries of numerous defense contracts, military bases, federal judgeships, and so on. Similarly, in disbursing funds for the Model Cities Program, Lyndon Johnson took pains to see to it that they were funneled into the hometowns of powerful committee leaders in Congress. As one Johnson aide recalls, the president was not reluctant to bestow federal largess on legislators who came to his aid on key votes:

> One day I was in the Oval Office on some business. The phone rang and it was Secretary [of Defense] McNamara. Johnson said, "Now, Bob, you do need a nuclear frigate . . . no, Bob, you *do* need another nuclear frigate and the ideal place that they're just ready to build it right now is in Baton Rouge, that's in Louisiana you know." He motioned to me to pick up the phone on the dead button, and there was Bob McNamara explaining how his cost benefit computers had all said he didn't need another nuclear frigate. And the president said, "Bob, you do need another nuclear frigate and you just *go right ahead* and get one, and Baton Rouge is just the place." He hung up and looked at me and said, "You know, Johnny, your liberal friends would have said that I was just immoral, but you know why we're going to have a nice brand new nuclear frigate? Because (and excuse my vulgarity), when there was a cloture vote on the Voting Rights bill, old Senator Allen Ellender (Dem., Louisiana) didn't vote. If he had, it would have taken two liberal votes to take him out. He just happened to go take a piss at that point and, as a consequence, we got cloture." Then he asked, "Which do your liberal friends think is more important, voting rights or a nuclear frigate?"[104]

In seeking to gain enough votes for his crucial tax cut legislation, President Reagan also used program and project bargaining chips to good advantage. Congressman Bill Goodling (R-Pa.), for example, agreed to support the tax cut after the Reagan administration promised not to close a military installation in his district and to support a $37 million program to clean up Three Mile Island.[105] Another congressman, Dave McCurdy (D-Okla.), saw a vote for the Reagan tax cut as a means of protecting military installations in his district: "The President said he would remember. I have three military bases in my district. I just want to know that if we come to a crunch over that, they're going to remember me."[106] Reagan also was not above reversing his position on existing federal programs in order to secure additional votes for his tax cut. For example, his farm legislation had called for phasing out price supports on both peanuts and sugar. This legislation was understandably opposed by legislators from peanut-growing Georgia and sugar-producing Louisiana. Many of these legislators, moreover, happened to be undecided or opposed to the tax cut proposal. Aware of their concern over price supports, Reagan decided that subsidies for peanuts and sugar deserved to be continued after all. Coincidentally, nearly all of the Georgia congressional delegation, along with two Louisiana legislators, were suddenly convinced that the Reagan tax cut proposal was worthy of support.[107]

President Clinton, too, saw an opportunity to use a federal project as leverage in securing a much-needed vote for his deficit reduction proposal from congressman Bill Sarpalius (D-Tex.). It so happened that Vice President Gore's Reinventing Government report called for terminating an 11,000-acre helium preserve located in the congressman's district. Now costing the federal government some $20 million a year, this preserve was established back in 1925 to provide fuel for a fleet of U.S. blimps. With the fleet having long since been eliminated, it seemed appropriate to shut down the helium preserve—a decision that did not sit well with Sarpalius because it would mean the loss of 220 federal jobs in his district. Unable to decide whether to vote for or against Clinton's deficit reduction plan, the congressman's quandry was quickly resolved following a chat with the president during which Sarpalius was promised that the helium preserve would be kept if he voted for the plan. He did.[108]

The Veto Power

The president's veto power is an effective tool not only for voiding congressional action after the fact but also for preventing Congress from passing certain legislation in the first place. As Table 3-1 clearly demonstrates, the potency of the veto as a persuasive tool lies in the fact that it is extremely difficult to override.

The president may employ the threat of a veto as a means of persuading Congress to make changes in legislation which in its present form is clearly unacceptable to him. President Nixon's warning that he would veto any congressional legislation authorizing Congress to approve executive agreements persuaded members of Congress to drop that provision from their legislation. On another occasion, Nixon informed Congress that he was displeased with the Senate version of a bill titled the Family Assistance Plan and made it known that unless Congress passed the House version of the bill, he would veto it. In the words of then-Senator Walter Mondale, who was a strong supporter of the Senate bill, "The practical and predictable result of this action was that no family assistance bill passed the Senate."[109]

Congress, however, is not powerless to thwart the use of the presidential veto. In addition to overriding a veto, Congress can also make use of another tactic. Under

TABLE 3-1   Presidential Vetoes and Overrides, 1932–1998

President	Number of Bills Vetoed	Number of Times Overridden
Roosevelt	633	9
Truman	250	12
Eisenhower	181	2
Kennedy	21	0
Johnson	30	0
Nixon	43	5
Ford	66	12
Carter	31	2
Reagan	78	9
Bush	44	1
Clinton	25	2

Source: Research Division of Congressional Quarterly, Inc., Washington, D.C.

its operating procedures, the Senate may attach an irrelevant amendment to a given piece of legislation. Such amendments are known as riders. In 1959, for example, a rider that called for extending the life of the Civil Rights Commission was attached to a foreign aid bill. In effect, this rider mechanism allows the Senate to attach an amendment that the president is against to a bill that he supports. Since the president's veto power does not permit him to veto only those parts of a bill he dislikes, he is faced with a dilemma: Either he must veto the entire bill, including those provisions he supports, or none of it, in which case the objectionable rider becomes law along with the rest of the bill. Needless to say, presidents do not like to be faced with such a dilemma, and consequently, they will attempt to use their influence to prevent the addition of objectionable riders to an otherwise acceptable piece of legislation.

Presidents have long wanted the authority to veto only those provisions of a bill they find objectionable. Known as an "item veto," this power is currently enjoyed by forty-three of the country's fifty governors. Ronald Reagan, believing that the item veto would help presidents root out pork in the federal budget, included in his 1984 State of the Union address a call for a constitutional amendment giving the item veto power to the president. The democratically controlled Congress, however, was not disposed to grant such authority to Reagan or Bush. Ten years later, however, over three hundred Republican House candidates signed on to a "Contract With America," which they pledged to implement if they gained control of Congress in 1994. The first plank in the ten-point contract called for giving the president the item veto power. Despite claims that such legislation would violate the Constitution and dangerously enhance presidential power, in 1996 Congress passed, and President Clinton happily signed, the Line Item Veto Act.

In a strict sense, the authority given to the president was not an item veto—a power that allows the executive to veto parts of a bill that are then returned to the legislature and subject to an override by a two-thirds vote in both Houses. Rather, the act gave the president "enhanced rescission" authority, which its authors believed would meet the test of constitutionality. Applicable to appropriations bills, new entitlement spending, or tax breaks narrowly targeted to one hundred people or less, the act provided that five days after signing a measure into law, the president could inform

Congress that he intended to cancel spending for certain items. Congress could then pass a bill reversing the cancellation. This bill, however, would be subject to a presidential veto, which would then require a two-thirds vote in Congress to override it.

For fiscal year 1998, Bill Clinton used the item veto to cancel $869 million, less than 1 percent of the $800 billion in spending appropriated by Congress.[110] While some complained that the president had been too timid in using his newfound authority, others who were directly affected by the cuts went into court charging that the item veto was unconstitutional. The case was appealed all the way to the Supreme Court, which in 1998 declared the Line Item Veto Act unconstitutional, noting that by allowing the president to cancel provisions that had already become law, Congress was unconstitutionally delegating to the president the power to repeal laws.

Campaign Assistance

A president recognizes that one of the common preoccupations of all politicians is securing reelection. Accordingly, he may decide to assist a member of Congress who is facing an especially tough fight in an upcoming election. Such assistance may result in the president taking special steps to ensure that he or she receives generous financial support from the party treasury. Or he may go further and offer to come into the representative's district and campaign on his or her behalf. Any representative will welcome such an offer—provided the president is popular in the district—for the chief executive's presence will ensure large crowds and extensive media coverage. Like the other tactics we have discussed, this one may be used by presidents to reward past behavior or to lay the groundwork for future support.

Appeal to the Public

With the exception of the veto power, all the tactics and tools of presidential persuasion discussed thus far are primarily geared toward influencing an individual legislator. But the president may also resort to a tactic designed to bring pressure to bear upon Congress as a whole. He does so by going over the heads of the members of Congress and taking his case directly to the American people. The hope, of course, is to generate enough public enthusiasm for his proposal that Congress will feel compelled to support it also. In an effort to mobilize the public in support of the president's budget cuts, for example, the Reagan White House enlisted the services of former President Ford; sent the vice president and six cabinet members on speaking tours around the country, arranging for them to appear on local television wherever they went; drafted twenty legislators and governors to stump for the budget cuts in thirty media center cities throughout the South; and finally, brought newspaper editors, corporate executives, local legislators, and mayors to the White House for briefings on the president's proposed budget.[111]

A president may also decide to take his case to the people through a nationwide address. Since frequent use of such a tactic would reduce its dramatic effect, it is likely to be reserved only for those issues that are of special importance to the president. No other elected office in our government is so well suited to making such a nationwide appeal. The visibility and prestige of the presidency guarantee the president an attentive audience, and his unequaled ability to command the use of the public airwaves ensures that he will be addressing a wide audience. Franklin Roosevelt proved a master at mobilizing public support for his programs through the use of a series of "fireside chats" with the American people on radio. On several occasions both Johnson and Nixon made televised addresses to the American people asking for their support on matters related to economic policy and the Vietnam War. Gerald Ford twice did the same in an effort to put public pressure on a Democratic Congress that proved unreceptive to his proposals for dealing with the problems of energy and recession; and Ronald Reagan's public offensive in support of his budget cuts also included a televised appeal to the American people: "I urge you again to contact your senators and congressmen. Tell them of your support for this bipartisan proposal. Tell them you believe this is an unequaled opportunity to help return America to prosperity and make government again the servant of the people."[112]

An appeal to the nation, however, does not in and of itself guarantee that a president will gain the public support he needs. Rather, the ultimate success of this tactic will hinge on his public prestige at the time, the nature of what he has to say, and his ability to communicate it effectively. President Carter's attempt to mobilize the American people behind his energy policies may serve to illustrate this point. After assuming office, he addressed the nation three different times regarding the energy crisis. Yet a Gallup poll taken in April 1978 indicated that he had not made any significant progress in educating the American people to the reality of this crisis.[113] To be sure, Carter was faced with a formidable task, because the "crisis" nature of the energy problem was not readily apparent. But it is just this fact that necessitates appeals to the public that are clear and inspiring. Unfortunately, the president's addresses to the nation lacked both these qualities; consequently, he was not able to mobilize the public behind his energy proposals. This explains, in part, why they languished so long in Congress. Ronald Reagan, on the other hand, proved to be a very able communicator, and he took full advantage of this talent in seeking to build public support for one of the key elements in his economic program, namely, a substantial reduction in federal spending. Shortly after his inauguration, he spoke to the American people from the Oval Office, emphasizing the need to cut the budget. He sounded this same theme nearly two weeks later in a televised address to Congress. Sensing that some of the momentum behind his proposals had been lost during his hospitalization, Reagan made yet another televised address to Congress just ten days before the House was scheduled to vote on his budget recommendations. The masterful delivery, combined with the fact that he was making his first public appearance since the attempt on his life, served to reinforce public and congressional support for his spending reductions. Thus, on May 7, 1981, the House gave its approval of them by a vote of 256 to 173. Approximately two months later, Reagan would once again take to the television airwaves—this time seeking to mobilize the American people behind his proposed tax cut. The success of his address was evidenced by the fact that members of Congress the next day reported being deluged with phone calls running six to one in favor of the tax cut. Several days later the Democrat-controlled House passed the president's tax cut proposal by a vote of 282 to 95.[114]

 ## THE QUEST FOR INFORMATION: THE PRESIDENT, CONGRESS, AND EXECUTIVE PRIVILEGE

One of the major responsibilities of Congress is to inquire into the operation of the executive branch. It does so for several reasons: to determine the effectiveness of the programs it has passed, to make sure that the executive branch is implementing legislation in keeping with congressional intent, and, to determine possible abuses of authority by the executive branch. The ability of Congress to exercise this investigative role is predicated upon its being able to secure the necessary information from the executive branch. Presidents, however, have not always been forthcoming in this regard, believing as they do that it is not in the public interest to disclose certain kinds of information to Congress. In refusing to do so, they have invoked what has come to be known as *executive privilege.* Although there is in fact no specific provision in the Constitution that accords them this right, presidents since the time of Washington have argued that the exercise of executive privilege is implied in the constitutional powers granted to the executive branch.

In the past, presidents have invoked executive privilege on matters concerning (1) foreign policy, (2) military security, (3) investigative files related to law enforcement, and (4) intragovernmental communications that are advisory in nature.[115] Washington, for example, argued that an element of secrecy must be maintained during delicate foreign policy negotiations. The same argument was made by presidents on matters related to national security. With respect to the third category, early presidents such as Jefferson and Tyler argued that release of investigative files related to law enforcement could damage innocent persons as well as compromise the integrity of the law enforcement process itself. Finally, presidents since the time of Jackson have viewed their personal communications with cabinet members and aides as privileged from congressional scrutiny on grounds that confidentiality is essential if presidents are to be assured of receiving frank and honest advice. Under the Eisenhower administration, however, this final category was greatly expanded to cover intragovernmental communications within *the entire* executive branch. Specifically, the umbrella of executive privilege extended to such executive branch communications as "interdepartmental memoranda, advisory opinions, recommendations of subordinates, informal working papers, material in personnel files."[116] Given this expanded view of executive privilege, it is hardly surprising that it was invoked more often during the Eisenhower administration than in the entire first century of American history.[117]

Neither Kennedy nor Johnson shared Eisenhower's broad view of this privilege. Indeed, each invoked it only twice during his administration. Although President Nixon's statements on the subject indicated that he shared the view of his two predecessors, his actions demonstrated otherwise. In his first term alone, he invoked the privilege four times personally. In addition, members of his administration refused congressional requests for information fifteen times.[118] Nor do these figures tell the whole story, for there were numerous occasions when members of the executive branch simply refused to hand over information to Congress without even bothering to invoke the doctrine of executive privilege. According to one Senate subcommittee study, between 1964 and 1974 there were 225 occasions when agencies of the executive branch refused to supply Congress with requested information, and over 90 percent of these came during the Nixon administration.[119] The difficulty experienced by Congress in securing information from the executive during the Nixon presidency was compounded by the president's refusal to permit his White House aides to testify before Congress. Although previous presidents had set restrictions on what their staff aides could say to Congress, they did not set down a blanket prohibition against appearing. President Nixon, however, prevented his staff aides from testifying on any subject whatever, including substantive policy questions.[120] In the past, Congress rarely had any need to question White House aides on policy matters because policymaking rested more with department heads, whom Congress was empowered to call for testimony. Under recent presidents, however, policymaking has moved away from department heads and into the White House. This tendency was accelerated during the Nixon presidency. During Nixon's first term, for example, the major force in shaping American foreign policy was not Secretary of State William Rogers, but rather the president's special assistant for national security affairs, Henry Kissinger. Yet, because Kissinger was a member of the White House staff, he was prohibited from testifying before Congress. Thus, Congress was denied the opportunity to probe the mind of the one man who, aside from the president, had the greatest impact upon the substance of American foreign policy.

Throughout our history, conflicts arising between the president and Congress over disclosure of information were ultimately resolved through a process of negotiation and accommodation. Such was not to be the case with the Nixon presidency. As the Watergate scandals unfolded, investigations began on three fronts. First, the Senate created a special Select Committee on Presidential Campaign Practices. Under the chairmanship of Senator Sam Ervin (D-N.C.), this committee was charged with investigating alleged campaign abuses during the 1972 election. As pressure mounted from both Congress and the public, the president also decided to appoint a special prosecutor to inquire into possible wrongdoing by members of the executive branch. And finally, as it began to appear that the president himself might be implicated in the Watergate scandals, the House Judiciary Committee initiated an inquiry to determine whether there were possible grounds for impeachment. All three of these investigative bodies repeatedly requested that the president provide them with information that was judged relevant in determining wrongdoing by members of the executive branch. The president refused to comply with certain of these requests, arguing that he alone had the ultimate right to determine what information could appropriately be turned over to Congress and the special prosecutor. Confrontation thus proved inevitable.

The House Judiciary Committee decided against taking the president into court because it felt the court had no constitutional role to play in the impeachment proceedings. Instead, the committee cited as one of the grounds for impeachment the president's repeated refusal to comply with committee subpoenas for information. No other president in our history had ever claimed that executive privilege could be used to withhold information requested in connection with an impeachment proceeding. Had the House Judiciary Committee acceded to this claim, it is clear that impeachment would have been rendered a meaningless instrument.

The Senate Watergate Committee, however, did decide to take the president into court over the issue of executive privilege. This was an act of considerable historical importance, because never before had Congress gone to court over this issue. The U.S. Appeals Court ruled that presidential conversations must be presumed privileged unless it can be shown that such information is "demonstrably critical to the performance of the committee's functions." In this particular case, the court concluded that the Ervin committee had not made such a showing. Although the court acknowledged that the Senate Watergate Committee had a legitimate "oversight" function with respect to the executive branch, it maintained that in this instance this function had been preempted by the House Judiciary Committee. Furthermore, while the court recognized that the committee's inquiry constituted a necessary part of its "legislative function," it concluded that such a function did not extend to "limitless fact finding."[121]

The special prosecutor also took the president into court because of his refusal to supply certain of the White House tapes that were deemed relevant in determining possible illegal activities in the executive branch. The lower courts ruled that the president was required to hand over the tapes in question, so Nixon appealed his case all the way to the Supreme Court. On July 24, 1974, the Supreme Court handed down its historic decision in *U.S. v. Nixon* concerning the issue of executive privilege. It ruled first that the president does indeed have a right of executive privilege. This in itself was a significant statement, for up to this time it had not been definitively established that the president enjoyed such a right. But the Court went on to say that this right was not absolute, as President Nixon had claimed, but rather was a "qualified privilege"; that is, the president's need for confidentiality had to be balanced against other compelling interests. In this particular case, the Court concluded that the need for the tapes in a criminal court proceeding outweighed the president's need for confidentiality. The Court did imply, however, that it might well have ruled differently if the president had based his claim of executive privilege on the "need to protect military, diplomatic or sensitive national security secrets."[122] Although this decision was a resounding defeat for President Nixon, it might be argued that it was a victory for the presidency, for it established that a president does have the right of executive privilege and that the Court may well defer to this right when it is exercised on sensitive matters related to military and foreign affairs. It is important to note, however, that the Court's ruling dealt only with the president's right to withhold information from the courts. The right to withhold information from Congress has still not been firmly determined, for the Supreme Court has never been asked to rule on this question.

Executive privilege became a controversial issue once again during the Ford presidency, but Congress took a more assertive position in responding to it. On one occasion, Secretary Kissinger refused to supply the House Select Committee on Intelligence with documents related to American covert operations abroad since 1961. The secretary argued that revealing such documents would violate the confidentiality of executive branch deliberations. In addition, former CIA Director William Colby refused to supply this same committee with subpoenaed documents dealing with the 1968 Tet offensive in Vietnam.[123] The House Select Committee on Intelligence made it clear that it was prepared to recommend that the House of Representatives find Kissinger and Colby in contempt of Congress. In theory, such a finding could have resulted in the House instructing its sergeant at arms to apprehend both secretaries and place them in the District of Columbia jail.[124] As has been the case throughout most of our history, however, direct confrontation was avoided through mutual accommodation. The House Intelligence Committee permitted Secretary Kissinger to give an oral report on the contents of the documents it had requested. Similarly, Director Colby agreed to hand over CIA documents in exchange for the committee's assurance that such documents would be held in the strictest confidence. In further disputes over the release of information, President Carter instructed Energy Secretary Charles Duncan to invoke executive privilege, as did Reagan in an order to Interior Secretary James Watt. Once again, however, congressional threats to hold these cabinet members in contempt ultimately brought a compromise similar to those already described. But one other such dispute that occurred during the Reagan years was not so easily settled and thus deserves more lengthy consideration.

In 1982, both the House Public Works Committee and the Energy and Commerce Committee had reason to believe that chemical companies might not be paying the full amount required of them in cleaning up toxic waste dumps. Accordingly, they instructed the head of the Environmental Protection Agency, Ann Gorsuch

Burford, to provide some 787,000 pages of documents related to the cleanup of hazardous waste sites.[125] On orders from President Reagan, she immediately invoked executive privilege, arguing that certain portions of the documents could not be revealed because they involved sensitive matters related to law enforcement. Unable to reach a compromise with the Reagan administration, the House followed the recommendation of its Public Works Committee and voted (259 to 105) to hold Burford in contempt of Congress. This was the *first* time in our nation's history that a government official had been held in contempt over the issue of executive privilege.[126] Following the contempt citation, House Speaker O'Neill asked the Justice Department to present the case to a grand jury for possible indictment. But the U.S. Attorney declined to do so. Instead, he asked a U.S. District Court to rule the contempt citation unconstitutional on the grounds that executive privilege entitled the president to withhold such information from Congress. The judge dismissed the case, ruling that both branches had failed to exhaust all possibilities for working out a compromise. The administration ultimately agreed to hand over the disputed documents in a three-step process, beginning with briefings, then edited versions, and finally the complete documents. Burford, meanwhile, resigned following allegations of misconduct, including perjury and conflict of interest.[127]

As Bill Clinton reached the midpoint of his second term he had invoked executive privilege in connection with two independent counsel investigations and four congressional inquiries. Independent counsel Donald Smaltz, charged with investigating potential wrongdoing by Secretary of Agriculture Mike Espy, subpoenaed communications between presidential advisers in connection with the White House's own internal investigation of Espy. The White House argued that these documents related to internal deliberations and thus were covered by executive privilege. A federal appeals court judge agreed, noting that executive privilege included communications among presidential advisers that were part of their preparation for advising the president. The claim of privilege could be disallowed only by demonstrating the documents' importance in a grand jury investigation, and by proving that the information in question could not be obtained elsewhere.[128]

The second and more notable dispute over executive privilege arose between President Clinton and independent counsel Kenneth Starr, who was charged with investigating several alleged presidential transgressions, including whether the president had lied under oath about having an affair with White House intern Monica Lewinsky and had encouraged her to lie as well. When Starr called White House aide Sidney Blumenthal and deputy counsel Bruce Lindsey to give grand jury testimony on the Monica Lewinsky affair, President Clinton barred them from responding to questions on grounds that White House deliberations on this subject were covered by executive privilege. Starr challenged this assertion in federal district court, maintaining that executive privilege applies only to the president's public responsibilities, not his private conduct. The White House countered by asserting that the Lewinsky case, even though a private matter, had "a demonstrable impact on the operations of the White House as an institution,"[129] and thus discussions about the subject were privileged. In ruling on the case, the district court acknowledged that deliberations related to private conduct could be privileged, but, following the reasoning in *U.S. v. Nixon,* it also noted that Clinton's claim of privilege had to be weighed against other compelling interests—in this case, the grand jury's need to determine possible criminal wrongdoing. In this instance, the court said, the information being sought by the independent counsel was essential to making such a determination and could not be obtained in any other way, because it was highly improbable that any matters related to perjury, suborning purjury or obstruction of justice would have been put in writing.[130]

The president also invoked executive privilege in connection with separate congressional inquiries into the administration's Haiti policy, antidrug program, and firings in the White House Travel Office. At one point Congress threatened to cite the White House for contempt of Congress when it refused to provide certain documents on the White House Travel Office, but an accomodation was ultimately reached in this case, and in the other inquiries.[131]

We may expect that compromise will continue to be the means by which the president and Congress resolve such disputes. A lower court has already sent a clear signal that it would prefer this approach. Moreover, since the Supreme Court has never been asked to rule on executive privilege as it relates to these two branches, both will likely be reluctant to take the matter all the way to the highest court and risk an adverse ruling.

 THE ULTIMATE CONFRONTATION: IMPEACHMENT

The Founding Fathers were fully cognizant of the fact that power may corrupt those who exercise it. Accordingly, in Article II, Section 4, of the Constitution they provided that "the President, Vice President and all civil Officers of the United States shall be removed from Office on Impeachment for and Conviction of, Treason, Bribery, or other High Crimes and Misdemeanors." Whether or not a president ought to be impeached was to be decided by the House of Representatives. Whether or not he should be convicted was to be determined by the Senate. In our entire history, only sixteen officers of the federal government have been impeached, and they included two presidents, a cabinet officer, a senator, and twelve federal judges. Only six were convicted, and they were all federal judges. The infrequent use of this formidable congressional power prompted Woodrow Wilson to refer to it as "little more than an empty menace." Lord Bryce, writing before the turn of the century, acknowledged that impeachment was indeed a formidable instrument, but maintained that it was precisely this fact that made it awkward to use.

> [It is] the heaviest piece of artillery in the congressional arsenal, but because it is so heavy, it is unfit for ordinary use. It is like a hundred-ton gun which needs complex machinery to bring it into position, an enormous charge of power to fire it, and a large mark to aim at.[132]

We now consider how this "heaviest piece of artillery" works, the drawbacks associated with such a process, and finally, whether there are realistic alternatives to it.

The Impeachment Process

Any member of the House of Representatives may introduce articles of impeachment against the president of the United States. In addition, independent counsels investigating possible wrongdoing by a federal official are also authorized by Congress to report to it acts that may constitute grounds for impeachment. Following such introduction, the common practice has been to refer the charges to the House Judiciary Committee for study, although the Speaker of the House may create a special committee for this task if he wishes. After examining the charges, the Judiciary Committee makes a recommendation to the full House. In the case of Richard Nixon, for example, the committee recommended that the House vote to impeach on only three of the five charges filed against him. With respect to Bill Clinton, the allegations outlined in the report of independent counsel Kenneth Starr were organized by the committee into four separate charges. Impeachment of a president requires only a *simple* majority of those present and voting. If the House does vote to impeach, the Senate is immediately informed so that preparations can be made for the trial. In the meantime, the House selects several of its members to prosecute its case against the president in the Senate. In the case of Clinton, thirteen managers were appointed— all Republican members of the House Judiciary Committee. Although these individuals are the only House members who participate in the Senate trial, the entire membership of the House may sit in on the proceedings as observers.

When federal officers other than the president are being tried, the president of the Senate—who is also the vice president—presides over the proceedings. When the president is on trial, however, the chief justice of the Supreme Court must preside. Regarding procedure, the Senate trial differs from a normal courtroom trial in several important respects. Whereas in a civil court proceeding lawyers can disqualify prospective jurors because of possible prejudice in the case, no senator may be disqualified from voting on the guilt or innocence of a president. During Andrew Johnson's impeachment trial, for example, his son-in-law was serving as a senator from the state of Tennessee, and he understandably voted against conviction of his father-in-law. In the Clinton trial, one senator (Tim Hutchinson, R-Ark.) was the brother of one of the House managers (Asa Hutchinson, R-Ark.) chosen to prosecute the case against the president in the Senate, and the daughter of another senator (Barbara Boxer, D-Calif.) was married to Hillary Clinton's brother. Second, in a civil court proceeding the presiding judge rules on matters of procedure and admissibility of evidence. In a Senate trial, the chief justice may initially rule on these questions, but his decisions can be overturned by a vote of the Senate. During the trial of Andrew Johnson, the rulings on evidence by the chief justice were overturned seventeen times. Third, in the American justice system an individual is free to appeal a trial verdict to a higher court. Most scholars agree that the Constitution does not allow the president to have his conviction in a Senate trial reviewed by the court. Fourth, in a civil court proceeding the standard of proof may, depending on the nature of the offense, require a preponderance of the evidence, clear and convincing evidence, or in a criminal case, evidence beyond a reasonable doubt. In a Senate trial, however, it is left up to each senator to decide what standard of proof he or she will apply to the evidence presented.

In order to remove a president from office, two-thirds of those senators present and voting must vote to convict. Should they do so, they must then vote on whether they want to prohibit the president from holding any federal office in the future. Finally, it should be noted that even after he is removed from office, a president is still subject to possible trial and punishment in the civil courts for his actions.

Impeachable Offenses

One of the major controversies concerning the impeachment process centers upon the question of what constitutes an impeachable offense. The Constitution states that a president may be impeached for "Treason, Bribery, or other High Crimes and Misdemeanors." While there is little dispute over the meaning of treason and bribery, there has been considerable disagreement over the meaning of high crimes and misdemeanors. Echoing the argument made by others before him, Richard Nixon's defense lawyer contended that this phrase refers exclusively to *criminal* offenses and not to *political* crimes. To interpret the phrase to include the latter, he argued, would mean that Congress could impeach a president for virtually anything.

Opposing this view are those who assert that the Founding Fathers fully intended high crimes and misdemeanors to include political as well as criminal offenses. They had, after all, borrowed the phrase from the British, who gave the term just that meaning. This position is certainly buttressed by historical precedent, for less than one-third of the eighty-three articles of impeachment drawn up by the House over the years have "explicitly charged the violation of a criminal statute or used the word 'criminal' or 'crime' to describe the conduct alleged."[133] Rather, most of the charges cited behavior that served to undermine public confidence in the office. Finally, it should also be noted that a restriction of the phrase "High Crimes and Misdemeanors" to mean only criminal activity would leave the Congress powerless to act against certain kinds of presidential behavior. For example, upon assuming office a president might decide to grant a free and open pardon to all individuals currently serving in federal prisons. Clearly, he would be doing nothing criminally wrong, for the Constitution empowers the president with the right to grant pardons. Yet most would agree that such an irresponsible act would constitute an extraordinary abuse of his constitutional powers.

In considering the charges against Richard Nixon, most of the members of the House Judiciary Committee adopted the broader view of the phrase "High Crimes and Misdemeanors," thus viewing it as encompassing political as well as criminal offenses. The committee ultimately passed three articles of impeachment against him. Article I charged him with *obstruction of justice.* He was accused of encouraging perjury, destruction of evidence, and making false and misleading statements. Article II cited him for *abuse of power.* Specifically, it was charged that Nixon (1) authorized agencies within the government (FBI and IRS) to harass private citizens for his own political advantage; (2) established a secret investigative unit within the White House, the purpose of which was to engage in unlawful and covert activity against private citizens; and (3) used the powers of his office to cover up these abuses. The final article of impeachment charged the president with *contempt of Congress.* The grounds for this charge were his continued refusal to comply with Judiciary Committee subpoenas for tapes and documents relevant to its impeachment investigation. Two additional articles were proposed, but the Judiciary Committee declined to vote in favor of them. One called for the president's impeachment because of the secret bombing initiated in Cambodia. This was rejected because some members of the Judiciary Committee felt that the president had authority to order such actions in his capacity as commander in chief. Others felt the charge was unjustified since Congress had acquiesced in the bombings. The other article rejected by the committee accused the president of income tax evasion. The reasons for voting down this charge were varied. Some believed that improper tax deductions were made by the president's lawyers, without the knowledge of the president himself. Other committee members felt that impeachment should be used for crimes against the integrity of the political system. In their judgment, tax evasion did not qualify as such a crime. Still others felt that enough was enough.

In the case of Bill Clinton, the major bone of contention in the House centered not on whether a president could be impeached for political as well as criminal offenses; rather, it focused on whether Bill Clinton's behavior rose to the level of impeachable offenses. Nearly all of the Democrats argued that his conduct was not impeachable, whereas almost all Republicans argued that it was. In votes that divided strictly along party lines, the Republican majority on the House Judiciary Committee reported out four articles of impeachment against the president. Article I charged him with giving "perjurious, false, and misleading testimony" to a grand jury (1) about his relationship with Monica Lewinsky, (2) about his testimony in a lawsuit brought against him for alleged sexual harassment of an Arkansas state employee (Paula Jones) while he was governor, and (3) by lying to his aides, anticipating that they would repeat those lies in their own testimony before the grand jury. Article II charged the president with lying in a civil deposition related to the Paula Jones sexual harassment suit. Article III accused the president of obstructing justice (1) by encouraging Monica Lewinsky to file a false affadavit, (2) by encouraging Lewinsky to give false testimony in the Paula Jones case, (3) by helping her to find employment in order to buy her silence, and (4) by attempting to influence the grand jury testimony of White House aides. Article IV alleged that the president abused the powers of his office by failing to comply with written congressional requests for information sought in its impeachment investigation and by making perjurious, false, and misleading statements in response to certain of these requests. Finally, in reporting these four articles of impeachment, the House Judiciary Committee also recommended that Clinton, if convicted, not be allowed to hold federal office again.

In votes that fell largely along party lines, the full House approved Article I (228–206) and Article III (221–212), while rejecting Articles II (229–205) and IV (285–148). The second article appeared less compelling because it involved presidential lying in a civil deposition, an offense for which individuals are rarely prosecuted. Moreover, his testimony in the deposition was ruled immaterial to the case, and the case itself was ultimately dismissed by the presiding judge. Article IV meanwhile, was most soundly defeated, with a majority of House members apparently concluding that the president was within his rights to invoke executive privilege in refusing to comply with certain requests for information made during the impeachment inquiry.

In the Senate trial, the votes to convict President Clinton fell well short of the two thirds required. The perjury charge went down to defeat by a vote of fifty-five to forty-five, while the vote on obstruction of justice was somewhat closer, with fifty senators voting for, and fifty against. Although a number of senators concluded that the charges were not proven to their satisfaction, there was a more fundamental concern that explained the vote—one that pertained to the gravity of the charges themselves. Simply put, the House managers failed to convince enough senators that Clinton's actions rose to the level of impeachable offenses. After all was said and done, the president was seen to have lied about an affair that had little to do with his public responsibilities, and posed no threat to our system of government.

The Impeachment Instrument: An Evaluation

Our experience with the Nixon impeachment process clearly demonstrates that it suffers from several severe limitations. In the first place, it consumes a great deal of time. More than nine months had passed from the time the House Judiciary Committee first began its inquiry until the day Richard Nixon resigned from office. If the president had permitted the process to run its full course, with a vote of impeachment on the House floor and a trial in the Senate, the process would probably have consumed an additional six months. The problem here is that the government is thrown into a state of paralysis over this extended period of time. Given the gravity of such an undertaking, Congress is not in a position to consider anything else. In addition, a president is severely weakened politically during this time and is unable to exert the necessary leadership over national affairs. Nor for that matter is he likely to be concerned with matters other than those related to his impeachment. Department heads not only complained about being unable to see the president, but also pointed to lack of direction from the White House in important policy areas. Moreover, it now appears that during Nixon's final year in office, his chief of staff acted as a surrogate president on many matters.[134]

Although the impeachment process moved more swiftly in the case of President Clinton, we should not necessarily take solace from this fact. Not only was his case considerably less complicated than the circumstances surrounding Nixon's wrongdoing, but the eight-month investigation of the Monica Lewinsky affair conducted by independent counsel Kenneth Starr spared the House Judiciary Committee from conducting its own lengthy inquiry.

Clinton, in contrast to Nixon, also appeared more engaged as president over the eleven-month period that included the Lewinsky investigation, impeachment deliberations in the House, and a trial in the Senate. That he was able to be so was no doubt made easier by the fact the charges against him were far less serious, and his popularity substantially higher, than Nixon's; and these realities, in turn, fostered the general impression that his removal from office was highly unlikely. Thus, as the House Judiciary Committee weighed the charges against him, Clinton brought the leaders of Israel and Palestine to the Wye Conference for painstaking negotiations and several weeks later ordered a four day bombing campaign against Iraq. He also gave a well received State of the Union Address before a joint session of Congress even as his trial was underway in the Senate. Significantly, however, Clinton's successes came in those areas where he was freest to act. The swamp of impeachment frustrated all of his major legislative initiatives, leaving him with a legislative success rate of 51 percent, the lowest on record for a sixth-year president, and the sixth lowest yearly success rating ever recorded for a sitting president.[135] Moreover, even though Clinton managed to remain more engaged than Nixon in the daily routine of being president, there were nevertheless complaints that foreign policy was adrift and domestic policy initiatives stymied by a White House preoccupied with scandal and the prospect of impeachment.[136]

The possibility that the impeachment process may lead to a protracted paralysis of governmental leadership is serious. Equally disturbing is the prospect that foreign governments may attempt to take advantage of this paralysis. During the week of October 14 to 20, 1974, Richard Nixon had to contend with a war in the Middle East, the firing of Archibald Cox as special prosecutor, and an impeachment inquiry in the House. Also that week the Soviet Union contemplated committing troops to the Middle East, a plan that compelled the United States to put its armed forces on "red alert." The Soviet Union may have considered such a dramatic move partly because it concluded that a weakened and preoccupied president would not be able to respond. In the final weeks of 1998, Saddam Hussein's decision to break off cooperation with UN weapons inspectors and Slobodan Milosvic's aggressive actions in Kosovo may indicate that Hussein and Milosevic believed they caught Clinton at a vulnerable moment.

If Richard Nixon's actions are any indication, a further problem that attends the impeachment ordeal is that a president, desperate to save his skin, may make decisions he would not otherwise make in an effort to bolster his support in Congress and/or the nation. Eager to placate the Goldwater wing of the Republican Party, whose support would be crucial in a Senate trial, Nixon abandoned his support of certain legislation and withdrew names of some nominees he had submitted to the Senate for confirmation. He also undertook trips to the Middle East and Soviet Union, neither of which had any substantive purpose beyond generating some positive news coverage. And some argued that his decision to place American forces on heightened alert constituted a contrived overreaction to the alleged possibility of Soviet intervention in the Middle East, designed to distract public attention from his domestic predicament.

Even if a president is not tempted to engage in such distortions of the policy process, the precarious political situation in which he finds himself invites the public, Congress, and the media to ascribe ulterior motives to his every action or inaction. Recall, for example, the skepticism that greeted President Clinton's decision to bomb terrorist camps in Sudan and Afghanistan shortly after his widely criticized apology to the nation for his behavior in the Monica Lewinsky affair, or his decision to launch an extended bombing strike against Iraq four days before the impeachment vote in the House. Such second guessing of presidential motives is not only debilitating to the political process, but it too could distort the policy process; presidents might decline to take timely action precisely because they fear a sinister interpretation will be given to their motives.

Our procedure for removing presidents from office suffers from another drawback, namely, that impeached presidents are likely to be rendered incapable of exerting political leadership even if they are not convicted. Let us suppose, for example, that Richard Nixon had been impeached in the House but had narrowly escaped conviction in the Senate by three or four votes. The country would have been left with a president whom a majority of both the House and the Senate deemed guilty of impeachable offenses. Such a president would scarcely be capable of leading the Congress under such circumstances. Nor is it likely that he would enjoy the confidence of the American people.

Finally, it should be noted that the impeachment process can be an extraordinary ordeal for presidents. Not only is the process prolonged, but presidents must also live with the prospect of being nationally disgraced and condemned by history. When these pressures are combined with the normal burdens of the office, one may well question the ability of some presidents to function rationally under such circumstances. Much has been written about Richard Nixon's state of mind during his last months in office, with his chief of staff allegedly telling the special prosecutor that "the President was unstable—in fact, out of control."[137] During Nixon's last week in office, the secretary of defense was so concerned about the president's emotional state that he took the unprecedented step of issuing an order to all U.S. military commands worldwide, instructing them to accept no direct orders from the White House unless they had been countersigned by the secretary of defense himself.[138] All of which suggests that if the impeachment process can impose such a severe emotional strain upon the occupant of the White House, then the country is in a very precarious position indeed. Accordingly, it may be argued that a swifter method of removal is necessary.

Identifying weaknesses in our current constitutional arrangements is, however, often far easier than coming up with solutions to remedy them. Throughout the

Nixon impeachment ordeal, many looked longingly at the British parliamentary system. If the prime minister receives a vote of "no confidence" in the House of Commons, parliament is dissolved, elections are held, and a new government installed. The entire process is consummated in seventeen days (excluding Saturdays and Sundays). Taking their cue from the British example, some have proposed that a president be removed if two-thirds of the Congress give him a vote of no confidence. Thereupon, a new election would be held for the presidency and both houses of Congress within thirty to sixty days following the no-confidence vote.[139]

The swiftness of the process makes it highly appealing, for it would minimize the pathologies already noted—government paralysis, policy distortions, the continuance of a politically traumatized leader in office, and the potential for erratic presidential behavior. But if the relative swiftness of removal renders a no confidence vote attractive, therein also lies its potential weakness. Although Richard Nixon would probably have been removed much sooner under such a system, it is also possible that Harry Truman would have been thrown out of office for his unpopular firing of General Douglas MacArthur. In short, the procedural ease with which a president could be removed from office would subject him to the whims and passions of the moment. The no confidence proposal also fails to take into account some important differences between the British political system and our own. In the first place, while a prime minister is assured of having a majority of his own party in control of Parliament, a president has no guarantee that his own party will control the Congress. A vote of no confidence would therefore be considerably more likely for those presidents who faced a Congress controlled by an unfriendly majority of the opposition party. Moreover, in removing the prime minister, the British are only getting rid of the head of government. The queen still remains as the head of state and as such represents an important symbol of continuity. In removing a president from office we are losing both the chief of state and the head of government. Third, holding new elections in Britain is managed with relative ease because of the country's small size. Given the size of the United States, elections constitute a formidable undertaking. It is highly questionable whether candidates could be nominated, campaign organizations created, adequate money raised, and an election held all within the thirty to sixty days following the removal of a president. Finally, and perhaps most important, unlike the prime minister, who is chosen by members of his party, the president is chosen by the people. Accordingly, it may be argued that any attempt to revoke their electoral judgment should be realized only with great difficulty.

It has occasionally been proposed that the Congress take action against a president who falls short of impeachment. Most often discussed is a vote of censure such as was used by the Senate against Andrew Jackson following his decision to remove the government's bank deposits from the Second Bank of the United States. Censure was also favored by House Democrats as an alternative to impeaching President Bill Clinton, and was seriously considered by some senators who, though unwilling to convict Clinton, nevertheless felt that some formal expression of disapproval should be registered against his behavior. The censure option is of questionable value, however, for it is not clear what kinds of actions would merit censure as opposed to impeachment. Andrew Jackson reminded the Senate that either he was guilty of impeachable offenses or he was not. If he was, the Senate would fail in its constitutional responsibilities by deciding not to impeach him. On the other hand, if he was not, then the Senate would be going beyond its constitutional responsibilities by censuring him.[140] The censure resolution drafted by House Democrats and offered as a substitute for articles of impeachment against Clinton stated that he "violated the trust of the American people, lessened their esteem for the office of the president and dishonored the office which they have entrusted to him." Given this littany of harsh judgments directed at the president, one might well ask why censure was judged to be more appropriate than impeachment?

Perhaps the most we can hope for is that a president, facing certain impeachment, will do as Richard Nixon did—resign and at least shorten the agony. Certainly presidents in Nixon's situation would have considerable incentive to throw in the towel. After all, no president in history has ever been convicted and removed from office, and thus any president might well want to avoid being the first. There is a more practical concern here as well, for presidents convicted of impeachable offenses lose their pension as well as the substantial sum awarded to them for transition expenses. But it is also true that in Nixon's case the evidence of wrongdoing was beyond dispute, for members of Congress were ultimately presented with a "smoking gun" in the form of highly incriminating White House tapes. In cases where the evidence is more ambiguous (e.g., Clinton's), presidents will—and probably should be—less likely to resign. In these circumstances, the failure of an impeachment inquiry to run its full course could well deny our political process the necessary cleansing that a full airing of the charges would bring, leaving instead a residue of resentment among a president's supporters that might endure for some time to come.

CONCLUSION: THE PROBLEM OF DEADLOCK

As the American people celebrated the bicentennial of the Constitution in 1987, our political system received more than the usual amount of scrutiny and reexamination. Since the relationship between the president and Congress is arguably the most significant institutional relationship in our Constitution, scholars and political observers understandably accorded it particular attention. Many were not altogether encouraged by what they observed. We now consider the nature of those concerns that persist more than a decade later.

As noted earlier in this chapter, separation of powers and checks and balances made a struggle between these two branches inevitable. This institutional antagonism could be softened to a considerable extent by political party, particularly if members of the president's party commanded majorities in both houses of Congress. Some observers, however, contend that party is no longer as effective in joining together what the Constitution divides. Increasingly, our national government has been subject to what the critics call "political gridlock" or "stalemate" in which the two branches appear unable to reach timely agreement on how to address critical national problems.[141] Energy, for example, emerged as a growing problem in the early 1970s, and yet not until 1979 did a president's energy legislation finally clear Congress. By 1980, the United States faced a hemorrhaging of illegal aliens across our borders. Legislation to deal with this problem was first introduced in 1981, but disputes between the Reagan administration and Congress delayed passage until 1987. Likewise, throughout the 1980s budget deficits grew to alarming levels while each branch blamed the other for failing to take the necessary corrective measures. And only after a thirteen-year impasse was the Clean Air Act of 1990 finally passed and signed into law. The list could go on.

The charge of stalemated government is not new. Indeed, as far back as 1950, a group of eminent political scientists produced a document entitled "Toward a More

Responsible Two Party System," criticizing the inability of our government to fashion and implement a coherent program.[142] A little over twenty years later, political columnist David Broder's book *The Party's Over* argued that as a result of the declining importance of political parties, "our government has suffered from crippled leadership, from a slowdown of decision making, an impairment of its vital processes. The result has been an accumulation of unresolved problems and a buildup of public frustration."[143] In recent years, however, the concern over stalemated government has taken on a greater sense of urgency, partly because the problems confronting the nation appear more severe and complex and also because the conditions giving rise to stalemate have become more pronounced. What are those conditions?

Under our Constitution it is possible for the presidency to be controlled by one political party, while the opposition party controls one or both houses of Congress. In approximately half of the elections in this century, one of the two houses of Congress was controlled by the opposition party. The most recent president to confront this circumstance was Ronald Reagan, who from 1981 to 1986 faced a Republican-controlled Senate and a Democrat-controlled House. More important, in the forty years intervening between 1952 and 1998 presidents have faced a Congress in which *both* houses were controlled by the opposition party over half the time—a condition that existed for only twelve years during all of the nineteenth century. The explanation for this phenomenon is quite simple. More Americans are splitting their tickets in presidential elections—behavior that is itself indicative of the diminished importance of party as a motivating factor in voting.

Political gridlock is not only the consequence of presidents confronting a Congress controlled wholly or in part by the opposition party. It is also compounded by the fact that they cannot necessarily count upon the support of their own party in Congress. Speaking to this problem, one critic observes:

> Whether or not the president has a majority in both Houses, he usually needs to form a coalition with a sizable bloc of the opposite party in order to enact most elements of his party's program. . . . With divided government and the lack of cohesion among each party's members, national policy has to be made one issue at a time. Each issue is decided by a cross-party coalition whose makeup shifts from one issue to the next. The result is a hodge-podge of ad hoc policy decisions that are usually inconsistent with one another.[144]

Though some scholars have long been critical of the lack of cohesion in our congressional parties, several circumstances have made the problem more severe. As noted earlier in this chapter, these include the reduced power of committee chairpersons, the declining importance of party within the electorate, reduced reliance of legislators on their party for getting elected, the growing influence of special-interest PACs, and the fact that Congress now conducts more of its business in public.

Although presidents Johnson and Reagan enjoyed considerable legislative success despite confronting some (Johnson) or nearly all (Reagan) of the liabilities discussed above, we paid a price for it. Johnson, for example, taking advantage of the overwhelming Democratic majorities in both houses following the 1964 election, pushed through one piece of legislation after another at a record-breaking pace. The result was some 181 new programs enacted into law in 1965 and 1966.[145] Quantitatively, this was one of the most remarkable legislative records in American history. Qualitatively, however, many of these programs left much to be desired. Several of them proved to be ill conceived because Congress did not have enough time to consider them carefully. Moreover, governors pointed out that Johnson's programs were being enacted so quickly that state and local officials did not have adequate time to gain an understanding of their complexities.[146] It must be remembered, however, that Johnson felt compelled to move quickly with Congress because he did not think he would be able to sustain continued support from members of his party: "I keep hitting hard because I know this honeymoon won't last. Every day I lose a little more political capital. That's why we have to keep at it, never letting up."[147] Although Reagan's legislative successes in 1981 have been characterized as legendary,[148] the reality of confronting a Democratic-controlled House, along with concerns about party cohesion within his own party, impelled him to move with far greater haste than prudence warranted. As Reagan's one-time budget director pointed out regarding the president's historic budget-cutting legislation, "The thing was put together so fast that it probably should have been put together differently. The reason we did it wrong— not wrong, but less than the optimum—was that we said, Hey, we have to get a program out fast . . . we didn't think it all through. We didn't add up all the numbers."[149]

If divided government and declining party loyalty within Congress have hampered cooperation between the two branches, this problem has, according to the critics, been further exacerbated by a constitutional element, namely, the two-year term for House members and the staggering of electoral terms.[150] With one-third of the Senate and all of the House up for election every two years, legislators' interests are less closely tied to those of the president. As the president starts his second year, members of Congress are already preoccupied with their own reelection prospects and less concerned about the president's program. Thus, presidents find it difficult to gain support for controversial but necessary legislation the benefits of which may not become apparent by midterm elections. Add to this the fact that since a president's party typically loses seats in Congress following midterm elections, he begins the final two years of his term in a weakened position.

Some scholars argue that the charge of gridlocked government is more apparent than real. Perhaps the most noteworthy study of the subject examined 267 important pieces of legislation passsed from 1946 to 1991 and found little difference in the number of bills passed under divided and unified governments.[151] Although these findings raise legitimate questions about the validity of the gridlock argument, this study is not without limitations. These include treating all 267 bills as equally important; not considering whether there might have been a greater need for legislation during some periods than others; ignoring excessive delay in the passage of legislation; and failing to include in the analysis legislation that was proposed but never passed. Indeed, one study that examines what did not pass, found that divided government had a significant impact on output: "Presidents oppose significant legislation more often under divided government and much more seriously considered, important legislation fails to pass under divided government than under unified government. Furthermore, the odds of such legislation failing to pass are considerably greater under divided government."[152]

Proposals for Change

Some of the proposals for fostering greater cooperation between the president and Congress are very drastic indeed. These include seeking to guarantee the president a party majority in Congress either by forcing voters to cast their ballot for a presidential-congressional team ticket or by providing the president's party with a requisite number of bonus seats in Congress.[153] Realistically, however, neither of these plans is likely to garner much support. In order for the team-ticket plan to guarantee a presidential party majority, the president and all of Congress would have to be elected every four years. Such a change would necessitate a constitutional amendment—one that would stand little chance of passage because most Americans would be offended by any attempt to limit their choice of candidates at the ballot box. Providing bonus seats would require a constitutional amendment as well. In addition, this proposal not only runs up against fundamental questions regarding equal representation but also, if implemented, could well create animosities between those legislators who had been elected and those who had been "bonused" into Congress through appointment.[154]

Other proposals for enhancing interbranch comity call for either allowing members of Congress to serve simultaneously in the president's cabinet or allowing cabinet members to serve as members of the House.[155] As with the other proposals, these would require constitutional amendments since the Constitution prohibits any individual from serving in Congress while holding another position in the federal government. Moreover, assuming that presidents were to decide which members of Congress would occupy cabinet posts, they would probably choose among the more senior members of Congress. Such decisions would no doubt leave deep scars with those senior—and powerful—members not selected. As for the other proposal, we may also question how welcome unelected cabinet members would be in an otherwise elected House of Representatives.[156]

More realistic changes have been suggested by the Committee on the Constitutional System, a group composed of distinguished scholars and practitioners of politics.[157] First, to enhance the likelihood that presidential candidates will have forged alliances in Congress *before* they are even elected, the committee proposes that each party's nominees for House and Senate races, along with senators not up for reelection, be made uncommitted delegates to the party's national nominating conventions. Second, to free legislators from the special-interest group pressures resulting from PAC campaign contributions, the committee recommends a system of public financing of congressional elections similar to the one now in effect for presidential campaigns. Only half of the money would be given directly to congressional candidates, however. The remainder would go to each party's congressional campaign committee, whose membership would consist of its congressional leaders. Allowing these party leaders to decide on which races to spend the money would give them greater leverage over party members when voting on legislation. Third, the committee calls for an amendment to the Constitution giving members of the House a four-year term and senators an eight-year term. Thus, the entire House and half the Senate would come up for election in presidential election years. This constitutional change would, according to the committee, "create a common political time horizon for all elected officials of at least four years. It would lengthen the 'honeymoon' period in which major but controversial legislation could be enacted, such as deficit reduction measures that may create unpopular pains within two years but produce popular benefits within four."[158] Finally, as a means of reducing the possibility of divided government, the committee calls for Congress to pass legislation that would require all states to include a line or lever on federal election ballots enabling voters to cast a straight-ticket vote, if they so choose. This option, incidentally, is already accorded voters in nineteen states.

Taken together, the reforms of the Committee on the Constitutional System offer some promise for elevating the level of cooperation between the president and his or her party in Congress. However, these proposals provide no guarantee that the president's party will constitute a congressional majority. And it is divided government, more than any other single factor, that poses the greatest impediment to cooperation between the two branches. Barring proposals designed to engineer a presidential party majority, the only remedy to this problem is the resurgence of party as a motivating factor in the voting decision. The evidence to date, however, suggests no significant movement in this direction.[159]

☆ NOTES

1. Emmet John Hughes, *The Living Presidency* (New York: Coward, McCann & Geoghegan, 1973), p. 208. Copyright © 1973 by Emmet John Hughes. Reprinted by permission of Coward, McCann & Geoghegan.

2. Cited in *New York Times Magazine,* April 20, 1975, pp. 112, 113. Copyright © 1975 by The New York Times Company. Reprinted by permission.

3. Cited in Richard Neustadt, *Presidential Power* (New York: Wiley, 1960), p. 84.

4. Cited in Theodore Sorensen, *Watchmen in the Night* (Cambridge, Mass.: MIT Press, 1975), p. 89.

5. Cited in Arthur Schlesinger, Jr., *The Imperial Presidency* (Boston: Houghton Mifflin, 1973), pp. 42, 151, 154.

6. Sarah A. Binder and Steven Smith, *Politics or Principle: Filibustering in the United States Senate* (Washington, D.C.: Brookings Institution, 1997), p. 11; Richard Reeves, *Running in Place: How Bill Clinton Disappointed America* (Kansas City: Andrews & McMeel, 1996), p. 7.

7. Roger Davidson, *The Role of the Congressman* (New York: Pegasus, 1969), p. 131

8. Cited in David Halberstam, *The Best and the Brightest* (New York: Random House, 1969), p. 516.

9. Cited in Ralph Huitt, "White House Channels to the Hill," in Harvey Mansfield, ed., *Congress against the President* (New York: Academy of Political Science, 1975), p. 83.

10. Harold Laski, *The American Presidency* (New York: Universal Library, 1940), p. 138.

11. Paul Light, *The President's Agenda* (Baltimore: Johns Hopkins University Press, 1982), p. 45.

12. Neustadt, *Presidential Power,* p. 90.

13. John Mueller, *War, Presidents and Public Opinion* (New York: Wiley, 1973), pp. 199, 201.

14. *The Gallup Opinion Index,* January 1974, p. 3; *The Gallup Opinion Index,* September 1974, p. 11.

15. For an extended discussion of the impact of public prestige on the president's legislative success, see George Edwards, *Presidential Influence in Congress* (San Francisco: Freeman, 1980), pp. 86–100.

16. Mueller, *War, Presidents and Public Opinion,* p. 202.

17. Booth Mooney, *LBJ: An Irreverent Chronicle* (New York: Crowell, 1976), pp. 19, 32. Copyright © 1976 by Booth Mooney. Reprinted by permission of Thomas Y. Crowell.

18. Cited in Hedrick Smith, "Taking Charge of Congress," *New York Times Magazine,* August 9, 1981, p. 17.

19. James Young, "The Presidency and the Hill," in Aaron Wildavsky, ed., *The Presidency* (Boston: Little, Brown, 1969), p. 418.

20. Cited in David Broder, *The Party's Over* (New York: Harper & Row, 1971), p. 6.

21. Cited in Hughes, *Living Presidency,* p. 63.

22. Cited in Broder, *Party's Over,* pp. 5, 6.

23. Cited in Broder, *Party's Over,* p. 34.

24. Taken from Lewis Paper, *The Promise and the Performance* (New York: Crown, 1975), p. 262. Copyright © 1975 by Lewis J. Paper. Used by permission of Crown Publishers, Inc.

25. Ibid., p. 261.

26. Ibid., pp. 260, 261.

27. Cited in Huitt, "White House Channels," p. 73.

28. Cited in Jack Valenti, *A Very Human President* (New York: Norton, 1975), p. 178.

29. Doris Kearns, *Lyndon Johnson and the American Dream* (New York: Harper & Row, 1976), pp. 222–32.

30. Joseph Califano, *A Presidential Nation* (New York: Norton, 1975), p. 215.

31. Rowland Evans, Jr., and Robert Novak, *Nixon in the White House* (New York: Vantage Books, 1971), p. 106.

32. Ibid., p. 109.

33. Cited in Randall Ripley, *Congress: Process and Policy* (New York: Norton, 1975), p. 233.

34. Cited in Huitt, "White House Channels," p. 76.

35. Haynes Johnson, *In the Absence of Power* (New York: Viking Press, 1980), pp. 23, 156, 165; see also Eric Davis, "Legislative Liaison in the Carter Administration," *Political Science Quarterly* 2 (Summer 1979), 294.

36. Cited in William Livingston, Lawrence Dodd, and Richard Schott, eds., *The Presidency and Congress: A Shifting Balance of Power?* (Austin, Tex.: Lyndon B. Johnson School of Public Affairs, 1979), p. 311.

37. Cited in Johnson, *In the Absence of Power,* p. 239.

38. *Washington Post,* November 13, 1977, p. B12.

39. Cited in Hedrick Smith, "Problems of a Problem Solver," *New York Times Magazine,* January 8, 1978, p. 36. Copyright © 1978 by The New York Times Company. Reprinted by permission.

40. Cited in *National Journal,* March 7, 1981, p. 384.

41. Godfrey Hodgson, *All Things to All Men: The False Promise of the Modern Presidency* (New York: Simon & Schuster, 1980), p. 31.

42. *Congressional Quarterly Weekly Report,* August 1, 1981, p. 1372.

43. Cited in ibid.

44. *Congressional Quarterly Weekly Report,* October 25, 1986, p. 2687; *Congressional Quarterly Weekly Report,* November 19, 1988, p. 3323.

45. *Congressional Quarterly Weekly Report,* October 17, 1992, p. 3247.

46. Cited in *Congressional Quarterly Weekly Report,* October 7, 1995, p. 3081.

47. Cited in Bob Woodward, *The Agenda: Inside the Clinton White House* (New York: Simon & Schuster, 1994), p. 125; see also Jeffrey Birnbaum, *Madhouse: The Private Turmoil of Working for the President* (New York: Times Books, 1996), pp. 209–10.

48. Cited in *Washington Post,* October 9, 1994, p. A21.

49. Kenneth Collier, *Between the Branches: The White House Office of Legislative Affairs* (Pittsburgh: University of Pittsburgh Press, 1997), pp. 262–63.

50. On this point, see Don Bond and Richard Fleisher, *The President in the Legislative Arena* (Chicago: University of Chicago Press, 1990), chap. 9; George Edwards, *At the Margins: Presidential Leadership of Congress* (New Haven: Yale University Press, 1989), chap. 9.

51. *Congressional Quarterly Weekly Report,* December 22, 1990, p. 4184.

52. *Congressional Quarterly Weekly Report,* December 21, 1996, p. 3427; *Congressional Quarterly Weekly Report,* January 3, 1998, p. 13; *Congressional Quarterly Weekly Report,* January 9, 1999, p. 75.

53. Figures for 1962 through 1978 taken from Frank Sorauf, *Party Politics in America,* 4th ed. (Boston: Little, Brown, 1980), p. 343. Figures for 1979 and 1980 were supplied to the author by the Research Division at Congressional Quarterly.

54. *Congressional Quarterly Weekly Report,* December 30, 1989, p. 3544; *Congressional Quarterly Weekly Report,* December 22, 1990, p. 4183; *Congressional Quarterly Weekly Report,* December 28, 1991, p. 3753; *Congressional Quarterly Weekly Report,* December 19, 1992, p. 3896.

55. These figures were provided to the author by the Research Division at Congressional Quarterly.

56. George Will, *Restoration: Congress, Term Limits and the Recovery of Deliberative Democracy* (New York: Free Press, 1992), pp. 77, 89.

57. On this point see Charles Jones, *The United States Congress: People, Place and Policy* (Homewood, Ill.: Dorsey Press, 1982), p. 234; Edwards, *Presidential Influence in Congress,* p. 191; Barbara Sinclair, "Coping with Uncertainty: Building Coalitions in the House and the Senate," in Thomas Mann and Norman Ornstein, eds., *The New Congress* (Washington, D.C.: American Enterprise Institute, 1981), pp. 178–220.

58. Cited in *Congressional Quarterly Weekly Report,* September 13, 1980, pp. 2696, 2698; see also *Congressional Quarterly Weekly Report,* September 4, 1982, pp. 2175–82.

59. Martin Wattenberg, *The Decline of American Political Parties, 1952–1980* (Cambridge, Mass.: Harvard University Press, 1984), chap. 1; William Flanigan and Nancy Zingale, *Political Behavior of the American Electorate,* 6th ed. (Boston: Allyn & Bacon, 1987), p. 31.

60. *National Journal,* November 15, 1986, p. 281; *Washington Post,* April 1, 1995, p. A8.

61. F. Christopher Arterton, "Campaign '92: Strategies and Tactics," in Gerald M Pomper, et al., *The Election of 1992* (Chatham, N.J.: Chatham House, 1993), pp. 87–88. See also Susan Hammond, Daniel Mulhollan, and Arthur Stevens, Jr., "Informal Congressional Caucuses and Agenda Setting, *Western Political Quarterly* 38 (December, 1985), 583.

62. Cited in *Washington Post,* May 23, 1977, p. 1.

63. Cited in *Washington Post,* November 11, 1983, p. A14.

64. Alexander Hamilton, "Federalist Paper No. 73," in Jacob Cooke, ed., *The Federalist* (Cleveland: World, 1961), p. 497.

65. Cited in Robert Dahl, *Pluralist Democracy in the United States* (Chicago: Rand McNally, 1967), p. 98.

66. Cited in Harold Laski, *The American Presidency* (New York: Grosset & Dunlap, 1940), pp. 126, 127.

67. Cited in John Johannes, *Policy Innovation in Congress* (Morristown, N.J.: General Learning Press, 1972), p. 3.

68. Ibid.

69. Ripley, *Congress,* p. 249.

70. Cited in James L. Sundquist, *The Decline and Resurgence of Congress* (Washington, D.C.: Brookings Institution, 1981), p. 402.

71. *Congressional Quarterly Weekly Report,* November 24, 1979, p. 2638.

72. William Mullen, *Presidential Power and Politics* (New York: St. Martin's Press, 1976), p. 79.

73. Walter Mondale, *The Accountability of Power* (New York: McKay, 1975), p. 126.

74. Ibid., pp. 126, 127.

75. *Washington Post,* November 28, 1994, p. A23.

76. *Congressional Quarterly Weekly Report,* July 13, 1985, p. 1380.

77. Cited in *New York Times,* January 9, 1974, p. E2. Copyright © 1974 by The New York Times Company. Reprinted by permission.

78. *Washington Post,* June 12, 1995, p. A17.

79. For an excellent discussion of the role of Congress in the budgetary process, see Allen Schick, *Congress and Money: Budgeting, Spending and Taxing* (Washington, D.C.: Urban Institute Press, 1981).

80. *Congressional Quarterly Weekly Report,* January 10, 1981, p. 63.

81. Jean Peters, "Reconciliation 1982: What Happened?" *P.S.* 14 (Fall 1981), 732, 733.

82. Louis Fisher, "In Dubious Battle? Congress and the Budget," *The Brookings Bulletin* 17 (Spring 1981), 9.

83. Peters, "Reconciliation 1982," p. 734.

84. Ibid., 735, 736.

85. Cited in *New York Times,* May 21, 1978, p. E4.

86. Howard Shuman, *Politics and the Budget* (Englewood Cliffs, N.J.: Prentice Hall, 1984), p. 184.

87. *Washington Post,* August 16, 1994, p. A8.

88. Cited in *New York Times,* June 19, 1994, p. E3.

89. For an excellent discussion of these various practices, see Louis Fisher, *Presidential Spending Power* (Princeton, N.J.: Princeton University Press, 1975). See also Timothy Ingram,"The Billions in the White House Basement," in Stanley Bach and George Sulzner, eds., *Perspectives on the Presidency* (Lexington, Mass.: Heath, 1974), pp. 333–47.

90. Schlesinger, *Imperial Presidency* p. 236.

91. Allen Schick, "The Battle of the Budget," in Mansfield, *Congress against the President,* p. 62.

92. Cited in Schlesinger, *Imperial Presidency,* p. 237.

93. Quoted on *The Advocates,* a program telecast on February 16, 1973, by the Public Broadcasting Service. This quote appears on p. 22 of the written transcript from this program.

94. Allen Schick, *Congress and Money,* p. 405; *Congressional Quarterly Weekly Report,* March 28, 1992, p. 792.

95. *National Journal,* May 24, 1986, p. 1261.

96. *Congressional Quarterly Weekly Report,* May 17, 1986, p. 1092; *Congressional Quarterly Weekly Report,* January 24, 1987, p. 145.

97. Howard E. Shuman, *Politics and the Budget,* 3rd ed. (Englewood Cliffs, N.J.: Prentice Hall, 1992), pp. 305, 306, 330–41.

98. Cited in Valenti, *Very Human President,* p. 194.

99. *New York Times,* March 8, 1993, A1.

100. Cited in Paper, *Promise and Performance,* p. 270.

101. Ibid., p. 272.

102. *Congressional Quarterly Weekly Report,* September 21, 1962, p. 1556.

103. Ripley, *Congress,* p. 229.

104. Cited in John Roche, "Comments on Part VI," in Marc Landy, ed., *Modern Presidents and the Presidency* (Lexington, Mass.: Heath, 1985), p. 188.

105. *Congressional Quarterly Weekly Report,* August 1, 1981, p. 1372.

106. Cited in *Washington Post,* July 30, 1981, p. A8.

107. *Congressional Quarterly Weekly Report,* August 1, 1981, p. 1372; *Washington Post,* August 10, 1981, pp. A1, 10; *Washington Post,* June 27, 1981, p. A1, A9; *Time,* August 10, 1981, p. 14.

108. *U.S. News and World Report,* September 13, 1993, p. 22.

109. Mondale, *Accountability of Power,* p. 82.

110. *Washington Post,* June 29, 1998, p. A13.

111. *New York Times,* April 26, 1981, p. E4.

112. Quoted in Samuel Kernell, *Going Public: New Strategies of Presidential Leadership* (Washington, D.C.: Congressional Quarterly Press, 1986), p. 120.

113. Cited in *Washington Post,* April 30, 1978, p. A15.

114. *Washington Post,* July 29, 1981, p. A1; *Congressional Quarterly Weekly Report,* August 8, 1981, p. 1431.

115. Robert Dixon, "Congress, Shared Administration, and Executive Privilege," in *Congress against the President,* p. 135.

116. Cited in Schlesinger, *Imperial Presidency,* p. 156.

117. Ibid., p. 158.

118. Dixon, "Congress and Executive Privilege," p. 134; Schlesinger, *Imperial Presidency,* p. 247.

119. Sorensen, *Watchmen in the Night,* p. 104.

120. Schlesinger, *Imperial Presidency,* p. 251.

121. Dixon, "Congress and Executive Privilege," pp. 136, 137.

122. Cited in *New York Times,* July 28, 1974, p. E2.

123. *New York Times,* December 14, 1975, p. E3; *Congressional Quarterly Weekly Report,* October 4, 1975, p. 2097.

124. Raoul Berger, "Congressional Subpoenas to Executive Officials," *Columbia Law Review* 75 (June 1975), 889.

125. *Congressional Quarterly Weekly Report,* December 31, 1982, p. 3162.

126. Ibid., p. 3163; Louis Fisher, *Constitutional Conflicts between Congress and the President* (Princeton, N.J.: Princeton University Press, 1985), p. 212.

127. Fisher, *Constitutional Conflicts,* pp. 212, 213; Carol Holt, "Executive Privilege," *Presidential Studies Quarterly* 16 (Spring 1986), 240.

128. Jeffrey Rosen, "Underprivileged: Why Clinton Deserves Executive Privilege," *New Republic,* April 13, 1998, p. 14.

129. Cited in *Washington Post,* May 28, 1998, p. A17.

130. *New York Times,* May 28, 1998, pp. A1, A20.

131. *Washington Post,* February 20, 1998, p. A9; *New York Times,* October 2, 1996, p. A12; *Washington Post,* September 26, 1996, p. A20.

132. Cited in Schlesinger, *Imperial Presidency,* p. 75.

133. Congressional Quarterly, *Impeachment and the U.S. Congress* (Washington, D.C.: Congressional Quarterly, 1974), p. 32.

134. Theodore White, *Breach of Faith* (New York: Atheneum, 1975), pp. 9, 13; see also Bob Woodward and Carl Bernstein, *The Final Days* (New York: Simon & Schuster, 1975), pp. 323, 324.

135. *Congressional Quarterly Weekly Report,* February 9, 1999, p. 75.

136. See, for example, *New York Times,* August 6, 1998, p. A23; *New York Times,* September 20, 1998, p. 1WK; *New York Times,* September 25, 1998, p. A6; *New York Times,* October 12, 1998, p. A8; *Washington Post,* November 4, 1998, p. A25.

137. Cited in Woodward and Bernstein, *The Final Days,* p. 249.

138. White, *Breach of Faith,* p. 23.

139. Cited in Erwin Hargrove, *The Power of the Modern Presidency* (New York: Knopf, 1974), p. 317.

140. Schlesinger, *Imperial Presidency,* pp. 411, 412.

141. See James L. Sundquist, *Constitutional Reform* (Washington, D.C: Brookings Institution, 1986), chap. 4; Donald L. Robinson, ed., *Reforming American Government* (Boulder, Colo.: Westview Press, 1985), parts II and III; Theodore Sorensen, *A Different Kind of Presidency* (New York: Harper & Row, 1984); Lloyd Cutler, "To Form a Government—On the Defects of Separation of Powers," *Foreign Affairs* 59 (Fall 1980), pp. 126–43; Gary Cox and Samuel Kernell, eds., *The Politics of Divided Government* (Boulder, Colo.: Westview Press, 1991).

142. "Toward a More Responsible Two-Party System: A Report of the Committee on Political Parties, American Political Science Association," *American Political Science Review* (Supplement: vol. 44, September 1950, no. 3, pt. 2).

143. Broder, *Party's Over,* p. xvii.

144. Lloyd Cutler, "Party Government under the Constitution (1985)," in Robinson, *Reforming American Government,* pp. 94, 95.

145. Joseph Califano, *A Presidential Nation* (New York: Norton, 1975), p. 20.

146. Broder, *Party's Over,* p. 64.

147. Cited in Valenti, *Very Human President,* p. 144.

148. Sundquist, *Constitutional Reform,* p. 109.

149. Cited in ibid.

150. *Washington Post,* February 1, 1987, p. D2.

151. David R. Mayhew, *Divided We Govern* (New Haven: Yale University Press, 1991), chap. 4. See also Charles Jones, *The Presidency in a Separated System* (Washington, D.C.: Brookings Institution, 1994), pp. 195–207; Morris Fiorina, *Divided Government* (New York: Macmillan, 1992), chap. 6.

152. George C. Edwards, III, Andrew Barrett, and Jeffrey Peake, "The Legislative Impact of Divided Government," *American Journal of Political Science,* 41 (April 1997), 561–62.

153. Robinson, *Reforming American Government,* pp. 177–82.

154. Sundquist, *Constitutional Reform,* pp. 98–103.

155. Robinson, *Reforming American Government,* pp. 143–48, 182–85.

156. Sundquist, *Constitutional Reform,* pp. 168–77.

157. *A Bicentennial Analysis of the American Political Structure,* Report and Recommendations of the Committee on the Constitutional System, Washington, D.C., 1987, pp. 8–12.

158. *Washingion Post,* February 1, 1987, p. D2.

159. On this point see Martin Wattenberg, "The Hollow Realignment: Partisan Change in a Candidate-Centered Era," *Public Opinion Quarterly* 15 (Spring 1987), 66; Morris Fiorina, "The Presidency and the Contemporary Electoral System," in Michael Nelson, *The Presidency and the Political System* (Washington, D.C.: Congressional Quarterly Press, 1984), pp. 209–24.

President, Public, and Press

Of all the constituencies with which presidents must interact, none is more important to him than the public. Only the people have the authority to renew or terminate his presidency, unless, of course, he is convicted of impeachable offenses by the Senate. And even that kind of drastic action would be highly unlikely unless the public was in favor of it. Also, presidents are less likely to encounter resistance to what they want if the public is firmly behind them. President Lincoln took note of this fact when he remarked, "In this and like communities, public sentiment is everything. With public sentiment nothing can fail, without it nothing can succeed."[1] Although Lincoln overstates the case, few would doubt that public support facilitates the president's ability to act. As was noted in Chapter 3, most of what a president wants to accomplish requires the acquiescence of Congress in one form or another. Moreover, given the constitutional restrictions on his power, as well as the absence of guaranteed support from members of his own party in Congress, the president is forced to enlist congressional support rather than command it. Since Congress is a popularly elected body, it must of necessity be sensitive to the level of public support the president can generate for his programs. Although public backing is not the only factor that can make a president an effective persuader, it is surely one of his most potent weapons.

In this chapter we shall examine how the public reacts to both the presidency and the president and consider what, if any, implications these reactions have for presidential power. For analytical purposes, public attitudes toward the office and the individual will initially be treated separately, but they are in fact interrelated. This interrelationship will constitute a second focus of this chapter. Here an effort will be made to assess the impact of President Nixon's Watergate involvement upon the public's attitudes toward the institution of the presidency. Finally, we shall examine how the president attempts to influence the public's attitude toward himself and his policies. In dealing with this matter, it will be important to discuss the president's relationship with the press, the primary instrument through which he communicates with the people.

PUBLIC ATTITUDES TOWARD THE OFFICE: PRE-WATERGATE

The Importance of the Office

That the American people attach extraordinary importance to the office of the presidency can be demonstrated in several ways, one of which is the number of people in the population who are able to identify the president of the United States. As Table 4-1 indicates, the president is by far the best-known public official in the country, with nearly all adults and young adults (98 percent) able to identify him. (Although it might be intriguing to speculate why the other 2 percent of the adult population apparently never got the word, this need not concern us here.) Moreover, not only is the president the most well known political figure on the national scene, but, with the exception of the vice president, other prominent public officials do not even approach this level of public recognition. Even schoolchildren in the primary grades can identify the president and correctly state his party identification. Furthermore, they also see him as the most important figure in their political world.[2]

It is hardly surprising that the president enjoys such widespread recognition among all segments of the public. He is, after all, the only nationally elected public official in our government. Equally important, he is the focal point of our political process, and thus the media's daily attention to his every word and action far exceeds the coverage given any other public figure.

A further indication of the importance of the presidency to the American citizenry is reflected in how their attitudes toward this particular institution affect their attitudes toward other institutions. Specifically, an increase or decrease in support for the presidency also appears to lead to an increase or decrease in support for other institutions such as Congress and the Supreme Court. One study showed, for example, that as public support for the presidency declined during the Watergate scandals, so too did support for Congress and the Court, although the declines for the latter were at a much slower rate.[3]

TABLE 4-1   Awareness of Political Leaders on the Part of Adults and Children, 1969–1970

	Percentage Correct by Age		
Office	*Adult*	*17*	*13*
President (Nixon)	98	98	94
Vice President (Agnew)	87	79	60
Secretary of State (Rogers)	16	9	2
Secretary of Defense (Laird)	25	16	6
Speaker of the House (McCormack)	32	25	2
Senate Majority Leader (Mansfield)	23	14	4
At Least One Senator from Own State	57	44	16
Both Senators from Own State	31	18	6
Congressman from Own District	39	35	11

Source: Fred Greenstein, "What the President Means to Americans," in James Barber, ed., *Choosing the President* (Englewood Cliffs, N.J.: Prentice Hall, 1974), p. 125.

Similarly, a study of children done during this same period demonstrated that their increasingly negative attitudes toward the presidency were accompanied by increasingly negative reactions toward other political objects.[4] Such a "fallout effect" suggests that for many Americans the presidency constitutes the most important and fundamental point of identification with the political system.

Finally, the population's reaction to the death of a president may also be taken as an indicator of the preeminent position the office holds in the public mind. Following the death of President Kennedy, for example, substantial numbers of the population reported physiological irregularities that exceeded the levels one would normally expect. A survey made by the National Opinion Research Center found that during the days immediately following the assassination, 43 percent of the adult population reported a loss of appetite, 48 percent experienced insomnia, 25 percent complained of headaches, 68 percent experienced nervousness and tension, 26 percent had rapid heartbeats, and 17 percent noted greater-than-normal perspiration. These symptoms of emotional strain were experienced by the president's detractors as well as his supporters. And the principal cause of such reactions appears to have had more to do with the fact that he was *the president* than with the nature of his death or his youth and personal appeal. The public's grief over President Kennedy was not a unique occurrence in our history. On the contrary, the historical evidence suggests that the public reacted in much the same way to the deaths of Lincoln, Roosevelt, McKinley, Garfield, and even such a marginal president as Warren Harding.[5] That the public has behaved in this way suggests that the president, regardless of who he happens to be, functions as perhaps the most important symbol of stability and national unity within our political system. When that symbol is suddenly taken away, the psychological effect upon the population is profound, even if only temporary.

The Office as an Object of Trust and Respect

In the past the population has exhibited a high degree of respect for and trust in the presidency. Such attitudes have taken root early in the lives of Americans, with grade-school children not only seeing the president as the most important public figure but also assessing him in highly positive terms. According to earlier studies, grade-school children viewed the president as "benevolent, dependable, trustworthy and infallible."[6] The following are examples of how he was characterized:

"[The President] gives us freedom." (Eighth-grade girl)

"[The President] deals with foreign countries and takes care of the U.S." (Eighth-grade boy)

"[The President] makes peace with every country but bad." (Fifth-grade boy)

"[The President] does good work." (Sixth-grade boy)

"[The President] is doing a very good job of making people safe." (Fourth-grade girl)[7]

These findings were based upon studies conducted during the relative tranquility of the late 1950s and early 1960s. Even leaving Watergate aside for the moment, most of the 1960s and early 1970s were characterized by political and social turmoil; there were racial riots in our major cities and student protests against the Vietnam War and, to some extent, against the political system itself. Thus, one might expect this turbulent era to have had profound effects upon attitudes toward political authority in general and the presidency in particular. Yet in a 1969–1970 study of British, French, and American children, Fred Greenstein concluded that the white American children "were extraordinarily positive in their spontaneous descriptions of the President."[8] Here are two typical responses:

> The President of the United States is a man or a woman or whatever, who is, like, picked by the people to lead the country. And they try to make the person almost perfect. I mean, if he does anything wrong they down him . . . because *if a person is going to be head of a country like the United States for years, he just has to be about perfect.*
>
> The President of the United States is a very important man that is trying to make the U.S. a better place and, well, he takes care of problems that just a few people won't be able to take care of, like the war in Vietnam and like the men who have been over there for a long time. And *he tries to make things equal and fair* so that you know you won't really get mad on the taxes. He's, well, he's trying to make the United States a better place and he's trying to solve a lot of problems.[9]

Black children in the group were far more inclined to give a negative response about the president than their white counterparts, but their responses were still more often favorable than unfavorable. As the following dialogue demonstrates, however, the negative responses were in some cases quite intense.

> **Respondent:** I'd say [of the president] he's stupid and he don't know what he's doing.
>
> **Interviewer:** What does he do?
>
> **Respondent:** He doesn't do . . . He doesn't let people do what they want to do. He always putting people in jail or somethin'. . . . He's supposed to keep peace in the world, but he isn't doing that. . . . He isn't trying to stop anything.
>
> **Interviewer:** Suppose a foreign child asks you what is the President of the United States?
>
> **Respondent:** A rat.
>
> **Interviewer:** Okay, try to give the foreign child an idea of what he does. What does he do?
>
> **Respondent:** I can name a lot of things. . . . He prejudiced. . . . He lousy. He picked Spiro Agnew. Spiro Agnew stinks and he ain't no good, none of them.
>
> **Interviewer:** What is the President's job?
>
> **Respondent:** To try and make people happy, but he's making them miserable.[10]

Although the reactions of both the black and white children were generally positive, it is important to note that the children in this study did *not* come from the more depressed areas of their community. The subgroups within our population who have not fared so well at the hands of society have shown demonstrably different feelings toward the presidency. Especially noteworthy in this regard is a study made of black and white children from grades five through twelve in the economically depressed area of Appalachia. It revealed that these children saw the president as more malevolent than benevolent. Although in the earlier grades they tended to idealize the president, their attitudes became increasingly negative toward him as they progressed toward the twelfth grade. By their senior year in high school, only 31 percent felt that the president "liked almost everybody while an equal percentage thought that he liked fewer people than most men."[11] Moreover, there was not even one twelfth grader who thought the president was the best person in the world; indeed, nearly one-third of them did not think he was a very good person at all. The decline in favorable responses to the presidency occurred more rapidly among the poor blacks than the poor whites, at least until the ninth grade. At this point, the attitudes of black children began to become more positive, a fact that may reflect their perception of the president as a visible spokesman for civil rights.[12]

In summary, although there are some marked exceptions among certain socio-cultural subgroups within our society, taken as a whole the evidence suggests that prior to Watergate the presidency was trusted and respected by the pre-adult population.

Not surprisingly, the indiscriminately positive attitudes shown toward the office by the pre-adult population do not persist into the adult years. Yet even though a more realistic appraisal replaces the idealization of the young, trust in the presidency has in the past remained quite high, even among adults. In 1966, for example, the Survey Research Center asked a national sample of adults what kinds of work they respected most highly. Included in the choices of occupations were a famous doctor, a bishop or other church official, president of a large corporation such as General Motors, a governor, senator, Supreme Court justice, and several other public officials. Also included, of course, was the president of the United States. The results were decisive, with 52 percent of the sample naming the president as their first choice. The next most respected occupations were those of physician and clergyman, but even these received only a little more than 10 percent of the first-choice responses.[13]

In another study conducted in 1966, 816 people were interviewed on their attitudes toward the presidency. Once again, the results suggested that in the past the office has been the respository of a high degree of respect and trust. Among other things, the authors constructed an "I Like Presidents" index, which appears in Table 4-2. All but two of the statements in the index received the support of a majority of those interviewed. It was also found that scores on the "I Like Presidents"

TABLE 4-2   "I Like Presidents" Index

		Percent Giving Support Responses
(1)	More nearly than any other person, the President stands for our country.	85
(2)	One sleeps better knowing that a President one trusts is watching over the country.	72
(3)	We are fortunate because our presidents usually make the right decisions.	69
(4)	Most people don't appreciate enough how hard Presidents work for the welfare of the country.	63
(5)	Since the President has the best information on public affairs, he is more likely than anyone else to know what is the best thing to do.	61
(6)	Just seeing or hearing a President makes one feel good.	38
(7)	Although he may have been an ordinary citizen before, when he becomes President he should be considered to be the wisest man in the world.	20

Source: From Samuel Kernell, Peter Sperlich, and Aaron Wildavsky, "Public Support for Presidents," in Aaron Wildavsky, ed., *Perspectives on the Presidency* (Boston: Little, Brown, 1975), p. 152. Copyright © 1975 by Little, Brown and Company, Inc. Reprinted by permission.

index were affected by certain background and psychological factors as well as by political attitudes about American government. More specifically, those scoring highest on the index tended to be individuals with authoritarian personalities, little education, and positive attitudes toward the American political system. This is not altogether surprising. The least educated tend to have little knowledge about the political system, and thus the president constitutes their only visible link to the government. Similarly, in contrast to nonauthoritarian types, those personalities who have a need for authority and order would understandably react more favorably to the authority the president represents. Finally, individuals with more positive attitudes toward the political system in general could also reasonably be expected to view the presidency more favorably.

If admiration may be taken as an indicator of trust and respect, then we find still further confirmation of the public attitude toward the office on these two dimensions. Since 1948 the Gallup poll has nearly every year (except 1975 and 1976) asked Americans, "What man that you have heard about, living today in any part of the world, do you admire most?" From 1948 through 1972, the president finished first in all but five of the twenty-five years. Truman came in third in 1950 and 1951 and was rated fourth in 1952. The other two years were 1967 and 1968, when President Johnson finished second, behind former President Eisenhower. As of the end of 1998, President Bill Clinton had finished first in the poll for six years running, despite his impeachment by the House in his sixth year.[14]

Attitudes about the Power of the Presidency

Although the public appears to feel that the powers of the presidency have grown while those of Congress have decreased, people do not have a naive impression of the office as all-powerful. In 1958, the Survey Research Center asked a national sample of Americans, "In general which do you think has the most say in the way our government is run—the Congress, the President, or are they about equal?" Fifty-two percent of the respondents felt that Congress had the most say, only 10 percent felt the president did, and 24 percent thought they were about equal.[15] In another national survey conducted approximately ten years later, only 10 percent of the population felt that the president had the power to get just about anybody to do what he wants.[16] A statewide poll taken in 1973 asked Minnesota citizens which institution had more power and control in relation to the government—Congress or the president. Although a substantial number came down on the side of the president (47 percent), Congress was still given the edge (49 percent).[17]

Given the trust and respect that have characterized public attitudes about the presidency in the past, one would expect that the population would be willing to accord the president considerable freedom of action in what he does. The preponderance of evidence does not confirm this expectation, however. After examining public opinion polls that, over a forty-year period, have dealt with various aspects of presidential power, one scholar concludes:

> A president would have few unchecked prerogatives if it were left to the American public. Whenever given a choice between congressional vs. presidential decision making, the people tend to trust Congress over the chief executive. Whether the issue pertains to specific domestic or military matters, or to authority in general, seems immaterial. Unsophisticated as the public may be in knowledge of constitutional provisions for the

separation of powers, they have systematically given implied consent to the principle of checks and balances or, at the least, have shown majority reluctance to grant too much power to one man, the president.[18]

In 1958, for example, the Survey Research Center asked a national sample of Americans the following question: "Some people say the President is in the best position to see what the country needs. Other people think the president may have good ideas about what the country needs, but it is up to Congress to decide what ought to be done. How do you feel about this?" Respondents came down decisively on the side of Congress (61 percent), with only 17 percent choosing the president. Among the remaining respondents, 7 percent said it depends, and 15 percent simply did not know how they felt on the matter.[19] Ten years later, a Harris poll asked a national sample of Americans whether they thought the president or Congress ought to have the major responsibility in making foreign, economic, and racial policy. The results, presented in Table 4–3, clearly demonstrate that a majority felt the president and Congress should play an equal role in all three policy areas. Also worth noting, however, is the fact that substantially greater numbers were willing to give Congress, rather than the president, the dominant policymaking role in all three policy areas.

One study in particular constitutes a notable exception to the findings presented above. In the early 1960s, two questions were put to a sample of Detroit citizens on the subject of presidential power. The first was a general question that asked whether they thought the president "should be able to make the people and Congress go along with him," or whether "it is up to the people through their congressmen to find solutions to the problems of the day," with the "President carrying out what the people and Congress have decided." A total of 51.5 percent felt that presidential leadership should be preferred, 39.6 opted for the combined leadership of the public and Congress, and 6 percent felt they should all be involved. A second question dealt specifically with a hypothetical matter of foreign policy: "Fighting has broken out abroad and the President thinks it is important to send troops there. Now, what do you think, should he send these troops, which he may legally do as President, or should he follow public opinion and keep them home?" An overwhelming 75 percent felt that he should go ahead and send the troops, while only 20.8 percent felt he should not.[20]

The discrepancy between these results and those of the Harris survey presented in Table 4-3 can perhaps be explained by two factors. In the Harris poll, respondents were asked to judge the role of the president and Congress in foreign policy; the Detroit study asked people to choose between the president's judgment and the public's. It may be that the public is sufficiently skeptical about its own knowledge of

TABLE 4-3   Public Views of Presidential and Congressional
Policymaking Responsibilities

	Foreign Policy	Economic Policy	Racial Policy
President	14	7	11
Equal	60	58	63
Congress	23	31	23
Not sure	3	4	3

Source: Louis Harris and Associates, Study No. 1900. Under contract to Roger H. Davidson and financed by the Social Research Council. Reprinted by permission of Professor Davidson.

foreign policy that it is willing to defer to the president. On the other hand, when the choice on making foreign policy is between the president and Congress, the public does have enough confidence in the judgment of Congress to want to include it in foreign policy decisions. Also, the time when each study was made may help to explain why the Detroit citizens—unlike those interviewed by Harris—preferred presidential leadership on matters in general and on the commitment of troops in particular. Whereas the Detroit study was done in the early 1960s, Harris made his survey in 1968. By this time the Vietnam War had become unpopular, and since the presidency had been responsible for getting us into it, the public may have concluded that Congress should have greater say in foreign policy. Similarly, rising inflation, racial unrest in the cities, and a general discontent with busing may also have led them to conclude that Congress should play a role in the making of economic and racial policy.

Although the public is not prepared to give the president the dominant role in the governmental process, it is nevertheless willing to give him strong support when he has made a decision. According to one study, for example, 56 percent of the respondents felt that the president should be supported even if they think he has made a wrong decision. At the same time, however, only 25 percent were willing to go so far as to say that he should be supported *no matter what he does*. During times of crisis, support for the president is even higher, with nearly two-thirds of the respondents feeling that the public should rally behind him. But even under crisis conditions, they do not favor blind and unquestioning support, for only 24 percent felt that people should *not* ask a lot of questions and demand a lot of answers at such times.[21]

To summarize briefly, prior to Watergate the public did not appear to believe that the presidency was an omnipotent institution. Nor, the evidence suggests, would they want it to be so. On the contrary, a majority of Americans favor a coequal partnership between the president and Congress in the making of policy. These findings suggest that although the public has in the past expressed considerable confidence in the presidency, this attitude has not overcome what is apparently an even stronger view—namely, that there should be a balance of power and responsibility within the government.

THE PUBLIC'S ATTITUDES TOWARD THE INDIVIDUAL

Thus far, our attention has been focused upon the public's pre-Watergate views of the presidency as an institution, without reference to the individuals who happened to occupy it. We now consider how and why the public reacts as it does to the people who serve in this office.

The Inevitable Decline in Support

Since the late 1930s, the Gallup poll has periodically tested the waters of public sentiment toward incumbent presidents. The question traditionally put to the public by Gallup has been, "Do you approve or disapprove of the way the President is handling his job?" The answers to this question over an expanse of some fifty years allow us to make some generalizations about the patterns of public support for presidents.

One thing is clear. A president's popularity typically begins to erode fairly soon after he assumes office. An examination of the public approval ratings of our last seven presidents is instructive in this regard. Table 4–4 gives their average public approval rating for each twelve-month period after they took office. (Prior presidents are excluded because so few poll readings were taken in the course of a given year.) Following their first twelve months in office, four of the nine presidents finished the year with an average approval rating below that received shortly after taking office. Upon completion of the second twelve months, however, the average approval ratings of all presidents except Bush were below their average for the previous year. Note also that of the eight presidents serving all or part of a third year, half suffered a further decline in their average approval rating over the previous year. The exceptions are Eisenhower, Reagan, Bush, and Clinton. Eisenhower experienced a seven-point increase, which is probably attributable to the termination of the Korean War in 1953. Reagan increased his public approval rating by a negligible one point, as did Clinton. Bush's approval rating, however, grew by a full thirteen points, making it the biggest year-to-year increase of any of the eight presidents. Of course, the circumstances of Bush's third year in office were highly conducive to such a favorable rating, for not only did the United States win the Gulf War, but it was accomplished in a relatively short period of time; the casualties were remarkably few (146); and the financial cost was borne largely by other countries.

The fourth year was a reelection year for all the presidents except Johnson. You will note that three of the four who won reelection experienced a significant increase in their average approval rating, with Nixon's climbing by thirteen points, Reagan's by eleven, and Clinton's by seven. This surge is understandable, however, since elections represent an intense effort to remobilize supporters. Although Eisenhower experienced a decrease, his drop represented a mere one point from an already high rating of 72 percent the previous year. Johnson's election to a full term occurred during his first twelve months in office. His average approval rating for 1964 was 75 percent, three points below his first rating upon taking office. But this finding should not occasion surprise either, for election year or not, it would be extremely difficult for any president to improve upon a public approval rating of 78 percent—the highest initial rating received by any of the last nine presidents and surely explained by a national desire to unite behind a new leader in time of crisis.

Two final points are worth emphasizing in connection with the data in Table 4-4. First, with the exception of Reagan and Clinton, in none of the years following election (Johnson) or reelection (Eisenhower, Nixon, Reagan, Clinton) did a president attain an average public approval rating equal to *any* of the prior years. Second, six of the eight presidents left office with a public approval rating substantially lower than the one they received upon taking office. Only presidents Reagan and Bush retired with a final public approval rating well above their first one—an achievement not altogether surprising given the fact that their initial rating (51 percent) was unusually low—lower, in fact, than for any president serving between 1953 and 1993. Note also that Reagan's average approval rating for his *entire* eighth year was five points below that of his first year; and Bush's fourth and final year rating was twenty-four points below his first year. To be sure, what a president does or fails to do may accelerate or retard an overall decline in support, but the decline itself appears to be inevitable.

Several factors may help to explain why this is so. In the first place, a president comes into office with the initial support of the majority coalition that gave him his election victory. He also picks up some additional support from those who, although not willing to support him as a candidate, now feel some obligation to unite behind

TABLE 4-4 Presidential Public Approval Ratings

	Support Upon Assuming Office	Average Approval 1st Year	Average Approval 2nd Year	Average Approval 3rd Year	Average Approval 4th Year	Average Approval 5th Year	Average Approval 6th Year	Average Approval 7th Year	Average Approval 8th Year	Support at Time of Death, Resignation, or Expiration of Term
Eisenhower	68	69	66	73	72	62	58	64	61	59
Kennedy	72	76	71	62*	—	—	—	—	—	58
Johnson	78	75	66	50	44	42	—	—	—	49
Nixon	59	61	54	49	62	40	26**	—	—	24
Ford	71	47	43	—	36	—	—	—	—	53
Carter	66	61	46	39	56	—	—	—	—	34
Reagan	51	57	44	45	56	60	60	47	52	63
Bush	51	64	66	79	40	—	—	—	—	56
Clinton	58	48	46	47	54	58	63	—	—	—

*Since Kennedy did not complete his third year, this figure represents the average of his third-year approval ratings up to the time of his death.

**Since Nixon did not complete his sixth year, this figure represents the average of his sixth-year approval ratings up to the time of his resignation from office.

Source: Data from 1945 to 1971 taken from George Gallup, *The Gallup Poll: Public Opinion 1935–1971* (New York: Random House, 1972). Data from 1972 on were taken from the monthly *Gallup Opinion Index.*

him as president. Thus, although Jimmy Carter defeated Gerald Ford by only three percentage points in the popular vote, a Gallup poll taken one month after he assumed office showed that 66 percent of the public approved of the way he was handling his job.[22] How long a president's "honeymoon" lasts depends upon how controversial his actions are, as well as upon the nature of events that he cannot always control. Gerald Ford's honeymoon ended abruptly when, one month after assuming office, he granted Richard Nixon a free and open pardon. This decision brought cries of outrage from the public, and his approval rating fell from 71 to 50 percent.[23] On the other hand, Reagan's honeymoon period, about to be cut short following his announcement of extensive budget cuts, was in fact extended as a result of the attempt on his life—an event that boosted his public approval rating by seven points.[24]

Although Gerald Ford's pardon of Nixon was undoubtedly more controversial than most presidential decisions made during the first few months in office, no president can avoid making controversial decisions for very long. All of the problems that come over his desk are important ones, and they are nearly always controversial as well. Each decision he makes will manage to dissatisfy some segment(s) of the population. As the number of controversial decisions increases, so too will the level of dissatisfaction, producing what one scholar has called a "coalition of minorities" opposed to the president.[25] In office only six months, Jimmy Carter made policy decisions that managed to stir up opposition in several quarters. Farmers were upset by his refusal to seek higher grain price supports. George Meany and the AFL-CIO were upset by his failure to give vigorous support to common situs picketing legislation as well as by his decision to seek a smaller increase in the minimum wage. The shoe industry was offended by Carter's refusal to raise tariffs on shoe imports. Both labor and industry strongly objected to certain portions of his energy program. And the liberal wing of the Democratic Party became increasingly disenchanted by Carter's determination to balance the budget even if it meant holding down expenditures for social programs. The president of the National Urban League charged that Carter had "betrayed" black people. Nor did Ronald Reagan win universal acclaim for the decisions he made during his first year in office. His reduction in spending for social programs brought with it the charge that he lacked compassion for the less fortunate in our society. A host of consumer and environmental groups alleged that his efforts to reduce government regulations constituted a sellout to the corporate establishment. Following his decision to fire air traffic controllers, most major labor unions in the country condemned his action as an assault on the labor movement. And the resumption of grain sales to the Soviet Union, though welcomed by farmers, angered conservatives who advocated a tougher stance toward the Soviet Union. The examples could go on, but these mentioned suffice to show that the necessity of making difficult decisions precludes a lasting honeymoon between the president and the public.

A president's declining public support is a consequence not only of what he does but also of what he fails to do. All presidential candidates have been prone to making extravagant promises during their campaigns. In part, this is a consequence of their desire to get elected; it also reflects a certain naiveté about the magnitude of the problems they must confront and the support that will be necessary from other power centers in government. Reagan, for example, despite some notable accomplishments, promised much more than he could deliver. No failure perhaps was more glaring than budget deficits. Throughout the 1980 election campaign, he promised to balance the federal budget, and yet the accumulated deficits during his presidency exceeded those of all previous presidents combined. He repeatedly promised no increase in taxes but in fact supported the 1982 tax increase legislation camouflaged as tax "reform." Throughout his campaign, he pledged vigorous support for legislation to outlaw abortion and restore prayer in the schools, but when push came to shove administration support on both issues proved to be less than wholehearted. Promises to abolish the Departments of Energy and Education and eliminate draft registration were also shelved, as was the pledge to push for a Family Protection bill.[26] Finally, despite numerous pledges never to negotiate with terrorists, his administration embarked upon a plan to trade arms for American hostages being held in Iran.

The overpromising syndrome forced Bill Clinton into a number of embarrassing retreats during his first year as president. In his campaign for the presidency, he had promised a middle-class tax cut only to back away from it once in office. On the other hand, he pledged not to raise the tax on gasoline or on corporations and yet increases on both were included in his deficit reduction package. There were also retreats from promises to end the ban on gays in the military, to present a health care plan to Congress during his first one hundred days, and to significantly increase spending in the fight against drugs. In the foreign policy area, meanwhile, he had inveighed against the Bush administration for granting most-favored-nation trade status to China, for inaction on Bosnia, and for denying fleeing Haitians the opportunity for a hearing. During his first year in office, however, Clinton renewed China's special trade status, turned away Haitian refugees, and left the Europeans to deal with Bosnia.[27]

Regardless of whether it results from political expediency or naiveté, the "overpromising" syndrome has a tendency to elevate public expectations beyond what is within reach. If presidents themselves come to realize the gap between what is promised and what is attainable, so too does the public. The result is a certain amount of disillusionment, which contributes to the decline in a president's support.[28] In assessing his first year in office, President Carter acknowledged that "my biggest mistake has been in inadvertently building up expectations too high."[29]

Finally, it has been suggested by Thomas Cronin that a president's declining public support may also be due in part to conflicting public expectations about what kind of person he ought to be. For example, Cronin points out that we seek a *gentle and decent* individual in the presidency, but these qualities must often conflict with our equally strong desire for someone who is *forceful and decisive.* We want someone who can exercise moral leadership in the office, but we also recognize the necessity of having an individual who realizes that *compromise* is essential if one is to get anything accomplished. We look for a president who can provide *innovative and creative* solutions, yet at the same time our democratic values have imbued us with the belief that presidents should be *responsive to public opinion.* We desire a leader who can *inspire us, elevate our hopes,* invite us to reach beyond our grasp, but we also insist that he should *not create false expectations.* We seek someone who can *unify* us, but our desire for creative, decisive, and courageous leadership makes it all but inevitable that he must *divide even as he leads.* These paradoxical expectations place a president in a no-win situation, for in attempting to fulfill some of them he cannot help but appear deficient in others.[30]

In addition to these general reasons why presidents suffer an overall decline in their popularity, certain circumstances and events appear to be especially important in accelerating or retarding this decline. The president appears to benefit from those situations in which he is acting as the symbolic leader of the nation.[31] President Nixon, for example, experienced increases in his popularity following his trips to China and the Soviet Union (see Figure 4-1), as did President Ford after returning

FIGURE 4-1   President Nixon's Public Approval Ratings, 1969–1974

Source: The Gallup Opinion Index, September 1974, p. 12.

from Europe and China (see Figure 4-2). Perhaps the most marked increases in public approval come on the heels of international crises involving the United States, especially when the president responds with bold and decisive action and accompanies it with an address to the nation.[32] Following the Cuban missile crisis, President Kennedy's popularity jumped by thirteen points. Likewise, President Ford's daring efforts to rescue the *Mayaguez* brought him an eleven-point rise in public approval, the single largest increase during his entire presidency (see Figure 4-2). Even when a presidential response to an international crisis appears unsuccessful, the public still exhibits a tendency to give support. Thus, following the embarrassing U-2 incident, which led to the collapse of the Paris summit meeting of the major world powers, Eisenhower's popularity still went up six points. The abortive Bay of Pigs invasion proved to be an even greater embarrassment to the United States in general and to the Kennedy administration in particular. Yet Kennedy's approval rating went up by

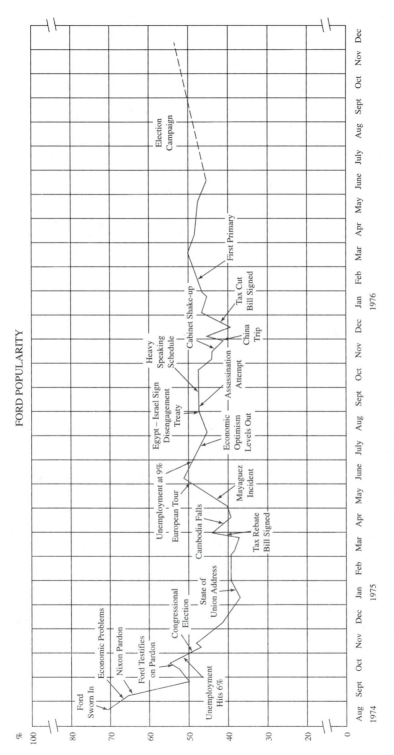

FIGURE 4-2 President Ford's Public Approval Ratings, 1974–1976

Source: *The Gallup Opinion Index*, January 1977, pp. 14, 15.

ten points. Jimmy Carter enjoyed a similar public response following the seizure of Americans in Iran and again after the unsuccessful attempt to rescue them (see Figure 4-3). Even if only temporary, this kind of supportive public response provides the president with some needed leverage in dealing with his critics. Finally, presidents benefit from events and actions that cannot be neatly categorized except to say that the public perceives them as "good news."[33] Such good news might take the form of a tax cut, the settlement of an international conflict, or a moon landing (see Figures 4-1, 4-2, 4-3, 4-4, 4-5, 4-6, and 4-7).

Among the circumstances that have a pronounced effect in reducing a president's popularity, a declining economy appears to be of major importance. Pollster George Gallup speaks to this point.

Nothing has so devastating an effect upon a president's popularity as do economic troubles. President Truman's popularity plunged 44 percentage points in just one year, between mid-1945 and mid-1946, largely as a result of the public's concern over economic matters. President Eisenhower's low point in popularity was recorded in the spring of 1958 during a period of recession. And all throughout the Watergate era, the public was actually more concerned about the economy than it was about Watergate.[34]

Reagan's and Bush's public approval records further reinforce Gallup's observation. Despite having been described as the "Teflon President" to whom nothing sticks, the teflon shield afforded Reagan little protection against a faltering economy. Indeed, the lowest public approval ratings of his presidency—on one occasion approaching 35 percent—came during the severe economic recession beginning in 1981 and continuing into the first part of 1983 (see Figure 4-4).[35] One study recorded a five-point decline in his popularity each time unemployment increased by one point.[36] Nor did the popularity heights to which Bush soared during and immediately after the Gulf War protect him as the economy grew steadily worse during his final year in office (see Figure 4-5). On the other hand, the highest approval ratings of Clinton's first six years in office (see Figure 4-7) came in the first two years of his second term as the economy grew at an unusually robust rate, producing the lowest unemployment, inflation, and mortgage rates rates seen in the last twenty-five to thirty years.[37]

At first blush the relationship between economic dislocations and presidential popularity seems readily explainable—people are merely reacting to the direct and immediate impact that economic adversity has on their pocketbooks. In fact, however, more recent evidence challenges this self-interested explanation. It suggests instead that while Americans hold the president accountable for the performance of the economy, they base their evaluation not on their *own* personal economic circumstances, but rather on how they think economic conditions are affecting the nation as a whole.[38]

In addition to being affected by an ailing economy, a president's popularity will be severely affected by public doubts about his integrity in connection with his public responsibilities. Of all the qualities that the public is searching for in a president, none appears to be more important than honesty.[39] While it is doubtful that this quality has ever enhanced a president's popularity to any great extent—one assumes, after all, that a president will be honest—its absence can certainly hurt him. In January 1973, Richard Nixon's popularity was at 68 percent, the highest level it had reached during his entire four years as president. Yet when the Watergate scandals began to unravel, his approval rating started to plummet and finally reached a low of

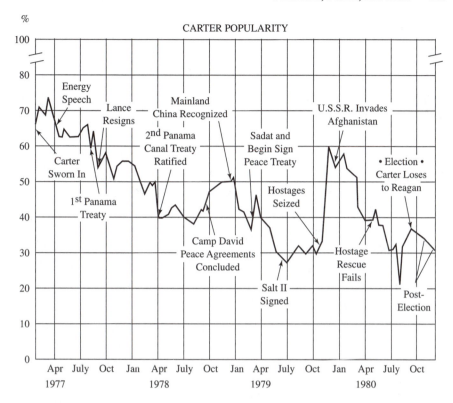

%

CARTER POPULARITY

FIGURE 4-3   President Carter's Public Approval Ratings, 1977–1980

Source: The Gallup Opinion Index, October/November 1980, pp. 6, 7.

25 percent shortly before he resigned from office (see Figure 4-1). This forty-three point decline was the sharpest recorded for a president since the presidency of Harry Truman. A sputtering economy was important in contributing to the rapidity of the decline, but so too was the public's ultimate conclusion that their president could not be trusted. No circumstance is likely to be more damaging to a president in the long run than an inability to maintain the public trust. Like innocence, once lost, it cannot be regained.

How then do we account for Bill Clinton who at the midpoint of his second term was enjoying relatively high approval ratings, despite a steady stream of allegations that ultimately led to his impeachment by the House of Representatives? From the time that the Monica Lewinsky scandal broke in mid-January 1998, all the way through to his impeachment some ten months later, Clinton's public approval ratings never dropped below 58 percent and even reached as high as 73 percent immediately after his impeachment. Did an unusually buoyant economy cause many Americans to simply look the other way? Prosperity undoubtedly played a role in deflecting some of the disapproval, but there was probably a more fundamental factor at work here. In contrast to Nixon, the major allegations surrounding Clinton's presidency related to

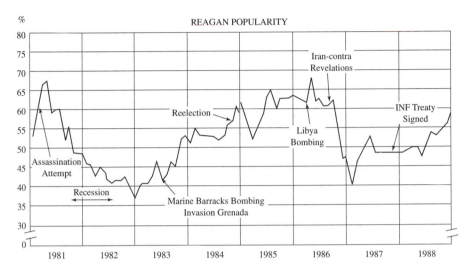

FIGURE 4-4   President Reagan's Public Approval Ratings, 1981–1988

Source: Adapted from *The Polling Report* 5 (January 30, 1989), p. 5.

private, not public behavior. Although an extramarital affair with a White House intern and the deceitful attempts to conceal it would have elicited a much harsher public reaction three decades ago, in today's more permissive society there is a greater willingness to tolerate such behavior. One suspects that Clinton also benefited from the fact that some of his accusers were not especially sympathetic figures and from an impeachment vote that divided so clearly along partisan lines.

The impact of war upon presidential popularity is less clear. In his exhaustive analysis of this subject, John Mueller found that the Korean War had a very definite effect in accelerating the decline of President Truman's popularity. On the other hand, while Johnson's declining popularity would appear to have been associated with the intensification of our war effort in Vietnam (see Figure 4-6), Mueller reports that the war actually had no substantial impact on the erosion of his public support. He suggests that one possible explanation for this anomaly is that Johnson managed to keep the Vietnam War above partisan politics, whereas Truman was not able to do so with the Korean War. Moreover, unlike Truman, Johnson faced a major domestic crisis at home in the form of racial unrest. Thus, it may be that dissatisfaction over this state of affairs was sufficient by itself to produce the marked decline in Johnson's popularity, leaving very little additional impact to be made by public discontent with the war.[40]

In summary, given the overall downward trend in a president's popularity as he moves through his tenure in office, it would seem appropriate for him to go after what he wants as soon as possible after assuming office. Unfortunately, this is more easily said than done. Presidential candidates have general notions about what goals they want to achieve and what directions they want to move in, but the details of how to do it are not worked out until after they take office. Even then, the process of formulating a major policy will usually require several months of evaluation, consultation,

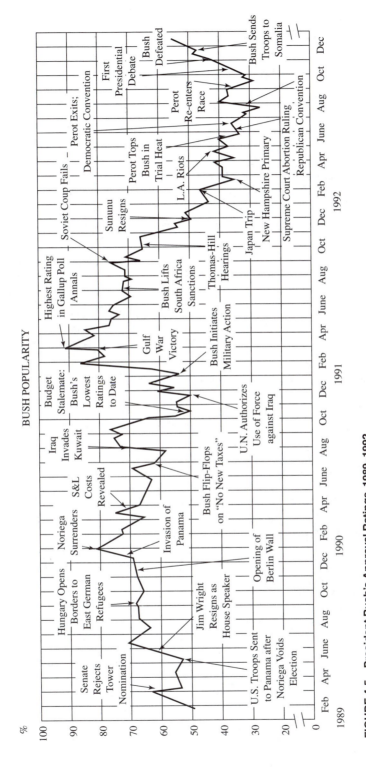

FIGURE 4-5   President Bush's Approval Ratings, 1989–1992

Source: Adapted from *The Gallup Poll Monthly*, January 1993, pp. 14, 15.

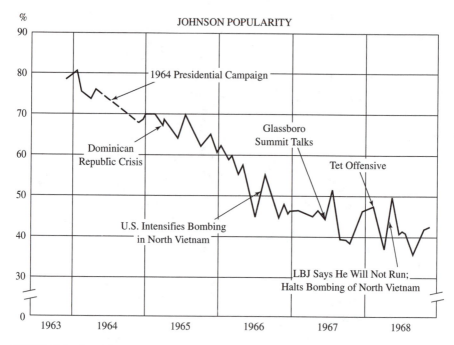

FIGURE 4-6   President Johnson's Approval Ratings, 1963–1968

Source: The Gallup Opinion Index, December 1968, p. 1.

and negotiation. In some cases, it may even be necessary to educate and shape public opinion, which, even though generally supportive of the new president, may nevertheless need some persuading on the specifics of what he wants to do.

In addition to acting sooner rather than later, the evidence also suggests that a president would do well to focus his attention on maintaining a stable economy. Unfortunately, this too is more easily said than done, for very few of the critical decisions related to the economy are his alone to make. Regulation of the money supply, for example, is the responsibility of the Federal Reserve Board, whose members will no doubt listen carefully to what the president says, but are under no obligation to do what he asks. As for fiscal matters, the president can make recommendations on both taxes and federal expenditures, but these must ultimately be approved by Congress. Nor can we overlook the fact that in an economic system dominated by private enterprise, most decisions made by corporations, labor unions, and consumers are beyond the purview of any government entity. Finally, of course, presidents have no direct control over economic decisions made by other governments—a limitation that is becoming all the more palpable as the economies of the world grow increasingly interdependent. Richard Nixon, for example, could do little to prevent the OPEC nations from increasing the price of oil in 1974, thereby precipitating a worldwide recession. Nor could Bill Clinton stop Japanese banks from making bad loans, or the Indonesian government from spending beyond its means, both of which actions did much to bring on the Asian financial crisis—a crisis that ultimately affected the U.S. economy as well.

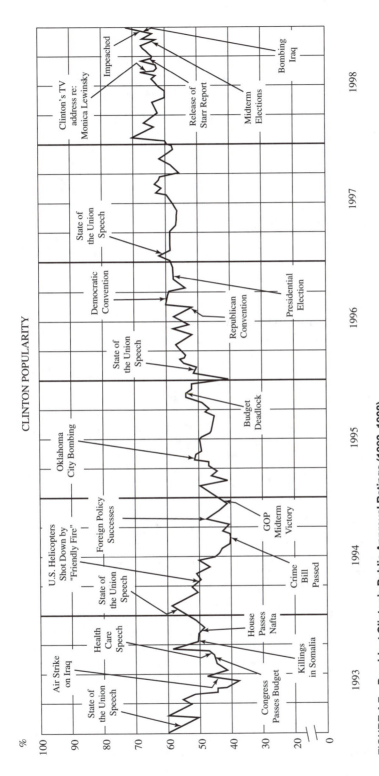

FIGURE 4-7 President Clinton's Public Approval Ratings (1993–1998).

Source: Adapted from *The Gallup Poll Monthly*, January 1993–December 20, 1998. http://www.gallup.com.

If worsening economic conditions have a pronounced impact upon a president's public support and if economic improvement is something that can occur only gradually over a period of many months, then what may presidents do to bolster their support in the interim? Since the use of force by a president provides him with the biggest positive kick in the polls, particularly when it is accompanied by a presidential address on the subject, might presidents be tempted, consciously or unconsciously, to resort to the use of force when the economy is in a slump? One of the most extensive examinations of public support for presidents suggests such a possibility: "The presidents are also more likely to engage in force of any kind as well as dramatic uses of force during bad economic times. The sharper the deterioration of economic conditions is, the much more likely will be the use of force. This curious and disturbing relationship is far stronger than could be expected by chance."[41] However, more recent investigations into this question find no significant relationship between adverse domestic conditions—including economic—and a president's propensity to use force.[42]

     ## THE INTERPLAY OF PUBLIC ATTITUDES TOWARD THE INDIVIDUAL AND THE OFFICE: THE CASE OF WATERGATE

Presidents benefit not only from the support the public gives them personally but also from the more generalized support it gives the presidency as an institution. As noted in an earlier section of this chapter, this generalized support has been fairly high in the past. How it converts into a president's personal popularity is difficult to say in precise terms, but it certainly helps. For example, the first Gallup poll taken after a president has been elected and reelected to the presidency has, with the exception of Reagan and Bush, shown a public approval rating substantially higher than the percentage of the popular vote that put him in office (see Table 4-5). Although Gallup poll ratings and popular vote percentages are not strictly comparable, the comparison does suggest that the public tends to unite around the newly elected leader, in part because he is *The President.* Even when a president's popularity declines below consensus levels—Truman's, Nixon's, and Carter's at one point dipped down into the twenties and Johnson's into the thirties—the residual support accorded the presidency itself allows a president to continue governing with at least some measure of effectiveness. This is not to say that support for the institution will always remain constant, unaffected by the actions of those who occupy it. If presidents behave in ways that seriously erode the public's confidence in them, one would also expect their actions to have an effect upon the public's confidence and trust in the office itself. And to the extent that the office commands less trust, its occupant will find it increasingly difficult to mobilize public opinion behind what he wants to do.

At this point, the scandals of Watergate become relevant to our discussion. Beyond any question, they disgraced the president involved in them to such a degree that he was compelled to resign from office or else face almost certain impeachment and conviction. But it is also important for us to know whether his actions reflected adversely upon the office as well. There was every reason to believe that they would, for Watergate was the greatest scandal in our political history—directly implicating a president in a systematic abuse of the powers and responsibilities of his office.

TABLE 4-5   Comparison of Popular Vote Percentage with Gallup Approval Percentage

	First Election		Second Election	
	Popular Vote[a]	Approval First Survey	Popular Vote[a]	Approval January Survey
Eisenhower	55.1	68	57.4	79
Kennedy	49.7	72	—	—
Nixon	43.4	59	60.7	68
Truman	—	—	49.6	69
Johnson	—	—	61.1	71
Ford	—	71	—	—
Carter	50.1	66	—	—
Reagan	50.7	51[b]	—	—
Bush	53.4	51	—	—
Clinton	43.2	58	—	—

[a]Percentage of total cast for all presidential candidates.
[b]It is worth noting here that while Reagan only received a 51 percent approval rating, only 13 percent expressed disapproval. The remaining 36 percent, which was an unusually large number, opted for no opinion.

Source: Figures for Eisenhower through Johnson taken from Elmer Cornwell, "The President and the Press: Phases in the Relationship," p. 60 in volume 427 (September 1976) of *The Annals* of the American Academy of Political and Social Science. Copyright © 1976 by the American Academy of Political and Social Science. Data for Ford and Carter taken from: *Gallup Opinion Index,* September 1974, p. 3; *Gallup Opinion Index,* April 1977, p. 3; Richard Scammon and Alice McGillivray, *America Votes* 12 (Washington, D.C.: Elections Research Center, 1977), p. 15. Data on Reagan taken from *Congressional Quarterly Weekly Report,* January 17, 1981, p. 138, and *Washington Post,* May 28, 1981, p. A12. Data on Bush and Clinton taken from Thomas R. Dye, *Politics in America* (Englewood Cliffs, N.J.: Prentice Hall, 1994), p. 725; *The American Enterprise* 4 (March/April 1993), p. 94; *The American Enterprise* 5 (January/February 1994), p. 82.

The Watergate scandals did indeed have an impact upon the public's attitudes toward the presidency. Table 4-6 shows the reactions of children in grades three through six to a question posed in 1962, 1973 (after the firing of Archibald Cox), and 1975 (after Watergate had run its course). The question did not refer to any specific president but instead asked, "Is the President your favorite?" Not surprisingly, in 1962 anywhere from 48 to 66 percent of the children were willing to say that the president was either their "favorite of all" or "almost their favorite of all." In 1973, however, the data available for grades three, four, and five clearly show that Watergate had a devastating effect. Indeed, only 5 to 23 percent were willing to consider him either as their "favorite of all" or almost so. On the other hand, between 47 and 64 percent acknowledged that he was *not* one of their favorites. By 1975, this negative attitude appears to have moderated significantly, but it is still closer to the 1973 reaction than it is to the reaction expressed in 1962. Also, even by 1975, anywhere from 29 to 35 percent of the children still gave the most negative response possible to the question.

Children in these same grades were also questioned on five different components of the presidential image—*attachment, benevolence, dependability, power,* and *leadership.* Predictably, all grades rated the president positively on all these components

TABLE 4-6   Comparison of 1962, 1973, 1975 Studies in Rating of the President for "Is the President Your Favorite?"

Grade and Year	He Is My Favorite of All	He Is Amost My Favorite of All	He Is More a Favorite of Mine Than Most	He Is More a Favorite of Mine Than Many	He Is More a Favorite of Mine Than a Few	He Is Not One of My Favorites
3rd, 1963	39%	27%	14%	8%	7%	6%
3rd, 1973	8	15	11	4	15	47
3rd, 1975	22	19	6	4	14	35
4th, 1962	28	30	17	11	7	7
4th, 1973	2	5	2	8	13	70
4th, 1975	7	9	22	20	13	30
5th, 1962	21	29	21	13	9	8
5th, 1973	2	3	8	13	11	64
5th, 1975	4	17	18	15	15	29
6th, 1962	22	26	20	14	9	7
6th, 1973	—	—	—	—	—	—
6th, 1975	5	8	18	16	25	29

Source: Adapted from F. Christopher Arterton, "Watergate and Children's Attitudes toward Political Authority Revisited," *Political Science Quarterly* 90 (Fall 1975), 481. Reprinted with permission from the *Political Science Quarterly.*[43]

in 1962, but in 1973 the reaction was strongly negative to all except two—power and leadership. By 1975, attitudes had once again moderated, but the president was just barely rated positively on dependability, continued to be rated negatively on attachment, and, for those above the third grade, still received a negative reaction on benevolence. Yet on the dimensions of power and leadership, the president appears to have been rated even more highly than he was in 1962. At the same time, however, the children in all of the grades studied were far less inclined to feel that the president *ought* to have such power.[43]

The immediate effects of Watergate upon adult attitudes toward the presidency appear to have been equally devastating. According to the Survey Research Center, in 1972 all major subgroups within the population except white Democrats expressed greater trust in the presidency than they did in either Congress or the Supreme Court. Yet by 1974 no subgroup rated it above the Supreme Court, and only independents trusted the presidency more than they did Congress. Indeed, for practically every major subgroup in the population, the decline in trust for the presidency was approximately 50 percent.[44] A survey of adults in the state of Wisconsin made in 1972 and again in 1974 also showed erosion in public support for the presidency. As Table 4-7 indicates, following the Watergate scandals the public appears to have had substantially less confidence in the performance capacity of the presidency (question 1). Moreover, its feeling of powerlessness toward the presidency increased (question 2), and so too did its belief that the office ought to be reformed (question 4). Question 3 was not asked in 1972, but responses to it in 1974 indicate that respect for the authority of

TABLE 4-7   Changes in Public Evaluation of the Presidency between 1972 and 1974

		Nov.–Dec. 1972	Mar.–Apr. 1974
Question 1	"Office of the President has done some good."	agree—52%[a] disagree—18	agree—33% disagree—27
Question 2	"People have a say in what the President does."	agree—19 disagree—58	agree—10 disagree—73
Question 3	"We should obey the President even if we disagree with him."	agree— disagree—	agree—49 disagree—27
Question 4	"Office of the President should be reformed."	agree—18 disagree—64	agree—45 disagree—35

[a]Percentages on each question do not add up to 100% because the "don't know" responses are not included.

Source: Adapted from Jack Dennis, "Who Supports the Presidency?" *Society* 13 (July/August 1976), 51, 52. Published by permission of Transaction, Inc. Copyright © 1976 by Transaction, Inc.

the office was below consensus levels, with only 49 percent believing that the president should be obeyed even if we disagree with him.

If Watergate did have an immediate and negative impact upon the public's attitudes toward the presidency, what about its long-range impact? Had trust in the office been permanently eroded for those generations of Americans who lived through Watergate? Did Richard Nixon, therefore, hand over a weakened institution to his successors? The available evidence provides some clues to this question. As already noted, the negative attitude of children toward the presidency had moderated considerably between 1974 and 1975. Moreover, there is some indication that the adult public was also recovering from its doubts about the office. According to a survey made by Potomac Associates, the number of people expressing a "great deal of confidence" in the executive branch (13 percent) did not change from 1974 to 1976. Yet the number expressing a "fair amount of confidence" rose from 29 to 46 percent; those expressing "not very much confidence" declined from 36 to 30 percent; and those having no confidence at all declined from 19 to 8 percent.[45] A Harris poll taken in March 1977 asked respondents how much confidence they had in the man running the White House, and 31 percent responded "a great deal," which constituted an eleven-point increase over the previous year.[46] Of course, this poll was asking the population to react to a particular president rather than to the institution, and thus it is at best only suggestive of a possible increase in confidence in the presidency. At the close of 1977, the University of Michigan's Institute for Social Research polled high school seniors on their attitudes toward various American institutions, one of which was the presidency. They were asked to rate them on a scale ranging from "very bad" to "very good." While only 20 percent of the nation's high school seniors had been willing to give the presidency either a "good" or "very good" rating in a similar poll conducted by the institute in 1975, 41 percent were willing to do so at the close of 1977.[47] Finally, it should be pointed out that even during the dark days of Watergate, confidence in the executive branch was far from being completely eroded. According to the Harris surveys, in 1973 only 34 percent of the public stated that they had "hardly any confidence at all" in the executive branch, and only 18 percent expressed this sentiment in 1974.[48]

In summary, if the president's relationship with the public is more crucial to him than anything else, it is equally true that trust is the cement necessary for holding it together. By virtue of his actions, Richard Nixon caused a near-total disintegration of this trust. This was his ultimate mistake.

The public has a relationship with the presidency as well as with the president. This relationship, too, is held together by trust. Having endured over the course of our history, it is a stronger, more durable bond and consequently not subject to erosion so easily. Thus, even though the behavior of Richard Nixon precipitated a near-total erosion of the confidence placed in him by the people, he did not manage to destroy completely their trust in the institution itself. But he did damage it all the same and to this extent handed over a weakened institution to his successor.

 ## PRESIDENTIAL EFFORTS TO INFLUENCE PUBLIC OPINION

We now shift the focus of our attention to how presidents attempt to influence public reaction to what they say and do. The necessity for them to do so is clear, first, because their reelection is contingent upon generating public approval, and second, because most of what a president wants to accomplish requires the support of other people in government. If his words and actions are perceived as commanding broad public support, they are more likely to be taken seriously.

Before a president can influence public opinion, he must first understand it. This understanding may be gained through a variety of sources, including personal contacts in and outside of government and reports by the national polling organizations, as well as by their own White House pollsters. All of this information, combined with his own intuitive feel for the public, will give a president some understanding of what is on the minds of the people and what is not.

In many instances, the president does not have to seek public support for what he does because it is fairly clear that his actions will be viewed favorably. It is only necessary that the public be made aware of them—such presidential activities as a trip abroad or an announcement of a proposed tax cut. Or they may include such seemingly trivial actions as Gerald Ford's calculated effort to phone celebrities and congratulate them on their achievements or Jimmy Carter's decision to spend the night in the private home of an average American citizen—all designed to enhance the presidential image and build up a reservoir of goodwill.

Even when a president earnestly desires public support on a given issue, he may deem it appropriate to lead by waiting, hoping that the unfolding of events will ultimately ripen public opinion to a conclusion he has already reached. Thus, despite recommendations that the United States should enter the Second World War, Franklin Roosevelt held off until events had convinced the American people of the necessity for doing so. While this strategy had its disadvantages, he felt they were outweighed by a more fundamental consideration, namely, that a decision to go to war must have broad public support. There are times, however, when a president cannot afford to wait for public opinion to ripen, either because time will not permit or because the issue he is concerned about has not yet entered the public's consciousness. Under such circumstances, he must ascend the presidential pulpit and seek to shape public opinion through education. This approach was best articulated by Theodore Roosevelt when he remarked, "People used to say of me that I was an astonishingly good politician and divined what the people were going to think. This was really not an accurate way of stating the case. I did not divine how the people were going to think. I simply made up my mind what they ought to think and then did my best to get them to think it." A more recent example of this approach was President Carter's decision to go before television cameras and educate the American public to the fact that the energy crisis was genuine and not contrived and that something had to be done about it now. His speech apparently had some impact, for according to a Gallup poll taken afterward, 54 percent of the American people agreed that the energy crisis was serious, whereas only 43 percent had thought so prior to the speech.[49]

Finally, there will also be occasions when the president must act contrary to public opinion, hoping that hindsight will bear out the wisdom of his decision. Truman faced just such a situation when he decided to fire General MacArthur, and so too did President Ford when he made the decision to pardon President Nixon. Understandably, presidents are least comfortable when faced with having to make an unpopular decision, and thus several factors will be carefully weighed before doing so: (1) Is adverse public reaction likely to have a temporary or a more lasting impact? If the former, he may decide that he can afford to ride it out. If the latter, he may conclude that such a decision poses an unacceptable threat to his future political leverage on other matters. (2) How critical is public support to the successful implementation of his decision? Gerald Ford's decision to pardon Nixon did not in any way depend upon public support. On the contrary, its success was contingent only upon Nixon's willingness to accept it. At the same time, however, a president might well be inclined to withhold a proposal that required public cooperation—such as gasoline rationing—if it was clear that the public was violently opposed to it. (3) Finally, in deciding whether or not to act, he must also assess what he considers to be his constitutional and statutory responsibilities in a given situation, both of which may preempt the other considerations.

The Media as Facilitators of Presidential Influence

Whether the president attempts to generate public support through direct appeals or through the mere reporting of his activities, he must do so via the national media. As one former White House aide put it, the media are "the daily national amplifier of the presidential voice."[50] As such, they can greatly facilitate the president's ability to communicate with and influence the public.

Making News. As noted earlier, one of the ways by which the president seeks to influence the public is by making them aware of what he is doing—a relatively easy task. More than any other public official, the president is assured of constant coverage by the media because the presidency is where the action is. Of equal importance is the fact that he has considerable leeway in determining *what* that action will be. Much of the information received by the press—both print and broadcast media—is based upon what the president and his administration choose to release. This is especially so in the area of foreign affairs, where news sources are more limited. In addition to reporting what the White House releases, the press also covers the activities of a president, be they as trivial as a Sunday visit to church or as significant as a trip abroad. Here again, when and how a president chooses to act is to a considerable extent his to control.

Regardless of how he chooses to make news, it is clear that the decision to do so is accompanied by careful planning and calculation. If it is bad news, every effort will be made to minimize its impact. Thus, it is common practice for the White House to break bad news late on Friday so that it makes Saturday's papers, which usually have the lowest readership. Moreover, whenever possible such an announcement will be made from a department in the executive branch rather than from the White House. The Clintons, for example, reserved for late Friday a statement disclosing that they had incorrectly calculated their income taxes on their Whitewater real estate holdings. The Bush White House usually reserved Fridays to announce controversial vetoes, including vetoes of legislation that would have raised taxes on millionaires and increased benefits for the unemployed. And for the Reagan administration, late Friday once again seemed an appropriate time to announce its controversial decision to retain tax-exempt status for Bob Jones University, despite abundant evidence of its discrimination against blacks.[51]

If the bad news comes not from the president but rather from his critics, the administration may try to overwhelm it by releasing a series of newsworthy announcements. Both Kennedy and Johnson, for example, planned a flurry of White House press releases whenever the Republican National Committee came to Washington to meet. Similarly, on the day that Robert Kennedy chose to deliver a speech critical of the Johnson administration's Vietnam policies, the White House orchestrated a whole series of news stories designed to minimize the coverage given to Kennedy: President Johnson called an impromptu news conference; announced that Soviet Premier Kosygin had agreed to negotiate limitations on antiballistic missiles; delivered an important civil rights speech at Howard University; and saw to it that both Secretary of State Rusk and General Westmoreland released statements critical of Kennedy's remarks.[52] Reagan aides, well aware that the day after his State of the Union addresses the press would be venturing over to Congress to get its reaction, made every effort to schedule a presidential trip.

When presidential actions are likely to meet with public approval, they are usually orchestrated in such a way as to have the maximum possible impact on both the media and the public. Recognizing that people often do not feel the impact of legislation until long after it has been implemented, President Johnson decided to draw public attention to the truth-in-packaging legislation he had proposed and that Congress had just passed. Accordingly, he instructed one of his aides to find the "biggest and most photogenic shopping center in the country" so he could fly there and sign the legislation into law. A suitable shopping center was finally located in Seattle, Washington. The president arrived and signed the bill, thereby producing an event that received considerable press and television coverage.[53]

Equal care went into the planning of President Nixon's historic visits to China and the Soviet Union. The decision to make the China trip in February 1972 came at a time when President Nixon's popularity was on the decline. Indeed, a Gallup poll taken in early February revealed that in a presidential race between Nixon and Senator Muskie, the president would win by only one percentage point.[54] The Chinese government was persuaded to permit live coverage of the presidential visit, and the president's schedule was arranged so that he would arrive in Peking during prime-time television hours in the United States. Similarly, on his return, Nixon purposely stopped over in Anchorage, Alaska, for nine hours so he and his entourage would arrive in Washington during prime time. Approximately one hundred million Americans saw at least some portion of the forty hours of network coverage given to the

China trip. Nor was it mere coincidence that all of this was happening as the president's Democratic opponents (Muskie and McGovern) were crossing swords in the New Hampshire primary. The trip to Moscow also came at a propitious time, as both Humphrey and McGovern were campaigning to win the large prize of delegates in California's winner-take-all primary. Once again, both the press and television accompanied the president; and once again, he returned to Washington during prime time, but on this occasion he proceeded directly to the Capitol and went before a joint session of Congress to report on his historic visit. The speech was carried live by all three networks. Not surprisingly, both the trip to China and the trip to the Soviet Union brought the president a needed boost in his public approval ratings.[55]

Of course, presidents cannot always be sure that what they propose to say or do will be favorably received by the various publics that make up the population. Thus, in order to avoid taking a position that could subsequently produce a strong negative reaction, they have frequently been known to send up a trial balloon, with the press acting as the vehicle for doing so. This tactic, which originated with Theodore Roosevelt, involves leaking a particular idea to one or more members of the press, who then proceed to report it as an idea rumored to be under consideration by the president. The ventilation of the idea in the press allows the president to gauge reaction to it both in and outside of government. If the reaction proves favorable, the president can go ahead and formally embrace the idea, but if the response is negative, he can disown the idea at no political cost to himself. Both the Ford and Carter administrations, for example, floated the rumor that a surtax on gasoline was one of the policies under consideration for dealing with the energy crisis. Each time the public reaction was immediate and intensely negative, thus leading both administrations to deny that the idea was being seriously considered.[56]

Influencing Opinion Makers.   In addition to securing the maximum media coverage of his own words and actions, a president also attempts to influence public opinion by trying to win the support of opinion makers. Although those connected with the media do not constitute the only people who influence thinking, they are surely an extremely important segment of that group. Well aware of this fact, President Kennedy embarked upon a policy known as Operation Publisher, which one journalist described as "the boldest and most successful instrument of Kennedy's press policy."[57] It entailed two-hour confidential meetings once a month with newspaper publishers from a given state. The purpose was to allow them to question Kennedy at length, thereby providing him with an opportunity to make a case for his policies, in hopes of gaining the publishers' editorial support. President Clinton pursued a similar strategy when, on the day before he presented his health care proposal to Congress, he invited to lunch several highly regarded columnists from the *New York Times, Washington Post, Los Angeles Times,* and *Wall Street Journal.* The president's sales pitch apparently had some impact, for all four journalists managed to find something good to say in their columns about the Clinton plan.[58]

This kind of presidential lobbying also takes place on a more informal level, with presidents seeking the support of those journalists with whom they enjoy a close personal relationship. Such relationships are not uncommon for politicians whose careers have brought them into close and frequent contact with the press. On one occasion, when he was meeting with little success in generating congressional and public support for his economic policies, President Kennedy contacted several of his friends in the press and encouraged them to write about the problems of the economy and how he planned to address them. As one White House correspondent recalls, "In the final months of 1962 there was a mysterious outbreak of stories about the balance of payments, new ideas for reporting the budget, and the need for tax reduction and reform, and many of them were traceable back to the President."[59] In return for such favors, journalists are also likely to benefit, whether it be an exclusive interview with the president, an invitation to dine with him, or early warning of a pending presidential decision.

Recently published transcripts of Lyndon Johnson's phone conversations in 1963 and 1964 reveal that he spoke frequently with members of the media, including noted print journalists (e.g., Walter Lippmann and James Reston), network executives, newspaper and magazine owners, and editors. In some instances he was making them aware of his own thinking, while in others he was picking their brains; in still others, he was complaining about what he viewed as inaccurate or unfair reporting about his administration.[60]

Press Conference.   Unlike attempts to influence public opinion through the orchestration of news or by appealing to opinion makers, the modern press conference allows the president to convey his views directly to the American people. First formally instituted by Woodrow Wilson, the press conference was originally conceived of as a means by which the press could question the president on current issues facing his administration. It was also an opportunity for the president to enunciate his views to the press. Hoover, Roosevelt, and Truman continued the practice, but during the Eisenhower presidency a new wrinkle was introduced. Perceiving that the press conference could provide an effective forum for a president to communicate with a wider audience, Eisenhower's press secretary decided to allow filming of the president's press conferences so that they could be run on television. President Kennedy introduced a further twist by deciding to hold *live* news conferences. Having come into office with most of the press against his presidential candidacy, he saw live news conferences as a means to communicate his views directly to the public without having them filtered through the press. Although President Nixon held them infrequently, his news conferences were also televised live, and he took the additional step of moving them to prime time. Whereas Presidents Ford and Reagan continued this practice, Carter, Bush, and Clinton were much more inclined to hold conferences at any time of day.

The press conference has been viewed as the only means by which the president is formally held accountable for his actions between elections. While this is true enough, the fact remains that a president risks little by participating. That he holds most of the cards in this confrontation was confirmed by a veteran member of the White House press corps in his assessment of the role of reporters during the Kennedy press conference: "[Reporters] became spear carriers in a great televised opera. We were props in a show, in a performance. Kennedy mastered the art of this performance early, and he used it with great effectiveness."[61] Even President Ford, who was hardly the equal of Kennedy in speaking ability, was able to use the forum of the press conference to good advantage. Indeed, a study of his news conferences commissioned by the National News Council concluded that they remained largely the "plaything" of the president.[62] Reagan, to be sure, proved less skillful than his predecessors in fielding questions from the press. Never known for having a firm grasp of details, he was given to factual errors and misstatements, which White House aides were forced to correct or clarify the following day. Even in Reagan's case, however, the advantages enjoyed by a president in the press conference enabled him to hold his own most of the time.

There are several reasons why the president enjoys a decided advantage in this formalized confrontation with the press. In the first place, the initiative for calling a press conference rests solely with the president. Lyndon Johnson's press secretary made this point quite bluntly: "It is the prerogative of the president to decide how he's going to make himself available to the press and how and when he makes certain information known to the press. It's to serve the convenience of the president, not the convenience of the press that presidential press conferences are held."[63]

The frequency of press conferences has varied widely among presidents. Woodrow Wilson stopped having them altogether once the United States became involved in the First World War. Franklin Roosevelt held more than any president in our history, averaging two a week for a total of 881 during his presidency. Richard Nixon, on the other hand, held only 39 nationally televised news conferences during the entire time he was in office, and at one point even went a full nineteen weeks without holding one. Although Jimmy Carter pledged to hold a news conference every two weeks, in actuality he held a total of 59, which averages out to 1.2 per month. Reagan, however, holds the record for the fewest number of press conferences given his time in office. In eight years, he held no more than 42—an average of 0.5 per month.[64] In marked contrast to his predecessor, Bush was highly accessible to the press, averaging 2.7 press conferences a month. Bill Clinton, on the other hand, was somewhat less accessible than Bush, holding 119 press conferences in his first term, for an average of 2.4 per month. If one includes his meetings with the press for the first five years of his presidency, then his total comes to 140 with an average of 2.3 a month.[65] During this period, moreover, only a very few of his press encounters were in prime time. Clinton's preference instead was to take questions from reporters during joint news conferences with visiting foreign dignitaries—occasions that, with the exception of C-SPAN, rarely received live coverage by the networks. Given that Clinton acquitted himself extremely well during press questioning, it is rather curious that he rarely opted for the prime-time format. Perhaps his strained relationship with the press, which dated back to his run for the presidency, combined with the alleged scandals swirling about his administration, caused his aides to conclude that prime-time encounters could be risky.

The format of the news conference is also determined by the president. Although the senior Associated Press correspondent is accorded the privilege of ending a news conference with the traditional "Thank you, Mr. President," the fact of the matter is that the president may, if he chooses, terminate it any time he wants. He also determines the questioning procedure. Herbert Hoover, for example, required that all questions be submitted in advance. He permitted no follow-up questions, answered only those he wished to, and even forbade the press to report those questions he refused to answer. Although no president since Hoover has required the submission of questions in advance, presidents Eisenhower, Kennedy, and Johnson declined to entertain follow-up questions. And no president has ever surrendered his right to decide which reporters he will call upon to ask a question.

Although the news conference is characterized by spontaneous questions, the president has a good deal more control over the agenda than it appears. He usually begins the conference with an opening statement, which frequently influences the subsequent focus of the questioning. Moreover, it is common practice for the president's press secretary to plant certain questions with friendly reporters to ensure that the president will have an opportunity to address the issues that concern him. Most important, the president does not come before the press unprepared. On the contrary, he is briefed by his aides on likely questions and appropriate answers. According to Eisenhower's press secretary, James Hagerty, the president and his staff are able to anticipate about 90 percent of the questions that will be asked.[66] Add to this the fact that the president alone decides who will get to ask a question, thus allowing him to avoid calling upon reporters known to be antagonistic to his administration. (Gerald Ford, for example, committed to memory a set of photographs of reporters classified as "unfriendly.") If the president gets an embarrassing question, he need not respond to it, and if he does not permit follow-up questions, there is little opportunity for a reporter to pursue an evasive answer. Finally, even in the setting of a press conference, the president benefits from the reverential attitude customarily shown toward the office. This is reflected in the tone of the questioning, which more often than not is deferential rather than combative.

All of these factors, then, serve to confirm a conclusion once reached by President Nixon's director of the Office of Communications, Herbert Klein: "The conference is the President's. This is undisputed."[67]

The Phone-In, Talk Show, and Town Meeting.   The Carter presidency brought a major innovation in presidential communication with the public. For two hours one Saturday afternoon the president participated in a national phone-in, which was broadcast on radio. Some seventy-six different callers got through to the president and questioned him on such wide-ranging subjects as the equal rights amendment, tax reform, consumer protection, the volunteer draft, and rising health costs, to name but a few. This format not only allowed the president to find out what issues were on the minds of the public, but it also provided him with an opportunity to express his views on these issues *directly* to the American people.

What Jimmy Carter began, Bill Clinton took to new heights. In a calculated effort to go over the heads of the Washington press corps, and recognizing that he was unusually effective when speaking and answering questions in an informal setting, Bill Clinton sought to communicate directly with Americans via radio and television talk shows, as well as in televised town meetings with groups of citizens.

The Presidential Address.   One final approach to influencing public opinion—considered by many to be the president's most effective weapon—is the televised address to the American people. His appearance live *on all three networks* during *prime time* assures him an audience of 70 to 80 million Americans to whom he can speak on virtually *any topic* he chooses, for as *long* as he wants, and *without any editing* of his remarks. The presidential address was first used by Franklin Roosevelt in his celebrated fireside chats to the American people. On twenty different occasions during his presidency, he went on radio both to inform the public of the problems facing the nation and to enlist their support for his programs. The advent of television has added a visual dimension to presidential communication and provided access to a much greater audience. Sensing the opportunities here, presidents have taken great pains to ensure an effective performance before the television cameras. Jimmy Carter, for example, hired a media consultant at a salary of $45,000 a year.[68] Presidents Johnson and Ford also hired media consultants.

All of our recent presidents have made use of the presidential address to the nation. Excluding inaugural and State of the Union addresses, Eisenhower made thirty-two; Kennedy, eleven; Johnson, fifteen; Nixon, thirty; Ford, eight; Carter, thirteen; Reagan, thirty-eight; Bush, twelve; and Clinton (1993–98), seventeen.[69]

But what is the impact of such addresses to the nation? One recent study examining presidential addresses from 1949 to 1980 indicates that they serve to boost a president's public approval rating, with Democratic presidents increasing their rating by 3 percent and Republican presidents by nearly 4 percent.[70] Another, examining addresses from 1949 through mid-1988 found an average jump in the polls of six percentage points.[71] In addition, Lou Harris has found that there is a definite "correlation between televised presidential speeches and increased public acceptance of the president's positions."[72] Following Lyndon Johnson's speech announcing his decision to order air strikes against North Vietnam in retaliation for their attacks on U.S. destroyers, public support for his Vietnam policy rose from 42 to 72 percent. During the U.S. bombing pause in 1966, 61 percent of the population favored a resumption of the bombing. But following the president's speech announcing a resumption of the bombing, public support for this action rose to 73 percent. Richard Nixon used the presidential address to maintain the support of the "silent majority" during the period when his Vietnam policies were drawing strong opposition from some segments of the population. He made a total of nine addresses to the nation on Vietnam, all during prime time. One of them, timed just prior to the peace moratorium in 1969, was viewed by 72 million Americans. According to one of Nixon's aides, the speech had precisely the desired impact: "Judging by the results, it was the most effective use of TV that's ever been done. You had the massively accelerating peace movement. But after the speech, the balloon just fizzled."[73] Some of Nixon's Vietnam addresses were used to announce and defend dramatic policy decisions. Following his speech outlining the beginning of a phased withdrawal of American troops from Vietnam, support for his Vietnam policy rose from 49 to 67 percent. Similarly, after the speech defending his controversial decision to invade Cambodia, public support for using American troops in Cambodia rose from 7 to 50 percent.[74]

Too Much Access?   The president's access to the media in general and television in particular has sparked concern in the political and journalistic communities for some time now. In just his first eight weeks in office, for example, President Carter averaged approximately one and a half hours of live coverage per week.[75] The presidential presence became even more pronounced in the spring of 1977, when the White House orchestrated a media blitz in connection with its energy program. The week of intense exposure began with an hour-long NBC special entitled "A Day in the Life of Jimmy Carter." Four days later the president gave a televised address to the nation outlining the country's energy problems. Two days later he outlined his energy program before a joint session of Congress in a speech covered live by the three television networks. And one day after that, he held a nationally televised press conference to answer questions about his energy proposals. President Reagan took a similar tack in seeking to sell the nation on the necessity for deep cuts in the federal budget. He began making his case in a televised address to the American people on February 5, 1981. This was followed by another televised address on February 18, this time before a joint session of Congress. A little over two weeks later, he held a televised news conference during which he once again pleaded his case for drastic cuts in the budget. And, on March 30, he returned to Congress for one final televised appeal on behalf of his budget. All of these appearances were covered by all three networks during prime time.

In the judgment of some, the president's ready access to television may serve to overwhelm and drown out the voices of opposition. In the words of one former director of the Federal Communications Commission, "Because he can act while his adversaries can only talk, because he can make news and draw attention to himself, and because he is the only leader elected by all the people, an incumbent President always has had an edge over his opposition in persuading public opinion. Presidential television, however, has enormously increased that edge."[76] Given the absence of highly organized and disciplined parties in Congress, the opposition party has traditionally lacked a single leader who could speak for it with one voice. These disadvantages have been compounded by the fact that the opposition party in Congress has not enjoyed the president's ready access to television. Although their views are reported in nightly news broadcasts, in the past they experienced considerable difficulty in acquiring television time to address the public the way a president can. For example, from January 1966 to October 1975, presidents requested airtime from the television networks forty-five times and were given it forty-four. In contrast, the Democratic leadership in Congress requested airtime on seven occasions during the Nixon and Ford presidencies and was granted it only three times.[77] Since the mid-1970s, however, the networks have become more accommodating. From 1975 to 1984 the opposition party was granted airtime on thirty-four different occasions.[78] Increased access to television has not neutralized the presidential advantage, however, for even though the networks typically accord the opposition party a prime-time slot, they have never given it command of all three networks. Thus, opposition party leaders, who are less known than the president to begin with and lack the aura surrounding the presidency, are destined to garner a much smaller viewing audience.

Come election time, the opposition party is especially disadvantaged, for the president can use his office to gain media coverage in ways that cannot be equaled by his opponents. The "equal-time" regulation states that if a radio or television station permits the use of its airtime to one candidate for elective office, it must grant all other candidates for the same office an equal opportunity to be heard. This regulation, however, applies only when the individual using airtime has already announced as a candidate. Thus, none of an incumbent president's television appearances is subject to a challenge for equal time until he announces that he is a candidate for reelection. Furthermore, the equal-time provision applies only to candidates for the same position. Accordingly, television appearances by a president/candidate before party nominating conventions have been held do not necessitate giving equal time to candidates seeking the presidential nomination in the opposition party. Finally, the Federal Communications Commission (FCC) has ruled that when an announced candidate is appearing on television in what is judged to be a *bona fide* news event, his or her opponent cannot make a claim for equal time. With specific reference to television appearances by a president or candidate, the FCC has ruled that his or her national addresses and news conferences fall under the classification of *bona fide* news events and thus are exempt from claims for equal time.

Finally, it should be noted that the president benefits from a form of media exposure that does not even involve his direct participation. This exposure comes by way of various media materials put out by the government. A report of the Office of Telecommunications Policy found that in 1972 alone government departments spent over $275 million "to produce radio, television and other media materials, much of it supportive of the incumbent administration."[79] Needless to say, the opposition party lacks the resources—financial and otherwise—to gain media exposure of this kind.

The networks have become sensitive to the concerns that have been voiced over the president's access to television, especially his ability to command the airwaves to address the American public directly, on any matter he chooses, without any editing of his remarks. In order to avoid giving the president a totally unchecked forum for the expression of his ideas, networks have for some time now provided analyses of presidential speeches following their delivery. Some would argue that the networks should go further and make a more rigorous determination as to the news value of a given presidential address. Where it lacks such value, live coverage by all three networks should not be given.[80] In actual fact, the practice of always acceding to presidential requests for television time has been followed only since 1966. From January 1964 through September 1965, for example, President Johnson requested television time on eight different occasions but was granted it only three times: "That is, at least one network declined to televise the message simultaneously with other networks or decided against any form of special news coverage."[81] Yet for a third party to decide when the president can communicate with the electorate is itself an unsettling prospect. Moreover, it is difficult to conceive of any presidential address as not being newsworthy, a conclusion the networks have also reached.

> It has become the routine practice of the networks to make television airtime available to a President when he requests it. Statements of network spokesmen suggest two bases for this practice: first, a presumption by the networks that any given Presidential address prepared solely for television almost surely will prove to be sufficiently newsworthy to justify preemption of regular network programming; second, a complementary premise that a Presidential address, regardless of its substance, has a unique inherent news value because of the importance of the Presidential office.[82]

Not only is it inappropriate to contemplate restricting the president's access to television, but there is reason to believe that his ability to command the airwaves is not all that alarming. In the first place, presidential television must be used sparingly or else it is likely to lose its impact. Franklin Roosevelt was keenly aware of this problem when he observed that "people tire of seeing the same name day after day in the important headlines of the papers, and the same voice night after night over the radio. Individual psychology cannot, because of human weakness, be attuned for long periods of time to constant repetition of the highest note in the scale."[83] President Carter's press secretary was sensitive to this problem during the media blitz on energy: "It's a calculated risk. It's an awful lot of exposure."[84]

Furthermore, it is not at all clear that television *per se* is responsible for the dramatic increases in public support for the president's *position* after some of his speeches. One might well argue that such increases have more to do with the nature of his remarks than with the medium through which he makes them. It is not altogether surprising, for example, that approval for President Johnson's Vietnam policies should have risen from 42 percent to 72 percent after he announced his decision to bomb North Vietnam in retaliation for its attacks on American destroyers. Americans have traditionally rallied around presidents at such times. Nor is it especially unusual that support for Richard Nixon's Vietnam policy should have increased after his address announcing the start of American troop withdrawals from Vietnam. Americans were eager to extricate themselves from a war they had grown tired of.

The Media as Complicators of Presidential Influence

If the media can facilitate a president's efforts to mobilize public opinion, they can also complicate these efforts. No one is more aware of this than the individual in the White House. Indeed, nearly every president in our history has at one time or another vented his spleen against those who reported on his actions and words. So enraged was George Washington by his press critics that he included an attack upon them in the first draft of his Farewell Address, noting that their publications "have teemed with all the Invective that disappointment, ignorance of the facts, and malicious falsehood could invent to misrepresent my politics and affections; to wound my reputation and feeling; and to weaken, if not entirely destroy the confidence you have pleased to repose in me."[85] Only at the insistence of Alexander Hamilton did Washington decide to eliminate these remarks from the final draft of his address. President John Adams became so disgruntled with press coverage of his administration that he proposed the establishment of a newspaper that would specifically reflect the views of the government. Even the great libertarian Thomas Jefferson underwent a change of heart toward the press. Prior to becoming president he had remarked that "were it left to me to decide whether we should have a government without newspapers, or newspapers without a government, I should not hesitate a moment to prefer the latter." Once in office, however, he wrote a friend, "Even the least informed of the people have learned that nothing in a newspaper is to be believed . . . and I therefore have long thought that a few prosecutions of the most prominent offenders would have a wholesome effect."[86]

Presidential antipathy toward the press has not been confined to earlier presidents who served at a time when the press was admittedly less responsible than it is today. Woodrow Wilson warned a friend, "Do not believe anything you read in the newspapers. If you read the papers I see, they are utterly untrustworthy. . . . Their lying is shameless and colossal."[87] Having always suspected that the eastern media could not abide a southerner as president, Lyndon Johnson bemoaned the fact that "they warp everything I do, they lie about me and about what I do, they don't know the meaning of truth. They are liars and cheats."[88] According to Bill Clinton's press secretary, Mike McCurry, the president saw the Washington press corps as embracing a "unique political culture" whose members have "never been able to accept him for what he is. That is why from the minute he arrived here they tried to destroy him."[89]

Among recent presidents, however, none felt a greater hostility toward the press than did Richard Nixon. It was summed up in one very brief warning to one of his aides: "Remember—the press is the enemy." As a symbolic indication of his low esteem for the press, he initially decided against even assigning the title of "press secretary" to anyone on his staff. Ron Ziegler prevailed upon Nixon to grant him the title, but the president signaled the low status of the position in another way. When he made his first trip to Europe, the press secretary was put at the bottom of the protocol list. Ultimately that too changed, not because Nixon had altered his views of the press, but because Ziegler had become a close adviser to him.[90]

An Adversarial Relationship.   Although some presidents have enjoyed more cordial relations with the press than others, the relationship remains an adversarial one because the interests of the president and the press are fundamentally in conflict. For his part, the president wishes to present the most favorable possible image of himself and his administration to the public. Doing so requires the orchestration of information and events. In the words of one seasoned Washington columnist, "Any good politician worth his salt will know that he must try to manage the news. An activist President will try to manage the news on the broadest scale of any politician, because his purposes are the largest."[91] Every effort will be made to ensure that good news will have maximum impact. Bad news will, in some cases, be repressed or else minimized. Needless to say, attempts to manage the news do not sit well with the press. Commenting on such efforts by the Kennedy administration, one noted columnist for the *New York Times* pointed out that its management of the news "was enforced more cynically and boldly than by any previous administration in a period when the United States was not at war."[92] This view was confirmed in a *Newsweek* poll of forty-three top Washington correspondents, forty of whom felt that the Kennedy administration had attempted to manage the news to a greater extent than any previous one.[93] When Lyndon Johnson became president, the phrase "news management" gave way to a new and more sinister characterization—the "credibility gap." The latter term grew out of such trivial incidents as Johnson's misleading statements about the heroics of his ancestors and more important ones dealing with our involvement in the Dominican Republic and Vietnam.[94] Today such attempts to manage the news, while continuing to irritate the media, scarcely surprise them. Indeed, reporters covering our presidents have routinely spoken of an administration's "spin" on a story, which is simply another way of saying that the White House is attempting to manage the news.[95]

The basic interests of the press are decidedly different from those of the president. While his interests require that he put the best possible face on what he says and does, the press feels it has a responsibility to report the negative as well as the positive about the president and his administration—where he has failed as well as succeeded, where he has been inconsistent as well as consistent, when he has been less than candid as well as when he has boldly stated the facts. Similarly, whereas the White House seeks to control the flow of news so that the timing of an announcement will have maximum or minimum impact, as the case may be, press competition requires that newspapers and television networks report significant developments as soon as they can find out about them. Acquiring information the president does not want released may come from extensive detective work, or a story may be leaked to some members of the press by a government official who is opposed to a policy currently under consideration by the president. Still another way for the press to pry information from the president is to report his intention not to make it public. Thus, when the press learned that President Ford did not intend to make public the Rockefeller Commission Report on the Central Intelligence Agency, it reported this fact. Reaction in Congress was so averse to keeping the report secret that the president was compelled to release it.

If the press reacts negatively to the presidential efforts at managing the news, it is equally clear that presidents have been angered by press attempts to frustrate these efforts. Given their egos, as well as the daily pressures of the office, it is not surprising that presidents have responded to negative or premature reporting as unfair. Nor have they always confined themselves to merely saying so. Reporters who write "unfriendly" stories about the administration may suddenly find their access to White House sources cut off. Theodore Roosevelt even went so far as to ban some reporters from the White House altogether. Occasionally, presidential reaction becomes even more heavy-handed. President Kennedy sought to have a *New York Times* reporter reassigned to another position because his stories from Vietnam were highly critical of administration policies there. In some cases, Kennedy even succeeded in squelching stories he thought would be damaging. He persuaded the *New York Times* not to print a story about U.S. intentions to invade Cuba. Similarly, in an effort to keep from further alienating the business community following his confrontation with the steel companies, he managed to persuade CBS news to air interviews with two members of his administration who were highly critical of business.[96] The press has since become less amenable to such requests, however. Jimmy Carter, for example, failed to dissuade the *Washington Post* from reporting a story alleging that foreign officials were being secretly paid by the CIA. Reagan's defense secretary, Caspar Weinberger, was similarly unsuccessful in his efforts to prevent the Associated Press and the three major television networks from reporting on a secret military shuttle mission involving a new spy satellite.[97]

Frustrated by leaks, some of our recent presidents have even gone so far as to order taps placed on the phones of certain reporters in order to determine their sources within the government. But the most concerted effort by an administration to intimidate the press came during the Nixon presidency. *Washington Post* columnist Joseph Kraft had his phone tapped, not because he was receiving leaked information, but because he was writing columns critical of the Nixon administration. CBS correspondent Daniel Schorr also felt the force of government intimidation by being subjected to an FBI investigation into his personal life, although he may not have been the first to face this kind of pressure.[98] Columnists Joseph Alsop and Stewart Alsop claim to have been subjected to the same form of harassment during the Eisenhower administration.[99] Perhaps the most notable difference between the Nixon administration and its predecessors with respect to influencing press coverage was its willingness to use the government's regulatory power in an effort to extract more favorable press treatment. In an Indianapolis speech, Nixon's director of telecommunications warned that local "station managers and network officials who fail to act to correct imbalance or consistent bias in the networks—or who acquiesce by silence—can only be considered willing participants, to be held fully accountable . . . at license renewal time."[100] The implication was clear.

The Public Broadcasting System (PBS), which is financed in part by the federal government, also became a target because of its allegedly liberal programming. Its director for program activities noted the Nixon administration's conviction that "until public broadcasting shows signs of becoming what this administration wants it to be, this administration will oppose permanent financing."[101] The White House also attempted to terminate certain PBS programs, but most were saved through private funding. Finally, the government's regulatory power was even used to intimidate a major newspaper, the *Washington Post*. In an effort to retaliate for the newspaper's repeated stories about the Watergate scandals, the administration let it be known that it might not renew the license of a Florida television station owned by the *Post*.

A president's efforts to influence the tone of press coverage meet with some success simply because he has something the press wants, namely, information about what he is thinking and doing. And since the networks and newspapers operate in a competitive environment, they are not unaware of the advantage they enjoy when the White House favors them with an inside scoop. But this carrot can only be used sparingly, and even then it fails as often as it succeeds. When, however, a president's attempt to influence reporting moves beyond his legitimate prerogative to grant and deny access to himself and his staff and escalates instead to using the power of government to intimidate, the payoff is likely to be a negative one. Such efforts will themselves be made a public issue by the press, which quite rightly sees them as a threat to its independence.

Aware, perhaps, that direct attempts to pressure reporters or media institutions could backfire, the Reagan administration sought to influence coverage by using a different tactic, namely, restricting media access to information. Although Reagan was certainly not the first to employ this tactic, no other recent president had done so on such a broad scale. Speaking to this point, the executive director of the Reporter's Committee for Freedom of the Press observed that the Reagan administration's "attitude toward government information and leaks is worse by far than anything since the voluntary censorship at the end of World War II."[102] Reagan's efforts to limit press access took several forms: reducing the number of presidential news conferences; excluding reporters from covering the early phases of the Grenada invasion in 1983; issuing an executive order that both authorized the use of polygraph tests on government officials suspected of leaking information and imposed lifetime censorship on governmental officials with access to classified information; issuing a presidential directive making it easier for government officials to give a "secret" classification to government documents; requiring top-level approval before senior officials in the Defense Department and some other agencies could give interviews to the press; and proposing legislation that would further restrict the kinds of information journalists could secure under the Freedom of Information Act.[103] Not all of these efforts met with success, however. Severely criticized for excluding journalists from the Grenada invasion, the Reagan White House agreed to a designated pool of reporters who would be included in any future such operations. Moreover, the president quietly rescinded the order on polygraph tests after senior cabinet officials balked at the idea. Nor would Congress have any part of White House proposals designed to dilute the Freedom of Information Act.[104]

Elevating Public Expectations.   Reporting the negative as well as the positive is not the only way by which the media complicate the president's attempt to maintain a favorable impression with the public. Ironically, they also do so by glorifying the office and—at least initially—the individual who occupies it.

While not alone in this practice, the journalistic community has traditionally celebrated the presidential office, pointing to it as *the* source of political and moral leadership. If significant changes are to be made, if we are to be led out of dark times, it is the presidency that will make it all possible. Even more important is the tendency for the media to paint a highly personalized and favorable image of the newly elected president. Articles appear extolling certain aspects of his character, and even the most trivial of his habits and tastes are somehow made to appear admirable. In a column written shortly after Gerald Ford assumed office, Joe McGinniss took note of this phenomenon with some dismay.

> At this stage of Gerald Ford's Presidency there is only one impression we are capable of receiving, and, unfortunately—both for him and for us—it is unrealistic.
> Consider what we know of him: he dances, he prays, he walks onto his front lawn in his bathrobe to get his morning paper. He makes his own breakfast, he swims, he holds meetings, he sleeps in the same bed as his wife.
> Hardly the stuff of which legends are made. Yet, since his elevation, each of these acts has been perceived as a source of hope and inspiration for the nation.
> And consider, for a moment, his words: Honesty is the best policy, practice the Golden Rule, God will provide. A month ago these were harmless platitudes, greeted with snickers and yawns, of a decent but docile Vice President. Now they are moving, simple, eloquent articulations of concepts so noble as to reduce brave columnists to tears.

> It does not matter, for now, who Ford is or what Ford does. He is the President, and simply by not having disgraced himself, or the office, he has become the recipient not only of the adulation and reverence which traditionally have been awarded the President; but also of that potent extra measure which had been repressed during the Nixon reign.[105]

Or consider the following testimonial to Reagan's leadership style:

> The banker's hours that Ronald Reagan is keeping bespeak a brand of measured leadership long absent from the Executive Mansion. . . . Jimmy Carter, Richard Nixon and other recent Presidents spent long hours immersing themselves in the details of problems—sometimes losing their sense of overall priorities in the process. Reagan's instinct, in contrast, is to keep his eye on the big picture at all times.[106]

Responding to panegyrics such as these written about Reagan, one columnist suggested to his colleagues that "out of fairness to the president, and the nation, let's suspend all beatification proceedings until at least next Labor Day."[107]

Of course, the media are simply reflecting and responding to the national desire to rally behind the newly elected leader. But there is a problem inherent in all of this. During the euphoria that accompanies and immediately follows the installation of a new president, expectations about him and what he can do are elevated beyond what is attainable. Then when presidential action falls short of these expectations—as inevitably it must—the public experiences a sense of disillusionment with the president. In the words of McGinniss, "In selling ourselves an ideal President who does not and never can exist, we are once again repeating the destructive process of buildup and letdown that we have suffered through so often in the recent past."[108] Presidents quite naturally enjoy being the beneficiaries of such adulation—indeed, they often encourage it—but they would do well to realize that these unrealistic appraisals may only serve to make their relations with the public more difficult over the long run.

Media Bias. In the judgment of some, the president's ability to mobilize public opinion behind his policies is complicated by an additional factor—media bias. The charge is not a novel one. Indeed, for years those on the right have accused the media of a liberal bias, while those on the left have been just as convinced that the media suffered from a decidedly conservative bias. Beginning in the late 1960s, however, the issue achieved heightened visibility because the White House entered the debate. In essence, the Nixon administration was contending that the television networks were dominated by individuals whose liberal ideology caused them to be openly hostile to the more conservative policies of the president and, for that matter, to the values of a majority of Americans as well. One of President Nixon's close aides stated the problem this way:

> An incumbent elite with an ideological slant unshared by the nation's majority has acquired absolute control of the most powerful medium of communication known to man. And that elite is using that media monopoly to discredit those with whom it disagrees, and to advance its own ideological objectives—and it is defending that monopoly by beating its several critics over the head with the stick of the First Amendment.
> Within the media, many will readily concede this bias and retort, "What else is new?" What is new is not the existence of the liberal bias. What is new, in the last decade, is the wedding of that bias to unprecedented power. Men who are taking an increasingly adversary stance toward the social and political values, mores, and traditions of the

majority of Americans have also achieved monopoly control of the medium of commmuication upon which 60 percent of these Americans depend as the primary source of news and information about their government and society. And these men are using that monopoly position to persuade the nation to share their distrust of and hostility toward the elected government.[109]

Vice President Agnew acted as the spear carrier for the administration on this issue as he took after the networks with such colorful phrases as the "super-sensitive, self-anointed, supercilious electronic barons of opinion." Nor was the press spared. Certain columnists for the *New York Times, Washington Post,* and national weekly magazines were chastised by the vice president for their "wild, hot rhetoric" and "irresponsibility and thoughtlessness."[110]

Although Agnew's remarks at times bordered on demagoguery, it is important to note that his concerns were shared by certain respected members of the journalistic and scholarly communities. Some, for example, acknowledge and are concerned by the increasing ideological homogeneity of the Washington press corps. Moreover, they attribute this development to the fact that more and more of the reporters covering Washington are middle- and upper-class individuals who have been educated at our elite institutions. Such institutions, it is argued, promote an idealistic liberalism.[111] Robert Novak, a syndicated columnist, even went so far as to specify some of the liberal attitudes that underlie the bias of the Washington press corps.

1. The immoral war in Vietnam was the result of our obsession with anticommunism.
2. The military-industrial complex is not to be trusted, and defense spending should be cut.
3. We should vigorously enforce pollution standards even at the risk of unemployment.
4. Integration of the races must be made a reality even if it means forced busing.
5. The forces of repression under the Nixon administration threatened our liberties.
6. National priorities must be reordered to bring about a massive infusion of funds into our cities for "social rebuilding purposes."
7. There must be a redistribution of wealth through reform of both the tax structure and fiscal policy.[112]

The political attitudes shared by members of the press would appear to suggest that the charge of liberal bias has some substance. In the most extensive study conducted on this subject, Robert Lichter and Stanley Rothman interviewed some 240 journalists employed by national newspapers and newsmagazines and the three major television networks. They found that 54 percent of these individuals characterized themselves as left of center, while only 19 percent saw themselves as to the right of the political spectrum. When asked to describe the political leanings of their fellow colleagues, 56 percent characterized them as left of center, and only 8 percent saw them as to the right of center. Furthermore, the voting behavior of these 240 journalists revealed that they cast their ballots overwhelmingly for Democratic presidential candidates, with 94 percent voting for Johnson in 1964, 87 percent for Humphrey in 1968, 81 percent for McGovern in 1972, and 81 percent for Carter in 1976.[113] A more recent study of 139 Washington bureau chiefs and congressional correspondents found that 89 percent had voted for Clinton in 1992.[114]

Even though the evidence suggests that members of the elite press congregate on the left of the political spectrum, this fact alone is not enough to demonstrate bias in reporting. The exclusion of personal views from the reporting function is, after all, one of the most widely held expectations within the journalistic profession and as such may override any personal inclination to bias the news. Thus, it is essential to examine how the news is reported. Let us first consider television reporting, which is the primary news source for most Americans.

The charge of a liberal news bias was bolstered by Edith Efron in her much-discussed book *The News Twisters,* which examined the news coverage accorded to Humphrey and Nixon by all three networks during the 1968 election campaign. Efron's conclusion was that the news departments of all three networks exhibited a flagrant bias against candidate Nixon.[115] Yet subsequent studies have cast some doubt upon the validity of her conclusion. CBS commissioned International Research Associates to undertake a similar study of its news coverage during the 1968 campaign. These results showed that 63 percent of the news stories mentioned Nixon and 61 percent mentioned Humphrey. With respect to favorable or unfavorable treatment in these stories, it was found that 19 percent of the stories were favorable to Nixon, 19 percent were unfavorable, and the remaining 62 percent were neutral. For Humphrey, on the other hand, 26 percent of the stories were judged favorable, 17 percent unfavorable, and the rest neutral.[116] While these results support Efron's general conclusion, they nevertheless show considerably less bias against Nixon than she found.

In still another study made of CBS coverage during the 1968 election campaign, researchers used the very same transcripts of the CBS evening news that Efron did. But whereas Efron had examined only the commentary about the candidates, these researchers also included the amount of time that the candidates themselves spoke before the cameras during news broadcasts. As Table 4-8 indicates, only with respect to *amount* of coverage did one candidate enjoy a substantial advantage over the other, with Humphrey getting 37.5 percent of the coverage and Nixon 28.6 percent. Converted into time, this amounted to an advantage for Humphrey of about three minutes per week. As for type of coverage, however, there was scarcely any difference between the two candidates.

Perhaps the most extensive investigation made of network news bias was Richard Hofstetter's study of the coverage given to Nixon and McGovern during the 1972 campaign. Whereas the studies mentioned above examined coverage only over a seven-week period, Hofstetter's study covered approximately twelve weeks of the campaign. Moreover, like Efron, he analyzed the coverage of all three television networks. His findings, however, do not support Efron's conclusion of a bias against

TABLE 4-8   CBS Treatment of the 1968 Presidential Candidates

	Nixon	*Humphrey*	*Other*
Amount of coverage	28.6	37.5	33.9
Type of coverage			
Favorable	24.5	23.5	17.8
Neutral	17.7	16.8	16.9
Unfavorable	11.7	11.0	15.1
Mixed	8.8	9.0	8.6
Candidate before camera	37.3	39.7	41.6
Total	100.0	100.0	100.0

Source: Adapted from Robert Stevenson et al., "Untwisting the News Twisters: A Replication of Efron's Study," *Journalism Quarterly* 50 (Summer 1973), 217, 218.

Nixon. On the contrary, he concludes that "it is not possible to make a persuasive case that partisan political bias was present in network television coverage of the 1972 presidential election campaign. Indeed, based on the evidence in this study, the objective reader would be forced to conclude that partisan bias was not a significant factor in news coverage."[117]

Finally, it is worth noting three more recent studies of network coverage, the first of which was undertaken in 1980. This investigation examined only news stories on CBS, but, unlike the studies discussed above, it focused on the nominating contest (January 1 through June 4) rather than on the general election campaign. The analysis of CBS Evening News during this period revealed that the three Democratic candidates received more coverage (176 stories) than all nine of the Republican candidates (145 stories). At the same time, however, the authors of this study found that for Republican candidates "more than one story in five was good press (the plurality was neither good nor bad, but neutral). For the Democrats the figure was not as good—only one in six."[118] Moreover, among the leading contenders in both parties, the percentage of favorable stories on each was as follows: Reagan—36 percent, Carter—35 percent, Kennedy—19 percent, Bush—6 percent. These figures hardly suggest a liberal bias on the part of the network. But what about the network's coverage of liberal Republican John Anderson, who was viewed by some as the darling of the media establishment? In terms of favorable stories, he ranked behind Reagan and Carter with 28 percent—a rather high figure considering that he failed to win a single primary. One might conclude that the treatment given Anderson lends some credence to the alleged liberal bias of the networks. Such a conclusion would not necessarily be warranted, however, for media coverage is typically much tougher on front-runners than it is on those who stand little or no chance of winning the presidency.[119]

The second study focused only upon the 1984 general election campaign (after Labor Day), but, in contrast to previous studies, it included coverage by all three television networks. These researchers found no bias either in amount of time on camera or in coverage of substantive policy issues. In addition, while they found the overwhelming majority (74 percent) of news stories to be neutral in tone, such was not the case for the remaining 26 percent. The Mondale/Ferraro ticket received 1,970 seconds of positive coverage and 1,450 seconds of bad press. Reagan and Bush, on the other hand, garnered only 730 seconds of positive coverage but a hefty 7,230 seconds of negative reporting.[120] Although one might attribute this substantial difference in positive coverage to liberal bias, there are other equally plausible explanations. For one thing, the media may have been attempting to create a closer contest out of what appeared to be a runaway election. A horse race, after all, is both more interesting for them to cover and more interesting for the public to follow. More crucially, as ABC political editor Hal Bruno points out, an incumbent president typically receives tougher treatment from the media because he has an established record to criticize.[121] Furthermore, the media may have been tougher still on this particular incumbent because he would never face an electorate again and also because he had been notoriously inaccessible to the press.[122] Finally, it is worth pointing out that had there been an underlying media antipathy toward the conservative Reagan candidacy, it should have been evident in 1980 as well.

A study of the 1992 election conducted by the Center for Media and Public Affairs once again found the treatment of the incumbent to be more critical. It examined 1,606 election stories on all three networks running from January through August and identified some 3,100 statements about the candidates that could be characterized as either positive or negative. Whereas 45 percent of the comments were praiseworthy of Bill Clinton, only 31 percent praised George Bush. The gap was even wider for their running mates, with Al Gore earning positive comments in 75 percent of the stories and Vice President Quayle in only 37 percent. S. Robert Lichter, co-director of the Center for Media and Public Affairs, concludes that "if any thread runs through these results, it is not liberal bias but anti-incumbent bias in presidential campaigns. We suggest a general rule: The stronger a candidate, the greater the media scrutiny."[123]

All of these studies have focused exclusively upon the question of television bias in a presidential election campaign. While, taken as a whole, they do not support the claim that the television networks showed a *pronounced and systematic bias* against Richard Nixon or Republicans in general, it might be argued that these studies still tell us nothing about bias *after* the election. Yet if the thesis of network bias is correct, it presumably ought to manifest itself during any given period of time. Indeed, one would expect such a bias to be especially pronounced during a presidential election campaign, given its crucial importance.

What of the charge that the *print* press is increasingly dominated by those of a liberal persuasion? Such noted publications as the *New York Times, Washington Post, Time,* and *Newsweek* have been cited as constituting the liberal axis of the print press. Although they have often espoused the liberal side on issues, it would be an oversimplification to say that these publications are characterized by a uniformity of positions. In 1972, for example, the *New York Times* endorsed George McGovern for president, while *Time* magazine supported President Nixon. Furthermore, the liberal persuasion does not by any means enjoy a monopoly on national publications. Publications such as the *Wall Street Journal, Daily News, U.S. News and World Report, Reader's Digest,* and *TV Guide* are generally considered to have a moderate-to-conservative orientation, and all enjoy a high circulation. Indeed, the *Wall Street Journal* and *Daily News* have the largest circulations of any newspapers in the country, and *TV Guide* and *Reader's Digest* the highest of any magazines.[124] While the *New York Times* and *Washington Post* are quite rightly considered to have substantial influence in governmental circles, it must be remembered that, taken together, their circulation still constitutes less than 1 percent of the population. The remaining readership is spread out among approximately 1,700 daily newspapers.[125] Moreover, of those newspapers with a policy of endorsing presidential candidates, an overwhelming majority have traditionally supported Republicans over Democrats. In 1984, for example, *Editor and Publisher* found that in a survey of 659 daily newspapers, 381 (18.3 million combined circulation) endorsed President Reagan. Mondale, however, was endorsed by only 62 dailies, with a combined circulation of 7.5 million.[126] Finally, it should be noted that most of the nation's daily newspapers get a large portion of their news from the Associated Press and United Press International news services. As one former presidential press secretary has pointed out, neither of these news organizations can be neatly classified into ideological categories.

> The largest audience remains, as it has for decades, with the Associated Press and United Press International—about 170 editorial employees who are not elitist by any definition other than competence. Neither are they liberal nor conservative. The *New York Times* and the *Washington Post* may dominate academic and governmental discussion, but the stories that move people in the mass usually bear the logotypes AP and UPI. Furthermore, the impact of these two wire services is far greater than the quality of the stories they write and distribute. In a very direct manner, they are more responsible than any other organization or group for establishing the pattern of daily news coverage not only for newspapers but for the television industry.[127]

In summary, biases do indeed exist within the nation's written press. The First Amendment was not drafted in the belief that newspapers would be objective. Indeed, the purpose of the amendment was in part designed to protect the right of newspapers not to be so. Having acknowledged the existence of bias, however, it is far less clear that it decidedly disadvantages a president of one ideological persuasion over another.

☆ AN ANTIPRESIDENCY BIAS

If it has yet to be proven that the media exhibit any systematic ideological bias against particular presidents, nevertheless, the evidence does suggest that the media are becoming more adversarial toward presidents in general. Grossman and Kumar, for example, examined presidential coverage by *Time* and the *New York Times* from 1953 to 1978. Although they found that favorable stories generally predominated over unfavorable ones during this entire time period, there were substantially more unfavorable stories from 1966 to 1978 than there were from 1953 to 1965.[128] Samuel Kernell used Grossman and Kumar's data to examine coverage of presidents only during their second and third years, thereby seeking to avoid "a possible halo effect during the first year, as presidents bask in victory, and during their fourth year, as they do what they can to win again." Favorable stories were once again more frequent overall, but the number of unfavorable stories grew with each succeeding administration.[129] In yet another study, Fred Smoller focused upon CBS news coverage from 1969 through 1984 and found that 55 percent of the stories were neutral, with the remaining 45 percent containing a positive or negative spin. Of this 45 percent, 27 percent were negative in tone, and only 18 percent were positive. In short, 60 percent of the stories having a spin were negative in nature. Smoller's findings also revealed that negative coverage had increased with each succeeding president.[130] More recently, two scholars from the Center for Media and Public Affairs examined how the three networks covered the Bush administration over a twenty-one month period, finding that only 44 percent of the stories about Bush himself and only 39 percent of the stories about his administration were favorable.[131] Meanwhile, their study of how the networks covered the first four months of the Clinton presidency found that no less than 64 percent of all the references to him were negative—a finding that, incidentally, scarcely seems compatible with the charge that the national media exhibit a liberal bias.[132]

Several factors may help to explain why presidents find it increasingly difficult to generate positive media coverage. For one thing, there has developed within the press what one noted columnist sees as a shift in attitude from "simple credulity to informed skepticism" about what the government says.[133] Several journalists mark the beginning of this change with the U-2 plane incident in May 1960. A high-altitude aircraft piloted by Francis Gary Powers was shot down over the Soviet Union while gathering intelligence information. The government initially issued a statement saying that the U-2 was probably a weather research plane. But after it was learned that the Russians had captured the plane intact, the Eisenhower administration acknowledged that it was a spy plane, but added that the flight had been undertaken without authorization from Washington. This statement also proved to be false, for President Eisenhower had approved both the U-2 program itself and the schedule for its flights over the Soviet Union. The president ultimately reversed his position and acknowledged that the spying flights had been authorized and indeed would continue.[134] The seed of skepticism planted by this incident continued to be nurtured by the lack of candor shown by subsequent presidents in dealing with such matters as the Bay of Pigs invasion, the sending of troops to the Dominican Republic, and the Vietnam War. Consequently, as Max Frankel has noted, the press is increasingly inclined to treat "virtually every official utterance as a carefully contrived rendering that needs to be examined for the missing word or phrase, the sly use of statistics, the slippery syntax or semantics."[135] Needless to say, the Watergate scandals did not do anything to diminish this skepticism. On the contrary, as two former Carter administration officials have observed, this event served only to increase press antagonism toward the presidency: "Although the media have traditionally been independent and critical of government, media attitudes now are unremittingly adversarial, especially after Watergate. . . . Given the unremittingly critical perspective that the press brings to the presidency, a disturbing but substantial question presents itself: namely, whether any president can be perceived as successful today unless his governing victories are overwhelming."[136] Reagan administration officials saw the problem as no less severe, with White House Deputy Press Secretary Larry Speakes stating before a Washington audience, "My question to you is, can the modern presidency survive the modern media? The steady denigration of the president has gone on for two decades. It has been directed not only at the president but at his use of presidential powers. . . ."[137] Although administration officials are admittedly not dispassionate observers, concern over the media's growing ill-temper has been voiced even in journalism circles:

> The Press has become so adversarial in its relationship with government that it threatens the democratic process.[138]
>
> > Michael J. O'Neil, president, American Society of Newspaper Editors, 1983

> The press now just chews everything to bits . . . I don't like this very much. Any new leader, policy, program or idea—because the press so abhors a vacuum—is simply chewn to bits before it has a chance to mature.[139]
>
> > Eric Severeid, former commentator, CBS

> Journalism is in a state of shrieking arrogance.[140]
>
> > Jim Lehrer, co-anchor, *MacNeil/Lehrer News Hour*

> The press is ravenous, ready to see scandal in a speck of dust. Its self-importance passes belief.[141]
>
> > Anthony Lewis, columnist, *New York Times*

Other developments related to media organization and personnel may also serve to increase the instability in the president's relationship with the press. The White House is being covered more and more by large news organizations, that is, reporters working for the three television networks, large national newspapers, and the weekly newsmagazines. Whereas smaller papers with limited resources must rely primarily on what the White House and the wire services provide them, the larger news organizations have the resources to monitor and investigate government activities in greater depth. The *Washington Post,* for instance, is staffed with a considerable number of researchers and librarians, in addition to reporters. The quality of the Washington press corps has also risen substantially. News organizations are not only insisting on higher educational qualifications, but they are also seeking reporters with special expertise in given policy areas. This puts them in a better position to evaluate complex policy issues independent of what the White House says about them.[142]

If the developments noted above have fostered a more critical cast to reporting among the national media in general, it is also the case that television's coverage of the president is even more critical than that of the print media.[143] This is due partly to the fact television news is driven by ratings. To ensure an attentive audience, the networks are disposed to present the news in the most alluring way possible. This means emphasizing drama and conflict, who is winning and who is losing, politics over policy, problems over solutions, and the exceptional over the normal.[144] In addition, time limitations on the evening news programs (twenty-two minutes, excluding commercials), combined with concerns about audience attentiveness, assure that stories will be oversimplified, with insufficient attention given to the complexities and nuances of governing.

The more critical tone of television journalism is also traceable to a perception on the part of TV reporters that they are being exploited by the White House. Television is, after all, the primary news source for a majority of Americans, and the networks give considerably greater attention to the presidency than do newspapers. Accordingly, the major preoccupation of the president's public relations establishment, as network correspondents well know, is to manipulate television coverage to the president's best advantage. As President Carter's press secretary (Jody Powell) put it: "They [reporters] recognize their vulnerability to manipulation and compensate like hell for it—in many cases, overcompensate for it. TV more, I think because they know . . . that they're being manipulated and so forth. And they're sensitive to criticism from other journalists . . . to protect themselves from that allegation."[145]

Possible Consequences of Media Negativism

Public support is a crucially important resource for a president to have as he seeks to persuade others to do his bidding. Increasingly negative media coverage, however, complicates his ability to maintain that support. This is not to say that the media are the initial cause of declining approval. The media are more often cue-takers than cue-givers. Accordingly, they typically become more negative after a president's popularity has already started to decline or after he begins to draw fire from others in government.[146] Once things do start to go wrong, however, the media serve as an *amplifier of presidential problems.* This amplification occurs in several ways. First, as already noted, television highlights the conflict dimension of presidential problems and oversimplifies them, providing little context regarding their complexity and treating them as *personal* failures.[147] Second, although the media provide the president with a formidable bully pulpit from which to speak, there are now unprecedented opportunities for presidential critics to use this bully pulpit as well—be it on the morning or late-night newscasts, an ever-growing number of public affairs news analysis programs, to say nothing of the TV studios that now exist in the House and Senate. Third, the negative coverage that presidents face when things do start to go wrong is compounded further because little differentiation exists within the national media regarding what stories are covered and how they are interpreted. Washington reporters readily admit that this rush to consensus, known as "pack journalism," is their most serious deficiency.[148] Fourth, as the president's declining public approval itself becomes the subject of news stories—a phenomenon that has become much more pronounced since the networks have developed their own polling operations—this attention causes his approval to fall further.[149] And finally, presidential efforts to reverse their declining fortunes through words or deeds are portrayed by an increasingly skeptical media as cynical attempts to manipulate the public.[150] For all of these reasons, then, the media may well accelerate a president's decline and complicate his ability to recover, thereby making him more dependent than ever upon fortuitous events or crises to turn things around.

The television networks began expanding their commitment to news programming in 1963 and since that time the presidency has been their star attraction. Presidential public approval ratings have not fared as well, however. As Table 4-9 reveals, only two presidents (Johnson and Bush) serving in the 1964–1992 period achieved public approval highs equal to or better than those achieved by Eisenhower and Kennedy. In each case, moreover, the circumstances that produced such high public approval were most unusual. Johnson's assumption to office in a time of national crisis understandably earned him a very high rating (83 percent)—equal to that achieved by Kennedy. Likewise, the unique circumstances surrounding the Gulf conflict—a *major* war won in a relatively *brief* amount of time and with *minimum* casualties—brought George Bush an unprecedented high rating of 89 percent. Note also, however, that neither Eisenhower nor Kennedy hit public approval lows that were even close to those reached by Johnson, Ford, Nixon, Carter, Reagan, Bush, and Clinton.

It is not being suggested here that the erosion of public support for presidents is primarily a function of media coverage. The circumstances dealt each president, and how he responds, ultimately determine his standing with the public. Kennedy and Eisenhower admittedly did not have to confront a highly unpopular war (Johnson, Nixon); urban unrest (Johnson); self-inflicted presidential scandal (Nixon); hyperinflation (Ford, Carter); or acute recession (Reagan). On the other hand, neither were their problems nor their critics so dramatically and continuously displayed on television. Nor were their declines in public support, when they occurred, as carefully monitored and highlighted in the news. Nor were their motives and purposes as subject to cynical interpretations by a media that has since grown more cynical.[151] As a consequence, when events turned against them or when they made a bad decision, their declines in public support were less severe and their ability to recover easier.

TABLE 4-9   Highs and Lows of Presidents' Public Approval Ratings

President	Tenure	High	Low
Clinton	1993–1996	60%	37%
Bush	1989–1992	83	32
Reagan	1981–1988	68	35
Carter	1977–1980	75	21
Ford	1974–1976	71	37
Nixon	1969–1974	68	24
Johnson	1963–1968	80	35
Kennedy	1961–1963	83	57
Eisenhower	1953–1960	79	49

Source: Gallup Report, No. 231, December 1984, p. 8; *Gallup Report,* No. 280, January 1989, p. 12; *Polling Report* 5 (January 30, 1989), p. 4; *Gallup Report,* No. 277, October 1988, p. 26; *American Enterprise,* March/April 1993, p. 94. Data on Clinton supplied to the author by the Gallup Organization.

Presidential Responses

Well aware of the growing negativism among the national media, presidents and their aides have tried to adapt to this reality. No administration, perhaps, did so with greater ingenuity than Reagan's. Seeking to influence what would get on the evening news programs and convinced that what viewers saw would impress them more than what they heard, Reagan media advisers went to great lengths to provide an irresistible "visual" of the president to accompany the major story they wanted to have covered each day. In addition, they carefully controlled how the president would be exposed to reporters, believing that ready access would only increase the likelihood that Reagan would be forced to deal with the media's agenda rather than his own. Accordingly, during his public appearances the press was kept at a considerable distance, news conferences were infrequent, and reporters were not allowed to ask questions of him during White House photo opportunities. Finally, in attempting to have their stories reported in as unadulterated a form as possible, the Reagan White House saw the regional media as its greatest target of opportunity. Journalists outside the beltway were judged more likely to go with the White House version of a story because they have fewer resources and, unlike the Washington press corps, are more likely to be awed by White House attention. Although it was the Nixon administration that first saw the potential of appealing to regional media, Reagan's press aides carried it to new heights. In its first three years alone, the Reagan administration held some 150 White House briefings for non-Washington media personnel. Other attempts to circumvent the White House press corps included electronically distributing press releases and supplying radio and video tapes to regional media, later followed by satellite distribution of Reagan videos to some 900 television stations across the country.[152]

Clinton and his aides made no secret of the fact that they too intended to go over the heads of the national media. Thus, it was nearly three months before he held his first formal news conference with the Washington press corps, and subsequent full-dress, prime-time news conferences have been few and far between. Considerable effort was also directed at media targets outside the Washington beltway. As one journalist notes:

> The staff attempts to tap every media outlet except the Washington correspondents. [White House director of media affairs Jeff] Eller has divided the country into four quadrants. Within each region, local radio stations, television stations and newspapers are called daily to see if they'd be interested in an interview with an administration official . . . Cabinet members are expected to be on call. On the fourth floor of the Old Executive Office Building, a television studio is in regular use. Aides estimate that they stage at least one major media event a day. . . . Press briefings and documents are constantly and instantly transmitted on computer networks like CompuServe and America Online. Presidential schedules are sent out on another computer network, U.S. Newswire. . . .[153]

Finally, in contrast to Reagan who appeared only in controlled settings, Clinton also sought to circumvent the Washington reporters by participating in TV town meetings, satellite news conferences, and radio and cable talk shows; and he was more than willing to remind journalists of the advantage of doing so: "You know why I can stiff you on the press conferences? Because Larry King liberated me by giving me directly to the American people."[154]

Whether these tactics paid significant dividends is far from clear. Clinton's first-year public approval average was 49 percent—lower than for any postwar president except Ford.[155] Moreover, as one might expect, his attempts to navigate around the national media served only to inflame further a relationship that had already become strained during his campaign for the presidency. Indeed, commenting on the unusually harsh treatment given Clinton by the press during his first year in office, *Newsweek* Bureau Chief Evan Thomas explained that there is "some overkill and a kind of meanness. And there is an element of revenge, because this particular crowd were smug, contemptuous of the press and thought they could go over our heads."[156]

 ## CONCLUSION

Few would dispute the necessity of having a vigorous and independent press. Scanning the governmental process with a watchful eye, it plays a crucial role in drawing public attention to error, inadequacies, and abuse of power. No historical example highlights its contribution in this regard better than the scandals of Watergate. Less appreciated but equally important is the role the press plays in preventing some abuses from occurring in the first place. In the words of one former White House aide, "The occasions on which presidents and their staff aides have decided not to cut corners because their action might be discovered by the press are legion."[157] However, in addition to watching for and pointing out what is wrong in government, the press also has a responsibility to identify the positive. In this connection, some have voiced the concern that for much of the national press a healthy skepticism about government has given way to a not-so-healthy cynicism. Such an orientation, it is argued, fosters a climate of negativism in which it becomes increasingly "hard for government to succeed and just as hard for government to appear to have succeeded when, indeed, it has done so."[158] The expression of this concern comes not from the lunatic fringe but rather from thoughtful observers of the political scene. The press would do well to ponder it.

 ## NOTES

1. Cited in Jack Valenti, *A Very Human President* (New York: Norton, 1975), p. 261.

2. Fred Greenstein, "Popular Images of the President," in Aaron Wildavsky, ed., *The Presidency* (Boston: Little, Brown, 1969), p. 290.

3. Jack Dennis, "Who Supports the Presidency?" *Society* 13 (July/August 1976), p. 51. See also Roger Davidson and Glenn Parker, "The Pattern of Support for Congress" (Paper presented at the 66th annual meeting of the American Political Science Association, Los Angeles, September 8–12, 1970); Kenneth Dolbeare and Phillip Hammon, "The Political Party Bias of Attitudes toward the Supreme Court," *Public Opinion Quarterly* 32 (Spring 1968), 16–30.

4. Christopher Arterton, "Watergate and Children's Attitudes toward Political Authority Revisited," *Political Science Quarterly* 90 (Fall 1975), 488.

5. Greenstein, "Popular Images," p. 228.

6. Michael Riccards, *The Making of the American Citizenry* (New York: Chandler, 1973), p. 70.

7. Fred Greenstein, "The Benevolent Leader: Children's Images of Political Authority," *American Political Science Review* 54 (December 1960), 939.

8. Fred Greenstein, "The Benevolent Leader Revisited:Children's Images of Political Leaders in Three Democracies," *American Political Science Review* 69 (December 1975), 1385.

9. Ibid., p. 1386.

10. Ibid.

11. Riccards, *American Citizenry,* p. 77.

12. Ibid., p. 79.

13. Fred Greenstein, "What the President Means to Americans," in James Barber, ed., *Choosing the President* (Englewood Cliffs, N.J.: Prentice Hall, 1974), p. 126.

14. *Gallup Report,* No. 231, December 1984, pp. 4, 5; see also Tom W. Smith, "The Polls: The Most Admired Man and Woman," *Public Opinion Quarterly* 50 (Winter 1986), 573–84; *Washington Post,* January 2, 1999, p. 192.

15. Hazel Erskine, "The Polls: Presidential Power," *Public Opinion Quarterly* 37 (Fall 1973), 491.

16. Cited in Thomas Cronin, *The State of the Presidency* (Boston: Little, Brown, 1975), p. 107.

17. Cited in Erskine, "The Polls," 491.

18. Erskine, "The Polls," 488.

19. Ibid., 492.

20. Roberta Siegel, "Image of the American Presidency: Part II of an Exploration into Popular Views of Presidential Powers," in Wildavsky, ed., *The Presidency,* pp. 300, 301.

21. Samuel Kernell, Peter Sperlich, and Aaron Wildavsky, "Public Support for Presidents," in Aaron Wildavsky, ed., *Perspectives on the Presidency* (Boston: Little, Brown, 1975), p. 153.

22. Cited in *Gallup Opinion Index,* April 1977, p. 3

23. *Gallup Opinion Index,* September 1977, p. 3; *Gallup Opinion Index,* November 1974, p. 19.

24. *Washington Post,* May 28, 1981, p. A12.

25. John Mueller, "Presidential Popularity from Truman to Johnson," *American Political Science Review* 64 (March 1970), 20.

26. Jeff Fishel, *Presidents & Promises* (Washington, D.C.: Congressional Quarterly Press, 1985), pp. 157, 159, 160, 161, 173.

27. *Washington Post,* April 29, 1993, p. A18; *Washington Post,* August 15, 1993, p. C2; *New York Times,* June 4, 1993, p. A12.

28. On this point, see Lee Sigelman and Kathleen Knight, "Why Does Presidential Popularity Decline?: A Test of the Expectation/Disillusionment Theory," *Public Opinion Quarterly* 47 (Fall 1983), 310–24; James Stimson, "Public Support for Presidents: A Cyclical Model," *Public Opinion Quarterly* 40 (Spring 1976), 1–21.

29. Cited in *National Journal,* January 14, 1978, p. 44.

30. Thomas Cronin, "The Paradoxes of the Presidency," *Skeptic,* No. 5 (September/October 1976), 20–23, 54–57.

31. Michael B. MacKuen, "Political Drama, Economic Conditions and the Dynamics of Presidential Popularity," *American Journal of Political Science* 27 (May 1983), 187–88.

32. Paul Brace and Barbara Hinckley, *Follow the Leader* (New York: Basic Books, 1992), p. 167.

33. See, for example, Richard Brody and Benjamin Page, "The Impact of Events on Presidential Popularity: The Johnson and Nixon Administrations," in Wildavsky, ed., *Perspectives on the Presidency,* pp. 136–46.

34. George Gallup, "Public Attitudes, Youth, and the Presidency," in John Hoy and Melvin Bernstein, eds., *The Effective President* (Pacific Palisades, Calif.: Palisades, 1976), p. 84.

35. See Gallup Polls in "Opinion Roundup," *Public Opinion* 10 (March/April, 1987), 34.

36. George Edwards, "Comparing Chief Executives," *Public Opinion* 8 (June/July 1985), 54.

37. *New York Times,* March 1, 1998, p. 5; *Washington Post,* June 6, 1998, p. 1.

38. Donald Kinder, "Presidents, Prosperity, and Public Opinion," *Public Opinion Quarterly* 45 (Spring 1981), 1–19; Richard Lau and David Sears, "Cognitive Links between Economic Grievances and Political Responses," *Political Behavior* 3 (No. 4, 1981), 279–302. For a somewhat different analysis, see George Edwards, *The Public Presidency* (New York: St. Martin's Press, 1983), pp. 228–37, who argues that presidents' public approval is influenced not by economic conditions as such but rather by what the public thinks the president is trying to do about them.

39. Mervin Field, "Public Opinion and Presidential Response," in Hoy and Bernstein, *Effective President,* p. 63. See also Siegel, "Image of the American Presidency," p. 303.

40. John Mueller, "Presidential Popularity," 29, 30.

41. Brace and Hinckley, *Follow the Leader,* p. 168.

42. See, for example, James Meernik and Peter Waterman, "The Myth of the Diversionary Use of Force by Presidents," *Political Research Quarterly* 49 (September 1996), 573–89.

43. Arterton, "Watergate and Children's Attitudes," 485, 486.

44. Arthur Miller, Jeffrey Brudney, and Peter Joftis, "Presidential Crises and Political Support: The Impact of Watergate on Attitudes toward Institutions" (Paper presented at the Midwest Political Science Association Convention, Chicago, May 1–3, 1975), pp. 27, 28.

45. Francis Rourke, Lloyd Free, and William Watts, *Trust and Confidence in the American System* (Washington, D.C.: Potomac Associates, 1976), p. 22.

46. Cited in the *Washington Post,* March 14, 1977, p. C9.

47. *Washington Post,* January 5, 1978, p. A8.

48. Cited in Everett Ladd, "The Polls: The Question of Confidence," *Public Opinion Quarterly* 40 (Winter 1976–1977), 546.

49. Cited in the *Wall Street Journal,* April 27, 1977, p. 1.

50. Joseph Califano, *A Presidential Nation* (New York: Norton, 1975), p. 102.

51. *New York Times,* August 29, 1997, p. A24; *Washington Post,* May 31, 1996, p. A21.

52. William Small, *Political Power and the Press* (New York: Norton, 1972), p. 114.

53. Califano, *Presidential Nation,* p. 109.

54. *Gallup Opinion Index,* March 1972, p. 5.

55. Newton Minow, *Presidential Television* (New York: Basic Books, 1973), p. 67; Martin Nolan, "The Re-Selling of the President," *Atlantic Monthly,* November 1972, pp. 79–81.

56. Michael Grossman and Martha Kumar, *Portraying the President: The White House and the News Media* (Baltimore: Johns Hopkins University Press, 1981), p. 173.

57. Taken from Lewis J. Paper, *The Promise and the Performance* (New York: Crown, 1975), p. 253. Copyright © 1975 by Lewis J. Paper. Used by permission of Crown Publishers, Inc.

58. *National Journal,* November 20, 1993, p. 2792.

59. Paper, *Promise and the Performance,* p. 254.

60. See Michael Beschloss, *Taking Charge: The Johnson White House Tapes, 1963–1964* (New York: Simon & Schuster, 1997).

61. Paper, *Promise and Performance,* pp. 323, 324.

62. Newton Minow and Lee Mitchell, "Incumbent Television: A Case of Indecent Exposure," *The Annals* 425 (May 1976), 77.

63. Cited in Small, *Political Power,* p. 185.

64. Lyn Ragsdale, *Vital Statistics on the Presidency* (Washington, D.C.: Congressional Quarterly, 1996), pp. 167, 168.

65. Figures for the first two years of Clinton's term taken from ibid., p. 168. Figures for 1995–1997 were calculated from the *Weekly Compilation of Presidential Documents* (Washington, D.C.: Government Printing Office, 1995–1997). Only those meetings with the press labeled as "News Conferences" were counted.

66. *New York Times,* March 11, 1977, p. A25.

67. Cited in Small, *Political Power,* p. 185.

68. Richard Reeves, "The Prime-Time President," *New York Times Magazine,* May 15, 1977, p. 18.

69. Ragsdale, *Vital Statistics on the Presidency,* p. 164. Data for 1995–1998 taken from *Television News Archive,* <http://tvnews.vanderbilt.edu.> January, 1998.

70. Lyn Ragsdale, "The Politics of Presidential Speechmaking, 1949–1980," *American Political Science Review* 78 (December 1984), 981.

71. Brace and Hinckley, *Follow the Leader,* p. 56.

72. Cited in Minow, *Presidential Television,* p. 19.

73. Cited in Paper, *Promise and Performance,* p. 208.

74. Denis Rutkus, *A Report on Simultaneous Television Network Coverage of Presidential Addresses to the Nation* (Washington, D.C.: Library of Congress, 1976), Appendix, pp. i–v.

75. *Washington Post,* March 20, 1977, p. 1.

76. Minow, *Presidential Television,* pp. 10, 11.

77. *New York Times,* January 18, 1976, p. 43.

78. Samuel Kernell, *Going Public: New Strategies in Presidential Leadership* (Washington, D.C.: Congressional Quarterly Press, 1986), p. 103.

79. Cited in Minow and Mitchell, "Incumbent Television," 78.

80. See, for example, Rutkus, *Report on Television Coverage.*

81. Ibid., p. 7.

82. Ibid., p. 1.

83. Cited in Paper, *Promise and Performance,* p. 234.

84. Cited in *Washington Post,* April 17, 1977, p. A5.

85. Cited in Small, *Political Power,* p. 58.

86. Cited in Peter Forbath and Carey Winfrey, *The Adversaries: The President and the Press* (Cleveland: Regal Books/King's Court Communications, 1974), p. 5.

87. Cited in Small, *Political Power,* p. 56.

88. Ibid., p. 109.

89. Cited in the *Washington Post,* November 18, 1996, p. C1.

90. William Safire, *Before the Fall* (Garden City, N.Y.: Doubleday, 1975), pp. 70, 351. Copyright © 1975 by William Safire. Used by permission of Doubleday & Company, Inc.

91. David Broder, "The Presidency and the Press," in Charles Dunn, ed., *The Future of the American Presidency* (Morristown, N.J.: General Learning Press, 1975), p. 264.

92. Arthur Krock, "Mr. Kennedy's Management of the News," *Fortune,* March 1963, p. 82.

93. Paper, *Promise and Performance,* p. 327.

94. David Wise, *The Politics of Lying* (New York: Vintage Books, 1973), pp. 27–75.

95. See, for example, John Anthony Maltese, *Spin Control: The White House Office of Communication and the Management of Presidential News* (Chapel Hill: University of North Carolina Press, 1992); Howard Kurtz, *Spin Cycle: Inside the Clinton Propaganda Machine* (New York: Free Press, 1998).

96. Paper, *Promise and Performance,* pp. 254, 255.

97. *Washington Post,* December 20, 1984, p. A15.

98. Theodore White, *Breach of Faith* (New York: Atheneum, 1975), pp. 121, 122.

99. Michael Grossman and Francis Rourke, "The Media and the Presidency: An Exchange Analysis," *Political Science Quarterly* 91 (Fall 1976), 459.

100. Cited in Wise, *Politics of Lying,* p. 403.

101. Cited in Walter Mondale, *The Accountability of Power* (New York: McKay, 1975), p. 205.

102. Cited in *Washington Post,* December 20, 1984, p. A15.

103. *New York Times,* March 24, 1985, p. F5; Steve Weinberg, "Trashing the FOIA," *Columbia Journalism Review* (January/February 1985), 25; *Washington Post,* December 20, 1984, p. A15; Steven Weisman, "The President and the Press: The Art of Controlled Access," *New York Times Magazine,* October 14, 1984, p. 34ff.

104. Weinberg, "Trashing the FOIA," p. 25; *Washington Post,* December 20, 1984, p. A15.

105. *New York Times,* September 8, 1974, p. E19. Copyright © 1974 by The New York Times Company. Reprinted by permission.

106. Quoted in Donna Cross, *Mediaspeak* (New York: Coward-McCann, 1983), p. 200.

107. *Washington Post,* February 21, 1981, p. A11.

108. *New York Times,* September 8, 1974, p. E19.

109. Patrick Buchanan, *The New Majority* (Philadelphia: Girard Bank, 1973), pp. 18, 20, 21.

110. Cited in Small, *Political Power,* p. 138.

111. Ithiel De Sola Pool, "Government and the Media," *American Political Science Review* 70 (December 1976), 1236. See also George Will, ed., *Press, Politics and Popular Government* (Washington, D.C.: American Enterprise Institute, 1972); Max Kampelman, "Congress, the Media and the President," in Harvey Mansfield, ed., *Congress against the President* (New York: Academy of Political Science, 1975), pp. 85–98.

112. Adapted from Robert Novak, "The New Journalism," in Harry Clor, ed., *The Mass Media and Modern Democracy* (Chicago: Rand McNally College, 1974), pp. 3, 4. Copyright © The Public Affairs Conference Center. Reprinted by permission of Rand McNally College Publishing Company.

113. Robert Lichter and Stanley Rothman, "Media and Business Elites," *Public Opinion* 4 (October/November 1981), 43. See also Stephen Hess, *The Washington Reporters* (Washington, D.C.: Brookings Institution, 1981), pp. 87–90.

114. *Washington Post,* May 7, 1996, p. A19.

115. Edith Efron, *The News Twisters* (Los Angeles: Nash, 1971), p. 47.

116. These figures cited in De Sola Pool, "Government and the Media," pp. 1236, 1237.

117. Richard Hofstetter, *Bias in the News* (Columbus: Ohio State University Press, 1976), p. 187.

118. Michael Robinson, with Nancy Conover and Margaret Sheehan, "The Media at Mid-Year: A Bad Year for McLuhanites?" *Public Opinion* 3 (June/July 1980), 42.

119. Ibid., pp. 42, 45.

120. Maura Clancey and Michael Robinson, "General Election Coverage: Part I," *Public Opinion* 7 (December/January 1985), 50; Michael Robinson, "The Media in Campaign '84: Part II, Wingless, Toothless and Hopeless," *Public Opinion* 8 (February/March 1985), 44, 45.

121. Clancey and Robinson, "General Election Coverage," 54.

122. Ibid.

123. *Washington Post,* September 6, 1992, p. C4.

124. Edwin Diamond, "New Wrinkles on the Permanent Press," *Public Opinion* 7 (April/May 1984), 4.

125. Philip Geyelin and Douglass Cater, *American Media: Adequate or Not?* (Washington, D.C.: American Enterprise Institute, 1970), p. 5.

126. *Editor and Publisher,* November 3, 1984, p. 9.

127. George Reedy, "Why Does Nobody Love the Press?" in Harry Clor, *Mass Media,* p. 29.

128. Grossman and Kumar, *Portraying the President*, p. 265.

129. Kernell, *Going Public*, pp. 180, 181.

130. Fred Smoller, "The Six O'Clock Presidency: Patterns of Network News Coverage of the President," *Presidential Studies Quarterly* 16 (Winter 1986), 40–42.

131. S. Robert Lichter and Richard E. Noyes, "In the Media Spotlight: Bush at Midpoint," *American Enterprise* 2 (January/February, 1991), p. 50

132. Cited in *New York Times*, June 17, 1993, p. A11.

133. Max Frankel, "The Press and the President," appearing under "Letters from Readers," *Commentary*, July 1971, p. 16.

134. Wise, *Politics of Lying*, pp. 47–50.

135. Frankel, "Press and the President," p. 16.

136. Ben Heineman and Curtis Hessler, *Memorandum for the President: A Strategic Approach to Domestic Affairs in the 1980's* (New York: Random House, 1980), p. 108.

137. *Washington Post*, January 29, 1983, p. A8.

138. Cited in Martin Linsky, *Impact* (New York: Norton, 1986), p. 15.

139. Quoted in Rudy Maxa, "Scribes, Mouthpieces Draw Sevareid's Ire," *Washington Post Magazine*, August 17, 1980, p. 2.

140. Spoken in a television interview with Charlie Rose that aired on June 1, 1993.

141. *New York Times*, May 28, 1993, p. Y15. For other discussions of the growing negativism on the part of the media, see Kenneth T. Walsh, *Feeding the Beast* (New York: Random House, 1996), chap. 20; David Paletz and Robert Entman, *Media Power Politics* (New York: Free Press, 1981), pp. 54–78; Austin Ranney, *Channels of Power* (Washington, D.C.: American Enterprise Institute, 1983), pp. 58–63, p. 179; Edwin Diamond, "From Patriotism to Skepticism: How TV Reporting Has Changed," *TV Guide* 30 (August 7, 1982), 5–8; Daniel Moynihan, "The President and the Press," in Rexford Tugwell and Thomas Cronin, eds., *The Presidency Reappraised* (New York: Praeger, 1974), pp. 148–67.

142. Grossman and Rourke, "Media and the Presidency," 468, 469.

143. Michael J. Robinson and Margaret A. Sheehan, *Over the Wire and on TV* (New York: Russell Sage Foundation, 1983), p. 103.

144. Hedrick Smith, *The Power Game* (New York: Random House, 1988), pp. 399–401; Grossman and Kumar, *Portraying the President*, pp. 306, 315, 324; Austin Ranney, *Channels of Power* (New York: Basic Books, 1983), p. 78.

145. Quoted in Robinson and Sheehan, *Over the Wire and on TV*, p. 201.

146. John W. Kingdon, *Agendas, Alternatives and Public Policy* (Boston: Little Brown, 1984), p. 62; Robert M. Entman, *Democracy Without Citizens* (New York: Oxford University Press, 1989), p. 69; Grossman and Kumar, *Portraying the President*, pp. 316, 317; and Brigitte Nacos, *The Press, Presidents and Crises* (New York: Columbia University Press, 1990), p. 183.

147. Grossman and Kumar, *Portraying the President*, p. 306; Entman, *Democracy Without Citizens*, pp. 76, 77.

148. Richard L. Rubin, *Press, Party and Presidency* (New York: Norton, 1981), p. 168; Grossman and Kumar, *Portraying the President*, p. 270; Benjamin Page, Robert Shapiro, and Glen R. Dempsey, "What Moves Public Opinion," *American Political Science Review* 81 (1987), 23–44; Stephen Hess, *Washington Reporters* (Washington, D.C.: Brookings Institution, 1981), pp. 130–31.

149. Brace and Hinckley, *Follow the Leader*, p. 166.

150. David L. Paletz and Robert M. Entman, *Media, Power, Politics* (New York: Free Press, 1981), p. 78; Roderick Hart, *The Sound of Leadership* (Chicago: University of Chicago Press, 1987), p. 124; and Grossman and Kumar, *Portraying the President*, p. 301.

151. On this point, see James Fallows, *Breaking the News: How the Media Undermine American Democracy* (New York: Pantheon Books, 1996), pp. 202, 203.

152. Hedrick Smith, *The Power Game* (New York: Random House, 1988), p. 406, 409; Mark Hertsgaard, *On Bended Knee* (New York: Farrar, Straus & Giroux, 1988), pp. 47, 37; Bradley H. Patterson, Jr., *The Ring of Power* (New York: Basic Books, 1988), p. 185.

153. Sidney Blumenthal, "The Syndicated Presidency," *The New Yorker*, April 5, 1993, p. 44.

154. Ibid., p. 42.

155. "Public Opinion and Demographic Report," *American Enterprise* 5 (January/February, 1994), p. 82.

156. *New York Times*, June 17, 1993, p. A11.

157. Califano, *Presidential Nation*, p. 102.

158. Daniel Moynihan, *Coping: On the Practice of Government* (New York: Random House, 1973), p. 337.

The President and the Bureaucracy

Although the president is admittedly the most important figure in the executive branch, he is by no means its sole member. The executive is composed of fourteen separate departments (see Table 5-1) and some 140 separate agencies, which together employ 2.8 million civilians. As such, it constitutes the largest and most complex entity in the federal government. Its size is a function of its responsibilities in the governmental process. These responsibilities include administering a myriad of federal programs—currently about 1,400 in number—that have an impact upon nearly every aspect of our national life. This function takes on added significance since the legislation enacting these programs is often written in rather general language. Consequently, the bureaucracy can exercise considerable discretion in deciding how such programs should be implemented. In addition to being an implementer of legislation, the bureaucracy is also a proposer. Indeed, most of the legislation annually submitted to Congress by the president is planned and drafted by the various departments and agencies in the executive branch. Finally, the bureaucracy also functions as a provider of information to both the president and the Congress. Its constant involvement in the day-to-day administration of federal programs, its abundance of trained experts in all policy areas, and its formidable capacity for data collection, all provide the bureaucracy with an unequaled capacity to inform decision makers.

As noted in Chapter 3, the president experiences considerable frustration in dealing with Congress. This is understandable, for the separation of powers and checks and balances serve to encourage a certain degree of antagonism. Each branch is organically distinct from the other, each exercises powers that can frustrate the will of the other, and each is elected by different constituencies and thus is subject to different pressures and expectations. On the other hand, the bureaucracy and the president are both members of the same branch of government. And even more important, it is the president who sits at the head of it. Thus, one might expect the president to encounter little difficulty in gaining the cooperation of those under him. Such an

TABLE 5-1   Executive Departments and Civilian Employees, 1998

Departments	Civilian Employees
Agriculture	94,169
Commerce	37,111
Defense	726,811
Education	4,637
Energy	16,292
Health and Human Services	59,046
Housing and Urban Development	9,849
Interior	66,240
Justice	118,972
Labor	15,738
State	24,412
Transportation	63,839
Treasury	158,447
Veterans Affairs	242,027

Source: Figures provided to author by the Work Force Analysis and Statistics Division of the Office of Personnel Management.

expectation would not be grounded in fact, however. Indeed, all of our more recent presidents have attested to the resistance they encountered from this vast bureaucracy over which they preside.

> The Treasury is so large and far-flung and ingrained in its practices that I find it almost impossible to get the action and results I want even with Henry [Morgenthau] there. But the Treasury is not to be compared with the State Department. You should go through the experience of trying to get any changes in the thinking, policy and action of the career diplomats and then you'd know what a real problem was. But the Treasury and State Department put together are nothing compared with the N-A-V-Y. The admirals are really something to cope with—and I should know. To change anything in the N-A-V-Y is like punching a feather bed. You punch it with your right and you punch it with your left until you are finally exhausted, and then you find the damn bed just as you left it before you started punching.
>
> Franklin Roosevelt

> I thought I was the President, but when it comes to these bureaucracies, I can't make them do a damn thing.
>
> Harry Truman

> Yea. One of the reasons, George, that you got to act on that SBA (Small Business Administration) guy—I don't care if he's a guy with eighteen kids—is that we have no discipline in this bureaucracy. We never fire anybody. We never reprimand anybody. We never demote anybody. We always promote the sons-of-bitches that kick us in the ass. That's true in the State Department. It's true in HEW. It's true in OMB, and true for ourselves, and it's got to stop. This fellow deliberately did not—I read the memorandum— he did not carry out an order I personally gave. I wrote the order out [unintelligible]. And the son-of-a-bitch did not do it. Now, I don't care what he is. Get him out of there.
>
> Richard Nixon

Before I became president, I realized and was warned that dealing with the federal bureaucracy would be one of the worst problems I would have to face. It has been even worse than I had anticipated.

Jimmy Carter

Although these remarks serve to highlight his sense of impotence in dealing with the bureaucracy, the president does have ways of exercising a measure of control over it. These include the power of *appointment,* the power to *reorganize the executive branch,* and the use of a coordinating procedure known as *central clearance.* As we shall see, however, these instruments of leverage are not absolute. Some are subject to constitutional, statutory, and political limitations. Moreover, none of these instruments is exercised in a vacuum, for the bureaucracy also has resources of its own, such as *expertise, permanence, and alliances* in and outside government, all of which may be used in an effort to countervail the resources of the president. To the extent that the bureaucracy is able to do so successfully, the president is precluded from being the master of his own house.

THE POWER OF APPOINTMENT

Kinds of Choices

Quite obviously, a president is not able to administer and supervise the operations of the executive branch by himself. Thus, he chooses what he believes to be a group of competent administrators to assist him in this task. These political appointees include department heads and those serving immediately under them, the members of independent agencies and regulatory commissions, and some bureau chiefs. While the power to fill these upper-level positions in the bureaucracy is surely an important one, it is also subject to several limitations. For one thing, presidents may not always be able to get the people they want. Some individuals do not choose to leave a high-paying job in the private sector to take a government job at much lower pay. Others may not be attracted to the particular position being offered. For example, Reagan's top choices to head the Department of Energy and Department of Education were, respectively, John Connally and Thomas Sowell.[1] Not finding the positions sufficiently enticing, both declined the offer. Still others are discouraged from accepting governent positions because of the stringent requirements contained in the Ethics in Government Act. Passed in 1978, this act requires cabinet officers and other top officials to disclose their income, liabilities, and assets; dispose of any holdings or debts that might be affected by their decisions in government; and refrain from having any dealings with a department or agency for at least one year after leaving it. (In connection with this last requirement, President Clinton required his appointees to sever all ties to a department or agency for five years). Clifford Hansen, for example, was forced to turn down the offer to serve as Reagan's secretary of the interior because he could not afford to comply with the second provision of the Ethics in Government Act. The Interior Department had granted Hansen's family a permit to graze their cattle in the Grand Teton National Park. Had he and his family surrendered the permit, they would have been put out of business. The husband of another prospective appointee had a small interest in a trust with holdings that could have represented a potential conflict of interest. The candidate was forced to withdraw even though neither she nor her husband had any control over the holdings.[2] President Bush's personnel office had to talk with nearly a dozen aerospace executives before they finally found one willing to serve as administrator of NASA. The others concluded that the divestments they would be required to make constituted too great a financial sacrifice.[3]

In filling top government positions, the president must take into account views other than his own. The Senate, for instance, has the constitutional responsibility for approving or rejecting the president's nominees to these posts. Accordingly, he is not likely to nominate an individual who enjoys little support among the Senate membership, for failure to win their approval would prove embarrassing to him and his nominee. Sometimes, of course, presidents will miscalculate, as Jimmy Carter did when he was forced to withdraw the nomination of Theodore Sorensen to be director of the Central Intelligence Agency. In this particular case, Carter's staff had apparently failed to gauge the degree of opposition to Sorensen in both the liberal and conservative wings of the Senate. In 1993, Clinton was likewise forced to withdraw the nomination of Lani Guinier to head the Justice Department's Civil Rights Division when it became clear that some of her academic writings contained ideas unacceptable to a considerable number of senators.

Various publics may also take a keen interest in a president's prospective appointment to a particular position, and their views cannot be easily ignored. It would be politically unwise, for example, for a president to nominate as secretary of labor an individual who was thoroughly unacceptable to the major unions. Similarly, he would be reluctant to fill the position of secretary of the treasury with an individual who did not enjoy the confidence of the business and financial interests in the country. It was for this reason that Clinton turned down the bid of his close friend Robert Reich to head the Treasury Department, placing him instead in the top position at the Department of Labor.

Number of Choices

The limitations on the presidential appointment power extend not only to the kinds of choices a president is able to make but also to the number of people he can appoint. In actuality, he has effective control over some 3,430 full- and part-time positions in the bureaucracy. The occupants of these positions serve at the pleasure of the president, which means they are subject to removal at his discretion. His right to do so was established by a Supreme Court ruling in the case of *Myers v. United States* (1926), and, as we shall see later, it has been modified only slightly since then. The remaining positions in the executive branch, however, are held by career civil servants, who are not appointed by the president but rather are selected in accordance with standards of merit determined by the Office of Personnel Management. Nor are they subject to removal by him except for malfeasance, neglect of duty, or inefficiency. Moreover, as we shall see shortly, prior to 1978 not only were the removal procedures extremely cumbersome, but presidents were also handicapped by their inability to use salary adjustments as a means of reward and punishment.

Although most career civil servants do not have policymaking responsibilities, approximately 125,000 have at least some, and an additional 7,000 have considerable responsibilities in this area. These individuals constitute part of the permanent government. They remain in their jobs while administrations come and go, and consequently their loyalties are likely to lie with their particular department or agency rather than with any given president. They are not likely to react favorably to presidential policies that seek to alter long-established agency procedures or that adversely affect the programs their agencies administer. Since these high-level career bureaucrats are charged with actual implementation of a president's policies, they may use their positions to frustrate rather than facilitate his wishes. Such resistance may take the form of delaying tactics, complying with the letter but not the spirit of a presidential policy, or failing to pass along an order received from above. Other tactics of resistance include "leaking" embarrassing information to the press and stirring up opposition to presidential policies among members of Congress and interest groups.

Because the major expansions in the bureaucracy have occurred as a result of massive social programs enacted under Democratic administrations, Republican presidents have long suspected that the career bureaucracy manifests a pronounced Democratic bias. Such suspicions are not entirely without foundation. Indeed, research undertaken on some eighteen government agencies found that among supergrade career bureaucrats working in these agencies, 17 percent classified themselves as Republicans, 47 percent as Democrats, and 36 percent as independents. And even those classifying themselves as independents exhibited attitudes that were more often characteristic of Democrats than Republicans. Furthermore, 79 percent of these high-level career civil servants favored maintaining or increasing the current level of government-provided services.[4] A still more recent study of 200 top-level bureaucrats further reinforces these findings. In addition to revealing that these individuals were typically "liberal reformist" in their attitudes, it found that a substantial majority of them had voted for the Democratic presidential candidate in each of the elections held from 1968 through 1976. In 1980, Reagan garnered only 36 percent of their vote, while 45 percent went to Carter and 18 percent to the independent candidacy of liberal Republican John Anderson.[5]

Although the president lacks authority to fill positions in the career bureaucracy, thanks to the Civil Service Reform Act of 1978 he now enjoys greater leverage over them than he once did. Proposed by President Carter, this legislation strengthens a president's hand in several respects. For one thing, it created a Senior Executive Service out of the 8,500 or so top administrative positions (grades 16, 17, and 18) in the government. The members of the Senior Executive Service can be moved within and between agencies, depending on where the administration thinks their talents are most needed. As one federal personnel administrator has pointed out, this flexibility is of considerable significance: "The new administration can move in somebody to replace a person who's resisting a new policy. And just the knowledge that you can be transferred—common sense tells you that people are going to do less blocking if they know that."[6] This transfer procedure is subject to certain limitations, however. While members of the Senior Executive Service can be moved at will *within* an agency, they cannot be transferred from one agency to another for at least 120 days after a president has taken office. Nor, theoretically, can such transfers be motivated by personal or political favoritism. In this connection, the president of the American Federation of Government Employees decided to provide the Clinton administration with a list of those career executives not fully supportive of Clinton policies so that the second-term transition team could move or transfer them. When the Senior Executives Association got wind of this plan, they asked the administration to refuse any such list. In a letter of reply the Clinton White House noted: "This administration does not request or make use of information on federal employees' support or non-support of agency missions for reassignment purposes. . . . The use of such information as a basis for personnel actions is expressly prohibited."

The Civil Service Reform Act also changed the criteria by which these top administrators receive salary increases. In the past, pay raises were exclusively a function of inflation and length of service, a practice that provided administrators with little incentive to improve performance. Under the new act, however, these automatic pay increases were replaced by a salary bonus system based upon performance. The bonuses do not become a permanent part of an administrator's base salary, but rather are a one-time payment. The act originally provided that such bonuses could not exceed 20 percent of an individual's base pay, but Congress has since lowered the percentage to 10. The act also provided for special presidential awards of $10,000 and $20,000 to those administrators whose performance has been truly exceptional over an extended period of time. The criteria for salary increases have also been changed for those occupying the 125,000 or so middle-management positions immediately below the Senior Executive Service. Rather than having their pay increases determined by inflation and length of service, these managers now receive only 50 percent of the increase due them for inflation, while the remainder is based upon job performance.

The Civil Service Reform Act also streamlined the procedures for the removal of incompetent and recalcitrant bureaucrats. Under former procedures, civil servants faced with removal could first seek redress through a review process established within their own agency. If they were not happy with the result, they could then go to the Civil Service Commission, which appointed an appeals officer to review the case. If dissatisfied with the finding of the appeals officer, they could take their case to the Appeals Review Board, which was directly responsible to the Civil Service Commission. If unhappy with the verdict of the Review Board, they could still make one final appeal to the Civil Service Commission itself. Since this lengthy appeals process often consumed up to three years, rather than seeking to remove employees, superiors would more likely try to get rid of them by transfer or even promotion. Not only was the removal process unduly cumbersome, but it also placed the Civil Service Commission in a conflict of interest, for the commission was charged with protecting federal employees on the one hand and promoting the efficient management of federal personnel on the other.

To overcome these problems, the Reform Act abolished the Civil Service Commission and replaced it with two new entities: (1) the Office of Personnel Management, charged with such responsibilities as administering Civil Service exams and making policy concerning salaries and benefits, and (2) the Merit System Protection Board, consisting of three members appointed by the president and confirmed by the Senate to serve staggered seven-year terms. The Merit System Protection Board has final authority to rule on recommended firings. Thus, an employee faced with removal now submits the case to a review process within his or her own agency. If dissatisfied with the outcome, the only other avenue of appeal is the Merit System Protection Board. To ensure protection of federal employees who "blow the whistle" on questionable practices in the bureaucracy, the act also provides that a special counsel be appointed to the board who is responsible for prosecuting political abuses and violations of the merit system.

Federal Regulatory Agencies

Within the executive branch several agencies are charged with the responsibility of regulating various aspects of our national life. The first of these, the recently abolished Interstate Commerce Commission, was created by Congress in 1887. These agencies, of which there are currently some twenty-three, establish and administer regulations as well as adjudicate disputes in such areas as communications, transportation, energy, finance, federal elections, and labor relations. The Civil Aeronautics Board, for example, regulates the air routes and safety standards of the airlines, and the Federal Maritime Commission performs similar regulatory functions for the shipping industry.

Although the president is vested with the power to appoint the members of these important regulatory agencies, this power is once again circumscribed in a variety of ways. In the first place, the terms of service in these agencies range from a minimum of three years to a maximum of fourteen. Moreover, the terms within each of the agencies are staggered. Both of these factors ensure that when a new president takes office, he will find many of the positions in the regulatory agencies held by individuals who were appointed by his predecessor. Of course, if a president is fortunate enough to serve two terms, his impact upon the regulatory agencies will be greater. During his five and a half years in office, for example, Richard Nixon was able to name every member in eight of the twelve agencies.[7]

Even when a president has the opportunity to fill vacancies, however, he is still constrained by the requirement that nearly all agencies must reflect some kind of partisan balance. Moreover, agency members usually assume a highly independent posture once they have been appointed. In the early 1960s, for example, the clearly stated position of the White House was that competition in the railroad and airline industries ought to be increased, yet the Civil Aeronautics Board and the Interstate Commerce Commission went ahead and approved railroad and airline mergers that served to reduce competition.[8] Lyndon Johnson likewise felt the sting of agency independence in 1965 when the Federal Reserve Board chairman, William MacChesney Martin, increased the discount rate over strong objections from the president. The president's irritation was all the greater because he had not only reappointed Martin to another fourteen-year term on the board but had also designated him as chairperson.

The independence of agency members is encouraged by two factors—first, the rather lengthy terms that characterize most agency positions, and second, the fact that members of the federal regulatory agencies do not serve at the pleasure of the president and thus cannot be arbitrarily removed by him. The basis for this limitation on the president's power was a ruling by the Supreme Court in the case of *Humphrey's Executor v. United States* (1935). In 1931, President Hoover reappointed William Humphrey to another seven-year term on the Federal Trade Commission (FTC). Shortly after becoming president, however, Franklin Roosevelt sought to remove Humphrey on grounds that the goals of his administration could best be served by allowing the president to pick the membership of the FTC. Roosevelt's reasons were in fact purely political, for he did not want a man of Humphrey's conservative views serving on the commission. The Court ruled that Congress had the right to establish agencies independent of executive control, and in this case the statute establishing the Federal Trade Commission had indeed specified that its members could not be removed except for malfeasance, neglect of duty, or inefficiency. Thus, the president's dismissal of Humphrey for political reasons was in violation of the law.[9] The scope of the president's removal power became an issue once again in the fifties, when President Eisenhower removed an individual from the War Claims Commission solely for political reasons. In this case, however, the circumstances were different because the statute creating the War Claims Commission did not specify the grounds for removing its members. The Supreme Court nevertheless ruled that since the War Claims Commission performed a judicial rather than an executive function, the president had no authority to remove its members (*Wiener v. United States,* 1958).[10] The independent character of the regulatory agencies continues to be a subject of some controversy. Those who support their current structure point out that the lengthy terms of service not only increase the expertise of agency members but also provide for continuity in policy. In addition, they argue that decision making by these bodies "provides both a barrier to arbitrary or capricious actions and a source of decisions based on different points of view and experience."[11] Finally, given the powerful political influence of the industries regulated by these agencies, it is absolutely essential that an agency be insulated from partisan influences. Critics are quick to point out, however, that agency independence often results in a lack of policy coordination between the president and the agencies on important economic matters. Furthermore, since many of the members in these agencies are in fact recruited from the industries that the agencies are supposed to regulate, the claim to agency impartiality is more fiction than fact. This charge was confirmed by a two-year congressional investigation (1975 to 1976) of nine regulatory agencies, which concluded that agency commitment to the interests of the regulated industries took precedence over their commitment to the public interest.[12]

Political Appointees: The Problem of "Going Native"

Thus far, our discussion has noted that the president's appointment power is limited by the availability of people willing to serve, by the acceptability of his nominees to groups in and outside government, by the relatively small number of people he is able to place in the bureaucracy, and by the restrictions upon his ability to remove some of them once they get there. His problems do not end here, however, for even those who serve at the pleasure of the president may not always be thoroughly supportive of his policies. Speaking to this point, Vice President Charles Dawes once remarked that "cabinet members are the natural enemies of the President."[13] To be sure, this remark is an exaggeration, but like all overstatements there is a kernel of truth in it. Even though the president's political appointees may assume their positions with every intention of expediting his policy goals, they soon discover that they must give an attentive ear to voices besides that of the president. These voices emanate from three major constituencies: the *career bureaucrats* within their own department, *members of Congress,* and various *organized interests* within society. Overresponsiveness to these groups by cabinet and subcabinet officials has frequently prompted White House aides to charge that cabinet officials "go off and marry the natives." We shall now consider why this happens.

As was noted earlier in this chapter, the loyalties of career bureaucrats tend to lie with the agency or department in which they work. Thus, they are not likely to be receptive to presidential policies that threaten their jobs or the agency's programs or organizational structure. Moreover, they will make every effort to impress their own views upon the head of their department or agency. And, as one former White House aide notes, they are often successful.

> The major problem is the lack of any identification [on their part] with the president's program priorities. At State they try to humor the president but hope he will not interfere in their complex matters and responsibilities. It is equally a problem with civil servants and Cabinet types. It is amazing how soon the Cabinet people get captured by the permanent staffs. Secretary ———— under Nixon, for example, was captured within days . . . and Nixon's staff didn't even try to improve things. They just assumed there was a great problem. Personally, I think you can't expect too much from the bureaucracy. It is too much to expect that they will see things the president's way.[14]

Given the formidable administrative task cabinet secretaries face, it is not surprising that they and their assistant secretaries come to rely heavily upon the career bureaucracy within their departments. Using the Department of Commerce as an example—and it is a relatively small department—the secretary of commerce is ultimately responsible for the actions of the following subunits within his or her department: Business and Defense Services Administration, Maritime Administration, Economic Development Administration, Environmental Services Administration, Office of Business and Economics, Office of Field Services, Bureau of the Census, Bureau of International Commerce, National Bureau of Standards, and the United States Travel Agency. And if the size and complexity of a department were not burden enough, a manager's task is further complicated by the fact that most of his or her time must be spent on other matters: "He spends 30 to 40 percent of his time testifying or meeting with Congress; the next block of his time meeting with constituency groups, speechmaking, etc.; the next block of time in committees—that leaves him about 10 percent of his time to devote to departmental matters if he's interested in doing so."[15]

To make matters worse, cabinet appointees and their assistant secretaries sometimes have very little expertise in the substantive concerns of their department. Furthermore, they are not likely to remain in their positions long enough to develop this expertise nor, for that matter, long enough to thoroughly grasp the internal operations of their department. For those cabinet members serving from 1952 to 1984, for example, the average tenure was only 2.5 years.[16] Similarly, a study made of undersecretaries and assistant secretaries during the Kennedy and Johnson administrations and the first four years of Nixon's revealed that nearly one-fifth served under twelve months and less than half served more than two years.[17] Consequently, cabinet secretaries and their assistants are forced to rely heavily upon the career bureaucrats, whose customarily long service in a department has provided them with a sophisticated understanding of the policy issues confronting it, as well as a thorough mastery of the department's internal operations.

The head of a department or agency must also be attentive to the views of Congress, especially those congressional committees having oversight responsibilities for that department. Committee judgments as to what programs and goals the department should pursue may not always accord with the president's. Moreover, because these committees are charged with authorizing programs and recommending appropriations for the departments, their policy preferences cannot easily be dismissed.

Finally, organized interests within the society constitute still another constituency requiring the attention of a cabinet secretary. Each of the domestic departments within the executive branch (Agriculture, Education, Energy, Interior, Labor, Commerce, Transportation, Health and Human Services, Housing and Urban Development, Veterans Affairs) provides services to one or more groups in the population. Quite understandably, these groups expect a department head to be an advocate for their own interests. Their expectations take on added importance because they are likely to have powerful support within Congress. Consequently, a cabinet secretary who chooses to ignore their pleas is likely to encounter rough going.

At the start of his second term, for example, President Nixon appointed the determined and conservative Caspar Weinberger to replace Elliot Richardson as secretary of what was then the Department of Health, Education and Welfare (HEW). Weinberger's marching orders were to cut back, as well as cut out, many of the expensive social service programs being administered by HEW. The new secretary soon made it clear that he was opposed to several of the department's goals and programs. Among them were higher Social Security payments; several forms of aid to elementary schools; federal grants used to train medical researchers, social workers, and educators; and direct programs of federal medical care.[18] His statements sparked a storm of opposition from medical school deans, college presidents, high school principals, social scientists, and other professional groups long served by these programs. Although Weinberger was not powerless to act, his actions were largely confined to what administrative discretion would permit, such as the tightening of eligibility requirements for federal grants and impounding a portion of the funds appropriated for certain programs (most of these impoundments were successfully challenged in the courts, however). But most of the cutbacks he sought to make required congressional approval, and Congress refused to cooperate. Indeed, even when Weinberger attempted to use his administrative authority to close eight Public Health Service hospitals, Congress promptly passed legislation revoking such authority. The opposition of both organized interests and their supporters in Congress ultimately forced Weinberger to abandon many of his original goals and turn instead to a policy of conciliation. He announced that HEW would increase aid to elementary and secondary schools by $500 million. An expensive vocational rehabilitation program opposed by the Nixon administration earlier in the year was soon signed into law by the president. In addition, HEW was now at work on a national health insurance plan, which was considerably more generous than the one earlier proposed by the Nixon administration. The secretary also announced that he was interested in lightening the Social Security tax burden on the poor. These reversals in position prompted one close observer of HEW affairs to comment that "they do show that even the most convinced conservative finds HEW's built-in pressures for activism hard to resist and the support of his constituents important, if not indispensable."[19]

Department and agency heads must thus perform a delicate balancing act among a variety of constituencies, only one of whom is the president. Of course, when and if a president concludes that the balancing is frustrating his own policy goals, he can remove his political appointees. But even here he does not have a completely free hand, for what he can do legally he may not be able to do politically. Some of his political appointees may be astute enough to build up a strong base of support within Congress as well as among various elements of the public. Accordingly, the president may incur high political costs if he removes them. For example, on numerous occasions Franklin Roosevelt's secretary of commerce adopted policy positions that were in direct conflict with the president's. Yet the secretary's excellent rapport with Congress and his strong support among powerful interests in the business community led Roosevelt to conclude that he stood to lose more by firing him than by keeping him on.[20]

J. Edgar Hoover is perhaps the classic example of a political appointee whose overwhelming support in and outside government rendered him invulnerable to presidential removal. Indeed, he was customarily the first individual to be reappointed by a succession of newly elected presidents. Although of late the reputation of the Federal Bureau of Investigation has been tarnished, for most of Hoover's long tenure as director the bureau enjoyed a reputation as the most professional law enforcement agency in the world. It was this reputation, established under his leadership, that afforded Hoover the ability to engage in independent political actions that presidents felt compelled to tolerate. In 1964, for example, the United States and the Soviet Union signed a consular treaty, which failed to receive Senate approval until three years later. One of the major obstacles to immediate ratification was none other than Mr. Hoover. Without consulting either his immediate superior in the Justice Department (the attorney general) or the president of the United States, the director appeared before a congressional committee and warned them that approval of the treaty would allow the Soviet Union to expand their intelligence operations in the United States. In September 1966, Secretary of State Rusk released his correspondence with Hoover, which revealed the director's refusal to entertain the secretary's request that he withdraw his opposition to the treaty. An editorial in the *New York Times* noted the significance of this exchange of letters.

> There can be few, if any, precedents for the spectacle that correspondence presents: the Secretary of State, in effect, asking a Federal police official of sub-Cabinet rank to stop blocking United States foreign policy, and then receiving a reply so cryptic and ungracious that it can only further encourage opponents of the Administration's policy. It is a reminder of the magnitude of Mr. Hoover's power with implications that go far beyond the immediate issue.[21]

Not all political appointees have enjoyed a base of support as broad as Hoover's, however. President Ford's dismissal of Defense Secretary James Schlesinger produced only minimal repercussions, for the secretary's aloof and sometimes arrogant style had not endeared him to very many members of Congress. Likewise, when Interior Secretary Hickel openly criticized President Nixon's administrative style, his swift removal was assured by the fact that he lacked any substantial following either in or outside government.

Political Appointees: The Problem of Getting Them in Place

As newly elected presidents seek to take control of the executive branch, it is quite obviously to their advantage to have their political appointees in place as quickly as possible. This goal is, unfortunately, becoming more and more difficult to achieve. Indeed, the time that elapses from the nomination announcement to completion of confirmation has been steadily increasing (see Figure 5-1).

There are several reasons for these delays. First, presidents have many more jobs to fill now. Scholar Paul Light notes that while Kennedy had to find appointees for only six layers in the bureaucracy, Clinton had to do so for fifteen layers.[22] Beyond this, the post-Watergate mentality has caused senators to approach the

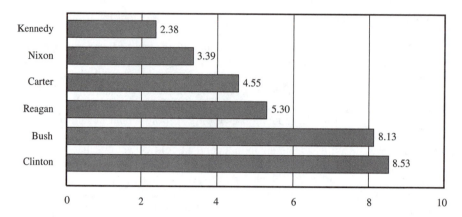

FIGURE 5-1   Average Months from Inauguration to Senate Confirmation, Initial Presidential Appointees

Source: "Obstacle Course: The Report of the Twentieth Century Fund Task Force on the Presidential Appointment Process" (New York: Twentieth Century Fund, 1996), p. 72.

confirmation process more carefully than used to be the case. Clinton, for example, was forced to withdraw the names of several nominees for high-profile positions in his administration. These included two individuals (Zoe Baird, Kimb Wood) nominated for attorney general, one (Lani Guinier) for assistant attorney general, and his nominees for CIA director (Anthony Lake), surgeon general (Henry Foster), and Air Force secretary (Daryl Jones). Third, given the tendency of political appointees to "go native" on the president, some presidents (Reagan and Clinton) have insisted that the White House play a much more active role in the selection of subcabinet appointees, rather than leaving those personnel decisions in the hands of department heads. Add to these factors the new ethics requirements that have substantially increased the paperwork and background checks that must be done on prospective appointees. Finally, in the case of Clinton at least, the appointments process was protracted even further by his strong commitment to achieve ethnic, racial, and geographical balance in the people he chose.

REORGANIZATION

Although the Constitution accords to Congress the responsibility for establishing, altering, or abolishing departments and agencies in the executive branch, for some time now the primary initiative in this area has rested with the president. The impetus for this change came during the presidency of Franklin Roosevelt. Concerned about the ability of the executive branch to function efficiently, Roosevelt created the Committee on Administrative Management, which has since come to be known as the Brownlow Committee. Acting upon the Brownlow Committee's recommendation that sound management required substantial reorganizations within the executive branch, Congress passed the Reorganization Act of 1939. This act empowered the president to transfer, abolish, or consolidate government agencies unless such plans were vetoed by *both* houses of Congress within *sixty days* after they were submitted to it. Following the substantial increase in the size of the bureaucracy during the New Deal and the Second World War, another study of the executive branch was commissioned under the chairmanship of former President Hoover. The first Hoover Commission's recommendations culminated in congressional passage of the Reorganization Act of 1949, which not only gave the president authority to reorganize government agencies but also granted him the power to create cabinet-level departments. Congress still maintained its ultimate control over executive reorganization, however, by stipulating that any reorganization plan could be killed if *either* house vetoed it within sixty days after it was submitted. The act has since been renewed periodically by Congress with only two major changes. The first came in 1964 when Congress amended it to prevent the president from using the reorganization power to create or abolish departments. The second change was made in the aftermath of the Supreme Court's 1983 decision declaring the legislative veto unconstitutional. No longer may a president's reorganization plan be vetoed by either house of Congress. Instead, a resolution of disapproval must be passed by both houses and then sent to the president for his signature or veto. Should the president choose to veto the resolution, Congress may override it with a two-thirds vote in both houses.

The reorganization initiative can be of great assistance to a president.[23] For example, by bringing under the control of one agency a variety of programs that were formerly administered by several agencies, he can achieve greater coordination over a particular policy area, eliminate possible duplication of effort, and more clearly establish lines of authority. These reasons undoubtedly accounted for President Carter's desire to combine all federal energy programs under one newly created Department of Energy. The reorganization initiative can also assist a president in other ways. If he has just implemented a new program and fears that it may become bogged down in the bureaucratic intransigence of an already existing agency, he may create a new one. That is, in part, why Lyndon Johnson decided to set up a special agency, the Office of Economic Opportunity, to administer many of his Great Society programs and—to highlight its importance—located it in the White House. Of course, reorganization may be used to downgrade as well as elevate the importance of an agency and its programs. Richard Nixon had little use for many of President Johnson's expensive social programs and thus moved the Office of Economic Opportunity out of the White House and into the large and cumbersome Department of Health, Education and Welfare. Finally, if an agency in a given department is proving resistant to presidential policies, the president may seek to transfer its functions to a department that is more controllable. That was the motivation behind President Nixon's unsuccessful attempt to eliminate the Interstate Commerce Commission and transfer its functions to the Department of Commerce.

On the Need to Reorganize

It is fair to say that the reorganization plans of recent presidents have been designed to bring greater coordination, accountability, and economy to the operations of the executive branch. Presidents have felt compelled to undertake such reorganizations because past decisions on where to locate new programs have not always been guided by a concern for efficient management.

The decisive factor in situating a new program in a particular department or agency often has little to do with rational concepts of management. One congressional committee may be considered more receptive to a proposed idea than another, or simply be less busy than another. One cabinet or agency head may have more influence with the President, the White House staff, or Congress; another may be more able as an administrator than those of his peers vying for the same program.[24]

These and other considerations have been responsible for locating programs and agencies in the most unexpected places. At various times in the past, for example, the Public Health Service, the Bureau of Narcotics, and the U.S. Coast Guard all came under the jurisdiction of the Treasury Department. Similarly, the government's current water-pollution control program is not to be found in the Department of Interior but rather in the Department of Health and Human Services. This kind of irrationality has, on occasion, made victims even of those who are closest to it. Thus, not long after Congress passed legislation permitting the president to declare certain areas of the country "wilderness areas," President Johnson decided he wanted to draw national attention to this project by making a public announcement of the first group of areas to be set aside. Accordingly, he instructed one of his aides to summon the secretary of the interior to the White House to brief members of the press on the project and announce the first selection of wilderness areas. After the press briefing, the president's aide received a phone call from Orville Freeman, the secretary of agriculture. With considerable irritation, Freeman inquired, "What in hell is going on over there? I just saw the wire service tickers saying that you and Udall briefed the press on the new wilderness areas. Wilderness areas fall within the jurisdiction of the Agriculture Department."[25] Yet neither the president of the United States, nor his aide, nor even the secretary of the interior was aware of this fact.

When functionally related programs are strung out over a variety of different departments and agencies, the president faces formidable difficulties in attempting to establish policy coordination and accountability. The following data should provide some appreciation of the problem: In 1977 nine different departments and twenty independent agencies administered programs related to education; seven departments and eight independent agencies dealt with health-related programs; three departments were involved in water resources; four agencies in two departments were involved in managing public lands; six agencies in three different departments were involved in federal recreation programs; seven agencies were involved in water and sewer systems; six departments were charged with compiling economic information; seven departments were involved in the area of international trade; seven departments and three independent agencies administered between twenty and thirty manpower programs.[26]

Difficulties of Reorganization

Recent presidents have commissioned groups of distinguished citizens to study the bureaucratic structure and come up with recommendations for making it more coherent and manageable. President Johnson established two task forces, with the first recommending the creation of a Department of Natural Resources and a Department of Housing and Community Development and the second calling for the establishment of a Department of Natural Resources and Development, a Department of Economic Affairs, and a Department of Social Services. Richard Nixon also established the

Advisory Council on Executive Organization, whose recommendations proved to be considerably more ambitious. Acting upon the belief that the federal government should be organized according to functions and goals rather than program, the council recommended retaining the departments of Justice, Defense, State, and the Treasury. At the same time, the remaining seven departments (Interior; Commerce; Labor; Agriculture; Transportation; Health, Education and Welfare; and Housing and Urban Development) were to be reorganized into the following four departments:

> *Department of Natural Resources*—land, recreation, water resources, energy and mineral resources, and marine resources.
>
> *Department of Human Resources*—health services, income maintenance and security, education, manpower, and social and rehabilitation services.
>
> *Department of Economic Development*—food and commodities, domestic and international commerce, science and technology, labor relations and standards, and statistical economic development.
>
> *Department of Community Development*—housing, community development, metropolitan development, and renewal development.[27]

Although some of the more modest recommendations of the Johnson and Nixon commissions have been approved by Congress, most of the far-reaching proposals outlined above have never been realized. To understand why this is so is to appreciate why the president's reorganization power is so severely limited.

Any time a president seeks to transfer, abolish, or consolidate government agencies, he is likely to face formidable opposition from three sources: those within the agency, those congressional committees exercising oversight over the agency, and finally, those clientele groups served by the agency. Lyndon Johnson's experience with the Maritime Administration illustrates the problem. One of his reorganization proposals called for combining this agency, along with several others, under what was to be a newly created Department of Transportation. This move seemed reasonable enough since the Maritime Administration was concerned with one form of transportation, namely, shipping. Opposition to this proposed change was not long in coming, however. Both organized labor and the shipping industry vigorously opposed the move and lobbied long and hard among members of Congress to defeat it. Their opposition was understandable. Such clientele groups have spent years establishing and cultivating relationships within an agency, and they do not want to see them disrupted by transferring the agency to another jurisdiction. Nor were they enamored of the prospect that their agency would now have to compete with several other agencies combined under the umbrella of the Department of Transportation. The move was also opposed by bureaucrats working for the Maritime Administration, because changing its jurisdiction could result in procedural and policy changes that might affect the nature of their jobs. The third major source of opposition came from the House Committee on Merchant Marine and Fisheries, which exercised oversight responsibilities over the Maritime Administration. Their objection stemmed from the fact that transferring the agency over to the Department of Transportation would take it out from under their committee's jurisdiction, thereby eliminating a major reason for the committee's existence. No committee's chairperson will support a proposal that will result in the liquidation of the committee's power base. Nor are other committee chairpersons likely to be receptive to such a proposal, as was made abundantly clear by the head of the House Committee on Merchant Marine and Fisheries during debate on the floor of the House: "If LBJ's transportation reorganization puts us out of business this year, then he may send up another proposal which will put your favorite committee out of business next year."[28] Ultimately the alliance of interest groups, bureaucrats, and legislators succeeded in handing President Johnson a resounding 260 to 117 defeat for his proposal in the House. Another of the president's proposals, combining the Departments of Labor and Commerce, faced a similar fate. In this case, however, opposition was so great in both the business and labor communities that the plan never even came to the floor of the House or the Senate for a vote.

Reorganizations that involve transferring or abolishing agencies are the hardest to bring off successfully. Once agencies are created and jurisdictions defined, a variety of interests develop a stake in maintaining things as they are. This is not to say that important reorganizations have never been realized, however. Among recent presidents, Eisenhower succeeded in creating the Department of Health, Education and Welfare, and Lyndon Johnson was able to get through Congress proposals establishing both a Department of Housing and Urban Development and a Department of Transportation. These plans succeeded in large part because committee jurisdictions were not altered by them. In the case of Housing and Urban Development, all of the agencies combined under it remained under the jurisdictions of the same congressional committees after the reorganization. Similarly, all but two of the agencies slated to be combined into the new Department of Transportation were to remain under the jurisdiction of the same congressional committees after the reorganization. The exceptions were the Maritime Administration and the Coast Guard. As noted earlier, the Maritime Administration ultimately was not incorporated into the Department of Transportation, in part because of strong objections from the House Committee on Merchant Marine and Fisheries. On the other hand, Congress did agree to move the Coast Guard, primarily because the Coast Guard wanted to be moved. But even though the lack of jurisdictional problems facilitated congresssional acceptance of Johnson's two reorganization plans, the job of gaining approval for them was not easy. In the words of Johnson's key aide on domestic matters, "The Transportation Department bill had been the toughest legislative fight of the 89th Congress."[29]

It is fair to say that Carter approached government reorganization with considerably more determination than any previous president. As a candidate he made it one of the cornerstones of his campaign, repeating time and again that he would reduce the number of government agencies and commissions from 1,900 to 200. Although he never even remotely approached this goal, he did undertake four *major* reorganizations of the federal bureaucracy. One called for reforms in the civil service system—a matter discussed earlier in this chapter. Of more immediate concern are the other three calling for the creation of a Department of Energy, a Department of Education, and a Department of Natural Resources.

Congress quickly approved Carter's proposal to consolidate the Federal Power Commission (FPC), Federal Energy Administration (FEA), and Energy Research and Development Administration (ERDA) under a Department of Energy. That this legislation sailed through Congress with relative ease is attributable to several factors. For one thing, the energy crisis had made it apparent to all concerned that a coordinated approach to this problem was essential. In addition, two of the agencies slated for consolidation, ERDA and FEA, had been viewed by Congress as only temporary at the time they were created. Third, since neither of these agencies had been in existence for more than three years, they had not yet built up a loyal clientele group. And last, all three agencies suffered from weak leadership and low morale. Consequently, they were in no position to make an effective challenge to Carter's consolidation effort.[30]

Although Congress also agreed to the creation of a Department of Education, President Carter ultimately received far less than he had requested. As originally submitted to Congress, the president's reorganization proposal specified that this new department was to house all education-related programs then in the Department of Health, Education and Welfare; the Department of Agriculture's school lunch, school breakfast, nutrition, and education programs; the Department of Housing and Urban Development's college housing program; the Department of Interior's Indian schools; the Department of Labor's education and training programs; the Defense Department's overseas schools; and certain science programs then being administered by the National Science Foundation. Numerous other programs that *ought* to have been incorporated into the new department were not even included in Carter's proposal because the administration thought they stood no chance of being approved by Congress. This strategic decision did not eliminate opposition to the president's plan, however. On the contrary, pressures from the bureaucracy, Congress, and clientele groups proved so great that the reorganization plan gained congressional approval only after Carter agreed to leave many of the programs right where they were. These included HEW's Head Start program, all the programs slated to be moved from the Department of Agriculture, the Department of the Interior's Indian schools, and the Department of Labor's education and training programs.[31]

Carter's plan to create a Department of Natural Resources met with even less success. Announced on March 1, 1979, this reorganization called for transferring the Forest Service from the Department of Agriculture and the National Oceanic and Atmospheric Administration from the Commerce Department. The reaction to this announcement was swift and intense. The forestry and home-building industries came out squarely against the plan and promptly mobilized their allies in Congress. The chairmen of the House and Senate committees with primary jurisdiction over the Forest Service stated that they would fight the reorganization plan every step of the way. Within the Forest Service itself, several key officials threatened to resign. Carter sympathizers within Congress also warned the president that if he pushed for this proposal, the resulting animosities could jeopardize the upcoming ratification of the SALT II treaty. Having finally concluded that the political costs would be too high, on May 15, 1979, the White House announced that it was abandoning the plan.[32]

In his campaign for the presidency, Ronald Reagan repeatedly inveighed against the growth of the federal government, and these attacks were frequently accompanied by a pledge to abolish the newly created Departments of Education and Energy. Once in office, he also added the Small Business Administration to the list, proposing, as several previous presidents had, that it be folded into the Commerce Department. In the final analysis, however, Reagan's ambitious reorganization plans failed to bear fruit. Terrence Bell, appointed to head the Department of Education and charged with carrying the fight for its abolition, soon became convinced that the department should be kept and made no secret of this belief in private conversations with members of Congress. Since this view was also shared by the educational establishment and most legislators, the administration was forced to shelve the plan.[33] The proposal to abolish the Department of Energy was likewise taken off the priority list. The administration thought it wise to continue the department long enough to reverse certain energy and environmental policies to which it was opposed; also the plan lacked the support of James McClure (R-Idaho), chairman of the Senate Energy Committee.[34] The administration did not fare any better when it went after a seemingly smaller fish, namely, the Small Business Administration. Although the president had been successful in reducing the agency's funding as part of the 1981 budget cuts, efforts in 1985 to eliminate the agency altogether were overwhelmed by the forces of Senate Small Business Committee Chairman Lowell Weicker (R-Conn.), small business lobbyists, and those within the agency itself.[35]

Reagan fared better with his second-term proposal calling for the elevation of the Veterans Administration to departmental status. This is not surprising, however. Veterans' organizations had long favored the change. Moreover, their clout with legislators, combined with the fact that no congressional committee jurisdictions would be altered, assured clear sailing through Congress.

The Clinton administration also tried its hand at reorganization but without much success. In an effort to reduce costs and increase efficiency, President Clinton charged his vice president with overseeing an exhaustive review of all government agencies. This initative, known as the "National Performance Review," culminated in some eight hundred recommendations, two of which entailed reorganizations. One called for transferring the law enforcement functions of the Drug Enforcement Administration (DEA) out of the Treasury Department and placing them under the supervision of the FBI in the Justice Department. This plan, however, was dropped two months after it was proposed, in the face of strong objections from Attorney General Janet Reno, officials within the DEA, and members of the House and Senate Judiciary committees. A second proposal recommended eliminating the Agriculture Department's Food Safety and Inspection Service, relocating this function in the Food and Drug Administration housed in the Department of Health and Human Services. This plan, too, appears to have died a quiet death. Not only did Clinton's own secretary of agriculture oppose having the program taken out of his department but, more important, so did members of the House and Senate Agriculture committees, who objected because moving the program from one department to another would take it out of their jurisdiction.[36]

A third Clinton reorganization initiative, unrelated to the National Performance Review, called for elevating the Environmental Protection Agency (EPA) to the status of a department. It too went down to defeat during Clinton's first year, clearing the Senate but not the House. There was little opposition to granting departmental status. On the contrary, the proposal has for some time commanded broad support within both Congress and the EPA, as well as among most environmental groups. The problem arose over efforts by some House members to attach to the bill amendments requiring the EPA to consider the economic costs that would be incurred by any of its proposed environmental regulations.[37]

The most extensive reorganization undertaken in the Clinton administration received its impetus more from Congress, and Senator Jesse Helms (R-N.C.) in particular, than from the White House. Helms, chairman of the Senate Foreign Relations Committee, favored abolishing the U.S. Information Agency (USIA), Arms Control and Disarmament Agency (ACDA), and the Agency for International Development (AID), and folding some of their programs into the State Department. He also let it be known that his cooperation on important administration foreign policy initiatives would be contingent upon the president's willingness to make these organizational changes in the foreign policy bureaucracy. Accordingly, the Clinton White House devised a plan that went a long way toward accommodating the senator from North

Carolina. It called for folding the USIA and ACDA into the State Department. AID, meanwhile, would retain its independent status, but its head would report to the secretary of state and a number of its administrative activities would be incorporated into the department. Personnel in all three agencies opposed the change, but they were not able to generate many allies elsewhere. Some relief agencies and foreign policy experts sympathized with their position, but others from these groups thought the reorganization plan had merit. In addition, congressional committees with jurisdiction over the agencies favored the move, as did Secretary of State Madeline Albright. Even the Clinton White House, though motivated in part by seeking to placate Senator Helms, believed that the plan would bring an end to managerial and administrative redundancies built into the foreign policy bureaucracy.[38]

 CENTRAL CLEARANCE

One of the most formidable instruments of presidential control over the bureaucracy is a procedure known as central clearance. Simply stated, it requires that all legislative proposals emanating from departments and agencies be cleared through the Office of Management and Budget, which is an administrative arm of the president. This procedure was begun in 1921, when President Coolidge issued a directive requiring all departments and agencies to clear their budget proposals with the Bureau of the Budget to ensure their compatibility with the president's own budget priorities. The clearing requirements became even more inclusive under Franklin Roosevelt, who insisted that not only budget proposals but all legislation coming from the bureaucracy must be subject to screening procedures. Subsequent presidents have followed suit. Given the volume of legislation coming out of the departments and agencies each year, the necessity for some coordinating mechanism seems clear. For example, the Department of Housing and Urban Development alone proposes approximately three hundred different bills annually.

In actuality, central clearance involves a series of clearing points. Following the annual request for budget proposals by the Office of Management and Budget, various agencies and bureaus within departments begin drafting legislative proposals. An agency proposal is then forwarded to the assistant secretary who has line responsibility over the agency. In consultation with the department's legislative counsel, the assistant secretary will decide which bills merit department support and recommend changes when necessary. The bills are then routinely sent to the head of the department, who is not likely to become directly involved unless the bill is of major importance or unless it has aroused controversy among the agencies within his department, in which case he will act as mediator. After clearance at the departmental level, a proposal will often undergo a form of interdepartmental clearance if its content will have an impact upon the concerns of one or more other departments. At this point, interdepartmental negotiating will take place, and wherever possible the necessary changes will be made in order to reflect the views and suggestions of these other departments.

The bill then moves to the central clearance point in the Office of Management and Budget (OMB). At this stage, OMB has several options open to it. First, it may give its approval, which may range from enthusiastic support to simply an acknowledgement that the bill is acceptable. Such varying degrees of support are to be expected, for even though a particular bill may not be in conflict with the president's program, it may not necessarily be at the top of the administration's list of priorities.

Thus, although the bill will be sent on to Congress, the president is not likely to work actively to secure its passage. A second course of action open to OMB is to return a legislative proposal to the department or agency with suggestions for changes. There then follows a process of negotiation between budget officials and the department in order to put the bill in a form acceptable to both. In some cases, the demand for changes may not come from OMB itself, but rather from other departments and agencies. Although these changes would normally be worked out at the interdepartmental clearing point, it is not always possible to reach an accommodation, and thus it falls to OMB to try to work out a settlement. The third option open to OMB is to return the proposal to a given department with a notation stating that it is simply not compatible with the president's program. Following such a rejection, the only option open to a department head in the past has been to make a direct appeal to the president. This approach has not proved very fruitful, however, for presidents have not been willing to undermine the credibility of OMB by frequently overruling it.

Since the early 1960s, White House staffs have become increasingly involved in the policymaking process. The net result of this development has been to reduce the role of OMB as the ultimate arbiter of the acceptability of a department's legislative proposals. As one government official notes, following a rejection of their proposals by OMB, departments are now taking their case to members of the White House staff with the hope of gaining a more favorable hearing: "There has got to be a way to go over OMB on a regular basis without going directly to the President. There is. That's the White House staff. Ted Sorensen and Joe Califano, in the Kennedy and Johnson administrations, respectively, were constantly available to mediate and arbitrate between the secretary of a department and the Director of the Budget."[39]

The End Run

Whether the final clearing point occurs at the level of OMB or the White House staff, rejection of some part or all of a department's proposal in theory means that it may not be submitted to Congress. In actuality, however, individuals within a department or agency will from time to time seek to reverse such a decision by making an end run around OMB and taking their case directly to Congress. Sometimes this ploy will have the tacit approval of a department head, and sometimes it will not. There is some risk, however, for the department that makes frequent use of this tactic may find OMB considerably less receptive to its future legislative proposals. For this reason, the end run usually involves working through informal channels. A department, for example, may enlist the support of its clientele groups, asking them to drum up support for the legislation among members of Congress. In addition, bureaucrats within the department may take advantage of their longtime contacts within Congress by paying them a private visit and pleading their case. Such efforts will often meet with a favorable reception, for departments and agencies take great pains to cultivate a good image in the minds of both Congress and the public. In 1972 alone, for example, departments and agencies spent $164 million on public relations, $37 million of which was spent by the Defense Department.[40] More important, departments attempt to ingratiate themselves with legislators by providing a variety of services and rewards. Requests for information are answered within twenty-four hours; drafting assistance is readily provided to a member of Congress who is sponsoring a bill of benefit to the department; speeches will be written for him or her upon request; federal facilities may be located in his or her district; transportation may be provided if he or she wishes to visit a federal installation at home or abroad.[41]

L. Mendel Rivers is perhaps the classic example of a congressman who benefited from such largess. During his long years of service on the House Armed Services Committee, part of which time as its chairman, Rivers proved to be a forceful and consistent supporter of a strong national defense. In appreciation of this support, the Defense Department made Rivers's congressional district the beneficiary of numerous federal facilities, including an Air Force base, an Army depot, a Marine Corps air station, an Air Force recreation center, a National Guard office, a Navy hospital, a radar station, an Air Force tank farm, and a national cemetery.[42] Needless to say, these and other rewards did not serve to diminish Mendel Rivers's enthusiasm for Defense Department programs.

The end-run strategy is used by the bureaucracy not only to gain favorable consideration of their own policy proposals but also to torpedo presidential policies they oppose. Kennedy's ultraconservative director of the Central Intelligence Agency, for example, happily lent members of his agency to the Senate Armed Services Committee in order to help conservative committee members make their case against the administration's proposed nuclear test ban treaty.[43]

Richard Nixon faced a similar problem with the commissioner of the Social Security Administration. According to one Nixon aide, "the President would make a policy and enunciate it but then Ball would go up to Congress, the doors to the committee room would close and he would say what he really thought. He was very persuasive. We couldn't have that."[44]

Determined department heads have tried to check this kind of behavior but have not met with much success. Kennedy's secretary of defense, Robert McNamara, became concerned that military officers were making public and written statements that were critical of U.S. military and foreign policies.[45] Accordingly, a procedure was instituted by which any remarks made to a public group by a military officer must first be screened by a committee in the Defense Department. Those parts of the speech that could prove embarrassing to the administration were then deleted from the prepared text. When the Senate Armed Services Committee got wind of this procedure, it promptly instituted an investigation, asking that the members of the screening committee appear before it. Secretary McNamara refused. The committee persisted in its demand until finally President Kennedy himself intervened and refused to disclose the names on grounds of executive privilege. In spite of the fact that the names were never revealed, the controversy created by the censoring procedure persuaded the administration to drop it.

HEW's Caspar Weinberger encountered similar resistance when he attempted to implement a slightly different procedure. Disturbed by the fact that career bureaucrats in HEW were going before congressional committees and speaking out against administration policies, he instituted a system of clearance and chaperones whereby all career officials in HEW not only had to gain prior approval before going to Capitol Hill, but they also had to be accompanied by someone "reliable" to ensure that their testimony would not be damaging to the administration. The policy was quickly dropped, however, when the powerful chairman of the Senate Finance Committee raised strong objections.[46] That members of Congress would oppose such muzzling procedures is quite understandable, for they place great value on the special expertise that career bureaucrats bring to the analysis of policy issues.

★ OTHER LIMITATIONS ON PRESIDENTIAL CONTROL

Our discussion thus far has focused upon identifying the three major ways by which the president attempts to exert a measure of control over the bureaucracy. We have made an effort to show how these instruments of leverage are restricted and resisted by the bureaucracy itself, as well as by Congress and organized interests outside government. At this point, however, it is important to note that the limitations on the president's capacity for control are also the result of other equally important factors that have little to do with any intentional efforts by bureaucrats to resist. They are (1) the size and complexity of the bureaucratic establishment and (2) the president's inability or unwillingness to make clear what he wants.

Size and Complexity

The bureaucratic establishment consists of some 2.8 million civilian employees, 87 percent of whom are not even located in Washington, D.C., but rather are spread out in various parts of the country and the world. At the top of this bureaucracy sits the president, and below him are several layers of officials through whom his directives must customarily pass before they are implemented. Depending on the department, these layers range anywhere from seventeen to thirty-two,[47] and their complexity ensures that presidential orders will occasionally be short-circuited during the process of transmission. In some instances, the order may be misconstrued; in others, it is simply not relayed to everyone who needs to know. As one former White House aide noted, "Departments are so big that it is difficult for anyone to get the 'message' around even when they want to do something about it."[48] This problem is further compounded when the number of people who need to know transcends the bounds of any one department or agency.

An incident that occured during the Kennedy administration may serve as an illustration of the communications problem. In the early stages of our involvement in Vietnam, President Kennedy became increasingly concerned over the Diem government's resistance to administration policies. Although several of his high-level advisers called for cutting off commodity aid to Vietnam in retaliation for its failure to cooperate, the president made it clear that he did not favor such a step at that time. As the recalcitrance of the Vietnam government increased, however, he finally decided to convene a group to reconsider the possibility of cutting off commodity aid. When the president raised the issue for consideration at the meeting, the director of the Agency for International Development (AID) informed the president that the decision had already been made. There followed this exchange:

> **President:** You've done what?
>
> **Director:** Cut off military aid.
>
> **President:** Who the hell told you to do that?
>
> **Director:** No one. It's automatic policy. We do it whenever we have differences with a client government.
>
> **President:** My God, do you know what you have done?[49]

The director of AID was not engaged in a deliberate effort to sabotage presidential policy, but rather was following the established policy of the State Department.

Unfortunately, officials at higher levels in the department apparently had failed to inform him of the president's earlier decision not to halt commodity aid. Such breakdowns can also occur as communications move up the bureaucracy to the president, as Gerald Ford discovered when he was put in the embarrassing position of having to withdraw his support from two sections of an antitrust bill submitted to Congress by his own Justice Department. The president had inadvertently not been informed of its content.[50]

Although more efficient organization would reduce the communications problem, it surely would not eliminate it. In a bureaucracy as large and complex as ours, such short circuits in the communications process are inevitable.

Lack of Clarity in Presidential Intent

The president's ability to secure bureaucratic compliance is also hampered by his unwillingness to make his position known. In some cases, for instance, he may intentionally withhold a given policy decision from the bureaucracy because he feels that it may encounter resistance at the lower levels. As former Secretary of State Kissinger has noted, however, such a strategy frequently leads to a situation where the White House and the bureaucracy are working at cross purposes.

> Because management of the bureaucracy takes so much energy and precisely because changing course is so difficult, many of the most important decisions are taken by extra-bureaucratic means. Some of the key decisions are kept to a very small circle while the bureaucracy happily continues working away in ignorance of the fact that decisions are being made, or the fact that a decision is being made in a particular area. One reason for keeping the decisions to small groups is that when bureaucracies are so unwieldy and when their internal morale becomes a serious problem, an unpopular decision may be fought by brutal means, such as leaks to the press or to congressional committees. Thus, the only way secrecy can be kept is to exclude from the making of the decision all those who are theoretically charged with carrying it out. . . . There is, thus, small wonder for many allegations of deliberate sabotage of certain American efforts, or of great cynicism of American efforts because of inconsistent actions. In the majority of cases this was due to the ignorance of certain parts of the bureaucracy, rather than to malevolent intent. Another result is that the relevant part of the bureaucracy, because it is being excluded from the making of a particular decision, continues with great intensity sending out cables, thereby distorting the effort with the best intentions in the world. You cannot stop them from doing this because you do not tell them what is going on.[51]

It is precisely this kind of presidential secrecy that accounted for the Nixon administration's embarrassment during the India-Pakistan War in 1971, when it was discovered that the White House was taking the side of Pakistan, while the State Department was supporting India. This policy conflict immediately brought the famous White House order instructing the State Department to "tilt" toward Pakistan.

Many times, of course, the president does make his position known but does so in a way that invites confusion and misinterpretation. Such ambiguity may result for a variety of reasons. If a given issue is especially controversial, political considerations may require that he phrase his decision ambiguously enough to satisfy those on both sides of the issue. Second, he may simply lack the time and knowledge necessary to work out the details of a decision. Finally, he may have made two policy decisions that are in direct conflict with each other.

It was the last situation that in part served to explain what many viewed as a classic case of bureaucratic intransigence. Within two years after he assumed office, President Kennedy ordered the State Department to negotiate the removal of U.S. Jupiter missiles from Turkey, for they had already become obsolete and were easy targets for Soviet missiles. It was not until the Cuban missile crisis in 1962 that Kennedy learned, in a letter from Nikita Khrushchev, that U.S. missiles were still in Turkey. Needless to say, the president was greatly irritated that his order had not been carried out, and even more so because he had to learn of it from none other than the head of the Soviet government. Yet the continued presence of missiles in Turkey was the consequence of bureaucrats' being faced with having to implement two conflicting presidential policies: One called for negotiating the removal of missiles from Turkey, but the other called for strengthening the NATO alliance. Kennedy had, after all, pledged to bolster the alliance during his campaign for the presidency, and after taking office he instructed the State Department to move in this direction. One former State Department official notes the dilemma faced by the bureaucracy in this situation.

> The officials who received the directive to remove the missiles from Turkey also felt themselves to be operating under a more general presidential directive to strengthen the troubled alliance. They did not believe that the order to remove the missiles from Turkey was meant to contradict the order to strengthen NATO. They raised the issue in a tentative way with the Turkish government. When that government registered strong objections, they held off obeying the order to remove the missiles.[52]

Presidents and their aides have a tendency to see lack of compliance as a deliberate attempt by various elements in the bureaucracy to subvert presidential policies. Such an assessment is understandable, for it is frequently correct. At the same time, however, presidents are far less inclined to acknowledge that problems with policy implementation may just as frequently be a product of their own making.

 ## ATTEMPTS AT GREATER CONTROL OVER THE BUREAUCRACY: THE CASES OF NIXON AND REAGAN

Although all of our recent presidents have remarked upon their inability to gain greater control over the reins of the bureaucracy, none made a more concerted and systematic attempt to correct this problem than presidents Nixon and Reagan. For this reason, their efforts in this area deserve our attention.

Nixon

Richard Nixon came into office claiming that, unlike his predecessor, he was not going to locate all policymaking in the White House. Instead, he would appoint competent administrators of independent mind and give them broad policymaking responsibilities.

> I would operate differently from President Johnson. Instead of taking all power to myself, I'd select cabinet members who could do their jobs, and each of them would have the stature and the power to function effectively. . . . Every key official would have the opportunity to be a big man in his field.[53]

I don't want a Cabinet of "Yes" men and I don't think you want a Cabinet of "Yes" men. Every man in the Cabinet will be urged to speak out in the Cabinet and within the Administration on all the great issues so that the decisions we will make will be the best decisions we can possibly reach.[54]

He further demonstrated their importance by his willingness to allow each department head to fill the subcabinet positions within the department. After his first six months in office, however, the president's enthusiasm for his cabinet started to wane as he saw his domestic secretaries slowly being captured by the career bureaucrats and clientele groups of their departments. HEW's Robert Finch was being pressured by his staff not to retrench on Johnson's Great Society programs. Equally disturbing were the actions of some of the liberal appointees Finch was placing in the subcabinet positions. Secretary of HUD George Romney had been persuaded by his department's housing experts to advocate expensive housing programs, which the president felt were a waste of money. Interior Secretary Walter Hickel had proved to be more responsive to environmental groups than the Nixon administration had expected or desired.

Developments such as these led the president to make some significant changes in his relations with domestic department heads. Cabinet meetings were held less and less frequently. Some cabinet secretaries, such as George Romney and Walter Hickel, found it increasingly difficult to gain access to the president. In addition, the White House began to play a much more active role in screening those being recommended for subcabinet-level positions in the various departments. Most important, policymaking was taken out of the hands of department heads and given to what were called *working groups*.[55] These groups were made up of some members of the White House staff and selected members of the bureaucracy. The White House staff clearly played the dominant role here, since they ultimately decided which individuals in a department would be brought into these working groups. This new procedure caused considerable irritation among department heads, for they were not always consulted on the makeup of the groups; nor were they always informed of the policy decisions reached by them.

As the White House staff became increasingly involved in policymaking, it quite naturally grew in size. This expansion continued as the staff began to involve itself in the actual administration of White House policies and programs. Thus, more and more decisions that would normally have been made within a given department or agency now had to receive clearance from the White House staff. Two consequences followed from these developments. First, the White House staff had become so large and unwieldy that in the process of trying to control one bureaucracy Richard Nixon had, in effect, created another one on top of it. Second, as the president's staff became increasingly involved in administering and overseeing programs, it ultimately found less and less time for the formulation of policy. Consequently, policymaking gradually shifted back to the bureaucracy, which was precisely what President Nixon was trying to prevent. One former government official speaks to this phenomenon as follows:

Operational matters flow to the top—as central staffs become engrossed in subduing outlying bureaucracies—and central policymaking emerges at the bottom. At the top minor problems squeeze out major ones, and individuals lower down the echelons who have the time for reflection and mischief-making take up the issues of fundamental philosophical and political significance.[56]

A Change in Approach

At the end of his first four years, President Nixon found that his attempts to get a handle on the bureaucracy had not proved successful. Following his reelection, therefore, he decided to deal with the problem in a more vigorous and systematic fashion. This decision was further encouraged by the fact that he had been returned to office with an overwhelming mandate from the people; accordingly, he was determined that no bureaucracy was going to frustrate the implementation of his policies.

Nixon's first goal was to populate the bureaucracy with people he could trust. To this end, he summoned his cabinet shortly after the election and asked them to submit *pro forma* resignations, some of which he accepted. Transportation Secretary Volpe, for example, was approached and told he had one half hour to decide if he wanted to become the next American ambassador to Italy. He accepted. His departure from the cabinet was occasioned by his frequent policy disputes during the previous four years with the president's chief domestic aide, John Ehrlichman. The secretary of commerce was informed that he was going to be made a roving ambassador specializing in U.S. trade relations. Although he suggested that it would be beneficial for him to remain in Washington for six months in order to work out his responsibilities with the State Department, he received word that he was to leave Washington as soon as possible. Only later did he learn that he was being replaced because he had been traveling in social circles known to be antagonistic to the president.[57] Other cabinet members—Romney, Laird, and Rogers—were leaving because they wished to do so.

The vacancies were to be filled by individuals who had little national following, thereby reducing their ability to act independently of the president. There was also some reshuffling within the cabinet. Suspicious of Elliot Richardson's cordial relationship with the HEW career bureaucracy but impressed nevertheless with his managerial skills, President Nixon decided to move him from HEW to secretary of defense. Richardson's replacement at HEW was Caspar Weinberger, who was transferred from his position as director of the Office of Management and Budget.

The change in Richard Nixon's attitude toward the cabinet proved to be remarkable. Whereas he had come into office stressing his desire to be surrounded by cabinet secretaries of independent mind, he now sought individuals who would give him unquestioning loyalty. This new attitude was best captured by Nixon's chief domestic aide, John Ehrlichman: "There shouldn't be a lot of leeway in following the President's policies. It should be like a corporation, where the executive vice presidents (the Cabinet officers) are tied closely to the chief executive, or to put it in extreme terms, when he says jump, they only ask how high."[58] In addition to reshuffling his cabinet, Nixon asked for the resignations of some two thousand other political appointees, including those at the deputy and assistant secretary level, and some high-level bureaucrats who enjoyed civil service status but whose jobs were not protected by statute. Some were simply fired outright, while others were transferred to positions where they could do little harm. The more important vacancies created by these firings were to be filled with people from the president's already bloated White House staff and by individuals from the Committee to Reelect the president (CREEP). It was felt that these Nixon loyalists could more effectively monitor the activities of the bureaucracy from positions within it than from the White House. In all, some eighty-four White House staffers and CREEP workers were strategically located in various departments and agencies throughout the bureaucracy. Even with these replacements, however, the firings had been so sweeping that many positions were still vacant several months later.[59]

Besides personnel changes, the president's plan for control also included a reorganization effort. In January 1973, Nixon announced that three of his cabinet secretaries—all with demonstrated track records of loyalty to the president—would enjoy the additional title of *counselor to the president.* In this capacity each would become responsible for coordinating policy areas that transcended the concerns of his own department. Thus, Secretary of Agriculture Earl Butz was given the area of *natural resources;* Secretary of HEW Caspar Weinberger, *human resources;* and Secretary of Housing and Urban Development James Lynn, *community development.* Secretary of the Treasury George Shultz had earlier been given an additional responsibility as special assistant to the president for *economic affairs.* These four "super" secretaries would see to it that the actions of departments involved in these four general areas were consistent with the policy goals of the president. Operating at a level above these supersecretaries were four individuals whom the president designated his principal White House assistants—Henry Kissinger, Roy Ash, John Ehrlichman, and H. R. Haldeman. Their responsibility would be "to integrate and unify policies and operations throughout the executive branch . . . and to oversee the activities for which the president is responsible."[60]

The Results

Unfortunately for President Nixon, he never had an opportunity to see how all of these changes would have affected his control over the bureaucracy, for shortly after they were implemented the scandals of Watergate engulfed his administration. His most important White House aides were forced to resign, and so too were some of the loyalists whom he had just appointed to positions in the bureaucracy. The president and his reconstituted White House staff soon became so preoccupied with avoiding impeachment that little attention could be directed toward monitoring the activity of the bureaucracy. With such a vacuum in leadership at the top, members of the executive branch from the cabinet on down found themselves with greater freedom of action.

Although the Watergate developments effectively cut short, and thus precluded, any definitive evaluation of Richard Nixon's strategy for control, the early indications were that it was meeting with less than complete success. Those White House staffers whom the president had sent out to colonize the bureaucracy were proving no match for the political and substantive expertise of the high-level career bureaucrats. Nor did the president's attempt to coordinate and oversee departmental activities through the use of supersecretaries prove workable. His transportation secretary, for example, made it quite clear that he was not going to take his marching orders from James Lynn, secretary of HUD and supersecretary for *community development.*[61] Such a reaction on the part of cabinet members should not have been surprising, for, as one former White House aide has noted, "Cabinet officers regard themselves as equals in their access and responsibility to the President and take seriously those laws that vest jurisdiction over certain matters to their department. . . . Nixon did not realize that cabinet officers will not take orders from one of their peers."[62] If Nixon was not initially sensitive to this fact, he soon became so, for he abolished the positions of supersecretaries only four months after creating them.

Reagan

Whereas President Nixon's attempt to get a handle on the bureaucracy did not take shape until the end of his first term, President Reagan and his aides made preparations for doing so well before they took office. The sum total of their efforts, both before and after their assumption of power, represented the most systematic and far-reaching effort ever made to take control of the executive branch.

This effort began as far back as April 1980, when Reagan aide Edwin Meese instructed Pendleton James to develop a process for the selection of executive branch personnel. James proved to be a judicious choice, for he had considerable experience as an executive talent scout in the private sector as well as in government during the Nixon administration. The formal transition process following Reagan's election was the most elaborate and expensive in history, consuming the $2 million appropriated by Congress for this purpose and an additional million that the Reagan people raised from private sources.[63] This money financed not only the appointments process itself but also close to one hundred special task forces made up of Reagan partisans. These groups were charged with going into various departments and agencies and getting a fix on their organizational structure, programs, problems, and personnel—an undertaking greatly facilitated by the Carter administration's decision to be as cooperative as possible.[64] Such advance detective work was designed to enable the Reagan administration to come into a given department or agency with a plan of action already developed.

Believing that personnel decisions were crucial to placing his stamp on the bureaucracy, Reagan approached the appointments process with greater care than any of his predecessors. The importance attached to this undertaking was signaled by the fact that Pendleton James was given an office in the White House and had direct access to the president, usually meeting with him twice a week during the early months of the administration.[65] The first order of business, selecting people for the all-important cabinet positions, was made by the president and his key aides, including James. Every effort was made to choose individuals who supported the president's goals and programs. Moreover, to minimize the possibility of capture by their departments, cabinet appointees were at the very outset "closeted with Budget Director-designate David Stockman and longtime Reagan aides and told what was expected of them. They were not allowed to bring agency staff members to these meetings, were assigned policy changes, and were told to 'hit the ground running.'"[66] The establishment of "cabinet councils" served as yet another means of tying Reagan's top appointees to his own interests. These councils were the brainchild of White House aide Edwin Meese; there were seven such councils, each responsible for making policy recommendations to the president in a given domestic policy area. Though most ultimately evolved into mechanisms for dealing with secondary rather than primary policy matters and were finally recast into just two councils in Reagan's second term, they nevertheless provided cabinet members with a sense of participation and an opportunity for input. The councils also gave the president a chance to reemphasize his agenda to the cabinet on a regular basis.[67]

President Reagan sought to use his appointment power to best advantage in filling subcabinet positions as well. Whereas Nixon and Carter had ceded this responsibility to cabinet members—a decision they would later regret—the Reagan White House made it abundantly clear to prospective cabinet secretaries that the White House would determine the criteria for filling second- and third-level positions in their departments and would have the final say on who was selected. Although Secretary of State Haig and Defense Secretary Weinberger chafed under this restriction and later managed to resist it to some extent, other department heads cooperated.[68] The criteria developed by Reagan and his aides were essentially three: Had the individual voted for Reagan? Was he or she a Republican? Was he or she a conservative? In addition, since Reagan policies were to represent a departure from business as usual, the lack of any previous Washington experience was viewed as more of an asset than a liability.

Screening procedures for subcabinet appointees were elaborate. Once the White House personnel office and a cabinet secretary had settled on a candidate, the name then had to be cleared by the president's national security or domestic policy adviser, depending upon the position; by political aide Lyn Nofziger, who was especially assiduous in checking for ideological purity; then by White House Counsel Fred Fielding. From there the candidate's name went to the White House Congressional Liaison Office, and then on to Reagan's three top staff aides (Baker, Meese, and Deaver) and, finally, to the president himself.[69] This protracted screening process caused a very considerable delay in making appointments,[70] but it also produced a coterie of subcabinet officials who, to an even greater extent than their bosses, evinced "an uncommon degree of ideological consistency and intensity."[71] Once selected, the Reagan White House also sought to ensure that subcabinet appointees would enter their respective departments with the "administration perspective." Accordingly, they were briefed not by career bureaucrats but rather by the Reagan task force that had been assigned to study their particular department. As a means of further reinforcing loyalty to Reagan, there were also plans to bring subcabinet appointees to the White House periodically to meet with the president. Whether this latter strategy was pursued, and if so how frequently, is unclear.[72]

Beyond placing loyalists in key positions throughout the bureaucracy, Reagan also sought to increase his control by reducing the number of career bureaucrats. Thus, his first official act upon assuming office was to issue an executive order instituting a hiring freeze. Furthermore, both administration budget cuts and voluntary departures by those disgruntled with cutbacks in domestic programs enabled the president to reduce the number of employees, particularly in those departments and agencies administering programs he opposed. In the Environmental Protection Agency, for example, the number of employees was reduced by 2,618 between January 1981 and March 1983. Similarly, at the Department of the Interior, James Watt closed seventeen field offices and eliminated dozens of federal mine inspectors. Such cutbacks made it much more difficult for these agencies to enforce federal regulations, many of which the administration was opposed to in the first place.[73] As to overall reductions across the federal bureaucracy, by 1983 there were 92,000 fewer career employees in domestic agencies (excluding the postal service) than there had been in 1981. Interestingly enough, however, those agencies targeted for reductions in career bureaucrats were the very same ones that enjoyed increases in the number of political appointees,[74] suggesting that the administration was seeking to install more malleable personnel in those agencies where they were attempting to make radical shifts in program priorities.

Yet another dimension to Reagan's assault on the bureaucracy was in the area of regulatory control. Having campaigned against intrusive government regulation of industry, Reagan was determined to lessen the burden of existing regulations and to curb the number churned out by government agencies in the future. The administration sought to neutralize regulations already on the books through a variety of means, including delays in implementation, selective enforcement, and reinterpretation.[75] Bear in mind that the reductions in personnel noted above, along with the refusal to fill vacancies, also lessened the capacity of agencies to enforce their regulations.

With respect to curbing future regulations, shortly after entering the White House, President Reagan issued an executive order imposing a sixty-day freeze on all new government regulations. In addition, he immediately established the President's Task Force on Regulatory Relief, chaired by Vice President Bush and charged with reassessing current regulations and making recommendations on the desirability of others being proposed. During his first month in office, Reagan also issued an executive order requiring all government agencies—except independent regulatory agencies—to submit to the Office of Management and Budget (OMB) a "regulatory impact statement" for any newly proposed regulation having an economic impact of $100 million or more. Although OMB lacked authority to compel an agency to alter a proposed regulation, the fact that it passed judgment on an agency's annual budget requests ensured that agencies would weigh carefully any concerns OMB might have about a given regulation. By June 30, 1983, OMB had reviewed some 6,700 regulations, with about one in nine being either revised or turned down. For the years 1985 and 1986, OMB figures indicate that roughly 23 percent of all proposed regulations were revised to make them consistent with administration goals.[76] In early 1985, Reagan issued yet another executive order enabling OMB to become involved in the rule-making process even earlier. This order required agencies to inform OMB of their *intention* to begin writing regulations in a particular area.

In attempting to expand his control over the bureaucracy, Reagan had one other arrow in his quiver, namely, the Civil Service Reform Act of 1978. In particular, his administration made considerable use of the provision that allows members of the Senior Executive Service to be reassigned. Intended to provide an administration with the ability to locate top career executives where their talents were most needed, this authority was in some instances used by Reagan's political appointees to rid agencies of bureaucrats deemed unfriendly to administration policies. In 1982 and 1983 the total number of reassignments were 1,226 and 1,100, respectively.[77] Some careerists were told they were being transferred to another part of the country, and, faced with this prospect, they chose to resign. Others were moved from positions of considerable responsibility and given only menial tasks to perform.[78]

As mentioned earlier, the Civil Service Reform Act was also intended to enhance presidential leverage over the bureaucracy by streamlining removal procedures and, at the upper levels of the civil service, predicating pay increases wholly or in part on merit. The Reagan White House reinforced this point in a memorandum sent to all department and agency heads, which noted that personnel performance appraisals constituted "an important vehicle to ensure that Administration initiatives and policies are appropriately carried out and that the primary objectives of the President are accomplished."[79] Although evidence is not available on how effective the Reagan administration was in using merit pay as a means of inducing cooperation, there are figures on the number of career bureaucrats fired *exclusively* for reasons of poor performance. This figure, which totaled 214 in 1980, grew steadily during the first four years of the Reagan administration, reaching 410 by 1985 and dropping slightly to 405 in 1986.[80] Despite the near doubling in number of people fired between 1980 and 1985, the absolute numbers seem surprisingly low.

The Results

It is clear that the Reagan administration expended an extraordinary amount of time and energy in seeking to create a more responsive bureaucracy. We must now ask, to what effect? The evidence suggests that the results were mixed. On the positive side, the care taken in the appointments process, along with efforts to socialize appointees into a White House perspective, did indeed yield appointees who were highly attuned to the president's objectives. To be sure, the turnover rate among cabinet members was high, with six departing the administration before the end of Reagan's first term. In contrast to the Nixon and Carter presidencies, however, only one of these departures (Education Secretary Terrence Bell) was rooted in philosophical differences with the president. Of the others, three left for personal reasons; another because he had become a political liability to the president; and the other, Secretary of State Alexander Haig, because his administrative control over foreign policy was less than he would have liked. At the subcabinet level, too, appointees appear to have been keenly supportive of the president's agenda. A study of political appointees in five agencies by Laurance Lynn revealed that "each appointee was acting as an agent for the president's policy preferences, and none showed much inclination to go into business for himself."[81]

But the Reagan approach to appointments carried a cost as well. For in seeking to make ideological compatibility and personal loyalty to Reagan the *sine que non* for appointment, particularly at the subcabinet level, the administration ended up appointing a good many individuals whose competence and experience left much to be desired. In this connection, one study conducted in the first half of 1981 found that nearly 60 percent of the individuals appointed to middle-level positions had no previous experience in the executive branch.[82] Laurance Lynn speaks to the consequences of this fact: "Presidential advisers might well have hoped for greater achievements from this group of officials. The Reagan administration is changing government, but not nearly to the extent that it might have if these officials as a group had been more capable. Opportunities were missed in at least four of the five agencies."[83]

In the regulatory area, the administration, by using OMB as a watchdog, appears to have been quite successful in limiting new regulations emanating from the bureaucracy. Even here, however, pressure finally began to build, with Congress, interest groups, and bureaucrats alike charging that OMB (1) kept no administrative records of its deliberations on regulations, (2) closed the meetings to the public, and (3) deliberately delayed action. These complaints in turn brought threats by Congress to cut off money for OMB's regulatory office unless it stopped sitting on proposed regulations and became more open in disclosing its decision-making procedures.[84]

The Reagan administration encountered more formidable obstacles in attempting to alter those rules already on the books. Congress declined to support Reagan proposals for legislative changes in health, safety, and environmental regulations. Although reductions in personnel enabled the administration to cut back on enforcement of existing regulations, efforts to eliminate enforcement altogether brought stiff resistance. In some instances, administration opponents turned to the courts, which, for example, overruled agency decisions to rescind the seat belt rule, to eliminate the requirement for ingredient labeling on liquor bottles, and to suspend the rule controlling toxic waste discharges.[85] In other instances, career bureaucrats leaked damaging information to Congress and the media. For example, EPA Director Anne Burford became the subject of revelations that accused her of failing to enforce toxic waste regulations against industries. She found her mismanagement subject to investigation by six congressional committees and was forced to resign, along with twenty other agency appointees. Under pressure from Congress and environmental groups, Reagan replaced Burford with William Ruckelshaus, who immediately corrected her excesses and sought and won from the administration a $165 million increase in the agency's budget.[86]

As for attempts to take advantage of newly won leverage granted under the Civil Service Reform Act of 1978, the administration was once again called to account. The House Post Office and Civil Service Subcommittee became a forum for airing frequent charges of arbitrariness in the transfer and firing of career bureaucrats. According to its chairwoman, Patricia Schroeder (D-Colo.), Reagan appointee Donald Devine, who headed the Office of Personnel Management (OPM) and was responsible for overseeing the civil service system, had "neutered OPM as an oversight agency. He has really allowed each agency to make whatever kind of personnel moves they want. They have deferred on their responsibility to give professional personnel advice. Instead, it's a 'wink, wink,' go ahead and do whatever you want."[87] When Devine appeared before the Republican-controlled Senate Governmental Affairs Committee to be confirmed for another four-year term as OPM director, he received a very chilly reception indeed. Committee members accused him of politicizing OPM, failing to execute personnel regulations in keeping with congressional intent, and undermining morale in the civil service. Recognizing that Devine stood little chance of being reconfirmed, the White House withdrew his name from consideration.[88]

In summary, although pressures from Congress, interest groups, and career bureaucrats, along with lack of experience among his own appointees, prevented Reagan from exercising as much control over the bureaucracy as he would have liked, nevertheless, he was more successful in this endeavor than any of his predecessors. That Reagan succeeded to the extent that he did is traceable to the care with which he approached the appointments process. He began the transition period early; retained White House control over subcabinet as well as cabinet positions; filled positions with individuals fully committed to his agenda; and reinforced that commitment through a rather elaborate socialization process that took the form of task force briefings and meetings with the president. There were, of course, other important elements in the administration's control strategy—regulatory control, aggressive use of personnel procedures, budget reductions—but their effectiveness was predicated upon having appointees in place willing to support them.

Future presidents could certainly benefit from emulating some of these practices, including an early start, White House control of subcabinet positions, and providing appointees with advance intelligence on the departments and agencies in which they will be working. But the most crucial element in the Reagan strategy—appointing individuals fully committed to the president's agenda—may prove more elusive. Reagan, after all, was a highly ideological president with clearly defined views on policy issues. Such clarity of goals and purpose in turn made it easier to identify those in sympathy with them. Less ideological presidents with more ambiguous views are likely to experience greater difficulty in screening personnel for policy compatibility.

✯ NOTES

1. *Washington Post,* December 19, 1980, p. A3; *Washington Post,* December 25, 1980, p. A3.

2. E. Pendelton James, "Lifting Barriers to Government Service," in *The Presidential Appointment Process: Panel Discussions on America's Unelected Government* (Washington, D.C.: National Academy of Public Administration, 1984), p. IV.

3. Constance Horner, "The Politics of Presidential Appointment: The Old and New Culture of Job Seeking in Washington," *American Enterprise* 4 (September/October, 1993), 24

4. Joel Aberbach and Bert Rockman, "Clashing Beliefs within the Executive Branch: The Nixon Administration Bureaucracy," *American Political Science Review* 70 (June 1976), 461.

5. Stanley Rothman and Robert Lichter, "How Liberal Are Bureaucrats?" *Regulation* (November/December 1983), 17, 18.

6. Cited in *Washington Post,* November 19, 1980, p. A1.

7. *Congressional Quarterly Weekly Report,* August 24, 1974, p. 2281.

8. Peter Woll and Rochelle Jones, "Bureaucratic Defense in Depth," in Michael Sego, ed., *Political Leadership in America* (Cleveland:Regal Books/King's Court Communications, 1974), p. 198.

9. *Rathbun (Humphrey's Executor)* v. *United States,* 295 U.S. 602 (1935).

10. *Weiner* v. *United States,* 375 U.S. 349 (1958).

11. This statement is taken from the report of the first Hoover Commission and cited in Emmette Redford, "The Arguments For and Against the Commission System," in Samuel Kristov and Lloyd Musolf, eds., *The Politics of Regulation* (Boston: Houghton Mifflin, 1964), p. 124.

12. *New York Times,* October 3, 1976, p. 21.

13. Cited in Harold Seidman, *Politics, Position and Power* (New York: Oxford University Press, 1970), p. 72.

14. Cited in Thomas Cronin, *The State of the Presidency* (Boston: Little, Brown, 1975), p. 161.

15. Remarks by Harold Seidman in Douglas Fox, ed., "A Mini-Symposium: President Nixon's Proposals for Executive Reorganization," *Public Administration Review* 34 (September/October 1974), 490.

16. Jeffrey Cohen, "On the Tenure of Appointive Political Executives: The American Cabinet, 1952–1984," *American Journal of Political Science* 30 (August 1986), 511.

17. *Watergate: Its Implications for Responsible Government,* a report prepared by a panel of the National Academy of Public Administration at the request of the Senate Select Committee on Presidential Campaign Activities (New York: National Academy of Public Administration, 1974), p. 107.

18. *Wall Street Journal,* November 13, 1973, p. 26.

19. Ibid.

20. Randall Ripley and Grace Franklin, *Congress, the Bureaucracy, and Public Policy* (Homewood, Ill.: Dorsey Press, 1976), p. 35.

21. *New York Times,* January 23, 1967, p. 42. Copyright © 1967 by The New York Times Company. Reprinted by permission.

22. *Washington Post,* January 11, 1993, p. A4.

23. For a useful collection of essays on why reorganizations are necessary, how they should be approached, and the problems that attend such efforts, see Peter Szanton, ed., *Federal Reorganization: What Have We Learned?* (Chatham, N.J.: Chatham House, 1981).

24. Joseph Califano, *A Presidential Nation* (New York: Norton, 1975), p. 21.

25. Ibid., p. 22.

26. *National Journal,* May 8, 1971, p. 978.

27. *Congressional Quarterly Almanac,* 1971, 27 (Washington, D.C.: Congressional Quarterly Press, 1972), p. 764.

28. Cited in Califano, *Presidential Nation,* p. 29.

29. Ibid., p. 51.

30. David Howard Davis, "Establishing the Department of Energy," *Journal of Energy and Development* 4 (Autumn 1978), 29–40.

31. Joseph Califano, *Governing America: An Insider's Report from the White House and the Cabinet* (New York: Simon & Schuster, 1981), pp. 282–85.

32. Godfrey Hodgson, *All Things to All Men: The False Promise of the Modern American Presidency* (New York: Simon & Schuster, 1980), pp. 81–85.

33. "Interview with Reagan's First Education Secretary," *Chronicle of Higher Education,* March 18, 1987, p. 27; *New York Times,* November 18, 1984, p. E2.

34. *Washington Post,* January 3, 1983, p. A4.

35. *National Journal,* August 10, 1985, pp. 1845–48.

36. *New York Times,* October 22, 1993, p. A8; *Congressional Quarterly Weekly Report,* September 11, 1993, p. 2385.

37. *Congressional Quarterly Weekly Report,* November 6, 1993, p. 3044.

38. *Congressional Quarterly Weekly Report,* April 19, 1997, p. 921; *New York Times,* April 18, 1997, p. A7; *Washington Post,* May 28, 1997, p. A17.

39. Cited in Robert Gilmour, "Policy Formulation in the Executive Branch: Central Legislative Clearance," in James Anderson, ed., *Cases in Public Policy Making* (New York: Praeger, 1976), p. 93.

40. Emmet John Hughes, *The Living Presidency,* p. 159. Copyright © 1973 by Emmet John Hughes. Reprinted by permission of Coward, McCann & Geoghegan.

41. James Davis, *The National Executive Branch* (New York: Free Press, 1970), pp. 132, 133.

42. Drew Pearson and Jack Anderson, *The Case against Congress* (New York: Simon & Schuster, 1968), p. 272.

43. David Halberstam, *The Best and the Brightest* (New York: Random House, 1969), p. 190.

44. *New York Times,* March 6, 1973, p. 20. Copyright © 1973 by The New York Times Company. Reprinted by permission.

45. Louis Gawthrop, *Bureaucratic Behavior in the Executive Branch* (New York: Free Press, 1969), pp. 162–65.

46. Richard Nathan, "The Administrative Presidency," *The Public Interest* No. 44 (Summer 1976), 44, 45.

47. Paul Light, *Thickening Government: Federal Hierarchy and the Diffusion of Accountability* (Washington, D.C.: Brookings Institution, 1995), pp. 7, 8.

48. Cited in Cronin, *State of the Presidency,* p. 171.

49. Cited in Halberstam, *Best and the Brightest,* p. 346.

50. *New York Times,* December 26, 1976, p. E1.

51. Cited in Morton Halperin, with the assistance of Priscilla Clapp and Arnold Kanter, *Bureaucratic Politics and Foreign Policy* (Washington, D.C.: Brookings Institution, 1974), p. 247.

52. Ibid., pp. 241–42.

53. Stephen Hess, *Organizing the Presidency* (Washington, D.C.: Brookings Institution, 1976), pp. 112, 113.

54. Cited in Richard Nathan, *The Plot That Failed* (New York: Wiley, 1975), p. 37.

55. Ibid., pp. 45–48.

56. Ibid., p. 52.

57. Theodore White, *Breach of Faith* (New York: Atheneum, 1975), pp. 176, 177.

58. Cited in *Watergate: Its Implications,* p. 46.

59. Lewis Beman, "President-Less Government in Washington," *Fortune,* January 1974, p. 84.

60. Cited in Nathan, *Plot That Failed,* p. 69.

61. Woll and Jones, "Bureaucratic Defense," p. 19.

62. Califano, *Presidential Nation,* pp. 30, 31.

63. Carl Brauer, *Presidential Transitions* (New York: Oxford University Press, 1986), p. 255.

64. Chester Newland, "Executive Office Policy Apparatus: Enforcing the Reagan Agenda," in Lester Salamon and Michael Lund, eds., *The Reagan Presidency and the Governing of America* (Washington, D.C.: Urban Institute Press, 1984), p. 143.

65. G. Calvin Mackenzie, "Cabinet and Subcabinet Personnel Selection in Reagan's First Year: New Variations on Some Not-So-Old-Themes" (Prepared for delivery at the annual meeting of the American Political Science Association, New York, September 2–5, 1981), p. 11.

66. Richard P. Nathan, "Institutional Change under Reagan," in John L. Palmer, ed., *Perspectives on the Reagan Years* (Washington, D.C.: Urban Institute Press, 1986), p. 129.

67. Newland, "Executive Office Policy Apparatus," pp. 153, 168; Terry Moe, "The Politicized Presidency," in John Chubb and Paul Peterson, eds., *The New Direction in American Politics* (Washington, D.C.: Brookings Institution, 1985), p. 262.

68. James P. Pfiffner, "The Carter-Reagan Transition: Hitting the Ground Running" (Prepared for delivery at the annual meeting of the American Political Science Association, Denver, September 1982), p. 21.

69. Mackenzie, "Cabinet and Subcabinet Personnel Selections in Reagan's First Year," p. 24; Brauer, *Presidential Transitions,* p. 230.

70. *National Journal,* December 4, 1985, p. 2869.

71. Cited in Lester Salamon and Alan Abramson, "Governance: The Politics of Entrenchment," in John L. Palmer and Isabel V. Sawhill, eds., *The Reagan Record* (Cambridge, Mass.: Ballinger, 1984), p. 46.

72. Moe, "'The Politicized Presidency," p. 260; Brauer, *Presidential Transitions,* p. 234.

73. Michael Kraft, "Environmental Policy Changes in the Reagan Presidency" (Prepared for delivery at the annual meeting of the American Political Science Association, Chicago, September 1–4, 1983), pp. 16, 18; Salamon and Abramson, "Governance: The Politics of Retrenchment," p. 47.

74. Edie N. Goldenberg, "The Permanent Government in an Era of Retrenchment and Redirection," in Salamon and Lund, *The Reagan Presidency,* pp. 390, 396; see also Robert F. Durant, *The Administrative Presidency Revisited* (Albany: SUNY Press, 1992), pp. 40, 41.

75. Kraft, "Environmental Policy Changes in the Reagan Presidency," pp. 27, 28; Salamon and Abramson, "Governance: The Politics of Retrenchment," p. 47; Martin Tolchin and Susan J. Tolchin, "The Rush to Deregulate," *New York Times Magazine,* August 21, 1983, p. 38.

76. *National Journal,* May 25, 1985, p. 1216; *Washington Post,* May 22, 1986, p. A17.

77. Goldenberg, "The Permanent Government," p. 397.

78. *National Journal,* April 9, 1983, pp. 735, 736; *U.S. News and World Report,* August 29, 1983, pp. 53, 54.

79. Cited in *National Journal,* April 4, 1983, p. 733.

80. These figures were provided to the author by the Office of Personnel Management.

81. Laurence Lynn, Jr., "The Reagan Administration and the Renitent Bureaucracy," in Salamon and Lund, *The Reagan Presidency,* p. 360.

82. Mackenzie, "Cabinet and Subcabinet Personnel Selection," p. 19.

83. Lynn, "The Reagan Administration," p. 369.

84. Kraft, "Environmental Policy Changes," p. 22; *Washington Post,* July 18, 1985, p. A21; *Washington Post,* August 16, 1986, p. A7; *Washington Post,* May 22, 1986, p. A17; *National Journal,* May 30, 1987, p. 1408.

85. *Washington Post,* January 29, 1984, p. D7.

86. *U.S. News and World Report,* August 29, 1983, p. 54; Kraft, "Environmental Policy Changes in the Reagan Presidency," pp. 21, 28.

87. *National Journal,* April 9, 1983, pp. 735, 736.

88. Bernard Rosen, "Crises in the U.S. Civil Service," *Public Administration Review* 46 (May/June 1986), 207–10.

Decision Making in the White House

 THE PARTICIPANTS

The president of the United States functions in several capacities in our political system. He is a foreign policymaker, legislator, party leader, manager of the economy, protector of the peace, and commander in chief. In performing all of those roles he is confronted with having to make decisions. This task is a formidable one. As Eisenhower informed the incoming President Kennedy, "There are no easy matters that will ever come to you as President. If they are easy, they will be settled at a lower level."[1] Moreover, the president cannot sidestep the problems that come over his desk. This reality was poignantly conveyed by a sign on President Truman's desk that read, "The Buck Stops Here." The president may act or refuse to act on a given matter, but in either case he will be making a decision; and whether the consequences be good or bad, he must ultimately accept the responsibility for that decision. Finally, the task of making presidential decisions is a challenging one because "all of the facts are rarely, if ever, available to a President at the time he must make most decisions. Those that are, often turn out to be half-facts or incorrect as they are subjected to careful analysis."[2] Lyndon Johnson demonstrated his sensitivity to this dilemma when he observed that the problem for presidents lies not so much in *doing* what is right, but rather in *knowing* what is right.

In this chapter we shall examine where and how the president gets the information and advice he needs in order to make decisions on the critical problems that come to him in the Oval Office. In the next chapter, five specific examples of presidential decision making will then be studied in order to determine how, in each case, the nature of the decision-making process affected the success or failure of that decision.

★ THE CABINET

There is no provision in the Constitution that calls for the establishment of a formal body known as the *cabinet.* The term itself was coined by newspaper reporters during the presidency of George Washington to refer to his four department heads, which at that time were the attorney general and the secretaries of state, war, and the treasury. Today, of course, the cabinet is considerably larger, with fourteen different departments within the executive branch. Moreover, recent presidents have typically accorded cabinet rank to the vice president and the U.S. representative to the United Nations. Reagan further expanded the size of the cabinet by awarding cabinet status to his White House counselor (Edwin Meese), CIA director (William Casey), director of the Office of Management and Budget (David Stockman), and U.S. trade representative (William Brock).

The president's cabinet has consisted of individuals who have built up considerable reputations based upon clearly demonstrated ability in a given field of endeavor. Accordingly, one would expect it to be a highly suitable group for the president to consult in seeking information and advice on critical problems. In actual fact, however, it has rarely been so. Andrew Jackson, for example, maintained that he could not find the "necessary standards of selflessness and candor" among his cabinet, and consequently he turned to an informal group of personal advisers who came to be known as his "Kitchen Cabinet." Abraham Lincoln showed his lack of concern for cabinet advice when, upon deciding to issue the Emancipation Proclamation, he convened it and said, "I have gathered you together to hear what I have written down. I do not wish your advice about the main matter. That, I have determined for myself."[3]

Throughout the First World War, Woodrow Wilson declined to include the cabinet in any major decision making, and when he did summon them together the issues discussed were, according to one cabinet member, essentially trivial in nature: "Nothing talked of at Cabinet that would interest a nation, a family, or a child. No talk of the war."[4] Nor did Franklin Roosevelt take the cabinet into his confidence. On the contrary, his secretary of the interior noted that "the cold fact is that on important matters we are seldom called upon for advice."[5] Unlike his predecessor, however, Harry Truman did initially make use of his cabinet, a fact that can perhaps be accounted for by his lack of confidence upon taking over the reins of the presidency. As he progressed through his term, however, the purpose of cabinet meetings became not so much to make important decisions as to ensure policy coordination. Among our recent past presidents, Eisenhower made the greatest use of the cabinet. He came into the presidency believing that the cabinet should be used to discuss matters of great public concern. Accordingly, he held frequent as well as long meetings with his cabinet. Agendas were prepared for each meeting, and he even went so far as to appoint a cabinet secretary. However, in spite of Eisenhower's effort to elevate the importance of the cabinet, one of his close advisers argues that he was not well served by it. Not only were the meetings for the most part noncontroversial, but cabinet members usually came unprepared, resulting in "unpremeditated, if not aimless discussions."[6] Kennedy's treatment of the cabinet provided a marked contrast to his predecessor. Although he began by holding regular cabinet meetings, he soon became frustrated with them, as his postmaster general recalls:

After the first two or three meetings, one had the distinct impression that the President felt that decisions on major matters were not made—or even influenced—at Cabinet sessions, and that discussion there was a waste of time. . . . When members spoke up to suggest or to discuss major Administration policy, the President would listen with thinly disguised impatience and then postpone or otherwise bypass the question.[7]

Kennedy ultimately concluded that the nature of the issue should determine which cabinet members needed to be consulted. It served little purpose, he thought, to convene the entire cabinet to discuss issues that might be of immediate concern to only one or two members. Thus, he abandoned regular meetings, and the few he did convene were for reasons of tradition rather than necessity.

Johnson made a serious attempt to use the cabinet after he took over the presidency. Regular meetings were scheduled, and a special assistant was appointed to think up topics for the group to discuss.[8] Like most other presidents, however, he gradually allowed the cabinet to fall into disuse, convening it only to give department heads "new political or personnel marching orders."[9]

Of all our recent presidents, none made a greater point of dramatically demonstrating the importance of the cabinet than did Richard Nixon. Indeed, he took the unprecedented step of having the group sworn in on live television. Moreover, he introduced each member, citing his accomplishments and qualifications for the post. Given such fanfare, it is especially ironic that Nixon ultimately sought to reduce the importance of his cabinet members, perhaps to a greater extent than any other recent president.

Bill Clinton followed in the footsteps of his predecessors, convening his cabinet a mere seven times during his first year in office and for purposes that were largely social and informational.[10] Midway into his second term, formal cabinet meetings continued to be a rarity, with one attendee noting that "Clinton cabinet meetings are informational, not deliberative. They occur when all the members need to be briefed on a particular initiative and told how much and how they will support it."[11]

If presidents do not rely heavily upon their cabinets for advice, it is important to know why. First of all, many critical matters must be discussed in secrecy, and presidents have found that the best way to maintain secrecy is to limit the number of people who will be privy to such matters. Consequently, they are reluctant to risk the chance of leaks by bringing sensitive issues before a cabinet consisting of fourteen or more individuals. Lyndon Johnson emphasized this point in a talk with his newly elected successor: "Let me tell you, Dick, I would have been a damn fool to have discussed major decisions with the full Cabinet present, because I knew that if I said something in the morning, you could sure as hell bet it would appear in the afternoon papers."[12]

Second, a president will place his confidence in people he can trust, and these are likely to be individuals whom he knows personally. Cabinet members, however, do not usually fall into this category. Political reasons often compel a president to settle for cabinet members who are not necessarily his first choice. Kennedy, for example, wanted McGeorge Bundy as his secretary of state. He decided not to appoint him, however, because he felt his newly appointed ambassador to the United Nations, Adlai Stevenson, would refuse to serve under Bundy. His second choice for the job was Senator William Fulbright. Again, however, Kennedy was dissuaded from choosing him because blacks objected to the senator's civil rights record, and Jewish groups took exception to his views on Israel.[13] Kennedy gave the position to Dean

Rusk, who, although highly recommended, was someone the president had never met. Nor had Kennedy ever met the men he selected to fill the posts of secretary of defense and secretary of the treasury, both of whom were Republicans as well as prominent members of the business community. Their appointments were motivated in part by Kennedy's desire to ease the fears of the conservative financial establishment, which viewed his presidency with considerable apprehension.

Political considerations also played a part in the choice of several of President Nixon's cabinet appointees. Daniel Patrick Moynihan was his personal choice for secretary of labor, but Nixon recognized the necessity of appointing someone who would be acceptable to the labor establishment. Accordingly, he decided against Moynihan for the job when he learned that the powerful president of the AFL-CIO objected to Moynihan's lack of administrative experience.[14] The position was given to George Shultz, a man the president had never met. The governor of Alaska, Walter Hickel, was picked to be secretary of the interior in part because President Nixon felt the western part of the country should be represented in the cabinet.[15] It was an appointment that Nixon would regret later on when Hickel openly criticized the president's administrative style. In an attempt to represent the liberal wing of the Republican Party in his administration, Nixon appointed his former political opponent, George Romney, as secretary of housing and urban development.[16] Recognizing that he did not, however, enjoy the full confidence of the president, Romney decided to leave the cabinet at the end of Nixon's first term.

The lack of complete trust that characterizes the relationship between the president and his cabinet appointees is not due merely to the fact that the president does not always get the person he wants. It also stems from the president's awareness that he does not command the total loyalty of many cabinet members. We have already dealt with this problem at length in an earlier chapter on the bureaucracy. Suffice it to say here that several departments in the executive branch (Agriculture, Commerce, Labor, Education, Interior, Health and Human Services, Housing and Urban Development, Energy, Transportation, and Veterans Affairs) represent powerful interest groups within our society, and these interests enjoy considerable support in Congress. Accordingly, department heads may be under considerable pressure from these interests to advocate and pursue policies that are not necessarily consistent with the president's program. Reacting vigorously to what he perceived as disloyal department heads, Richard Nixon began his second term by demanding the resignation of two cabinet members and reshuffling two others. In response to a question on this shake-up, Nixon's chief of staff, H. R. Haldeman, replied: "You're goddamned right we're cleaning house, we're going to have loyal people now, who take their marching orders from the White House, no Cabinet officer is going to be able to make his own deal with Congress."[17] This same concern was the primary motivation behind Carter's now-famous cabinet purge, the likes of which had not occurred since the presidency of John Tyler. Distressed at the apparent disarray within his administration, Carter in July 1979 summoned individuals in and outside government to Camp David for the purpose of reassessing his administration. Among the several problems identified at these meetings was an absence of loyalty among certain of his cabinet members.[18] Accordingly, upon his return to Washington, he promptly asked for the resignations of his entire cabinet, five of which he accepted. These included Joseph Califano (health, education, and welfare), Michael Blumenthal (treasury), James Schlesinger (defense), Brock Adams (transportation), and Griffin Bell (attorney general). With the exception of Bell, who had expressed a desire to leave the administration, the others were removed because the president and his aides had concluded that their behavior reflected less than wholehearted support for his policies. This was an ironic turn of events for a president who took office promising to give his cabinet members primary responsibility for policy formulation and implementation: "I believe in Cabinet administration of our government. There will never be an instance while I am President where members of the White House staff dominate or act in a superior position to the members of our Cabinet."[19]

Finally, if the president is reluctant to trust the counsel of cabinet members because of the reasons stated above, it must also be acknowledged that cabinet members are themselves reluctant to provide frank and honest advice.

> There is no such thing as adversary discussion in a cabinet meeting. Men do not pound the table, contradict each other, challenge contrary opinions. . . . What follows is a gentlemanly discourse conducted on an extremely "high" level, and enveloped in the maximum dullness conceivable. And every word is addressed to one man and one man only. A Cabinet meeting is not a marketplace of thought where ideas undergo crucial tests.[20]

More important, cabinet secretaries are reluctant to disagree openly with the president. Indeed, one of Kennedy's closest aides, Theodore Sorensen, warns that a president must take care not to make his position known too early in such meetings, for once it is detected, there is a rush by the others to register their agreement with him.[21] Robert Kennedy described this phenomenon.

> His office creates such respect and awe that it has almost a cowering effect on men. Frequently I saw advisers adapt their opinions to what they believed President Kennedy and, later, President Johnson wished to hear. I once attended a preliminary meeting with a cabinet officer, where we agreed on a recommendation to be made to the President. It came as a slight surprise to me when, a few minutes later, in the meeting with the President himself, the cabinet officer vigorously and fervently expressed the opposite point of view, when from the discussion, he quite accurately learned that it would be more sympathetically received by the President.[22]

Even such a forceful and independent personality as Secretary of State Dean Acheson acknowledged that he found it extremely difficult to stand up to President Truman when he disagreed with him.[23]

Cabinet Member Influence

Although we have mentioned several factors that serve to reduce the impact of cabinet appointees upon presidential thinking, it should be noted that under certain circumstances individual members may come to exercise considerable influence. Specifically, those individuals whose ability, loyalty, and personality are judged favorably by a president will gain entry to his inner circle. Eisenhower, for example, never disguised the fact that he valued highly the judgment of his treasury secretary, George Humphrey. Similarly, having developed great respect for the abilities of Defense Secretary McNamara and Treasury Secretary Dillon, President Kennedy frequently sought out their counsel on a variety of matters. On the other hand, while he regarded Secretary of State Rusk as able and hardworking, he never felt comfortable around him. Their relationship was a very formal one—indeed Rusk was the only member of the Kennedy cabinet whom the president never addressed by his first name.[24] Johnson, however, had no difficulty in developing a free and easy relationship with Rusk. In addition, his confidence in the loyalty and judgment of both Rusk and McNamara ensured that they would be influential figures in foreign policy deliberations. In the Nixon administration, John Connally stood out as one of the most influential members of the cabinet. Although prior to Connally's appointment as treasury secretary, the president had only a passing acquaintance with the Texan, Connally's ability, loyalty, and style impressed Nixon to such a degree that he even seriously considered the former Texas governor as a running mate in the 1972 election.[25]

Other things being equal, the influence of certain cabinet members over the president also stems from the nature of their responsibilities. Those members who deal with matters of greatest concern to the president will have greater access to him. Given the fact that presidents have increasingly focused their attention on matters of foreign policy, national security, the economy, and justice, it is not surprising that the secretaries of state, defense, and the treasury and the attorney general are the cabinet members with whom he has the most frequent contact. Indeed, these secretaries have come to be known as the *inner* cabinet. The *outer* cabinet members (notably the secretaries of agriculture, education, labor, commerce, interior, transportation, health and human services, housing and urban development, energy, and veterans affairs) may from time to time gain access to the president when an important issue arises relevant to their departments, but their access is not likely to be consistent over time. Moreover, as noted earlier, these *outer* cabinet departments represent strong clientele groups in the population. And to the extent that heads of these departments develop loyalties to such groups, their loyalty to the president is suspect, and consequently he is less likely to take them into his confidence.[26]

Reagan and Cabinet Government

Having noted that presidents typically do not rely very heavily upon their cabinet in making decisions, it must also be said that Ronald Reagan took office determined to reverse this historical pattern. For this reason, it is worth considering his attempt to do so.

That Reagan should have opted for Cabinet government is not surprising, for he practiced this collegial form of decision making as governor of California. In the words of Caspar Weinberger, one-time aide to Governor Reagan and subsequently his secretary of defense:

> In California, the governor used this system with good effect. He had regular weekly meetings of his Cabinet. Prior to the meetings, short memoranda summarizing and focusing the points to be discussed were circulated. These memoranda were backed up with lengthy position and background papers, and each Cabinet officer was expected to participate fully in the debate on all subjects, even though some of them were miles away from any of that Cabinet member's specific responsibilities. The system worked well; it promoted active, vigorous and informed discussion; numerous different viewpoints were presented to the governor; he had ample opportunity to consider which positions he wished to adopt; and his decision, sometimes after vigorous argument, was not only expected to be supported, but was supported, by his Cabinet members.[27]

In the Reagan presidency, cabinet government was to take the following form: First, the president was to meet weekly with his entire cabinet, and, according to White House Counselor Edwin Meese, such meetings would be reserved solely for "broad issues affecting the entire government . . . and overall budgetary and fiscal matters."[28] Second, in dealing with more discreet policy issues, the president would, depending upon the issue, meet with one of seven cabinet councils, each focusing on a specific policy area and all but one chaired by a member of the cabinet.

> *Economic Affairs:* Secretaries of Treasury (chair), Commerce, State; Chairman of the Council of Economic Advisers, Director of Office of Management and Budget; *ex officio* members: Vice President, chief of staff, Counselor to the President.
>
> *Commerce and Trade:* Secretaries of Commerce (chair), Treasury, State, Agriculture, Transportation, and U.S. Trade Representative; *ex officio* members: Vice President, chief of staff, Counselor to the President.
>
> *Human Resources:* Secretaries of Health and Human Services (chair), Labor, Agriculture, Education, Housing and Urban Development, Attorney General; *ex officio* members: Vice President, chief of staff, Counselor to the President.
>
> *Natural Resources and Environment:* Secretaries of Interior (chair), Agriculture, Transportation, Energy, Housing and Urban Development; *ex officio* members: Vice President, chief of staff, Counselor to the President.
>
> *Food and Agriculture:* Secretaries of Agriculture (chair), Interior, Commerce, Transportation, U.S. Trade Representative; *ex officio* members: Vice President, chief of staff, Counselor to the President.
>
> *Legal Policy:* Attorney General (chair); Secretaries of State, Treasury, Interior, Commerce, Labor, Health and Human Services, Housing and Urban Development; Director of OMB; *ex officio* members: Vice President, chief of staff, Counselor to the President, Legal Counsel to the President.
>
> *National Security Council* (created in 1947); President (chair); Vice President; Secretaries of State, Defense; Director of CIA, Chairman of Joint Chiefs of Staff, chief of staff, Counselor to the President.[29]

Of course, organizing the cabinet more fully into the presidential decision-making process does not by itself ensure that department heads will keep the president's interests in mind rather than those of their own department. As noted in the previous chapter, however, Reagan took great pains to minimize the possibility that cabinet members would stray from the reservation. In addition, the heavy White House staff presence in Reagan's cabinet government system ensured that his key aides would be guiding the policymaking process. White House Counselor Edwin Meese was charged with setting the agenda of cabinet meetings; Meese and Chief of Staff James Baker were ex officio members of all the cabinet councils and were responsible for preparing council agendas and calling meetings; and finally, the staff arm of these councils—the National Security Council staff and the Office of Policy Development—were both lodged in the White House and came under Meese's direct supervision.

How did Reagan's model of cabinet government work in practice? The weight of the evidence suggests that it met with only limited success. As with his predecessors, Reagan's enthusiasm for full-fledged cabinet meetings as a mechanism for reaching important policy decisions began to wane very quickly. Following a flurry of such meetings during his first few weeks in office, the president and his aides concluded that they were time-consuming; that certain cabinet members voiced opinions on issues they knew little about; and that the substance of such meetings was frequently leaked to the press.[30] As for the elaborate system of cabinet councils, its greatest benefit appears to have been as a morale booster. During Reagan's first term, department heads averaged three or four meetings a week at the White House, with the president in attendance about one-third of the time. These opportunities to meet with the boss and his staff appear to have provided cabinet secretaries with some sense of participation and inclusion. To some extent, moreover, they served to mute as well the customary strains between the cabinet and White House staff.[31] With respect to the shaping of policy, however, the influence of the domestic councils was confined largely to secondary issues.[32] White House staffers quickly concluded that this system was simply too cumbersome and time-consuming for the consideration of pressing top-priority issues. Thus, most of the critical first-term domestic policy initiatives were fashioned not through the council network but rather by White House Chief of Staff James Baker's Legislative Strategy Group and by OMB Director David Stockman.[33]

The councils' limited utility is also suggested by Donald Regan's decision to eliminate most of them when he became the chief of staff in early 1985. Having convinced Reagan that they were "cumbersome and redundant,"[34] he immediately reduced the domestic councils to two—the Economic Policy Council and the Domestic Policy Council. The former was to be chaired by Treasury Secretary James Baker (with whom Regan had just traded jobs), and the latter by the attorney general, a post that was now held by former White House aide Edwin Meese. Yet it is far from clear that these two remaining cabinet councils enjoyed any greatly enhanced influence over policy. Baker declined to use the Economic Policy Council for the most significant second-term economic initiatives (tax reform, realignment of the dollar, international debt), relying instead on ad hoc groups that he himself brought together. A more active role for the Domestic Policy Council, meanwhile, was inhibited by Meese's growing preoccupation with his own legal difficulties and their impact upon the Justice Department.[35]

 THE EXECUTIVE OFFICE OF THE PRESIDENT

Concerned that the administrative responsibilities of the president had become too overwhelming for one man, President Franklin Roosevelt in 1936 established the President's Committee on Administrative Management, which was charged with evaluating the administrative procedures of the executive branch. The committee's evaluation concluded that "the President needs help."[36] Accordingly, in 1939, the Executive Office of the President (EOP) was established by Executive Order 8248. It was to consist of six administrative assistants to the president, along with three advisory bodies: the National Resources Planning Board, the Liaison Office for Personnel Management, and the Office of Government Reports. For thirty-eight years after its establishment, the EOP expanded steadily; at the time President Carter assumed office the EOP included some 1,991 full-time staff members.

This expansion occurred for a variety of reasons. In part, it was a response to crises of one sort or another. Following the abortive Bay of Pigs invasion, for example, President Kennedy concluded that the information that had guided the planning of this undertaking was seriously deficient, and consequently he decided to expand the size of the National Security Council staff.[37] Similarly, President Ford established the Economic Policy Board, the Council on Wage-Price Stability, and the Labor Management Committee, all of which were designed to assist him in dealing with the economic recession that befell the nation in 1974 and 1975. He also added the Energy Resources Council in response to yet another crisis—energy. Another cause for EOP expansion was the realization that certain problems facing our industrialized society are of such complexity that the president needs a group of experts readily available to assist him in dealing with them. This consideration motivated the creation of such units as the Council of Economic Advisers and the Office of Science and Technology.

Finally, of course, the creation of Executive Office units in the White House resulted from a desire to bring about greater policy coordination. Given today's large federal programs, which in many cases involve the participation of several departments and agencies throughout the bureaucracy, there has developed a need for a higher-level body that can coordinate administrative activities and settle interdepartmental conflicts.

Most of our recent presidents have come into office promising to reduce the size of government and have sought to demonstrate their own willingness to sacrifice by reducing the size of the Executive Office of the President. Jimmy Carter, for example, ordered the Office of Management and Budget to undertake a study to determine how the EOP might be reduced in size. Based on recommendations from OMB, the president implemented a reorganization of the EOP that reduced its staff from 1,712 to 1,459; cut back its operating units from 21 to 12; and created two new EOP operations, the Domestic Policy Staff and the Office of Administration. The staff reductions proved to be short-lived, however, for the EOP grew in size each following year and by 1980 employed some 1,900 individuals.[38] The Reagan administration did manage to reduce the Executive Office staff, which was down to 1,272 six months before he left office.[39] By the time George Bush left office, the EOP had increased somewhat to 1,394—a level that Bill Clinton reduced to 1,044 during the first year of his presidency. The projected figure for 1998 was 1,015 full-time staff, with an additional 170 individuals detailed to the Executive Office from other agencies.[40]

The current composition of the Executive Office of the President is shown in Figure 6-1. Several units within the EOP are of sufficient importance to deserve special attention.

National Security Council

The National Security Council (NSC) was established in 1947 for the purpose of providing the president with advice and policy coordination on matters related to national security. Many representatives and senators who were upset with Roosevelt's personal direction of war strategy in the Second World War felt the NSC would ensure that presidents would be presented with a wider range of views on military and diplomatic matters. Its statutory members include the president, vice president, secretary of state, and secretary of defense. Congress also specified certain individuals who would serve as statutory advisers to the council, notably the chairman of the Joint Chiefs of Staff, the director of the CIA, and the director of the Arms Control and Disarmament Agency (added in 1975). Presidents were also authorized to appoint additional advisers to the council as they saw fit. And, in fact, the number of advisers has increased considerably over the years. At the start of his second term, for example, President Reagan decided to make his secretary of the treasury, attorney

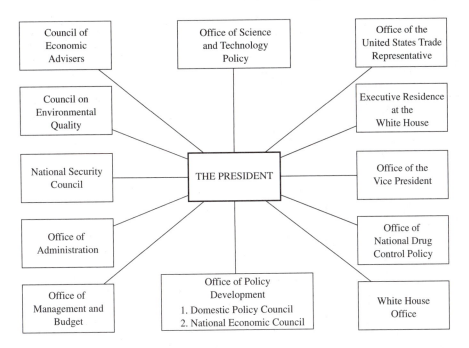

FIGURE 6-1 **Executive Office of the President**

Source: U.S. Government Manual (Washington, D.C.: Government Printing Office, 1997–1998), pp. 90–108.

general, and chief of staff members of the council. Although this was the first time a treasury secretary had ever held membership, the attorney general and staff chief had been granted observer status on the council in some previous administrations.[41] President Clinton likewise expanded the number of NSC participants, asking his chief of staff and two other special assistants to sit in on meetings.[42]

Like all advisory groups to the president, the National Security Council has been important only to the extent that presidents have been willing to let it become so. The council appears to have received greatest use during the Truman, Eisenhower, and Reagan years. Truman sought the advice of the NSC frequently following the outbreak of the Korean War. His successor called the NSC together almost once a week, not a surprising development given the fact that Eisenhower's military background had accustomed him to operating through formal channels. Yet even though Eisenhower relied on this body more than any president before or since, it was still not the dominant force in shaping foreign policy during his administration. Eisenhower wanted the council to deal with long-range policies rather than the day-to-day happenings in the world; in addition, he had a forceful secretary of state, John Foster Dulles, who was not about to surrender the foreign policy initiative to anyone else in the government.[43]

Although President Kennedy met with the members of the National Security Council during his first few months in office, he ultimately found it to be too large a group for making policy on delicate matters of national security. Johnson shared Kennedy's view, preferring to rely on a few select individuals whom he knew well and felt he could trust.[44] Thus, in planning strategy related to the Vietnam War, he chose to deal primarily with a small group of advisers who met with him every Tuesday for lunch. On occasion, he would even bring in trusted friends from outside government. A meeting of the full National Security Council was convened by Johnson only for "educational, ratification and ceremonial purposes."[45] Ironically, Richard Nixon came into office criticizing his predecessors for their failure to utilize the NSC, and although he did indeed meet more frequently with the group during his first two years in office, the meetings became increasingly infrequent as the influence of his national security adviser, Henry Kissinger, grew. Moreover, like his two predecessors, Nixon preferred to deal with foreign policy crises by bringing together a small group of advisers. This group, created after a United States reconnaissance plane was shot down over North Korea, came to be known as the "Washington Special Actions Group." Although the NSC enjoyed some resurgence under President Ford, its role was decidedly secondary to the one played by Henry Kissinger. Rather than meeting with the National Security Council on any regular basis, Carter preferred to breakfast once a week with a small group of foreign policy advisers—the vice president, secretary of state, aide Hamilton Jordan, and National Security Adviser Zbigniew Brzezinski. For handling foreign policy crises, the president established the Special Coordination Committee, presided over by Brzezinski. This group was composed of the NSC membership, energy and treasury secretaries, and six of Carter's top White House aides.

Given President Reagan's commitment in principle to cabinet government, it is not surprising that the National Security Council assumed greater importance in his administration. During his first four years, for example, Reagan participated in some 225 NSC meetings. In contrast, Nixon attended only 86 in a little over five years; Ford, 39 in two years; and Carter, 41 over a period of four years.[46] Before an issue was brought before the full council and President Reagan, however, it was typically addressed first by one of three senior interdepartmental groups, each chaired by a member of the National Security Council: foreign policy (secretary of state, chairman), military and defense (secretary of defense, chairman), intelligence policy (director of CIA, chairman).[47] In dealing with unforeseen foreign policy crises, however, Reagan followed the lead of his predecessors and created a "crisis management group," chaired by the vice president.

Bill Clinton chaired only eight National Security Council meetings during his first ten months in office, an indication that it was not destined to be a primary forum for him in addressing foreign policy issues. Not only did he prefer informal groups and consultations over more formalistic approaches to policymaking, but his policy interests ran much more to domestic issues.[48]

If the Security Council's role in shaping foreign policy has been variable, the same cannot be said of its staff. The NSC staff was originally conceived of as a career staff that would carry over from one administration to the next. During the Kennedy administration the staff developed into an instrument of the incumbent president, primarily because Kennedy had become increasingly frustrated with the lack of initiative and imagination at the State Department. Accordingly, he sought to move foreign policymaking into the White House, and the National Security Council staff provided a ready instrument for developing this capability. He expanded the size of the staff considerably and ordered the creation of a "Situation Room" in the White House, which would receive all cable traffic coming into the State Department, CIA, and Defense Department, thus providing the NSC staff with its own intelligence capacity.

He also gave his ambitious national security adviser, McGeorge Bundy, responsibility for directing the activities of the staff.

The NSC staff continued to be an important force in foreign policy under President Johnson, but it had to share the spotlight with Secretary of State Rusk, who stood much higher in Johnson's esteem than he had in Kennedy's. It was in the Nixon administration, however, that the staff of the NSC came into its own. Three circumstances made this inevitable: first, a president whose primary interests lay in the area of foreign affairs; second, a national security adviser (Henry Kissinger) whose foreign policy expertise and sense for bureaucratic politics were unequaled; and third, a secretary of state whose talents in both of these areas were limited.

Under President Ford, the NSC staff continued in its prominent role, while Henry Kissinger simultaneously held the positions of national security adviser and secretary of state. Ultimately Kissinger was asked to give up his role as national security adviser, which meant he was no longer director of the NSC staff. While this change did not diminish Kissinger's role in foreign policy, one suspects that it lessened the importance of the NSC staff.

The powerful role played by Henry Kissinger as national security adviser evoked considerable criticism. Such a development, it was argued, undercut the authority of the secretary of state and often produced conflicting signals on the direction of American foreign policy. This criticism reached a crescendo during the Carter administration, with some—including Kissinger himself—calling for the abolishment of the position of national security adviser.[49] It is particularly ironic that Carter's national security adviser should have played such a pivotal role in the formulation and articulation of foreign policy, for the president vowed to make Secretary of State Cyrus Vance the undisputed spokesman on America's relations with the rest of the world. The reality proved to be considerably different, however, for it was not long before Carter's flamboyant national security adviser, Zbigniew Brzezinski, was undertaking sensitive diplomatic missions, meeting with ambassadors and heads of state, holding press conferences, and appearing on television. Indeed, Brzezinski even went so far as to designate a member of the NSC staff as his press secretary. Nor did Brzezinski's high profile encounter any significant challenge from Cyrus Vance, a man with a profound distaste for political infighting. Ultimately, Vance chose to resign his post when Brzezinski and other White House aides persuaded the president to go ahead with the rescue of Americans held hostage in Iran—a decision that offended Vance, not only because he thought it imprudent but also because he felt the State Department had not been adequately consulted on the matter. Although it was thought that his more assertive successor, Edmund Muskie, would present a greater challenge to Brzezinski's foreign policy role, Muskie soon learned that the national security adviser's proximity to the president puts the secretary of state at a distinct disadvantage in attempting to influence the president's thinking on world affairs. As one former national security adviser observed: "The national security adviser is right down the hall, and likely to see the president several times a day. The president is likely to trust him because he has no institutional interest, such as a big department to run, and nobody to serve but the president. And he always has the opportunity for the last word—a cover note on a memo, or personal comment when he takes it into the Oval Office. This is where the power lies."[50]

In view of the growing criticism leveled at the role of the national security adviser during the Carter years and given as well Reagan's commitment to the primacy of his cabinet members in formulating policy, Reagan took steps to reduce the role of his own national security adviser, Richard Allen. Not only was Allen ordered to keep a low profile and eliminate the press secretary on the NSC staff, but he also came under the direct supervision of White House aide Edwin Meese. This change marked a break with the long-standing tradition of having the national security adviser report directly to the president. Allen suffered a further diminution in stature when, after six months on the job, he was advised to provide daily national security briefings to Reagan in written form rather than orally. Allen, it should be noted, was not in much of a position to reverse the more downgraded role that had been carved out for him. Administration figures did not perceive him as a heavyweight thinker in foreign policy and were similarly unimpressed with the quality of people he had hired for the NSC staff. To make matters worse, reports circulated in the press alleging that Allen had improperly accepted gifts from a Japanese magazine and had failed to provide certain pertinent information in his financial disclosure statement. Although the Justice Department cleared Allen of any illegal actions, the president decided that Allen had become a political liability. In January 1982, he was replaced.

As President Reagan and his aides discovered, however, the diminution of the national security adviser's role carried a price, for Allen lacked the clout to forge a consensus out of the foreign policy differences developing within the administration—most notably between the State and Defense departments. Thus, in a reversal of position, the decision was now made to elevate the stature of national security adviser. This change was signaled by placing Reagan's close friend Assistant Secretary of State William Clark in the position and authorizing him to report directly to the president rather than to Meese and to resume the practice of briefing the president each day in person. Under Clark the White House did indeed become more assertive in directing foreign policy, prompting the strong-willed Secretary of State Alexander Haig to resign on the grounds that White House aides were preempting his self-proclaimed role as the "vicar" of foreign policy.

Following Clark's brief stint as national security adviser, the post was held by Robert McFarlane, who would ultimately resign after two years over differences with Reagan's staff chief, Donald Regan. Not a conceptual thinker in the mold of a Kissinger or Brzezinski, McFarlane did not seek to shape the broad dimensions of foreign policy but rather saw his function as one of "policy facilitation and coordination."[51] In this role, he enjoyed some limited success in muting the policy conflicts between the secretaries of state and defense, as well as calming the waters on Capitol Hill. His successor, John Poindexter, handicapped by no previous experience in government, proved to be notably less capable in these areas.

McFarlane and Poindexter may not have achieved the influence of Kissinger and Brzezinski across the broad range of foreign policy issues, but they did outdistance their predecessors in one respect. Both took the NSC staff beyond a purely policy role and into the domain of covert operations. These activities, which have been collectively characterized as the Iran-contra affair, will be examined more thoroughly in the next chapter. Suffice it to say here that the NSC staff, with the acquiescence of both McFarlane and Poindexter and apparently without the specific knowledge of the president, raised money for the contras from both foreign governments and private sources and became involved in coordinating military support for contra guerrilla operations. With the president's general approval, the NSC staff in 1985–1986 also managed the negotiations and logistics for selling the Iranian government arms in return for the release of American hostages. On his own initiative, Poindexter subsequently authorized the diversion of some monies from Iranian arms sales to the contras.[52] When these activities became public, Poindexter was forced to resign and was replaced by Frank Carlucci and then by General Colin Powell.

The national security adviser during the Reagan years was probably destined to become a less formnidable figure than in most previous administrations even after White House efforts to reinvigorate the role. Several factors help to explain why this was so. First, two of the administration's key foreign policy actors, Defense Secretary Weinberger and CIA Director William Casey, were longtime personal friends of the president. Consequently, they had ready access to him and were not about to subordinate themselves to a White House staff aide. Second, no Reagan security adviser held the post long enough—there were six different advisers in eight years—to develop a truly close working relationship with the president. Finally, and most decisive, given the president's rather passive management style, he had little inclination to focus foreign policymaking in the White House under a strong national security adviser. Rather, he was content to delegate broadly, exhibiting little interest in follow-up and apparently little disturbed by the frequent foreign policy scuffles that broke out among his cabinet members.[53] Ironically, however, this very same passivity probably encouraged McFarlane and Poindexter to go beyond any of their predecessors by involving themselves and the NSC staff in a series of covert actions, many of which were undertaken without presidential approval. Subordinates, after all, take their cues from their superiors. Had Reagan been a sterner taskmaster, supervising his aides more closely and insisting on being kept fully informed of what they were doing in his name, McFarlane and Poindexter may not so easily have taken to such freelancing.

Under George Bush, National Security Adviser Brent Scowcroft was an important player in the foreign policy process but did not achieve the influence of Kissinger and Brzezinski. This is readily understandable given that Bush's secretary of state, James Baker, was not only a strong personality with a keen grasp of bureaucratic politics but also the president's closest confidant. The two national security advisers (Anthony Lake, Samuel Berger) who served under Clinton were more low-key as well. Neither possessed a big ego; both served a president for whom foreign policy was not a primary interest; and in the case of Samuel Berger, Clinton's second-term national security adviser, served with a secretary of state (Madeline Albright) who was not reluctant to assert her prerogatives.

In summary, the record to date suggests that the role of national security adviser is likely to assume greatest influence when all of the following conditions are present: a president who is an activist in foreign policy; a secretary of state who is relatively weak; and a national security adviser assertive enough to fill the vacuum.

Council of Economic Advisers

Established under a provision of the Federal Employment Act of 1946, the Council of Economic Advisers was created in response to the belief that presidents needed expert advice on such complex economic matters as employment, tax policy, and inflation. Although Franklin Roosevelt had several economists on his staff who informally provided him with information and advice about the economy, many members of Congress were not pleased with the advice he was receiving; nor did they appreciate the fact that no attempt was made to share this information with Congress. Consequently, while Congress stipulated that the president could appoint the three members of the Council of Economic Advisers, it also required that council membership be approved by the Senate. Furthermore, Congress stipulated that the council must report to Congress from time to time. In point of fact, however, the council has had a great deal more influence upon presidential thinking when it has attempted to serve the president alone than when trying to serve both president and Congress.[54]

Members of this council are by no means the only individuals that advise the president on the economy. Typically, the secretaries of the treasury, commerce, labor, and agriculture, as well as the director of OMB and the president's White House adviser on domestic policy, all play key roles. Indeed, during the Reagan presidency the council played a decidedly secondary role in shaping economic policy, with OMB Director David Stockman and Treasury Secretary Donald Regan exercising the dominant influence in the first term and Treasury Secretary James Baker during the second. That the president attached less importance to the council was vividly symbolized by the fact that following the resignation of its chairman, Martin Feldstein, the vacancy was allowed to languish for months before being filled.

Office of Management and Budget

The Office of Management and Budget is among the most important units in the Executive Office of the President. This is evidenced by the fact that in 1973, Congress passed a law requiring that the director and deputy director of OMB be confirmed by the Senate. Created in 1921 as the Bureau of the Budget, and originally located in the Treasury Department, it was moved to the Executive Office in 1939.[55] As part of President Nixon's reorganization efforts, the bureau was renamed the Office of Management and Budget in 1970. Its responsibilities include (1) assisting the president in drawing up the budget he submits to Congress each year; (2) acting as a clearinghouse for all legislation coming from the various departments to ensure that no department sponsors legislation that might be in conflict with the president's policy objectives; and (3) monitoring the implementation of presidential programs to see that they are administered economically and efficiently. This last responsibility reflected President Nixon's desire to have the bureau focus more directly on managerial efficiency in government—thus the change in name to Office of *Management* and Budget. Specifically, Nixon wanted OMB to become more involved with evaluating and coordinating programs, improving the organization of the executive branch, establishing more effective information and management systems, and considering ways of developing better executive talent. Although OMB made some effort in these areas during the Nixon and Ford administrations, the results were not especially noteworthy. Carter, however, having campaigned on the issue of improving government management, made a greater attempt to develop the management mission of OMB. Accordingly, his first OMB director, Bert Lance, devoted a considerable portion of the office's resources to this matter, concentrating particularly on government reorganization.[56]

Although the Office of Management and Budget has been of critical importance in all administrations, it became even more so during the Reagan presidency. Budget and tax cuts constituted the very centerpiece of the president's domestic legislative program. In addition, David Stockman, a former congressman and Reagan's first OMB director, not only was well versed in budgetary politics from a legislative perspective but exhibited a command of the executive budget unequaled by any other Reagan appointee. Consequently, as Reagan's first treasury secretary attests, Stockman's role proved decisive in shaping the president's first-term budget cuts; "very few ideas except Stockman's were ever expressed. Everyone was singing from his sheet of music."[57] OMB's importance was enhanced still further by the president's decision to press it into service as a clearinghouse for all regulations proposed by government agencies—a matter that we examined at some length in the previous chapter.

Although the Bush administration continued OMB's aggressive watchdog role in connection with federal regulations, Bill Clinton introduced some important modifications. Responding to criticisms that OMB assessment of proposed regulations was too heavily driven by purely quantitative indicators, he ordered that more qualitative factors (e.g., issues of equity) be considered as well. Moreover, Clinton sought to reduce White House encroachment on agency decisions by instructing OMB to confine its review to those proposed regulations that have a significant impact (i.e., $100 million dollars or more). Finally, seeing merit in the charge that OMB review in some instances produced lengthy delays in getting needed regulations in place, Clinton ordered that OMB must in most instances complete its review of a regulation within ninety days.[58]

Domestic Policy Council

Originally named the Domestic Council, this unit was a creation of the Nixon administration. It was viewed as the domestic counterpart to the National Security Council and charged with formulating and coordinating policy related to domestic matters. The membership of the council included the president, vice president, director of the Office of Economic Opportunity, and all department heads except the secretaries of defense and the treasury. It was also provided with a staff under the directorship of John Ehrlichman, Nixon's special assistant.

In actuality, the Domestic Council did not function in the manner that was intended. It rarely met as a group, primarily because its size was considered too unwieldy for a fruitful discussion of issues. Its staff, on the other hand, did become an important force in the shaping of domestic policy. Under the direction of John Ehrlichman, it grew to sixty-six people in just two years and devoted most of its time to establishing domestic priorities and providing the president with options for dealing with pressing domestic problems.[59] During those first two years, the procedure for handling a given domestic issue typically involved the creation of a cabinet committee from among the department heads serving on the Domestic Council. In addition, a task force was established consisting of individuals from the various departments and agencies concerned with the issue under consideration. Significantly, Ehrlichman and his staff determined the composition of the task force. Moreover, they were careful to select individuals whose views were clearly in tune with those of the administration. This practice upset some cabinet members, who saw individuals being picked from their departments whose views were not always consistent with their own. The task force was chaired by a member of the Domestic Council staff, and its final recommendations were presented to the cabinet committee or frequently to the president himself.

The important role played by the Domestic Council staff from 1970 to 1972 was significantly diminished in 1973. Several factors contributed to this decline. For one thing, Ehrlichman was elevated to the position of counselor to the president, and a considerably less influential administration official, Kenneth Cole, was placed at the head of the Domestic Council staff. More important, President Nixon realized that the efforts of this staff to supervise the coordination and implementation of domestic policy had resulted in a bloated White House bureaucracy. Thus, he decided to shift most of this responsibility to three trusted cabinet members, giving each the additional title of counselor to the president. Each of these "super" secretaries would be given responsibility for supervising the formulation and coordination of domestic policy in one of three major areas: natural resources, human resources, and community development. In addition, the Domestic Council would now consist of three committees based upon these three major areas, with the supersecretary in charge of each area acting as the committee's chairperson.

As noted in Chapter 5, Nixon's effort to establish supersecretaries did not prove workable, and he dispensed with them after a few months. Moreover, it was at precisely this time that the Watergate scandals began to break, and as Nixon became increasingly preoccupied with trying to save his presidency, he had no time to spend on domestic initiatives. Needless to say, this state of affairs left both the Domestic Council and its staff with little direction.

Upon the recommendation of his transition team, President Ford decided to maintain the Domestic Council but expanded its membership to include additional representatives from several units within the Executive Office, as well as from certain government agencies. In addition, he placed Vice President Rockefeller in charge of the council. Neither the council nor its staff proved to be an effective force in the formulation of domestic policy, however. To some extent, this was simply because the Ford administration undertook comparatively few domestic policy initiatives. Also, some of President Ford's top aides had objected to placing Rockefeller in charge of the council. Consequently, the relations between the Ford staff and Rockefeller's Domestic Council staff were not as cordial as they might have been. Rockefeller finally asked to be relieved of his supervisory responsibility after concluding that the amount of time he was investing in this endeavor was yielding little payoff.

Carter's reorganization team recognized the necessity for coordinating domestic policy, but they were also aware of the president's desire to deal with issues through ad hoc groups rather than formal structures. Accordingly, the Domestic Council was eliminated and replaced with a Domestic Policy Staff headed by the president's assistant for domestic affairs and policy, Stuart Eizenstat. In dealing with domestic issues, the Domestic Policy Staff followed a procedure that began with an "issue definition memorandum" drafted by Eizenstat either on his own initiative or at the request of a particular department or agency. This memorandum contained the questions that needed to be addressed concerning a given issue; specified an ad hoc coordinating committee whose membership included cabinet or subcabinet members from all of the departments and agencies involved with the issue; and designated an agency to take the lead in analyzing the issue and making recommendations. Before the issue definition memorandum was written up by Eizenstat, however, he first consulted with the vice president, senior White House aides, and the departments and agencies affected. When the memorandum was completed, he took it to the president for approval. If Carter gave the go-ahead, the issue was discussed in the coordinating committee, after which the lead agency prepared a "response memorandum" detailing its recommendations for dealing with the issue in question. Other departments and agencies could also add their own views to the response memorandum. The Domestic Policy Staff then summarized all of these opinions and recommendations and sent them on to the president, along with its own analysis and recommendations.[60]

This rather intricate process reflected the president's desire to give departments and agencies greater input into the policymaking process than they had in the past. It was also designed to provide Carter with input from a wide range of sources. Eizenstat explained, "The notion is to involve all Cabinet Secretaries in the early stages; no one feels left out and can throw a monkey wrench in the review at the last minute. There is a cross fertilization of ideas and the president gets all views."[61] As Carter's enthusiasm for cabinet government declined, however, the role of the Domestic Policy Staff in formulating domestic policy proposals increased markedly, and Eizenstat, himself a member of Carter's inner circle of Georgians, became the chief spokesman for the administration's domestic programs.

Although the Domestic Policy Staff was renamed the Office of Policy Development (OPD) by the Reagan administration, it continued to focus on domestic issues. However, in keeping with the president's intention of according his cabinet primary responsibility in policymaking, the OPD from the very outset was slated to play a less prominent role than its counterpart had in the Carter White House. The OPD staff was reduced by approximately half at the beginning of the Reagan presidency and cut again in subsequent years. Moreover, unlike Stuart Eizenstat who reported directly to Carter, Reagan's domestic policy adviser reported to White House Counselor Edwin Meese, until he became attorney general in the second term. The major function of OPD was to serve as a staff arm for the cabinet councils,[62] but even after these councils began to wane in importance, OPD never managed to assert itself. In the first term, White House Chief of Staff James Baker took a skeptical view of the Meese domestic policy shop, viewing it as long on ideology and short on pragmatism.[63] And by the time Baker left at the start of the second term, White House attention was increasingly dominated by foreign policy issues. Add to these disadvantages frequent turnover in the position of domestic policy adviser—four changes in all—which itself may have reflected frustrations over the limited role of OPD.

The Office of Policy Development under the Clinton administration consisted of a revived domestic council (now named the Domestic Policy Council) and a newly created National Economic Council, the latter to be discussed later.

Twenty members strong, the Domestic Policy Council included all cabinet secretaries except state and defense, the heads of the Environmental Protection Agency and OMB, the director of the Office of National Drug Control Policy, the AIDs policy coordinator, and four senior domestic policy advisers to the president.[64] Its purpose was to oversee the development and implementation of the president's domestic policy agenda and facilitate coordination and communication among the heads of relevant federal offices and agencies. Unfortunately, the Domestic Policy Council performed none of these functions particularly well. Carol Rasco, the director of the council and Clinton's assistant for domestic policy, saw the most important domestic policy issues captured by other entities. The deficit and NAFTA, for example, gravitated to the National Economic Council; health care became the preserve of Hillary Clinton and presidential assistant Ira Magaziner; Senator Patrick Moynihan (D-N.Y.) was allowed to take the lead on welfare reform; political reform and crime were taken over by the president's Office of Legislative Affairs; and government reform was handed over to the vice president.[65] Furthermore, once it became apparent that the Domestic Policy Council was not a significant player, policy coordination suffered as cabinet members on their own began to push program proposals that were not necessarily consistent with Clinton's goals.[66] A more effective director of the Domestic Policy Council and its staff might have been able to forestall, or at least lessen, these problems. Unfortunately, Carol Rasco lacked the experience for such a role, was not assertive enough in laying claim to issues, and ultimately lost the confidence of the president.[67] Nor, of course, did it help that her boss was someone who did not place a high premium on a structured decision-making process.

National Economic Council

Having developed a more sophisticated understanding of the economy and economic policy than any of his predecessors, Bill Clinton was convinced that the White House needed the equivalent of a national security council "to coordinate and formulate advice across the whole range of national and international economic issues."[68] Accordingly, in campaigning for the presidency he promised to create an "Economic Security Council." In its final incarnation, the name would be altered slightly to the National Economic Council (NEC). Headed by his national economic adviser, a newly created staff position within his administration, its functions are to provide economic advice to the president, coordinate economic policy throughout the executive branch, and monitor the implementation of economic policies. Toward these ends, its core membership included the secretaries of labor, commerce, and the treasury as well as three individuals from within the Executive Office of the President, notably, the chairman of the Council of Economic Advisers, the head of the Office of Management and Budget, and the head of the Office of the U.S. Trade Representative.

By most accounts the council established itself as an important player in the White House policymaking process during Clinton's first term, thanks in no small part to the talents of the president's first national economic adviser, Robert Rubin. Having come to Washington following a highly successful stint as cochairman of the Goldman Sachs investment banking firm, he had instant credibility in financial circles as well as within the White House. This fact, combined with his considerable brokering skills, enabled him to bring coherence and coordination to the various strands of thinking within the administration on such important matters as the budget deficit, trade with China, and NAFTA. In recognition of his abilities Clinton tapped Rubin to head the Treasury Department in 1995, replacing him with Laura D'Andrea Tyson, former chairwoman of the Council of Economic Advisers. The NEC subsequently experienced some diminution in importance, in part because Rubin carried his influence with him; partly also because Clinton's new chief of staff, Leon Panetta, formerly director of OMB and one-time chair of the House Budget Committee, took over the leadership role on the president's budget.[69]

Panetta, however, left government at the start of Clinton's second term, as did Clinton's second national economic adviser, Laura D'Andrea Tyson. Whether Tyson's replacement, Richard Sperling, would be able to retain a significant role for the NEC was unclear. On the one hand, he was highly knowledgable in budgetary matters, which augured well for his influence, especially given Panetta's departure. On the other, he lacked the reputational weight of his two predecessors and would have to work with a treasury secretary (Robert Rubin) whose stature continued to grow, and whom Clinton dubbed "the captain of our economic team."[70]

The White House Staff

For the president's purposes, the White House staff (White House Office) is perhaps the most important unit in the Executive Office. It consists of numerous personal advisers who may hold the title of assistant, counselor, or aide to the president. Usually among the more important staff members are the assistant for national security affairs, assistant for domestic affairs, counsel to the president, appointments secretary, assistant for communications, assistant for legislative affairs, press secretary, and chief of staff, if he has one. With a few exceptions, individuals holding these positions are largely unknown to the American public. It is doubtful, for example, that most people would recognize the names of Sandy Berger, Erskine Bowles, and Bruce Lindsey, all of whom occupied important positions on President Clinton's White House staff. Nor is it likely that people outside of government would have recognized the names of Bob Haldeman, John Ehrlichman, Chuck Colson, and John Dean had it not been for the scandals of Watergate. The fact that a president's senior staff members operate in relative obscurity should not cause us to view them as inconsequential figures, however. On the contrary, they are among the most powerful people in government. Their importance derives from their immediate and direct access to the president. They enjoy this access because most of the senior staff, having usually been longtime associates of the president, command his total confidence.

Among the more notable developments in the White House staff has been its gradual expansion over the years. Thomas Jefferson administered the government with a personal staff of one messenger and a secretary, whose services he paid for with his own money. Grant had only three staff assistants, and, despite our involvement in the First World War, Wilson maintained a rather small staff of seven. Gradually, however, the White House staff began to expand. Roosevelt had an immediate staff of 11; Truman, 13; Eisenhower, 37; Kennedy, 23; Johnson, 20; Nixon, 48; Ford, 56; Carter, 48; Reagan, 83; Bush, 77. But these figures do not tell the whole story, for nearly all of these aides had support staffs of their own.[71] Thus, when we include all the full-time employees serving in the White House Office, the average staff size for each of these presidents becomes Roosevelt, 51; Truman, 272; Eisenhower, 351; Kennedy, 422; Johnson, 304; Nixon, 506; Ford, 583; Carter, 412; Reagan, 371; Bush, 380, and Clinton, 415 (through 1995).[72] Even these figures may not give a complete picture, however, since the White House commonly borrows employees from the various departments and agencies and details them for service on the president's business.

Given the complexity of the problems we face today, plus the fact that we look increasingly to the president for solutions, it is not surprising that the White House staff has grown considerably. But there are other reasons for its expansion. Increasingly frustrated over the unresponsiveness of the bureaucracy from department heads on down, presidents have moved policymaking into the White House and given it to aides they could trust. With some regret, Senator Hollings (D-S.C.) took note of this development during the Nixon administration.

> It used to be if I had a problem with food stamps, I went to see the Secretary of Agriculture whose Department had jurisdiction over that program. Not any more. Now, if I want to learn the policy, I must go to the White House and consult John Price. If I want the latest on textiles, I won't get it from the Secretary of Commerce, who has the authority and responsibility. No, I am forced to go to the White House and see Mr. Peter Flanigan. I shouldn't feel too badly. Secretary [of Commerce] Stans has to do the same thing.[73]

The increase in staff is also attributable to the president's desire to monitor the activities of the various departments and agencies to make sure they are implementing his policies.[74] This factor accounts in part for the especially large increase in the White House staff during the Nixon administration. Convinced that the bureaucracy had a liberal Democratic bias, President Nixon wanted to make sure that his more conservative programs were not being sabotaged by the bureaucracy.[75]

The changes in the *size and responsibilities* of the White House staff have evoked legitimate concern among people both in and outside government.[76] A staff grown so large becomes difficult to supervise, with the result that staff members run about demanding action in the name of the president, but not always with the president's authorization. Nor has the transfer of responsibility for policymaking and implementation away from department heads and into the White House been viewed as altogether desirable. For one thing, it has been argued that, with few exceptions, the technical skills and expertise necessary to formulate policy proposals reside in the departments and not in the White House and Executive Office staffs. Second, even with its increased size, the White House staff cannot hope to oversee the implementation of presidential programs effectively, for there are too many, and they are frequently so complex that several departments and agencies are involved. Third, to the extent that cabinet members are excluded or minimally involved in the formulation of policy, they have less of an incentive to see that those policies are implemented effectively. Fourth, if cabinet members rather than the White House were visibly identified with generating and articulating policy proposals, some of the controversy that may surround such proposals could be deflected away from the president and toward department heads.[77] Finally, there is the issue of accountability. At the expense of departments, the White House staff has been given a vastly increased role in the formulation and implementation of policy, and yet, unlike cabinet secretaries, they are subject neither to Senate confirmation nor to periodic questioning by Congress.

Sharing many of these concerns, the Reagan administration vowed to reduce the size of the White House staff and increase the role of the cabinet in policymaking. While cabinet government was indeed realized to a greater extent than under previous presidents, as noted earlier, it fell well short of what Reagan and his aides had promised. So too did White House staff reductions. The Reagan White House claimed that between 1981 and 1987 it had reduced the White House staff from 351 to 318, but neither of these figures included employees detailed to the White House from other government agencies. According to the General Accounting Office, the number of employees so assigned during this six-year period reached 380.[78]

In keeping with his promise to shrink the overall size of the executive branch by 10 percent, President Clinton promised to reduce the White House staff by 25 percent. In his first year he did in fact cut the size of the White House staff from 461, which it had reached in the final year of the Bush administration, down to 419.[79] The reductions did not last, however. By 1997, the Clinton White House had abandoned its promise of a 25 percent reduction, arguing that the drug control office and the legal counsel's office required an increase in personnel. The White House also reported in 1997 that over the course of the previous four years its staff had been enhanced by forty-one "paid volunteers," some financed by the Democratic National Committee and others by nonprofit entities. This was in addition to the thirty individuals who had been detailed to the White House staff from other federal agencies.[80]

The notion that presidents should manage with smaller staffs may have some resonance with newly elected presidents, but its importance is likely to recede rather quickly as presidents set about the task of governing.

THE WHITE HOUSE STAFF AND THE PROBLEM OF PRESIDENTIAL ISOLATION

Although one may question the increasingly powerful role played by the White House staff in the administrations of our more recent presidents, clearly there are certain critical functions that any White House staff must perform. In the first place, it must see to it that important information and advice get to the president from people both in and outside government. A president is constantly besieged by people who wish to see him. In addition, letters, memoranda, and reports are sent to him for his attention. Quite obviously, there are not enough hours in the day for a president to honor all these requests; consequently, it falls to the White House staff to determine which people and material are important enough to deserve his personal attention. Second, the staff itself should act as a source of information, advice, and ideas for a president. Third, it should function as a critic and evaluator of the president's own ideas and judgments, as well as those coming from other people in and outside government. Finally, it should act as a channel through which the president can convey his own wishes to those in the bureaucracy, Congress, the press, opinion leaders, and the public.

While all of these functions are important, the first three are especially so, since they bear directly on the acquisition of information and advice—the essential ingredients for informed decision making. The degree to which the staff can perform these three functions successfully depends upon (1) how the staff is organized, (2) staff attitudes toward the president, and (3) the president's attitude toward his staff. Let us now examine each of these three factors in greater detail.

Staff Organization

The organization of the White House staff defies precise generalization, for its form and structure are inevitably a reflection of the style and personality of the person it is serving. However, we can say that staffs have ranged on a continuum, from structured to unstructured. Perhaps the best example of the unstructured type was the White House staff of Franklin Roosevelt. He functioned as his own chief of staff, handing out assignments to staff members and requiring them to report directly to him. There was no rigid chain of command on the Roosevelt staff. On the contrary, all of his staff members had direct access to him. He also sought to surround himself with generalists, that is, people whose breadth of knowledge was such that they could be put to work in a variety of different policy areas. By doing so, Roosevelt avoided the possibility of a staffer developing so much influence in a given policy area that the president would be forced to rely exclusively upon him as a source of information. Nor was he content to delegate a given task to only one staff aide, but instead would often give the same assignment to several aides. This practice frequently caused competition and conflict among his staff, but it also ensured that several channels of information would be open to him on a given problem. While to some, Roosevelt's staff appeared to be in a state of chaos, this method of operation accomplished Roosevelt's purpose, namely, to avoid the presidential isolation that can result from restricted channels of information.[81] The Kennedy and Johnson staffs were similar to Roosevelt's. Each president functioned as his own chief of staff, each was accessible to staff members who wished to see him; and while both assigned their staff members to a given area of responsibility, they did not hesitate to assign them to a problem outside their specialty area if the need arose.[82]

Both Eisenhower and Nixon provide examples of presidents who had highly structured staffs, although each had different reasons for making them so. Eisenhower had spent most of his life in the military and was thus accustomed to staffs that operated according to a rigid chain of command with clearly specified rules and procedures. It is not surprising, therefore, that he followed this model upon becoming president. He gave his staff members specific areas of responsibility. As his chief of staff he appointed Sherman Adams, who was regarded by many as the most powerful man in government next to the president himself. Adams was charged with handing out assignments to staff members. More important, it was Adams who decided which individuals and what materials would gain entry to the Oval Office. Moreover, if reports and memoranda were to have any chance of gaining the personal attention of the president, they normally had to be reduced to one page.[83] Thus, whereas Roosevelt had a variety of information channels, Eisenhower had essentially one—Sherman Adams. This rigidity in staff organization and procedures did moderate somewhat in 1958, when Adams was succeeded by the less autocratic Jerry Persons.

President Nixon's staff was perhaps even more structured than Eisenhower's. H. R. Haldeman functioned as the president's chief of staff, and the rest of the staff were each given a specific area of responsibility. A staff member who went beyond his responsibilities was severely reprimanded. Jeb Magruder, for example, one day wrote a memorandum proposing a new idea for the president's attention. It was quickly returned with a note from Haldeman saying, "Your job is to do, not to think."[84] Similarly, in drafting a speech for Nixon on Vietnam, one of his speechwriters proposed that no more draftees be sent to fight in Vietnam. He was promptly taken off the speech.[85] Any person wishing to see the president or any material marked for his attention nearly always had to gain the approval of Haldeman before gaining entry to the Oval Office. Haldeman was strongly criticized by staffers, members of Congress, and department heads for building a "Berlin Wall" around the president. However, he was merely accommodating himself to the style of his chief, for, as one White House aide noted, "Nixon did not like to see many people, and wanted to see still fewer privately."[86]

Even among Nixon's personal staff, access was restricted to only a very few aides. Former President Johnson detected the isolation of President Nixon while visiting him at the White House. The former president was astounded to observe that Nixon had one little phone with just three buttons on it, which could connect him with only Haldeman, Ehrlichman, and Kissinger.[87] In contrast, when Johnson was president he had a telephone with an elaborate set of buttons that could put him in direct contact with any member of his staff or the cabinet.

Haldeman's deputy assistant testified before the Senate Watergate Committee that "60 percent of the time that the President spent with any staff member in 1972 was spent with his chief of staff, and that for 90 percent of that time they were alone."[88] Nixon speechwriter William Safire recalls that the only time the staff saw Nixon was when they were asked to show up for the arrival of Nixon's helicopter on the White House lawn. More frequently than not, people were told that if they had something to say to the president they should put it down on paper. Contrary to popular belief, some Nixon aides contend that Haldeman, being sensitive to the president's isolationist tendencies, took great pains to see that Nixon was presented with a full range of opinion.[89] But even if several options were presented to the president, either on paper or by Haldeman himself, such a procedure still foreclosed the opportunity for give-and-take between the president and his aides, where he could probe and challenge their ideas and vice versa.

Nixon's isolation from his staff no doubt explains why he was unaware of some of their Watergate-related activities. Whether such activities would have been avoided if Nixon had not remained so isolated seems doubtful, however, for the White House staff takes on the coloring of the person it serves.

Even before taking office, Jimmy Carter had made it clear that his staff would be organized in the tradition of Roosevelt, not Nixon. He would function as his own chief of staff. All of his senior aides would be treated equally, and each would report directly to him. Indeed, in characterizing the organization of the White House staff, Carter associates likened it to a bicycle wheel, with staffers representing spokes that lead directly to the center—the president. The analogy did not originate with the Carter administration, however. Rather, it was borrowed from President Ford's White House aides, who had tried to arrange his staff along the same lines—but failed. In the words of Ford's chief of staff, "The spokes of the wheel concept is a nice concept, but it won't work. . . . Somebody has to make certain that before the President signs off on a decision that he has all the relevant information and that he has taken into consideration economic, political, domestic, foreign, and all other factors involved. Somebody has to police the process."[90]

During his first twelve months in office, Carter remained accessible not only to his nine senior staff aides but also to the vice president and the cabinet. Those members of the staff who could not get in to see him personally were nevertheless able to present their views in writing. In place of a chief of staff, senior staff aides, who met three times a week, handled staff coordination. As time passed, these meetings gradually dropped off to only twice a week, and senior aides increasingly sent deputies to attend in their places.

After the first year, however, it became apparent to both President Carter and his top advisers that the White House staff operation was not functioning as effectively as they had hoped. Carter found himself inundated with detail, and apparently neither he nor anyone else was making any effort to discriminate between matters that could be handled at a lower level and those that could not. In addition, the absence of any single point of coordination frequently resulted in the left hand not knowing what the right hand was doing.[91] This problem was highlighted, for example, when the United States decided to issue a joint communique with the Soviet Union calling for a resumption of Geneva talks on the Middle East. In taking such a step, the United States appeared to be inviting the Soviet Union to play an active role in dealing with the Middle East problem. But, despite the fact that this decision had weighty implications in terms of its impact on American Jewish opinion, none of the president's domestic advisers was consulted before the decision was made.

In January 1978, President Carter issued two orders to his senior staff, the first of which authorized his top political adviser, Hamilton Jordan, to become more actively involved in the substance of foreign policy decisions. More directly relevant to our discussion here, however, was the second order, which stated that Jordan would henceforth have responsibility for coordinating staff activities. He would chair the weekly staff meetings, hold any additional ones he deemed necessary, and report discussions and recommendations directly to the president.[92] Although Jordan continued to insist that he was not really functioning as chief of staff in this new role, it was nevertheless clear that an effort was being made to provide more structure to the White House staff operation. These steps did not prove sufficient, however, for when Carter undertook an agonizing reappraisal of his administration a year and a half later, much of the criticism voiced was directed at the White House staff operation. It was argued that its activities were not well coordinated; that its follow-through on presidential directives left much to be desired; and that it did not effectively organize the president's time for more important matters. Ultimately, although it ran contrary to his natural inclinations, Carter formally designated Hamilton Jordan as his chief of staff.

Moreover, since Jordan was not noted for his organizational ability, the White House brought on board Alonzo McDonald, a corporate executive with a reputation for efficient management. Aside from holding more meetings among members of the senior staff, it is not altogether clear how the structure of the White House staff changed once Jordan and McDonald assumed their new roles. McDonald did insist, however, that his efforts to bring greater efficiency to the president's staff did not have the effect of rendering Carter less accessible to his aides.[93]

Reflecting Reagan's disposition to delegate authority and hold himself aloof from the details of decision making, Reagan's staff structure in his first term was more reminiscent of Eisenhower's than Carter's. Unlike Eisenhower, however, who placed supervision of the White House operation solely in the hands of Sherman Adams, Reagan initially divided this responsibility among his three top aides: James Baker, Edwin Meese, and Michael Deaver. These three men handed out White House assignments and, along with his national security adviser and personal assistant, were the only staff members who had direct access to Reagan. Baker, designated chief of staff, oversaw the day-to-day operations of the White House, including press, congressional, public relations, personnel, and intergovernmental affairs. By all accounts, the organizational and political skills that Baker brought to these tasks were of a very high order. Meese, meanwhile, had overall responsibility for the policymaking apparatus, and Deputy Chief of Staff Michael Deaver was charged with advance scheduling and overseeing the First Lady's staff.[94] This troika arrangement was by no means free of tensions. On the contrary, disagreements soon developed among the three, with the pragmatists Baker and Deaver typically facing off against the more ideological Meese, who strenuously resisted efforts to dilute the conservative Reagan agenda.[95] On the whole, however, this system worked reasonably well, providing the president with valuable channels of information and a healthy clash of views.[96]

At the start of Reagan's second term, however, the staff organization underwent an abrupt change. Chief of Staff James Baker traded places with Treasury Secretary Donald Regan. Meese and Deaver soon left as well, the former to become attorney general and the latter to enter the consulting business. Regan, who had been the chief executive officer of Merrill Lynch, found the existing White House staff organization untidy and moved to institute the kind of rigidly hierarchical operation to which he had been accustomed in the corporate world. With no objection from the president, all functions that had previously been performed by the troika were now lodged with Regan, who was responsible for "personnel, the coordination of information, the choice of issues, the flow of paper, and the schedule that controlled the President's travel and other movements and determined who would see him and who would not."[97] In addition, only three individuals now had direct access to the president—the chief of staff, the national security adviser, and the president's personal assistant. With these sweeping changes, Regan achieved a concentration of power in the chief of staff equaled only by Sherman Adams after Eisenhower's heart attack in 1955.[98]

Reagan does not appear to have been well served by these changes, however. Given the fact that he was already inclined toward disengagement from the policymaking process, these organizational changes, by further restricting access to him, merely reinforced his passivity. Thus, it may be more than coincidental that during the first half of his second term, the president appeared even less well briefed on matters related to his administration than he had during his first four years. Investing so much authority in Regan proved to be imprudent on other grounds as well. Regan lacked the political savvy of his predecessor, and consequently relations with Congress suffered, as did White House ability to anticipate such political minefields as the president's visit to Bitburg, inadequate preparation for the Reykjavik summit, and the Iran-contra affair. Indeed, with respect to the last debacle, Regan's stewardship came under such heavy criticism that he was forced to resign. His successor, former U.S. Senator Howard Baker (R-Tenn.), wasted no time in forging a more decentralized staff organization, reserving for himself the role of presidential adviser while dispersing other chief of staff functions among five aides.[99]

In summary, the Roosevelt approach to the White House staff would appear to be far more conducive to maximizing the flow of information into the Oval Office than were the hierarchically organized staffs of Eisenhower and Nixon. And yet a staff as unstructured as Roosevelt's is simply not feasible in the contemporary presidency. Roosevelt, after all, sat at the top of a staff that was relatively small because it had limited responsibilities in formulating legislation and overseeing presidential programs. Consequently, the task of functioning as his own chief of staff was more manageable. On the other hand, both Ford and Carter came into the presidency after the White House staff had undergone a remarkable expansion during the Nixon years. Not surprisingly, both ultimately concluded that they needed a chief of staff. All of this is not to say that presidents must adopt a rigid Nixonian staff organization. Rather, it is to suggest that a balance must be struck, one that results in enough structure to achieve adequate coordination and free the president from unnecessary detail, and yet at the same time has enough flexibility to provide the president with sufficiently varied channels of information and advice.

For the first two and a half years of his presidency it is not at all clear that Bill Clinton struck that necessary balance. By all accounts, there was little structure to his White House staff. He granted Oval Office walk-in rights to at least twelve aides; the responsibilities attached to various staff positions were often ill defined; to an unprecedented degree, friends and associates with no official White House titles were issued White House passes and used for special assignments; and Clinton's chief of staff (Thomas "Mack" McLarty), an individual with no previous experience in politics, lacked the temperament and stature to forge some degree of discipline within the White House decision-making process, leaving the president to function essentially as his own chief of staff.[100]

Clinton aides maintained that the fluidity of the staff structure was tailored to the style of their boss: "The President is into everything, wants to decide everything, wants the details of everything."[101] This approach, as noted earlier, has the advantage of exposing the president to many sources of information and advice, but it also runs the risk of overburdening the president with detail, impeding coordination, and blurring lines of accountability. In addition, given the fact that Clinton had a tendency to procrastinate on making decisions, a staff organization that lacked some semblance of hierarchy merely increased the likelihood that reaching closure on issues would be difficult to achieve. Thus, rather than compensating for the president's weaknesses, Clinton's staff structure served to reinforce them.

The pathologies associated with Clinton's approach to White House management were much in evidence during his first two and a half years in office. White House aides testified to endless and often directionless meetings. Nominations to fill positions in the Executive and Judiciary proceeded at an excruciatingly slow pace and were not always preceded by careful staff work. Some one hundred White House staffers, though they had been in their positions for over a year, still had not taken the necesssary steps to receive security clearances; and inadequate supervision of staffers led to the clumsy handling of several White House personnel matters, most notably those relating to the White House Travel Office and to the suicide death of the president's deputy legal counsel (Vincent Foster).[102] Nor, finally, were any of the problems plaguing Clinton's staff helped by the excessively high rate of turnover among its members. During the first year alone, the president had named four deputy chiefs of staff, two directors of congressional liaison, two communications directors, two scheduling directors, two directors of intergovernmental relations, and two political directors.

That greater organization, discipline, and coordination were required was recognized midway into 1994 when the president replaced Chief of Staff Mack McClarty with OMB Director Leon Panetta. To his astonishment, Panetta learned that there existed no White House staff organization chart outlining who did what. Moreover, he discovered that the president was spending 22 percent of his time sitting in staff meetings and was vastly overscheduled for public events of one kind or another. Accordingly, Panetta took control of the president's calendar, more than halved the amount of time Clinton spent in staff meetings, increased his "thinking time" to 35 percent, eliminated free-floating advisers, and allowed into the Oval Office only those individuals who had his or the president's specific approval.[103] With Panetta's departure at the beginning of Clinton's second term, the president's former deputy staff chief, Irskine Bowles, was persuaded to return to Washington to head the White House staff. Having worked with Panetta and helped to shape the staff changes, Bowles did not embark upon any significant changes in staff operations.

Clinton's early management problems, it should be stressed, were traceable not only to how the staff was structured but also to the people he placed on it. The fact is that Clinton did not take adequate care in deciding how he would staff the White House—an oversight he would later come to regret: "I spent all my time before I took office choosing my Cabinet. . . . But I didn't spend the time I should have choosing my staff. I just reached out and took the people who helped me get elected and put them on the staff. It was a mistake."[104] Thus, the president found himself surrounded mostly by bright, young, and largely untested individuals. Indeed, only his national security adviser, Anthony Lake, had served in the White House under a previous administration.[105] Bear in mind too that Clinton hailed from a relatively small, one-party state and was himself without any previous Washington experience. Accordingly, it was imperative that he choose individuals who would make up for this deficit, not reinforce it.

Staff Attitudes toward the President

A less rigidly structured staff does not by itself maximize the possibility that the person in the Oval Office will get all the information he needs. Those staff members who have access to the president must be willing to speak candidly with him. When necessary, they must be capable of telling him things he may not want to hear. This may take the form of presenting him with disquieting information or being openly critical of his ideas. This staff function is *especially* important because they are the people whose judgment the president trusts most and because others in government are often reluctant to speak frankly with the president.

In spite of their relatively close relationship with the president, however, staff members also have a tendency to be overawed by the presidency. This reaction serves to restrain them from challenging the president. Robert Kennedy noted that this office has an "almost cowering effect on men."[106] Another of Kennedy's aides, Theodore Sorensen, notes its effect in the following way:

> I saw no halo, I observed no mystery. And yet I found that my own personal, highly informal relationship with him changed as soon as he entered the Oval Office.
>
> He was the same human being with the same faults and virtues with whom I had worked, joked, argued, and traveled, almost night and day, for eight years. Yet my attitude was instantly characterized by a greater degree of not only deference but awe. Addressing him at all times, at play as well as work, as "Mr. President" instead of the former Jack was but a symbol of this change. I noted a similar alteration in the attitudes of his other staff members, his old friends, his seniors in Congress, and even his political enemies.[107]

In a similar vein, Charles Colson admits that even after he came to know Richard Nixon well, "I never lost my reverent awe of the President, or the Presidency, which for me were synonymous."[108] This attitude could not help but affect what he characterized as his relationship with Nixon. "During the time I served in the White House, I rarely questioned a Presidential order. Infrequently did I question the President's judgment. I had one rule—to get done that which the President wanted done."[109]

There is yet another reason why staff aides are often disinclined to speak candidly with the president. Not unlike other government officials, White House advisers seek to maintain, and hopefully increase, their power. As a former presidential adviser noted, power is defined in terms of one very important factor.

> Power in Washington is measured by a stern gauge: the direct proportion of access to the President, for the asset of the realm is information that flows only from the President. If you were to fluoroscope the brain and conscience of any top official within the government, you would be able to chart the flight of agony caused by lost intimacy with the President, or denial of access to him.[110]

Daniel Moynihan was not insensitive to the importance of access when he was taken on as a Nixon adviser. He decided to forego a spacious office in the Executive Office Building across the street from the White House and instead took a tiny office in the White House basement because it put him closer to the president. Although Henry Kissinger had considerable access to the president, he nevertheless bemoaned the fact that it was not enough. One Nixon speechwriter recalls an incident in which Kissinger acknowledged his distress.

> I was writing the President's opening toast for the first night in Moscow at the end of the State dinner in Granovit Hall. Henry glanced at my four-page draft and said, "You need two more pages." I said, no, Haldeman told me one thousand words tops, and Kissinger exploded: "Foreign policy decided by flacks." . . . He called Haldeman to get the President to change to fifteen hundred words. . . . The fact that he had to deal with Haldeman and could not go direct to the President irritated him immensely. It was Nixon putting him down again. "A week ago," Henry said with passion, "he would have done anything I asked, he was on his *knees—God!* And now I have to talk to Haldeman."[111]

If power is defined in terms of access to the president, how then do White House staffers gain and maintain such access? By flattering him, agreeing with him, withholding unpleasant thoughts from him. Woodrow Wilson's close aide Colonel

House frankly admitted that he constantly flattered his boss, on one occasion telling him that he was the "one hope left to this torn and distracted world. Without your leadership, God alone knows how long we will wander in the darkness."[112] During Kennedy's presidency, one of his closest advisers gave a speech in which he compared the president favorably with such notables as Apollo, Charlemagne, Roland, and St. Francis. Similarly, one of Lyndon Johnson's senior staff members was criticized in the press for giving a rather syrupy speech in which he stated, "I sleep each night a little better, a little more confidently because Lyndon Johnson is my President. For I know he lives and thinks and works to make sure that for all Americans, and indeed, the growing body of the free world, the morning shall always come."[113]

The President's Attitude toward Staff

Staff behavior that takes the form of flattery as well as ready agreement with the president can succeed only if presidents are willing to encourage it. There is, in fact, a tendency for presidents to do so, and the reasons grow out of the effects the office has upon the individual as well as the effect the individual has upon the office.

To understand how the office may influence the individual, consider for a moment how we treat this institution. For years the scholarly and journalistic communities have sung the praises of this office, pointing to it as the only place in our political system capable of leadership and innovation. Not only have the media romanticized the presidency, but they have also personalized it, informing us of the president's habits, tastes, and hobbies, many of which have become national fads. Nor should we minimize the symbolic trappings surrounding the office. The president is the only democratically elected chief executive in the world who is hailed by a special song ("Hail to the Chief") when he appears at public events. Men and women alike stand when he enters and leaves a room. Upon becoming president, he is henceforth referred to as "Mr. President" even by his closest friends. This fact was impressed upon Eisenhower when, shortly after assuming the presidency, he placed a call to his friend Omar Bradley, chairman of the Joint Chiefs of Staff. After the conversation was over, Eisenhower turned to his secretary and with great surprise remarked, "He called me Mr. President, and I've known Brad all my life."[114] While the prime ministers of Great Britain are referred to by their cabinet as Prime Minister on formal occasions, in cabinet meetings they are called by their first names. Members of the president's cabinet, however, would never think of referring to him by anything other than "Mr. President," regardless of the circumstances.

Custom-made automobiles, planes, bodyguards, and houses are all placed at his disposal. Extraordinary efforts are made to fulfill his every wish. One day, for example, while President Eisenhower was putting on his special green on the White House lawn, a squirrel ran in front of the ball and he casually remarked, "Get that goddamned squirrel out of here." Lo and behold, the next day he discovered the corps of the Parks Department rushing about the White House lawn trapping squirrels. Attention and reverence are accorded presidents even after they leave office. When a former president takes ill, we receive hourly bulletins on his condition, and when he dies, a national day of mourning is declared, and he is usually laid to rest in an elaborate state funeral. Clearly, the respect for this institution has changed markedly from the time of Thomas Jefferson, who, after being inaugurated, returned to his boardinghouse for dinner and had to wait in line until there was a vacant place at the table.

It is difficult for a president to escape being affected by the reverential treatment accorded to the office he occupies. One of Kennedy's longtime friends recalls that when sailing on the presidential yacht, Kennedy became quite annoyed if other boats failed to recognize and salute him. On one occasion, after giving a speech on a military base, President Johnson headed out onto the landing strip full of planes. While proceeding to where he thought his plane was situated, he was approached by a soldier, who told him his plane was off in the other direction. Johnson took him by the shoulder and said, "Son, I want to tell you something—just so you never forget. All of them, those over there *and* those over there—are my planes." Only after Richard Nixon was severely ridiculed by the press did he abandon the regal, fancy-dress uniforms he had ordered for the White House guards. And as Charles Colson notes, Nixon was also quite insistent that traditional symbolic trappings be maintained. One evening, for example, President Nixon decided to pay an unannounced visit to the Kennedy Center to hear a concert given by the military bands. Shortly before entering the presidential box, Colson recalls, "The President turned and said, 'Have you made arrangements for them to play the you-know-what, Chuck?' He didn't come right out and say it, but I knew he meant 'Hail to the Chief.'"[115]

These examples of presidential behavior may seem inconsequential, but they are symptomatic of a more fundamental presidential attitude that is of concern to us. Presidents have a tendency to become intoxicated by the deference and veneration shown to the office they hold. They begin to see themselves as deserving of praise and come to view challenge and disagreement as an affront.[116] In order to preserve their access to the president, staff members accommodate themselves to this presidential tendency. One of Franklin D. Roosevelt's closest aides contends that those advisers who lasted the longest with him were the ones who did not challenge his thinking, but rather gave unquestioning service.[117] Even the seemingly unpretentious Harry Truman was not enamored of the prospect of having an individual on his staff whose sole job would be to act as a critic of presidential thinking. In fact, one of his advisers made just such a suggestion, although he noted that such an individual would probably last only six months. Truman replied, "Six *months?* I would not have him around six *minutes.*" Similarly, one of Eisenhower's senior aides notes that in the closing years of the Eisenhower presidency, the White House staff agreed informally not to bring him any upsetting news.[118]

The isolation of presidents from the disquieting advice of staff members was especially pronounced in the Johnson and Nixon administrations. Both men were deeply insecure, and consequently they were especially susceptible to the arrogance generated by the intoxicating atmosphere of the presidency. In Johnson's case, his style of bullying staff members and his obsession with loyalty further encouraged advisers not to challenge him. One participant in White House decision making during the Johnson presidency describes how this timidity manifested itself.

> The President, in due course, would announce his decision and then poll everyone in the room—Council members, their assistants, and members of the White House and NSC staffs. "Mr. Secretary, do you agree with the decision?" "Yes, Mr. President!" "Mr. X, do you agree?" "I agree, Mr. President." During the process I would frequently fall into a Walter Mitty–like fantasy: When my turn came I would rise to my feet slowly, look around the room and then directly at the President, and say very quietly and emphatically, "Mr. President, gentlemen, I most definitely do *not* agree!" But I was removed from my trance when I heard the President's voice saying, "Mr. Cooper, do you agree?" And out would come a "Yes, Mr. President, I agree."[119]

As we shall see in the next chapter, those aides who did ultimately stand up and challenge Lyndon Johnson's Vietnam policy either lost their access to him or, more frequently, were let go.

Of all our presidents, Richard Nixon was perhaps the most isolated. As noted earlier, he simply did not like to see people. Moreover, like his predecessor, he did not take kindly to disagreeable advice from his staff. Indeed, when possible, he sought to avoid seeing advisers who he knew were about to bring him "bad news or unpalatable recommendations."[120] Those who did challenge him with disturbing facts thought twice before doing so again. One aide, for example, recalls complimenting the president on one occasion for becoming more accessible to the press. Having held a rather antagonistic attitude toward the press, Nixon proceeded to deny that he was becoming any more accessible. When the evidence was produced to show that he was in fact granting more interviews to newspeople, the president promptly canceled a news conference that had been scheduled for the next day. As for the aide who brought the disquieting information to Nixon and even refuted the president's challenge to its validity, he recalls that, "for three solid months I did not receive a speech assignment from the President, or a phone call, or a memo, or a nod in the hall as he was passing by."[121] As further punishment, he was one of two longtime advisers not invited to the White House wedding of the president's daughter.

If accounts of Carter's White House staff are correct, it behaved no differently from those of previous presidents. Indeed, after his administration was only three months old, Carter received a confidential memo from Hamilton Jordan expressing concern over the tendency of advisers to anticipate what the president wanted to hear instead of providing him with candid appraisals.[122] Although a sense of awe for the office no doubt fostered this kind of behavior, there is evidence to suggest that Carter's personality may also have been a contributing factor. Charles Kirbo, who was one of the president's closest confidants, readily acknowledged that the president "has a strong personality that tends to intimidate some people."[123] This assessment was confirmed by another White House assistant: "The office, of course, is so damned intimidating in itself and Carter is such an intimidating man that it's just very difficult to disagree with him."[124] Other individuals in the Carter administration remarked about being ignored or receiving an "icy look" from the president when they dissented too strongly from his views.[125] Even the dissent of Carter's closest adviser, Hamilton Jordan, was reportedly cut short on one occasion after the president bluntly replied: "When you read as much as I do, then maybe you'll have the right to disagree."[126] Yet, unlike Johnson's and Nixon's, Carter's impatience with dissent does not appear to have been rooted in feelings of insecurity, but rather in a supreme sense of confidence in his own judgments.

By way of style and temperament, Gerald Ford and Ronald Reagan were quite different from the other presidents discussed here. Both lacked the powerful ego and insecurity of a Johnson or Nixon. Nor was their inner self-confidence so overpowering as to engender the kind of arrogance that sometimes characterized the Carter personality. Consequently, they appear to have been much less influenced by the monarchical trappings of the presidency, less inclined to feel the need for praise or agreement from those around them. And yet the awe of the presidency was still there and, according to Ford's chief of staff, served to inhibit his advisers from being completely candid with him.

I can think of many instances where individuals who have been long-time associates and colleagues of the President's have been in a meeting with the President, addressed an issue with him, and then slipped down to my office after the meeting and said, "Now, what I really wanted to say was this." And they took the bark off, and there was something that had a very different feel.[127]

Nor was it any different under Reagan, who, if anything, was an even more affable and less threatening personality than Ford. Indeed, one Reagan adviser, commenting on the effectiveness of the cabinet council system, observed that "the effect of having the president there is to suppress most meaningful controversy. This is too bad. The participants seem to be much less willing to express their views forcefully if the president is there than if he isn't."[128] Or consider White House Chief of Staff Donald Regan—hardly viewed as a shrinking violet within the Washington community— seeking to explain why he failed to challenge a critical decision that he thought Reagan had made too hastily: "It is one thing to brashly speak your mind to an ordinary mortal and another to say 'Wait a minute!' to the President of the United States. The mystery of the office is a potent inhibitor."[129]

OUTSIDE ADVISERS

In discussing whom the president consults for information and advice, we have thus far focused upon individuals and groups within the executive branch. But the president seeks the counsel of people outside of government as well. Such individuals often include former government officials. Lyndon Johnson, for example, sought the advice of former presidents Truman and Eisenhower. Indeed, in the case of the latter, Johnson on many occasions had him flown by a Jetstar from his farm in Gettysburg to Andrews Air Force Base outside Washington. Johnson then helicoptered to Andrews, where he met in secret with Ike aboard the Jetstar. He also sought the assistance of former Secretary of State Dean Acheson in dealing with the Cyprus problem.[130] Similarly, in September 1979, Jimmy Carter brought together fifteen former government officials (including Henry Kissinger, Clark Clifford, Dean Rusk, William Rogers, and McGeorge Bundy) to advise him on how to respond to the presence of Soviet troops in Cuba.

Presidents also turn to old and trusted friends for advice. Johnson, for example, brought his longtime friend Clark Clifford into the deliberations on Vietnam long before he finally appointed him as secretary of defense. Similarly, his lawyer friend Abe Fortas was consulted on a variety of matters before, as well as after, he appointed him to the Supreme Court. Even a president's family has been reputed to exercise considerable influence over presidential opinion. Eisenhower sought out his brother Milton, and Kennedy was known to consult with his father. In the cases of Roosevelt, Carter, Reagan and especially Clinton, the judgment of their wives was frequently solicited on a variety of matters. Indeed, to an unprecedented degree Hillary Clinton has been a major player in both personnel and policy decisions.

Other outsiders consulted by presidents include recognized experts in a given field. Both Kennedy and Johnson, for example, sought the expertise of economist John Kenneth Galbraith and foreign policy expert Henry Kissinger. Moreover, presidents may from time to time bring a whole group of experts together to examine a critical problem or formulate policy proposals. Lyndon Johnson made use of several such informal presidential task forces that were charged with developing legislative proposals for his Great Society program. These groups were made up of academi- cians, economists, scientists, doctors, businesspeople, labor leaders, and lawyers from all over the country.[131] Nixon continued the practice, setting up seventeen different task forces for purposes of developing legislative programs for 1970 and beyond.[132]

In attempting to deal with certain highly visible and controversial issues, presi- dents may decide to establish more formalized groups, known as commissions, whose members are appointed directly by the president. Following the urban riots of the mid-1960s, for example, Johnson established the National Commission on the Causes and Prevention of Violence, and toward the end of his administration he cre- ated the National Commission on Obscenity and Pornography. Similarly, in response to the increasing concern among Americans over the use of drugs, Richard Nixon established the National Commission on Drug Abuse. Following the revelations about CIA activities in and outside the United States, President Ford decided to clear the air by appointing an eight-member commission charged with determining whether or not the CIA had exceeded its statutory authority. Of these eight members, seven were private citizens and the eighth was Vice President Rockefeller, whom Ford designated as chairman of the commission. During his first term in office, Bill Clinton created eight different commissions on such varied subjects as entitlement programs, Gulf War veterans' illnesses, consumer protection and quality in the health care industry, U.S.-Pacific trade investment policy, infrastructure protection, bioethics, HIV/AIDS, and sustainable development.

Relying upon individuals who are not officially connected with the government can be very beneficial to a president. Given their separation from the machinations of government, as well as the fact that their livelihood is in no way dependent upon the favor of the president, they are more likely to provide him with a candid assessment. Seeking the advice of distinguished private citizens is not without its risks, however, for they may ultimately come up with conclusions and recommendations that run contrary to the views of the president. Thus, it was undoubtedly somewhat embar- rassing for President Nixon when he felt compelled to refute publicly the findings of both the National Commission on Obscenity and Pornography and the National Commission on Drug Abuse. Nor was it likely that the distinguished citizens sitting on these commissions were pleased that he did so.

Finally, it should be noted that presidents may also seek the counsel of individ- uals who, although not outside of the government, are nevertheless outside of the executive branch. I refer to members of Congress, many of whom are recognized experts in certain policy areas. President Kennedy had great respect for the foreign policy expertise of former Senator William Fulbright, who was chairman of the Sen- ate Foreign Relations Committee. Accordingly, he included him in the White House deliberations on the Bay of Pigs invasion of Cuba. Similarly, Lyndon Johnson always sought the advice of then-Senator Wayne Morse on important matters concerning labor because of the senator's knowledge of labor relations. However, according to Lyndon Johnson's former press secretary, George Reedy, the counsel provided to presidents by members of Congress is often not what it should be. For them, just as for others in government, frank advice is often muted by their awe for the office.

I can recall an occasion about six or seven months after I had left the White House, when I met Senator Russell at a party in Washington. I said to him: "Senator, do things look as bad as I think they do?" and he said "Yes, they do, George." And I said, "Senator, you used to be quite effective in talking to the President. Why don't you make a trip down to the White House and have a heart-to-heart talk?" And his response was, "George, I can't talk to a President the way I can talk to a Senator." And this to me was the key. There *is* a difference in status which separates the President from his peers because if a United States Senator is not the peer of a President, who is?[133]

Reedy also notes his surprise at the behavior of Senator Barry Goldwater and Governor George Wallace when they came to the White House in 1964. As presidential candidates, they had been traveling about the country excoriating the president and his policies, and Reedy fully expected that they would have some strong words for the president. Yet when these two rather independent and blunt individuals were confronted with his presence, "they were the mildest, meekest Casper Milquetoasts I've ever seen in my life. Those men were not afraid of Lyndon Johnson. It was the president who overawed them."[134]

 NOTES

1. Taken from Lewis J. Paper, *The Promise and the Performance* (New York: Crown, 1975), p. 138. Copyright © 1975 by Lewis J. Paper. Used by permission of Crown Publishers, Inc.

2. Joseph Califano, *A Presidential Nation* (New York: Norton, 1975), p. 218.

3. Cited in Kenneth Cole, "Should Cabinet Departments and Agencies Be More Independent?" in Charles Roberts, ed., *Has the President Too Much Power?* (New York: Harper's Magazine Press, 1974), p. 126.

4. Cited in Emmet John Hughes, *The Living Presidency* (New York: Coward, McCann & Geoghegan, 1973), p. 148. Copyright © 1973 by Emmet John Hughes. Reprinted by permission of Coward, McCann & Geoghegan.

5. Ibid.

6. Cited in Charles Hardin, *Presidential Power and Accountability* (Chicago: University of Chicago Press, 1974), p. 38.

7. Cited in Thomas Cronin, *The State of the Presidency* (Boston: Little, Brown, 1975), p. 166.

8. From George E. Reedy, *The Twilight of the Presidency,* p. 74. Copyright © 1970 by George E. Reedy. Reprinted by arrangement with the New American Library, Inc., New York.

9. Cited in Cronin, *State of the Presidency,* p. 186.

10. Fred Barnes, "Cabinet Losers," *New Republic,* February 28, 1994, p. 22.

11. Cited in *Washington Post,* July 5, 1998, p. C7.

12. Cited in Richard Nixon, *The Memoirs of Richard Nixon* (New York: Grosset & Dunlap, 1978), p. 357.

13. David Halberstam, *The Best and the Brightest* (New York: Random House, 1969), pp. 40, 41.

14. Theodore White, *Breach of Faith* (New York: Atheneum, 1975), p. 103.

15. From William Safire, *Before the Fall* (Garden City, N.Y.: Doubleday, 1975). Copyright © 1975 by William Safire. Used by permission of Doubleday & Company, Inc.

16. Richard Nathan, *The Plot That Failed* (New York: Wiley, 1975), p. 39.

17. Cited in White, *Breach of Faith,* p. 179.

18. *Wall Street Journal,* July 20, 1979, p. 1; *Time,* July 30, 1979, p. 10.

19. Cited in Ben Heineman, Jr., and Curtis Hessler, *Memorandum for the President: A Strategic Approach to Domestic Affairs in the 1980s* (New York: Random House, 1980), p. 118.

20. Reedy, *Twilight of the Presidency,* pp. 77, 78.

21. Theodore Sorensen, *Decision-Making in the White House* (New York: Columbia University Press, 1963), p. 60.

22. Cited in Hardin, *Presidential Power,* p. 41.

23. Ibid., p. 35.

24. Paper, *Promise and Performance,* pp. 158, 159.

25. Safire, *Before the Fall,* pp. 497–508.

26. Cronin, *State of the Presidency,* pp. 191, 197, 198.

27. *Washington Post,* December 1, 1980, p. A19.

28. *National Journal,* March 3, 1981, p. 399.

29. *Washington Post,* February 16, 1981, p. A4; *National Journal,* March 3, 1981, p. 399.

30. *Washington Post,* February 15, 1981, p. 1; *U.S. News and World Report,* March 16, 1981, p. 18.

31. *National Journal,* June 28, 1986, p. 1583; Colin Campbell, S.J., *Managing the Presidency* (Pittsburgh: University of Pittsburgh Press, 1986), pp. 75, 76, 217.

32. Peter M. Benda and Charles H. Levine, "Reagan and the Bureaucracy: The Bequest, the Promise, and the Legacy," in Charles O. Jones, ed., *The Reagan Legacy* (Chatham, N.J.: Chatham House, 1988), p. 110.

33. *National Journal,* June 28, 1986, p. 1583.

34. Donald T. Regan, *For the Record* (New York: Harcourt Brace Jovanovich, 1988), p. 235.

35. *National Journal,* June 15, 1985, p. 1418.

36. Cited in Clinton Rossiter, *The American Presidency* (New York: New American Library, 1956), p. 122.

37. Cronin, *State of the Presidency,* p. 121.

38. U.S. Bureau of the Census, *Statistical Abstract of the United States* (Washington, D.C.: Government Printing Office, 1980), p. 281.

39. This figure was provided to the author by the Research Division of Congressional Quarterly, Inc.

40. *New York Times,* February 10, 1993, p. A10; *Washington Post,* March 13, 1997, p. A21.

41. Regan, *For the Record,* pp. 238, 239.

42. *Washington Post,* October 31, 1993, p. C7.

43. I. M. Destler, "National Security Advice to U.S. Presidents," *World Politics* 29 (January 1977), 147, 148.

44. Keith Clark and Laurance Legere, *The President and the Management of National Security* (New York: Praeger, 1969), p. 60.

45. Ibid., p. 88.

46. Leslie Gelb, "Taking Charge," *New York Times Magazine,* May 26, 1985, p. 30.

47. *Washington Post,* February 26, 1980, p. A1.

48. *Washington Post,* October 31, 1993, p. C7. See also Colin Campbell, "Management in a Sandbox: Why the Clinton White House Failed to Cope with Gridlock," in Colin Campbell and Bert Rockman, eds., *The Clinton Presidency: First Appraisals* (Chatham, N.J.: Chatham House, 1996), pp. 75, 76.

49. *Washington Post,* November 13, 1979, p. A19; I. M. Destler, "A Job That Doesn't Work," *Foreign Policy* 38 (Spring 1980), 80–88.

50. Cited in *Washington Post,* May 4, 1980, p. A8.

51. Joseph G. Bock and Duncan L. Clarke, "The National Security Assistant and White House Staff—National Security Policy Decisionmaking and Domestic Political Considerations, 1947–1984," *Presidential Studies Quarterly* 16 (Spring 1986), 271.

52. U.S. Congress, U.S. Senate Select Committee on Secret Military Assistance to Iran and the Nicaraguan Opposition, U.S. House of Representatives Select Committee to Investigate Covert Arms Transactions with Iran, *Report of Congressional Committees Investigating the Iran-Contra Affair,* Senate Report No. 100–216, House Report No. 100–433, 100th Cong., 1st sess., 1987, pp. 3–22.

53. On foreign policy disagreements within the Reagan administration, see, for example, *National Journal,* February 28, 1987, pp. 470, 471; *Washington Post,* December 8, 1986, p. A15.

54. Erwin Hargrove, *The Power of the Modern Presidency* (New York: Knopf, 1974), p. 85.

55. For a useful discussion of OMB, see Larry Berman, *The Office of Management and Budget and the Presidency* (Princeton: Princeton University Press, 1980).

56. *National Journal,* October 1, 1977, pp. 1518, 1519.

57. Regan, *For the Record,* p. 153.

58. William F. West and Andrew W. Barrett, "Administrative Clearance under Clinton, *Presidential Studies Quarterly* 26 (Spring 1996), p. 527.

59. Ronald Moe, "The Domestic Council in Perspective," *The Bureaucrat* 5 (October 1976), 257, 258.

60. "Presidential Domestic Policy Review System," *Weekly Compilation of Presidential Documents XIII,* No. 38 (September 19, 1977), 1343–44.

61. *National Journal,* April 5, 1978, p. 586.

62. *National Journal,* December 10, 1983, p. 2567; *National Journal,* April 4, 1987, p. 825.

63. *National Journal,* May 9, 1981, pp. 824–27.

64. Shirley Anne Warshaw, *The Domestic Presidency: Policymaking in the White House* (Englewood Cliffs, N.J.: Prentice Hall, 1997), p. 194.

65. Warshaw, *The Domestic Presidency,* pp. 197, 200, 202, 209.

66. Ibid., pp. 202, 203.

67. Elizabeth Drew, *On the Edge: The Clinton Presidency* (New York: Simon & Schuster, 1994), p. 348; Campbell, "Management in a Sandbox," p. 78; Warshaw, *The Domestic Presidency,* pp. 208, 209.

68. M. Stephen Weatherford and Lorraine M. McDonnell, "Clinton and the Economy: The Paradox of Policy Success and Political Mishap," *Political Science Quarterly* 111 (Fall 1996), p. 419.

69. *National Journal,* June 29, 1996, pp. 1417, 1418; *Washington Post,* December 8, 1996, pp. 1, 26; *National Journal,* December 21, 1996, p. 2753.

70. Cited in *National Journal,* December 12, 1996, p. 2753.

71. Arthur Schlesinger, Jr., *The Imperial Presidency* (Boston: Houghton Mifflin, 1973), p. 221. Copyright © 1973 by Arthur Schlesinger, Jr. Reprinted by permission of Houghton Mifflin Company. The figures on Ford taken from *1976 Congressional Directory,* 94th Cong., 2nd sess. (Washington, D.C.: Government Printing Office, 1976), pp. 483, 484. Figures for Carter and Reagan taken from Shirley Warshaw, *Powersharing: White House–Cabinet Relations in the Modern Presidency* (Albany: SUNY Press, 1996), pp. 111, 154. Figures for Bush compiled from *The Capitol Source* (Washington D.C.: National Journal, Spring 1998), pp. 8–11.

72. Compiled from Lyn Ragsdale, *Vital Statistics on the Presidency* (Washington D.C.: Congressional Quarterly Press, 1996), pp. 258–61.

73. Cited in John Anderson, "A Republican Looks at the Presidency," in Charles Dunn, ed., *The Future of the American Presidency* (Morristown, N.J.: General Learning Press, 1975), pp. 214, 215.

74. Hugh Sidey interviews Bill Moyers, *The White House Staff vs. The Cabinet* (Washington, D.C.: Washington Monthly, 1969), p. 4.

75. Nathan, *Plot That Failed,* pp. 37–54, 82.

76. See, for example, Heineman and Hessler, *Memorandum for the President,* pp. 122–24; National Academy of Public Administration, *A Presidency for the 1980s* (Washington, D.C.: National Academy of Public Administration, 1980), p. 12; Stephen Hess, *Organizing the Presidency* (Washington, D.C.: Brookings Institution, 1976), chaps. 8–11.

77. For a useful discussion of how some cabinet members have served this function for presidents, see *Richard J. Ellis, Presidential Lightning Rods: The Politics of Blame Avoidance* (Lawrence: University Press of Kansas, 1994).

78. *Washington Post,* March 21, 1988, p. A9.

79. *Washington Post,* February 10, 1993, p. A10.

80. *Washington Post,* March 13, 1997, p. A21; *Washington Post,* March 12, 1997, p. A10.

81. Arthur Schlesinger, Jr., "The Dynamics of Decision," in Aaron Wildavsky, ed., *The Presidency* (Boston: Little, Brown, 1969), pp. 133–50; Alex Lacy, "The White House Staff Bureaucracy," *Transaction* 7 (January 1969), 52, 53.

82. Paper, *Promise and Performance,* pp. 146, 147; Lacy, "White House Staff," p. 55; Califano, *Presidential Nation,* p. 48.

83. Lacy, "White House Staff," p. 54.

84. Cited in Paper, *Promise and Performance,* p. 120.

85. Safire, *Before the Fall,* p. 274.

86. Ibid., p. 281.

87. Paper, *Promise and Performance,* p. 113.

88. Cited in John Kessel, *The Domestic Presidency* (North Scituate, Mass.: Duxbury, 1975), p. 114.

89. Safire, *Before the Fall,* pp. 283, 277; see also Robert Woodward and Carl Bernstein, *The Final Days* (New York: Simon & Schuster, 1976), p. 31.

90. Cited in Robert Shogan, *Promises to Keep* (New York: Crowell, 1977), p. 202.

91. Samuel Kernell and Samuel L. Popkin, eds., *Chief of Staff* (Berkeley: University of California Press, 1986), pp. 71, 72.

92. *The New Republic,* February 11, 1978, p. 11.

93. Herman Nickel, "Can a Managerial Maestro End the White House Cacophony?" *Fortune,* October 22, 1979, pp. 58–75.

94. *National Journal,* January 17, 1981, p. 89; *Washington Post,* May 24, 1981, pp. A1–A3; Hedrick Smith, "Troika," *New York Times Magazine,* April 19, 1981, p. 15; Regan, *For the Record,* p. 234.

95. See, for example, *Wall Street Journal,* March 3, 1983, p. 1; *National Journal,* May 28, 1983, pp. 1100–1103.

96. Richard P. Nathan, "Institutional Change under Reagan," in John L. Palmer, ed., *Perspectives on the Reagan Years* (Washington, D.C.: Urban Institute, 1986), p. 124; James Best, "Presidential Learning: A Comparative Study of the Interactions of Carter and Reagan," *Congress and the Presidency* 15 (Spring 1988), 38.

97. Regan, *For the Record,* p. 234.

98. Hedrick Smith, *The Power Game* (New York: Random House, 1988), p. 327.

99. David Eisenhower, "Fighting the President's Final Battles," *New York Times Magazine,* September 6, 1987, pp. 38, 43; *National Journal,* April 4, 1987, pp. 824, 825.

100. *Washington Post,* November 9, 1993, p. A8; *Time,* June 7, 1993, p. 25; *Washington Post,* April 13, 1994, p. A1.

101. Cited in *Washington Post,* November 9, 1993, p. A8.

102. *Washington Post,* November 9, 1993, p. A8, A9; *U.S. News and World Report,* October 25, 1993, pp. 29, 32; *Washington Post,* March 21, 1994, p. A19; *Washington Post,* April 3, 1994, p. A1. See also Richard Haas, "Bill Clinton's Adhocracy," *New York Times Magazine,* pp. 40, 41; Bob Woodward, *The Agenda* (New York: Simon & Schuster, 1994); and Jeffrey Birnbaum, *Madhouse: The Private Turmoil of Working for the President* (New York: Times Books, 1996).

103. *Washington Post,* January 4, 1997, pp. A1, A11; *Washington Post,* November 9, 1996, p. A1; *New York Times,* August 17, 1995, p. A12.

104. Cited in Dick Morris, *Behind the Oval Office* (New York: Random House, 1997), pp. 97, 98.

105. Elizabeth Drew, *On the Edge: The Clinton Presidency* (New York: Simon & Schuster, 1994), p. 130.

106. Cited in Hardin, *Presidential Power,* p. 41.

107. Theodore Sorensen, *Watchmen in the Night* (Cambridge, Mass.: MIT Press, 1975), p. 140.

108. *Family Weekly,* March 28, 1976, p. 4.

109. Cited in Paper, *Promise and Performance,* p. 119.

110. Jack Valenti, *A Very Human President* (New York: Norton, 1975), p. 66; see also Reedy, *Twilight of the Presidency,* p. 88.

111. Safire, *Before the Fall,* p. 437.

112. Cited in Hughes, *Living Presidency,* p. 144.

113. Valenti, *Very Human President,* pp. 95, 96.

114. Cited in Charles Murphy, "Eisenhower's White House," in Nelson Polsby, ed., *The Modern Presidency* (New York: Random House, 1973), p. 89.

115. Charles Colson, *Born Again* (Lincoln, Va.: Chosen Books, 1976), p. 53. Copyright © 1976. Published by Chosen Books Publishing Co., Ltd., Lincoln, Virginia 22078. Used by permission.

116. See Bruce Buchanan, *The Presidential Experience: What the Office Does to the Man* (Englewood Cliffs, N.J.: Prentice Hall, 1978), chap. 4.

117. Cited in Hardin, *Presidential Power,* p. 25.

118. Hughes, *Living Presidency,* p. 143.

119. Cited in Russell Baker and Charles Peters, "The Prince and His Courtiers: At the White House, the Kremlin, and the Reichschancellery," *The Washington Monthly,* February 1973, p. 36.

120. Woodward and Bernstein, *Final Days,* p. 31.

121. Safire, *Before the Fall,* p. 350.

122. Shogan, *Promises to Keep,* p. 200.

123. Ibid., p. 249.

124. Cited in *New York Times,* April 25, 1977, p. 53.

125. Hedrick Smith, "Problems of a Problem Solver," *New York Times Magazine,* January 8, 1978, p. 38.

126. Cited in *New York Times,* April 25, 1977, p. 53. Copyright © 1977 by The New York Times Company. Reprinted by permission.

127. Interview with Donald Rumsfeld on "Firing Line," telecast on the Public Broadcasting System, November 1975. Transcript from Southern Educational Communications Association, P.O. Box 5966, Columbia, S.C. 29250.

128. Cited in Campbell, *Managing the Presidency,* p. 75.

129. Regan, *For the Record,* p. 267.

130. Valenti, *Very Human President,* pp. 308, 380.

131. Califano, *Presidential Nation,* p. 239.

132. "The Office of the President: Formulation and Implementation of Domestic Policy," *The White House: Organization and Operation,* Proceedings of the 1970 Montauk Symposium, vol. I (New York: Center for the Study of the Presidency, 1971), p. 82.

133. George Reedy, *The Presidency in Flux* (New York: Columbia University Press, 1973), p. 30.

134. Ibid., p. 32.

Five Cases in Presidential Decision Making

Quite obviously, the essential ingredients for informed decision making are information and advice. The latter includes varying perceptions as to how the facts ought to be interpreted, judgments about what options are available for dealing with a particular issue, and judgments about what consequences are likely to follow from the implementation of any given option. Of course, even if the president is in possession of the best information and advice he can hope to get, there is still no guarantee that he will make the right decision. The facts and advice he receives may prove to be wrong. Or his own biases may be so strong that he misperceives the realities of a situation and thus ignores the advice he receives. Or perhaps circumstances may arise that could not have been anticipated at the time a decision was made. Yet even if access to information and advice do not always ensure the right decision, it is even more likely that their absence will produce a bad one.

Whether or not the flow of information and advice to the president is maximized will depend most directly upon two factors, the first of which is the number of sources he is willing to seek out. To the extent that he restricts his information channels, he risks becoming the captive of what a few people tell him. For not only are government actors capable of misjudgments, but in most instances they have a stake in how a given policy issue is to be resolved, and thus, consciously or unconsciously, they may provide the president with a biased assessment. Though by no means foolproof, the president's willingness to expose himself to a variety of sources acts as a corrective against biased or faulty information.

The accumulation of the necessary facts and advice for informed decision making is also dependent upon the degree to which the president encourages a frank and open exchange of views from among those he does consult. Indeed, he must make a special effort in this regard, for as already noted, presidential advisers are too much inclined toward ready agreement with their boss. Moreover, if scholars such as Irving Janis are correct, there is still another reason for him to do so—cohesive decision-making groups have a tendency to engage in "groupthink." Among other things, this phenomenon involves an effort by the group to maximize amicable relations by minimizing differences and emphasizing areas of agreement: "The group leader and the members support each other, playing up the areas of convergence in their thinking, at the expense of fully exploring divergences that might disrupt the apparent unity of the group. Better to share a pleasant, balmy group atmosphere than to be battered in a storm."[1] Both the excessive deference and "groupthink" phenomena can only be further encouraged if the president conveys the impression that he does not take kindly to those who dissent from his and the group's point of view.

Having stressed how important it is for the president to consult widely, it is also important to recognize that this task is rendered easier or more difficult by the nature of the decision. The decisions the president makes may be viewed along two dimensions, one dealing with their *substance* (foreign ⟷ domestic) and the other with their *importance* (routine ⟷ crisis).

Substance.   Although the president has more freedom to act in foreign policy, his informational constraints are also greater. To the extent that foreign policy involves issues exterior to the United States, the problems in acquiring necessary information about them are increased. Quite obviously, getting information is less difficult in the domestic area, where the proximity of an issue renders its nature and consequences more readily observable.

Also, the president's informational problems are likely to be greater in the area of foreign policy because there are fewer participants in the foreign policymaking process, and thus the sources of information are fewer. At the upper levels, the participants in foreign policy in most instances include the Departments of State and Defense, the CIA, and the National Security Council. Although Congress certainly has an impact upon foreign policy, its role in domestic policy is more direct and persistent. The president's information base on foreign policy is superior to that of Congress; the committee organization of Congress is far less developed in the foreign policy area than in the domestic area; and the interests of most representatives incline toward domestic issues because the political payoff is likely to be greater. While interest groups are more in evidence on those foreign policy issues that have immediate and direct domestic implications, their involvement is far less apparent as the issues become more discretely foreign in their impact. This is in marked contrast to the domestic policymaking process, where a whole panoply of interests are constantly operating at both the executive and congressional levels.

Finally, it should be noted that, unlike the domestic policymaking process, the limited number of actors in foreign policy will often be reduced still further because many foreign issues involve delicate matters of national security.

Importance.   The president's problems with information relate not only to the substance of a given issue but also to its importance. While in the strict sense every issue that requires a presidential decision qualifies as important, some issues are clearly more important than others; given the considerable demands on his time, the president must reserve his own energies for the more critical ones. Thus, on the more routine issues—whether domestic or foreign—he is not likely to become directly involved in the decision-making process until the final stage. This means that he is far more reliant upon what his advisers tell him regarding the deliberations up to that point. On the other hand, when dealing with issues of great moment, the president's involvement in the decision-making process is likely to be more persistent and direct. Consequently, he is in a position to hear *firsthand* the facts presented, the options considered, and the consequences weighed. Moreover, as the most prominent actor in the decision-making process, he is in a better position to force consideration of all possibilities—if he is of the mind to do so.

Yet, although the president has the advantage of more intimate involvement on the more critical issues, it should be pointed out that such issues may impose an informational constraint that is not likely to be present on more routine matters. For among the more critical issues the president must confront are those characterized as "crises." By their very nature, crises customarily require timely action, which may sometimes prevent him from making as extensive a search for information as he might like.

FIVE CASES OF PRESIDENTIAL DECISION MAKING

In the remainder of this chapter, we shall examine five examples of presidential decision making. Four (Bay of Pigs invasion, Vietnam, Iran-contra affair, and shoe import quotas) attempt to show how and why the flow of information to the president was not maximized, whereas the other (Cuban missile crisis) demonstrates an apparently successful effort at information maximization. Before looking at these examples, however, the reader should be apprised of their limitations. Four of the five fall decidedly in the realm of foreign policy. The absence of more examples on the domestic side is dictated by the state of the literature on presidential decision making, which unfortunately has focused almost exclusively on the analysis of foreign policy decisions.[2] Also, while it is hoped that the following examination of these five decisions identifies the major factors that bear on the decision-making process, this cannot be said with complete certainty. As one president himself admitted, "There will always be the dark and tangled stretches in the decision-making process—mysterious even to those who may be most intimately involved. . . ."[3]

The Bay of Pigs Invasion

The plan to invade Cuba had its genesis in the Eisenhower administration. Acting upon a proposal made by Vice President Nixon, Eisenhower instructed the Central Intelligence Agency to organize and train Cuban exiles for the purpose of engaging in guerrilla warfare against the government of Fidel Castro. As the plan began to take shape, the CIA's confidence grew to the point where it decided to abandon the more modest goal of guerrilla warfare and opted instead for a full-scale invasion of Cuba. This invasion, which occurred approximately three months after John Kennedy took office, may be justly characterized as one of the greatest foreign policy blunders in American history.

Upon landing at the Bay of Pigs, the invasion force of 1,400 men was put at a severe disadvantage, for Castro's air force sank two of the four ships that were supposed to provide the invaders with munitions and other supplies. Following these sinkings, the other two ships promptly departed the scene and sought safer waters. Although all reports suggest that the invaders fought valiantly, by the third day they were surrounded by Castro's army and forced to surrender or else be killed. The costs resulting from this debacle were high for both the president and the country. Kennedy and his administration appeared inept. Moreover, charges of American imperialism and aggression were heard in the United Nations and in foreign capitals around the world. After it was all over, President Kennedy turned to an aide and mused aloud, "How could I have been so far off base. . . . How could I have been so stupid to let them go ahead?"[4] Others were asking the same question.

The pressures upon Kennedy to go ahead with the invasion had been considerable. While he personally did not think that Castro posed any security threat to the United States, the presence of a Communist regime only ninety miles off our coast was a constant source of irritation. In addition, during his election campaign Kennedy had pledged to support anti-Castro rebels. By refusing to do so, he would be not only reneging on a promise but also abandoning a tradition of American support for anti-communist forces around the world. There was also the problem of what to do with the Cuban exiles if the plan were called off. If brought to the United States, they would undoubtedly reveal the plan and make known their dissatisfaction with the president's refusal to go through with it. Furthermore, Kennedy was advised that a decision to go ahead or to abort the invasion plan could not be delayed, for the Soviet Union would soon be providing Castro's army with armaments and training, thus making it a more formidable opponent. With all of these factors in mind, the president gave the go-ahead but also made one major change in the plan—there was to be no overt U.S. involvement in the operation. As he would later recount to one of his aides, he thought the United States had everything to gain and nothing to lose. The invasion, after all, had a good chance of succeeding, and even if it failed, the Cuban exiles could retreat to the mountains and carry on guerrilla warfare against the Castro regime.[5] Moreover, all of this could be achieved without any direct involvement on the part of the United States.

Given the nature of the facts and advice he received, it is not surprising that Kennedy's initial skepticism about the invasion plan was ultimately overcome by a more optimistic attitude. Unfortunately, most of the information provided him proved to be erroneous or inadequate. The CIA's Richard Bissell had, for example, assured him that no one would ever be able to trace the invasion plan back to the U.S. government. The exiles were being trained in secret camps in Nicaragua and Guatemala, and the American B-26s that were to be used for air cover in the invasion would be painted to look like Castro's own B-26 bombers, thus creating the impression that his own men had defected to the other side. Despite these precautions, however, stories about an impending invasion of Cuba began to appear in the press as early as one week prior to the event.

That both the invasion and our covert involvement in it could have been kept secret seems naive, considering that the plan was known to some 1,400 Cuban exiles as well as to officials in the Nicaraguan and Guatemalan governments. This miscalculation may have arisen from the CIA's lack of experience in planning large-scale clandestine operations.[6] Kennedy's advisers also appeared confident that camouflaged American B-26 bombers could knock out Castro's allegedly ill-equipped air force immediately before the landing of the invasion force at the Bay of Pigs. This assessment also proved to be a gross misjudgment. The B-26s were obsolete. Many of them developed engine trouble, and on the first day alone, half of them were shot down by Castro's planes. Contrary to what Kennedy had been told, the Cuban dictator's air force proved to be well trained and well enough equipped to meet the invasion challenge. Even those American planes that managed to escape being shot down proved to be limited in their effectiveness. Their flight from Nicaragua to Cuba had required a considerable amount of fuel; consequently, in order to ensure enough fuel for the return to Nicaragua, the planes were limited in the amount of time they could spend over the combat area.

Kennedy had repeatedly inquired about the morale of the invasion brigade, and CIA officials assured him that it was high. This evaluation represented an exaggeration of considerable proportions, however. Many of the Cuban exiles had little use for their commanding officers. The latter were left over from the Batista regime, which had governed Cuba ruthlessly before Castro came to power. At one point prior to the invasion, there was a full-fledged mutiny among the Cuban exiles, and the ringleaders were spirited off to a Guatemalan prison camp by CIA agents. The morale of the invasion brigade would no doubt have been even lower had not the CIA deceived them into believing that other brigades were also being trained for the invasion, that American marines would be assisting in the operation, and finally, that landings would be made on other parts of the island so as to draw some of Castro's forces away from the Bay of Pigs.[7] These false promises were apparently made without the knowledge of President Kennedy.

The ability of the invasion brigade to establish a beachhead on the shores of Cuba was predicated on the assumption that it would be facing a poorly trained and ill-equipped Cuban army. While Kennedy had received assurances from the CIA that Castro's army would pose no serious threat to the invaders, in actual fact the training and military equipment of Castro's forces proved to be more than adequate to the task of thwarting the invasion. The CIA had been told as much by experts in the State Department and British Intelligence but chose to ignore these estimates and failed to pass them along to the president.

Certainly one of the most costly miscalculations concerning the Bay of Pigs invasion dealt with the role of the Cuban underground and the likelihood of a revolt against Castro by the Cuban people themselves. Given the small number of people in the invasion force, the overthrow of Castro would be contingent upon carefully coordinated sabotage efforts by the Cuban underground and upon armed uprisings among the populace. As one Kennedy adviser noted, this view was universally shared by those advising the president: "We all in the White House considered uprisings behind the lines essential to the success of the operation; so, too, did the Joint Chiefs of Staff."[8] The CIA reported that the Cuban underground consisted of some 2,500 individuals plus another 20,000 or so sympathizers. Once the invasion force landed, these indigenous anti-Castro forces would swing into action and internal uprisings would follow.

Here, too, the CIA assessment was more a reflection of hope than of the realities of the situation. In actuality, the CIA had not made any hard intelligence estimates as to the capability of the Cuban underground or the likelihood of popular uprisings. Indeed, CIA Director Allen Dulles later admitted that his agency never really expected much support from the Cuban underground because, as it turned out, the underground distrusted the CIA and vice versa. Consequently, there was little coordination between the invasion planners and the leaders of the underground. Moreover, the CIA never provided the underground with the supplies they needed to carry out sabotage operations. These factors alone made it all but inevitable that the internal resistance movement would lack any substantial punch. Furthermore, after the invasion began, Fidel Castro proved to be highly efficient at rounding up potential dissidents, and his support among the Cuban people proved to be far greater than the CIA had estimated. Thus, the possibility of overthrowing the Castro regime through indigenous uprisings was doomed to failure.[9]

The safety of the invasion brigade had been a constant source of concern to Kennedy. In the event that the invasion did not succeed, he wanted to be sure that the exiles would be able to escape. On several occasions the top men at the CIA assured the president that they would, noting that if necessary the brigade could retreat into the Escambray Mountains, which were only a short distance from the landing site. Once in the mountains, they could join up with other anti-Castro forces and assist them in guerrilla operations against the regime. Unfortunately, this plan would work only so long as the brigade landed at Trinidad, which was the original site selected for the invasion. On the grounds that Trinidad was too conspicuous for such a landing, the site was later changed to the Bay of Pigs. With this change, the Escambray Mountains were now some eighty miles away, and in order to get to them the invading force would have to traverse terrain consisting largely of swamps and jungle. Consequently, the CIA made no preparation for an escape to the mountains, and instead instructed the exiles to fall back on the beaches if the invasion effort failed. While Kennedy knew of the change in the landing site, he was not told that this change eliminated the possibility of an escape to the mountains.[10] Nor did it occur to Kennedy or any of his advisers to look at a map of Cuba; had they done so, they would have seen immediately that the escape option was not feasible.

In the decision-making process that led up to the Bay of Pigs invasion, Kennedy was clearly the victim of faulty and inadequate information. In part this resulted from his almost exclusive reliance upon one channel of information—the CIA. Since this agency had planned the invasion, it is not altogether surprising that it proved to be a forceful advocate of the benefits and less than forthcoming on the risks involved in such a venture. Had other units in the government been more intimately involved in evaluating the plan, its limitations may well have been exposed. Unfortunately, the operations division of the CIA kept close control over the plan. Neither the Cuban desk at the State Department nor even the intelligence-gathering division at the CIA was consulted on the invasion plans. Moreover, when the head of the State Department's intelligence branch later asked permission to scrutinize the plan, he was refused.[11] The severe restriction put on the number of people involved in the planning and evaluation of the invasion was motivated by a desire to maintain complete secrecy, but, as one Kennedy adviser noted, "the 'need-to-know' standard—i.e., that no one should be told about a project unless it becomes operationally necessary—thus had the idiotic effect of excluding much of the expertise of government at a time when every alert newspaper reporter knew something was afoot."[12] Therefore, with the cat out of the bag, the continued concern for secrecy served little useful purpose in this particular case.

Of course, a president may indeed be forced to restrict his channels of information when he is dealing with highly sensitive matters, but it is precisely on these occasions that both he and his advisers must be especially vigilant in probing and challenging the few experts on whom they are relying. In this respect, both Kennedy and some of his key advisers failed. During the deliberations with the CIA and the Joint Chiefs of Staff, Kennedy's advisers expressed few doubts about either the feasibility or desirability of the invasion. There appears to have been no serious examination of the most fundamental question of all—Was the invasion necessary in the first place? Also absent was any serious probing of the CIA about how it knew that Castro's army was ill equipped and poorly trained, or on what grounds it concluded that his political strength was weak. Nor were the Joint Chiefs thoroughly questioned on the military aspects of the invasion. That key advisers failed to raise vigorous challenges should not be interpreted to mean that no doubts existed, however. In fact, one of the participants in the group, Arthur Schlesinger, wrote a lengthy memorandum to the president which argued that Castro was too strong to be overthrown by this small-scale invasion. Yet at no time did he voice these misgivings during the deliberations. Likewise, according to one State Department official, Secretary of State Rusk raised incisive questions about the plan with his aides at the State Department but declined to do so during meetings at the White House. Moreover, one undersecretary who had attended one of the meetings in Rusk's place subsequently wrote an extensive memorandum criticizing the proposed invasion. But when he asked Rusk's permission to present these arguments to the president, he was refused. Even the CIA and the Joint Chiefs apparently had some doubts regarding the plan's feasibility after the president stipulated that there could be no *overt* U.S. involvement, yet they too failed to voice them to the president.[13] They might have, however, had they been pressed more forcefully by Kennedy and his advisers.

Thus, despite lingering doubts, the meetings took place in what Arthur Schlesinger describes as a "curious atmosphere of assumed consensus." Several factors may help to explain why this occurred. For one thing, to the *newly* installed president and his advisers, the CIA and the Joint Chiefs appeared as formidable and impressive advocates of the plan, thus discouraging any serious challenge to their assessments. As Kennedy later remarked, "You always assume that the military and intelligence people have some secret skill not available to ordinary mortals."[14] Second, some Kennedy advisers apparently felt that opposition to the plan would be interpreted as being "soft on communism," a label that might destroy their credibility in future White House councils.[15] Finally, Kennedy's own handling of the deliberations was not as effective in encouraging debate and thorough analysis as it might have been. In the interest of security, he permitted the printed information distributed by the CIA to be collected at the end of each session; thus there was little opportunity for advisers to digest and critically evaluate it. He made no effort to circulate the memo he had received from Schlesinger criticizing the plan; nor was he especially vigilant in encouraging those in attendance to voice their opinions. Undersecretary of State Chester Bowles attended one of the meetings in Rusk's place and was appalled by what he heard. Unfortunately, the president did not call upon him to express his views; nor could he volunteer them, since protocol dictates that undersecretaries may not speak at meetings unless asked by the president. The president also knew of Arthur Schlesinger's misgivings about the invasion but apparently made no effort to force him to voice them before the group. To his credit, it should be noted that Kennedy did invite Senator William Fulbright to come before a final meeting of the group and express his strong opposition to the plan, a view he had already communicated to the president in a memorandum. After the senator finished his presentation, however, Kennedy failed to stimulate a discussion about it. Instead, he continued what he had begun before Fulbright came into the meeting—going around the table and asking each member of the group for a final opinion on whether to go ahead with the plan. Following a unanimous vote in favor of the invasion, Kennedy gave the final go-ahead, assuming a consensus among his advisers that proved to be far less real than it appeared.[16]

The Cuban Missile Crisis

As a foreign policy problem, the Cuban missile crisis differed from the Bay of Pigs invasion in two important respects. For one thing, the stakes were much higher. The United States was now in a direct "eyeball-to-eyeball" confrontation with the second greatest nuclear power in the world. President Kennedy estimated the chances of a resulting nuclear war at one in three. Second, whereas there was ample time to consider the plan for the Bay of Pigs invasion, the placing of missiles in Cuba by the Soviet Union was unexpected and required an immediate response by the United States.

The Soviet Union had repeatedly asserted that there was little reason for it to place nuclear weapons on foreign soil. As the Soviet news agency put it, "There is no need for the Soviet Union to shift its weapons for the repulsion of aggression, for a retaliatory blow, to any other country, *for instance Cuba.* Our nuclear weapons are so powerful in their explosive force . . . that there is no need to search for sites for them beyond the boundaries of the Soviet Union.[17] Yet the increase in the shipment of Soviet arms and personnel to Cuba caused Kennedy considerable concern. Through private diplomatic channels, he sought and was given assurances by the Soviets that no offensive missile capability would be placed in Cuba. But as the buildup in arms continued, the president felt it necessary to issue a public warning to the Russians, noting that if Cuba became an "offensive military base of sufficient capacity for the Soviet Union, then this country will do whatever must be done to protect its own security and that of its allies."[18] At this point, the United States still had no hard evidence that the Russians had in fact placed offensive missiles in Cuba. Indeed, in September 1962 a National Intelligence estimate concluded that it was unlikely that the Soviets would make such a move. This assessment proved to be inaccurate, however, for one month later photographs taken by a U-2 reconnaissance plane provided incontrovertible evidence that missile sites were indeed being constructed there.

The president summoned a group of advisers to the Cabinet Room, informed them of the news, and stated that under no conditions could the United States accept the Soviet Union's bold action. He then instructed the group to consider a course of action that would lead to the removal of the missiles from Cuba. That Kennedy immediately eliminated one option—doing nothing—was dictated by several considerations. He saw the Soviets' action as a probe designed to test American will in general and his own in particular. He feared that Premier Khrushchev had perceived him as a man lacking in resolve. There were indeed some grounds for Khrushchev to think so, for when the two met in Vienna in June 1961, Kennedy appeared indecisive and intimidated by the Soviet leader.[19] Moreover, Khrushchev apparently had been surprised that the United States did not respond more forcefully when the Soviet Union erected the Berlin Wall in August 1961. If Kennedy once again appeared weak in the face of this latest Soviet initiative, the Russians would feel free to become even more daring in the future. Also, Kennedy felt that regardless of whether the missiles in Cuba would significantly alter the balance of power, they would appear to have done so. As he himself remarked, "Appearances contribute to reality." Finally, he had to take domestic political considerations into account as well; if he failed to take action, the Republicans would be handed an explosive campaign issue in the upcoming midterm elections. Nor could he ignore the possibility that inaction might even lead to his impeachment.

Rather than relying only upon the National Security Council as he had done in the Bay of Pigs invasion, this time Kennedy reached out to a wider group, which would later be dubbed the Executive Committee of the National Security Council (ExComm). From his White House staff he included not only his special assistant for national security affairs but also his close aide Theodore Sorensen. In addition, his appointments secretary and personal confidant Kenneth O'Donnell were invited to some of the meetings. Although neither Sorensen nor O'Donnell had any special expertise in foreign policy matters, the president nevertheless respected their judgment. Besides, the Bay of Pigs fiasco had already taught him that experts could be wrong. Naturally, the chairman of the Joint Chiefs, the secretaries of defense and state, and the director of the CIA were also included in ExComm. But this time Kennedy also made a special effort to reach out for capable individuals further down in the bureaucracy. Thus, from the Department of State he brought in Undersecretary George Ball, Deputy Undersecretary Alexis Johnson, Assistant Secretary Edwin Martin, the U.S. Ambassador to the United Nations Adlai Stevenson, and Soviet expert Llewellyn Thompson. Likewise, he included both the deputy and assistant secretaries of defense. Although neither the Justice nor Treasury Department had any direct involvement in the crisis at hand, the president asked Attorney General Robert Kennedy and Treasury Secretary Douglas Dillon to attend the meetings—again, because he valued their judgment. Also tapped for the group was the deputy director of the U.S. Information Agency. In addition to reaching down into the government, Kennedy sought the wisdom of prominent individuals outside of government. Included were Dean Acheson (former secretary of state), Robert Lovett (former defense secretary), and John McCloy (former high commissioner of Germany), all of whom were present at several of ExComm's meetings. Kennedy also communicated by phone with former presidents Hoover, Truman, and Eisenhower, although none of them participated in the deliberations.

In summary, in dealing with the Cuban missile crisis the president was clearly seeking to expand his channels of information and advice. In contrast to the group that had deliberated on the Bay of Pigs invasion, ExComm included more people from the White House staff, more from the various departments and agencies, and a third group of individuals from outside the government. While the numbers involved increased the risk of a leak, Kennedy apparently felt that an even greater risk lay in limiting his sources of information. At this point it is worth noting that the president sought to enhance his access to information in still another way. Following the Bay of Pigs debacle, he decided to set up a Situation Room in the basement of the White House, which would be tied into all of the cable traffic coming into the Departments of State and Defense and the CIA. The White House would thereby gain the information in these cables firsthand, rather than having to rely on the departments to relay it.

In order to avoid the illusory consensus that had developed in connection with the Bay of Pigs invasion, President Kennedy took several steps to ensure that ExComm would rigorously consider all the options available to his administration. First, he absented himself from several of the earlier meetings. Robert Kennedy later commented, "This was wise. Personalities change when the president is present, and frequently even strong men make recommendations on the basis of what they believe the president wishes to hear."[20] When the president was present, he took special pains to elicit the views of lower-level advisers, for he had learned that "lower-ranking advisers . . . would not voluntarily contradict their superiors in front of the President, and that persuasive advisers such as McNamara unintentionally silenced less articulate men."[21] In his absence, Kennedy charged his brother and Theodore Sorensen with the responsibility for drawing out the views of all members of the group and encouraging a contentious discussion of the issues. To further foster a free exchange of opinion, the members of ExComm were told not to confine their remarks to their own area of expertise. Instead, military experts were to feel free to comment on the political aspects of the issue, and political experts were to feel equally free to address the military aspects. In addition, the group was told that the customary rules of protocol would be set aside, thus freeing undersecretaries and assistant secretaries from having to wait until they were called upon before offering their views. Lastly, the meetings were conducted without prearranged agendas so members of the group would feel free to raise any issue they thought appropriate.

Virtually all recollections of the ExComm deliberations suggest that the president's efforts to avoid a premature consensus were successful. Theodore Sorensen, for example, has noted:

> Indeed, one of the remarkable aspects of those meetings was a sense of complete equality. Protocol mattered little when the nation's life was at stake. Experience mattered little in a crisis which had no precedent. . . . We were fifteen individuals on our own, representing the President and not different departments. Assistant Secretaries differed vigorously with their Secretaries; I participated much more freely than I ever had in an NSC [National Security Council] meeting; and the absence of the President encouraged everybody to speak his mind.[22]

In commenting on the participants in the deliberations, Robert Kennedy wrote, "It is no reflection on them that none was consistent in his opinion from the very beginning to the very end. . . . For some there were only small changes, perhaps varieties of a single idea. For others there were continuous changes of opinion each day."[23] Despite the fact that in his initial charge to ExComm the president appeared to have ruled out a nonmilitary response to the situation, some members of the group forced consideration of it anyway. McNamara, for example, initially raised the possibility that perhaps no action was necessary at all, for the presence of the missiles did not materially alter the nuclear balance of power. Moreover, whether we were killed by a missile from the Soviet Union, or from a Russian submarine, or from Cuba made little difference; the end result was the same. This view was rejected by the others, who argued that missiles launched from Cuba would give us less warning time to react and that the accuracy of offensive missiles would be substantially increased if launched from nearby Cuba rather than from thousands of miles away in the Soviet Union. McGeorge Bundy and Adlai Stevenson argued that our response should be diplomatic rather than military. They reasoned that we had nothing to lose by taking the diplomatic route first; even if this approach failed, it had the advantage of not foreclosing other options. At least in Bundy's case, it is not clear that he really favored this approach as much as he wanted the president to consider all options: "I almost deliberately stayed in the minority. I felt that it was very important to keep the President's choices open."[24] Although Stevenson proved to be an advocate of the diplomatic approach throughout the deliberations, others rejected that approach on the grounds that it would allow Khrushchev to stall long enough to permit the missiles to become operational.

Thus, there developed a consensus on the necessity for military action, but the group was still sharply divided as to what form it should take. Six options were considered:

1. Blockade Cuba and thereby deny entry to Soviet ships carrying armaments.
2. Bombard the missile sites with pellets that would neutralize the missiles without causing casualties.
3. Surgically bomb the missile sites but forewarn the Cubans and Soviets in the area.
4. Surgically bomb the sites without any forewarning.
5. Bomb all military targets in Cuba.
6. Undertake a full-scale invasion of Cuba.

The military argued that a surgical strike was not feasible and pushed for a bombing of all military targets in Cuba. During the second week of deliberations, however, civilian experts learned that a surgical strike was in fact possible, and it was restored as an option. The group continued to debate the blockade option versus some kind of attack upon Cuba itself. Indeed, ExComm appeared to be so far from reaching a consensus on what to do that President Kennedy grew frustrated. Accordingly, he instructed both his brother and Sorensen to bring the group to a recommendation. Their efforts were not successful, however, as the group continued to debate the possibilities. Finally, eight of the fourteen agreed that the blockade was the most desirable course of action to follow.[25]

A blockade had several advantages. First, it was drastic enough to convey our determination, and yet not so drastic as to invite a military response from the Soviet Union. Second, even if the blockade should produce a military confrontation off the coast of Cuba, our naval superiority would be overwhelming. Third, a blockade would leave the next move up to the Russians, while still providing them with some time to consider what that move should be. Fourth, the blockade did not foreclose other, more drastic options. Finally, this response was more appealing to the president when viewed against the alternative of a military strike. Both he and some others were troubled by the morality of a sneak attack on Cuba. In addition, the Air Force could not guarantee that a strike on the missile sites would incapacitate all of the missiles. Then, too, a direct strike on Cuba would possibly be drastic enough to elicit a military response from the Soviets in a place such as Berlin where their conventional forces were superior to our own.

Whether or not President Kennedy handled the Cuban missile crisis deftly is a matter of some debate. Some would contend that it was indeed his finest hour—that he judiciously selected a course of action that, while forceful enough to convince the Russians we meant business, was nevertheless not so reckless as to precipitate a military response from the Russians. Others argue that the president needlessly took us to the precipice of nuclear war—that domestic political considerations caused him to adopt a stance far more severe than was warranted by the presence of missiles in Cuba. Still others point out that the blockade did not in and of itself prove sufficient to force the Russians into removing their missiles from Cuba; rather, they agreed to do so only after Robert Kennedy privately warned Soviet Ambassador Dobrynin that unless the Soviet Union removed the missiles, we would. Yet if President Kennedy did make the wrong decision, it was not for want of having the necessary facts and options placed before him. On the contrary, not only did he reach out to a variety of sources for information and advice, but he also structured the deliberations so as to maximize the expression and evaluation of all points of view. Clearly, the president who faced the Cuban missile crisis was far wiser in the ways of decision making than the man who, one year earlier, had ordered the abortive Bay of Pigs invasion. He had, in short, learned from his mistakes.

The Vietnam War

Regardless of what standard one chooses to employ, the Vietnam War qualifies as perhaps the greatest foreign policy blunder in American history. Not only did it fail, but the costs exacted upon the nation during the process were extraordinary. First and foremost was the cost in lives, with some 46,000 Americans killed and three times as many wounded. There were social and political costs as well, for as the war became more unpopular, protests grew increasingly more violent and public confidence in government began to erode. The war also imposed a heavy burden on our economic resources as hundreds of millions of dollars were diverted into an ever-expanding war effort. And to all of this must finally be added the loss in our international prestige, especially among nations of the Third World.

Although U.S. involvement in Vietnam had its beginnings in the Kennedy administration, the full-scale commitment of our human and material resources to this Southeast Asian country was made under the stewardship of President Johnson. As Johnson prepared for the election campaign of 1964, he found himself confronted with a rapidly deteriorating situation in South Vietnam. Its government was unstable; the rising number of desertions in the armed forces was a clear indication of declining morale; the North Vietnamese had increased the movement of troops and arms into the South; and the Vietcong (South Vietnamese Communists) had become more daring in its military operations there, the most recent of which had been an attack on an American military base at Bien Hoa. Having been apprised of these developments, Johnson ordered his advisers to review our policy toward Vietnam and recommend a course of action. Since his own energies were focused on the election campaign, he did not involve himself directly in these policy discussions but accepted the recommendation that flowed from them, namely, a continuation of retaliatory strikes.

The most critical decision came in 1965 when Johnson sent the chairman of the Joint Chiefs and Defense Secretary McNamara to South Vietnam on a fact-finding mission. Their report to the president pointed out that the South Vietnamese were in desperate straits. Reinforcements for the Vietcong were pouring into the South, and without a substantial commitment of U.S. forces the South Vietnamese army would be incapable of preventing a takeover of its country. It was clear to the president that he was now at the crossroads. To assist him in deciding which way to turn, he summoned together a vast array of individuals from inside the government: Dean Rusk, George Ball, and William Bundy from the State Department; Robert McNamara, Cyrus Vance, and John McNaughton from Defense; members of the Joint Chiefs and the secretaries of the Army, Navy, and Air Force representing the military; Admiral Raborn and Richard Helms from the CIA; Carl Rowan, director of the U.S. Information Agency; McGeorge Bundy, Special Assistant for National Security Affairs, and his aide Leonard Unger; and Jack Valenti and Bill Moyers from his White House staff. From outside the government, Johnson brought in Henry Cabot Lodge, who had recently retired as U.S. ambassador to South Vietnam, and Clark Clifford, who had been an adviser to several presidents. While not all of these individuals were present at all of the meetings that took place from July 21 to 27, each attended at least one of them.

At the first meeting, Secretary McNamara proceeded to inform the group of recommendations made by William Westmoreland, the general in charge of U.S. military operations in South Vietnam.

1. An initial commitment of 175,000 troops would be necessary by the end of 1965 in order to repel the advances of the enemy.

2. Another 100,000 troops would be necessary in 1966 so the United States would be able to take the offensive.

3. Still another increment of troops (*unspecified*) would be necessary if war were to be brought to a successful conclusion by the end of 1967.

McNamara noted that he concurred with these recommendations and suggested that Johnson call up 235,000 reservists.[26] Following this presentation, the president put some tough questions to the group.

> Have we wrung every single soldier out of every country that we can? Who else can help us here? Are we the sole defenders in the world? Have we done all we can in this direction? What are the compelling reasons for this call-up? What results can we expect? Again, I ask you what are the alternatives? I don't want us to make snap judgments. I want us to consider all our options. We know we can tell the South Vietnamese we are coming home. Is that the option we should take? What would flow from that?"[27]

The president then asked for reactions from those who disagreed with McNamara. George Ball said he thought we were getting ourselves into a quagmire that would inevitably lead to a greater and greater expansion of the war. Carl Rowan stated that more troops would do no good as long as the South Vietnamese government remained so unstable. In the afternoon session, the president began by asking Ball to elaborate on his opposition to increased U.S. involvement. Ball argued that American conventional forces could not successfully fight a guerrilla war in an Asian jungle, and he noted also that as we became bogged down, the temptation to expand the war into North Vietnam would become irresistible. In a protracted war, he said, world opinion would ultimately turn against us. After Ball finished, the other side began to weigh in. First, there was Secretary of State Rusk, who pointed out that our failure to stand firm in Vietnam would only serve to encourage further communist aggression in other parts of the world. Ambassador Lodge concurred with Rusk, reminding the group that our lack of resolve in Vietnam would be analogous to the capitulation to Hitler at Munich. After further discussion, the president adjourned the group and told them that on the following day he wanted them to hear what the military had to say on the matter.

At the opening of the next meeting, Johnson outlined to the military his own view of what the alternatives were: (1) cut our losses and leave the country; (2) continue at our current level of commitment and slowly lose; or (3) increase our commitment, with the risk that the war might escalate and last a long time. All of the military spokesmen appeared confident of our ability to win if our troop commitment was significantly increased. The president probed them further, asking if we were starting something that in two or three years we would not be able to finish. Wouldn't the Chinese and the Russians come in on the side of the North Vietnamese?[28] The spokesmen did not think either of these possibilities likely. Johnson then asked his special adviser for national security affairs to present some disquieting arguments that were being made by some representatives and senators: "What Bundy will now tell you is not his opinion or mine, but what we hear. I think you ought to face up to this too."[29] Bundy proceeded to raise the following concerns:

1. Everything we have done in Vietnam thus far has failed.
2. How can conventional forces be sent to fight a guerrilla war?
3. We are ignoring General MacArthur's long-accepted warning that the United States should never become involved in a land war in Asia.
4. How can we win a war for a country that does not appear to want to help itself?
5. Is not the problem in Vietnam essentially political rather than military?

Johnson asked the group to ponder these questions and be prepared to discuss them at the next meeting. In the subsequent meetings these doubts were apparently answered to his satisfaction.

In the final analysis, Johnson seemed strongly persuaded by the argument that if we backed down in Vietnam, the Communists would be encouraged to become aggressive in other parts of Asia, Africa, the Middle East, and Latin America.[30] No doubt this view took on added credibility for Johnson because it was shared by the two advisers he respected most: secretaries Rusk and McNamara. He therefore decided to increase our troop commitment by 100,000, as General Westmoreland had suggested. At the same time, however, he refused to go along with the recommendation to call up the reservists, fearing that such drastic action would both alarm the country and perhaps force the Russians and Chinese to enter the conflict. At the final meeting, which was held at Camp David, the president went around the table asking his advisers if they were in agreement with his decision. Only George Ball and Clark Clifford expressed skepticism. He then called the congressional leadership together to get their reaction to his decision, and although they posed several questions, only Senator Mansfield expressed serious doubts about the president's proposed course of action.

In retrospect, it is clear that both Johnson and his advisers made a grave miscalculation. The North Vietnamese and Vietcong proved to be a far more formidable foe than they had anticipated, and the South Vietnamese less capable and committed than they had hoped. But if this initial decision to increase our involvement in Vietnam was a bad one, it cannot be attributed to Johnson's failure to reach out for information, nor to his unwillingness to push for examination of all points of view. At this stage, at least, he appears to have encouraged consideration of the costs and benefits associated with getting out, continuing what we were doing, or escalating our involvement. The short circuit in the decision-making process lay, rather, in the kind of information and advice he was given.

Several factors may help to explain why the advice proved inadequate. Some would surely argue that Johnson and his advisers were captives of an outmoded anticommunist ideology, which called for the United States to stop the spread of communism anywhere in the world. So strong was this view, it is argued, that it blinded them to both the political and the military realities of the situation in Vietnam. Second, those advising the president may have fallen victim to overconfidence. In the words of Johnson's close aide Bill Moyers, "There was a confidence, it was never bragged about, it was just there—a residue, perhaps of the confrontation over the missiles in Cuba—that when the chips were really down, the other people would fold."[31] Third, the quality of advice that Johnson was getting was hampered by the lack of expertise on Southeast Asia. As Dean Rusk would later point out, the government had few experts on this area of the world because most had left the State Department after being discredited as a result of our problems with China in the 1950s.[32] Fourth, the information base on which Johnson and his advisers were operating may not have presented an altogether accurate appraisal of the military picture in Vietnam. Those in the field were committed to the view that the United States belonged in Vietnam, and the information relayed back to Washington was frequently designed so as not to discourage this belief.

David Halberstam, for example, tells of assessments submitted in 1965 by the CIA regarding future prospects in Vietnam. One was written by an individual who had been studying that country for over ten years. Among other things, he pointed out in his conclusions that the enemy was possessed of an enormous capacity to escalate the war if the United States decided to bomb; it was his judgment that the enemy would not hesitate to make full use of this capability. However, before this CIA assessment was sent back to the United States, the pessimistic portions were deleted from the report by Ambassador Taylor's office in Saigon. Another assessment had been requested by General Westmoreland, who wanted a study on the ability of the North Vietnamese to reinforce their troops in the South. When the study was completed, he voiced amazement at the results and asked that the figures be rechecked. After being informed that the figures were indeed accurate, he replied, "If we tell this to the people in Washington we'll be out of the war tomorrow. We'll have to revise it downward."

One final respect in which the advice received by Johnson proved to be inadequate lay in the failure of the military to voice its objections to the nature of his escalation decision. While firmly supportive of an increased commitment to Vietnam, the Joint Chiefs did not feel that the president had gone far enough. In addition to dispatching 100,000 troops, they felt a successful prosecution of the war required calling up the reserves as well as placing the country on a war footing. Yet when Johnson, during that final meeting at Camp David, asked the chairman of the Joint Chiefs if he agreed with the decision, General Wheeler answered yes.[33] Had Wheeler voiced his strong doubts about Johnson's decision on the grounds that it was not enough, the president might have heeded this advice by further escalating our commitment. On the other hand, he may also have concluded that the costs of our involvement were going to be too high and thus moved toward a reduction in our commitment. Why Wheeler failed to voice his objections is unclear. Possibly he feared he would be overruled anyway, or perhaps he was afraid that by calling for more drastic action he would scare Johnson out of making any increase at all in our commitment to Vietnam.

Unfortunately, the lengthy review of our Vietnam policy during July 1965 was really the only one to take place until the Vietcong launched their famous Tet offensive in 1968. After the initial commitment to increase our efforts, subsequent decisions were largely tactical in nature and involved little reevaluation of underlying objectives and costs, despite the fact that greater and greater involvement on our part seemed to have little impact upon bringing the war to a successful conclusion. Although it may indeed be argued that the failure to reconsider our Vietnam policy was simply a reflection of the fact that both Johnson and his advisers were convinced of its soundness, other factors appear to have been at work also. For one thing, President Johnson himself can hardly be said to have encouraged an atmosphere conducive to a reexamination of our policy toward Vietnam. As the war began to go badly and public criticism mounted, Johnson became more irascible and increasingly prone to equate dissent with disloyalty. On one occasion, for example, when the White House was holding a banquet for students who had been selected as Presidential Scholars, Johnson sought to bar the parents of one girl from attending the banquet because they had spoken out against the war.[34] It is not surprising, therefore, that he appeared to be equally distraught with those inside the government who voiced similar doubt about our presence in Vietnam. As a result of this attitude, many aides were reticent about disagreeing with the president openly. John McNaughton, the chief assistant to Defense Secretary McNamara, repeatedly voiced his opposition to the bombing in the presence of his boss at the Defense Department; he even went over to the White House in the evenings to secretly argue his point of view with a White House aide. Yet when Johnson on one occasion went around the table asking aides if they agreed with the decision to bomb oil depots in North Vietnam, McNaughton merely replied, "I have nothing to add sir."[35] According to George Ball, even McNamara himself harbored doubts about the bombing long before he voiced them publicly. As David Halberstam notes:

> When it came right down to it, McNamara had doubts about the bombing in his mind, but those doubts were not reflected in the meetings. He was forceful, intense, tearing apart the doubts of the others, almost ruthless in making his case. . . . He was, Ball found, quite different in private sessions than in the major meetings where Johnson presided. When Ball prepared paper after paper for Johnson, he would first send them to the other principals, and occasionally McNamara would suggest that he come by and talk the paper over before they went to see the President. Ball would find McNamara surprisingly sympathetic.[36]

Those within the administration who did voice disagreement with Vietnam policy might find themselves frozen out of the decision-making process or else invited to leave. At one of the strategy meetings in 1965, for example, Vice President Humphrey voiced strong opposition to the bombing; thereafter, he was systematically excluded from discussions on the war and bypassed in the memo traffic relating to Vietnam policy. Similarly, in an appearance before a Senate committee in 1967, Secretary McNamara for the first time publicly voiced his doubts about the bombing. Subsequently, he was progressively bypassed in the deliberations. To one senator, the president remarked, "No don't go see Bob—he's gone dovish on me."[37] The final straw came when McNamara delivered a speech in Montreal in which he voiced his misgivings about our whole involvement in Vietnam. To his surprise, he read in the papers a few days later that President Johnson had appointed him to head the World Bank.

Despite Johnson's apparent disdain for dissent, there were a few within his administration—Bill Moyers, Harry McPherson, George Ball—who were willing to voice their criticisms. But apparently they were tolerated because they kept their views within the "family" and never challenged the fundamental assumptions of our Vietnam policy.[38] Yet one suspects that the role of critic within the administration was not a pleasant one, for both Moyers and Ball resigned their positions in 1967.

In addition to Johnson's own failure to encourage an atmosphere conducive to independent thinking, the apparent unwillingness to reassess our Vietnam policy may have also been fostered by the development of "groupthink" among the president's senior advisers. These individuals, who typically met with the president every Tuesday for lunch, became known as the Tuesday Cabinet. The membership included Dean Rusk; Robert McNamara; Earle Wheeler, chairman of the Joint Chiefs; Richard

Helms, director of the CIA; Bill Moyers, press secretary; and the president's special adviser for national security affairs, McGeorge Bundy (later to be replaced by Walt Rostow). Several factors may help to explain why this group sought to minimize differences and maximize agreement. For one thing, their relationships with each other appear to have become personal as well as professional. As Bill Moyers recalls:

> The men who handled national security affairs became too close, too personally fond of each other. They tended to conduct the affairs of state almost as if they were a gentlemen's club, and the great decisions were often made in that warm camaraderie of a small board of directors deciding what the club's dues are going to be for the members next year. . . . So you often dance around the final hard decision which would set you against . . . men who are very close to you, and you tend to reach a consensus.[39]

The inclination toward group cohesion may also have been enhanced by the fact that the group's policy decisions on Vietnam were coming under severe attack from people in Congress and the country at large. In his analysis of the Tuesday Cabinet, for example, Henry Graff notes that as members of the group "felt increasingly beleaguered, they turned toward one another for reassurance."[40] Perhaps most important of all, Johnson insisted on making decisions by consensus—an idiosyncrasy that was in evidence even during his years in Congress. This desire to have everybody on board could only serve to further increase the pressures toward a convergence of views.

In addition to the factors already mentioned, Johnson's failure to reconsider our commitment to Vietnam—at least up until 1968—may also have been due in part to the fact that he was not being given a fully accurate picture of how the war was going. Perhaps the president's most critical source of information on the war was his national security adviser, Walt Rostow, an avowed hawk. Rostow's briefings to the president were frequently selective, as he sought to accentuate the positive and minimize the negative. Moreover, he was also successful in persuading the CIA officer (George Carver) charged with briefing the White House to become more optimistic in his reports. Indeed, by 1967 it had become quite clear that Carver's briefings on the war appeared far more optimistic than assessments by other intelligence analysts within the CIA.[41]

That Johnson had not been told all became painfully apparent during the deliberations in 1968. It was in January of that year that the enemy launched its Tet offensive—a massive, coordinated assault upon the major population centers of South Vietnam, including Saigon. Needless to say, the ability of the enemy to strike at will in areas that were thought to be safely in the control of the South Vietnamese stunned Washington. No less was the shock when the president learned that General Westmoreland was now asking for an additional 200,000 American troops. Quite obviously, this would represent a substantial increase in our commitment, necessitating a call-up of the reserves and placing the country on a semiwar footing. Before taking such a drastic step, Johnson asked his newly appointed secretary of defense, Clark Clifford, to undertake a study as to the desirability of such a course of action.

Clifford was in a unique position among Johnson's advisers. As the new man on board, he was able to view Vietnam more objectively than the others. In addition, since he had reluctantly accepted the job of secretary of defense and was already a man of considerable stature, he felt no pressure to temper his own views to those of Johnson. Clifford's own soundings within the bureaucracy, as well as the studies made by his task force, convinced him that the United States was accomplishing neither its military nor its political objectives in Vietnam. The Clifford task force concluded that additional troop commitments would serve no useful purpose unless the South Vietnamese government was able to win the support of its people and carry the fight to the Vietcong more aggressively. The pessimism of the report startled the president, and for the moment he decided to give Westmoreland only an additional 22,000 troops.[42]

Clifford became convinced that the United States should now move in an entirely different direction, namely, negotiations; moreover, a halt to the bombing might prove to be a necessary first step in leading to them. Rusk had proposed a limited bombing pause (no bombing north of the twentieth parallel) on the grounds that the rainy season was approaching in North Vietnam and thus the bombing would achieve only limited results anyway. Clifford argued for a more extensive halt to the bombing, but he was outnumbered by those who believed that such action would not bring the North Vietnamese to the negotiating table. Although the president decided to scrap the idea of a bombing pause, Clifford was able to prevail upon him to hold off on a final decision until he met with a group of distinguished citizens: "I thought it was going to take something very substantial to shift the president's attitude. I needed some stiff medicine to bring home to the president what was happening in the country."[43]

This group of citizens, dubbed the Wise Men, included individuals who had been involved in earlier policy decisions on Vietnam: George Ball, McGeorge Bundy, Henry Cabot Lodge, and Maxwell Taylor. Also brought in were respected individuals who had served in earlier administrations: Dean Acheson, Douglas Dillon, Arthur Dean, John McCloy, Cyrus Vance, and Robert Murphy. Representing the military were retired generals Omar Bradley and Matthew Ridgway. The president also invited both his close friend Abe Fortas, who was currently sitting as a member of the Supreme Court, and Arthur Goldberg, the U.S. ambassador to the United Nations.

At the first meeting, the Wise Men met with senior officials in the government, but with Johnson absent. Questions were asked about the viability of the South Vietnamese government, the capability of their armed forces, the success of the pacification program, and so on. The senior officials then left and the group was briefed by individuals from the Departments of State and Defense and the CIA. When the Wise Men finally met with the president the next day, all but three expressed grave concern over the course of the war itself as well as the divisions it was causing among the American people. They felt that a further increase in American troops was out of the question. On the contrary, the consensus of the Wise Men was that the South Vietnamese should shoulder a greater share of the burden, thereby allowing for a substantial cutback in our commitment. The pessimism of the group stunned the president and, according to Clifford, his first reaction was that "somebody had poisoned the well."[44] The next day Johnson insisted on meeting with the government officials who had briefed the Wise Men, and, according to Townsend Hoopes, Johnson wanted to know, "What did you tell them that you didn't tell me?" The briefers insisted that there were no discrepancies. But the president continued, "You must have given them a different briefing; you aren't telling me what you told them because what you're telling me couldn't account for the inferences they drew."[45] No explanations were forthcoming.

The advice of this distinguished group of American citizens appears to have been instrumental in causing Johnson to alter his approach, for only one week later he went before the American people and announced a halt to the bombing of North Vietnam (except in the area north of the Demilitarized Zone). Furthermore, he informed the North Vietnamese that he was designating a special representative who would be willing to meet with them at any time and at any place in order to discuss an end to the conflict. Clearly the efforts of an independent-minded Clark Clifford had paid off, but it is worth noting that they came at a cost to his personal relationship with the president.[46] Although Johnson was ultimately willing to alter an unsuccessful policy, his ego would not permit him to honor the man who had been instrumental in bringing him to do it.

In summary, the president's initial decision to increase our commitment to Vietnam was probably an unwise decision, but it resulted not from his failure to reach out for information but rather from the kind of information and advice he was given. Yet once our policy toward Vietnam was set in motion, the president's demeanor and style did little to foster a frank and rigorous reexamination of this policy. Of course, we cannot be sure that a less intimidating presidential style would necessarily have caused Johnson and his advisers to alter their course any earlier, but it certainly would have made such a possibility more likely.

The Iran-Contra Affair

As President Reagan approached the halfway mark of his second term in office, his administration had been free of foreign policy setbacks severe enough to have a lasting impact on his public standing. To be sure, the terrorist attack on the Marine barracks in Lebanon, the visit to Bitburg, West Germany, and the breakdown of the Reykjavik summit all generated considerable controversy, but none left the president permanently damaged. Indeed, prior to public exposure of the Iran-contra affair, Reagan was riding high in the polls, having achieved a public approval rating of 67 percent. His decision to trade arms for hostages, however, would change all that.

Following revelations of the Iran-contra affair, the president's public approval fell by twenty-seven points, making it the most precipitous one-month decline ever recorded for a president.[47] The scandal understandably raised doubts about the president's judgment and credibility. It was he, after all, who had inveighed so persistently against negotiating with terrorists under any circumstances. Subsequent to the revelations, moreover, his credibility was further damaged when he and other White House spokesmen were repeatedly forced to change their stories concerning the chain of events and motivations behind the arms-for-hostages trade. The damage also went well beyond Reagan's relations with the American people. Members of Congress were outraged by both the trade of arms and the diversion of funds to the contras; these actions were in apparent violation of laws passed by Congress—the Arms Export Control Act, the Boland Amendment, and the Accountability for Intelligence Activities Act. Nor could the trading of arms for hostages help but prove a major blow to American credibility in the world community, for the Reagan administration was simultaneously pursuing "Operation Launch"—a program it had launched in 1983 designed to discourage other nations from selling arms to Iran.[48] Moreover, within the Middle East itself, existing doubts about American reliability were further reinforced, since the sale of arms to Iran appeared completely at odds with our announced policy of not taking sides in the war then going on between Iran and Iraq.

The revelations surrounding the Iran-contra affair would ultimately spawn three separate investigations: a preliminary inquiry by the Senate Select Committee on Intelligence; another by the Tower Commission, which was appointed by the president; and an investigation lasting several months by a joint committee of the House and Senate. The testimony given to these three bodies will serve as the primary source of information in analyzing the deliberations that led to selling arms for hostages.

Believing that the United States must begin to consider the nature of its relations with Iran after the Ayatollah Khomeini, National Security Adviser Robert McFarlane asked for an interagency study of this question in August 1984. The findings from this study were not encouraging. The State Department concluded that there was little we could do to open doors with Iran, and the CIA reported that it had little ability to influence events there. These assessments were apparently viewed by NSC staff members as unduly defeatist.[49]

By early 1985, the U.S. intelligence community believed the situation in Iran to be sufficiently volatile that fighting among various factions could occur at any time. Donald Fortier and Howard Teicher, both members of the NSC staff political/military section, worked closely with CIA officials to provide an updated Special National Intelligence Estimate of the situation in Iran. Noting that the Soviets were in a position to take advantage of Iran's unstable situation and observing that the United States had little leverage there, this estimate suggested that our European allies could protect Western interests by providing military assistance to Iran.[50] This assessment ultimately became a draft presidential decision document that was submitted to National Security Adviser McFarlane in June 1985. He, in turn, sent the draft to Secretary of State Shultz, Defense Secretary Weinberger, and CIA Director Casey for their reactions. Shultz characterized as "perverse" the proposed course of action recommended in the draft. Weinberger was even less charitable in his reaction, writing on the draft that "this is almost too absurd to comment on." Only Casey was generally sympathetic with the desire to improve relations with Iran, although he did not specifically address the issue of military assistance. Given the chilly reception, McFarlane decided to let the matter drop and did not send the draft on to the president.[51]

In the next several weeks, two developments conspired to strengthen the hand of those NSC members who wanted the Reagan administration to become more proactive in its relations with Iran. First, the spectre of terrorism once again came to the forefront on June 29, when a TWA jetliner with 135 passengers aboard was hijacked on route from Athens to Rome. One of the American passengers was executed. Second, in early July an Israeli government official met with McFarlane at the White House, informing him that Iran was ready to engage in a political dialogue with the United States. The Israeli went on to note that Iran was willing to demonstrate its good intentions by bringing its influence to bear in gaining the release of American hostages being held in Beirut; however, the Iranians involved would need to demonstrate some tangible results—such as military assistance—in return for embarking upon this dialogue with the United States. McFarlane reported this conversation to President Reagan, who decided that the possibility of a dialogue ought to be explored.[52]

Some ten days later, Michael Ledeen, consultant to the NSC staff, was visited by an emissary of Israeli Prime Minister Shimon Peres. Reiterating the desire of certain elements within the Iranian government to improve relations with the United States, the emissary went on to inform Ledeen that these Iranian contacts could secure the release of all American hostages if Iran were given one hundred TOW missiles by Israel. Both McFarlane and Chief of Staff Regan reported this conversation to the president, who was in the hospital recuperating from a cancer operation. Although Reagan later told the Tower Commission that he did not recall this conversation,

McFarlane testified that the president said, "Go ahead. Open it up." Regan also confirms that such a meeting took place, with the president inquiring about the reliability of the Iranians who had been in contact with Israel.[53]

In the next couple of weeks yet another meeting took place between the Israeli emissary and McFarlane. In this conversation, McFarlane was told that the Iranians inquired whether the U.S. government would supply Iran with arms, to which McFarlane responded in the negative. He was then asked how the United States would respond if Israel shipped weapons to Iran and whether we would be willing to provide Israel with replacements for any such shipments. The specific plan called for Israel to ship one hundred TOW missiles to Iran, an action that, according to the Israeli emissary, would both establish the good intentions of the United States and result in the release of all the hostages.[54]

In order to determine how the Reagan administration should respond to these questions and proposals, a meeting of the National Security Council was convened on or around August 8. It is important to note at this point that the decision to hold this meeting violated the normal policymaking process for dealing with national security issues. Typically such issues are first addressed by an interagency group (IG), of which there are some fifty-five in the national security policymaking structure. These groups consist of professionals from the Departments of Defense and State, the CIA, and other national security agencies. After an issue is studied by this group, it is then taken up by one of some twenty-five senior interdepartmental groups (SIGs). And from here, it goes to the National Security Council.[55] In the interest of maintaining secrecy, however, both interagency stages were bypassed by McFarlane and Poindexter throughout the seventeen months during which relations with Iran were considered by the president. In addition, the Iran initiative was completely withheld from three Middle East experts (Stark, Rahir-Keli, and Ross) on the NSC staff itself. Nor was Admiral Crowe, chairman of the Joint Chiefs of Staff and a member of the National Security Council, informed of the initiative until July 1986.[56] As the Tower Commission would later point out, the effect of drawing the circle of decision makers so narrowly was to deny the president valuable expertise on a host of relevant considerations, including intelligence on the factions in Iran, Israeli motivations, the reliability of the Iranian intermediaries, how to approach the opening with Iran, how the Iran-Iraq military balance might be affected, and what U.S. laws might be violated by such an initiative.[57]

The first NSC meeting took place without the participants having had the benefit of any advance preparation. Nor, given the fact that interagency groups had been excluded, did the participants have before them any analytical paper outlining potential problems, benefits, or options. Both Shultz and Weinberger opposed the Israeli request, arguing that it could not be kept secret, would constitute trading arms for hostages, and would run contrary to our government's embargo on arms to Iran. According to McFarlane, the initiative was approved by Chief of Staff Regan, CIA Director Casey, and Vice President Bush. Subsequent to this meeting, President Reagan gave the go-ahead to transferring some arms from Israel to Iran, with the United States agreeing to replenish the Israeli arsenal. The president stipulated, however, that the amount of arms shipped must not be enough to alter the military balance in the Iran-Iraq war.[58] It should also be noted here that McFarlane, in view of the opposition from both Shultz and Weinberger, subsequently instructed the CIA not to provide the two men with intelligence on Iran. Weinberger would later learn of this order and countermand it.[59]

On August 20, Israel shipped 96 TOWs to Iran, but this delivery was not followed by the release of any hostages. The Israelis were then told by the Iranian intermediary (Ghorbanifar) that one American hostage would be released if an additional 400 TOWs were shipped. Actually, Iran received another 408 on September 15, and the following day one hostage was released.[60] Thus, after being promised that all hostages would be let go for 100 missiles, the United States ended up with one hostage for 508 missiles.

During the next three months a series of meetings between NSC staff members, Israeli officials, and the Iranian intermediary led to another arms shipment agreement—this one calling for 80 HAWK missiles to be delivered on November 24. The arms were to be flown from Israel to a third country and then on to Iran. If all went well, the hostages were to be released by Thanksgiving. The president was informed of this pending shipment while at the Geneva summit, as was George Shultz, who continued to object that it constituted "a straight arms for hostages swap."[61] Unlike in the previous transfers, however, the United States became more directly involved in the HAWK shipment. Problems developed with respect to the transport of HAWKs by plane through the third country, at which point McFarlane instructed Lt. Colonel Oliver North to resolve the problem. (North had been detailed from the Defense Department to the NSC staff.) After a series of flight arrangements had fallen through, North resorted to having the CIA transport the arms. This action necessitated a Covert Action Finding, granting presidential authorization for the CIA's involvement. Accordingly, it was drafted by the CIA and given to Assistant National Security Adviser John Poindexter. This finding, incidentally, did not refer to the arms shipment as an attempt to improve diplomatic relations with Iran but rather portrayed the motive of the arms transfer as a purely arms-for-hostages operation.[62] Indeed, it was for this reason that Poindexter would destroy the document after the Iran-contra affair became public nearly a year later.[63] The finding was notable in other respects as well. For one thing, it was an after-the-fact authorization, with Poindexter taking it to the president for his signature nearly two weeks after the shipment of HAWKs. As Poindexter himself admitted, he presented the finding to the president without first having subjected it to the normal staffing and review. Nor were all members of the National Security Council informed of the finding, as required by a 1982 national security directive signed by the president. In fact, Poindexter recalls having discussed it only with Casey and his deputy director.[64]

As for the shipment of HAWKs, only 18 of 80 were on the plane when it landed in Iran. Contrary to McFarlane's orders, they were shipped before any hostages were released, and, to the considerable consternation of Iran, they proved to be the wrong model of HAWK. Again, no hostages were released.[65]

On December 4, 1985, the day that Poindexter replaced McFarlane as the president's national security adviser, Oliver North informed Poindexter of yet another arms-for-hostages proposal—this one calling for 3,300 Israeli TOWs and 50 HAWKs in exchange for release of all the hostages. In discussing this latest deal, North on his own also informed Israeli officials that our government wanted to divert profits from this next sale to help the contras in Nicaragua.[66] On December 7, the president held a formal meeting of the National Security Council to discuss this latest proposal. According to Secretary of State Shultz, this was the first meeting where the participants had an opportunity to prepare for the discussion in advance.[67] Shultz wasted no time in voicing his opposition. He argued that the trade of arms for hostages would undermine our policy against dealing with terrorists and that the trade would ultimately become public, thereby jeopardizing our position with moderate Arabs and our allies. Shultz also maintained that the action would not provide us with any influence over moderate elements in Iran. Weinberger echoed these sentiments and pointed out that such a trade would be illegal, violating both our arms embargo against Iran and the Arms Export Control Act. Deputy CIA Director McMahon, who attended in place of Casey, contended that the long-range goal of improving relations with Iran by allying ourselves with moderates was ill conceived because there were no moderates in that country. Moreover, call it what you might, the plan still amounted to an arms-for-hostages trade. Finally, McMahon noted that there were grounds for doubting the reliability of the Iranian intermediary. White House Chief of Staff Regan also weighed in against any more arms sales. McFarlane and Poindexter, on the other hand, argued for continuing the initiative, as did the president, whose concern for the hostages was so palpable that he appeared little concerned about the legal issues raised by Weinberger. Strong opposition from the others, however, put the matter on hold pending a visit by McFarlane to London, where he was to check on the reliability of the Iranian intermediary and to explore the possibility of freeing the hostages without resorting to arms sales.[68]

Upon his return, McFarlane reported to the president and several members of the National Security Council that his conversations with the Iranian intermediary led him to conclude that the intermediary was an unsavory character in whom no confidence could be placed. For this reason, McFarlane recommended against the latest proposed arms sale, but noted that such a decision might imperil the lives of the hostages.[69] President Reagan concurred with this recommendation, but it was also clear that the hostages had become a preoccupation with him. According to one participant in the meeting, the president noted that "he was looking powerless and inept because he was unable to do anything to get the hostages out."[70] In later testimony, both McFarlane and Poindexter would confirm this concern, noting that the president would begin practically every daily national security briefing by asking whether there was any news on the hostages.[71] Poindexter, concluding that the president had not totally foreclosed keeping the Iran initiative alive, instructed North to keep exploring the possibilities.[72]

Based upon talks with a new Israeli intermediary, North presented yet another plan to Poindexter, in which Israel would provide Iran with a total of 4,000 TOW missiles. Following the shipment of the first 500, all U.S. hostages would be released, and Israel would simultaneously secure the release of twenty to thirty Hizballah prisoners being held by the Israeli-supported Lebanese Christian forces. Following these transactions, the remaining TOWs would be shipped to Iran by Israel, and the United States would replenish the Israeli arsenal.[73] Because the Israeli sale of U.S. military equipment would violate the Arms Export Control Act, Poindexter concluded that a presidential Covert Action Finding would be necessary. Thus, at a morning national security briefing on January 6, 1986, Poindexter informed the president of the plan—and gave him a first draft of the finding. Reagan was sympathetic to the plan—indeed, he even signed the first draft of the finding—and called for a National Security Council meeting the next day to consider it. Apparently without any advance notice of the subject, the matter was discussed, with only Shultz and Weinberger voicing their opposition to a plan the president now clearly supported.[74]

In the next week or so, the proposed plan was to be altered in two significant respects. The first change was in response to the legal opinions of Attorney General Meese and CIA lawyers, who concluded that shipment of American arms from

Israeli stocks would violate the Arms Export Control Act. In their judgment, however, a violation could be avoided if U.S. military equipment were first purchased by the CIA and then sold to Iran and if such action were also accompanied by a presidential finding. Poindexter and North now advocated just such an arrangement. At North's request, William Secord, who was taken on as a consultant to the NSC staff, was to act as a CIA agent and handle the financial transaction.[75]

At his daily national security briefing with the president on January 17, 1986, Poindexter presented for Reagan's signature a final draft finding authorizing the arms sales to Iran. Also in attendance were the vice president, Donald Regan, and another member of the NSC staff (Donald Fortier). Needless to say, this was a critical meeting because a decision to go ahead with the plan would now involve the United States in the *direct* sale of arms to Iran. Yet the deliberations were scarcely designed to maximize the flow of information and advice to the president on this pending decision. For one thing, none of Reagan's senior foreign policy advisers (Shultz, Weinberger, Casey) was in attendance. (Indeed, Shultz was never even informed of the decision in the months that followed.) Moreover, as the president would later testify, at no time was he apprised of how the plan would be implemented or of the possible risks involved in having the NSC staff, which had no experience in covert operations, assume operational control of the plan. Finally, the president appears to have been misled on a point that he regarded as essential to approving the arms sale, namely, that it must not alter the military balance between Iran and Iraq. Poindexter's memorandum accompanying the finding was reassuring on this point, for it noted that the Israelis believed Iran was losing the war and that steps should be taken to restore the balance. In actuality, however, this assessment ran contrary to CIA and State and Defense Department intelligence estimates—estimates of which Poindexter was surely aware.[76]

After the meeting of the National Security Council on January 7, the Iranian initiative was never again subject to a full-scale review by the president's principal foreign policy advisers. What the president learned of subsequent developments, which we shall consider shortly, came in his daily national security briefings from Poindexter.[77] Reliance upon Poindexter, however, was surely problematical, for he was a staunch advocate of the very policy on which he was supposed to be providing neutral counsel. That he lacked a dispassionate perspective, moreover, would become apparent in the coming months when he failed to apprise Shultz and Weinberger of continuing arms deals and actively sought to exclude them from meeting with the president to discuss the matter.

By the time this latest plan was put into effect, Oliver North had, without presidential approval, added a sweetener for the Iranians, namely, providing them with U.S. military intelligence on Iraq. The first 500 TOWs were shipped to Iran on February 17, but, contrary to the agreement, the shipment was not followed by the release of any hostages. Even so, the second 500 were delivered following the president's authorization given during one of his morning national security briefings.[78] There soon followed a new series of Iranian demands, which called for a meeting of senior U.S. and Iranian officials in Iran and the delivery of spare parts for their HAWK missiles—all in return for the release of the hostages. Although Chief of Staff Regan was now counseling against sending any more weapons, the president nevertheless gave his approval to dispatch McFarlane to Iran in a plane containing some of the spare parts requested. Following McFarlane's meeting there and the release of the hostages, the spare parts were to be unloaded and others shipped. When North requested that

Poindexter now convene a meeting of the president, Casey, Weinberger, and Shultz for the purpose of discussing the proposed trip, Poindexter vetoed the idea, informing North that "I don't want a meeting with RR, Shultz, and Weinberger."[79] As it turns out, after several days of meetings in Iran characterized by misunderstandings, additional Iranian demands, and no release of hostages, McFarlane refused to order the full shipment of spare parts and departed—not, however, before the Iranians had removed the small number of spare parts that were on McFarlane's plane.[80]

Upon his return to Washington, McFarlane recommended to the president that all arms transfers be stopped. Reagan concurred. In July one hostage was finally released. Believing that failure to ship the remaining spare parts might endanger the lives of the remaining hostages, Poindexter recommended that the president approve the shipment of the remaining spare parts. Reagan did so at the end of July. Meanwhile, some of the money received from all of the arms sales to date was being diverted by North to support the contras in Nicaragua—a reason, no doubt, why he pushed so hard for a continuation of arms sales even when they failed to lead to release of all the hostages.[81]

The release of a hostage in mid-July now brought to two the number freed since the Iran initiative began. If this represented progress, it was soon offset by the kidnapping of another American in September and yet another in October. Optimism was soon rekindled, however. After the breakdown of McFarlane's discussions in Iran, Poindexter had at long last concluded that the Iranian intermediary was not reliable. Accordingly, back in June he had instructed North to cast about for a new channel through which the United States could deal. North and Secord found such an individual, who turned out to be a member of the Iranian Revolutionary Guard Corps.[82] While this new emissary promised to assist in release of the hostages, his wish list embraced a far broader range of demands than his predecessor's. Under an agreement negotiated with North, the United States would sell Iran 500 TOW missiles and HAWK spare parts, as well as provide updated military intelligence and free medical supplies. In addition, the United States would provide a plan for bringing about the release of seventeen Iranian terrorists being held in Kuwait. (This portion of the agreement, incidentally, ran totally contrary to official U.S. policy regarding the Kuwaiti prisoners and was negotiated by North without the knowledge of the president or State Department.) One or two hostages would then be released. Nine days later an additional 1,000 TOWs would be shipped. Finally, the Iranian contacts would continue their efforts toward creating the conditions necessary to bring about the release of the remaining hostages.[83]

On October 27, Reagan authorized the shipment of the first 500 TOWs, which were delivered to Iran on the next day. Five days later just one American hostage was released. On the next day, however, the arms sale initiative was exposed in a Lebanese magazine. These events precipitated a meeting of the National Security Council, where Secretary Shultz for the first time received official confirmation of the direct U.S. arms sales. In a private meeting with the president four days later, Shultz urged him not to sell any more arms. Reagan, however, remained noncommittal and rejected Shultz's proposal that the State Department now be allowed to assume control over the Iran initiative. Only after the diversion of funds to the contras became public more than a week later, followed by Poindexter's resignation, did the president authorize the State Department to take over. When Shultz heard of North's negotiated nine-point plan—particularly the part relating to the release of Iranian terrorists held by Kuwait—he immediately went to the president. Reagan, astonished at what he was hearing, authorized Shultz to repudiate the nine-point plan and to inform the Iranians that there would be no more arms sales.[84]

Thus, after nearly a year and a half of secret negotiations and meetings, during which time the Iranians had been sold some two thousand TOW missiles, eighteen HAWK missiles, and millions of dollars worth of spare parts, all the United States had to show for its efforts was the release of three hostages and the kidnapping of two more by Iranian terrorists.

It would be difficult to conjure up a set of circumstances more hospitable to minimizing the flow of information and advice to the president than those present in the arms-for-hostages deliberations. From the very outset, the desire for secrecy not only excluded expertise from other departments and agencies but also Middle East experts within the NSC staff itself. Even for those few who did participate, the opportunities to discuss and review the initiative were infrequent—a mere three meetings of the National Security Council in a seventeen-month period. Nor were these meetings themselves designed to maximize informed discussion. Two of the three were convened without the participants having had the benefit of advanced preparation; no analytical material was distributed; formal minutes that might have provided guidance at future meetings were never recorded;[85] and by the time the second and third meetings took place, Shultz and Weinberger had already been denied information about intervening developments. The most critical decision (January 17 meeting) of the entire eighteen months—the direct sale of weapons to Iran—was taken without the participation of the president's three senior foreign policy advisers—Shultz, Weinberger, and Casey. While Casey, to be sure, would prove a strong supporter of the plan, clearly the other two were not. Once the division of opinion among the president's advisers had become clear, supporters of the plan not only denied information to opponents but also sought to exclude them from the deliberations. Finally, subsequent to the third NSC meeting in early January 1986, the president's primary source of information thereafter was his national security adviser, John Poindexter—the major advocate for continuing the initiative. Moreover, since Poindexter and other NSC staff members and consultants were responsible for implementing the arms sales, the president lacked an independent base of information for following and evaluating their performance. As it turns out, of course, not only did North and Poindexter divert money from the sales to the contras, but they also provided military intelligence to the Iranians and promised U.S. pressure to force both the release of Kuwaiti-held terrorists and the ouster of Saddam Hussein of Iraq—all this undertaken in the president's name but without his knowledge.

How can we account for the fact that the arms-for-hostages decision was made in such a lackadaisical fashion? Certainly part of the blame can be laid at the doorstep of Reagan's national security advisers, whose personal policy views overrode their obligation to provide the president with as complete a base of information and advice as possible. The ultimate responsibility for this debacle, however, falls on the shoulders of President Reagan himself. Simply put, he failed to help himself secure the best possible information and advice needed to make an informed judgment. The Tower Commission Report speaks to this very point:

> The NSC system will not work unless the President makes it work. After all, this system was created to serve the President of the United States in ways of his choosing. By his actions, by his leadership, the President therefore determines the quality of its performance.

... [Reagan] did not force his policy to undergo the most critical review of which the NSC participants and the process were capable. At no time did he insist upon accountability and performance review. Had the president chosen to drive the NSC system, the outcome could well have been different. As it was, the most powerful features of the NSC system—providing comprehensive analysis, alternatives and follow-up—were not utilized.[86]

Clearly, Reagan could have insisted that the NSC meet more frequently than it did and that the meetings be preceded by better preparation. He could have insisted that the most critical decision in this whole affair, the direct sale of arms to Iran, not be made in the absence of Shultz, Weinberger, and Casey. Furthermore, although later testifying that he was never apprised of how this decision would be implemented or what risks attended having the NSC staff assume operational responsibility, there is nothing in the record to suggest that he probed these matters. Indeed, in the three investigations into the Iran-contra affair, one does not find a single instance where witnesses recounted the president having asked searching, probing questions on any aspect of the arms-for-hostages trade. Such apparent passivity throughout this whole affair also startled the members of the Tower Commission; one member, Edmund Muskie, observed, "We were appalled by the absence of the kind of alertness and vigilance to his job and to these policies that one expects of a president."[87] Nor, as the president's chief of staff, Donald Regan, recounts, was Reagan's disengagement unique to this particular decision:

He trusted his lieutenants to act on his intentions, rather than on his spoken instructions. . . . Never—absolutely never in my experience—did President Reagan really lose his temper or utter a rude or unkind word. Never did he issue a direct order, although I, at least, sometimes devoutly wished that he would. He listened, acquiesced, played his role, and waited for the next act to be written.[88]

Of course, it is possible to argue that even had the decision-making process been more systematic and thorough, the same decision would have been made. Reagan did, after all, approve the initial plan in the face of opposition from two of his most trusted advisers, the secretaries of state and defense, and he continued to approve additional sales despite repeated Iranian bad faith and even after his chief of staff counseled against it. The fundamental problem with this decision, it might then be argued, was not the process itself. Rather, it was simply bad presidential judgment fueled by an overpowering impulse to free the hostages. While this line of reasoning certainly has some merit, the point is that the decision-making process failed to provide the systematic information and advice that could have served to test and challenge Reagan's own impulses and predispositions on this issue. Had it done so, Reagan might well have decided not to trade arms for hostages. The fact that it did not merely increased the likelihood that he would.

Shoe Import Quotas

The decision-making problem that the Carter administration faced on shoe import quotas differs from the previous cases in two important respects. In the first place, it involved an issue that was domestic in nature every bit as much as it was foreign. Thus, there were many *more interests in and outside government participating in the decision-making process* than was the case in the decisions just analyzed.

Second, unlike the Bay of Pigs, the Cuban missile crisis, the Vietnam War, or the Iran-contra affair, the issue of shoe import quotas was relatively *routine* in nature, and thus the president's involvement was less direct.

Since the time that tariffs on shoes were lowered in 1968, countries such as Taiwan, South Korea, Spain, Italy, and Brazil have been exporting large quantities of shoes to the United States. Because the cost of labor in these countries is substantially cheaper than it is here, they have been able to sell their products at prices well below those of American shoe companies. Consequently, by 1976 these countries had managed to corner 46 percent of the American shoe market—up from 22 percent in 1968.[89] This development led to the closing of some three hundred shoe factories in the United States, as well as a loss of 70,000 jobs. In the early part of 1976, the American Footwear Industries Association sought relief from the International Trade Commission. Created by Congress under the Trade Act of 1974, this commission is charged with considering trade complaints and making recommendations for dealing with them. After receiving the commission's recommendations, the president has sixty days in which to accept or reject its report. If he should decide to reject their recommendations and come up with his own, they are still subject to a congressional override by concurrent resolution. In this particular case, the International Trade Commission ruled by a three-to-two vote that import quotas should be raised in order to provide some relief to the beleaguered shoe industry. Given the closeness of the vote, however, as well as pressure from the Departments of State, Commerce, and the Treasury, President Ford decided to reject the commission's recommendation. Instead, he decided to provide "trade adjustment assistance" to the shoe industry. In essence, this amounted to raising the benefits to unemployed shoe workers and increasing loans to the shoe industry so it might modernize and diversify.

Upset with President Ford's decision, in September 1976 the Senate Finance Committee asked the International Trade Commission to reopen its inquiry into the financial plight of the shoe industry. The commission did so and issued its report on January 6, 1977, this time solidly backing the imposition of import quotas on shoes. Specifically, it recommended that for the next five years some twenty different countries be permitted to export 265 million pairs of shoes at a tariff rate of 10 percent. For all shoes over this amount, the tariff rate would be raised to 40 percent. Rather than acting on the commission's recommendations, President Ford decided to leave the matter to the man who would be succeeding him on the twentieth of January.

Clearly, the issue of quotas posed a dilemma for the incoming President Carter. For one thing, he had campaigned on a free-trade plank, declaring that if industries were hurt by imports then they should be helped with federal aid. In addition, the United States was on record as wanting to help the economies of the underdeveloped countries by reducing trade barriers. Third, a decision by the largest free trader in the world to raise tariff barriers would serve to trigger a similar reaction among other nations. And finally, President Carter had pledged to do everything he could to bring inflation under control. By putting a tariff on foreign shoes, he would be forcing Americans to pay higher prices for the shoes they bought. If all of these points constituted compelling reasons for not instituting quotas, there were also some strong reasons why he should. Most important of all was the fact that a significant part of his electoral support had come from labor, a group to whom he had promised more jobs. Furthermore, there was strong support for quotas among those members of Congress who represented the thirty-nine states where shoes were produced.

The day after he took office, Carter received Presidential Review Memorandum

No. 7 from the National Security Council. Its substance consisted of an analysis of trade issues in general as well as the foreign policy implications of shoe import quotas in particular. On February 4, the Office of the Special Trade Representative—a unit within the Executive Office of the President charged with advising the president on trade matters—sent a background memo to President Carter's Economic Policy Group, which was to meet on February 7. Chaired by Treasury Secretary Michael Blumenthal, this group was responsible for coordinating Carter's economic policy. The other members of the group were the vice president, five cabinet officers, and the heads of five different units within the Executive Office of the President. The memo sent to this group outlined five options for dealing with the shoe problem. Three involved the imposition of some kind of tariff or quota; one called for the continuation of our free-trade policy, but with an increase in "trade adjustment assistance" to the shoe industry; the fifth option was to negotiate Orderly Marketing Agreements (OMAs) with the major exporters of shoes. OMAs are formal contracts between an importing and exporting country. While they are more stringent than voluntary restraints, they are less so than quotas. In addition to reviewing the substance of this memo at their February 7 meeting, the Economic Policy Group examined a second memo, which contained State Department objections to the recommendations of the International Trade Commission. In essence, the State Department argued that the commission's quota recommendations were too restrictive and thus potentially damaging to our relations with the countries involved.[90]

Throughout February and March, interested parties made their case to various government agencies, including the Economic Policy Group. The shoe producers spoke out strongly in favor of quotas, and they had a strong ally in the person of George Meany. Speaking for the AFL-CIO, Meany insisted that without quotas on shoes, the industry would face "slow but certain death." The president received further pressure to move in this direction from the nation's governors, thirty-six of whom signed a petition asking the president to "provide effective import relief to the footwear industry before more jobs are lost, more plants are closed and more communities are afflicted by the current tidal wave of footwear imports." These sentiments were echoed by various representatives and senators. Weighing in against quotas, however, were other industry officials, consumer groups, major U.S. allies, the chairman of the Federal Reserve Board, and the president's national security adviser. Speaking on behalf of U.S. retailers, the Volume Retailers Association of America cited a study they had commissioned which showed that quotas would cost the American consumer $500 million annually. In an address to the National Press Club on March 22, the Japanese prime minister voiced grave concern over the possibility that the United States might move in a protectionist direction: "Surely we have learned that such a course can only exacerbate world economic conditions."[91] Similar sentiments were voiced on the same day by Federal Reserve Board Chairman Arthur Burns in testimony before a Senate committee. In a memo sent to the president on March 16, National Security Adviser Brzezinski added his voice to the chorus, noting the importance of a "free trade" position to our relations with other nations.[92]

On March 21 the president's Economic Policy Group met to consider a course of action. While agreeing that the shoe industry should be provided with some additional federal relief assistance, the group was divided on what other steps should be taken. Those within the group representing the State Department, the Treasury Department, HUD, and the Council of Economic Advisers were opposed to any kind of quotas, whereas those from the Departments of Labor, Commerce, and Agriculture, as well as from the Office of Management and Budget and the Office of the Special Trade Representative, came down on the side of a three-year Tariff Rate Quota. Although the middle option—Orderly Marketing Agreements—was raised as a possibility by domestic policy adviser Stuart Eizenstat, apparently it was not given very serious consideration.[93] Following the meeting, Special Trade Representative Robert Strauss sent the president a memo outlining the views of the Economic Policy Group but failed even to mention the possibility of OMAs as an option. In addition, through inadvertence the Strauss memo was not sent to the head of Carter's Domestic Policy Staff, who thus was not able to provide the president with an assessment of the memo. Fortunately, a Strauss aide, who was apparently disturbed by what he had heard at the meeting of the Economic Policy Group, happened to send a memo to the vice president in which he pointed out that a no-relief stance on the part of the Carter administration could seriously jeopardize the president's relations with Congress. He further noted that the OMA option might well be the best compromise under the circumstances. On Monday, March 28, the president met with the Economic Policy Group, and the OMA option was raised as a possible solution. This course of action seemed most appealing to Carter, but because the group had neglected to give it serious consideration in the prior meeting, there had been no staff work done on it.[94] Thus, the president found himself in a meeting where he lacked the information necessary to make a decision on the OMA option. Accordingly, he immediately instructed his special trade representative to prepare a memo on the feasibility of OMAs.

Strauss's memo came to the president on March 30, and it recommended the OMA approach. It was preceded by another memo from the head of Carter's Domestic Policy Staff, which also came down on the side of OMAs. On the same day, President Carter also received considerable advice from other interested parties. The State Department, for example, sent the president an extensive memo criticizing the OMA option as too protectionist and potentially damaging to U.S. relations with other nations. In addition, a communication came to the president from an American official who was planning the president's upcoming economic summit in London. Fearing that any form of trade restrictions might hamper trade discussions with Western leaders, he asked the president to reject OMAs and instead to request that other nations voluntarily restrict their shoe imports. Finally, the Labor Department also chimed in with a memo arguing that voluntary restraints were inadequate and the OMA approach not much better.[95]

Having been pressured by those in and outside of government who were either for or against instituting quotas, it is not surprising that President Carter ultimately chose a middle course, namely, Orderly Marketing Agreements (OMAs). Specifically, these agreements were to be negotiated with Taiwan and South Korea, the two countries that had been exporting the largest number of shoes. Carter also decided to increase federal aid to the beleaguered shoe industry. Pursuant to this decision, the Commerce Department decided to spend $56 million in the form of advice, loans, and loan guarantees to American shoe producers.

The shoe import quota decision serves to highlight two important points. First, it is essential that a president's advisers carefully consider all of the options available to him on a given issue. In this instance, Carter's Economic Policy Group did not appear to have done so. Indeed, the option that the president finally chose (OMAs) had been quickly dismissed at the group's second meeting. Although the OMA option was reintroduced into the deliberations at a later meeting, the president was not able to make a decision on it at that time because his advisers had not prepared any assessment of OMAs. This case study also serves to illustrate that on more routine decisions the president is particularly dependent upon his advisers—at least to the extent that he must rely upon their characterizations of the deliberations on a given issue. Because the Bay of Pigs invasion, the Cuban missile crisis, and the Vietnam War were issues of considerable magnitude, the president's involvement in the decision-making process was more persistent and direct. Thus, he had a greater firsthand knowledge of the deliberations. In contrast, the issue of shoe import quotas was certainly a more routine issue, and consequently President Carter was not directly involved in the deliberations until their final stage. For this reason, he was dependent upon what his advisers relayed to him concerning what had transpired during the earlier stages of the decision-making process. In this particular case, he was not adequately informed in this regard. Indeed, Strauss's memo to the president summarizing the meeting of the Economic Policy Group failed even to mention the OMA option, let alone explain why the group did not seriously entertain it as a possible solution.[96]

MAXIMIZING THE FLOW OF INFORMATION TO THE PRESIDENT

In the last several years, numerous proposals have been put forth to expand the president's sources of information. Many, no doubt, have been motivated by our dismal experience with the Vietnam War and the Iran-contra affair. The common theme running through these proposals is the establishment of some kind of advisory council to the president. This approach is not a novel one. Indeed, the Founding Fathers considered but ultimately rejected the proposal to establish a Council of State, whose membership would possibly include the Speaker of the House, president of the Senate, chief justice of the Supreme Court, and the heads of the various executive departments. Samuel Rosenman, an adviser to two presidents, recalls that he and Bernard Baruch tried unsuccessfully to persuade presidents Roosevelt and Truman to create a "think board" whose purpose would be "to consider the future, travel the country and come back to the White House to say: 'There is this or that situation. I think it is serious or critical. You should consider taking some action.' "[97]

In 1975 two separate groups came up with recommendations that an advisory group be established to advise the president on matters of foreign policy. The one group consisted of scholars, jurists, and other respected figures, all of whom had come together for a conference on the powers of the presidency. This group called for the establishment of an executive council made up of four or five distinguished private citizens who would be appointed by the president and subject to confirmation by the Senate. Another group, the Commission on the Organization of the Government for the Conduct of Foreign Policy, called for the establishment of a Council on International Planning. It too would be composed of private citizens knowledgeable in foreign affairs and would be available to the president to use as he saw fit. Such ideas surfaced again following the Iran-contra affair, with *Time* magazine editor Walter Isaacson calling for "appointment of a panel of 'wise men,' an outside group of elder statesmen to give regular foreign policy advice to a foundering president."[98] The eminent scholar and diplomat George Kennan went further, arguing that such a group should be created by constitutional amendment and should be available to advise both Congress and the president.[99]

One other proposal deserves our attention here, for unlike those already mentioned, it calls for bringing together certain individuals already in government. Graham Allison and Peter Szanton have proposed that the National Security Council be abolished and replaced by a group they call ExCab, whose permanent membership would include the secretaries of state, defense, the treasury, and health and human services, as well as the head of either labor or commerce. In their judgment, such a group would be more reflective of the overriding reality of today's world, which is that issues of foreign and domestic politics are increasingly intertwined. They point out that ExCab would have the potential to "widen the circle of advisers that the president normally consulted before taking major decisions, thus improving the odds that major decisions would be taken with an eye to both their domestic and foreign effects. It would put those advisers directly in touch not only with the president but with each other, helping to generate a collegial comprehension of the varied dimensions of the issues confronting the president."[100] The National Academy of Public Administration sounded a similar theme in calling for the establishment within the Executive Office of an Economic Affairs staff, which would be charged with integrating the economic aspects of domestic and foreign policies.[101]

While all of these proposals have merit, they all suffer from a common weakness. In the final analysis, presidents make decisions as they wish to make them. Thus, the mere creation of an advisory body is no guarantee that it will be used. Moreover, proposals that call for establishing advisory councils of *outside* experts suffer from an additional disadvantage. Few would doubt the desirability of a president consulting knowledgeable people outside government. Since their interests are not directly tied to his and since they have no stake in the decision, it is more likely that their views will reflect greater objectivity and candor. Indeed, the "Wise Men" consulted by Johnson in 1968 served a highly useful function in this regard. But if we institutionalize such a group within the government, do we not thereby tie its interests more directly to those of the president? Of course, one might argue that provisions could be made for the group's independence, but surely presidents would strongly resist any efforts in this direction.

With respect to whom the president should consult, we might also suggest that he seek to include in the decision-making process more people whose political experience has been rooted in *domestic politics*. According to Richard Neustadt, this need is especially critical in the foreign policy area, where for years important decisions have been dominated by nonpolitical experts, thus resulting in a lack of appreciation for the domestic implications of foreign policy decisions.[102]

Other suggestions for improving presidential decision making have focused not so much on creating additional sources of information as on making better use of the ones that already exist.[103] For one thing, presidents should avoid getting themselves into a position where they are dependent on only one source of information. Second, although it may be appropriate for the president to have policy advocates on his White House staff, this role should not be performed by staffers whose major function is to provide the president with facts and advice coming in from other sources. Clearly, Johnson and Reagan were not well served by their national security advisers, whose views on Vietnam and the arms-for-hostages trade, respectively, significantly influenced the kinds of information and advice to which they exposed their presidents. Third, given the tendency of presidential advisers to adopt what they perceive to be the president's position on an issue, it may be advisable for presidents to refrain from making their own inclinations known initially. Fourth, it may also be desirable for presidents to absent themselves from deliberations during the early stages of the decision-making process. Truman, for example, on the grounds that his presence might hamper frank discussion, absented himself from meetings of his National Security Council when it was deliberating on possible responses to the Berlin blockade. Similarly, those close to the decision-making process during the Cuban missile crisis have noted that Kennedy's absence from the earlier meetings made for a much more candid discussion among the participants. Of course, if a president chooses to employ this tactic, it is absolutely essential that his advisers provide him with a complete picture of what took place in his absence. Theodore Sorensen and Robert Kennedy, both of whom were highly attuned to the president's interests, performed this function well during the Cuban missile crisis. Fifth, in the interests of preventing a premature consensus, the president (and in his absence, someone from his staff) should foster an atmosphere that is conducive to a thorough airing of views. Among other things, this means encouraging the participation of all those present, accentuating the disagreement that arises among the various participants, taking care to see that someone presents the case for what may be an unpopular position, and, perhaps most important of all, avoiding any impression of impatience with views that do not coincide with his own. Presidential advisers, who often are overly deferential to begin with, will only become more so if they see that their boss is not comfortable with dissenting points of view.

Of course, it is one thing to suggest how presidents may better maximize the flow of facts and advice from the people around them, and quite another to persuade them to implement such suggestions. A president's decision-making style is to a considerable extent a reflection of his personality, and consequently, it is not readily subject to change. Thus, given Johnson's intimidating style, his intolerance for those who disagreed with him, and his obsession with reaching a consensus, it is difficult to imagine that he would feel comfortable with several of the suggestions made above. Moreover, even presidents who are more open and flexible in their decision-making styles are likely to become less so the longer they remain in office. One reason for this may be that presidential egos, which are usually considerable to begin with, are bolstered still further by the undue reverence accorded the office they hold. Consequently, presidents become increasingly arrogant and less tolerant of those who would challenge their judgments. Another reason may be that as pressures build and opposition mounts, presidents have a tendency to turn toward those who will provide unquestioning support. As Stephen Hess has noted, "Outside opposition generally forces internal consensus as administration officials begin to huddle together for comfort. And a president, feeling increasingly threatened, turns more and more to those who give him the most loyal support."[104]

Given these realities, one final and more drastic proposal may be in order, namely, *requiring* the president to appear before Congress periodically and answer questions in much the same way as the prime minister is compelled to do in the British House of Commons. (House Majority Leader Richard Gephardt suggested a variation of this proposal to President-elect Clinton, namely, that he *voluntarily* come to the well of the House to answer questions).

Having the president defend his policies and actions before Congress would have several benefits, the first being to reduce the regal, "untouchable" nature of the presidency. Presently, the only time the president is held accountable for his actions between elections is when he holds a press conference. Even here, however, he is not questioned by his peers; nor is he even required to hold press conferences. Second, appearances before Congress might serve to reduce the isolation that results as presidents increasingly surround themselves with people of like mind. Finally, the fact that presidents would be compelled to justify his actions before Congress in person might also provide some additional incentive for him to consult more systematically with the legislature on important policy issues.

As for the weaknesses of this proposal, one may question whether members of Congress would be any less deferential than presidential advisers. Certainly no serious challenges were raised against President Ford when he voluntarily testified before the House Judiciary Committee concerning his pardon of President Nixon. But perhaps that was to be expected, since presidents have rarely appeared before Congress to justify their actions. If such appearances were institutionalized, as this proposal suggests, the tendency to be overly deferential to the president would probably decrease considerably after the first several encounters. A more serious objection to this proposal, however, might be that very little in the way of meaningful interaction could take place in an encounter between the president and 535 members of Congress. (As a way around this problem, it might be more appropriate for the president to meet with a smaller group of individuals selected from the total membership of Congress. This group should probably not exceed forty people; the president should meet with it once a month on Capitol Hill; its membership should consist of an equal number of Republicans and Democrats from the House and an equal number from the Senate; and to ensure that all would have an opportunity to participate in the meetings, the membership of the group would be determined each month through a system of random selection.) One final objection to this proposal may be raised on the grounds that it is simply out of touch with reality. After all, to require presidents to appear before Congress would necessitate a constitutional amendment, and such a process is customarily a long and tedious one. Moreover, although students of the presidency may be properly concerned over the potential for presidential isolation in decision making, it is highly doubtful that this concern has yet permeated the national consciousness.

Alas, all of the proposals suggested here may be found wanting in terms of their feasibility, desirability, or both. Thus, in all probability, we shall have to content ourselves with identifying the problem areas in presidential decision making, hoping all the while that the person in the Oval Office will take cognizance of them.

☆ NOTES

1. Irving L. Janis, *Victims of Groupthink* (Boston: Houghton Mifflin, 1972), p. 39. Copyright © 1972 by Houghton Mifflin Company. Reprinted by permission.

2. Hugh Heclo, *Studying the Presidency: A Report to the Ford Foundation* (New York: Ford Foundation, 1977), p. 22.

3. Cited in Theodore Sorensen, *Decision-Making in the White House* (New York: Columbia University Press), p. xiii.

4. Cited in Theodore Sorensen, *Kennedy* (New York: Harper & Row, 1965), p. 309.

5. Ibid., pp. 295–97.

6. Janis, *Victims of Groupthink,* pp. 20, 21.

7. Ibid., p. 22.

8. Ibid., p. 24.

9. Ibid., pp. 24–26.

10. Sorensen, *Kennedy,* p. 302.

11. Roger Hilsman, *To Move a Nation* (Garden City, N.Y.: Doubleday, 1964), p. 31.

12. Arthur Schlesinger, Jr., *A Thousand Days* (Boston: Houghton Mifflin, 1965), p. 248.

13. Janis, *Victims of Groupthink,* p. 42; Sorensen, *Kennedy,* p. 306.

14. Cited in Schlesinger, *Thousand Days,* p. 258.

15. Sorensen, *Kennedy,* p. 306.

16. Janis, *Victims of Groupthink,* pp. 43–46; Peter Wyden, *Bay of Pigs: The Untold Story* (New York: Simon & Schuster, 1979), pp. 146–52.

17. Cited in Graham Allison, *Essence of Decision* (Boston: Little, Brown, 1971), p. 40.

18. Ibid., p. 41.

19. James Nathan, "The Missile Crisis: His Finest Hour Now," *World Politics* 27 (January 1975), 266.

20. Robert Kennedy, *Thirteen Days* (New York: Norton, 1969). p. 11.

21. Sorensen, *Kennedy,* p. 679.

22. Ibid.

23. Kennedy, *Thirteen Days,* p. 9.

24. Cited in Allison, *Essence of Decision,* p. 196.

25. Nathan, "Missile Crisis," p. 260.

26. Herbert Y. Schandler, *The Unmaking of a President: Lyndon Johnson and Vietnam,* p. 28. Copyright © 1977 by Princeton University Press. Reprinted by permission of Princeton University Press.

27. Cited in Jack Valenti, *A Very Human President* (New York: Norton, 1975), pp. 326, 327.

28. Ibid., pp. 346, 348.

29. Ibid., p. 351.

30. Lyndon Johnson, *The Vantage Point* (New York: Holt, Rinehart and Winston, 1971), pp. 148, 151, 152.

31. Cited in Janis, *Victims of Groupthink,* p. 125; see also David Halberstam, *The Best and the Brightest* (New York: Random House, 1969), pp. 640, 774.

32. Erwin Hargrove, *The Power of the Modern Presidency* (New York: Knopf, 1974), p. 152.

33. Halberstam, *Best and Brightest,* pp. 610, 661, 728.

34. Eric Goldman, *The Tragedy of Lyndon Johnson* (New York: Knopf, 1968), pp. 501, 502.

35. Cited in Halberstam, *Best and Brightest,* pp. 447–49.

36. Ibid., p. 625.

37. Ibid., p. 783.

38. Janis, *Victims of Groupthink,* p. 120.

39. Ibid., pp. 105, 106.

40. Ibid., p. 105.

41. Ibid., p. 775; see also Townsend Hoopes, *The Limits of Intervention* (New York: McKay, 1969), p. 218. For other examples of misinformation, see Leslie Gelb, *The Irony of Vietnam: The System Worked* (Washington, D.C.: Brookings Institution, 1979), pp. 309–10.

42. Schandler, *Unmaking of a President,* pp. 174, 177, 180.

43. Ibid., pp. 254, 255.

44. Ibid., p. 264.

45. Cited in Hoopes, *Limits of Intervention,* pp. 217, 218.

46. Schandler, *Unmaking of a President,* p. 267.

47. *New York Times,* December 7, 1986, p. E5.

48. *Washington Post,* December 10, 1986, p. A22.

49. *Report of the President's Special Review Board* (Washington, D.C.: Government Printing Office, 1987), p. III-3. This document will be cited as the *Tower Commission Report* in the remainder of this chapter.

50. *Tower Commission Report,* pp. III-3, 4.

51. U.S. Congress, U.S. Senate Committee on Secret Military Assistance to Iran and the Nicaraguan Opposition, U.S. House of Representatives Select Committee to Investigate Covert Arms Transactions with Iran, *Report of Congressional Committees Investigating the Iran-Contra Affair,* Senate Report

No. 100–216, House Report No. 100–433, 100th Cong., 1st sess., 1987, p. 165 (this document will be cited as the *Iran-Contra Report* in the remainder of this chapter); *Tower Commission Report,* p. III-4.

52. *Tower Commission Report,* pp. III-4, 5.

53. Ibid., pp. III-5, 6; U.S. Congress, Senate Select Committee on Intelligence, *Report of the Select Committee on Intelligence,* Senate Report No. 100–7, 100th Cong., 1st sess., p. 5.

54. *Tower Commission Report,* p. III-6.

55. *Washington Post,* June 21, 1987, p. B2; James Bamford, "Carlucci and the N.S.C.," *New York Times Magazine,* pp. 26, 76.

56. Bamford, "Carlucci and the N.S.C.," p. 76; *Washington Post,* June 21, 1987, p. B2; *Iran-Contra Report,* p. 247.

57. *Tower Commission Report,* p. III-4.

58. Ibid., pp. III-6, 7, 8; *Iran-Contra Report,* p. 6; *Report of the Select Committee on Intelligence,* p. 7.

59. *Iran-Contra Report,* p. 169.

60. Ibid., pp. 168, 169.

61. Ibid., p. 178.

62. Ibid., p. 186.

63. Ibid., p. 197.

64. Ibid., pp. 197, 195; *Washington Post,* December 11, 1986, p. 1.

65. *Iran-Contra Report,* pp. 175, 187.

66. *Tower Commission Report,* p. III-10; *Iran-Contra Report,* p. 197.

67. *Tower Commission Report,* p. III-10.

68. *Iran-Contra Report,* pp. 198, 199; *Tower Commission Report,* p. III-11.

69. *Iran-Contra Report,* p. 200.

70. *Tower Commission Report,* p. III-11.

71. Ibid.

72. *Iran-Contra Report,* p. 200.

73. Ibid., p. 201.

74. Ibid., p. 203.

75. Ibid., pp. 205, 206, 208.

76. *Tower Commission Report,* pp. III-12, 13; *Iran-Contra Report,* pp. 17, 18, 208, 209.

77. *Tower Commission Report,* p. III-3.

78. *Iran-Contra Report,* p. 227; *Tower Commission Report,* p. III-14.

79. *Iran-Contra Report,* p. 237; *Tower Commission Report,* p. III-16; *National Journal,* August 8, 1987, p. 2043.

80. *Tower Commission Report,* pp. III-16; *Iran-Contra Report,* p. 238.

81. *Iran-Contra Report,* pp. 193, 246, 247.

82. Ibid., p. 249,

83. Ibid., pp. 257, 258.

84. Ibid., pp. 259, 262, 263.

85. *Tower Commission Report,* pp. III-6, 10, 11, 12.

86. Ibid., p. IV-10.

87. Cited in *Washington Post,* July 16, 1987, p. A17.

88. Donald Regan, *For the Record* (New York: Harcourt Brace Jovanovich, 1988), p. 268. See also Hedrick Smith, *The Power Game* (New York: Random House, 1988), pp. 627, 628.

89. *Washington Post,* March 21, 1977, p. A1.

90. Office of Management and Budget, *Decision Analysis Report: Case Study, Footwear Import Agreements,* pp. 84, 85. This study was supplied to the author by Robert J. Cunningham of the Office of Management and Budget.

91. Cited in *Wall Street Journal,* March 23, 1977, p. 44.

92. Office of Management and Budget, *Decision Analysis Report,* p. 88.

93. Ibid.

94. Ibid., pp. 89, 90.

95. Ibid., pp. 90–92.

96. President Reagan subsequently terminated the OMAs on the grounds that the American shoe industry had once again become competitive with other countries.

97. Cited in John Stegmaier, "Toward a More Effective Presidency," *Presidential Studies Quarterly* (Spring/Summer 1977), 149.

98. *New York Times,* December 7, 1986, p. E29.

99. *New Republic,* January 26, 1987, p. 23.

100. Graham Allison and Peter Szanton, *Remaking Foreign Policy: The Organizational Connection* (New York: Basic Books, 1976), p. 79. Copyright © 1976 by Basic Books, Inc., Publishers, New York.

101. National Academy of Public Administration, *A Presidency for the 1980s* (Washington, D.C.: National Academy of Public Administration, 1980), pp. 17–18.

102. *Washington Post,* September 7, 1977, p. A15.

103. See, for example, Alexander George, *Presidential Decisionmaking in Foreign Policy: The Effective Use of Information and Advice* (Boulder, Colo.: Westview Press, 1980), chaps. 6, 11; Irving Janis, *Victims of Groupthink,* pp. 209–19.

104. Stephen Hess, *Organizing the Presidency* (Washington, D.C.: Brookings Institution, 1976), p. 163.

The Presidency
and Emergency
Powers

Consideration of the presidency and emergency powers has been deferred until this point because it involves the functioning of the office under *abnormal* circumstances; however, the occurrence of emergencies has not been so rare as to render emergency powers a topic too exotic for consideration. On the contrary, over the course of the last forty years or so, many Americans have lived a good part of their lives under national emergencies of one kind or another. Roosevelt declared a state of emergency in 1933 in order to forestall the collapse of the American banking system. In 1939, he announced a "limited" national emergency in the wake of the outbreak of war in Europe and an "unlimited" one in 1941 as the Nazi threat grew more imminent. Truman put the nation on an emergency footing in 1950 after our entry into the Korean War. Thereafter, no national emergencies were declared until the country was well into the first term of the Nixon administration, when President Nixon made two emergency proclamations, one in March 1970 as a result of the halt in the postal service and the other in August 1971 in response to the dangerously high deficit in the United States balance of payments. A number of national emergenices have been declared subsequently, but these have been very narrowly defined and usually related to an issue of foreign policy. Bill Clinton, for example, made five national emergency declarations during his first term. These included prohibiting certain economic transactions with Angola (1993); preventing U.S. companies from any involvement with the petroleum industry in Iran (1995); ordering the release of food grain from the U.S. disaster reserve to assist farmers in the Southwest (1996); restricting movement and anchorage of U.S. vessels in Cuban territorial waters (1996); and limiting trade and other transactions with Serbia and Montenegro (1996). Since there is no reason to believe that the future will treat us any more kindly than has the past, emergencies of varying severity will no doubt continue to intrude into our national life at one time or another.

There is a second and even more compelling reason why the topic of emergency powers deserves our close attention, namely, the fact that the nature of these powers is indeed awesome. Upon declaration of a national emergency, there are currently some 470 emergency statutes that become operative. Depending upon the nature of the emergency, the president may invoke some or all of these statutes to regulate the political and economic freedoms to which we are normally accustomed. Powers granted the president under these statutes may be broken down into three broad categories: (1) powers over individuals, (2) powers over the control and regulation of property, and (3) powers over communications.[1] Listed below are just some of the relevant powers that fall under each of these categories.

I. Powers over Persons

Can order the confinement of any individual deemed to be a threat to the security of the United States.

Can restrict travel abroad as well as travel to the United States.

Can restrict access to U.S. citizenship.

Can restrict the movement of individuals *within and over* (air flight) the United States.

Can require that certain individuals—by nature of their backgrounds, associations, activities, or ownership of certain articles—register with the government.

Can restrict freedom of association; for example, (1) can prevent individuals deemed a threat to the national security from being employed in certain critical industries, (2) can remove any federal employees deemed a threat to the national security.

Can suspend writ of habeas corpus.

Can declare martial law.

Can assign armed forces "to assist in military matters in any foreign country."

II. Powers over the Control and Regulation of Property

Can order the stockpiling of certain strategic materials.

Can impose restrictions on the export of U.S. goods.

Is authorized to allocate materials in ways he thinks necessary in order to promote the national defense.

Can require industries to give priority to government contracts and seize by any means necessary those industries that fail to comply.

Can fix wages and prices.

III. Powers over Communications

In carrying out his obligations to report to Congress, the president may withhold information he deems damaging to the national security.

If he concludes that the nation is under threat of attack, he may refrain from publishing his regulations in the *Federal Register.*

During war or threat of war he may establish procedures for censoring mail, cable, radio, or other means of communication between the United States and any foreign country.

Can require those engaging in propaganda activities on behalf of foreign governments to register with the U.S. government.[2]

Given the far-reaching nature of these powers, it is worth considering whether their exercise is ever appropriate in a democracy. If it is, then what safeguards are necessary to protect against the abuse of these powers? Finally, to what extent have these safeguards been present in the American experience with emergency powers? These questions will constitute the major concerns of this chapter.

THE FOUNDERS, THE CONSTITUTION, AND EMERGENCY POWERS

At the time the Founding Fathers undertook the formidable task of constructing a new government, the practice of investing government with emergency powers was not without precedent. Aristotle, for example, noted in his writings that the Greek city-states had resorted to elective tyrannies on those occasions when civil strife threatened law and order within the community. The elaborate constitutional framework of the Roman republic also made provision for emergency situations. Executive authority was normally vested in two consuls, but during times of "grievous wars or serious unrest" the Roman Senate could initiate a proposal asking the consuls to select an individual who would function as a temporary dictator. It was also possible for the consuls themselves to initiate a proposal for dictatorship, which had subsequently to be approved by the Senate.[3]

To these historical examples must be added the writings of such eminent political thinkers as Rousseau and Locke, both of whom addressed the appropriateness of granting emergency powers to government. Notwithstanding his strong commitment to a democratic order, Rousseau felt that circumstances might necessitate the suspension of the normal constitutional processes.

> The inflexibility natural to laws, which hinders their bending to events, may in certain cases be pernicious, and, in a crisis, even occasion the ruin of the State. The order and slowness of legal forms require a space of time which circumstances sometimes refuse. . . . [F]or this reason it is advisable not to establish political institutions so strongly as to prevent a possibility of suspending their operation.[4]

Accordingly, Rousseau called for the creation of a "supreme magistracy," which in times of grave crisis could exercise dictatorial powers—but only on a temporary basis. Locke took a similar position. While acknowledging that limited government was essential to democracy, he remained cognizant of the fact that dire circumstances might warrant the assumption of extraordinary powers by the government. Specifically, he argued that the sovereign should have the *prerogative* "to act according to discretion for the public good, without the prescription of the Law and sometimes even against it." Moreover, since the legislature was so unwieldy and unable "to foresee, and so by laws to provide for, all Accidents and Necessities, that may concern the public," this prerogative would be most appropriately lodged with the Executive.[5]

As men of considerable learning, it seems likely that the Founding Fathers were acquainted with how earlier peoples had attempted to cope with emergency situations. They certainly were not unaware of what Locke had to say about prerogative, for his writings constituted an important part of the intellectual baggage they brought to the Constitutional Convention. Yet as one peruses the convention debates, *The Federalist,* and the ratifying debates, there is scarcely any indication that the Founding Fathers felt it would be necessary to alter constitutional arrangements in times of emergency. In the Constitution itself, there is only one provision that explicitly calls for altering the existing constitutional order in times of crisis: "The Privilege of Writ of Habeas Corpus shall not be suspended, unless when in Cases of Rebellion or Invasion the Public Safety may require it" (Article 1, sec. 9). Aside from this exception, however, the delegates apparently felt that the provisions they wrote into the Constitution were adequate to deal with any crisis the nation might face. Those parts that may be viewed as contemplating emergency situations are (1) the right of the United States to guarantee to every state a republican form of government and to protect each state against invasion, and upon its request, against domestic violence (Article 4, sec. 4); and (2) the right of Congress to declare war, raise armies, "provide for calling forth the Militia to execute the Laws of the Union, suppress Insurrections and repel Invasions" and to make all Laws which shall be necessary and proper for carrying into Execution the foregoing Powers" (Article 1, sec. 8). The only constitutional provisions having any direct relevance to the president's ability to act in emergencies are (1) his designation as "Commander in Chief of the Army and Navy of the United States and of the Militia of the several States when called into the actual Service of the United States" (Article 2, sec. 2); (2) his right to convene one or both houses of Congress on extraordinary occasions (Article 2, sec. 3); and (3) his right to protect states, upon their request, against domestic violence when Congress cannot be convened (Article 4, sec. 4). Excepting these provisions, it appears that any additional emergency actions taken by the president would have to come through a statutory delegation granted to him by the Congress.

 ## ON THE NECESSITY FOR EMERGENCY POWERS

That the Founding Fathers declined to make special provision for suspending constitutional requirements in times of emergencies is not altogether surprising. Their generally skeptical view of human nature, as well as their experience with living under a tyrannical British king, made them reluctant to concentrate power in any institution. On the contrary, they went to great lengths to create a constitutional structure that would diffuse power. It was first divided between the states and the national government. At the national level, legislative, judicial, and executive power were placed in three separate institutions. Since the Founding Fathers considered the legislative branch the most powerful of the three, they sought to diffuse its power further by dividing it into two chambers, the House and Senate. Nor was this enough, for they feared that each branch might attempt to infringe upon the powers and responsibilities of the other. Consequently, each was given powers (checks) over the other two branches. As Madison noted, each department must be given "the necessary constitutional means, and personal motives, to resist encroachments of the others." Finally, having become convinced that certain additional safeguards were necessary to protect the citizenry from the power of government, the first Congress proposed and the states ratified a series of amendments that have come to be known as the Bill of Rights.

Although under normal conditions, federalism, separation of powers, checks and balances, and the Bill of Rights all function as formidable and necessary roadblocks to the abuse of governmental power, under conditions of emergency they may function as an impediment to the preservation of the polity itself. All Western democracies have at one time or another faced emergencies that seriously threatened their very existence. In some cases the threat has come from without, in the form of an attack from a foreign power. In other instances, the threat has come from within, perhaps from a severe economic depression or domestic violence and subversion. But regardless of the source, such crises have required swift and decisive action. In a democracy like ours, where power is both diffused and restricted, the government is ill suited to acting efficiently in times of crisis. Thus, we are confronted with a dilemma that was best articulated by Abraham Lincoln over one hundred years ago: "Is there in all republics this inherent and fatal weakness? Must a government of necessity be too *strong* for the liberties of its people, or too *weak* to maintain its own existence?"[6]

Most would probably agree that this dilemma should be resolved in favor of according the government some additional capacity to deal with crisis situations. This additional capacity must typically involve both a *concentration and expansion* of power. Since most major crises are national in scope, this means concentrating power at the national level. But where at the national level? Clearly the Supreme Court, by virtue of its function, is not a suitable agency; nor is the legislative branch, given its size. Thus, the most logical choice is the executive, for it alone has the capacity to act with dispatch. In addition to being concentrated, governmental power must also be expanded. To deal successfully with crises of great magnitude, the government must have the capacity to mobilize and coordinate the human and material resources of the nation. This may require that we give government the power to impose restrictions upon certain political and economic freedoms to which we are normally accustomed. The nature and scope of these restrictions have been illustrated at the outset of this chapter.

ON THE NECESSITY FOR SAFEGUARDS

If the government must be accorded expanded powers when the nation faces emergency situations, then appropriate safeguards are necessary to forestall their misuse. Extraordinary powers, after all, create the potential for extraordinary abuses. In this section, we shall consider what scholars have acknowledged as essential safeguards[7] and to what extent these safeguards have been present or wanting in the American experience with emergency powers.

Essential Safeguards

Emergency powers should be invoked only when there is a genuine emergency.

That emergency powers should only be employed in a real emergency is obvious enough. But how does one ensure this? One could resort to a definitional safeguard, thereby specifying the circumstances that may be defined as emergency situations. In following this approach, however, there is always the risk that such a list will fail to encompass all possibilities. Alternatively, it has been suggested that a broader definition is more appropriate—one that would define an emergency as any situation that threatens the continued existence of the prevailing constitutional order. But even this more general definition may prove too restrictive. Suppose, for example, that terrorists were running about the country poisoning the water supply. Although such a circumstance might not necessarily pose a threat to the very existence of the nation, one might nevertheless argue that this kind of activity could be classified as an emergency situation. Thus, rather than having to contend with the problems created by attempting to define an emergency, a more suitable safeguard may lie in *who* is empowered to declare that an emergency exists. This leads us to the next point.

> *The decision to declare an emergency should not rest with the agency that will exercise emergency powers.*

As already noted, the exercise of emergency powers must of necessity be lodged in the executive. At the same time, however, to allow the executive to make the sole determination as to when they should be invoked is to face the risk that he may resort to them prematurely. Accordingly, the ultimate authority for declaring a national emergency should be vested in the legislature. The word *ultimate* is an important and necessary qualifier here, because it is possible to conceive of circumstances where the executive will not have enough time to seek a declaration of national emergency from the legislature. Thus, he must be free to make the *initial* determination himself, subject to a later ratification or rejection by the legislature. At the same time, however, not all emergencies are of equal magnitude; consequently, when circumstances permit, the president should ask the legislature for a declaration.

Within the American experience, declarations of national emergency always have been made by the president. Moreover, Congress has willingly passed all kinds of statutes empowering the president to take extraordinary action when, in his judgment, an emergency situation existed. And only in rare instances have these statutes reserved to Congress the right to review a presidential declaration.[8] In no instance has the president ever asked Congress to issue a formal declaration of national emergency—even when the circumstances would have permitted him to do so. In 1950, for example, circumstances were not so grave that Truman lacked the time to seek a declaration from Congress following our entry into the Korean War. Nor would it appear that the balance of payments deficit was so critical in 1971 that President Nixon did not have time to gain a congressional declaration before he imposed currency restrictions and enforced controls on foreign trade.

The autonomy accorded the president in declaring national emergencies is in marked contrast to the procedures followed in several other contemporary Western democracies. In both Canada and West Germany, for example, a declaration of national emergency by the prime minister is subject to ratification by the legislature.

> *Emergency powers should not be initiated without provision for their termination, and the decision to terminate should not rest with the agency exercising such powers.*

Since the assumption of emergency powers greatly facilitates the president's ability to act, the possibility exists that he will want to hold onto them beyond the time required to meet a given crisis. Thus, when the legislature itself declares an emergency or gives its approval to one announced by the president, it should stipulate a termination date. To be sure, emergencies are not always so discrete that one can precisely determine when they shall cease to exist. But if the period of time should prove too short, the legislature can extend it. Likewise, if the grant of emergency authority proves to be longer than is necessary, the legislature may nullify its original termination date.

In providing for the creation of the role of "dictator," the Romans clearly specified a limitation on it of six months. Similarly, during the Second World War, the British Parliament was even more stringent, allowing Prime Minister Churchill grants of emergency powers for only thirty days at a time. By comparison, the American approach to this issue has at best been shoddy and unsystematic. In none of the six national emergencies proclaimed by presidents over the last half century has a termination date been specified. Nor, with rare exceptions, has Congress written any provisions for termination into its statutory grants of emergency powers to presidents. This is not surprising, given the fact that the legislation providing these grants of authority has customarily been drafted in the executive branch and then submitted to Congress for passage. Since the executive was not interested in stipulating any conditions for congressional review or termination of these powers, no such provisions were included.[9] Nor was it uncommon for Congress to rush these drafts through to passage, with little thought given to their substance. This kind of perfunctory approval reached the outer extreme in an emergency economic measure passed by Congress in 1933. This particular bill was subjected to a total of only eight hours of debate in both houses. Moreover, there were no committee reports, and when the bill came onto the floor of the Senate for consideration, only one copy was available.[10]

As already noted, there have been six major national emergencies declared by presidents in the last six decades. Three were declared by Franklin Roosevelt (1933, 1939, 1941), one by Truman (1950), and two by Nixon (1970, 1971). Although in 1952, Truman issued a proclamation terminating Roosevelt's emergencies of 1939 and 1941, the other four (1933, 1950, 1970, 1971) had still not been terminated as of 1976. Finally, in September of that year, Congress passed legislation wiping them off the books. But the point is that during the entire period from 1933 to 1976, the United States was legally in a state of emergency and thus a president could have invoked emergency powers under the 470 emergency statutes on the books. Indeed, in some instances, emergency powers were exercised during nonemergency circumstances, and such actions were judged legal because a national emergency was technically still in effect. In 1970, for example, a U.S. court of appeals upheld the Cuban Assets Control Regulations on the grounds that they were consistent with the authority granted to the executive under the Korean emergency—this despite the fact that the justification for the Korean emergency had long since passed.[11]

Actions taken in times of emergency should be grounded in constitutional or statutory provisions.

Because the country is faced with a grave crisis does not mean that the executive may arrogate powers to himself without any regard to their legality. To allow him to do so would, in essence, be to vest in him legislative and judicial as well as executive authority. And as James Madison warned us over two hundred years ago, previous experience has shown that "the accumulation of all powers legislative, executive and judiciary in the same hands . . . may justly be pronounced the very definition of tyranny."[12] Of course, it may well be the case that during emergency situations the legislature will have to delegate more of its own power to the executive. Moreover, there may also be instances where the severity of the crisis is such that presidential action cannot be deferred, and consequently, the statutory grant of authority may have to come after the fact. But regardless of when it comes, if the president's actions cannot be justified on constitutional grounds alone, they must be legitimized by statute. And even then, they may ultimately be subject to review by the courts. Richard Nixon's contention that "when the president does it, that means it is not illegal" is political nonsense.

In seeking to ground their emergency actions in *constitutional or statutory authority,* some presidents have moved more cautiously than others. Clearly Lincoln's handling of the Civil War stands out as the most arbitrary use of emergency powers. Following the secession of the South from the Union, Lincoln unilaterally increased the size of the army, spent unappropriated funds from the U.S. Treasury, and suspended the writ of habeas corpus. The first two actions were in direct violation of the Constitution, for Congress is given the exclusive authority to regulate the size of the armed forces and spend money. Although the Constitution does not specify who may suspend habeas corpus, few doubted that this was a power the Founding Fathers had intended to reserve exclusively to Congress.[13] At the time Lincoln took these actions, Congress was not in session, and although he could have called a special session, he did not see fit to do so until a full eleven weeks after the South had seceded. This unusual delay was, no doubt, designed to give him a free hand in responding to events. When Congress was finally convened on July 4, 1861, Lincoln did acknowledge some doubt as to the constitutionality of his actions: "These measures, whether strictly legal or not, were ventured upon under what appeared to be a popular demand and a public necessity, trusting then, as now, that Congress would readily ratify them. It is believed that nothing has been done beyond the constitutional competency of Congress."[14] In short, he was espousing John Locke's doctrine of the sovereign's prerogative—the right to act, when necessity requires it, in the absence of the law and sometimes even against it. Presented with a *fait accompli* and sympathetic with his purposes as well, Congress readily blessed Lincoln's actions: "All the acts, proclamations and orders of the President respecting the army and navy of the United States . . . are hereby approved and in all respects made valid . . . as if they had been issued and done under the previous express authority and the direction of Congress of the United States."[15]

Although Congress proceeded to grant the president additional statutory authority, there were nevertheless many instances where Lincoln continued to act independently. In some cases, he took initiatives that clearly fell within the purview of the legislative branch. These included the issuance of the Emancipation Proclamation; the making of rules and regulations for the armed forces, a power explicitly reserved to Congress in the Constitution (Article 1, sec. 8); the declaration of martial law behind the lines; seizure of property; suppression of newspapers; arresting without a warrant; and prohibiting the use of the postal service for "treasonable correspondence."[16] The extent of the powers assumed by Lincoln was vividly captured in a remark made by his secretary of state to the British minister: "My Lord, I can touch a bell on my right and order the imprisonment of a citizen of Ohio, I can touch a bell again and order the imprisonment of a citizen of New York; and no power on earth, except that of the President, can release them. Can the Queen of England do so much?"[17]

In justifying his authority to take such extraordinary actions, Lincoln cited several parts of the Constitution, most notably the president's authority as commander in chief; his obligation "to take care that the laws be faithfully executed"; and the oath of office, which pledges the president to "preserve, protect, and defend the Constitution of the United States." That any or all of these provisions entitled him to arrogate such far-reaching powers to himself is highly questionable, to say the least. But because his actions enjoyed broad support in both Congress and the general population, no challenges were forthcoming—at least not until after the war. In his defense, it must be noted that no president before or since has faced a crisis of such magnitude as the Civil War, and thus in this particular instance swift and extraordinary action may well have been necessary. Yet, as Clinton Rossiter observed, "There is, however, this disturbing fact to remember: he set a precedent for bad men as well as good. . . . If Lincoln could calmly assert: 'I conceive that I may, in an emergency, do things on a military ground which cannot constitutionally be done by Congress,' then some future President less democratic and less patriotic might assert the same thing."[18]

In the twentieth century, the most notable crises have been precipitated by either war or a faltering economy. In meeting these crises, however, the approach of both presidents Wilson and Roosevelt was decidedly different from that of Lincoln. In preparing the country to cope with the First World War, Wilson did not strike out on his own as Lincoln had done, but rather, with rare exception, he sought statutory authorization for what he wanted to do. Congress promptly responded by passing the Overman and Lever acts, which together provided him with a variety of emergency powers. These included the authority to take over and operate the railroad, water systems, and telephone and telegraph networks; redistribute the functions of agencies in the federal government; regulate the foreign language press and censor communications into and out of the United States; regulate or seize all shipbuilding operations; regulate exports; and establish restrictions on the actions of enemy aliens. Roosevelt was also careful to gain legisiative authorization for dealing with the Great Depression, although such grants of authority did not always precede his own actions. In 1933, for example, he declared a national emergency and immediately suspended all financial transactions by ordering all banks to close their doors to the public. While he based his authority on the Trading with the Enemy Act (1917), this justification was dubious at best, since the act authorized the president to regulate trade and financial actions between the United States and foreigners, and only in time of war. Yet this justification, questionable though it was, nevertheless demonstrated Roosevelt's concern for cloaking his actions in legality. Moreover, the president quickly asked Congress to pass legislation that would provide a more solid legal base for what he had done. This legislation came just three days later in the form of the Emergency Banking Act.

Because of either increasing confidence or a greater sense of urgency, Roosevelt behaved far more independently of Congress as he faced up to his second major crisis. In 1939, he declared a "limited" national emergency, thereby clearing the way for invoking certain statutes that would enable him to prepare the nation for almost certain involvement in the Second World War. The term *limited* was used to prevent the population from becoming unduly alarmed. By May 1941, however, the situation in Europe had steadily worsened, and Roosevelt elevated the emergency to an "unlimited" one. In the months ahead, he proceeded to create more than twenty government agencies whose purpose was to deal with the domestic impact of the war. Moreover, he did so without any authorization from Congress. Aware that there was no constitutional precedent for this action, he attempted to skirt the constitutional issue by grouping agencies under the Office of Emergency Management, an agency that had been authorized by Congress in 1940.[19]

Roosevelt's exercise of prerogative was also apparent in other areas. From the time the war began up to 1943, the president seized no fewer than eleven industrial facilities and justified his action in "the Constitution and the laws."[20] Precisely what part of the Constitution and what laws he had in mind was never made clear. In February 1942, he issued an executive order removing Americans of Japanese ancestry from the West Coast on the grounds that they posed a threat to the security of the United States. Although his action was ratified by Congress one month later, it is far from clear that circumstances required him to act prior to congressional authorization. There had, after all, been no known instances of sabotage by Japanese Americans. By far, Roosevelt's most far-reaching claim to presidential prerogative came in a speech given to Congress in September 1942. He asked the membership to repeal a certain provision of the Emergency Price Control Act (1942) dealing with farm parity and then went on to warn that unless Congress did so, he would repeal it himself! In asserting his authority on this matter he noted that "the President has the powers, under the Constitution and under congressional acts, to take measures necessary to avert a disaster which would interfere with the winning of the war. . . . When the war is won, the powers under which I act automatically revert to the people—to whom they belong."[21] Quite obviously, if one accepted this line of reasoning, it would be difficult to conceive of any limits that could be imposed upon presidential actions in time of war. Not even Lincoln, who frequently acted in the absence of congressional authorization, ever contended that he could unilaterally nullify legislation that had been duly passed by Congress and signed into law by a president. As it turned out, Roosevelt's preposterous warning was never put to the test, for Congress quickly took action to repeal the parity provision. Indeed, given Roosevelt's astuteness in political matters, it hardly seems likely that he would have issued such a challenge unless he was certain that the votes were there for repeal.

Emergency Powers and the Courts

We have noted that the exercise of emergency powers should be grounded in constitutional or statutory authority. With the exception of Lincoln, who acknowledged the doubtful constitutionality of his *initial* actions taken after the South seceded, in all the cases cited above presidents attempted to legitimize their actions through appeals to the Constitution or the statutes, or both. While this should hardly come as a surprise, nevertheless the mere assertion of legality does not necessarily make it so. In the American political system, the final judgment on the legality of presidential as well as congressional acts rests with the Supreme Court. Thus, the Court functions as the ultimate safeguard against the abuse of emergency powers. As we shall see shortly, however, its record in this area has been mixed.

As one peruses American constitutional history, only two cases stand out as attempts by the Supreme Court to limit the president's emergency powers. The first case was *Ex parte Milligan* (1866). L. P. Milligan and his associates were arrested in Indiana on October 5, 1864, by the military commander of the district. Shortly thereafter, Milligan was tried in Indianapolis by a military commission that had been created by the sole authority of President Lincoln. The commission found him guilty of aiding a group of rebel forces who were preparing to invade Indiana. Although Milligan was sentenced to be hanged in May 1865, President Andrew Johnson commuted his sentence to life in prison. In the meantime, however, Milligan sued the government on the grounds that his constitutional rights had been violated. The Supreme Court finally heard the case in 1866 and, in a unanimous opinion, ruled that President Lincoln had been without the constitutional authority to set up military commissions behind the lines as long as the civil courts were still operating. In this particular instance, the civil courts were still functioning (in fact, Indiana had not been invaded by rebel forces). In its opinion, the Court set forth a stinging indictment of the right of the president to act independently of the Constitution.

> The Constitution of the United States is a law for rulers and people, equally in war and in peace, and covers with the shield of its protection all classes of men, at all times, and under all circumstances. No doctrine, involving more pernicious consequences, was ever invented by the wit of man than that any of its provisions can be suspended during any of the great exigencies of government. . . . The theory of necessity on which it is based is false; for the government, within the Constitution, has all the powers granted to it, which are necessary to its existence. . . .
> . . . It could well be said that a country, preserved at the sacrifice of all the cardinal principles of liberty, is not worth the cost of preservation.[22]

Yet one cannot help but wonder whether the vigor of the Court's decision was not in large part a consequence of the circumstances under which it was rendered. In the first place, the justices heard the case after the crisis of the Civil War had been ended; second, President Lincoln was dead by this time. Would the Court have so readily challenged Lincoln's authority had they been forced to decide the case while he was still president, embroiled in the greatest national crisis of our political history, and with a public and Congress strongly supportive of the actions he took? The opinion of the Court itself causes one to be doubtful.

> During the late and wicked Rebellion, the temper of the times did not allow that calmness in deliberation and discussion so necessary to a correct conclusion of a purely judicial question. [F]eelings and interests prevailed which are happily terminated. Now that public safety is assured, this question as well as all others, can be discussed and decided without passion.[23]

The case of *Youngstown Sheet and Tube Co. v. Sawyer* (1952) provides a more meaningful effort by the Court to challenge the president's exercise of emergency powers, since the decision was rendered against a sitting president. Briefly, the circumstances surrounding this historic case were these: On December 31, 1951, the contract between the major steel companies and their employees ran out before agreement was reached on a new one. At President Truman's behest, the steelworkers continued to work without a contract while the matter was turned over to the Wage Stabilization Board. The negotiating process continued for over three months, to no avail. Finally, the frustrated United Steel Workers of America announced that they would strike on April 9, 1952. Two hours before the announced strike deadline, President Truman issued an executive order authorizing the secretary of commerce to seize the steel mills. The steelworkers were asked to resume work—this time as government employees—and they complied. Truman contended that the seizure was absolutely necessary, because a strike would have seriously impaired the war effort and damaged the economy as well. Yet he took this extraordinary action in the absence of any statutory authority. Both the Selective Service Act (1948) and the Defense Production Act (1950) authorized presidential seizure of industrial facilities, but only if industries failed to give priority to defense contract orders. Neither of these acts granted the president any seizure authority in the event of an unresolved labor dispute. To deal with this latter problem, Congress had passed the Taft-Hartley Act (1947), part of which authorized the president to seek an eighty-day injunction against a strike. Moreover, in drafting this legislation, Congress had specifically considered and rejected the option of providing the president with authority to seize industrial facilities in the event of a strike. Notwithstanding all of this, Truman went ahead and took over the steel mills "on the authority vested in me by the Constitution and laws of the United States, and as President of the United States and Commander in Chief of the armed forces of the United States."[24] In a later defense of his decision, he put the matter more bluntly, noting that, "the President has very great inherent powers to meet national emergencies."[25]

Upon issuing his executive order, Truman promptly informed Congress of what he had done and acknowledged its right to overrule him if it so chose. Congress failed to respond, however, and this led Truman to write a letter to the Senate, once again asking Congress either to support or oppose what he had done. There was still no response. Meanwhile, the steel companies decided to take the government to court and sue for the return of their property. In the lower courts, the government boldly argued that the president had "inherent" emergency powers, and that was that. This defense was not received sympathetically by the district court, however, so when the case reached the Supreme Court, the government changed its tack. It contended that a genuine emergency did indeed exist and now argued that "the aggregate of his constitutional powers" as president and commander in chief entitled Truman to act in the absence of congressional authorization until such time as Congress itself decided to act. The government brief also noted that there were abundant historical precedents for presidential seizure of industrial facilities.

In arguing their side of the case, the steel companies acknowledged the president's right to take emergency actions and even took cognizance of the fact that in some cases his actions might have to precede congressional authorization. But they went on to insist that the president cannot act at such times without at some point gaining congressional ratification; nor can he act contrary to the expressed or implied will of Congress. In this particular instance, they argued, not only had the president's actions failed to be ratified by Congress, but Truman had failed to employ the remedy (Taft-Hartley Act) that had been legislated by Congress for dealing with labor disputes.

In a six-to-three decision, the Supreme Court found in favor of the steel companies. Writing the opinion for the majority, Justice Black rejected the notion that a president had *any* inherent prerogative in times of emergency; nor did he feel that the role of commander in chief invested the president with any special domestic powers. Therefore, in the absence of any valid constitutional justification for his actions, the president's authority would have to come from a statutory authorization. In this instance, Black noted, there was "no statute that expressly authorizes the president to take possession of property as he did here," and thus his seizure of the steel mills constituted a usurpation of the legistature's power.

Although Truman lost in this particular case, it is far less clear that the Court was rejecting any presidential claim to prerogative in times of emergency. Indeed, each of the five justices who sided with Black wrote a concurring opinion, suggesting that while they agreed with his overall conclusion, they did not fully share his reasoning. Four of the six justices on the majority side either implied or explicitly stated that the president did indeed have some degree of executive prerogative in times of emergency.[26] By far the most thoughtful concurring opinion came from Justice Jackson, who delineated three major types of presidential action.

1. When the president acts in accordance with the implied or expressed will of Congress; in this situation his authority has the greatest presumption of legitimacy, "for it includes all that he possesses in his own right plus all that Congress can delegate."

2. "When the President acts in the absence of either a congressional grant or denial of authority"; in this instance, he must rely solely on his own independent powers, and thus his actions would have to be judged on "the imperatives of events and contemporary imponderables rather than abstract theories of law."

3. When the president acts contrary to the implied or expressed will of Congress; here Jackson argued the president's power "is at its lowest ebb, for then he can rely only upon his own constitutional powers minus any constitutional powers of Congress over the matter." Accordingly, under these circumstances, his action must be subject to the most careful judicial scrutiny, for "what is at stake is the equilibrium established by our constitutional system."[27]

Since Truman's seizure of the steel mills violated the expressed will of Congress embodied in the Taft-Hartley Act, his action fell into the third category.

In addition to their being troubled by Truman's failure to comply with the expressed will of Congress, another, perhaps more telling, current of thought ran through the opinions of the justices. Specifically, they simply were not convinced of Truman's claim that the steel crisis represented one of the gravest crises this nation had ever faced. Nor for that matter was the country as a whole convinced. Indeed, during the two months that intervened between the time of the seizure and the hearing of the case by the Supreme Court, it had become abundantly clear that neither Congress, the public, nor the nation's leading newspapers felt the strike was grave enough to justify Truman's drastic actions. On the contrary, in many quarters the steel seizure was viewed as an abuse of power sufficient to warrant impeachment.[28] On the other hand, had there existed a national consensus on the presence of a genuine emergency, the Court would more than likely have ruled in Truman's favor, given the fact that several of the justices acknowledged some degree of executive prerogative.

Although the Court's decision in the steel seizure case served notice that the president's powers were not limitless in times of emergency, it is important to note that Truman's actions lacked the support of both the public and Congress. Would the Court be equally willing to challenge a president's exercise of emergency powers if his actions had the strong backing of both Congress and the American people? The case of *Korematsu v. United States* (1944) provides a possible—and disturbing—answer to this question. This particular case had its origins in an executive order issued by President Roosevelt in February 1942. It instructed the "Secretary of War, and the Military Commanders who he may from time to time designate . . . to prescribe military areas in such places and of such extent as he or the appropriate Military Commander may determine, from which any or all persons may be excluded, and with respect to which, the right of any person to enter, remain in, or leave shall be subject to whatever restrictions the Secretary of War or the appropriate Military Commander may impose in his discretion."[29] This order was specifically aimed at the large concentrations of Japanese Americans on the West Coast. Since many of the nation's defense industries were located in this area of the country, it was feared that Japanese Americans might engage in sabotage and other subversive activities out of loyalty to their homeland. This fear—bordering on hysteria—was dramatically revealed in the final recommendation made by the general of the Western Defense Command to the secretary of defense in which he called for the removal of the Japanese from the West Coast.

In the war in which we are now engaged, racial affinities are not severed by migration. The Japanese race is an enemy race and while many second and third generation Japanese born on United States soil, possessed of United States citizenship, have become "Americanized," the racial strains are undiluted. . . . It therefore follows, that along the vital Pacific Coast over 112,000 potential enemies, of Japanese extraction, are at large today. There are disturbing indications that these are organized and ready for concerted action at a favorable opportunity. The very fact that no sabotage has taken place to date is a disturbing and confirming indication that such action will be taken.[30]

As a consequence of Roosevelt's executive order, 112,000 individuals of Japanese descent, 70,000 of whom were full-fledged American citizens, were summarily separated from their homes, jobs, and property and relocated in detention camps, where they were held for periods of up to four years. Even if one allows for the fact that the United States was at war, this action still constituted an appalling abuse of emergency powers. Not only had the Japanese Americans historically been model citizens, but more important, there was no evidence to suggest that they had or were about to engage in sabotage. As is apparent above, the recommendation of the general of the Western Defense Command was able to cite no evidence of sabotage by Japanese Americans. Rather, the general was reduced to arguing that "the very fact that no sabotage has taken place to date is a disturbing and confirming indication that such action will be taken." This was a curious bit of logic, to say the least.

Instead of presuming guilt by reason of race, surely a more judicious approach would have been to handle each individual on a case-by-case basis whereby only those found to be disloyal would be detained. Although the government argued that time would not permit such an approach, this justification is far from persuasive. In the first place, thousands of enemy aliens throughout the country had already been investigated on a case-by-case basis. Second, Japanese Americans of questionable loyalty were in most cases already known to both the FBI and military intelligence, and thus they could have been weeded out from the rest of the group by the same procedure the government was using with German American and Italian American minorities. Finally, it is worth noting that even the British, who were considerably more hard-pressed than the United States, managed to investigate some 74,000 enemy aliens within a period of a few months.

By the time the Court was called upon to rule on the constitutionality of President Roosevelt's executive order, it was abundantly clear that his action commanded broad support in and outside of government. Congress had passed legislation ratifying the executive order one month after it was issued. Moreover, the nation's leading opinion makers had called repeatedly for some kind of government action against the Japanese American community. Such an eminent and respected columnist as Walter Lippmann, for example, felt compelled to write a column entitled "The Fifth Column on the Coast," in which he noted that "the Pacific Coast is in imminent danger of a combined attack from within and without." One of Lippmann's newspaper colleagues was even more direct: "The Japanese in California should be under armed guard to the last man and woman right now—and to hell with habeas corpus."[31]

The case that came before the Court was *Korematsu v. United States*. It involved a Japanese American who had been convicted of remaining in a region from which the Japanese had been excluded. In a six-to-three decision, the Court upheld the exclusion order. Speaking for the majority, Justice Black argued that the government's action was well within "the combined federal war powers of Congress and the Executive." He went on to note that military necessity required that the army be able to take such action in wartime. While acknowledging that the exclusion of Japanese Americans from the West Coast created considerable hardship for them, he pointed out that "hardships are a part of war and war is an aggregation of hardships." In short, life is tough. Justice Black said nothing at all about the constitutionality of detaining Japanese citizens in camps, a matter he did not consider to be at issue in this case. Three of the justices issued strong dissents from Black's ruling. Justice Roberts contended that the issue of exclusion could not be divorced from the issue of detention. Moreover, he also reminded the Court that it was upholding the conviction of Korematsu in the absence of *any* evidence demonstrating his disloyalty. Justice Murphy argued that the exclusion policy was, by itself, one that "goes over the 'very brink of constitutional power' and falls into the ugly abyss of racism." Justice Jackson's dissent was motivated not by a repulsion over what the government had done, but rather by the belief that the Court should not be ruling on cases of this sort. He saw war as an extraconstitutional activity and thus not subject to constitutional constraints.[32]

On the same day that the Court ruled on *Korematsu,* it rendered another decision that bore directly on the constitutionality of *detaining* Japanese Americans. In this particular case, *Ex parte Endo,* the Court found that since the loyalty of Mitsuye Endo had already been established beyond any doubt, the War Relocation Authority had no right to detain her at the Tule Lake War Relocation Camp. Yet in rendering the majority opinion, Justice Douglas refused to confront the issue of whether detention itself was constitutional. This can only be viewed as an astonishing bit of judicial behavior, given the fact that neither Roosevelt's executive order nor the legislation subsequently passed by Congress ratifying the order specifically authorized the creation of detention camps. It is even more astonishing when viewed in the context of the *Ex parte Milligan* decision. As the you will recall, the Court ruled here that an individual accused of a crime could not be arrested by the military and tried by a military tribunal unless the civil courts were not functioning. Was it not also unconstitutional, then, to confine individuals who had not committed any crime at all, and who had not had the benefit of any trial, military or otherwise? Douglas contended that the Milligan case was not applicable here, because the Japanese were being confined by civil authorities rather than military. However, it may well be argued that Douglas was making a distinction without a difference here, since the civilian authorities were acting pursuant to orders given by the military.[33] The Court's failure to come to grips with the obvious and fundamental constitutional issues in the case was more than likely motivated by a desire to avoid a direct confrontation with the president and Congress. Although this strategy may have been astute politically, this was hardly the Court's finest hour as defender of the Constitution.

In summary, the effectiveness of the Court in checking the possible abuse of emergency powers is likely to depend upon the circumstances. If Congress and the public remain unconvinced that the exercise of the presidential prerogative is justified by circumstances, the Court is not likely to be convinced either. On the other hand, if the public and Congress are firmly persuaded that an emergency does indeed exist, and if they are strongly supportive of whatever actions the president may take to meet it, the Court is not likely to risk a confrontation with the president, Congress, and the public at such a critical time. Thus, there is considerable merit in Clinton Rossiter's observation that "the Court's power of judicial review is least useful when most needed."[34] For it is in times of grave emergency that the government will be most prone to take drastic action, and as the relocation and detention of Japanese Americans demonstrates, such action may on occasion stray far from both the letter and the spirit of the Constitution.

CONGRESSIONAL ACTION ON EMERGENCIES

In June 1972, the Senate decided to create a Special Committee on National Emergencies and Delegated Powers. The impetus for this action came as a result of testimony given by Secretary of Defense Melvin Laird before the Senate Foreign Relations Committee. His appearance had been occasioned by the recent introduction of U.S. troops into Cambodia. At one point in the hearings, Secretary Laird was asked what would happen if Congress voted to cut off funds for the Cambodian invasion. To the astonishment of all, he replied that the president could continue the funding under a Civil War emergency statute passed by Congress in 1861, which was still on the books. Known as the Feed and Forage Act, it allowed the president to spend unappropriated funds for purposes of clothing, feeding, and otherwise supplying the cavalry in the American West. In actuality, Laird was wrong about the date, for the act was not a Civil War statute but in fact dated all the way back to 1799.[35] Erroneous or not, his testimony threw a scare into the senators present, and the Senate decided it was time to investigate precisely what emergency powers Congress had granted to the president over the course of our political history. To its surprise, the special committee discovered that nowhere in the government was there a catalog of the emergency statutes passed by Congress. Instead, the statutes were scattered throughout the voluminous United States Code along with all the other federal statutes. With the assistance of the Air Force, which fortunately had put the entire United States Code on computer tapes, the committee was finally able to track down some 470 emergency statutes. During the course of their inquiry, they also learned that four separate national emergencies were still in effect at the time of their investigation. Having apprised itself of the sloppy handling of national emergencies as well as of the scope of powers granted to presidents under such conditions, Congress concluded that corrective legislation was necessary. No doubt the intervening events of Watergate further heightened its commitment to act. Accordingly, it passed the National Emergencies Act, which was signed into law by President Ford in September 1976. The major provisions of this legislation are outlined below.

I. Termination of Existing National Emergencies

Terminates two years from the date of enactment of this act emergency powers and authorities possessed by the president or any other federal officer or executive agency that were still in effect as a result of previously declared emergencies.

II. Declaration and Termination of Future National Emergencies

All future national emergencies declared by the president can be terminated by Congress through a concurrent resolution (concurrent resolution provision ruled unconstitutional by Supreme Court in 1983) or by a presidential proclamation.

Not later than six months after an emergency has been declared, and not later than the end of each six-month period thereafter, Congress shall be required to consider whether that emergency shall be terminated.

If the president has declared a national emergency, and if it has not been terminated by Congress (in accordance with the provision stated above), it shall be terminated at the end of one year unless the president informs Congress that it is still in effect.

III. Procedures Relating to the Use of Emergency Powers

When the president declares a national emergency, he must specify to Congress the provisions of law under which he will act.

The president and all federal agencies shall keep and report to Congress a record of all rules and regulations issued during an emergency. The same applies to all expenditures for emergency actions.[36]

In order to eliminate the possible use of dilatory tactics as a means of preventing a vote on termination, the act specifies the following procedures for handling the concurrent resolution:

1. It shall be referred to the appropriate committee in the House and reported out within fifteen calendar days.
2. It shall then become the pending business on the floor of the House and must be voted on within three calendar days.
3. The resolution will then be sent to the other House, where the same procedures shall be followed.
4. If the two Houses should disagree on the concurrent resolution, a conference committee will be formed, which shall report a recommendation back to both Houses within six calendar days.

Unlike the War Powers Resolution, the National Emergencies Act makes no provision for any kind of presidential consultation with Congress *prior* to the declaration of a national emergency. To set down an absolute requirement that he consult Congress would quite obviously be unrealistic, for the necessity of timely action may preclude that possibility. Yet it might be argued that not all emergencies are of equal severity, and thus it would have been appropriate to call upon the president to at least consult with Congress when the circumstances permit.

Clearly, the provisions of the act do indeed render the president more accountable in the exercise of his emergency powers. At the same time, however, neither this act nor anything else one might contemplate is likely to prevent an abuse such as that inflicted upon Japanese Americans. If the president, Congress, and the American people are convinced that the circumstances are so grave as to require drastic action, that action will be taken and, in all probability, will be upheld by the Court as well. James Madison was well aware of this political reality when he observed that it is "vain to oppose constitutional barriers to the impulse of self-preservation."[37]

⭐ NOTES

1. J. Malcolm Smith and Cornelius Cotter, *Powers of the President During Crises* (Washington, D.C.: Public Affairs Press, 1960).

2. Ibid., pp. 26–92; see also U.S. Congress, House, Subcommittee of the Committee on the Judiciary Hearings, on H.R. 3884, *National Emergencies Act,* 94th Cong., 1st sess., 1975, pp. 22, 23.

3. Clinton Rossiter, *Constitutional Dictatorship* (Princeton, N.J.: Princeton University Press, 1948), p. 19.

4. Jean Jacques Rousseau, *The Social Contract* (New York: Hafner Press, 1947), p. 110.

5. Peter Laslett, *Locke's Two Treatises of Government* (Cambridge: Cambridge University Press, 1967), pp. 392–93.

6. Cited in Rossiter, *Constitutional Dictatorship*, p. 3.

7. See, for example, Rossiter, *Constitutional Dictatorship*, pp. 297–306; Carl Friedrich, *Constitutional Governments and Democracy* (Waltham, Mass.: Blaisdell, 1968), pp. 557–81.

8. "The National Security Interest and Civil Liberties," *Harvard Law Review* 85 (April 1972), 1291.

9. *Hearings on National Emergencies Act, 94th Cong.*, 1st sess., 1975, p. 35.

10. Frank Church, "Ending Emergency Government," *American Bar Association Journal* 63 (February 1977), 198.

11. Gerhard Casper, *On Emergency Powers of the President: Every Inch a King?* (Andover, Mass.: Warner Modular Publications, 1973), p. 4.

12. James Madison, Federalist Paper No. 47, in Jacob Cooke, ed., *The Federalist* (Cleveland: World, 1961), p. 324.

13. This view was upheld in the case of *Ex parte Merryman* (1861). Chief Justice Taney, who was performing in his role as circuit judge, ruled Lincoln's suspension of habeas corpus unconstitutional. Lincoln, however, chose to ignore the ruling.

14. Cited in Rossiter, *Constitutional Dictatorship*, p. 229.

15. Cited in John Roche, "Executive Power and Domestic Emergency: The Quest for Prerogative," *Western Political Quarterly* 5 (December 1952), 598–99.

16. Arthur Schlesinger, Jr., *The Imperial Presidency* (Boston: Houghton Mifflin, 1973), p. 58. Copyright © 1973 by Arthur H. Schlesinger, Jr. Reprinted by permission of Houghton Mifflin Company.

17. Ibid., pp. 58, 59.

18. Rossiter, *Constitutional Dictatorship*, p. 239.

19. Edward Corwin, *The President: Office and Powers*, 4th ed. (New York: New York University Press, 1957), pp. 242, 243.

20. Roche, "Executive Power," p. 607.

21. Ibid., p. 609.

22. *Ex parte Milligan*, 71 U.S. (4 Wall.) 2, 18 L. Ed. 281 (1866).

23. Ibid., p. 109.

24. Cited in Smith and Cotter, *Powers of the President*, p. 134.

25. Cited in Schlesinger, *Imperial Presidency*, p. 142.

26. *Youngstown Sheet and Tube Co.* v. *Sawyer*, 343 U.S. (1952), pp. 582–89.

27. Ibid., pp. 635–38.

28. See, for example, Roche, "Executive Power," p. 613; Maeva Marcus, *Truman and the Steel Seizure Case* (New York: Columbia University Press, 1977), pp. 83–101.

29. Cited in Roger Daniels, *The Decision to Relocate the Japanese Americans* (Philadelphia: Lippincott, 1975), p. 113.

30. Cited in Eugene Rostow, "Our Worst Wartime Mistake," *Harper's*, September 1945, pp. 195, 196.

31. Cited in Daniels, *Japanese Americans*, pp. 47, 48.

32. *Korematsu* v. *United States*, 323 U.S. (1944), pp. 215–48.

33. *Ex parte Endo*, 323 U.S. (1944), pp. 284–307.

34. Clinton Rossiter, *The American Presidency*, 2d ed. (New York: New American Library, 1960), p. 53.

35. See Louis Fisher, *Presidential Spending Power* (Princeton, N.J.: Princeton University Press, 1960), p. 240.

36. Public Law 94–412 (National Emergencies Act), 94th Cong., Sept. 14, 1976, p. 1.

37. James Madison, Federalist Paper No. 41, in Cooke, *The Federalist*, p. 270.

Personality
and the Presidency

So far we have been concerned with how the president interacts with the environment around him. The major components of his environment include the international situation; political, social, and economic conditions in our own society; institutional actors such as Congress, the bureaucracy, the courts, the press, and organized interests; and the general public. In assessing how the president interacts with these various elements, we have dealt with the role of his personality in only a passing fashion. We shall now deal with it directly, first by considering to what extent an understanding of a president's personality can help us to explain his behavior as he attempts to shape and respond to his environment. We shall then address the question of whether some personality types may be more suited to the demands and responsibilities of the presidency than others. Finally, we shall consider if it is possible to do a better job of screening the personalities of candidates who seek the office. Of course, all of these considerations presume that the personality variable can have a major impact upon presidential conduct—a matter to which we now turn.

CONDITIONS CONDUCIVE
TO THE EXPRESSION OF PERSONALITY

The likelihood that an individual's behavior will give expression to his personality depends not only upon the degree to which a given circumstance elicits his strong beliefs, feelings, and needs, but also on whether he finds himself in a structured or unstructured situation. That is, to the extent that certain norms and expectations prescribe what is expected of an individual in a given situation, the opportunity for personality to have an impact is lessened. This is especially so when a violation of prescribed behavior results in sanctions. These expectations may be formalized to the point where they are codified in law—a 65-mile-per-hour speed limit on interstate highways, for example—or they may be of an informal nature. Thus, although it is not written into the rules of the U.S. Senate that members must treat their colleagues with utmost courtesy, there does exist an informal institutional consensus that requires it. Regardless of whether expectations operate at a formal or an informal level, sanctions may result from noncompliance. If caught exceeding the 65-mile-per-hour speed limit, a driver will be subject to a traffic ticket. Similarly, if a senator fails to adhere to the norm of senatorial courtesy, he or she is likely to be ostracized by the rest of the membership.

When an individual is put into a less structured environment, there is greater likelihood that personality will surface in his behavior. Thus, he might find himself faced with a new situation that may be largely free of any expectations or cues regarding behavior; or he might be involved in circumstances where there are indeed expectations for behavior, but they are contradictory; or he may find himself in a situation where the cues from the environment allow for a variety of different, yet acceptable, modes of conduct.[1]

Of the three branches of government, the presidential environment is perhaps the most unstructured of all. Within both Congress and the Supreme Court there have evolved numerous informal norms of behavior that the ongoing membership instills in its new members. But the presidency is something quite different. Since only one person occupies the office, there is no ongoing membership there to socialize him into any particular set of behavior patterns. Rather the expectations for presidential conduct are, to a considerable extent, the creation of the person who happens to occupy the office at any given time. His behavior is, to be sure, circumscribed by constitutional requirements as well as by public expectations, but both tend to be rather broadly defined, allowing him considerable leeway in responding to his environment. The style he chooses to adopt in dealing with such constituencies as Congress, the bureaucracy, the public, and the press is largely his to determine. So too is the manner in which he organizes and interacts with his staff. Furthermore, while he is charged with making decisions, how he does so will be largely shaped by his own needs and inclinations. Moreover, *what* he decides may also invite the intrusion of personality, for in some cases the issue he faces may be new, or ambiguous, or possibly one on which there is sharp disagreement.

ANALYSIS OF PRESIDENTIAL PERSONALITY

There have been numerous attempts to psychoanalyze historical figures. Among the more notable efforts have been Freud's analysis of Leonardo da Vinci and Erik Erikson's case studies of Martin Luther and Gandhi. Only within the last twenty years or so, however, have scholars begun to focus their attention on assessing the personalities of presidents. Indeed, prior to this time the only systematic analysis of a president's personality was the psychobiography of Woodrow Wilson by Alexander and Juliette George. Not surprisingly, the especially fascinating personalities of Johnson and Nixon have spawned several attempts to fathom their psychological makeup—for example, Doris Kearns's *Lyndon Johnson and the American Dream* (1976), Hyman Muslin and Thomas Jobe's *Lyndon Johnson, The Tragic Self: A Psychohistorical Portrait* (1991), Blema Steinberg's, *Shame and Humiliation:*

Presidential Decisionmaking on Vietnam (1996), Bruce Mazlish's *In Search of Nixon* (1973), Eli Chesen's *President Nixon's Psychiatric Profile* (1973), David Abrahamsen's *Nixon vs. Nixon* (1977), Fawn Brodie's *Richard Nixon: The Shaping of His Character* (1981), and Vamik D. Volkan et al.'s *Richard Nixon: A Psychobiography* (1997). These and several other psychoanalytic case studies have attempted to construct a president's personality by looking for persistent behavior patterns as he responds to his environment over the course of his private and public life. These psychobiographies also make an effort to explain why an individual's personality develops as it does. Since psychoanalytic theory posits that personality is shaped by psychological needs that develop during the formative years, such explanations have necessitated piecing together a president's childhood experiences.

Psychoanalytic inquiries into presidential behavior, however, are not without their limitations. For one thing, there is the problem of data. No president has ever surrendered himself to the psychoanalyst's couch and submitted to prolonged in-depth questioning. (The closest we have come to this were the extensive conversations Doris Kearns had with Lyndon Johnson over a four-year period after Johnson left the presidency.) Thus, the researcher is forced to rely upon biographies, letters, diaries, and interviews with family, friends, and associates, as well as upon what presidents write about themselves. Richard Nixon's book *Six Crises* provides valuable insights into how he attempted to cope with his environment. But most presidents have not chosen to write books of this kind. Nor have they chosen to write their own life story—Jimmy Carter being a notable exception.

The data problem may be especially acute when the scholar is attempting to reconstruct the formative years of a president's life. Although biographies may be of assistance, there is no way of knowing that a biographer has recorded all the facts that a psychoanalyst might deem important. Interviews with family and friends may fill in the gaps, but even here one is faced with the problem of recall. In addition to the problem of adequate data, there is also the matter of interpretation. One observer, for example, may see rigid or inflexible behavior as a sign of some underlying insecurity, whereas another may view it as a dedication to principle. Since there is an absence of agreed-upon standards of evidence and inference within psychoanalytic theory, no interpretation can be demonstrated with certainty.

Finally, some object to the fact that psychoanalytic theory places such great stress on childhood experiences as the determiner of an individual's personality. Such reductionism, it is argued, fails to take account of adolescent and adult experiences that may influence the development of personality. While all of these limitations should not cause us to dismiss the psychohistorical approach out of hand, they should invite us to view such explanations as suggestive rather than definitive. Much of what follows in the remainder of this chapter should be viewed in the same light.

Barber's Analysis

James David Barber's *The Presidential Character: Predicting Performance in the White House* deserves our special attention for several reasons. First, his analysis of the personalities of fifteen twentieth-century presidents shows a careful concern for marshaling evidence. Second, the inferences made from this evidence are, for the most part, formulated with appropriate caution. Third, although Barber's analysis of presidential personalities places considerable stress upon childhood experiences, he does not ignore the impact of adolescent and adult experiences on the development of personality. Fourth, his work represents the first attempt to move from a case-study examination of individual presidents to a classification of presidential personalities into types. Finally, Barber has suggested what factors may account for the development of each type, thus providing us with some assistance in predicting presidential personalities.

Barber's conceptualization of personality consists of three components, the first of which is *character.* Character is "the way the President orients himself toward life—not for the moment—but enduringly"; how he "confronts experience"; and how he views himself. This facet of personality is largely determined during the formative years of one's life. Of the three personality components, it is clear that Barber views this first as the most important for understanding presidential behavior. The central message of his book, he states, is "look to character first." The second component of personality is *worldview,* which consists of the individual's "primary, politically relevant beliefs, particularly his conceptions of social causality, human nature, and the central moral conflicts of the time." This belief system, according to Barber, takes its shape during the period of adolescence. The third component is *style,* which he defines as the way a political leader performs three roles: "rhetoric, personal relations, and homework." How an individual's style develops will be a function of his needs, skill, and the opportunities that present themselves. Barber is quick to point out that personality does not operate in a vacuum. Rather, the manner in which character, worldview, and style influence presidential behavior will also depend on what kind of "power situation" the president finds himself in as well as on the "climate of expectations" existing within the population.[2]

Barber's personality types are derived from what he considers to be two fundamental orientations toward life. The first is an *active-passive dimension,* which is concerned with how much energy an individual expends on what he does. Does he seek to influence his environment, or is he largely content to be influenced by it? The second dimension is one of *positive-negative* affect, and it relates to how an individual feels about what he does. Specifically, is he happy and optimistic or sad and pessimistic? Combining these dimensions, Barber comes up with four personality types, which he uses to classify fifteen twentieth-century presidents from Taft to Reagan (see Figure 9–1).

	POSITIVE	NEGATIVE
ACTIVE	Franklin Roosevelt Harry Truman John Kennedy Gerald Ford Jimmy Carter George Bush	Woodrow Wilson Herbert Hoover Lyndon Johnson Richard Nixon
PASSIVE	William Taft Warren Harding Ronald Reagan	Calvin Coolidge Dwight Eisenhower

FIGURE 9–1 **Barber's Classification of the Personalities of American Presidents (Taft-Bush)**

The major attributes that Barber finds present in each of these four types are briefly summarized below.

Active-positive: self-confident; flexible; creates opportunities for action; enjoys the exercise of power, does not take himself too seriously; optimistic; emphasizes the "rational mastery" of his environment.

Active-negative: compulsive; expends great energy in what he does but derives little enjoyment from it; preoccupied with self in terms of whether he is failing or succeeding; low self-esteem; has problems with self-definition; inclined toward rigidity; pessimistic.

Passive-positive: compliant; low self-esteem, which he attempts to overcome by being an ingratiating personality; reacts rather than initiates; reluctant to act decisively; superficially optimistic.

Passive-negative: involved in politics out of a sense of duty and not because he enjoys it; compensates for low self-esteem by being of service to others; responds rather than initiates; avoids conflict and uncertainty; emphasizes principles and procedures and demonstrates an aversion to engaging in politicking.[3]

Of course, personalities are rarely so discrete that they can be neatly identified as wholly one type or another. Barber readily admits this, noting that some presidents may manifest the characteristics of more than one of his four types. Thus, the classification of presidents is based upon the general tendency for a president's behavior to conform to the attributes of a given type, although it must be recognized all the while that the fit may not be a perfect one.

In this chapter, we shall focus primarily on the active-positive and active-negative types since—as we hope will become apparent—the former shows the greatest promise of successfully coping with the responsibilities and pressures of the presidency, whereas the latter has the potential for doing the greatest harm. This is not to say that the passive-positive or passive-negative president cannot be either harmful or beneficial. But we shall defer a discussion of these matters until later in the chapter.

LYNDON JOHNSON AS AN ACTIVE-NEGATIVE

Many of the problems that surrounded the Johnson presidency may be traced back to a psychological state that appears to be characteristic of all active-negative presidents, namely, a profound sense of insecurity. Before discussing its impact upon Johnson's presidential behavior, however, it is first helpful to know what factors may have engendered this condition.

Johnson's Youth

The environment in which Johnson grew up was not an altogether happy one. Throughout most of his childhood, his family experienced financial hardship, with his father going bankrupt three different times. All of Lyndon's clothes were homemade, and the food on the table was characteristic of the rural poor—bacon fat on cornbread, grits, turnip greens, and the like. To his father's apparent embarrassment, young Lyndon at one point even became a bootblack in order to earn extra money.[4]

Johnson's relationship with his parents was another source of unhappiness during his early years. His attachment to his mother was a strong one. Indeed, in later years he would characterize her as "a saintly woman, I owe everything to her."[5] Rebekah Baines Johnson was a cultured and intelligent woman whose father had at one time been editor of a newspaper and later became the secretary of state for Texas. Her marriage to Sam Johnson was a step down for her on the social ladder, and the financial situation of the Johnson family was a source of disappointment and concern to her. She was determined that young Lyndon would do better. By the time he was two years old she had taught him the alphabet, and at the age of four she had him reading and enrolled in the first grade. Lyndon was also taught to recite the poetry of Longfellow and Tennyson, and by the time he was seven his mother had him taking dancing and violin lessons. When Johnson excelled in the tasks his mother had laid down for him, he received an outpouring of love and affection from her. "I'll never forget how much my mother loved me when I recited those poems. " By the same token, when he failed to live up to her expectations, her love was withdrawn completely. "For days after I quit those lessons she walked around the house pretending I was dead. And then to make it worse, I had to watch her being especially warm and nice to my father and sisters."[6] Later on, when Lyndon initially decided not to attend college, his mother once again retaliated with a freeze-out of affection: "We'd been such close companions, and, boom, she'd abandoned me."[7] When he ultimately did decide to go to college at San Marcos, his mother even traveled there to help him study for his math entrance exam. All of this suggests that the pressures on Lyndon to succeed were considerable, and the consequences that followed when he did not were often traumatic.

If Lyndon's relationship with his mother imposed a psychological strain on him, so too did his relationship with his father. In first grade, Lyndon wrote a poem entitled, significantly perhaps, "I'd Rather Be Mamma's Boy." None of the evidence on Johnson's youth suggests that he felt close to his father. Sam Johnson's drinking, as well as his failure to provide adequately for the family, caused considerable suffering for the person Lyndon loved most—his mother. He would never forget the time he came across his mother crying in the living room because Sam had been out drinking all night. Lyndon put his arms around her and told her not to worry because he would always be there to take care of her.

Another source of tension grew out of the fact that Sam Johnson was constantly raising doubts about his son's manliness. Lyndon Johnson vividly recalled the time his father accused Rebekah of making a sissy out of their son because he was still wearing curls at the age of four. After his wife had repeatedly refused to cut his hair, Sam took it upon himself to do so one day while she was at church. As a youth, the matter of masculinity appears to have preyed upon Lyndon's mind. He was noticeably concerned when his school friends began making fun of him because he was engaged in such "feminine" activities as dancing and playing the violin.[8] Of greater concern, however, were the gnawing doubts raised by his father. Lyndon would often go hunting with his friends but always returned empty-handed because he could not bring himself to pull the trigger. One day his father asked him if he was a coward. Lyndon promptly picked up his gun and went out and shot a rabbit. On another occasion, he wrecked the family car and was afraid to return home and tell his father about it. Instead, he went to his uncle's house, where he received a call from his father on the following day. Sam said he had bought a new truck and wanted Lyndon to go get it. He then added, "I want you to drive it around the courthouse square, five times, ten times, fifty times, nice and slow. You see there's some talk around town this morning that my son's a coward, that he couldn't face up to what he'd done, and that he ran away from home. Now I don't want anyone thinking I produced a yellow son. So I want you to show up here in that car and show everyone how much courage you've really got."[9]

So determined was Johnson about demonstrating his manliness to his father that it appears to have been his major reason for initially deciding against continuing with his education after high school. He feared that if he decided to go to college, "it would make me a sissy again and I would lose my daddy's respect."[10]

Considering the tensions that existed in his relationship with both parents, it is not surprising that Lyndon ran away from home after he finished high school. But after spending two difficult years out in California, he grew weary of fending for himself and returned home. His mother continued to press him on going to college, but to no avail. Instead, he turned to working on a road gang and began drinking heavily. He got into several fights, and on one occasion returned home with a bloodied face. Reduced to tears at the sight of her son, his mother remarked, "To think that my eldest born should turn out like this."[11] Such a statement of dispirited resignation from the one person he loved and admired most weighed heavily on Lyndon. He decided to go to college.

In describing the environment of Johnson's youth, a plausible argument can be made that his experiences fostered the development of a low sense of self-esteem. He received little love and affection from his father, nor could he always count on receiving it from his mother. At times his mother gave affection effusively, but at other times she denied it completely. In addition, there were self-doubts concerning Lyndon's ability to meet the high expectations his mother had for him. Finally, there were the gnawing uncertainties Johnson experienced about his own masculinity. All of these factors created within him an emotional tension that could not be released against a father whom he feared or against a mother whom he loved. Instead, this emotional energy was directed toward achievement, for in this way he would be able to demonstrate his self-worth.

In college, the driving, self-disciplined, achievement-oriented Johnson began to show. He got a part-time job collecting trash at Southwest Texas Teachers College. Despite the menial nature of the job, he tried to collect more trash than any of his fellow workers. When this job did not prove challenging enough, he went to the college president's office and asked for something better. He was then given the position of assistant janitor, but that did not satisfy him for long either. He returned to the president's office and said he wanted to help him. The president obliged by making Johnson an assistant in his office. Lyndon was ultimately given the responsibility of answering some of the president's mail, assisting him with his reports, and accompanying him to the Texas legislature. Nor were his college activities confined only to working for the president. When he failed to gain entry into the prestigious campus honorary known as the Black Stars, he created his own honorary and dubbed it the White Stars. He became editor of the college newspaper and developed into a prize debater. Although he never managed to become president of the student body, he was nevertheless instrumental in picking the president and helping him win. Finally, even with all of this activity, he managed to graduate from college with honors.

Johnson Enters Politics

That Johnson would ultimately enter politics is understandable. His mother had always had a keen interest in national politics, and his father was involved in politics on both a local and state level. Furthermore, Johnson's involvement in campus politics had demonstrated a real talent for dealing with people. But his own explanation suggests a more profound reason for choosing a political career.

> I still believed my mother the most beautiful, sexy, intelligent woman I'd ever met and I was determined to recapture her wonderful love, but not at the price of my daddy's respect. Finally, I saw it all before me. I would become a political figure. Daddy would like that. He would consider it a manly thing to do. But that would be just the beginning. I was going to reach beyond my father. I would finish college; I would build great power and gain high office. Mother would like that. I would succeed where her own father had failed; I would go to the Capitol and talk about big ideas. She would never be disappointed in me again.[12]

Thus, a political career would serve to confirm Johnson's feeling of manliness. Politics would also provide him with the power necessary to achieve, and through achievement he would gain the love and respect of his mother and others as well. The need for affection and respect ran deep in Johnson, but because his own sense of self-esteem appears to have been low, this respect and affection of necessity had to come from others. He craved and reveled in the cheers of approval he received while campaigning: "Oh boy, listen to that." Following lengthy speeches, he was always able to state correctly the number of times he had been applauded.[13] Especially revealing in this regard were the feelings he expressed about his landslide victory over Goldwater in 1964: "It was a night I shall never forget. Millions upon millions of people, each one marking my name on their ballot, each one wanting me as their President. . . . For the first time in all my life I truly felt loved by the American people."[14] But if politics carried with it the opportunity to receive approval from others, it also brought the possibility of losing it. So strong was his fear of rejection and failure that periods of despondency set in before nearly all of his decisions to run for or seek reelection to public office.[15]

Worldview and Style

It was during Johnson's years in Congress that two other facets of his personality began to manifest themselves, namely, his worldview and style. If he was determined to achieve, it is equally clear that the direction of his achievements would be guided in part by a genuine compassion for the less fortunate. While it is probable that his hero, Franklin Roosevelt, influenced this aspect of Johnson's worldview, a more significant factor was his own firsthand experience with poverty. Although the Johnson family had not been dirt-poor, life had not been easy. More important, he saw the full impact of real poverty when he taught Mexican American children in Cotulla, Texas: "My students were poor and they often came to class without breakfast, hungry. They knew even in their youth the pain of injustice. . . . I often walked home late in the afternoon, after the classes were finished, wishing there was more I could do."[16] Johnson's view of the world beyond the boundaries of the United States was to a considerable extent determined by his experience of living through the Second World War, a war that he thought might have been avoided had political leadership been more resolute against aggression.[17] His actions in Congress and later in the presidency would reveal his firm conviction that the surest way to stop aggression was to challenge it head-on and without delay.

Johnson rose quickly to positions of power in Congress, with the crowning achievement being his selection as Senate majority leader. It was in this position that his political style became apparent. As in all active-negative types, his inner drive to achieve created an almost inexhaustible reservoir of energy. Johnson worked longer and harder than others. He expected the same from his staff, which was generally acknowledged to be the most overworked and harassed group of individuals in the Senate. He learned to master the details of both legislative procedure and substantive policy issues, a talent no doubt helped by his unusually keen intelligence. Perhaps his greatest talent was an uncanny ability to decipher the motives, needs, strengths, and weaknesses of others. Having done so, he would then play upon them in order to achieve the result he wanted. As one aide noted, "The senator was indeed persuasive, to say the least, but the principal reason he prevailed so often was that when he talked to a man he almost invariably knew more about him than the man himself knew."[18] Johnson was most effective in one-on-one situations, and his tactics nearly always included excessive flattery and, when the occasion warranted it, tears or anger. Although the following description by Johnson relates to members of the press, it nevertheless provides some indication of the care and calculation that went into the "Johnson treatment."

> You learn that Stewart Alsop cares a lot about appearing to be an intellectual and a historian—he strives to match his brother's intellectual attainments—so whenever you talk to him, play down the gold cuff links which you play up with *Time* magazine, and to him, emphasize your relationship with FDR and your roots in Texas, so much so that even when it doesn't fit the conversation you make sure to bring in maxims from your father and stories from the Old West. You learn that Evans and Novak love to traffic in backroom politics and political intrigue, so that when you're with them you make sure to bring in lots of details and colorful description of personality. You learn that Mary McGrory likes dominant personalities and Doris Fleeson cares only about issues, so that when you're with McGrory you come on strong and with Fleeson you make yourself sound like some impractical red-hot liberal.[19]

In addition to hard work and the manipulation of others, there were several other dimensions to Johnson's style. He had an obsession with secrecy and a passion for developing a consensus around issues. According to one aide, "He loved unanimous committee reports."[20] Finally, he insisted upon complete and total loyalty from those immediately around him and sought to ensure it through fairly persistent intimidation.

These particular elements of his style are perhaps explainable to some extent by the active-negative's belief that he lives in a dangerous world. Certainly those who knew Johnson best acknowledged that he viewed other people with a certain degree of suspicion.[21] Accordingly, secrecy could provide him with the option of surprise and the room to maneuver right up to the time of decision. The careful search for consensus forestalled the possibility of an ambush against what he wanted to accomplish. And a staff whose loyalty was beyond question provided him with at least a few people whom he could trust implicitly. In short, all of these stylistic qualities enhanced his sense of control over an otherwise uncertain and dangerous world.

The Johnson Presidency

The Johnson presidency was characterized by extraordinary activity. The rigorous schedule Johnson had maintained during his Senate years continued in the White House. Any attempts to get him to relax were to no avail. The results of his driving energy were evident in the myriad legislative proposals sent to Congress, which included programs dealing with the cities, civil rights, education, medical care, crime, consumer protection, jobs, housing, and conservation. Indeed, it was one of the most formidable legislative records of any president in our history, although some argued that in his effort to accomplish things he sacrificed quality for quantity.

Yet there were several unsettling aspects to the Johnson presidency, and these were ultimately traceable to the nature of his personality. The active-negative seeks to confirm his self-worth through achievement, but in order to achieve, one must have control. Fear of losing control had always preoccupied Johnson. He frankly admitted that throughout his political career he frequently had dreams with a recurring theme— *paralysis.* Following the heart attack he suffered while serving as Senate majority leader, he dreamed that he was paralyzed in bed and could hear others in the next room deciding how to divide up his power. As vice president, he dreamed of being seated at a desk where, once again, he was paralyzed.[22] In the White House, his obsession with control manifested itself in the trivial as well as the important. When a member of his staff undertook the task of putting together the president's speeches for publication in a book, Johnson insisted on approving such aspects of the book as the margins, the type, and the cover design. One day, while cruising down the Potomac on the presidential yacht *Sequoia,* he passed Vice President Humphrey, who was cruising on another one of the presidential yachts. The president promptly informed Humphrey that henceforth, if he wanted to take out one of the yachts, he must first receive permission from Marvin Watson, the president's aide.[23]

The desire to control extended to more important matters as well. Johnson held a close rein over the personnel and budgets of the various executive departments. He would not permit any of his cabinet to make disclosures to the press. Rather, all information released by the government would come from the White House. As in his Senate days, Johnson insisted upon complete subservience from those around him, cabinet as well as staff members. Attempts to challenge or question his politics brought either a freeze-out or dismissal. Everybody had to be on board. On one occasion, for example, when a member of his staff presented Johnson with the name of a possible staff replacement, the first question the president asked was, "How loyal is that man?" His aide replied, "Well, he seems quite loyal, Mr. President." Johnson responded, "I don't want loyalty. I want *loyalty.*"[24] Although Johnson's penchant for loyalty, secrecy, and consensus may have given him a greater sense of control over his environment, these aspects of his style did not serve him well when he confronted the issue of Vietnam. His insistence upon loyalty and consensus stifled debate and encouraged others to tell him only what he wanted to hear. The demand for secrecy often restricted the consultation process to only a small group of individuals.

One of the most disturbing features of the Johnson presidency was his inclination to sacrifice means for ends. This aspect of his political style may also be rooted in the active-negative's sense of insecurity. Since a confirmation of self-worth is dependent upon achievement, the risk of failure becomes intolerable. Consequently, the active-negative may go to extraordinary lengths to avoid it. Johnson was apparently so determined that nothing would get in the way of his election to the presidency in 1964 that he sent a group of FBI agents to the Democratic Convention. Ostensibly their purpose was to collect information on militants, but in fact it was to provide him with political intelligence on his political opponents.[25] Even though he was well ahead of Goldwater in the polls, it now appears that he practiced some of the "dirty tricks" that would later be repeated in spades by the Nixon administration.[26]

Johnson's lack of concern for *means* was also reflected in his willingness to play freely with the truth. As was often the case, this behavior pattern manifested itself in trivial as well as important matters. Johnson once pointed to a Lincolnesque log cabin in Texas and told reporters that he was born there. On another occasion, he told a group of soldiers that his ancestors had fought at the Alamo. Whether he was attempting to add some glitter to his roots—about which he had always felt insecure—is not clear. But the fact of the matter is that both statements were totally false. More damaging, of course, was his tendency to mislead on issues of consequence. Thus, when he came under heavy criticism for sending 22,000 American troops into the Dominican Republic, he justified his actions on the grounds that he was protecting American lives, and at a news conference he proceeded to paint a tragic picture of the situation Americans found themselves in there. Both the description and the justification proved to be false. There was no evidence to suggest that American lives were in grave jeopardy. Moreover, as Johnson acknowledged privately, his real reason for committing the troops was to prevent a communist takeover of the government.[27]

At no time was Johnson's deception more clearly shown than in dealing with the Vietnam War. He knew that the major achievement of his administration would be its vast array of social programs. As Johnson later recalled, the passage of this legislation would realize his "youthful dream of improving life for more people and in more ways than any other political leader, including FDR. . . . I was determined to keep the war from shattering that dream."[28] Fearing that Congress would cut back money for his Great Society programs if the projected cost of the war was too high, Johnson informed Congress that the war's projected cost for 1967 would be only $10 billion. In actuality, his secretary of defense had told him that the cost could run as high as $17 billion. It happened that at this particular time Congress was considering the possibility of a tax increase as a means of cooling down the economy. Had Congress known that the war might cost $17 billion, it would certainly have decided in favor of a tax increase. Operating on the $10 billion figure, however, Congress decided that the tax increase was not necessary. As it turned out, the cost of the war came closer to $21 billion, and for want of a tax increase the economy was started on an inflationary spiral that plagued us for a number of years. In addition to deceiving Congress about the cost of the war, the president misled the country on the extent of our involvement as well. Secretary McNamara, who had been sent to Vietnam on a fact-finding mission, returned to Washington and informed the president that the United States would have to commit anywhere from 100,000 to 125,000 troops. Johnson gave the go-ahead for 100,000 troops, but he also realized that such a massive infusion of troops might spark a negative reaction in the country. Accordingly, he decided to tell the American people about only 50,000 of the 100,000 or so troops he intended to send.[29]

Johnson's handling of the Vietnam War brought out two other disturbing aspects of the active-negative's personality, a tendency toward rigidity and the displacement of personal frustrations upon others. No doubt, Johnson's decision to commit American troops to the defense of South Vietnam grew out of a worldview that was shaped by the belief that aggression must be met head-on. Yet he persisted in his Vietnam policy even when it became apparent that it was failing and was exacting extraordinarily high human, economic, and psychological costs on the American public. This kind of inflexibility appears to be rooted in the active-negative's self-esteem, which is so impoverished that he finds it extremely difficult to admit the possibility of failure. Johnson's associates had long observed his reluctance to admit error, even when it merely involved apologizing to someone for something he had done.[30] Acknowledging the possibility of failure becomes even more unlikely on an issue in which the active-negative has invested so much of himself. Vietnam appears to have been such an issue for Johnson, for any sign of retreat would have signaled his failure to measure up on a quality about which he had always been highly sensitive—his manliness. In the following statement he reveals this concern.

> For this time there would be Robert Kennedy out in front leading the fight against me, telling everyone that I had betrayed John Kennedy's commitment to South Vietnam. That I had let a democracy fall into the hands of the Communists. That I was a coward. An unmanly man. A man without spine. Oh, I could see it coming all right. Every night when I fell asleep I would see myself tied to the ground in the middle of a long, open space. In the distance, I could hear the voices of thousands of people. They were all shouting at me and running toward me: "Coward! Traitor! Weakling!" They kept coming closer. They began throwing stones. At exactly that moment, I would generally wake up . . . terribly shaken.[31]

Thus, Johnson steadfastly pursued his policy of expanding troop commitments and accelerating the bombing of North Vietnam. As the picture grew bleaker, he began to blame his problems on others. Most notable among the villains was the eastern establishment. As he later recalled, he thought they were deliberately creating dissension over his Vietnam policy because of his Texas background, because he had never gone to Harvard, because his Great Society programs had far outshone the accomplishments of the Kennedy administration. "You see, they had to find some issue on which to turn against me and they found it in Vietnam."[32] Then there was the press, which, he reasoned, had turned against him because it was more interested in winning Pulitzer Prizes than in printing the truth. Then too there was his most vocal and articulate critic in Congress, Senator William Fulbright, who had turned dovish only because Johnson failed to make him secretary of state.

In no instance did Johnson entertain the possibility that dissent might be grounded in any motive other than self-interest. Nor, as he would later recall, was he above ascribing communist influence to the thinking of his critics and even his advisers.

> Two or three intellectuals started it all, you know. They produced all the doubt, they and the columnists in the *Washington Post,* the *New York Times, Newsweek* and *Life.* And it spread and it spread until it appeared as if the people were against the war. Then Bobby Kennedy began taking it up as his cause and with Martin Luther King on his payroll he went around stirring up the Negroes and telling them that if they came out into the streets they'd get more. Then the Communists stepped in. They control the three networks, you know, and the forty major outlets of communication. It's all in the FBI reports. They prove everything. Not just about the reporters but about the professors too.
>
> Isn't it funny that I always received a piece of advice from my top advisers right after each of them had been in contact with someone in the Communist world? And isn't it funny that you could always find Dobrynin's [Soviet Ambassador to the United States]

car in front of Reston's [newspaper columnist] house the night before Reston delivered a blast on Vietnam?[33]

Dovish senators were also perceived by Johnson as being under the communist spell. He noted, for example, that they frequently attended receptions at the Russian Embassy, that some of the senators' daughters were dating the sons of embassy officials, and that some of the senators were even having their dovish speeches written at the embassy. Indeed, so suspect did he become of his critics' motives that he ordered various government agencies to keep dossiers on certain members of Congress, journalists, and various other critics.[34] As protest to his politics mounted, so too did his paranoia. Aides who expressed disagreement with his Vietnam policy were let go. To one he remarked, "I can't trust anybody! What are you trying to do to me? Everybody is trying to cut me down, destroy me!"[35] On another occasion, he opened up a cabinet meeting by asking, "Why aren't you out there fighting against my enemies? Don't you realize that if they destroy me, they'll destroy you as well?"[36] In short, as Lyndon Johnson surveyed his environment, he increasingly saw himself as a man under siege by conspiratorial elements whose only purpose was to do him in.

In 1968, Johnson was finally prevailed upon to make an important change in his Vietnam policy. His intensive bombing of North Vietnam had not brought the North Vietnamese to the negotiating table as he had hoped. Therefore, with great reluctance, he finally accepted the advice of those who argued that the North Vietnamese would be more likely to negotiate if the bombing were halted. Does this change in position not indicate that he could be flexible? Certainly it does. Rigidity is not a condition like pregnancy, where one is either pregnant or not pregnant; rather, it may be spoken of in terms of degrees. To the extent that Johnson was ultimately able to alter his position, he appears less rigid, for example, than Woodrow Wilson, who refused to compromise on any aspect of his proposal for a League of Nations. But if the active-negative's rigidity results from an unwillingness to admit failure, was not Johnson's reversal of position on the bombing in effect an admission of failure? Apparently he was able to convince himself that he had not lost the love and respect of the American people, despite his disastrous Vietnam policy: "No matter what anyone said, I knew that the people out there loved me a great deal. . . . Deep down I knew—I simply knew that the American people loved me. After all that I'd done for them and given to them, how could they help but love me?"[37] Of course, the true test of whether or not he was still liked would have been his reelection in 1968. But at the very time he announced a halt to the bombing, he also stated that he would not seek reelection. Although he maintained that his decision was based upon a desire to keep politics out of our Vietnam policy, one cannot help but wonder if it was also motivated by a fear that he might be rejected.

 RICHARD NIXON AS AN ACTIVE-NEGATIVE

Nixon's Youth

Like Johnson, Richard Nixon did not have a very happy childhood. As he would later recount, "We were poor. We worked hard. We had very little. We all used hand-me-down clothes. I wore my brother's shoes and my brother below me wore mine and other clothes of that sort."[38] There was little time for play.

Young Nixon also experienced problems of a physical nature. As a baby he had fallen out of a buggy and severely gashed his head; thereafter he appears to have suffered constantly from motion sickness. At the age of four he contracted a severe case of pneumonia and nearly died. He was plagued by hay fever as well, and in high school contracted a case of undulant fever, causing him to miss most of a school year. He also went through the traumatic experience of watching two brothers die of tuberculosis and feared that he too would succumb to the same fate.[39] With respect to his family relationships, young Richard did not find in his father a man with whom he could easily identify. It is fair to say that Frank Nixon had never been very successful at anything he did. He lost his job as a trolley car operator after crashing a trolley car into an automobile. His father-in-law gave him the land to plant an orange grove, which ultimately failed. He became foreman of a citrus ranch, but this job lasted for only a few months. Once again, his father-in-law stepped in and helped him to purchase land for another orange grove, but Frank Nixon chose property with depleted soil, and this venture fizzled out also. He finally ended up supporting the family by operating a small grocery store.

Frank Nixon was an irascible sort, prone to violent outbursts of temper and ridicule of others. Richard and his brothers often bore the brunt of his wrath. Indeed, one of the neighbors recalls that Frank "could be hard and he could be beastly . . . like an animal. He could be very hard on the children—spank them freely and give them cracks."[40] Thus, if young Richard was to be the object of affection, it would have to come from someone other than his father.

Nixon's mother appears to have been the most significant figure in his life while he was growing up. In his final public remarks as president, he harkened back to the memory of both parents, but his warmest remarks were reserved for his mother: "Nobody will ever write a book probably about my mother. Well, I guess all of you would say this about your mother: my mother was a saint."[41] In stark contrast to her husband, Hannah Nixon was the epitome of self-control, and she sought to instill this quality in her children. Moreover, it was from her that Richard received care and affection. But the security gained from her affection could not always be counted on, for there were extended periods when they were separated from each other. At one point, for example, Hannah Nixon was away from the family for two years when she took one of their tubercular sons to Arizona. On another occasion, when Richard was twelve, he was sent away from home to live with his aunt for six months. Precisely what necessitated his departure is still obscure. Despite these separations, however, the relationship between Nixon and his mother was a very close one. He constantly helped her with chores around the house and as a teenager spent considerable time assisting her in the family store. But the closeness of the relationship also appears to have caused him some anxiety about his masculinity. His brothers teased him for being a "mama's boy." Thus, when he helped his mother with "woman's work" around the house, he took the precaution of closing the blinds so that no one would see him.[42] This concern also manifested itself in school, where he made a point of stressing his dislike for girls. Especially noteworthy in this regard is an essay he wrote about his brother Arthur, who had died of tuberculosis. As the following excerpt demonstrates, the essay is replete with references to Arthur's distaste for things feminine. That Richard chose to emphasize this aspect of a brother he greatly admired suggests that establishing a masculine identity was much on his mind.

There was one time when he was asked to be a ring bearer at a wedding. I remember how my mother had to work with him for hours to get him to do it, because he disliked walking with the little flower girl. Then I remember the grief he experienced over his hair. My parents had wanted him to be a girl in the first place; consequently, they attempted to make him one as much as possible. Each day he begged my mother for a boy's haircut, and when he finally did get it, there was not a happier boy in the state. . . . He was doing exceptionally well in all things except drawing. He absolutely would not take interest in anything he thought common to girls."[43]

As with the case of Johnson, one can hypothesize that the seeds of Nixon's insecurity were sown within his childhood experiences: lack of affection from a dominating and ridiculing father; sporadic affection from a mother who was separated from him for extended periods of time; doubts about his masculinity arising from a close identification with his mother and perhaps from his physical frailty as a youth. The confluence of all these factors produced in Nixon a low sense of self-esteem. Since his self-worth could not be confirmed by what he was, it would have to be confirmed as a result of what he did.

Achievement requires self-discipline and hard work. Hannah Nixon had instilled in Richard the necessity for self-control, and his own determination to demonstrate his worthiness provided the energy to work hard. Indeed, Nixon approached every task with extraordinary intensity. One college classmate recalls that "it wasn't uncommon for him to work himself ill." According to the recollections of his history professor, "He was out to win. . . . He was a brute for discipline."[44] His lack of coordination prevented him from making the first football team, but what he lacked in physical prowess was made up for by his competitive spirit. Although athletics did not turn out to be his forte, Nixon did discover that he had a way with words, a talent he put to good use on the college debating team as well as in the classroom. He also took up acting and became sufficiently proficient at it to be able to produce tears when a given scene required it. Apparently he commanded the respect of his fellow students, for he helped found and became the first president of a college club known as the Orthogonians. More important, he also managed to get himself elected student body president. But respect did not convert to close personal friendships. Nixon was an intensely private person and did not relate to others easily. One classmate recalled him as "lonely, and so solemn at school. He didn't know how to mix."[45]

Despite the fact that he graduated second in his class from college, his strong desire to succeed caused him considerable anxiety when he went to law school: "I'm scared. I counted thirty-two Phi Beta Kappa keys in my class. I don't believe I can stay up top in that group."[46] At the completion of his second year in law school, he was afraid that his grades would not be good enough to retain his ranking of third in his class and his scholarship as well. Indeed, so great was his anxiety on this matter that he and some other students broke into the dean's office to sneak a look at the grades. Had he been caught, he almost certainly would have been dismissed from school, but his compulsive fear of failure apparently outweighed the possibility of expulsion. His fears of not achieving in law school proved to be unwarranted, for he graduated third in his class. Once again, it was success born of hard work, with little apparent enjoyment. As his roommate recalled, "Nixon had a quality of intensity in him, worked hard, pretty intense guy—he had a sense of privacy and not terribly strong on humor."[47]

Nixon Enters Politics

After law school Nixon tried to secure a position with a prestigious New York law firm but was turned down. He took a job with the Office of Price Administration in Washington but tired of it and decided to enlist in the Navy. Unlike Johnson, Nixon does not appear to have consciously planned a political career. While stationed in Maryland, he received a call from a banker friend in California who asked him if he wanted to run for Congress. Nixon accepted. Certainly his intelligence, capacity for hard work, and rhetorical ability would suit him well to politics. But as Nixon himself noted, he was an "introvert in a highly extroverted profession."[48] This aspect of his personality was evidently overcome by a deep psychological need to confirm his self-worth. As one longtime associate later recalled, "It's a case of cold respect, he wants respect."[49]

The respect Nixon so earnestly sought would be gained by facing up to political challenges and meeting them successfully. Indeed, one cannot read the comments and writings of Richard Nixon without coming away with the clear impression that he viewed life in general, and politics in particular, as a struggle, a battle in which he was to be *tested.*

> I believe in the battle, whether it's the battle of the campaign or the battle of this office, which is a continuing battle. It's always there wherever you go. I perhaps, carry it more than others because that's my way.[50]

> Anybody in politics must have a great competitive instinct. He must want to win. He must not like to lose, but above everything else, he must have the ability to come back, to keep fighting more and more strongly when it seems that the odds are the greatest. That's the world of sports. That's the world of politics. I suppose you could say that's life itself.[51]

> [To members of the press] Don't give me a friendly question. Only a hard, tough question gets the kind of an answer—you may not like it—but it is the one that tests the man. And that is the responsibility of members of the press to test the man. . . . I can only say I benefit from it.[52]

> Eisenhower demonstrated a trait that I believe all great leaders have in common: they thrive on challenge; they are at their best when the going is hardest.[53]

> No one really knows what he is capable of until he is tested to the full by events over which he may have no control.[54]

> I don't know what the future brings, but whatever it brings, I'll be fighting.[55]

As Nixon noted in his book *Six Crises,* facing up to the struggle and the challenge is a difficult emotional experience for him, something he does not enjoy doing. In addition, when confronting the difficult decisions that challenge brings, he inevitably sees himself as doing the difficult but also the *right* thing. In discussing his Vietnam decisions, for example, he points out that "the President of the United States, when he was under unmerciful assault at the time of Cambodia, at the time of May 8th, when I ordered the bombing and mining of North Vietnam . . . still went ahead and did what he thought was right."[56] Later on, when he first went on television to discuss Watergate, he would make the same point.

Who then is to blame for what happened in this case? For specific criminal actions by specific individuals, those who committed those actions must of course bear the liability and pay the penalty. For the fact that alleged improper actions took place within the White House or within my campaign organization, the easiest course would be for me to blame those to whom I delegated the responsibility to run the campaign. But that would be a cowardly thing to do.

I will not place blame on subordinates, on people whose zeal exceeded their judgment and who may have done wrong in a cause they desperately believed in to be right. In any organization the man at the top must bear the responsibility.

That responsibility, therefore, belongs here in this office, I accept it.[57]

His emphasis on lack of enjoyment in facing up to challenges and his stress upon taking the difficult but correct course of action in resolving them seem designed to convince himself that he is genuinely being tested.

Worldview and Style

In certain respects, the Nixon worldview is elusive, for it was often adapted to what the political circumstances required. In fact, a close adviser to President Eisenhower maintains that this was one of the reasons Ike considered dropping him from the ticket in 1956. He seemed "too political without holding a genuine point of view."[58] Yet two dimensions of Nixon's worldview stood out glaringly: strong anticommunism (although this too would moderate) and a pessimism that was rooted in a suspicion of other people. So apparent was this latter facet of his personality that his classmates in law school gave him the nickname of Gloomy Gus. Nixon did not take an optimistic view of his fellow men and women. He expressed the belief that most people are "mentally and physically lazy." Moreover, people in politics were seen by him as ingrates and opportunists: "One of the hardest lessons for those in political life to learn is that the rarest of all commodities is a political friendship that lasts through time of failure as well as success."[59] The depth of his suspicion comes through most clearly, however, in an interview he gave to Stewart Alsop while vice president.

Nixon: The more you stay in this kind of job, the more you realize that a public figure, a major public figure, is a lonely man—the President very much more so, of course. But even in my job you can't enjoy the luxury of intimate personal friendships. You can't confide absolutely in anyone. You can't talk too much about your personal plans, your personal feelings. I believe in keeping my own counsel. It's something like wearing clothing—if you let down your hair, you feel too naked.

. . . You know I try to be candid with newspapermen, but I can't really let my hair down with anyone.

Alsop: Not even with old friends, like Jack Drowns, say?

Nixon: No, not really with anyone, not even with my family.[60]

As for political style, his campaigns reflected one of its hallmarks—hard work. Nearly all campaigns appear to have been grueling experiences, with Nixon working himself almost to the point of exhaustion. He prepared carefully and mastered the details of issues. The rhetorical skills he had demonstrated in college were incorporated into this political style. His speeches were hard-hitting and were able to touch the underlying concerns—and frequently fears—of the public. Indeed, it was his rhetorical talents that came to his aid in facing up to some of the events he labeled as "crises" in his political career—his emotional television defense of his political slush fund in the 1952 election campaign, and his famous "kitchen debate" with Nikita Khrushchev. Later on, he would once again employ rhetoric—this time unsuccessfully—in his attempt to explain away the scandals of Watergate.

Still another manifestation of the Nixonian political style was his insistence on being in complete control of things. In writing about Nixon's bid for the presidency in 1960, Theodore White observed that "no other candidate of the big seven operated in 1960 with fewer personnel or kept more of the critical decisions in his own hands."[61] This assessment is confirmed by one of Nixon's closest political advisers, who recalls that "he was the hardest candidate of all to manage."[62] This feature of the Nixon style was once again in evidence during the 1968 campaign, when he restricted his television appearances to formats over which he had complete control. There were no appearances on talk shows or public affairs programs such as *Meet the Press* and *Face the Nation.* Given his character, this aspect of Nixon's style is quite understandable; if one is obsessed with avoiding failure, he must maintain his power to control his environment, especially when that environment is perceived as dangerous and uncertain.

Considering Nixon's introverted and suspicious nature, it is not surprising that reclusive tendencies were also manifested in his political style. One of his close aides during the vice presidential years recalls that only rarely did he meet with Nixon. Most of the time the vice president preferred to communicate with him through memoranda. Similarly, during Nixon's presidential campaigns, he would not join the politicians and reporters who were traveling on his plane, but preferred to sit at the back of the plane by himself. If someone had something to say to him, the message was conveyed through a close aide. Of course, if a candidate wants to get elected, he quite obviously must get out and meet people. Nixon did so, but the experience was not an enjoyable one for him. During the 1968 campaign, one aide recalls that "on the way out, as we were landing, I asked Nixon if he was enjoying the campaign. 'Never do,' he said, looking out at the crowd lined up along the fence, the signs, the mike on the podium, the local politicians waiting to shake hands. 'Campaigns are something to get over with.'"[63] This reaction is in stark contrast to a Johnson or a Humphrey, both of whom experienced a sense of rejuvenation from getting out to meet the people.

One final aspect of Nixon's prepresidency style deserves mention here, namely, his willingness to "play rough." Even his closest aide, H. R. Haldeman, has readily acknowledged this facet of Nixon's personality: "Nixon rarely spared the rod or the knife in his speeches and, to put it mildly, he wasn't averse to using all possible means to try to defeat his opponents. I believed in tough campaigning too, but even from my hard-line standpoint, Nixon went too far at times."[64] In one way or another, this trait insinuated itself into nearly all of Nixon's campaigns for public office. In his first campaign for Congress, he ran against a moderate liberal by the name of Jerry Voorhis. Making the most of his rhetorical ability, he gave a series of hard-hitting speeches in which he accused Voorhis of being associated with an organization alleged to have communist ties. Apparently voters were called on the phone and actually told that Voorhis was a communist. Although it was never demonstrated that there was any substance to Nixon's charges, these scare tactics worked. Nixon was elected by a 15,000-vote margin. He took the same tack in his subsequent campaign for election to the U.S. Senate, but this time his opponent was Helen Gahagan Douglas. Once again, his rhetoric implied that his opponent had communist sympathies; he sarcastically dubbed her the "Pink Lady" and noted that her voting record was written on a pink piece of paper. His margin of victory this time was 680,000 votes. Even as Eisenhower's running mate in 1952, the cloud of questionable tactics hung over him. Not only was there the issue of his secret "slush fund," but many people were shocked by the nature of his attacks against the incumbent administration. He took after the State Department, characterizing it as the "Kollege of Kommunism, Kowardice, and Korruption." He also accused Secretary of State Acheson of "color-blindness—a form of pink eye toward the Communist threat to the United States."[65] By the time he ran for governor of California in 1964, public fears of communism had subsided, and thus he made no effort to play upon them in his campaign. Yet even in that campaign there was some doubt raised about his tactics, as evidenced by the fact that a California court found the Nixon campaign organization guilty of violating the state's election laws.

Nixon himself once remarked that "I play to win."[66] But the pattern of conduct described here suggests that the desire to win took precedence over *how* he won. Several features of his personality may help to explain why this was so. First, the active-negative's self-esteem, impoverished to begin with, cannot tolerate failure; consequently, he may be under especially strong pressures to sacrifice means for ends to avoid it. Second, Nixon's view of the world may also have been a contributing factor here. If an individual perceives himself as surrounded by a hostile world, then he must play rough or else be victimized by others.[67] Finally, one cannot help but wonder if Nixon's rough tactics were also designed to erase doubts about his manliness. Clearly a concern for toughness appears to have been much on his mind throughout his political life. One longtime observer of Nixon's career notes "the captivating iridescence he saw in any invitation to toughness."[68] Nixon was fascinated by New York, in part because it was "very cold and very ruthless." He had great respect for people like Nikita Khrushchev, Spiro Agnew, John Mitchell, and John Connally because they were tough. At the same time, he expressed reservations about some of his aides—Len Garment and Robert Finch, for example—because he did not think they were mean enough. Even during the darkest hours of his presidency, his preoccupation with manliness was in evidence. On the eve of his departure from the White House, he met late into the night with Henry Kissinger. It was an emotional encounter. At one point, Nixon broke into tears and asked Kissinger to kneel down and pray with him. Fearful of the impression he might have left, he called Kissinger on the phone afterward and made a request: "Henry, please don't ever tell anyone that I cried and that I was not strong."[69] In his departing remarks to the White House staff the following day, he spoke of Theodore Roosevelt, noting that he too had faced hardship and disappointment during his life. More important, however, he pointed out that Roosevelt had "served his country, always in the arena, tempestuous, strong, sometimes right. But he was a *man*."[70] Nixon sounded the same theme in a conversation with Ken Clawson, a White House aide who visited the former president just two weeks after he resigned from office.

> "You see, don't you?" the Old Man [Nixon] said. "You've got to be tough. You can't break, my boy, even when you know there's nothing left. You can't admit, even to yourself, that it is gone. Now, some people we both know think that you go stand in the middle

of the bullring and cry, 'mea culpa, mea culpa,' while the crowd is hissing and booing and spitting on you. But a man doesn't cry," he said, clenching the stem of his pipe between his teeth. "I don't cry. You don't cry."[71]

The Nixon Presidency

Whereas Johnson retreated into isolation only when things started to go badly for him, reclusiveness was a persistent element of the Nixon style. Nixon came into the presidency believing that "I must build a wall around me."[72] He did precisely that. Only Haldeman, Ehrlichman, and sometimes Kissinger had ready access to him. When faced with important decisions, he frequently went into seclusion and pondered his options. Had he consulted more widely, had he taken more people into his confidence, might he have avoided the scandals of Watergate? Had he reached beyond the counsel of Haldeman and Ehrlichman, might he have decided to respond to the initial Watergate revelations by means other than a cover-up? It seems doubtful, but he might have.

It has already been suggested that the active-negative's special need for control may result from both his obsession with avoiding failure and his belief that he lives in a dangerous world. Although we could see manifestations of this need in Nixon even prior to his taking office, it was most apparent during his presidency. As with Johnson, it extended to the trivial as well as the important. In his testimony before the Senate Watergate Committee, one Nixon aide recalled the president's involvement in the following kinds of matters:

> The President was concerned with whether the shades were closed or open. Social functions were always reviewed with him. . . . He debated whether we should have a U-shaped table or a round table. He was deeply involved in the entertainment business, whom we would get for what kind of group. . . . He was very interested in meals and how they were served and the timing of the serving by the waiters.
>
> He debated receiving lines and whether or not he should have a receiving line prior to the entertainment for those relatively junior people in the Administration who were invited to the entertainment portion of the dinners only and not to the main dinner. . . . He wanted to review the musical selections himself. He was interested in whether or not a salad should be served and decided that at small dinners of 80 or less, the salad course should not be served.
>
> He was very interested in who introduced him to guests and he wanted it done quite properly. . . . He wanted a professional producer to come and actually produce the entertainment. . . . Guest lists were of great interest to him. . . . He would review all of these lists personally and approve them personally. . . .
>
> Ceremonies—he was interested in—the details of the drive up the walkway, whether the military would be to the right or left, which uniforms would be worn by the White House Police, whether or not the Secret Service would salute during the Star Spangled Banner and sing.[73]

The desire for control was also evident on more substantive matters. Although all presidents have felt frustrated by their lack of control over the bureaucracy, Nixon, along with Reagan, made a more systematic effort to correct this problem. Nor was Nixon's motive for doing so merely to facilitate the implementation of his policies. Thus, when he learned that the IRS was dragging its feet on investigating his political enemies, he remarked, "I look forward to the time that we have agents in the

Department of Justice and the IRS under our control after November 7."[74] He also sought to enhance his control by keeping a tight rein over the flow of information. News releases were to come from the White House and not from other departments and agencies in the government. He held fewer news conferences—some thirty-seven in all—than any president except Ronald Reagan. Furthermore, the ability of Congress to exercise its constitutional responsibility for overseeing the executive branch was seriously impaired by the president's broad-sweeping use of executive privilege. And as noted in Chapter 3, in many cases the Nixon administration's refusal to provide Congress with requested information was done without even bothering to invoke executive privilege. But nowhere was Nixon's control over information more evident than in foreign policy, for not only was Congress frequently not consulted, but on several occasions it was not informed—the secret bombing of Cambodia being the most glaring example of this. Finally, it should be noted that in addition to withholding information, Nixon also sought to nullify the constitutional responsibilities of Congress through his abuse of impoundment and the pocket veto.

Unfortunately for Nixon, the gradual unraveling of the Watergate scandals proved uncontrollable, a fact that caused him considerable exasperation: "I hate things like this. We're not in control."[75]

Of all the elements in Richard Nixon's personality, none proved to be more damaging in the presidency than his inclination to sacrifice means for ends. In the spring of 1972, the Gallup polls had shown Nixon running only slightly ahead of Senator Edmund Muskie (D-Maine), while the Harris polls actually gave Muskie a slight lead. Since the election had to be won at all costs, all manner of "dirty tricks" became the order of the day. The sign hanging over the office door of the Committee to Reelect the President (CREEP) told it all: "WINNING IN POLITICS ISN'T EVERYTHING, IT'S THE ONLY THING." To this end, the Democratic National Committee headquarters was broken into by members of what was later dubbed the White House "Plumbers" unit. Spies were hired and planted in the campaign organizations of presidential candidates Hubert Humphrey, George Wallace, and Edmund Muskie. Various dirty tricks were played on the Democratic candidates by CREEP, the most famous of which was its release of a completely false story alleging that Muskie had referred to Americans of French Canadian extraction as "Canucks." Because Senator Ted Kennedy (D-Mass.) was also perceived as a potential political threat to the president, a member of the Plumbers was charged with investigating his sex life, family, and drinking habits in an effort to uncover embarrassing information.

Whether or not Richard Nixon authorized these and other such activities is not of primary importance here. What does matter is that he appears to have fostered an atmosphere among his subordinates that served to encourage this kind of behavior. Moreover, there were other Watergate-related activities of which Nixon did approve—none more disturbing than his willingness to use the resources of the federal government to harass his political opponents. Thus, shortly before the 1972 election and despite the fact that Nixon's victory was assured, he issued the following instructions to John Dean:

> I want the most comprehensive notes on all those who tried to do us in. They didn't have to do it. If we had a very close election and they were playing the other side I would understand this. No—they were doing this quite deliberately and they are asking for it

and they are going to get it. We have not used the power in this first four years as you know. We have not used the Bureau and we have not used the Justice Department but things are going to change now.[76]

Certain individuals were singled out as special objects of the president's wrath. One such person was Edward Bennett Williams, a noted liberal and lawyer for the *Washington Post,* about whom Nixon made the following remark: "I wouldn't want to be in Edward Bennett Williams' position after this election. We are going to fix the son of a bitch, believe me. We are going to. We've got to, because he is a bad man."[77] That Nixon should have taken such a vindictive attitude is not altogether surprising. It has already been noted that he had always been suspicious of other people's motives. But under the pressures of the presidency, this suspicion increasingly developed into a siege mentality, as evidenced by a remark he made to John Dean: "Nobody is a friend of ours. Let's face it." Critics were defined not merely as opponents but rather as "enemies." As such, they posed a threat to the one thing that concerns an active-negative most—his ability to succeed. Consequently, they had to be dealt with ruthlessly. Nowhere was Nixon's determination to do so more disturbingly revealed than in a statement he made in the presence of his close aides: "One day we will get them—we'll get them on the ground where we want them. And we'll stick our heels in, step on them hard and twist . . . get them on the floor and step on them, crush them, show no mercy."[78]

If Watergate reflected Nixon's willingness to sacrifice means for ends, it also highlighted another dimension of the active-negative personality—rigidity. This may come as somewhat of a surprise, since Nixon often exhibited remarkable flexibility in his views. Given the fact that anticommunism had been the hallmark of his political beliefs throughout most of his public career, few would have expected Richard Nixon to be the first president to embark upon a policy of *détente* with both China and the Soviet Union. Nor, given his earlier antipathy toward wage and price controls, would one have anticipated that he would ultimately institute them. Yet as Barber notes, rigidity in the active-negative is likely to set in when he faces a situation that makes him *"seriously vulnerable to public exposure of personal inadequacy"* or that threatens his power.[79] The uncovering of Watergate threatened to do both. Accordingly, in the interests of avoiding failure at all costs, means were once again sacrificed for ends. The immediate solution was a cover-up, which in the first instance was designed to avoid implicating the president and his immediate associates. When that failed, the president decided to blame the scandals on "overzealous" aides, but he continued to insist that he was involved in neither the scandals themselves nor the efforts to cover them up. As the evidence continued to mount against him, he saw himself as being victimized by those whose only goal was to bring him down. As he would later recount in his interviews with David Frost, "It was a five-front war with a fifth column. I had a partisan Senate committee staff. We had a partisan special prosecutor staff. We had a partisan media. We had a partisan Judiciary Committee staff in the fifth column."[80] It was Richard Nixon confronting still another struggle, another challenge in which he saw himself faced off against a constellation of forces whose hatred of him was so great that they were incapable of viewing the evidence objectively. He appears to have viewed this challenge like all the other challenges in his life—as another test of his self-worth.

This view was poignantly revealed by Nixon in remarks made at a press conference following one of the most harrowing weeks of his presidency—a week during which the Senate Watergate hearings were in session; the House Judiciary Committee was preparing for its impeachment inquiry; the president fired Archibald Cox, which in turn led to the resignation of Attorney General Richardson and the dismissal of Assistant Attorney General William Ruckelshaus; and, to make matters worse, war broke out in the Middle East, and the United States armed forces were put on red alert.

> I have never heard or seen such outrageous, vicious, distorted reporting in twenty-seven years of public life. I'm not blaming anybody for that. Perhaps what happened is that what we did brought it about, and therefore the media decided that they would have to take that particular line. But when people are pounded night after night with that kind of frantic, hysterical reporting, it naturally shakes their confidence. And yet I should point out that even in this week when many thought that the President was shellshocked, unable to act, the President acted decisively in the interests of peace and interests of the country, and I can assure you that whatever shocks gentlemen of the press may have, or others—political people—these shocks will not affect me and doing my job.

Later in the press conference:

> *Reporter:* Mr. President, Harry Truman used to talk about the heat in the kitchen, and . . .
>
> *President:* I know what he meant.
>
> *Reporter:* A lot of people are wondering how you are bearing up under the emotional strain of recent events. Can you discuss that?
>
> *President:* Well, those who saw me during the Middle East crisis thought I bore up rather well. . . . I have a quality which is—I guess I must have inherited it from my Midwestern mother and father—which is that the tougher it gets the cooler I get. Of course it isn't pleasant to find your honesty questioned. . . . But as far as I'm concerned, I have learned to expect it. It has been my lot throughout my political life, and I suppose because I have been through so much, that may be one of the reasons . . . I have what it takes.[81]

Nixon remained inflexible on his involvement in the Watergate scandals right up to the end, despite a substantial body of evidence to the contrary. His resignation speech contained no mention of guilt, not even by implication. Rather, he was resigning, he said, because he no longer enjoyed enough political support in Congress. Even upon receipt of his pardon, he issued a statement in which he acknowledged certain errors in judgment but made no admission of intentional wrongdoing. He continued to maintain this posture two years later when he granted a series of interviews to television personality David Frost. When asked, for example, why he had authorized such illegal actions as wiretappings and burglaries, he responded, "Well, when the President does it, that means that it is not illegal." When invited to explain those portions of the White House tapes that showed him rehearsing Haldeman in the false testimony that would later be given before the Grand Jury, Nixon replied that he was merely playing the role of defense lawyer for a good friend. Only in the final interview (which was the first one to be aired on television) did Nixon begin to come to grips with the full implications of what he had done.

It is ironic that a president who was obsessed with avoiding failure should ultimately be judged as one of the greatest failures of any president in our history. This irony is further increased by the fact that, but for Watergate, the Nixon presidency might well have received high marks. Certainly the case can be made that much of his foreign policy demonstrated creativity and insight. Even on the domestic side, his program of revenue sharing marked a fundamental—and in the judgment of many, a favorable—change in federal-state relations. Unfortunately, his own insecurities gave rise to a pattern of conduct so disgraceful that it dwarfed his accomplishments. Moreover, the American people paid an exceedingly high price for these insecurities: presidential abuse of power, obstruction of justice, and governmental paralysis for more than a year as both Congress and the president were preoccupied with impeachment. But the highest price paid was best articulated by Richard Nixon himself: "I let down the country. I let down our system of government and the dreams of all those young people that ought to get into government, but think it's all too corrupt and the rest."[82]

FRANKLIN ROOSEVELT AS AN ACTIVE-POSITIVE

Roosevelt's Youth

Concerning Franklin Roosevelt's early years, one scholar of the Roosevelt family has remarked that "in the long shelf of biographies of American presidents, one searches in vain for the story of a childhood more serene and secure." The financial hardship experienced by both Johnson and Nixon was totally absent from Roosevelt's childhood. His family were members of the aristocracy, with a style of living in keeping with their social position: a country estate, servants, horses, frequent trips abroad. More important, young Franklin did not suffer any want of affection from his mother and father; an only child, he was the center of their attention. At the same time, however, he was not given free rein. Both parents set down definite expectations for his behavior and intellectual development, but they enforced their standards with a sense of understanding. In the words of his mother, "We never were strict merely for the sake of being strict. In fact, we took a secret pride in the fact that Franklin instinctively never seemed to require that kind of handling."[83] Although James Roosevelt had an air of formality and reserve about him, this does not appear to have hampered his relationship with his son. Indeed, the evidence suggests that father and son were frequently in each other's company—boating, swimming, hunting, riding horses, or touring the family estate. Franklin's relationship with both parents was a close one, but he could not become completely dependent upon them because they were frequently traveling and did not always take him with them.

The Roosevelt who left home to face the outside world was full of self-confidence and optimism—qualities fostered not only by a happy and loving environment but also by his family's high social position and accomplishment. At fourteen he was sent off to boarding school for four years, where he adjusted to a highly regimented existence without any problem. His gregariousness and personal charm proved of great assistance to him in getting along with his classmates. At Harvard he became involved in a variety of activities ranging from participating in athletics and social clubs to writing for the *Harvard Crimson*. He was elected to official positions in some of these campus organizations, but his most significant achievement was his selection as editor in chief of the *Crimson*. The key to his leadership ability appears to have been grounded in his winning personality. As one editor of the newspaper observed, "In his geniality was a kind of frictionless command."[84] In Roosevelt's senior year, his class saw fit to nominate him for class marshal and select him as permanent chairman of the Class Committee. But there was one profound disappointment for Roosevelt during his college career: his failure to gain entry into Porcellian, Harvard's most exclusive club. Yet it is interesting to note how his reaction differed from Johnson and Nixon, both of whom found themselves in a similar situation. When Johnson failed to be selected for the most exclusive club (Black Stars) on his college campus, he organized another club known as the White Stars. On Nixon's college campus, the most exclusive club was the Franklins, noted for its snobbishness. Nixon was instrumental in forming another club known as the Orthogonians. Roosevelt was undoubtedly hurt over his rejection by Porcellian, but his high sense of self-esteem enabled him to take the disappointment in stride. In the case of Johnson and Nixon, however, it may well be that their fear of rejection spurred each of them to organize his own club and thus ensure acceptance into it.

Entry into Politics; Worldview and Style

After graduation from law school, Roosevelt entered a prominent New York law firm, where for four years he worked on matters he found thoroughly uninspiring. Finally, in 1910 politics sought him out. A local politician visited him and asked him to run for the New York Assembly, and Roosevelt accepted. Several factors made politics an appealing prospect to Roosevelt. He was gregarious by nature, a quality that would be highly suited to the extroverted profession of politics. In addition, he appears to have wanted personal power, but unlike the ambitions of Johnson and Nixon, this desire was rooted in self-confidence rather than insecurity. Finally, the attraction of politics was strongly reinforced by a worldview that emphasized service. This perspective had been shaped by several forces. There were his parents, who had instilled in him the aristocracy's sense of noblesse oblige—the responsibility of the more fortunate to serve the community. And the involvement of James Roosevelt in community activities, many of which were charitable, demonstrated that the preachments of service were more than empty words. In addition, these views were powerfully reinforced by Roosevelt's headmaster at boarding school, a man who apparently had an extraordinary influence upon Roosevelt's thinking: "As long as I live, the influence of Dr. and Mrs. Peabody means and will mean more to me than that of any other people next to my father and mother."[85] Endicott Peabody saw his mission as one of instilling within the wellborn of Groton a commitment to both Christian values and service, especially public service. A further incentive to serve was provided in the example set by Roosevelt's ancestors. While he was at Harvard, Franklin wrote a paper on the history of the Roosevelt family and noted that "they have never felt that because they were born in a good position they could put their hands in their pockets and succeed. They have felt, rather, that, being born in a good position, there was no excuse for them if they did not do their duty by the community."[86]

For Johnson and Nixon, politics was fraught with anxieties. The political world was a dangerous one. Both were preoccupied with avoiding failure. On the other hand, Roosevelt's confidence and optimism led him to approach the challenges of politics with joyous expectation. Upon election to the New York State Assembly, he found himself battling the political bosses of Tammany Hall, and he relished it: "There is nothing I love as much as a good fight. I never had as much fun in my life as I am having right now."[87] When he was presented with the opportunity to become assistant secretary of the Navy, he approached the job with his characteristic ebullience and confidence, expressing no hesitation, no doubts about his ability to handle it. Although he now found himself dealing with a ponderous military bureaucracy, his enthusiasm was in no way dampened: "I have loved every minute of it."[88]

It was during Roosevelt's stint as assistant secretary of the Navy that his political style began to emerge. He was first of all a man of action. Problems were there to be understood and solved; if one solution did not work, he would try something else. At the same time, however, his decisions were preceded by a careful mastering of the details of a problem as well as the political environment surrounding it. This information was garnered through frequent contact with people, another hallmark of his political style. There was a constant flow of people into his office, precisely because he encouraged it: "I want you all to feel free that you can come to me at any time in my office, and we can talk matters over. Let's get together for I need you to teach me your business and show me what is going on."[89] According to the then secretary of war, the constant meeting with people, the constant probing and listening, appeared to have accomplished their purpose: "I should think he'd wear himself out in the promiscuous and extended contacts he maintains with people. But as I have observed him, he seems to clarify his ideas and teach himself as he goes along by that very conversational method."[90] Of course, Roosevelt's frequent contacts with people were designed to persuade as well as to learn. Roosevelt proved highly effective at such persuasion, for like Johnson, he seems to have had a keen understanding of human nature, an ability to read people and appeal to them in terms of their own needs. As one of his White House assistants would later remark, "It is probably safe to say that during 1933, 1934, and 1935 a record-breaking number of men of some political eminence went to the President's office in a state of incipient revolt and left it to declare to the world their subscription to things that they did not subscribe to."[91] No doubt this aspect of Roosevelt's style was greatly enhanced by his special personal charm, congeniality, humor, enthusiasm, and obvious interest in the person with whom he was talking.

When Roosevelt moved on to become governor of New York, another aspect of his political style surfaced, namely, his rhetorical skills. Faced with a Republican legislature that often proved unreceptive to his programs, he took his case to the people of New York through personal appearances and radio addresses. Just as he had proved effective in appealing to people on an individual level, so too did he have a talent for appealing to them *en masse*. His rhetoric conveyed a genuine sense of concern and empathy with his audience, and his points were stated in a manner that made them readily comprehensible to the average citizen.

The Roosevelt Presidency

Whoever stepped into the presidency in 1933 would find himself confronting an economic crisis the likes of which the country had never experienced. Yet as Roosevelt took over the reins of power he exuded his customary self-confidence. In the words of

Richard Neustadt, "His image of the office was himself-in-office. The memoirs left by his associates agree on this if nothing else: he saw the job of being President as being F.D.R. He wanted mastery, projected that desire on the office and fulfilled it there with every sign of feeling he had come into his own."[92] He enjoyed being president.

Convinced of the necessity for action and confident in his ability to make it happen, Roosevelt moved with dispatch: "One thing is sure. We have to do something. We have to do the best we know how to do at the moment. . . . If it doesn't turn out right, we can modify it as we go along."[93] The first hundred days of his administration were a bustle of activity, producing the greatest waterfall of legislation of any president in our history. Especially notable among his legislative accomplishments during this initial period were the Farm Relief Act, Banking Act, Economy Bill, Securities Act, Federal Relief Act, Railway Reorganization Act, National Recovery Act, and Agricultural Adjustment Act. His decisions about what to do and when to do it, as well as his assessments of actions already taken, were arrived at through his exposure to wide-ranging channels of information. This necessitated making himself accessible. He met frequently with members of Congress. He met twice a week with members of the press, answering questions as well as asking them. Approximately one hundred people within the government had direct access to him by phone. Nor was it uncommon for him to pick up the phone and summon to the White House some bright young bureaucrat he had heard about. When people came to see him in his office, he would often take the opportunity to probe their minds on a variety of issues, not simply on the one they had come to discuss with him. Recognizing that his own staff was one of his most crucial sources of information, he structured it in ways that would enhance its performance of this task. As noted in Chapter 6, all staff members had direct access to him. The same assignment was given to more than one person, and Roosevelt deliberately played personalities off against each other. All of this produced a kind of creative conflict that, although exasperating for his staff, served to maximize the flow of information and ideas to him.[94] Roosevelt was well aware of the provincialism in Washington and thus exhorted members of his staff to seek out information as he did: "Go and see what's happening. See the end product of what we are doing. Talk to people; get the wind in your nose."[95]

There was also an element of secretiveness in the Roosevelt style. During the process of accumulating information about an issue, he rarely revealed what his own inclinations might be. With one person he might imply that he leaned in one direction, while with the next he would create an entirely different impression. The purpose, of course, was to keep his options open. He was constantly assessing the political realities of a situation, biding his time until the most propitious moment for making a decision. He recognized that success was in part dependent upon timing. Yet, unlike Johnson and Nixon, he did not extend his secrecy to restricting the number of people involved in the decision making; nor did he keep important decisions secret after they had been made. It is unlikely, for example, that Roosevelt would have disguised our increasing commitment to Vietnam or that he would have secretly bombed Cambodia. Such secrecy would not have been necessary, for it was his custom not to make such crucial decisions until he had prepared both the public and Congress to accept them.

In seeking to persuade, Roosevelt drew upon two very effective elements of his political style: his skills in personal relations and in rhetoric. Much of his success with Congress was attributable to his ability to manipulate them: "Roosevelt's leadership talents lay in his ability to shift quickly and gracefully from persuasion to cajolery to flattery to intrigue to diplomacy to promises to horse-trading—or to concoct just that formula which his superb instincts for personal relations told him would bring around the most reluctant congressmen."[96] When necessary, he would exert further pressure by taking his case to the American public. The primary instrument for doing so was the "fireside chat," and its effectiveness lay in its informality as well as in Roosevelt's ability to convey his ideas clearly and with a sense of genuine concern.

Although Roosevelt's personality was to a large extent responsible for his political success, it also led to the major miscalculation of his presidency—his decision to pack the Supreme Court. We have already noted that Roosevelt was an activist, a man interested in results. Given this disposition, one can understand his frustration with a conservative Supreme Court that repeatedly declared important parts of his New Deal programs unconstitutional. The legislation voided by the Court included the Railroad Pension Act, Farm Mortgage Law, Agricultural Adjustment Act, Bituminous Coal Act, and a portion of the National Industrial Recovery Act.

A man of great self-confidence to begin with, Roosevelt became even more so following his landslide reelection victory in 1936. Accordingly, he took the brash step of proposing legislation to Congress that would permit the president to add an additional member to the Supreme Court for every judge who reached the age of seventy and did not avail himself of the opportunity to retire. Since there were six judges who fell into this category, Roosevelt would be able to add six additional members and thus break the conservative hold on the Court. He argued that the purpose of this legislation was to allow the Court to operate with greater efficiency. Such a flimsy and demonstrably false justification was, by itself, sufficient to spark outrage from both Congress and the American public. However, the cold reception given his proposal was heightened by Roosevelt's failure to employ some of the hallmarks of his political style—reaching out for information and advice, carefully assessing the political environment, preparing the public for what he wanted to do. In this particular instance, the proposal came as a surprise to all concerned. Neither Congress nor the cabinet was consulted. Moreover, the president made no attempt to reveal, let alone explain, his proposal to the people during his campaign for reelection.[97] The result was a stunning defeat for a man who had allowed his overconfidence and impatient desire for results to distort his view of political reality.

Yet if the court-packing episode highlighted Roosevelt's weaknesses, it also demonstrated his strengths. The president did not adopt a rigid stance by converting his proposal into a do-or-die proposition. When failure became apparent, he accepted it and moved on to something else. He was able to joke about his blunder, and apparently he even concluded that the proposal itself had been ill conceived. In putting together his public papers he titled the volumes in the following fashion: 1935—"The Court Disapproves," 1936—"The People Approve," 1937—"The Constitution Prevails."[98] When the 1938 congressional elections came, Roosevelt campaigned against those senators who had failed to support his plan, but he did not convert them into "enemies" who must be punished by any means, fair or foul. In short, he responded to his defeat with a sense of proportion, and he was able to do so because of his self-confidence. He was not obsessed with avoiding failure; he did not see his performance in the political world as a constant struggle to test his self-worth. As he once remarked to an aide, "You'll have to learn that public life takes a lot of sweat, but it doesn't need to worry you. You won't always be right, but you mustn't suffer from being wrong. That's what kills people like us."[99]

RONALD REAGAN: AN IMPERFECT PASSIVE-POSITIVE

Earlier in this chapter, it was noted that personalities are rarely so discrete as to fall neatly into one of four types. Although Barber readily acknowledges this point, noting that some presidents evinced characteristics of more than one type, he appears little inclined to see much ambiguity in the Reagan personality. Shortly before Reagan assumed the presidency, Barber predicted that the one-time movie actor would be a "conserver of his energies, a take-it-easy type. And, as everyone everywhere has noticed, he is an optimist, a booster, a smiler, a genial fellow. In my jargon, that combination makes Reagan a 'passive-positive,' that is, the receptive, compliant, other directed character whose life is a search for affection as a reward for being agreeable and cooperative rather than personally assertive."[100] Nothing in Reagan's first-term performance caused Barber to alter that assessment. Although much of the evidence would indeed appear to support Barber's characterization of Reagan, some does not. We now consider the Reagan personality in greater detail.

Reagan's Youth

Ronald Reagan's childhood and adolescence were largely full of happy memories, despite circumstances that at times placed a burden on him and other family members. Although not destitute by any means, the Reagans certainly were not financially comfortable: "We were poor but we didn't know we were poor."[101] Reagan's father, Jack, was plagued by a rather serious drinking problem. This fact, combined with a constant search for greener pastures, led Jack to move the family from one Illinois community to another, finally settling down in the town of Dixon when Ronald was nine. Here Jack was moderately successful as a shoe salesman, until he was let go at the onset of the Great Depression. Undeterred, he campaigned hard for Franklin Roosevelt in Dixon, and after Roosevelt's election he was appointed head of the local welfare office. His drinking could have easily engendered harsh feelings on the part of the Reagan children, but his wife, Nelle, was instrumental in preventing such attitudes from developing. She taught the children to view their father's drinking as a sickness deserving of compassion, not contempt. Nor was her compassion confined to the family. The hungry, sick, and unwanted in Dixon were regularly beneficiaries of Nelle's generosity, in the form of food, clothing, or other assistance.[102]

Unfailingly optimistic in her outlook, Nelle encouraged Ronald to "take a broad and happy view of life."[103] Even Jack Reagan, despite his setbacks, continued to believe that success would ultimately come to those who had the energy and capacity for hard work.[104] The sense of optimism inculcated in young Ronald was not in any way diminished by the experiences of his high school years. On the contrary, his affable nature enabled him to make friends easily and no doubt contributed to his selection as football captain and class president. In his high school yearbook, the picture of each graduating senior was captioned with a motto that captured what was most distinctive about that individual. Significantly, under Reagan's picture appeared "Life is just one grand sweet song, so start the music."[105] The sweet song continued at Eureka College.

Not captivated by his classroom studies, Reagan's energies were instead focused in the areas of sports, drama, and student government. He was the school's number-one swimmer for three years; the primary cheerleader for the basketball team; a participant in many of the school plays; and a member of the Student Senate for two years, during one of which he served as its president. He was exceedingly popular, with one friend describing him as "having a personality that would sweep you off your feet" and another recalling that "I can't think of anyone who disliked him."[106]

In retrospect, one of the most critical events of Reagan's college career came in his freshman year. Given Eureka's desperate financial condition, the college's newly selected president decided that it would be necessary to cut back on the faculty and course offerings. This decision galvanized faculty as well as students, and Reagan was appointed to represent the freshman class on the campus strike committee. When faculty and students met in the college chapel one evening to take a vote on whether to strike, freshman Reagan was chosen to address the group. His speech proved so compelling that all present rose to their feet cheering, and the vote to strike passed by acclamation. One week later the college president resigned, and the plan to reduce the number of faculty and courses was dropped. In later recalling the event, Reagan would observe: "I discovered that night that an audience has a feel to it and, in the parlance of the theater, that audience and I were together. . . . It was heady wine. Hell, with two more lines I could have had them riding through 'every Middlesex village and farm'—without horses yet."[107] Here for the first time, the young Reagan began to sense both his rhetorical skills and the considerable satisfaction he derived from pleasing an audience. These sentiments, subsequently reinforced by performances in several school plays, steered Reagan into the acting profession after a brief stint as a radio sportscaster.

Worldview and Style

With the hardships of the Depression having been visited upon his family and his father an avid Roosevelt fan, it is not surprising that Reagan became a New Dealer as well. Indeed, he elevated FDR to the status of hero, memorizing the most memorable lines from his speeches and aping his mannerisms. Nor did this support wane after the president's passing. Reagan went on to join the American Screen Actors Guild, peopled largely by Roosevelt supporters; helped found the California chapter of Americans for Democratic Action, an organization that carried the torch for New Deal values; and in 1948, headed a group of actors supporting the election of Harry Truman, and two years later campaigned against a California Republican candidate for the U.S. Senate by the name of Richard Nixon. On international matters, meanwhile, his experience with fighting communist infiltration of the Screen Actors Guild and other actor-affiliated organizations engendered in him a loathing of communism that he would carry the rest of his life.

Circumstances and events, however, would ultimately dampen Reagan's enthusiasm for activist government and unions. Five years after the dissolution of his first marriage in 1947, he married Nancy Davis, the stepdaughter of a prominent and highly conservative surgeon. Reagan began to move in her social circles, meeting people for whom Roosevelt was anathema. By this time also, his Republican brother Neil had become a business executive and took every opportunity to convince his younger brother of the error of his ways. Most critical in explaining his change of heart, however, was an eight-year contract that he signed with General Electric as host of its television program *General Electric Theatre.*[108] More than simply a host, he traveled the country speaking at various GE plants and before a host of business groups. Rubbing elbows with corporate types on a daily basis, he enthusiastically adopted a pro-business and antigovernment stance. Moreover, while not equating liberalism with communism, he did contend that liberal government programs represented "a foot in the door."[109] Over time Reagan's antigovernment rhetoric became so strident and controversial that when his contract came up for renewal in 1962, GE informed him that he must henceforth confine his activities exclusively to promoting its products. Reagan refused and the relationship ended.[110]

Barber argues, plausibly, that the striking turnabout in the Reagan worldview was not rooted in careful reflection but rather in the passive-positive personality's desire to please significant others: "To put it plainly, Reagan's conservatism has been circumstantial, not visceral."[111] Thus, once his marriage and affiliation with GE placed him in new social and business circles, he sought to please by recasting his beliefs to suit them; in the case of GE, he sought so hard to please that he ultimately espoused an antigovernment stance that even the GE corporate structure found excessive. The desire to please, incidentally, was apparently important to him in his acting as well. Of the fifty-three films that he made during his Hollywood years, he played the villain only once and has repeatedly voiced his regret at ever having done so.[112]

As for Reagan's political style, it revealed itself in both his run for and service in the governorship of California. This office, significantly, was not one that he sought. On the contrary, the most perceptive chronicler of his political career notes that Reagan, "usually the reactive man, would never have sought elective office except for the insistence of those who came to him and the absence of any other untarnished Republican candidate available to run against Governor Brown. Certainly he would not have taken the initiative in seeking office."[113]

Continuing to speak before a host of different business and professional groups after leaving GE and campaigning in support of Barry Goldwater's presidential quest in 1964, Reagan quickly gained a national reputation as a highly effective exponent of conservative Republican philosophy. In the domestic area, he now saw nearly all problems as traceable to federal intervention in the social and economic lives of the citizenry. Free the population from such intrusions and success would elude only those who lacked the ambition to seek it. As for the world beyond our shores, he preached that the United States was locked in a life-and-death struggle with the Soviet Union, whose sinister hand lay behind all manifestations of political instability. These views caught the eye of some wealthy, conservative businessmen who prevailed upon Reagan to run for governor. The advertising firm of Spencer Roberts was given the task of packaging his image and issue positions. As political aide Lyn Nofziger would later recall, Reagan was largely a passive figure in this endeavor: "He didn't even run his own campaign. His campaign was run by hired people who then walked away and left it."[114]

The passive posture evinced by Reagan during his campaign carried over into the governorship. Little involved in transition planning, he preferred instead to turn the whole matter over to his campaign manager and a group of wealthy business executives who had backed his candidacy.[115] After assuming the reins of power, moreover, he delegated authority so liberally that he was frequently unaware of what his own administration was doing. During his first term, for example, when asked by a reporter to name any single item in his legislative program, Reagan proved unable to do so.[116] Likewise, in meetings with his cabinet, major issues would come up for decision only to find that the governor was learning about them for the first time.[117] John Sears, who would for a time manage Reagan's bid for the presidency in 1980, recalls that Governor Reagan "seldom came up with an original idea, and often, like a performer waiting for a writer to feed him his lines and for a director to show him how to say them, he waited for others to advise him what to do."[118] Yet for all of his passivity, when his convictions were engaged by an issue, he was not averse to asserting himself. Particularly in his second term, he took on student protesters, the educational establishment, and such highly charged issues as tax and welfare reform.

Reagan and the Presidency

Although Ronald Reagan would ultimately run for the presidency four times (1968, 1976, 1980, 1984), it was not an office he initially sought. Indeed, when the idea was broached by Tom Reed, one of the millionaires who had urged him to run for governor, Reagan expressed no interest at all. But as biographer Lou Cannon notes, "Reed, meanwhile, was banking on Reagan's desire *to please* [emphasis added]. He knew the governor, out of politeness, if nothing else, was unlikely to close the door completely to visiting supporters who urged him to run for president."[119] Reagan finally agreed to have his name entered for the nomination but not until the week of the convention, and by that time it was too late.

In his victorious campaign for the 1980 presidential nomination, Reagan was largely content to take direction from his campaign staff, much as he had done in the race for the governorship. Moreover, he allowed to fester a debilitating internal squabble between his campaign manager (John Sears) and other key aides. As would so often prove the case, he was prodded into action only after his wife, Nancy, intervened and demanded a resolution of the conflict. Sears was fired.[120] Even one of the most celebrated events of the 1980 campaign—the dispute between Reagan and Bush in the New Hampshire primary debate in which Reagan came across as assertive and in charge—proved to be more apparent than real. Reagan and Bush had agreed to debate each other, but not until the day of the debate was the former governor told that his campaign manager had invited the other presidential contenders to the debate as well. Viewing this change as violation of the ground rules, Bush refused to debate if the others participated. As Reagan took to the stage, he asked one of his campaign aides, "What am I supposed to do? What exactly am I supposed to do?" An aide, James Lake, answered, "We're going to go up there. You're going to make this statement that these guys should be allowed to speak. If they leave, you've got to stay and debate." Once on stage, Lake sent a note up to Reagan saying, "Give 'em hell, Governor. The whole place is with you." Reagan did precisely that, insisting that the other candidates be allowed to participate. Because Reagan's demand represented a violation of the agreed-upon ground rules, the moderator asked that his microphone be turned off, at which point Reagan shouted the now-celebrated rejoinder, "I paid for this microphone, Mr. Green."[121] It was a stellar performance by the former governor, but one that had been scripted and directed by others.

According to his campaign manager, Edward Rollins, Reagan was no more engaged when he ran for reelection in 1984: "The president was never really involved in any of the planning or strategy of the campaign. He would make small talk some of the time relative to what was going on with Mondale or [Democratic candidate] Gary Hart. But there was never any real inquisitive effort to get to the nitty-gritty on his part. I don't think he ever focused on it. The truth of the matter is that Ronald Reagan is the perfect candidate. He does whatever you want him to."[122]

We now consider the passive dimension of the Reagan personality as it relates to the presidency. That he would not be investing the energy of a Johnson or a Nixon as president was forecast in his 1980 bid for the office. Complaining that his campaign schedule required him to get up too early, an aide replied, "You'd better get used to it, Governor. When you're President, that fellow from the National Security Council will be there to brief you at 7:30 every morning." To which Reagan replied, "Well, he's going to have a helluva long wait."[123] True to his word, Reagan arrived at the Oval Office around 9:15 A.M. and received his national security briefing at 9:30. Nor was it uncommon for him to leave the office by 4:00 P.M. Moreover, if the length of Reagan's workday was leisurely compared with that of other recent presidents, neither can it be said that he packed more into fewer hours. On the contrary, according to one account of his presidency, many Reagan aides were astounded by his inattentiveness.

> They found that Reagan was not just passive, he was sometimes entirely disengaged. He did not delegate in the usual sense; he did not actively manage his staff by assigning tasks and insisting on regular progress reports. Instead, he typically gave his subordinates little or no direction. Usually, he provided the broad rhetoric and left them to infer what he wanted. When it came to the fine points of governing, he allowed his staff to take the lead. "He made almost no demands and gave almost no instructions," conceded former adviser Martin Anderson. "Essentially, he just responded to whatever was brought to his attention." He seemed to have unquestioning trust in many of the small and large decisions others made for him—and when his staff could not reach a decision, he frequently made none either unless events forced him to do so.[124]

Nor were the above perceptions confined to White House advisers or members of the cabinet. Republican members of Congress who met regularly with Reagan expressed shock at his lack of knowledge on major issues, with the House Republican leader commenting on one occasion that "the president's really not as well posted on the specifics and on the machinery as Johnson, Nixon and Ford who used to be more intimately involved in how it all worked. Sometimes I think, 'My Gosh, he ought to be better posted. Where are his briefing papers?' "[125] Similarly, in public appearances before the press and other audiences, Reagan's misstatements of fact were so frequent and at times so egregious as to prompt a book titled *There He Goes Again: Ronald Reagan's Reign of Error*, which documented some three hundred factual errors after only two years in office.[126] Seeking to avoid such public displays of ignorance, his staff moved to limit his exposure to the press and carefully programmed the president's remarks at other public occasions. As a consequence of these efforts, references to Reagan aides as his "handlers" and "managers" soon became commonplace in daily accounts of the Reagan presidency.[127]

It should be noted, however, that there were limits to Reagan's passivity. He was not a Warren Harding, whom Barber describes as "a man of no political convictions who would do what he was told."[128] On the contrary, Reagan entered the White House with certain stubbornly held views and once in office would develop others. These included lowering taxes; increasing defense spending; pursuing the Strategic Defense Initiative (Star Wars); aiding the Nicaraguan contras; selling arms to Iran; visiting Bitburg, West Germany; and attending the Reykjavik Summit.[129] On matters such as these, Reagan could not be "handled" or "managed." Rather, as his former Chief of Staff Donald Regan attests, if the president's fundamental convictions were engaged by an issue, he was not averse to overruling a chorus of advice: "It was not uncommon for him to render courageous decisions on domestic economic questions in the face of nearly unanimous advice and pressure to do the opposite."[130] And yet, while Reagan's strongly held views defined the parameters beyond which his aides could not go on certain policy questions, he remained remarkably passive concerning how his goals would be realized.

As for the positive dimension of the Reagan personality, he certainly appears to have had a decidedly favorable reaction to the leisurely presidency that he defined for himself. Ruminating about what he would want students to know of his presidency, he remarked, "I would also tell students that I've enjoyed the job. And some nights you go home feeling ten feet tall. . . . I've had a fair sprinkling of them."[131] Absent from his public remarks were any complaints about the loneliness and pressures involved in making tough decisions.[132]

Barber tells us that passive-positives go about their work with "an appearance of affectionate hopefulness"—a disposition not altogether surprising for a personality that seeks to please.[133] Few presidents have evinced this attitude in so compelling and consistent a fashion as did Ronald Reagan. Characterized by one White House aide as an "absolutely unstoppable optimist,"[134] he rarely lost an opportunity in his formal addresses to celebrate America's past and its future. Such ebullient optimism proved a welcome tonic to a population emerging from the Carter presidency having been told that it suffered from a "crisis of confidence." Even Reagan's former presidential opponent, Walter Mondale, willingly acknowledged this point: "He's uncanny in his ability to create a sense of feeling good, of enhancing the American spirit, of pumping up the American sense of self-worth."[135] Accompanying his optimism was a self-confidence that suggests Reagan was thoroughly comfortable with who he was. This feature of his personality would appear to be at variance with Barber's passive-positive profile. Barber tells us that passive-positive presidents suffer from a low sense of self-esteem: "The contradiction is between low-self esteem (on grounds of being unlovable, unattractive) and a superficial optimism."[136] In Reagan's case, however, such an assertion would appear difficult to sustain, for nowhere in his background does one find the gnawing self-doubt that consumed Johnson and Nixon. In the words of one longtime friend, "He is the most secure man, emotionally and psychologically, that you'd ever want to meet. He has his own solid feeling of self-worth."[137] This view is echoed by two more neutral observers who undertook an assessment of the president's second term: "Reagan's self-confidence was an important part of his appeal. In a complex world, he trusted his instincts, frequently to surprisingly successful effect. . . . Reagan simply wasn't agonized by self-doubt."[138] His inner confidence revealed itself in a host of different ways. To the astonishment of many, he was willing to entertain the possibility of placing a former president (Gerald Ford) on the ticket as his running mate in 1980; he freely employed his sense of humor to poke fun at his own shortcomings; and, unlike both Johnson and Nixon, he remained largely unaffected by the trappings surrounding the presidency and felt no need to inflate his own ego by intimidating those around him.[139] On the contrary, geniality was one of the salient features of both the public and private Reagan. Moreover, as the cochairman of the Republican Party noted, this geniality was extended to opponents as well as friends: "There is no hatred in him, no vindictiveness, no grudges, no desire to get back."[140]

Although Reagan's unremitting optimism buoyed the public spirit and his inner confidence freed us from the rigidity and vindictiveness evidenced in the Johnson and Nixon presidencies, the passive dimension of his personality was not without costs. Clearly, his "hands off" management style allowed policy disputes in his administration to fester for extended periods of time, thereby creating an impression of drift, conflicting signals, and a lack of coherence. This problem was most apparent in foreign policy, where for five years the president's secretaries of defense and state, along with their subordinates, locked horns on a host of issues, including the presence of American troops in Lebanon, how to fight terrorism, our strategy in Central America, how to negotiate with Moscow, and interpretations of existing arms treaties with the Soviets.[141] Reflecting on this persistent policy discord, one astute Washington columnist observed, "The present turmoil in Washington can only be understood in this context of an unrefereed foreign-policy struggle that goes well beyond the ordinary and often useful competition between agencies and individuals. Reagan from the very beginning has countenanced, indulged it to an amazing degree. The result is that nothing is ever quite settled."[142]

The problems associated with Reagan's passivity went well beyond policy drift, however. Presidential aides who perceive their boss as little interested in supervising and holding them accountable for what they do may be tempted to take liberties with their positions. Thus, after the first day of meetings between Reagan and Gorbachev at the Geneva Summit, White House Deputy Press Secretary Larry Speakes took it upon himself to issue a press release quoting the president as having made certain remarks to the Kremlin leader. Not only did Reagan never make these statements, but Speakes did not even bother to clear the release with the president.[143] The alleged remarks, to be sure, caused no embarrassment to Reagan. Yet the fact that a White House aide would have felt free to take such liberties in connection with an event as sensitive as this suggests that he felt no threat of being called to account by his boss—and indeed he was not. We saw the same freelancing by White House aides in connection with the Iran-contra scandal. More specifically, in the course of negotiations with Iranian intermediaries, Oliver North made representations that ran totally contrary to U.S. policy;[144] and even more important, National Security Adviser William Poindexter unilaterally authorized the diversion of funds from Iranian arms sales to the contras. In this instance, of course, the president paid a very high price indeed for the actions of his overzealous aides.

Finally, there is yet another dysfunction that may befall those presidents predisposed toward a more passive posture. Accurate information and sound advice are the building blocks of informed decision making. A president whose innate passivity renders him little inclined to reach out and probe for information and advice risks denying himself those essential building blocks. For Ronald Reagan, the consequences of this deficiency were nowhere more apparent than in the ill-fated decision to trade arms for hostages. Although his role in these deliberations was addressed at some length in Chapter 7, the assessment made by Tower Commission member Edmund Muskie is worth quoting again: "We were appalled by the absence of the kind of alertness and vigilance to his job . . . that one expects of a president."[145]

PERSONALITY QUALITIES SUITABLE TO THE PRESIDENCY

Although one could, no doubt, think of a variety of personality attributes that would be desirable in a president, our discussion throughout this chapter suggests that some appear to be especially necessary. In the first place, a president should be an activist in the sense that Barber defines the term—that is, someone who creates opportunities for action, someone who initiates rather than responds. One might object to this assertion on the grounds that the country cannot tolerate a steady diet of activism. Occasionally it needs time to consolidate and take stock of itself, and a president of the more passive type can perform this needed function. This argument has a certain validity to it, but on balance the passive president would seem to be a luxury we can no longer afford. Like it or not, the United States has been thrust into the dominant leadership position on the international stage, and at home we are faced with problems of formidable proportions—health care, drugs, crime, environmental pollution, urban decay, to name but a few. When and if these problems are solved, there is every reason to believe that others will take their place, if only because today's solutions often become tomorrow's problems. Under a passive president we run the risk of being overtaken by events. To be sure, there may also be an element of risk in the activist president, for in his desire to achieve results he may try to do too much too fast, as Carter did in his first year. But if this should happen, at least Congress has the ability to slow him down—even if it has not always chosen to do so. On the other hand, if we are faced with a passive president, the problem of compensating for this becomes more difficult, because Congress is far better suited to checking overzealous leadership than it is to filling the vacuum that results from its absence.

It would also seem desirable to have someone in the White House whose orientation is positive rather than negative. It makes sense, after all, to expect that we are more likely to get a better performance from someone who enjoys what he is doing than we are from someone who does not. Moreover, if the latter is the case, we must ask why? Does he not enjoy the politicking that is the lubricant of the governmental process and so essential to getting things done? Or is his lack of enjoyment rooted in a sense of insecurity arising from self-doubt or fears that he is surrounded by a hostile environment?

In this chapter, much has been made of the necessity for having a president with a high sense of self-esteem—a quality that appears to be present in the active-positive and lacking in the active-negative. Here too, however, one might argue that low self-esteem in a president is not without its blessings, for in an effort to confirm his self-worth such a person would have an especially high motivation to achieve. Unfortunately, the presidencies of both Johnson and Nixon demonstrate that low self-esteem may carry costs as well as benefits. So impoverished is the active-negative's sense of worth that the prospect of failure becomes intolerable. Moreover, in order to avoid it, he may engage in behavior that can prove detrimental to the political system. Such behavior could include a tendency to seek greater and greater control over his environment, an inclination toward rigidity, and a willingness to sacrifice means for ends. This latter aspect of behavior is perhaps the most disturbing. As already stated, for both Johnson and Nixon it took the form of deliberate deception, and in the case of Nixon, harassment of political opponents as well.

Two qualifications must be attached to what has been said here. First, it is not inevitable that a president with low self-esteem will sacrifice means to ends, for his sense of morality may intrude—an attribute that is also essential in the presidential personality. Woodrow Wilson, for example, is generally regarded as a man who experienced severe self-doubt, yet his deep sense of morality was apparently strong enough to fend off any temptations to employ the heavy-handed tactics characteristic of Johnson and Nixon. Moreover, despite his inflexibility, Wilson's presidency was one of notable achievement. Thus, we may not want to exclude an individual from the presidency solely for want of self-esteem, provided that we also discern in his character a strong sense of morality. Second, a president with high self-esteem is not necessarily immune to sacrificing means for ends. John Kennedy, for example, may be viewed as an active-positive president, yet when the steel companies raised their prices in 1962, he threatened to use antitrust laws against them unless they rescinded the increase. Moreover, he took the additional step of sending a personal emissary to Pittsburgh to inform steel executives that their personal tax returns would be audited if they refused to roll back prices.[146] This hardly constitutes an example of admirable presidential behavior. Yet the major point to be made here is this: Although there is no reason to believe that the moral standards of the active-positive are any greater or less than those of the active-negative, the active-positive will nevertheless be under much less pressure to compromise those standards because he is not laboring under the compulsive fear of failure.

In considering personality attributes desirable in a president, we should also be attentive to how he relates to people. Does he enjoy interacting with people, and is he effective at doing so? This is an important question for two reasons. First, much of a president's success will depend upon his ability to be an effective persuader. This frequently requires that he meet personally with individuals and groups. Presidents who feel uncomfortable around others are likely to resist interaction to whatever extent possible and thus are apt to be less effective at persuasion as well. Richard Nixon's problems with Congress were, at least in part, the result of his failure to maintain adequate contact with its membership. Johnson and Roosevelt, on the other hand, showed no such reluctance. Moreover, their ability to persuade was enhanced further by a keen understanding of the motives and needs of other political actors.

The president's readiness to interact with others is important for another reason. His primary responsibility, after all, is to make decisions, and in order to do so effectively he needs information. Frequent contact with people is an invaluable means for accumulating information and ideas. No president was more sensitive to this fact than Franklin Roosevelt, who structured his environment so as to maximize his exposure to others. Of course, doing so came naturally to him, because he was by nature a gregarious person. Richard Nixon, on the other hand, provides a stark contrast to Roosevelt. In the words of one Nixon aide, he "did not like to see many people, and wanted to see still fewer privately." Accordingly, he structured his environment in such a way as to minimize his exposure to others. The result was a severe reduction in the channels of information open to him.

In addition to a president's willingness to interact with others, we should be equally concerned about how he perceives others. In other words, does he appear to be trusting of the other people in his environment, or does he view them with suspicion? A president who harbors deep suspicions about his environment may engage in behavior that is damaging both to the office and to the political system. For example, if he is already inclined toward isolation, a suspicious nature may only serve to make him more so. One can also hypothesize that such an attitude would lead to a style of excessive secrecy, with the result that the number of people involved in decision making will be kept small, and those in and outside government will be denied information that they have a right to know. A distrusting nature may also cause a president to become so concerned with the loyalty of those around him that he equates dissent with disloyalty, and consequently the healthy conflict of opposing views becomes stifled. Finally, one cannot help but wonder whether a deep suspicion of the world around him may also encourage a president to sacrifice means to ends. For if he is to succeed in what he perceives as an unscrupulous world, it may be necessary for him to adopt what he perceives to be the tactics of his adversaries.

The Case of Jimmy Carter

Although nearly all of the desirable personality characteristics identified above are associated with the active-positive type, we should not suppose that an active-positive personality ensures an effective presidency. To demonstrate that this is not necessarily the case, one need look no further than Jimmy Carter, whose stewardship will now be considered in more detail.

By way of style and program, Jimmy Carter was an activist. He worked extraordinarily long hours and immersed himself in the details of policymaking to a far greater extent than most presidents. His domestic programs sought to address a broad range of problems, including election, welfare, and tax reform; consumer protection; government reorganization; hospital cost containment; and energy. In the foreign policy realm he moved to elevate the importance of human rights, improve relations with the Third World, reduce tensions in the Middle East, and achieve some meaningful reductions in nuclear armaments. Carter also experienced a positive reaction to the job of being president and exhibited a sense of proportion regarding its frustrations: "I am at ease. When we have difficulties, I don't withdraw. I am not paranoid. I recognize that some of the controversy and difficulties and failures are because of the ambitious nature of some of our undertakings. There has never been an evening when I went to bed that I didn't look forward to the next day. If I do the best I can with something and then fail, I don't have any second thoughts or post-regrets. Some of the limitations I have found in the job are frustrating but I have accepted them."[147]

It is equally clear that Carter assumed the presidency with an extraordinary confidence in his own abilities. While some have argued that his apparent self-confidence masks an underlying feeling of vulnerability,[148] most are convinced that he is comfortable with himself: "Basically he has a secure sense of self. He knows who he is."[149] Indeed, those who observed Carter at close range were invariably struck by his self-assurance. On the campaign trail in 1976, during bad times as well as good, "he possessed a quiet self-confidence that could be almost irritating in its stolidness."[150] This assessment is echoed by a Washington correspondent who, after interviewing Carter at some length, reported that "my only personal session with him then left an impression of cold, even disturbing, self-assurance."[151]

Although a reputation for stubbornness had preceded his arrival in Washington, actually, as governor of Georgia he had shown a repeated willingness to compromise on his programs.[152] In the presidency also he would ultimately agree to settle for less than he wanted on legislation dealing with such issues as federal water projects, energy, farm price supports, and the Panama Canal treaties. Nor was Carter reluctant to acknowledge that his administration was not functioning as effectively as it should. Twice, for example, he retreated to Camp David to consider how things might be improved, the first time meeting primarily with aides and the second reaching out to public officials and private citizens from around the country. And even though the accumulation of problems surrounding his presidency evoked some of the most virulent and sustained criticism ever directed at a sitting president regarding his competence, Carter did not respond by converting opponents into enemies or by retreating into isolation.

Yet despite the fact that Carter appears to have related to his environment in the manner of an active-positive, both the Washington establishment and the American people concluded that he had not mastered the job of being president. That he failed to do so may be attributed to several factors, not the least of which was his lack of experience. Having previously held no elected or appointive position in the federal government, he assumed the presidency with little knowledge of the power relationships, personalities, and ways of proceeding in the capital city. Second, this shortcoming was exacerbated by the fact that he surrounded himself with aides who were just as deficient as he was in this respect. Their combined lack of experience was, as noted in Chapter 3, especially evident in their approach to Congress. While lack of knowledge regarding Washington politics quite obviously became less of a problem as the president moved through his term, Carter labored under other limitations that could not be so easily corrected by the mere passage of time. For one thing, in his personal relations Carter was at once both open and remote. To his credit, he made himself readily accessible to members of Congress, the press, and those within his administration. At the same time, however, he was an introverted, shy individual. Thus, when interacting with people in groups or one-on-one, he came across as aloof and distant.[153] This remoteness unfortunately prevented him from establishing close personal relationships with power brokers in Washington—relationships that could have helped to defuse opposition. As one Southern senator put it, "He hasn't a single friend up here. Not one soul."[154] Carter also never really developed a strategic political sense. He was not very adept at factoring political considerations into his policy positions and actions—for example, when to move on an issue, or how a proposed course of action would affect his future political leverage. Also, Carter never succeeded in conveying a clear sense of direction to those in and outside of government. To be sure, he submitted a large number of proposals to Congress on a broad range of issues, but he failed to articulate his priorities or to explain how his programs fit into his larger vision for American society. Commenting on this deficiency, one of his former aides concluded: "I came to think that Carter believes fifty things, but no one thing. He holds explicit, thorough positions on every issue under the sun, but he has no large view of the relations between them, no line indicating which goals (reducing unemployment? human rights?) will take precedence over which (inflation control? a SALT treaty?) when the goals conflict. Spelling out these choices makes the difference between a position and a philosophy."[155] Finally, although few failed to be impressed by Carter's grasp of the problems facing the nation, his uninspiring rhetorical style impeded his ability to educate the population on the nature of these problems and generate public support on behalf of his programs.

There were, of course, some substantial achievements during the Carter presidency, notably a peace accord between Egypt and Israel, the Panama Canal treaties, the formal recognition of China, and the beginnings of an energy policy. But, in the final analysis, these successes were not sufficient to overcome a growing impression expressed most succinctly by one of the president's own aides: "Carter does good things badly."[156]

☆ PREDICTING PRESIDENTIAL PERSONALITIES

If, as this chapter has tried to suggest, a president's personality can have a considerable impact upon how he conducts himself while in office, then it would appear that we ought to give closer scrutiny to this facet of a presidential candidate. James David Barber has proposed that "we need a new program of research aimed at assessing—before the choice is narrowed to a few—the probable course each emerging candidate would follow in the White House. Such a program could draw on the talents of psychologists, historians, journalists, politicians, political scientists, and others."[157]

Various proposals have been suggested regarding how this assessment might be made. Two scholars, for example, have developed a quantitative measure for determining a president's *power and achievement* need based upon a content analysis of his inaugural address.[158] They have suggested that this approach might also be applied to the campaign speeches of presidential candidates. Yet this proposal is fraught with difficulties. For one thing, candidates do not always write their own campaign speeches. Nor do they always adhere to what they say in them. On several occasions during his campaign for the presidency in 1968, Richard Nixon stated that he would run an open administration and would show no reluctance to delegate power. Nothing could have been farther from the truth. Finally, while this approach is designed to give us some understanding of a candidate's need for power and achievement, it tells us nothing about what motivates these needs. In the case of Nixon, for example, we would also want to know that these needs were rooted in a deep sense of insecurity.

Other proposals call for subjecting candidates to some kind of psychological testing. As far back as 1948, Harold Lasswell proposed the establishment of a National Personnel Assessment Board, which would administer tests to candidates in order to identify those with "nondestructive, genuinely democratic characters."[159] This proposal should also give us pause for thought. Quite obviously, a serious and perhaps fatal blow would be dealt to the candidacy of any individual who failed to receive the stamp of approval from such a board. To whom do we want to give the power to render such a judgment? How would the judges be selected? What if these experts cannot agree on what interpretation should be given to the evidence? How would they deal with the problem of predicting the *likelihood* that a given candidate would engage in destructive behavior? For remember, these experts will not be studying psychotics whose capacity for irrationality can be predicted with a high degree of certainty. Rather, they will be dealing with individuals who have demonstrated an ability to cope with their environment. Although some may demonstrate tendencies toward destructive behavior, these are only possibilities. But how much of a possibility? Do we exclude those with a 50 percent chance of engaging in destructive behavior in the presidency? Do we include a candidate if there is an 80 percent chance that he will not engage in destructive behavior?[160] Finally, even if all of these problems could be adequately dealt with, there is still the possibility that this kind of screening process could be undermined. Presidential contenders receive expert advice on a variety of matters related to their candidacy. Public relations experts advise them on what appeals should be made to the people; policy specialists advise them on issues; speech coaches help them with their delivery. More than likely, if an assessment board were established, some candidates would also hire consultants to advise them on matters related to their psychological examination, such as what kinds of questions should be anticipated and what kinds of responses would be most appropriate.

For those who eschew any efforts to submit candidates to psychological testing, the psychohistorical approach to assessing candidates may prove more appealing. As noted at the outset of this chapter, the psychohistorical approach attempts to discover the psychological makeup of an individual by scrutinizing his or her past. But even here we are confronted with some formidable difficulties. As Barber himself has noted, of the three components that make up personality (*character, style,* and *worldview*), it is character that appears to be most important to understanding a president's behavior: "Most strikingly for the active-negative (compulsive-tending) presidents, but also for the other types, character is the most important predictor."[161] Barber further states that character takes shape in childhood, and herein lies the problem, for although an examination of a candidate's childhood may provide us with the best clues to his character, the evidence is likely to be the leanest for this period of his life experience. Candidates do not usually write their own biographies. Thus, we have no systematic evidence on how *they* viewed *their* childhood experiences, except as they may choose to discuss them in interviews. While scholars can attempt to reconstruct a candidate's childhood through interviews and biographies—if there are any—the end product is still likely to be a sketch rather than a detailed picture. Thus, the conclusions drawn and the inferences made are of a highly tentative nature.

Despite these limitations, this chapter has tried to show that psychohistorical explanations may be of some assistance in providing another perspective from which to view presidential behavior. Yet it may be argued that it is one thing to make use of a psychohistorical explanation in seeking to gain additional insight into why presidents behave as they do, but it is quite another to apply it to candidates in quest of the presidency. In short, might we possibly do an injustice to both the candidates and the voters by making use of this approach in the screening process? If the answer is no, there is still another problem to be faced, for Barber has suggested that the assessment of candidates should take place before the field has been narrowed to only a few. But surely his meticulous inquiry into the characters of presidents was a time-consuming task. This raises the following question: Will there be enough time between when a candidate declares candidacy and when the nomination is made to conduct a careful inquiry into his character? The magnitude of the task becomes even greater if we are faced with the kind of situation we had in 1976, when there were initially fourteen candidates seeking the Democratic nomination for president.

In attempting to gain some kind of insight into a presidential candidate's personality, it may make more sense to focus our attention on his public career, for the evidence here is likely to be easier to come by. Such an approach would involve examining and accumulating information about his behavior in the political arena from the start of his political career right up to and including his campaign for the nomination. Does he invest considerable energy in politics, and does he appear to enjoy doing so? How does he perceive his environment? Does he interact freely with those around him—press, staff, fellow politicians? Is he flexible? How does he respond to criticism and to those who give it? Does he appear to show concern for means as well as ends? Of course, even this approach is not without its limitations. For one thing, its usefulness will depend to a large extent upon how long a candidate has been in political life. In the case of Richard Nixon, the record available for examination was extensive. At the time he ran for president in 1968 he had already been in politics for over twenty years, first as a congressman, then as a senator, then as vice president, then as a presidential candidate, then as a candidate for governor of California. Add to this the book he wrote (*Six Crises,* 1968), which detailed how he coped with the major crises of his political career. In contrast to Nixon is the case of Jimmy Carter, whose only political experience prior to assuming office was four years in the Georgia legislature and four years as governor. This more restricted time span of political activity obviously complicates the task of trying to detect patterns in a candidate's behavior. But even if we are fortunate enough to be presented with a candidate whose political career spans a number of years, there is still no guarantee that he will have revealed the full range of his personality. Barber himself admits that those on their way to the presidency are likely "to respond more fully to external pressures and demands, to conform more closely to the expectations of those around them. The preliminary roles are all much more restrictive than the Presidency is, much more set by institutional requirements. One need only consider the legislative performance of Senators who became Presidents to see how contradictory and misleading the signs can be."[162]

Yet relative to the other approaches we have discussed, this one would appear to be the most promising. That it may not tell us all we need to know about a candidate's personality is no reason for abandoning it altogether. On the contrary, we should scrutinize the political careers of presidential contenders with far more care than we have shown in the past. Where scholars and journalists uncover behavior patterns that are a source of either concern or confidence, the results of their inquiry should be thoroughly reported. But this effort must be preceded by something else of equal importance—an attempt to better educate the public as to why personality is such an important factor in assessing presidential candidates.

★ NOTES

1. Fred Greenstein, *Personality and Politics* (Chicago: Markham, 1969), pp. 46–47.
2. James David Barber, *The Presidential Character: Predicting Performance in the White House,* 2d ed. (Englewood Cliffs, N.J.: Prentice Hall, 1972), pp. 7, 8, 445. Copyright © 1972 by James David Barber.
3. Ibid., pp. 12, 13, 95–97, 146, 172, 174, 206, 210, 211.
4. Cited in ibid., pp. 129, 130.
5. Ibid., p. 129.
6. Cited in Doris Kearns, *Lyndon Johnson and the American Dream* (New York: Harper & Row, 1976), p. 25. Copyright © 1976 by Doris Kearns. Reprinted by permission of Harper & Row, Publishers, Inc.
7. Ibid., p. 40.
8. Ibid., p. 33.
9. Ibid., p. 38.
10. Ibid., p. 40.
11. Cited in Barber, *Presidential Character,* p. 135.
12. Cited in Kearns, *Lyndon Johnson,* p. 44.

13. Eric Goldman, *The Tragedy of Lyndon Johnson* (New York: Knopf, 1968), p. 47.

14. Cited in Kearns, *Lyndon Johnson,* p. 209.

15. Booth Mooney, *LBJ: An Irreverent Chronicle* (New York: Crowell, 1976), pp. 112, 156, 157. Copyright © 1976 by Booth Mooney. Reprinted by permission of Thomas Y. Crowell, Inc. See also Kearns, *Lyndon Johnson,* p. 49; Michael Beschloss, ed., *Taking Charge: The Johnson White House Tapes, 1963–1964* (New York: Simon & Schuster, 1997), pp. 468–70.

16. Cited in Kearns, *Lyndon Johnson,* p. 65.

17. Lyndon Johnson, *The Vantage Point* (New York: Holt, Rinehart and Winston, 1971), pp. 46, 47.

18. Mooney, *LBJ,* p. 31.

19. Cited in Kearns, *Lyndon Johnson,* pp. 127, 128.

20. Mooney, *LBJ,* p. 101.

21. Ibid., p. 276.

22. Kearns, *Lyndon Johnson,* pp. 33, 167.

23. David Halberstam, *The Best and the Brightest* (New York: Random House, 1969), p. 648.

24. Cited in ibid., p. 526.

25. Nick Thimmesch, "The Abuse of Richard Nixon," *The Alternative* 9 (April 1976), 7.

26. Theodore White, *Breach of Faith* (New York: Atheneum, 1975), pp. 99, 100, 325.

27. David Wise, *The Politics of Lying* (New York: Vantage Books, 1973), pp. 60, 61. See also Arthur Schlesinger, Jr., *The Imperial Presidency* (Boston: Houghton Mifflin, 1973), p. 178.

28. Cited in Kearns, *Lyndon Johnson,* p. 282.

29. Halberstam, *Best and Brightest,* pp. 727, 736–38.

30. Mooney, *LBJ,* p. 27. See also Jack Valenti, *A Very Human President* (New York: Norton, 1975), p. 273.

31. Cited in Kearns, *Lyndon Johnson,* p. 253.

32. Ibid., p. 313.

33. Ibid., pp. 316, 317.

34. Halberstam, *Best and Brightest,* pp. 757, 758.

35. Cited in Barber, *Presidential Character,* p. 53.

36. Cited in Kearns, *Lyndon Johnson,* p. 317.

37. Ibid., p. 315.

38. Cited in David Abrahamsen, *Nixon vs. Nixon,* p. 50. Copyright © 1976 by David Abrahamsen. Reprinted with the permission of Hill and Wang (now a division of Farrar, Straus & Giroux, Inc.).

39. Ibid., p. 142.

40. Ibid., p. 91.

41. Cited in *New York Times,* August 10, 1974, p. 4. Copyright © 1974 by The New York Times Company. Reprinted by permission.

42. Earl Mazo and Stephen Hess, *Nixon: A Political Portrait* (New York: Popular Library, 1968), p. 10.

43. Cited in Bela Komitzer, *The Real Nixon: An Intimate Biography* (Chicago: Rand McNally, 1960), p. 79.

44. Cited in Abrahamsen, *Nixon vs. Nixon,* pp. 28, 110.

45. Ibid., p. 103.

46. Cited in Barber, *Presidential Character,* p. 409.

47. Cited in Abrahamsen, *Nixon vs. Nixon,* p. 116.

48. Ibid., p. 148.

49. Cited in Theodore White, *The Making of the President 1968* (New York: New American Library, 1969), p. 177.

50. Cited in Erwin Hargrove, *The Power of the Modern Presidency* (New York: Knopf, 1974), p. 47.

51. Cited in Abrahamsen, *Nixon vs. Nixon,* p. 83.

52. Cited in William Small, *Political Power and the Press* (New York: Norton, 1972), p. 126.

53. Excerpts from Richard M. Nixon, *Six Crises* (Doubleday, 1962) Copyright © 1962 by Richard M. Nixon. Reprinted by permission of Doubleday & Company, Inc.

54. Cited in Bruce Mazlish, *In Search of Nixon* (Baltimore: Penguin Books, 1972), p. 110.

55. Cited in *Washington Post,* May 26, 1977, p. A13.

56. Cited in *New York Times,* October 27, 1973, p. 14. Copyright ©1973 by The New York Times Company. Reprinted by permission.

57. Cited in *New York Times,* May 1, 1973, p. 31. Copyright © 1973 by The New York Times Company. Reprinted by permission.

58. Cited in Arthur Woodstone, *Nixon's Head* (New York: St. Martin's Press, 1972), p. 33.

59. Cited in Nixon, *Six Crises,* p. 394; see also Richard Nixon, *The Memoirs of Richard Nixon* (New York: Grosset & Dunlap, 1978), p. 110.

60. Cited in excerpt from Stewart Alsop, *Nixon and Rockefeller* (New York: Doubleday, 1960). Copyright © 1960 by Stewart Alsop. Reprinted by permission of Doubleday & Company, Inc.

61. Theodore White, *The Making of the President 1960* (New York: New American Library, 1961), p. 81.

62. Cited in Barber, *Presidential Character,* p. 374.

63. William Safire, *Before the Fall* (Garden City, N.Y.: Doubleday, 1975), p. 70. Copyright © 1975 by William Safire. Used by permission of Doubleday & Company, Inc.

64. H. R. Haldeman, with Joseph DiMona, *The Ends of Power* (New York: Times Books, 1978), p. 50. Reprinted by permission of The New York Times Book Company. Copyright © 1978 by H. R. Haldeman, with Joseph DiMona.

65. Cited in White, *Breach of Faith,* p. 64.

66. Cited in Safire, *Before the Fall,* p. 601.

67. See Nixon, *Memoirs,* pp. 646, 682.

68. White, *Breach of Faith,* p. 163.

69. Cited in Bob Woodward and Carl Bernstein, *The Final Days* (New York: Simon & Schuster, 1976), p. 424.

70. Cited in *New York Times,* August 10, 1974, p. 4. Copyright © 1974 by The New York Times Company. Reprinted by permission.

71. Cited in *Washington Post,* August 9, 1979, p. D3.

72. Cited in White, *Breach of Faith,* p. 63.

73. Cited in Fred Greenstein, "A President Is Forced to Resign: Watergate, White House Organization, and Nixon's Personality," in Allan Sindler, ed., *America in the Seventies: Problems, Policies, and Politics* (Boston: Little, Brown, 1977), pp. 89, 90.

74. Cited in J. Anthony Lukas, *Nightmare: The Underside of the Nixon Years* (New York: Viking Press, 1976), p. 26.

75. Cited in Haldeman, *Ends of Power,* p. 19.

76. Gerald Gold, ed., *The White House Transcripts* (New York: Bantam Books, 1974), p. 63.

77. Cited in Woodward and Bernstein, *Final Days,* p. 88.

78. Cited in Charles Colson, *Born Again* (Lincoln, Va.: Chosen Books, 1976), p. 72. Copyright © 1976. Published by Chosen Books Publishing Co., Ltd., Lincoln, Virginia 22078. Used by permission.

79. Barber, *Presidential Character,* p. 387.

80. Richard Nixon, the Nixon-Frost interviews, 1977. By permission of Syndicast Services.

81. *New York Times,* October 27, 1973, p. 14. Copyright © 1973 by The New York Times Company. Reprinted by permission.

82. Richard Nixon, the Nixon-Frost interviews, 1977. By permission of Syndicast Services.

83. Cited in Frank Freidel, *Franklin D. Roosevelt: The Apprenticeship* (Boston: Little, Brown, 1952), p. 23.

84. Cited in Erwin Hargrove, *Presidential Leadership: Personality and Political Style* (London: Macmillan, 1966), p. 55.

85. Cited in Barber, *Presidential Character,* p. 218.

86. Cited in Allen Churchill, *The Roosevelts* (New York: Harper & Row, 1965), p. 180.

87. Cited in Barber, *Presidential Character,* p. 225.

88. Ibid., p. 230.

89. Ibid., p. 227.

90. Cited in Frances Perkins, *The Roosevelt I Knew* (New York: Viking Press, 1956), p. 21.

91. Cited in James MacGregor Burns, *Roosevelt: The Lion and the Fox* (New York: Harcourt Brace Jovanovich, 1956), p. 348.

92. Richard Neustadt, *Presidential Power,* 1st ed. (New York: Wiley, 1960), p. 162.

93. Cited in Arthur Schlesinger, Jr., "The Dynamics of Decision," in Aaron Wildavsky, ed., *The Presidency* (Boston: Little, Brown, 1969), p. 139.

94. Ibid., pp. 134–38.

95. Cited in Barber, *Presidential Character,* p. 234.

96. Burns, *Roosevelt: The Lion and the Fox,* p. 348.

97. Ibid., p. 314.

98. Barber, *Presidential Character,* p. 245.

99. Cited in Schlesinger, "Dynamics of Decision," p. 139.

100. *Washington Post,* Special Supplement, "Inauguration '81," January 20, 1981, p. 8.

101. Cited in Lou Cannon, *Reagan* (New York: Putnam, 1982), p. 22.

102. Ibid., pp. 24, 25, 27, 28.

103. Ibid., p. 27.

104. Ibid., pp. 26, 32.

105. Ibid., p. 30.

106. Ibid., pp. 38, 40.

107. Ibid., pp. 35, 36.

108. Ronnie Dugger, *On Reagan: The Man and His Presidency* (New York: McGraw-Hill, 1983), p. 15.

109. Ibid., p. 269.

110. Cannon, *Reagan,* p. 96.

111. James David Barber, *The Presidential Character: Predicting Performance in the White House,* 3d ed. (Englewood Cliffs, N.J.: Prentice Hall, 1985), p. 472.

112. Robert Dallek, *Ronald Reagan: The Politics of Symbolism* (Cambridge, Mass.: Harvard University Press, 1984), p. 20.

113. Cannon, *Reagan,* p. 102.

114. Cited in ibid., p. 119.

115. Ibid., pp. 120, 121.

116. Jane Mayer and Doyle McManus, *Landslide* (Boston: Houghton Mifflin, 1988), p. 10.

117. Cannon, *Reagan,* p. 126.

118. Dallek, *Ronald Reagan: The Politics of Symbolism,* p. 12; see also Bill Boyarsky, *Ronald Reagan: His Life and Rise to the Presidency* (New York: Random House, 1981), p. 11.

119. Cannon, *Reagan,* p. 158.

120. Ibid., p. 239.

121. Barber, *Presidential Character,* 3rd ed., p. 491.

122. Mayer and McManus, *Landslide,* p. 7.

123. Cannon, *Reagan,* p. 304.

124. Mayer and McManus, *Landslide,* pp. 27, 28.

125. Cited in Hedrick Smith, "Taking Charge of Congress," *New York Times Magazine,* August 9, 1981, p. 47.

126. See Mark Green and Gail MacColl, *There He Goes Again: Ronald Reagan's Reign of Error* (New York: Pantheon Books, 1983).

127. See, for example, *Washington Post,* January 6, 1986, p. A2; *National Journal,* June 13, 1987, p. 1538.

128. Barber, *Presidential Character,* 2d ed., p. 205.

129. Hedrick Smith, *The Power Game* (New York: Random House, 1988), p. 304.

130. Donald Regan, *For the Record* (New York: Harcourt Brace Jovanovich, 1988), p. 250.

131. *Time,* April 7, 1986, p. 27.

132. Bernard Weinraub, "The Reagan Legacy," *New York Times Magazine,* June 22, 1986, p. 14; see also Regan, *For the Record,* p. 271.

133. Barber, *Presidential Character,* 3rd ed., p. 150.

134. Cited in Steven Weisman, "Magic Prevail?" *New York Times Magazine,* April 29, 1984, p. 46.

135. Weinraub, "The Reagan Legacy," p. 20.

136. Barber, *Presidential Character,* 3rd ed., p. 9.

137. Cited in Frank van der Linden, *The Real Reagan* (New York: William Morrow, 1981), p. 21.

138. Mayer and McManus, *Landslide,* p. 27.

139. Cannon, *Reagan,* p. 305.

140. Cited in *Washington Post,* Special Supplement, "Inauguration '81," p. 8.

141. Smith, *The Power Game,* p. 580.

142. *Washington Post,* December 8, 1986, p. A15.

143. Mayer and McManus, *Landslide,* p. 160.

144. U.S. Congress, U.S. Senate Committee on Secret Military Assistance to Iran and the Nicaraguan Opposition, U.S. House of Representatives Select Committee to Investigate Covert Arms Transactions with Iran, *Report of Congressional Committees Investigating the Iran-Contra Affair,* Senate Report No. 100–216, House Report No. 100–433, 100th Cong., 1st sess., 1987, pp. 227, 257, 258.

145. Cited in *Washington Post,* July 16, 1987, p. A17.

146. Joseph Califano, *A Presidential Nation* (New York: Norton, 1975), pp. 135, 263.

147. Cited in *New York Times,* October 23, 1977, p. 36. Copyright © 1977 by The New York Times Company. Reprinted by permission.

148. Betty Glad, *Jimmy Carter: In Search of the Great White House* (New York: Norton, 1980), p. 494.

149. Bruce Mazlish and Edwin Diamond, *Jimmy Carter: An Interpretive Biography* (New York: Simon & Schuster, 1979), p. 254.

150. Jules Witcover, *Marathon* (New York: Viking Press, 1977), p. 143.

151. Haynes Johnson, *In the Absence of Power: Governing America* (New York: Viking Press, 1980), p. 13.

152. Gary Fink, *Prelude to the Presidency* (Westport, Conn.: Greenwood Press, 1980), p. 172; Glad, *Jimmy Carter,* p. 168.

153. Mazlish and Diamond, *Jimmy Carter,* p. 248; Glad, *Jimmy Carter,* p. 498; Fink, *Prelude to the Presidency,* p. 178.

154. Cited in Johnson, *In the Absence of Power,* p. 282.

155. James Fallows, "The Passionless Presidency," *Atlantic* (May 1979), p. 42.

156. Cited in Johnson, *In the Absence of Power,* p. 300.

157. James Barber, "President Nixon and Richard Nixon: Character Trap." Reprinted from *Psychology Today Magazine,* October 1974, p. 118. Copyright © 1974 by Ziff-Davis Publishing Company.

158. Richard Donley and David Winter, "Measuring the Motives of Public Figures at a Distance: An Exploratory Study of American Presidents," *Behavioral Science* 15 (May 1970), 227–36.

159. Cited in Alan Elms, *Personality in Politics* (New York: Harcourt Brace Jovanovich, 1976), p. 174.

160. Ibid., pp. 173–74.

161. Barber, "President Nixon and Richard Nixon," p. 113.

162. Barber, *Presidential Character,* 2d ed., p. 99.

Presidential Leadership

In a society as competitive as our own, it is not surprising that considerable effort is expended in evaluating performance. We face such evaluation throughout our years of schooling. We face it again as we pursue our careers. While these assessments take place on a daily basis as we interact with those around us, more formalized mechanisms will be used periodically to evaluate our on-the-job performance. Therefore, it comes as no surprise that public officials face a similar scrutiny. The importance and visibility of the presidency, however, make the evaluation process far more intense and persistent. Almost from the day the president assumes office, newspapers, magazines, and periodicals carry articles and editorials that seek to assess whether the president is leading well or poorly. Moreover, in addition to assessments by the journalistic and scholarly communities, George Gallup, Louis Harris, and the television network pollsters provide the nation with almost monthly reports on what kind of job the American public thinks the president is doing. Should a president choose to seek a second term, his performance will once again be subject to the judgment of the American people. Nor does the evaluation process end when his tenure in office is terminated. On the contrary, books and articles then start to appear, which seek to assess his overall performance or some aspect of it. To take just one example, within three years after Kennedy's assassination, some eight books were published on his presidency. Moreover, as both the passage of time and new information have presumably brought a better perspective, a second and third generation of books have been published on the assassinated president. These include Henry Fairlie, *The Kennedy Promise* (1972); Lewis Paper, *The Promise and the Performance* (1975); Bruce Miroff, *Pragmatic Illusions* (1976); Joan and Clay Blair, Jr., *The Search for JFK* (1976); Gary Wills, *The Kennedy Imprisonment* (1982); Herbert S. Parmet, *JFK: The Presidency of John F. Kennedy* (1983); Thomas Reeves, *A Question of Character* (1991); Irving Bernstein, *Promises Kept* (1991); Richard Reeves, *John Kennedy* (1993); and Seymour Hersh, *The Dark Side of Camelot* (1997). No doubt there will continue to be books written on Kennedy, as well as on other past presidents, for the judgment of history is an ongoing process.

The evaluation of presidents inevitably leads to a comparison of performances. Indeed, considerable discussion and debate have been devoted to identifying the "great" and "not so great" presidents in our history. Some scholars have written on the subject, and others have polled their fellow academicians to learn what ranking they gave to the men who have occupied the White House. Certainly the most notable efforts to rate presidents were the polls conducted by historian Arthur Schlesinger, Sr. (see Table 10-1). In his 1948 poll, he surveyed fifty-five outstanding authorities on American history. He conducted another poll in 1962, this time surveying some seventy-five persons representing a variety of fields, including historians, political scientists, and journalists. As to the standards by which presidents were to be judged, Schlesinger specified only one—performance while in office.

As Table 10-1 indicates, the interest in ranking presidents continues unabated. In 1970, for example, Gary Maranell and Richard Dodder sought the judgments of 571 historians, asking them to rate our presidents on the basis of (1) accomplishment, (2) strength in shaping government and events, (3) an active or passive approach to their administrations, (4) idealism, and (5) flexibility. On the heels of this survey came another one in 1972 by Malcolm Parsons, who asked 146 economists and 120 political scientists to rate presidents from Franklin Roosevelt to Nixon on the basis of their (1) idealism, (2) flexibility, (3) activism, and (4) accomplishment. His purpose was to determine whether political scientists as a group differed from economists in their rankings of these five presidents and to see whether the ideological orientation of the respondents influenced their evaluations. In 1975, a random sample of the American public got a chance to express their views when George Gallup asked what three presidents they considered to be the greatest. This poll was followed six years later by a *Chicago Tribune* poll in which the paper's White House correspondent, Stephen Neal, queried 49 historians and political scholars on whom they considered to be our ten greatest and ten worst presidents. Neal, now writing for the *Chicago Sun-Times,* repeated the exercise in 1995, this time asking fifty-eight presidential scholars to rate presidents on political leadership, foreign policy, domestic policy, character, and impact on history. Certainly the most ambitious and careful inquiry into the ranking of presidents was a lengthy study in 1983 by Robert Murray and Tim Blessing in which they asked nearly 900 historians to respond to 125 questions entailing 400 separate responses. These questions were targeted not only at presidents and the criteria for rating them; they were also designed to elicit information about the historians themselves, in order to determine whether their own backgrounds and subject matter specialities affected their ranking of presidents.

As we moved through the last decade of the century, there were two additional studies of note. In 1996, the *New York Times* asked historian Arthur Schlesinger, Jr., to replicate the polls conducted by his father in 1948 and 1962. He asked a group (thirty-two) of mostly scholars to rate the presidents, on the very general criterion of "performance in office." While Jefferson and Wilson dropped slightly, the results otherwise differ very little from the 1962 poll, with the notable exception of Eisenhower, who climbs from twentieth to tenth. The most recent entry into the presidential rating game comes from William Ridings and Stuart McIver who asked 917 scholars, public officials, political activists, and attorneys to rate presidents along five dimensions—leadership qualities, accomplishments and crisis management, political skills, appointments, and character and integrity. No doubt, the fascination with judging and comparing presidents will remain with us.

TABLE 10-1 Evaluations of Presidential Performance

Schlesinger Poll 1948	Schlesinger Poll 1962	Maranell-Dodder Poll 1970	Gallup Poll 1975	U.S. Historical Society Poll 1977	Chicago Tribune Poll 1982	Murray-Blessing Poll 1983	Chicago Sun-Times Poll 1995	Schlesinger, Jr. Poll 1996*	Ridings-McIver Poll 1997
Great	*Great*	*Overall Prestige*	*What Three U.S. Presidents Do You Regard as the Greatest?* (%)	*Ten Greatest Presidents* Votes	*Ten Greatest Presidents*	*Great*	*Ten Best Presidents*	*Great*	
(1) Lincoln	(1) Lincoln	(1) Lincoln	Kennedy 52	Lincoln 85	(1) Lincoln	Lincoln	(1) Lincoln	(1) Lincoln	(1) Lincoln
(2) Washington	(2) Washington	(2) Washington	Lincoln 49	Washington 84	(2) Washington	F. Roosevelt	(2) F. Roosevelt	(2) Washington	(2) F. Roosevelt
(3) F. Roosevelt	(3) F. Roosevelt	(3) F. Roosevelt	F. Roosevelt 45	F. Roosevelt 81	(3) F. Roosevelt	Washington	(3) Washington	(3) F. Roosevelt	(3) Washington
(4) Wilson	(4) Wilson	(4) Jefferson	Truman 37	Jefferson 79	(4) T. Roosevelt	Jefferson	(4) T. Roosevelt	*Near-Great* (4) Jefferson	(4) Jefferson
(5) Jefferson	(5) Jefferson	(5) T. Roosevelt	Washington 25	T. Roosevelt 79	(5) Jefferson	*Near-Great* T. Roosevelt	(5) Jefferson	(5) Jackson	(5) T. Roosevelt
(6) Jackson	*Near-Great* (6) Jackson	(6) Wilson	Eisenhower 24	Wilson 74	(6) Wilson	Wilson	(6) Truman	(6) T. Roosevelt	(6) Wilson
Near-Great (7) T. Roosevelt	(7) T. Roosevelt	(7) Truman	T. Roosevelt 9	Jackson 74	(7) Jackson	Jackson	(7) Wilson	(7) Wilson	(7) Truman
(8) Cleveland	(8) Polk	(8) Jackson	L. Johnson 9	Truman 64	(8) Truman	Truman	(8) Jackson	(8) Truman	(8) Jackson
(9) J. Adams	(9) Truman	(9) Kennedy	Jefferson 8	Polk 38	(9) Eisenhower	*Above Average* J. Adams	(9) Eisenhower	(9) Polk	(9) Eisenhower
(10) Polk	(10) J. Adams Cleveland	(10) J. Adams	Wilson 5	J. Adams 35	(10) Polk	L. Johnson	(10) Reagan	*High Average* (10) Eisenhower	(10) Madison
Average (11) J.Q. Adams	*Average* (11) Madison	(11) Polk	Nixon 9	L. Johnson 24	*Ten Worst Presidents (with Worst No. 1)* (1) Harding	Eisenhower	*Ten Worst Presidents (with Worst No. 1)* (1) Grant	(11) J. Adams	(11) Polk
(12) Monroe	(12) J.Q. Adams	(12) Cleveland	All others 9	Cleveland 21	(2) Nixon	Polk	(2) Tyler	(12) Kennedy	(12) L. Johnson
(13) Hayes	(13) Hayes	(13) Madison	Don't know 3	Kennedy 19	(3) Buchanan	Kennedy	(3) Harrison	(13) Cleveland	(13) Monroe
(14) Madison	(14) McKinley	(14) Monroe		Madison 16	(4) Pierce	Madison	(4) Taylor	(14) L. Johnson	(14) J. Adams
(15) Van Buren	(15) Taft	(15) J.Q. Adams		J.Q. Adams 14	(5) Grant	Monroe	(5) Fillmore	(15) Monroe	(15) Kennedy
(16) Taft	(16) Van Buren	(16) L. Johnson		Eisenhower 14	(6) Fillmore	J.Q. Adams	(6) Arthur	(16) McKinley	(16) Cleveland
(17) Arthur	(17) Monroe	(17) Taft		Monroe 7	(7) A. Johnson	Cleveland	(7) A. Johnson	*Average* (17) Madison	(17) McKinley
(18) McKinley	(18) Hoover	(18) Hoover		Hoover 6	(8) Coolidge	*Average* McKinley	(8) Pierce	(18) J.Q. Adams	(18) J.Q. Adams
(19) A. Johnson	(19) Harrison	(19) Eisenhower		McKinley 4	(9) Tyler	Taft	(9) Buchanan	(19) Harrison	(19) Carter
(20) Hoover	(20) Arthur Eisenhower	(20) A. Johnson		Van Buren 2	(10) Carter	Van Buren	(10) Harding	(20) Clinton	(20) Taft
(21) Harrison	(21) A. Johnson	(21) Van Buren		Arthur 2		Hoover		(21) Van Buren	(21) Van Buren
		(22) McKinley		Tyler 1					(22) Bush
		(23) Arthur		Buchanan 1					(23) Clinton
		(24) Hayes		Grant 1					(24) Hoover
		(25) Tyler		Hayes 1					(25) Hayes
		(26) Harrison							(26) Reagan
									(27) Ford
									(28) Arthur

Below Average
(22) Tyler
(23) Coolidge
(24) Fillmore
(25) Taylor
(26) Buchanan
(27) Pierce

Failure
(28) Grant
(29) Harding

Below Average
(22) Taylor
(23) Tyler
(24) Fillmore
(25) Coolidge
(26) Pierce
(27) Buchanan

Failure
(28) Grant
(29) Harding

(27) Taylor
(28) Coolidge
(29) Fillmore
(30) Buchanan
(31) Pierce
(32) Grant
(33) Harding
(W. Harrison and Garfield not included due to brevity of tenure)

Taft	1
Coolidge	1
Nixon	0
W. Harrison	0
Taylor	0
Fillmore	0
Pierce	0
A. Johnson	0
Garfield	0
B. Harrison	0
Harding	0
Ford	0

Hayes
Arthur
Ford
Carter
B. Harrison

Below Average
Taylor
Fillmore
Coolidge
Pierce

Failures
A. Johnson
Buchanan
Nixon
Grant
Harding

Not Rated
Reagan
W. H. Harrison
Garfield

(22) Taft
(23) Hayes
(24) Bush
(25) Reagan
(26) Arthur
(27) Carter
(28) Ford

Below Average
(29) Taylor
(30) Coolidge
(31) Fillmore
(32) Tyler

Failure
(33) Pierce
(34) Grant
(35) Hoover
(36) Nixon
(37) A. Johnson
(38) Buchanan
(39) Harding

(29) Taylor
(30) Garfield
(31) B. Harrison
(32) Nixon
(33) Coolidge
(34) Tyler
(35) W. Harrison
(36) Fillmore
(37) Pierce
(38) Grant
(39) A. Johnson
(40) Buchanan
(41) Harding

*William Harrison and James Garfield not rated.

Sources: Arthur Schlesinger, Sr., "The U.S. Presidents," *Life* (November 1, 1948), p. 65, *Life Magazine*, © 1948 Time Inc. Reprinted with permission; Arthur Schlesinger, Sr., "Our Presidents: A Rating by 75 Historians," *New York Times Magazine*, July 29, 1962, pp. 12ff.; Gary Maranell and Richard Dodder, "Political Orientation and Evaluation of Presidential Prestige: A Study of American Historians," *Social Science Quarterly* 51 (September 1970), 418; *The Gallup Opinion Index*, February 1976, pp. 14, 15; U.S. Historical Society provided the author with results of its survey; *Chicago Tribune Magazine*, January 10, 1982, p. 9; Robert Murray and Tim Blessing, "The Presidential Performance Study: A Progress Report," *Journal of American History* 70 (December 1983), 540, 541; *Chicago Sun-Times*, November 19, 1995, pp. 30, 31; Arthur M. Schlesinger, Jr., "The Ultimate Approval Rating," *New York Times Magazine*, December 15, 1996, pp. 48, 49; William Ridings and Stuart McIver, *Rating the Presidents* (Secaucus, N.J.: Citadel Press, 1997), p. XI.

EVALUATING PRESIDENTIAL LEADERSHIP: THE PROBLEMS

If evaluating presidential performance is something we all do, laypeople and scholars alike, it is also important to bear in mind that such an exercise is not as easy as it might appear, for one must confront the difficult question of how performance is to be measured. In response to just such a question, one student of the presidency remarked that "in the final analysis the basic yardstick is the achievement of that individual and his (or her) administration."[1] Although few would dispute this statement, we are still faced with a variety of factors that complicate the task of determining *what constitutes achievement*. Let us examine some of these factors more closely.

Achievement Is in the Eye of the Beholder

All of us carry around a cargo of values, beliefs, and orientations that influence our perceptions of the world around us. These values and beliefs determine the yardsticks by which we choose to measure presidents. For example, in their study of how 571 historians ranked presidents, Maranell and Dodder found that liberal historians valued *flexibility and idealism* in presidents, whereas conservative historians did not.[2] To take another example, Clinton Rossiter suggests that one of the standards for assessing presidential greatness must be a president's philosophy of presidential power. He argues that effective leadership is, in part, dependent upon an activist view of presidential power: "Indeed, if he is not widely and persistently accused in his own time of 'subverting the Constitution,' he may as well forget about being judged a truly eminent man by future generations."[3] Some would readily share Rossiter's expansive view of presidential power. Others, however, would reject it as too permissive and instead concur with President Taft, who maintained that the president could exercise only those powers specifically granted or reasonably implied to him: "There is no undefined residuum of power which he can exercise because it seems to him to be in the public interest." Still others may not be philosophically opposed to an expansive view of presidential power as such, so long as it is used for purposes consistent with their own values and beliefs. No doubt many of those who are opposed to the spending of vast sums of money on social welfare programs applauded Nixon's vigorous use of the impoundment power to cut back on such programs. On the other hand, those who feel that the federal government has an obligation to look after the less-well-off parts of the population surely saw Nixon's bold impoundments as callous and unwarranted. In short, what one sees depends to a considerable extent upon where one stands.

The Situational Problem

The task of evaluating presidential leadership is further complicated by the fact that our presidents have not all entered the White House confronting the same set of circumstances, opportunities, and expectations. On the contrary, if one views the presidency in a broad time frame, it is clear that during most of this century presidents have had to function in an environment decidedly different from that faced by presidents in the eighteenth and nineteenth centuries. Our earlier presidents did not have to contend with a large and complex federal bureaucracy or with such a large, culturally diverse, and urbanized population. Moreover, since they served at a time when the role of the federal government was minimal, public expectations regarding the role of the president were limited also. As we have gradually looked more and more to the federal government to solve the nation's economic and social problems, inevitably we have also expected more of our presidents in these areas. Our earlier presidents likewise faced a very different international environment. The United States had not yet had thrust upon it the responsibility of leading the free world; our economic and security interests were not yet so intimately tied to those of other nations; and, finally, neither we nor any potential adversary had the capacity to incinerate the planet with nuclear weapons.

If the presidential environment varies over centuries, it may also be said to vary from one presidency to the next. George Washington, for example, was faced with the unique task of starting a newly constituted government off on the right foot. In presiding over a divided nation, Abraham Lincoln confronted the greatest internal crisis in the history of our republic. Woodrow Wilson was the first president to take the nation into a world war. Franklin Roosevelt had to guide the country during another world war abroad as well as lead us through an unprecedented economic crisis at home. Truman had to ponder not only the future of the European nations devastated by the war, but also the use of a weapon with a destructive capacity qualitatively different from anything the world had ever known. Eisenhower presided over the nation at a time when we no longer had a monopoly on nuclear weapons. Rather, the new reality of international politics was that the Soviet Union had the capacity to inflict devastating damage upon the United States and its allies. Lyndon Johnson took over the presidency at a time of rising expectations among blacks and at a time when urban decay had reached crisis proportions. His successor had to find a way to get us out of what had become the most unpopular war in our history, as well as try to bind up the social wounds caused by it. Gerald Ford came into office without having been chosen by a national constituency, and both he and his successor had to confront two problems heretofore unknown to presidents—stagflation and an energy crisis. Reagan and Bush, meanwhile, faced unprecedented budget deficits; and Bush and Clinton had to feel their way in an international environment no longer defined in terms of the Cold War.

In judging presidential performance, it may be argued that we must take into consideration not only the nature of the times in which a given president served, but also the political constraints—legal and otherwise—under which he governed. For example, given the fact that a president customarily enjoys a decided advantage by having his own party in control of Congress, should we not expect more from presidents who enjoy this advantage? Likewise, since 1951 all presidents have labored under the Twenty-Second Amendment, which limits a president to only two terms. As noted in Chapter 3, this limitation undoubtedly has a significant effect upon the president's political leverage as he moves through his second four years. Given this fact, we may well decide that expectations should be higher for those presidents who did not labor under this restriction.

One final aspect of the situational problem deserves mention here. To what extent is our evaluation of a president's performance conditioned by the momentous nature of the times in which he served? Clinton Rossiter states the answer bluntly: "A man cannot possibly be judged a great President unless he holds office in great times. . . . This standard may work unfairly on Presidents who live under sunny skies, but that is the way that history is written."[4] Certainly the available evidence gives some credence to this view. Note that of the top five presidents appearing in each of the polls reproduced in Table 10-1, a majority served during times of great moment. In the case of Washington, it was his fate to be the first to lead the country under a wholly new set of constitutional arrangements. Lincoln, Wilson, Franklin Roosevelt, and Truman led the nation in wartime. Yet, although governing during a period of great crisis enhances the chances of being judged a great leader, it does not ensure it. James Madison, for example, presided over the nation during the War of 1812, and yet his performance in office has generally been appraised as mediocre. Nor did Herbert Hoover benefit from the fact that he occupied the presidency during the greatest economic crisis in our history. Quite the contrary. He has been roundly criticized for his failure to respond to the crisis. Great times only provide the opportunity for leadership. The wherewithal necessary to meet such challenges must come from the person in the White House.

Of course, our discussion here presumes that the greatest test of leadership comes during times of crisis. This presumption is open to some question. Indeed, we may have every right to expect greater things from the president who serves under "dark" as opposed to "sunny" skies. By their very nature, great crises bind the country and the government together behind the president, thereby greatly facilitating his ability to act. Both Abraham Lincoln and Franklin Roosevelt took some extraordinary initiatives in meeting their respective crises. Some were of doubtful constitutionality, and, in the case of Lincoln, some were clearly unconstitutional. But all had the support of both the public and Congress. In more tranquil times, however, mobilizing support is not so easily accomplished. To do so, therefore, may require that a president be even more skilled and resourceful in seeking to unite Congress and the public behind his purposes.

The Problem of Perspective

Another factor that complicates the task of evaluating presidential performance is *time*. With its passage inevitably comes the uncovering of new information that may alter judgments of a presidency in either a favorable or an unfavorable direction. Assessments of John Kennedy's performance provide one of the most dramatic examples of this. The appraisals that appeared not long after his death were, for the most part, highly favorable. In the last several years, however, the glitter surrounding Kennedy has been tarnished by a series of revelations. Some concerned his personal life. Others related to certain government activities undertaken during his stewardship: for example, the tapping of Martin Luther King's telephone by the FBI, and the CIA's attempt to assassinate Patrice Lumumba, as well as its use of Mafia connections in an effort to assassinate Fidel Castro. Even if it has not been firmly established that Kennedy was aware of such activities, the fact is he should have been. These revelations, coupled with claims that the Kennedy years were long on style and short on substance, have led even one of his most ardent admirers to acknowledge "there's no doubt about it: the idea that Kennedy was a minor figure of limited achievement is widely held today and can be supported in a depth not possible in 1964."[5] Reflecting this changed assessment, Kennedy dropped from a rating of ninth in 1970 to nineteenth in a 1977 poll (see Table 10-1). In the most recent presidential rating, however, his reputation has enjoyed a mild resurgence, finishing twelfth (1996) and fifteenth (1997), respectively, in the Schlesinger, Jr. and Rydings-McIver polls (see Table 10-1).

If the uncovering of new information has reduced the stature of Kennedy, it has had the opposite effect on assessments of Eisenhower. Previously, though he was admired for his integrity, most scholars viewed Ike as an inarticulate, passive president, who left most major policy decisions to his cabinet members. Archival materials made available to scholars in the mid-1970s, however, reveal a decidedly more forceful and calculating leader. Among other things, they show a president who clearly called the signals on the direction of foreign and domestic policy; who, in the interest of preserving his own personal popularity, intentionally let his cabinet members take the lead in articulating administration policies so that any resulting controversy would be directed at them rather than him; and who deliberately uttered incoherent statements to the press in order to befuddle his listeners, believing as he did that on some matters the less said the better.[6]

In addition to new information, our initial perspective on a given presidency may also be altered by intervening events. Thus, when viewed in the context of the Watergate squalor, or when compared with the imperial tones that characterized the Johnson and Nixon presidencies, the openness and simplicity of Truman and Eisenhower assume greater significance. The Vietnam War provides another example of an event that has altered our perspective on the past. The nation was much moved by President Kennedy's inaugural address, in which he made a seemingly boundless commitment to the defense of freedom: "Let every nation know, whether it wishes us well or ill, that we shall pay any price, bear any burden, meet any hardship, support any friend, oppose any foe, in order to assure the survival and the success of liberty. This much we pledge—and more." This policy, which was responsible for our initial involvement in Vietnam under the Kennedy administration, now appears excessive, to say the least.

On the other hand, the protracted war in Vietnam appears to have brought some luster to the Eisenhower presidency. When the French suffered a resounding defeat at the hands of the North Vietnamese in 1954, Eisenhower was under considerable pressure from his advisers to commit American forces to the area. Keenly aware, however, of how large a commitment would be necessary to do the job, Ike decided against any U.S. involvement. Although in the past this decision never loomed large among his accomplishments, in light of our subsequent experience in Southeast Asia it now takes on considerably greater meaning. Indeed, in commenting on the reassessment of Eisenhower, one commentator points out that we have only recently begun to appreciate his astuteness in foreign affairs: "We were at war when he came to office, and six months later we were out of it, and we did not enter another war during his tenure. . . . Eight years of Eisenhower: seven and a half of peace. Ten years of Kennedy, Johnson, Nixon: almost ten solid years of war."[7]

The impact of new information and intervening events on Eisenhower's fortunes in the presidential rankings has been dramatic. Finishing no better than twentieth in the 1962 Schlesinger poll, in the three most recent scholarly rankings Ike moves into the top ten among presidents (see Table 10-1). No other president has improved his ranking so dramatically.

The Matter of Unanticipated Consequences

If a given presidential decision proves to be an especially wise one, we are inclined to chalk it up as a plus for his performance record, regardless of what a president's motives might have been at the time the decision was made. The purchase of Alaska in 1867 may serve as an illustration of this. At the initiative of Secretary of State William Seward, President Andrew Johnson authorized the purchase of Alaska from the Russians for the sum of $7.2 million. At the time this decision was made and for years afterward, it was generally viewed as a waste of money. Indeed, in many quarters the Alaskan territory was derisively characterized by such expressions as "Seward's Icebox" and "Johnson's Polar Bear Garden." Quite obviously, no one would share this assessment nowadays, given the events that have intervened since then. On the contrary, in the words of historian Thomas Bailey, "Now that Alaska has panned out with gold, fish, and furs, and has become a state of enormous economic and strategic value, we think more highly of Andrew Johnson's floundering administration for having brought off the coup. It will probably stand as the most significant single act of the ex-tailor's troubled four years, even though it was conceived and carried through by his expansionist Secretary of State."[8] Yet one may well question whether Johnson should reap the praise for such a decision if only because, as Bailey implies, Seward originated the proposal and was largely responsible for engineering its approval by Congress. But there is an even more fundamental consideration, namely, that the acquisition of Alaska has proven *most* beneficial for reasons that neither Johnson nor Seward could have anticipated. Although Seward was aware of some of Alaska's resources, his primary motive for the purchase was to allow the United States to develop its commerce on the Pacific Ocean. As he once remarked, "Japan, China, and Australia are . . . commercially bound to the American Pacific coast"; on another occasion, he noted that "the extension of American invention and enterprise into Japan, China, Australia, and India are worthy of consideration equally with international commerce between the United States and the countries of Western Europe."[9] No one at that time could have known that Alaska housed vast oil reserves; nor, more important, could they have known that Russia—with whom we enjoyed cordial relations at the time—would one day constitute our major adversary on the international stage.

While we may well want to credit presidents for decisions that demonstrate a sense of vision and foresight, we must also be careful to distinguish such decisions from those that prove highly beneficial largely because of fortuitous circumstance.

Achievement Versus Agenda Setting

In assessing presidential performance, we must also consider the question of whether presidents are to be given credit only for what they accomplished or whether we are also to recognize them for what they *tried* to accomplish. In 1948, for example, President Truman addressed the Democratic National Convention and proclaimed that it was time for the government to correct the injustices that had for so long been inflicted upon blacks. Accordingly, he announced that he would call Congress into special session to consider civil rights legislation. No such legislation was ever passed by Congress, but Truman nevertheless had begun the process of elevating into the public mind an issue that had long been ignored by his predecessors. Moreover, he did so not only by calling for legislation but also by creating a Commission on Civil Rights and issuing an executive order calling for the desegregation of the armed forces.

Civil rights legislation was passed in 1957 and 1960, but it was not the result of vigorous presidential leadership. Indeed, active presidential involvement in civil rights did not come again until the presidency of John Kennedy. Although he trod gingerly on the civil rights issue at first, in the spring of 1963 Kennedy introduced into Congress the most sweeping civil rights bill to date and threw the full weight of the presidency behind it. Yet at the time of his death, Kennedy had still not succeeded in getting his civil rights legislation passed; nor, for that matter, had he been successful in gaining passage of other important pieces of his New Frontier legislation—Medicare, for example. It took instead the subtle political skills of Lyndon Johnson to engineer congressional approval of civil rights legislation, Medicare, and several other Kennedy programs. No doubt Johnson must be given credit for his ability to get things done. But is Kennedy to receive no recognition merely because he failed where Johnson succeeded? Some will surely argue that credit is also due those presidents who identify certain crucial issues and raise them to the level of national visibility, thereby compelling the nation to take notice of them. Even though Kennedy was unsuccessful in realizing his goals in such areas as civil rights and health care, he did succeed in placing these issues on the national agenda. Had he not done so, the needed legislation in these areas may well have come even later.

The Matter of Who Gets Credit

Given the fact that the presidency constitutes the focal point of our political system, we have a tendency to identify a given president with whatever successes or failures may have occurred during his tenure in office. In doing so, we may be making judgments about presidents that, in some instances, are either overly generous or unduly harsh. We should not, for example, give credit for an accomplishment that was realized despite a president rather than because of him. In this connection, it is worth noting that the Reconstruction Finance Corporation, though created during the final year of the Hoover administration, was nevertheless strongly opposed by Hoover himself. Similarly, although the Federal Deposit Insurance Corporation is generally regarded as one of the major accomplishments of Franklin Roosevelt's administration, the fact is he came out against the legislation.[10]

There may be other accomplishments realized during a given president's tenure that, though not necessarily opposed by him, nevertheless were realized for reasons having very little to do with his own leadership. Thus, while it so happens that we landed a man on the moon during the presidency of Richard Nixon, he scarcely deserves any of the credit for such an achievement. Rather, if there is any recognition to be given, it must go to President Kennedy who, back in 1961, committed the resources of the nation to the goal of putting a man on the moon by the end of the decade. Similarly, we generally credit Franklin Roosevelt with pulling us out of the greatest economic crisis in our history, and yet his own programs had relatively little to do with it. To be sure, the economy did improve in 1935 and 1936, but this was only temporary. By 1937, the unemployment rate had reached 20 percent, and the index of business activity was down by thirty-five percentage points—the most rapid decline ever recorded. The major factor ultimately responsible for lifting us out of the economic doldrums was our entry into the Second World War.[11] All of this is not to say that Roosevelt deserves no credit for his efforts. His programs may not have succeeded in taking us out of the depression, but many of them did alleviate its consequences. Moreover, the very fact that Roosevelt was doing *something* undoubtedly provided a psychological boost to a population long frustrated by the inaction of his predecessor. The fact remains, however, that our economic recovery was due primarily to events rather than to Roosevelt's own initiatives.

One final aspect of the "who gets credit" problem is also worth considering here. We value the ability of a president and his administration to come up with new ideas and approaches for dealing with pressing problems. But should the recognition we give to such creative approaches be tempered by a consideration of *where* they originated? In 1950, for example, the Truman administration sought and received congressional approval of the Food for Peace program. This called for shipping surplus grain to needy countries. In the early 1960s, the Kennedy administration established the Peace Corps and secured Senate ratification of the Nuclear Test Ban Treaty. Yet the ideas for these efforts did not originate with the Truman or the Kennedy administrations. Rather, they were all first proposed by Senator Hubert Humphrey.[12] Thus, while both Truman and Kennedy may deserve considerable credit for having the discernment to seize upon a good idea, whatever points are to be awarded for originality and creativity must go to the late senator from Minnesota.

 ## QUALITIES OF LEADERSHIP

Thus far, we have focused on some of the factors that complicate the task of evaluating presidential leadership in terms of achievement or, if you will, results. I do not propose here to resolve all of these difficulties. Instead, in the remaining pages of this chapter I would like to identify a number of qualities and skills that seem necessary to gain results. Before doing so, however, several qualifying remarks are in order. First, one will not find universal agreement on what qualities are deemed essential to effective leadership. Thus, some would no doubt want to add or subtract from the ones identified here. Second, given the absence of a firmly based empirical literature on this subject, our discussion is admittedly impressionistic. Third, when viewing the qualities and skills identified here, we should bear in mind the enduring context in which a president must function. Under a different set of political and institutional arrangements, some of these qualities and skills might not be necessary in the same degree; others might not be necessary at all. Finally, while the following qualities and skills seem—to this writer—essential to effective presidential leadership, some will be needed to a greater extent under some circumstances than under others.

Empathy with the Public

In the final analysis, there are two constituencies that are most important to a president—Congress and the public. As already noted, much of what a president wants to accomplish requires the cooperation of Congress. Yet unlike parliamentary democracies, ours does not guarantee that a president will have the support of his party in Congress, let alone have a majority. Thus, in attempting to persuade Congress to do his bidding, the president needs the additional leverage that broad public support can provide. For to the extent that a president is perceived as having a wide following in the population, other elected officials will be considerably more receptive to his programs. In the words of Woodrow Wilson, "Let him once win the admiration and confidence of the country, and no other single force can withstand him, no combination of forces will easily overpower him."[13]

To gain this needed support, however, the president must know the people he seeks to lead. He must have the capacity to understand their hopes and aspirations, their fears and anxieties; he must be able to sense their moods. If he lacks this "feel" for his people, he will have difficulty not only in knowing how to respond to them but also in getting them to respond to him.

The development of such an understanding is undoubtedly facilitated by the nature of our electoral process. The nominating and election campaigns, grueling though they may be, provide an important means of educating presidential candidates about the nation and its people. Former presidential aspirant Walter Mondale readily acknowledges this fact.

> A Presidential campaign requires a candidate to speak throughout the nation, to listen carefully, and to learn about the problems of regions and communities. All of this is an essential part of the education of potential Presidents about this country. I think only candidates can realize how incredibly vast and varied America is. It is only this way that candidates can become familiar with this country, with its people and their leaders, with its problems. In this way, they can come to respect the differences that exist in our country. And through this educational process a truly national leader, capable of dealing intelligently, responsibly and respectfully with our nation's problems, can be developed.[14]

This education process cannot end on the campaign trail. It must also continue in the White House. Yet no elective office in this country removes an individual further from the people than the presidency does. Keeping in touch, therefore, requires a special effort. It will help for a president to surround himself with people of diverse backgrounds, with people who have varied contacts with different segments of the community. It will also help if some of these people have themselves been directly involved in elective politics. Most important, the president must make himself accessible not only to those within his immediate circle but also to others both in and outside government. No president did so to a greater degree than Franklin Roosevelt, and none was more skillful at sensing the pulse of the nation.

The costs for failing to comprehend the public mood can be high indeed. Woodrow Wilson suffered the major defeat of his presidency when he stubbornly refused to accept Senate changes in the treaty creating the League of Nations. He insisted that such changes were opposed not only by himself but also by the American people. In actuality, the public overwhelmingly supported them.[15] Hoover was soundly trounced in the 1932 election because he persisted in preaching against government intervention to help a faltering economy, erroneously believing that the American people shared his view.[16] Although Franklin Roosevelt was usually masterful at gauging public sentiment, he failed to do so accurately when he presented his court-packing proposal. The result was one of the most embarrassing political blunders of his presidency. Apparently Richard Nixon also failed to grasp the limits of public tolerance when he executed the famous "Saturday Night Massacre," an act that produced more letters and telegrams of protest to members of Congress than any presidential action in our history.

An Ability to Communicate

William Allen White made a telling point when he observed that "a democracy cannot follow a leader unless he is dramatized. A man to be a hero must not content himself with heroic virtues and anonymous action. He must talk and explain as he acts—drama."[17] Few would dispute the fact that the towering political figures of this century were exceptionally skillful at communicating with those they sought to lead. This skill in part involves a manner of expression that moves and inspires; in part, an ability to take the people into one's confidence; and in part a talent for stating issues and goals in a way that makes them readily comprehensible. Of Churchill, for example, it was said that he "marshalled the English language and sent it into battle." Indeed, his skill in this regard both comforted and inspired the British people as they faced the relentless destruction heaped upon them by the Nazi war machine. Among American presidents, Theodore Roosevelt, Woodrow Wilson, John Kennedy, and Ronald Reagan were all captivating speakers, as was Bill Clinton when speaking extemporaneously. Others, such as Eisenhower, Johnson, Ford, and Carter were notably less effective. None excelled in this area more than Franklin Roosevelt, however. His gift for communicating lay first in his ability to create a sense of intimacy with his audience, whether it was large or small. His radio talks to the American people were indeed "chats" rather than addresses. In addition, Roosevelt was unusually adept at reducing issues to their essence, so that the public had little difficulty in grasping their meaning. Thus, following Roosevelt's first fireside chat, which announced the bank holiday, Will Rogers commented that "Roosevelt explained the banking situation so well even the bankers understood it." FDR's skill in this regard was best exemplified in the simple but effective analogy he used to explain the Lend-Lease program to the American people.

> Suppose my neighbor's home catches on fire and I have a length of garden hose four or five hundred feet away. If he can take my garden hose and connect it up with his hydrant, I may help him to put out his fire. Now what do I do? I don't say to him before that operation, "Neighbor, my garden hose cost me $15; you have to pay me $15 for it." What is the transaction that goes on? I don't want $15—I want my garden hose back after the fire is over. All right. If it goes through the fire all right, intact, without any danger to it, he gives it back to me and thanks me very much for the use of it.[18]

Roosevelt's communicating style was also characterized by a flair for the dramatic when the circumstances required it. Moreover, the president was well aware of this talent, noting to one aide that he and Orson Welles were the two best actors in the country. In contrast to FDR, presidents Taft and Hoover did not seek to dramatize their leadership through words or action. Taft concluded, "I have made up my mind . . . that I will not play a part for popularity. . . . I cannot be spectacular." Similarly, Hoover appeared committed to the belief that the presidency "is not a showman's job." But as Emmet Hughes has aptly pointed out, in taking this approach to leadership both of these presidents were ignoring a reality recognized even by our very first president, who once remarked: "The truth is the people must *feel* before they will *see*."[19]

That communication skills can facilitate the task of leadership may be seen with dramatic clarity in the contrast between two of our more recent presidents, Jimmy Carter and Ronald Reagan. Clearly, Reagan's talent in oral expression proved to be one of his greatest assets. He spoke with disarming sincerity, employed a conversational style of presentation that allowed him to establish a sense of intimacy with his audience, and made his major points forcefully and clearly. On the other hand, although Jimmy Carter was a reasonably able extemporaneous speaker, his formal addresses were uninspiring. Lacking was the apt phrase, example, or analogy that might have served to drive a point home. Moreover, Carter's tone was sometimes condescending, and his modulation often was not appropriate to the substance of what he was saying.

The difference in their speaking ability was reflected in the results each achieved when he put it to the test. Reagan's televised addresses to the American people on his proposed budget cuts and on his tax cut proved instrumental in generating the public support necessary to ensure congressional approval. Carter, however, never fully galvanized the nation behind his energy program, despite the fact that he spoke to the American people on energy more times than on any other topic. In his first year he gave three nationally televised addresses on this issue. The first sought to demonstrate that the energy crisis was real, with the president noting that we must declare the "moral equivalent of war" on the problem. Two days later, he appeared before a joint session of Congress to outline his proposed solutions to the problem. This appearance was followed the next day by a nationally televised news conference during which he elaborated on his earlier remarks. Although these speeches had some impact initially, Carter was still not able to develop sustained public support for his program. Sensing this, he gave another televised address to the American people some six months later. Unfortunately, by way of both content and style it proved to be the most ineffective speech he had given to date. Indeed, Carter's lack of success in dramatizing the crisis nature of the energy problem was reflected in a Gallup poll taken in February 1978, which found that only 23 percent of the American people felt that the energy shortage was *the* most important problem confronting the nation. In July 1979, Carter gave what was to be his final televised address on energy. Although this speech appears to have increased from 37 percent to 47 percent the number of people who thought energy was a "very serious problem," he still had not succeeded in persuading a majority of Americans to accept this point of view.[20]

With the advent of radio and television, the ability of a president to communicate effectively through the spoken word has quite obviously assumed even greater importance. But there are also more recent developments that render communication skills even more indispensable for the person who occupies the White House at this point in time. For one thing, in recent years the overall trend in party identification has been downward; even among those who identify with a political party, the "weak" identifiers outnumber the "strong."[21] This trend suggests that the president's hard-core base of support within the population is not only smaller but also less committed. Therefore, it may erode even more quickly than in the past unless the president is especially effective at explaining and justifying to the people what he has done, what he wants to do, and why.

Presidents also must compete with the communications media, which in the aftermath of Watergate have become decidedly more skeptical and questioning about what the government is doing. Speaking to the problems he faced during his first year, for example, President Carter took note of the media's tendency to "separate the component parts of an overall objective, to emphasize failure, that does make it very difficult for me as President to keep before the public consciousness what we hope to achieve."[22] One observer of the Washington scene sees this tendency in even more severe terms: "It is beginning to seem as if, once America elects a leader, it immediately sets about demolishing him, sprawling him across its front pages like an insect on a windshield. How can its allies trust the United States not to pull a President down into the gutter on the smallest pretext?"[23]

Finally, in seeking to articulate what he perceives to be in the public interest, the president must speak above the voices of an ever-growing chorus of well-organized and well-financed special interests, all seeking to get their share of government benefits. Moreover, to the extent that domestic and foreign issues are increasingly intertwined, his voice must now compete with those of the special interests in foreign as well as domestic policy.

Credibility

Whatever skills a president may have at expressing his views and purposes, they will do him little good if the people are not prepared to believe what he has to say. In a democracy, trust is the vital link between the leaders and the led. While the citizenry may forgive varying kinds of presidential ineptitude, it will not forgive those who have violated the public trust or who have surrounded themselves with others who did. Nor, apparently, is the judgment of history much more tolerant. Note, for example, that in four (1948, 1962, 1970, 1983) of the six surveys (rating all the presidents) appearing in Table 10-1, the two lowest rankings are reserved for those presidents (Grant and Harding) whose administrations were characterized by widespread corruption. In the other two surveys (1996, 1997), Harding again comes in dead last and Grant not far behind. President Grant freely appointed his own relatives to a variety of different government positions and allowed himself to be manipulated by people around him whose activities ranged from graft to defrauding the government. During the Harding administration the discovery of bribery in connection with the sale of government-owned oil lands produced the great Teapot Dome scandal. In addition, corrupt practices were uncovered in both the Veterans' Bureau and the Office of the Attorney General. Nor was that all, for three of Harding's cabinet officers were forced to resign, with one suffering the added indignity of going to prison. Yet, given the fact that neither Grant nor Harding was directly involved in the scandals around him, the judgment of history might have been more charitable had there been some overriding achievement in other areas of their administrations. Such was not the case, however.

The scandals of the Truman administration in no way approached those of Grant and Harding, but they were significant enough to be made a major campaign issue in 1952. Indeed, a Gallup poll taken in February/March 1952 revealed that 57 percent of those surveyed agreed with the statement that "the Democratic party is loaded down with graft and corruption."[24] Although Truman was not involved in any of the corruption uncovered at the Bureau of Internal Revenue, the Reconstruction Finance Corporation, and the Department of Justice, he was far less sensitive to these problems than he should have been. Thus, despite the fact that he did not discourage investigations into any of these agencies, he defended far too long some of the people involved. Truman's popularity ultimately slipped all the way down to 23 percent. Although the Korean War and the firing of MacArthur were important contributing factors, the fact remains that Truman's popularity reached its lowest ebb after the scandals broke into the news. In the words of one Truman scholar, "The moral fiber of the Truman administration had been called into question by the highly publicized revelations of spoilsmongering. The personal authority of the president had been undermined."[25]

History, however, has taken a far more favorable view of Truman than did his contemporaries (Table 10-1). No doubt this assessment has been due not only to Truman's lack of personal involvement in the scandals that tarnished his administration but also to such formidable achievements as the Marshall Plan, NATO, and the Truman Doctrine.

The scandals of Watergate differ from the others just mentioned in two important respects. First, the primary motive was not a monetary one, but rather a desire to use the power of the federal government to harass and intimidate "enemies" of the Nixon administration. Second, the escapades of Watergate directly implicated the president of the United States. In some instances, Nixon gave his approval to certain activities; in others, he tried to cover them up; in still others, he did both. Had Nixon himself not been directly involved, he might well have survived his second term, although in a dramtically weakened position, to be sure. But as soon as the public became firmly convinced that he and those around him had violated the public trust on a massive scale, his public support rating underwent one of the most precipitous declines of any president on record. His trip to Moscow and his tumultuous reception in Egypt did little to slow it. Nor were attempts to defend himself in television addresses and televised news conferences enough to reverse it.

In the aftermath of Watergate, we may well ponder whether presidents and their associates will be more hard-pressed to maintain the public trust than they have been in the past. Some fear that after having lived through an administration (Nixon's) in which standards of moral conduct were almost nonexistent, we may now have gone to the opposite extreme and imposed standards that are too high. Irving Kristol speaks to this point.

> Though Americans have always been cynical about political corruption and petty abuses of official prerogatives, they have also been aware—deep down—that it is not really so trivial a matter. . . .
>
> Unfortunately, however, the other side of American political cynicism is American self-righteous moralism. The demand for "clean government" becomes an insistence on a degree of political purity which, in the real world, is either not within human reach or is itself self-destructive. At the moment, this kind of moralistic fervor is in full swing, and is notable in the vigilantelike passion with which the news media track down every sort of misdemeanor committed by officials, no matter how trivial or ambiguous or even nonexistent.[26]

A Sense of Timing

Victor Hugo once remarked that "there is no force on earth greater than an idea whose time has come." Those presidents who have been especially successful in realizing their goals were also skillful at knowing when the time was ripe for action. They tested the winds of public and congressional sentiment. If the winds were blowing in the right direction, they moved ahead; if not, then they would bide their time, perhaps waiting for unfolding events to take hold and push the public to the point of receptivity. Or, if events could not speak louder than words, they might take to the hustings and try to educate the population to their purposes. But whether through events or their own actions, or both, when the propitious moment arrived, they acted.

By all accounts, Lincoln appears to have been a master at timing. James Russell Lowell, in his essay on Lincoln, testifies to this fact.

> Time was his prime minister, and, we began to think, at one period, his general-in-chief also. At first he was so slow that he tired out all those who see no evidence of progress but in blowing up the engine; then he was so fast, that he took the breath away from those who think there is no getting on safely while there is a spark of fire under the boilers. God is the only being who has time enough; but a prudent man, who knows how to seize the occasion, can commonly make a shift to find as much as he needs. Mr. Lincoln, as it seems to us in reviewing his career, though we have sometimes in our impatience thought otherwise, has always waited, as a wise man should, till the right moment brought up all his reserves. *Semper nocuit differre paratis* is a sound axiom, but the

really efficacious man will also be sure to know when he is *not* ready, and be firm against all persuasions and reproach till he is.[27]

Nowhere was his skill in this area more apparent than in his decision regarding the Emancipation Proclamation. Despite constant pressure to free the slaves, Lincoln deferred. There was no doubt in his mind that such a time would eventually come, however: "I can see emancipation coming; whoever can wait for it will see it; whoever stands in its way will be run over."[28] Indeed, he had drafted the proclamation well before he decided to issue it. But his delay in doing so was motivated by several considerations. For one thing, he wanted to hold off until he was sure that the slaveholding border states would remain in the Union. Second, he wanted to wait until he had firmly cemented the support of the British, for if they had recognized the Confederacy, the Union cause would have been dealt a serious blow. Finally, he was also looking for a dramatic event on the battlefield that would give greater import to the proclamation. He ultimately succeeded in gaining the support of the border states as well as the British. Moreover, the Battle at Antietam supplied him with the dramatic event he was awaiting, for even though the casualties were heavy on both sides, this historic confrontation demonstrated Lee's inability to penetrate the North successfully. Shortly thereafter, Lincoln issued the Emancipation Proclamation.

Among presidents in this century, few were as adept at identifying the propitious moment as Franklin Roosevelt. He was not speaking lightly when he remarked, "I cannot go any faster than the people will let me." In seeking to determine just how fast that was, he constantly tested the waters of public opinion, one of his favorite tactics being to ask a cabinet member to give a speech on an idea that was currently under consideration. If the speech produced a favorable reaction, Roosevelt would take the idea and run with it. If it fell on deaf ears, he would disown the idea or try to educate the public toward acceptance. His sensitivity to the public mood on occasion caused considerable frustration among his advisers. In 1940 and 1941, for example, several of them pleaded with him to ask Congress for a declaration of war. Although Roosevelt was well aware that the United States would inevitably have to enter the Second World War, he also recognized that the public was not yet ready for such a bold step. Accordingly, throughout 1940 and 1941, he gradually increased our commitment to the British and the Russians, sensing all the while how much of an escalation the public would tolerate, and helping to prepare them for it as well. Thus, he ensured that when we did enter the war, we would do so as a united nation. As he knew only too well, such had not been the case when we entered the First World War.[29]

Although Lyndon Johnson was hardly the equal of Roosevelt in communicating with the public and preparing them for what he wanted to do, he did have a keen sense for how events could set the stage for what he hoped to accomplish. Moreover, no president in our history had a more subtle understanding of how and when to move on Congress. If the public was Roosevelt's compass, then Congress was Johnson's.

Following the assassination of Martin Luther King, Jr., for example, Johnson immediately reintroduced into Congress his legislation designed to prevent discrimination in housing. This legislation had been defeated on two previous occasions, but this time it passed both houses of Congress and was immediately signed into law by the president. While some may have seen Johnson's timing as a crass attempt to play upon emotions, others no doubt saw it as a stroke of political genius. So too was his timing on the crucially important Voting Rights Act of 1965. Having just achieved passage of the 1964 Civil Rights Act, Johnson initially concluded that 1965 would not be an appropriate year to ask Congress to consider voting rights legislation. In his judgment, both Congress and the nation needed a breather. The movement of events, however, caused him to alter his appraisal. On March 7, 1965, Martin Luther King, Jr., led a march from Selma to Montgomery, Alabama, as a protest against infringement upon black voting rights. On the evening news programs, a shocked nation witnessed unarmed blacks being attacked by clubs, cattle prods, and police dogs. The reaction was immediate. Demonstrators assembled outside the White House and demanded that the president take action; telegrams and phone calls coming into the White House expressed the same sentiment. Instead, Johnson held off, realizing that a premature use of federal force would make a martyr of George Wallace among the states' rights advocates in Congress and throughout the nation. When he finally did commit troops, it was perceived not as an arbitrary use of federal power but rather as a last-ditch effort to avoid further violence.[30] Moreover, Johnson was now convinced that the brutality of the last several days had united Congress and the American people behind a commitment to guarantee black voting rights. Accordingly, on March 14 he pledged to send a voting rights bill to Congress. On March 15 he took the dramatic step of appearing personally before a joint session of Congress to demand that it act. On March 17 he formally submitted his voting rights legislation, which was signed into law some three and a half months later. Had it not been for the events of Selma and Johnson's ability to discern their meaning, action on the rights of blacks would have been delayed still longer.

Jimmy Carter, on the other hand, never fully grasped the strategic importance of timing. In the words of the chairman of the powerful House Ways and Means Committee, "That's one thing I think the President has not understood. Timing is *critical*. It's absolutely essential."[31] In February 1978, for example, Carter's legislation calling for the establishment of a Consumer Protection Agency was soundly defeated in the House of Representatives. Given the fact that he had repeatedly taken a vigorous stand in favor of greater consumer protection during the campaign, the defeat of this bill constituted a significant setback for his legislative program. Although several factors were responsible for his defeat, certainly one of the major reasons was Carter's decision to submit the bill without having first generated the necessary support within Congress and among the American people. Indeed, his failure to mobilize public opinion for this particular bill was especially unfortunate, because a Harris poll found that Americans were in favor of a Consumer Protection Agency by a two-to-one margin.[32]

Carter might also have taken a lesson from Lyndon Johnson on how to pace the introduction of his legislative programs to Congress. Although Johnson kept the members of Congress extremely busy, he was usually careful to avoid sending them a whole series of major proposals all at once: "It's like a bottle of bourbon. If you take it a glass at a time, it's fine. But if you drink the whole bottle in one evening, you have troubles."[33] In his first year, Carter made the mistake of sending a whole cluster of major proposals to Congress in a relatively brief span of time, thus forcing him to contend with many different pockets of opposition *all at once*. Vice President Mondale expressed the problem best when he noted that Carter's legislative program suffered from "fratricide, the concept in missilery where you fire too many missiles too close together and they kill each other off."[34]

The obstacles to be faced in getting legislation through Congress are formidable enough to begin with. Presidents cannot afford the additional disadvantages that follow from their failure to identify the propitious moment for action.

Courage

Among the qualities necessary for effective leadership, few probably command as much admiration as courage. And, for a democratically elected leader, the ultimate test of courage is to go ahead and make a decision knowing full well that he will incur the public's wrath by doing so. It is the president acting as statesman rather than as politician. Of course, presidents must be both. Indeed, in discussing the necessity for a keen sense of timing, we were in fact identifying a skill of an astute politician. At the same time, however, a president cannot always postpone doing what he thinks is right until he has mobilized public opinion. On some questions, the public may not be persuadable; on others, they may not be persuadable soon enough. Thus, although the president must always weigh anticipated public reaction, he cannot be eternally ruled by it. As Winston Churchill once observed, "Nothing is more dangerous than to live in the temperamental atmosphere of a Gallup poll, always feeling one's pulse and taking one's temperature. . . . There is only one duty, only one safe course, and that is to try to be right and not to fear to do so or say what you believe to be right."[35]

Over the course of our history several examples may be pointed to that, in varying degrees, qualify as courageous presidential actions: Washington's steadfast commitment to negotiating the Jay Treaty despite a torrent of public criticism; Lincoln's decision to relieve General McClellan as commander of the Army of the Potomac; Woodrow Wilson's decision in the face of widespread prejudice to nominate the first Jew to the Supreme Court. Several more recent examples could also be identified, but two stand out as especially courageous. The first was Truman's decision to remove General Douglas MacArthur from his post as United Nations Supreme Commander in South Korea.

Truman and MacArthur.   After the invasion of South Korea by North Korea, American forces succeeded in pushing the invasion force out of the South. In fact, they were so successful that the Truman administration altered its original goal of simply containing the communists and decided instead to push ahead into North Korea in the hope of reunifying the two countries. Although there was always the risk that the Chinese communists would come into the war on the side of North Korea, this was not considered likely. We miscalculated, however, for the Chinese did intervene on the side of the North Koreans, and together they drove the American forces a considerable way down the South Korean peninsula. After four months of heavy fighting, the Chinese and the North Koreans were driven out of the South. At this point, the Truman administration decided that a negotiated settlement would now be the most judicious course to follow. MacArthur, on the other hand, was calling for an expansion of the war into China, arguing that we should bomb its major industrial and communications facilities and blockade its coast. When Truman rejected this recommendation, MacArthur decided to go public. On March 25, 1951, he released to the press a statement demanding the surrender of the enemy. This action proved to be especially inappropriate, because it was at just this time that Truman had planned to issue a statement implying our interest in a negotiated settlement. Some two weeks later the minority leader of the House of Representatives stood up before that body and read a letter from MacArthur that decried the president's war policy. Five days later, Truman relieved MacArthur of his command.[36]

Both the Joint Chiefs and our European allies agreed that MacArthur's plan to carry the war into China was not feasible. By doing so, we would have run the grave risk of bringing the Soviet Union into the conflict on the side of China; and in order to attain the required force levels for such an undertaking, it would have been necessary to take troops from Europe, thereby leaving our allies exposed to any military ventures that the Soviet Union might undertake there. Given the Soviet threat in Europe, neither Britain nor France was prepared to commit any of its military strength to Asia. Thus, we would have had to go it alone.

But there was another issue at stake here aside from the rightness or wrongness of MacArthur's views. Under our constitutional arrangements, the military is subordinate to civilian authority, a principle reflected in the constitutional provision making the president commander in chief of the armed forces. Had Truman permitted MacArthur to continue in his open defiance of the president's policies, civilian control over the military would have been seriously undermined. It was for this reason that Truman relieved the general of his command.

There was relatively little Truman could have done to avoid the negative public reaction that followed this decision. MacArthur was, after all, a national hero. Add to this the fact that his "Let's go get 'em" approach toward the Chinese had wide popular appeal. And, finally, add also the fact that Truman's popularity had been declining even prior to the MacArthur firing. Given all of these factors, it is hardly surprising that MacArthur returned to the United States not in disgrace but rather as a conquering hero. He was given a ticker-tape parade down Fifth Avenue and accorded the honor of addressing a joint session of Congress. As for Truman, several Republicans in Congress announced that they would seek to impeach him; various state legislatures condemned his action as excessive; and in communities throughout the land he was burned in effigy.[37]

The judgment of history, however, has come down on the side of Truman rather than MacArthur. For not only was he right, but he was willing to be so knowing full well that it would bring him the condemnation of most of the nation.

Ford and Nixon.   Gerald Ford's pardoning of former President Nixon provides a still more recent example of extraordinary presidential courage. Surely Ford could not have doubted that such a decision would bring an early end to his honeymoon with Congress, the press, and the public. And that it did, for 61 percent of the American public expressed their disapproval of the pardon. This disapproval was reflected in Ford's popularity rating, which prior to the pardon was 66 percent and afterward dropped to 50 percent. Nor did the population mellow very much on this issue, for as Ford entered the 1976 election campaign, 57 percent of the American public still felt that the pardon was wrong.[38]

If the decision to pardon Nixon for his unlawful behavior created the impression that not all were treated equally before the law, nevertheless there is no evidence to suggest that President Ford's action was guided by any motive other than getting Watergate behind us. The accomplishment of this goal would not have been possible if Richard Nixon had been brought to trial. For one thing, in view of the climate of opinion at the time, he could not have received a fair trial."[39] Thus, there would probably have been a delay in the trial of two or three years, and perhaps even longer. Moreover, if Nixon had come to trial and lost, the lengthy appeals process that would have inevitably followed would probably have kept Watergate on the front pages for an additional two years. Certainly a credible argument can be made that another five years of Watergate would have been debilitating to the national psyche.

While we may still be too close to the happenings of Watergate to assess the correctness of Ford's decision objectively, one suspects that history will judge it to have been not only courageous but also wise.

Decisiveness

There is, to be sure, a relationship between courage and decisiveness. Yet they are not one and the same, for even though acts of courage may also be characterized as decisive, it does not necessarily follow that all acts of decisiveness are courageous as well.

Although presidents perform a variety of different functions in our political system, in the final analysis we elect them to make decisions. The president who fails to act resolutely and unambiguously when the occasion requires runs the risk of being overtaken by events; he invites others to misinterpret his intentions; and he invites a loss of confidence in his leadership as well. Even though decisiveness alone does not ensure public support, the appearance of indecision will almost certainly lead to an erosion of it. Thus, as was clearly demonstrated in the 1932 election, the public's perception of Herbert Hoover as indecisive in responding to a rapidly deteriorating economy brought about a loss of confidence in his leadership. On the other hand, even though Franklin Roosevelt's bold new programs were not by themselves sufficient to lift us out of the Great Depression, he showed no reluctance to deal with the crisis: "One thing is sure. We have to do something. We have to do the best we know how at the moment. . . . If it doesn't work out right, we can modify it as we go along."[40] His take-charge approach earned him the confidence and admiration of the American people.

This same resolve was also evidenced in his successor, Harry Truman, as he faced such difficult issues as the use of the atomic bomb on Japan, the revitalization of Europe, the commitment of U.S. forces to South Korea, the firing of General MacArthur, and the desegregation of the armed forces. Indeed, to a greater extent than for any other modern president, decisiveness appears to have been the hallmark of the Truman leadership style.

Among the several criticisms leveled at Jimmy Carter's leadership, none perhaps was heard more frequently than the charge of indecisiveness. The problem here was not so much the president's failure to take a position but rather his failure to maintain it. Early in his administration, for example, the president sought congressional support for a fifty-dollar tax rebate. No sooner had some members of Congress been prodded into publicly endorsing the proposal, than they were informed that Carter had decided against it. In an address on energy given in April 1978, the president announced that he intended to decontrol the price of oil. During a visit to Iowa shortly thereafter, he was asked how he would respond if Congress passed legislation blocking decontrol. To the astonishment of decontrol advocates, Carter stated that he would *not* veto such legislation.[41] Needless to say, the apparent conflict between this statement and his energy speech raised serious doubts about the president's commitment to lifting price restrictions on oil. The growing frustration over White House inconstancy was reflected in Congressman John Dingell's (D-Mich.) reaction to a sudden administration shift on legislation creating an Energy Mobilization Board:

"I am incapable of describing to you this administration's position on anything. . . . It seems to change . . . depending on the time of day and who you talk to."[42]

The frequent changes in direction were also apparent in matters related to foreign policy. Thus, after persuading reluctant allies to endorse the production of the neutron bomb and its deployment in Europe, in March 1978 Carter stunned European leaders by deciding against deployment. In August 1979 the administration revealed that Soviet troops were stationed in Cuba. Both the president and his secretary of state initially responded by declaring that the presence of these troops was unacceptable, but in the following weeks they retreated from this hard-line position—a retreat that, some feared, would only encourage the Soviet Union to doubt American resolve in responding to communist penetration of the Western Hemisphere. Perhaps the most embarrassing instance of administrative fickleness came in March 1980, when Donald McHenry, U.S. Ambassador to the United Nations, voted to support a Security Council resolution condemning Israeli settlements in Arab-occupied territories and East Jerusalem. Within twenty-four hours, however, McHenry was instructed by the White House to change his vote from "yes" to "no." Whether this reversal was the result of a breakdown in communications or administration misgivings regarding the possible negative political fallout that would attend a vote against Israel has never been firmly established.

In summary, while some of the above examples may have been the consequence of poor coordination rather than genuine indecision, the fact remains they all fostered the perception that the president was a man uncertain of what he wanted.

Vision

Although presidents lead at a discrete period in time, it cannot be said that their actions are similarly confined. On the contrary, the present is significantly shaped by what presidents have done in the past and the future by what presidents do in the present. Accordingly, it is important for a president to have a sense of vision—an ability to appreciate the implications that present events and circumstances have for the future. Lyndon Johnson made the point well.

> One of the hardest tasks that a President faces is to keep the time scale of his decisions always in mind and to try to be the President of all the people. He is not simply responsible to an immediate electorate, either. He knows over the long stretch of time how great can be the repercussions of all that he does or that he fails to do, and over that span of time the President always has to think of America as a continuing community.
>
> He has to try to see how his decisions will affect not only today's citizens, but their children and their children's children unto the third and fourth generation. He has to try to peer into the future, and has to prepare for that future.
>
> . . . Irresistible forces of change have been unleashed by modern science and technology, and the very facts dissolve and regroup as we look into them. To make no predictions is to be sure to be wrong. . . .
>
> The President of this country, more than any other single man in the world, must grapple with the course of events and the directions of history. What he must try to do, try to do always, is to build for tomorrow in the immediacy of today.[43]

Despite the fact that Wilson's stubbornness prevented Senate approval of the League Covenant, his forward-looking concept of a League of Nations embodied a recognition of the world as a community and the preservation of peace as a global responsibility. Franklin Roosevelt "grasped at once the political implications of the news of advances in Germany" and thus marshaled the nation's resources for the purpose of developing an atomic bomb.[44] When Europe lay devastated after the Second World War, it was apparent that only the United States possessed the capacity to help it rebuild. Sensing that the military and economic security of our country would continue to be tied closely to that of Europe, President Truman had the foresight to approve the Marshall Plan—a program that called for a massive infusion of American economic aid to help revitalize Europe. Despite subsequent strains in the relationship from time to time, the Marshall Plan was instrumental in creating an enduring bond between the United States and Europe. Considerable credit is also due to President Eisenhower, whose spirit of "rapprochement" with the Soviet Union reflected a belief that the futures of both nations depended upon a reduction in tensions. Kennedy, too, was looking to the future when, despite uncertainty as to how the public would react, he called upon the Soviet Union to join the United States in banning all nuclear testing in the atmosphere, a call that ultimately resulted in the Nuclear Test Ban Treaty. If the initiatives of both Eisenhower and Kennedy did not make the subsequent move toward détente inevitable, they certainly made it more likely.

We must also credit Kennedy for calling upon the nation to probe the frontiers of outer space, a challenge that he issued in his 1961 State of the Union Address to Congress.

> If we are to win the battle that is now going on around the world between freedom and tyranny, the dramatic achievements in space which occurred in recent weeks should have made clear to us all, as did the Sputnik, in 1957, the impact of this adventure on the minds of men everywhere who are attempting to make a determination of which road they should take.
>
> ... Now is the time to take longer strides—time for a great new American enterprise—time for this nation to take a clearly leading role in space achievement which, in many ways, may hold the key to our future on earth.
>
> ... I believe that this nation should commit itself to achieving the goal, before this decade is out, of landing a man on the moon and returning him safely to earth. No single space project in this period will be more impressive to mankind or more important for the long range exploration of space.[45]

Although Kennedy, nor anyone else for that matter, could fully comprehend what lay beyond the confines of our own planet, he nevertheless was able to grasp the fact that no great nation could ignore the challenge to explore it.

In addition to having a sense of vision, effective leadership also requires that the person in the White House have *a* vision. After all, in order to lead a population, *you* must know where you want to take them and you must be sure that *they* know also. For Wilson, this vision was embodied in the New Freedom; for Franklin Roosevelt, the New Deal; for Kennedy, the New Frontier; for Johnson, the Great Society; for Nixon, A Generation of Peace; for Reagan, A New Beginning. Even if phrases such as these could hardly capture all of what these presidents had in their minds, nevertheless they did convey a general sense of direction. The difficulties Jimmy Carter experienced in office were due, at least in part, to his failure to convey to Congress and the public where he chose to take us. In January 1978, Carter aide Jody Powell frankly acknowledged this problem: "If there is one area that I see the biggest failure, it is exactly in that area. We haven't clearly enough articulated that overarching, unifying theme or presentation of what we're about or the way we're approaching things. We spent so much time in getting under way on the Administration's work that we did not spend enough time in explaining it in an understandable way to the public."[46] Even at the end of four years in office, however, Carter had not succeeded in articulating his vision for America. That he failed to do so suggests the absence of any such vision on his part rather than the administration's neglect in trying to explain it.

George Bush faced the same problem throughout his four years in office as he found himself constantly having to answer the charge that he did not stand for any-thing—a charge that he disparagingly referred to as "the vision thing."

Few presidents, on the other hand, have assumed office with a clearer sense of purpose and direction than Ronald Reagan. Although the desirability of his New Beginning has been the subject of heated debate, Reagan's elucidation of this vision left little doubt as to its meaning—namely, a systematic effort to drastically reduce the role of the federal government in the social and economic lives of the citizenry.

Flexibility

Flexibility is used in two senses here, one *cognitive* and the other *tactical*. Re-garding the first, it is essential that presidents be open to new ideas and approaches. Circumstances and knowledge change too quickly for a political leader to cement himself into rigid and unalterable views of the world around him. Hoover, for exam-ple, had long been philosophically opposed to federal intervention in the life of the nation, believing instead that our economic and social ills could be eradicated most effectively through voluntarism and governmental assistance at the state and local levels. Unfortunately, he clung rigidly to this view even as the economy slid steadily downhill: "Each community and each State should assume its full responsibilities for organization of employment and relief of distress with that sturdiness and indepen-dence which built a great Nation."[47] He maintained this position even though it had become abundantly clear that neither the states nor voluntary organizations pos-sessed the capacity to combat the widespread unemployment and hunger befalling the American people.

Richard Nixon, on the other hand—for all of his other shortcomings—demon-strated a capacity for intellectual flexibility. Few political figures on the national scene had been more doggedly anticommunist than he. Yet he was not so rigidly tied to this view that it prevented him from grasping the changing circumstances in the relationship between China and the Soviet Union, as well as how these changes could be exploited in moving toward détente with both countries. Nor did his long-standing opposition to wage and price controls prevent him from instituting them in 1971, after he was persuaded of their absolute necessity.

Presidents must show flexibility not only in their openness to new ideas but also in how they go about trying to realize their goals. The person in the White House, after all, does not hold all the chips in the political game. Rather, more often than not he must compete with Congress, the bureaucracy, and various organized interests within the society, all of which have formidable resources of their own that may be brought to bear in the policymaking process. Accordingly, at times he must be prepared to compromise with these other power centers, for a rigid insistence upon getting the whole loaf may lead to getting nothing at all. This is not to say that he must readily abandon his goals and principles. It does mean, however, that he must be prepared to settle for results that move him *closer* to his goals—even though not as close as he might like. The point is well made by James Russell Lowell.

> It is loyalty to great ends, even though forced to combine the small and opposing motives of selfish men to accomplish them; it is the anchored cling to solid principles of duty and action, which knows how to swing with the tide, but is never carried away by it—that we demand in public men, and not obstinacy in prejudice, sameness of policy, or a conscientious persistency in what is impracticable. For the impracticable, however theoretically enticing, is always politically unwise, sound statesmanship being the application of that prudence to the public business.[48]

Perhaps in no instance were the costs of inflexibility more apparent than in Woodrow Wilson's efforts to gain approval for the League of Nations. The idea to establish such an organization was his own, and he personally attended the Paris Peace Conference, where he helped draft the provisions of the League Covenant. When ratification of the covenant came before the U.S. Senate, however, several senators expressed reservations concerning certain provisions. Wilson, unfortunately, would not even entertain the possibility of compromise on any aspect of the covenant. Thus, by rigidly insisting on getting everything, he ended up getting nothing. The Senate refused to ratify the covenant, and Wilson suffered the greatest defeat of his presidency.

In contrast to Wilson, John Kennedy's actions in the area of civil rights provide us with an example of a president who showed considerable flexibility in pursuit of his goals and principles. He had campaigned strongly on behalf of civil rights for blacks, frequently noting the indifference of the Eisenhower administration in this area. Once in office, however, he began to see that the articulation of such a goal was far easier than its realization, for the civil rights issue now had to be considered within the political context of his presidency. For one thing, Kennedy's narrow election victory greatly restricted his political leverage over both Congress and the public. For another, he now found himself confronted with a Congress in which Southerners held a disproportionate share of the power. Thus, even if he pushed hard and early for a civil rights bill, there was every chance that he would still fail. Moreover, he would no doubt alienate many Southern representatives and senators whose support was necessary to realize other parts of his legislative program. Accordingly, he temporarily placed civil rights legislation on the back burner.

Even in areas where the cause of blacks could be advanced through executive action alone, Kennedy also compromised. For example, he appointed more Southerners to the federal bench than either he or blacks would have liked, but he felt that building southern support in Congress dictated this compromise. At the same time, however, executive action in other areas clearly demonstrated a concern for blacks. Thus, even though Kennedy did not appoint as many blacks to executive positions as some had wanted, the fact remains that from 1961 to 1963 the number of blacks in the upper levels of the civil service rose 88 percent.[49] He ordered the Justice Department to step up its prosecution of cases dealing with school desegregation and voting rights violations, and he petitioned the Interstate Commerce Commission to eliminate segregation in bus terminals that were providing interstate bus service. After some delay, he also issued an executive order prohibiting racial discrimination in the sale or rental of federally financed housing. To be sure, for economic, legal, and political reasons, he decided to exempt some housing from this order. These exceptions included housing already built, houses not in commercially developed areas, and FHA loans given for home improvements. Yet if this executive order did not go as far as many had hoped, it is also important to note that the Eisenhower administration had not been willing to go any of the distance at all in this area. When blacks seeking entry to the universities of Mississippi and Alabama were harassed, Kennedy dispatched federal marshals to protect them. Finally, it should be pointed out that through private persuasion, the Kennedy administration succeeded in bringing about voluntary desegregation in some 256 southern cities and managed to establish biracial committees in 185 of them.[50]

As blacks became increasingly demonstrative in drawing attention to their deplorable condition in American society, the threat of a violent response by whites increased also. Accordingly, in June 1963, Kennedy went before the American people and announced that he would shortly submit civil rights legislation to Congress. Eight days later Congress received the most comprehensive civil rights bill ever to be placed before it.

The argument that there should be no timetable on civil rights for blacks is a compelling one. If one accepts this principle, then Kennedy's actions may indeed appear to have been overly timid. Yet the fact remains that, even with all the compromises, Kennedy still advanced blacks further toward the goal of full civil rights than had any of his predecessors. Moreover, we cannot overlook the political and social constraints under which he was required to lead. Had he pushed for more earlier and harder, he may well have accomplished less in the way of civil rights and jeopardized some of his other legislative programs as well. It is well to recall here an observation of the late Hubert Humphrey: "Compromise is not a dirty word. . . . There are times, of course, when it is better to lose than to be partially successful. . . . But to make losing a habit in the name of moral principle or liberal convictions is to fail to govern."[51]

A Sense for Power

Harry Truman once remarked, "I sit here all day trying to persuade people to do things they ought to have sense enough to do without my persuading them. . . . That's all the powers of the President amount to." This rather simple statement in fact makes a profound point about the role of the president in our political system. For, despite the attention focused on the office, despite the powers granted it and the pomp surrounding it, the fact remains that presidents are most often in a position where they must enlist the support of others rather than being able to command it. The separation of powers, checks and balances, the independent power bases within the executive branch as well as in the society at large—all of these ensure that it could not be otherwise. At the same time, however, if the president must persuade more often than command, he nevertheless has considerable resources at his disposal that can make him a formidable persuader. At various points in this text, these resources have been discussed. They include (1) constitutional authority, (2) information, (3) the status of the office, (4) control of federal projects and patronage, and (5) ready access to the public through the media. Depending upon circumstances, other resources may include (6) high popularity, (7) a party majority in Congress, and (8) the nature of the times. Yet if all of these factors can affect the president's ability to influence outcomes, it must be remembered that they can do so only if he *recognizes* them as such, for power comes to those who sense what power is made of.[52]

But the president's potential for influence does not lie only in the factors identified above. It is also a function of the kinds of decisions he makes. As Richard

Neustadt notes, "A President's own choices are the only means *in his own hands* of guarding his own prospects for effective influence."[53] The president with a keen sense for power will be attentive to how any given decision he makes will affect his ability to exert influence in the future. On this score, one may well question how sensitive Jimmy Carter was to the power stakes involved in his decisions to invoke the Taft-Hartley Act against striking coal miners in March 1978. The act, after all, had long been anathema to organized labor in general and to coal miners in particular. Indeed, the miners had been ordered back to work under Taft-Hartley in 1948 and 1950, and on both occasions they had refused to comply. The miners also made it clear that they would ignore any such order given by President Carter. Yet even though all the evidence indicated that the miners would not obey, the president still went ahead and ordered them back to work under the provisions of the Taft-Hartley Act. Under the best of circumstances, a president should be wary of putting his prestige on the line by giving an order that he knows will not be obeyed and that he knows cannot be readily enforced (it simply was not possible to arrest all of the coal miners who were in violation of the back-to-work order). It is all the more perplexing that Carter would have made this decision at a time when, in the absence of any major successes in his administration, his leadership ability was already being questioned in many quarters. Finally, one cannot help but wonder whether the miners' flagrant violation of Carter's back-to-work order might have undermined his leverage in dealing with future strikes, had there been any.

Of course, to say that a president must be sensitive to the power implications of his decisions does not mean that power considerations can always be uppermost in his mind. At times a president will be forced to make decisions that, although highly unpopular and injurious to future influence, are nevertheless deemed to be in the public interest as he sees it. At the same time, however, there are many issues concerning which the president has some latitude about how he responds. In the case of Carter and the coal miners, for example, some would surely contend that the president should have sought congressional authorization to seize the mines, especially since the miners indicated a willingness to return to work under such an arrangement. Others would argue that more drastic measures could have been avoided had Carter personally intervened in the strike earlier and "jawboned" both parties, much as Johnson did in the 1964 railroad strike.

Up to this point, it has been suggested that a sense for power is the ability of a president to discern what gives him influence. But a sense for power also entails something more, namely, *a willingness to make effective use of that influence.* The leader who is unwilling to take advantage of the resources at his disposal invites others to conclude there is little to fear from opposing him. The limited accomplishments of the Carter administration during its first year were, in part, the result of the president's failure to use all of the resources at his command. In the words of press secretary Jody Powell, "We've learned that just being an honest and decent and friendly sort of chap is not sufficient to make things happen the way they're supposed to happen, that people aren't going to do what you think they should do because they think you're a nice guy. It may be to our discredit that it took us a year to learn that."[54]

There is indeed some evidence to suggest that the Carter White House had learned. In December 1977, for example, the House voted (191 to 161) to appropriate money for the very B-1 bomber that the president had earlier decided to scrap. Fortunately for the president, this bill was defeated in the Senate. The House supporters of the B-1 did not give up, however. Shortly thereafter, they managed to get $462 million for two B-1 bombers written into a $7.8 billion appropriations bill. The Carter administration was determined to have the appropriation for the B-1 deleted from the bill. In pursuance of this goal, several key members of Congress were informed that sewer grants and disaster loans for their districts would be slow in coming unless they voted to delete the B-1 appropriation. The vote to delete carried. As one congressman noted, this application of pressure by the Carter White House was decidedly different from its tactics on previous occasions: "On earlier B-1 votes there was almost a reluctance to use the power of the Presidency. You almost got the feeling that they were somehow not involved."[55] There were also reports that Carter was willing to make trades in exchange for votes on the crucially important Panama Canal treaties. For example, although the administration had been strongly committed to closing several military bases around the country, some senators who came out in support of the treaties were happy to learn that the bases in their states would probably be taken off the list of closings. Carter also decided to drop his opposition to a $2.3 billion emergency farm bill. Subsequently, Senator Herman Talmadge (D-Ga.), a strong advocate of the emergency measure, announced his support for the first Panama Canal treaty. Similarly, Carter gave his approval to government stockpiling of copper—a reversal of his earlier position. And coincidentally, Democratic Senator Dennis DeConcini, who represents the copper-mining state of Arizona and whose support of the first Panama Canal treaty was uncertain, came down on the side of ratification.

From the very beginning, Reagan and his aides demonstrated that they fully appreciated how to employ the resources of the presidency. This appreciation was revealed most clearly in their lobbying efforts on behalf of the crucially important tax cut bill. This carefully orchestrated offensive included, first of all, personal lobbying by the president himself. Thus, fifteen Democratic members of Congress were courted with an invitation to picnic with Reagan at his Camp David retreat and to discuss the tax proposal with him. Upon his return to Washington, the president also met individually or in small groups with another fifty-three legislators, most of them Southern Democrats. He then turned his attention to prominent leaders in the business community, 200 of whom were invited to the White House to hear his pitch on the necessity of reducing taxes. A second dimension of the administration's lobbying effort consisted of bringing pressure to bear upon representatives from within their own districts. In fifty-one swing congressional districts, the White House mobilized local organizations and major campaign contributors, asking them to convey their support of tax cut legislation to their respective representatives. Where additional enticements were necessary to persuade reluctant legislators, Reagan and his aides showed a ready willingness to horse-trade. Several Democratic members of Congress from Georgia, for example, decided to side with the president after he agreed to drop a provision in his farm bill dealing with peanut allotments; a congressman from Pennsylvania also came on board after being told that a military base in his district would not be closed after all; and still others decided to cast their lot with the Reagan tax cut in return for his support of sugar price supports and more funds for Conrail, Medicaid, and energy subsidies to the poor.[56] All of these efforts were topped off by a twenty-three minute nationally televised presidential address, in which Reagan not only appealed for public support but also asked that citizens convey this support to their elected representatives. As a consequence of bringing presidential influence to bear in all these different ways, a tax bill whose fate initially appeared uncertain passed the House by a comfortable margin of forty-three votes.

To suggest that presidents must have a sense for power will no doubt raise a red flag in the minds of some. It can certainly be argued that the most dangerous presidency in our history was the result of a president who was intoxicated by power. This leads us to one final point in our discussion, namely, that to have a sense for power is to appreciate not only its potential but also its limits—limits dictated in part by the Constitution and in part by public expectations. Whether due to his own insecurities or lack of moral purpose, the ultimate tragedy of Richard Nixon lay in his inability to discern these limits. And for this failure both he and the nation paid dearly.

☆ CONCLUSION

Of the three branches of government, the presidency stands out as the institution with the greatest capacity to lead the nation. Clearly, the Supreme Court is ill suited to such a role; it can speak only when spoken to, and its reply must necessarily be confined to the particular case before it. Although Congress may focus upon any issue it wishes, both its size and the multiplicity of its local interests guarantee that it will speak with many voices. The president alone has the ability to speak with one voice on any matter he chooses. This does not mean, however, that whoever happens to occupy the presidency will be an effective leader. While many of us cling to the notion that the office somehow ennobles the person, this view must remain more a hope than an expectation. To be sure, the presidential experience can develop and refine qualities of leadership, but it cannot create them; the qualities identified here are, to varying degrees, sown within the individual.

The American people will no doubt continue to look to the president to take the lead in addressing the problems facing our nation, and world leaders are likely to expect no less on matters of international concern. It is equally clear, however, that new realities promise to make the task of leading a formidable one. As the economy globalizes, foreign policy issues will become much heavier with domestic implications, and consequently, the president will have to compete with many more voices in and outside government as he seeks to work his will in foreign affairs. This burden will be made even heavier given that the president no longer stands as protector of the free world—a role that endowed him with added stature at home and abroad when he spoke on matters of international importance.

With the reduced importance of party in Congress, power in that body has become more widely diffused, thereby complicating the president's attempts to forge a consensus around his legislative programs. The American public, too, may prove more difficult to mobilize, for even though confidence in the presidency has enjoyed some resurgence in the aftermath of Watergate, it has not yet returned to the levels attained in the early 1960s. Nor, given the deeply seated cynicism of the national media, is such a prospect likely in the foreseeable future. In addition, for the public as for Congress, party appears less effective as a mechanism for forging unity out of diversity. Fewer people now identify with our political parties, and even among those who do, the weak identifiers outnumber the strong. Accordingly, presidents now find themselves with a hard-core base of support that is both smaller and less committed.

Finally, the problem of budget deficits is still with us. Admittedly, a particularly buoyant economy brought an unexpected budget surplus in 1998 and enabled Clinton to submit a balanced budget for 1999. But as the economy slows down, the surpluses will disappear, and the task of avoiding future budget deficits will require hard choices on spending reductions. Thus, whereas presidents were once in a position of being able to promise more, they must now convince the American people to accept less—hardly an enviable task.

★ NOTES

1. R. Gordon Hoxie, "Presidential Greatness," in Philip Dolce and George Skau, eds., *Power and the Presidency* (New York: Scribner, 1976), p. 261.

2. Gary Maranell and Richard Dodder, "Political Orientation and the Evaluation of Presidential Prestige: A Study of American Historians," *Social Science Quarterly* 51 (September 1970), 421.

3. Clinton Rossiter, *The American Presidency* (New York: New American Library, 1960), pp. 138, 139.

4. Ibid., p. 138.

5. Tom Wicker, "Kennedy without End, Amen," *Esquire,* June 1977, p. 65.

6. For recent reassessments of Eisenhower, see John P. Burke and Fred Greenstein, *How Presidents Test Reality* (New York: Russell Sage Foundation, 1989); Richard Melanson and David Mayers, eds., *Reevaluating Eisenhower* (Urbana: University of Illinois Press, 1987); Fred Greenstein, *The Hidden Hand Presidency* (New York: Basic Books, 1982); Robert Divine, *Eisenhower and the Cold War* (New York: Oxford University Press, 1981); William Ewald, Jr., *Eisenhower the President: Crucial Days, 1951–1960* (Englewood Cliffs, N.J.: Prentice Hall, 1981).

7. Cited in Vincent De Santis, "Eisenhower Revisionism," *Review of Politics* 38 (April 1976), 198.

8. Thomas Bailey, *Presidential Greatness* (Englewood Cliffs, N.J.: Prentice Hall, 1966), p. 41.

9. Cited in Ernest Paolino, *The Foundations of the American Empire* (Ithaca, N.Y.: Cornell University Press, 1973), pp. 117, 118.

10. Bailey, *Presidential Greatness,* pp. 104, 105.

11. Thomas Cochran, *The Great Depression and World War II* (Glenview, Ill.: Scott, Foresman, 1968), p. 78.

12. *Congressional Quarterly Weekly Report,* January 21, 1978, p. 111.

13. Taken from *The Promise and the Performance* by Lewis J. Paper (New York: Crown, 1975), p. 201. Copyright © 1975 by Lewis J. Paper. Used by permission of Crown Publishers, Inc.

14. Walter Mondale, *The Accountability of Power* (New York: McKay, 1975), p. 260.

15. Paper, *Promise and Performance,* p. 215.

16. Ibid., p. 204.

17. Cited in Emmet John Hughes, *The Living Presidency* (New York: Coward, McCann & Geoghegan, 1972), p. 101. Copyright © 1973 by Emmet John Hughes. Reprinted by permission of Coward, McCann & Geoghegan.

18. Cited in Paper, *Promise and Performance,* p. 218.

19. Cited in Hughes, *Living Presidency,* pp. 94, 101.

20. *Washington Post,* September 2, 1979, p. A12.

21. John Kessel, *Presidential Campaign Politics: Coalition Strategies and Citizen Response* (Homewood, Ill.: Dorsey Press, 1980), p. 224.

22. Cited in *New York Times,* October 23, 1977, p. 36. Copyright © 1977 by The New York Times Company. Reprinted by permission.

23. *Washington Post,* September 18, 1977, p. B8.

24. George Gallup, *The Gallup Poll, Public Opinion, 1935–1971,* vol. II (New York: Random House, 1972), p. 1051.

25. Bert Cochran, *Harry Truman and the Crisis Presidency* (New York: Funk & Wagnalls, 1973), p. 386.

26. Irving Kristol, "Post-Watergate Morality: Too Good for Our Good?" *New York Times Magazine,* November 14, 1976, p. 35. Copyright © 1976 by The New York Times Company. Reprinted by permission.

27. James Russell Lowell, *Political Essays* (Boston: Houghton Mifflin, 1871), pp. 188, 189.

28. Cited in Hughes, *Living Presidency,* p. 111.

29. See remarks by Samuel Rosenman and Benjamin Cohen in Hughes, *Living Presidency,* pp. 322, 360.

30. Doris Kearns, *Lyndon Johnson and the American Dream* (New York: Harper & Row, 1976), pp. 228, 229. Copyright © 1976 by Doris Kearns. Reprinted by permission of Harper & Row, Publishers, Inc.

31. Cited in *Washington Post,* February 5, 1978, p. A3.

32. *Washington Post,* February 12, 1978, p. A3.

33. Cited in Eric Goldman, *The Tragedy of Lyndon Johnson* (New York: Knopf, 1969), p. 259.

34. Cited in Hedrick Smith, "Problems of a Problem Solver," *New York Times Magazine,* January 8, 1978, p. 33. Copyright © 1978 by The New York Times Company. Reprinted by permission.

35. Cited in Leo Bogart, *Silent Politics* (New York: Wiley, 1972), p. 47.

36. See John Spanier, *American Foreign Policy since World War II,* 2nd ed. rev. (New York: Praeger, 1962), pp. 86–93; Richard Neustadt, *Presidential Power* (New York: Wiley, 1960), pp. 13, 92, 93.

37. Spanier, *American Foreign Policy,* p. 96.

38. Arthur Miller and Warren Miller, "Partisanship and Performance: 'Rational' Choice in the 1976 Presidential Election" Paper presented at the annual meeting of the American Political Science Association, Washington, D.C., September 1–4, 1977, p. 72.

39. Leon Jaworski, *The Right and the Power* (New York: Reader's Digest Press, 1976), pp. 237, 238.

40. Cited in Arthur Schlesinger, Jr., "The Dynamics of Decision," in Aaron Wildavsky, ed., *The Presidency* (Boston: Little, Brown, 1969), p. 139.

41. Elizabeth Drew, "A Reporter at Large (Washington, D.C.)," *The New Yorker,* August 27, 1979, p. 63.

42. Cited in *Washington Post,* September 13, 1979, p. A6.

43. Cited in James MacGregor Burns, *Presidential Government* (Boston: Houghton Mifflin, 1965), pp. 323, 324.

44. Herman Finer, *The Presidency: Crisis and Regeneration* (Chicago: University of Chicago Press, 1960), p. 130.

45. *New York Times,* May 26, 1961, p. 12. Copyright © 1961 by The New York Times Company. Reprinted by permission.

46. Cited in Smith, "Problems of a Problem Solver," pp. 44, 45.

47. Cited in Harris Warren, *Herbert Hoover and the Great Depression* (New York: Norton, 1959), p. 193.

48. Lowell, *Political Essays,* pp. 196, 197.

49. Carl Brauer, *John Kennedy and the Second Reconstruction* (New York: Columbia University Press, 1977), p. 319.

50. Ibid., pp. 208, 320.

51. Excerpt from Hubert H. Humphrey, *The Education of a Public Man* (Garden City, N.Y.: Doubleday, 1976), pp. 136–37. Copyright © 1976 by Hubert H. Humphrey. Reprinted by permission of Doubleday & Company, Inc.

52. Neustadt, *Presidential Power,* p. 120.

53. Ibid., p. 57.

54. Cited in Drew, "A Reporter at Large," p. 80.

55. Cited in *Washington Post,* February 27, 1978, pp. A1, A7.

56. *Congressional Quarterly Weekly Report,* August 1, 1981, pp. 1372, 1373; Hedrick Smith, "Taking Charge of Congress," *New York Times Magazine,* August 9, 1981, p. 17.

The Vice Presidency

In establishing the vice presidency, the Founding Fathers created an office that has pleased few people. Presidents have usually seen fit to ignore it; those who served in the office have nearly always suffered through it; and, following the general election, the public typically forgets about it. Not surprisingly, therefore, some contend that the vice presidency must be reformed, while others insist that the most judicious course of action would be to abolish the office altogether.

There have, in the past, been two fundamental problems associated with this, the second highest office in the land. The first has to do with the manner in which its occupant is chosen. The second problem is that there is so little for the vice president to do. Although for analytical purposes we shall address each of these problems separately, it will become apparent that the two are not unrelated.

★ VICE PRESIDENTIAL SELECTION

That we should be concerned about how the vice president is chosen seems obvious enough for, as John Adams observed, "I am the Vice President. In this I am nothing. But I may be everything." And indeed, during the course of our political history, vice presidents have become "everything" with disturbing frequency. Of our last forty-two presidents, nine succeeded directly to the presidency upon the death or resignation of a president—and it would have been as high as fourteen had would-be assassins succeeded in their attempts on the lives of presidents Jackson, Truman, Ford, Reagan, and president-elect Franklin Roosevelt. An additional five vice presidents advanced to the presidency through election. For John Adams, Jefferson, Van Buren, and Bush, election to the presidency came immediately after their service in the vice presidency, whereas for Nixon it required a wait of eight years. In short, one way or another, fourteen (nearly one-third) of our last forty-two presidents have come from the office of vice president.

Even though there is a good chance a vice president may become president, the care taken in selecting him has left a great deal to be desired. The original Constitution stipulated that the vice presidency would be awarded to the individual who received the second-highest number of electoral votes for president. The Twelfth Amendment (1804) dispensed with this procedure and replaced it with one whereby members of the electoral college would vote for the vice president separately. Interestingly enough, during the congressional debate on this amendment, the Federalists in Congress strongly opposed its adoption. They reasoned that the office held little appeal and thus no one of high caliber would seek it. Consequently, they argued, "mediocre characters would be nominated for the place and it would be awarded solely from the viewpoint of gaining votes for the president."[1] Rather than face such a prospect, the Federalists called for a constitutional amendment abolishing the office. Needless to say, their proposal failed to attract the necessary support within Congress.

The concerns of the Federalists proved to be well founded, for throughout the 1800s and the early part of the nineteenth century both parties chose marginal types as their vice presidential nominees, and even some of them had to be prodded into accepting the nomination. The list of nobody-knows-who included such names as George Clinton, Daniel Tompkins, George Dallas, Hannibal Hamlin, William Wheeler, Levi Morton, and Garret Hobart. The political parties themselves seem to have had second thoughts about their judgment, for throughout the 1800s only one vice president was renominated for a second term. Moreover, those who succeeded to the presidency upon the death of a president were passed over for their party's nomination in the next general election.[2] Finally, it is worth noting here that some of the parties' choices for vice president may be characterized as particularly irresponsible. As a running mate for Franklin Pierce, the Democrats in 1852 nominated Rufus King—known to be fatally ill with tuberculosis and who succumbed soon after taking office. In 1904, the Democrats selected eighty-one-year-old Henry Gassaway Davis for the number-two spot, a man distinguished for little other than his advancing years. Likewise, in 1912, the Republicans renominated Vice President James Sherman to run for reelection with President Taft against Democratic challenger Woodrow Wilson, even though Republican party leaders knew Sherman was gravely ill at the time—indeed, he died six days prior to the November election.

The 1942 Democratic convention marked a significant change in how the vice presidential nominee was selected. Whereas prior to this time the decision had been made by party leaders at their respective national conventions, Franklin Roosevelt now insisted that he be allowed to designate his own running mate, in this instance, Henry Wallace. Although Wallace was by no means the favored candidate among convention delegates, Roosevelt let it be known that he would turn down his own renomination for an unprecedented third term unless Wallace were chosen.[3] The convention deferred to Roosevelt, and thereafter both parties accorded presidential nominees the prerogative of naming their running mates—if they chose to do so—and the conventions routinely ratified them.

This change did not significantly alter the criteria by which vice presidents were picked, however. The primary considerations continued to be political—choosing someone who would give an ideological or geographical balance to the ticket, thereby enhancing the prospects for election victory in the fall. Richard Nixon, for example, appears to have been chosen as Eisenhower's running mate primarily because he was young, conservative, and from the state of California. Similarly, Kennedy gave the nod to Lyndon Johnson because he would help the ticket in the South in general and the state of Texas in particular. Some Kennedy confidants suggest that there was a more subtle reason for his choice—to get Johnson out of the Senate, where, as the powerful majority leader, he would be in a position to obstruct Kennedy's legislative programs.[4] Richard Nixon's personal choice for a running mate in 1968 was his good friend Robert Finch, but he settled on a little-known governor from the state of Maryland by the name of Spiro Agnew because Finch declined to be considered and it was thought that Agnew would help the ticket in the border states. More recently, Ronald Reagan turned to George Bush, but only after he failed to entice Gerald Ford onto the ticket. Although the two men had little affection for one another, Reagan aides felt that the selection of Bush would help to appease the moderate wing of the Republican Party and further strengthen the chances of carrying the crucially important state of Texas.

Although it is certainly true that some presidential running mates have been individuals of considerable capability, it is far less clear that competency to assume the presidency has been the primary criterion in selecting a running mate. As one congressman put it, presidential nominees "will not, in the final analysis, choose their Vice-Presidential candidate to succeed them. They will choose them to help them succeed."[5] There is, of course, an irony in all of this, for there exists very little empirical evidence on precisely how vice presidential candidates have contributed to an election victory. Moreover, what little evidence there is suggests that the person in the number-two slot is of only marginal importance.[6]

If the preeminence of political criteria in choosing the vice president has fostered skepticism about the selection process, so too has the haste with which the decision has been made. Because presidential contenders are primarily concerned with securing their nomination, they scarcely have time to engage in a systematic search for a running mate prior to the convention. Moreover, given the fact that the vice presidential nominee has been picked *no later than one day after the selection of the presidential nominee,* the latter has often had little opportunity to screen potential running mates. In addition, following a fight to secure the presidential nomination, the nominee and his staff are likely to be thoroughly exhausted both emotionally and physically—a condition hardly conducive to careful deliberation. In 1952, for example, there was only a three-hour recess between the balloting for president and vice president. Eisenhower immediately assembled his aides and gave them a list of seven names from which to choose. The aides, who were "tired to the point of exhaustion," proceeded to deliberate, rejecting the first two individuals put forward, Taft and Dirksen: "Nixon's name was offered third, and Paul Hoffman spoke well of him and implied that Dewey favored him. No one had any objections. Without debate, the consensus was that Nixon would be satisfactory. The Eisenhower list of seven names was never produced or mentioned. Eisenhower was immediately called and told that the caucus had decided on Nixon, and he replied, 'That's fine by me.'"[7] In 1968, Richard Nixon set about choosing his running mate in a manner hauntingly similar to the way he himself had been chosen in 1952. While the convention was in the process of nominating him, aides were hurriedly called together to consider the choice of his running mate. Since Nixon had promised to reveal his choice by 11:00 A.M. the next morning, he had to move quickly. Two meetings were held that afternoon, two the next morning, and out of these deliberations finally emerged the name of Spiro Agnew.[8] It is possible that if Nixon and his aides had had more time to check into the background of the Maryland governor, they might have uncovered some of the problems that led to Agnew's resignation as vice president some five years later. George McGovern's choice of Senator Thomas Eagleton as his running mate in 1972 provides an even more poignant example of the uncertainties associated with such a truncated selection process. Locked in a heated struggle with Hubert Humphrey for the Democratic presidential nomination, McGovern and his aides had no time to consider a vice presidential candidate either before or at the convention. With the nomination finally in hand, McGovern went to bed, after telling his aides to convene the next morning for the purpose of selecting a running mate. An exhausted staff quickly settled on Eagleton, a man who appeared sixth on the list of possibilities and whom McGovern had met only briefly on two earlier occasions.[9] Once again, had more time been available to them, they might well have discovered Eagleton's past emotional problems before, rather than after, he was approved by the convention. As it was, McGovern was placed in the embarrassing position of having to drop Eagleton from the ticket and replace him with Sargent Shriver, whose candidacy was ratified by the Democratic National Committee one month after the convention.

It is worth noting here that the selection of Walter Mondale as Jimmy Carter's running mate constitutes a notable exception to the haphazard approach usually taken in selecting vice presidential candidates. Carter's staff devoted well over a month to screening the backgrounds of prospective candidates, and Carter himself had lengthy talks with each of those who appeared on the final list of possibilities. But we must also remember that Carter came into the 1976 Democratic convention with his own nomination safely in hand, and thus both he and his staff had the time to make a careful search for a vice presidential candidate. Unfortunately, those presidential contenders who find themselves in a close contest for the nomination do not have the luxury of being able to shop around for a running mate.

Although more time enhances the likelihood that greater care will be taken and, consequently, that a better choice will be made, such an outcome is by no means assured. To demonstrate this point, we need look no further than George Bush's selection of a running mate in 1988. Like Carter, Bush had the Republican nomination sewn up well before the convention, and he too spent several weeks searching for a running mate. All his vice presidential possibilities were required to fill out an elaborate, probing questionnaire. Bush aide Robert Kimmitt then conducted extended interviews with each candidate. And before making his decision, Bush either directly or indirectly consulted a wide circle of individuals, including family, staff, members of Congress, governors, and state party leaders.[10] In the final analysis, however, and to the astonishment of a good many Washington hands, he selected an individual, J. Danforth Quayle, whose qualifications for the office were widely regarded as seriously deficient—so much so, in fact, that they became a campaign issue. Why Bush made such a choice is still a matter of speculation. In the judgment of some, the screening process was not structured to ensure that Bush would learn all he needed to know about his running mate. Bush himself never interviewed any of the candidates, nor did any key Bush advisers, other than Kimmitt, have access to the background checks done on each vice presidential aspirant.[11] But even if one allows for these limitations, it still seems unlikely that someone as widely connected as Bush would have been unaware of the most worrisome aspect of Quayle, namely, his reputation as an intellectual lightweight. A more probable explanation, as Quayle himself acknowledges, is that political considerations were paramount.

> George Bush selected me, I think, for three major reasons. The first reason was generational: I belonged to the "baby boomer" generation, an enormous segment of our voting population. The second reason was ideological: I came more from the conservative wing of the party, as did Ronald Reagan. And the third reason was geographical: I was from the Midwest, and that region was going to be a battleground in the election campaign.[12]

Bill Clinton also had the good fortune of having the nomination sowed up before he went into the convention and thus was able to make a careful search for a running mate. Following the Carter approach, which included interviews with the finalists, he ultimately tapped Senator Albert Gore (D-Tenn.), a centrist Democrat who commanded wide respect among fellow politicians. Although Gore appeared to replicate Clinton rather than complement him—both, after all, were young and from the South—there were good reasons for such a choice. Not only did both men project Clinton's theme of a new generation of thinking; they also further reinforced the ticket's roots in a region that had not been especially hospitable to Democratic Party nominees in the last three presidential elections.

Reforming Vice Presidential Selection

The Eagleton debacle in 1972, along with the resignation of Vice President Agnew, generated a spate of proposals designed to improve upon the way we select our vice presidential candidates.[13] One calls for moving from an elected to an appointive vice president who would be nominated by the newly elected president and confirmed by both houses of Congress. While such a plan would foster a more rigorous scrutiny of a prospective vice president, it could also give us a president who was not elected. Moreover, such a change would require going through the lengthy and cumbersome process of amending the Constitution. A second proposal calls for having candidates run for the vice presidency in the primaries and caucuses, just as presidential candidates do now. Implementation of this change would surely provide an extended period of time during which to take the measure of vice presidential aspirants, but it would also deny the presidential nominee any role in the selection of his or her running mate, probably not attract individuals of high caliber, and preclude the possibility of choosing a presidential contender as vice president. A third plan would automatically award the vice presidency to the runner-up in the presidential contest, thereby increasing the likelihood that the vice president would be someone of reasonably high quality. Perhaps, but we have no guarantee that the runner-up would accept the vice presidential nomination, and there exists the real possibility that the party could be left with two individuals who were ideologically incompatible. Add to these drawbacks the fact that such a method would remove any discretion on the part of the convention. A fourth proposal would require the presidential nominee to submit a list of acceptable candidates to the convention, which would then choose from among them. There is little to recommend this change in procedure, for a presidential nominee could well be denied his or her top choice. Furthermore, one may question whether, in the brief amount of time available, a convention of several thousand delegates could consider the candidates any more carefully than the presidential nominee and his staff do now. These same kinds of problems would attend a fifth proposal, which calls for a completely open convention whereby the delegates would be free to nominate anyone they wished for the vice presidency.

Still another plan, advanced by a Harvard Study Group on Vice-Presidential Selection, calls for reordering national convention business so that forty-eight hours, instead of the present twenty-four, would intervene between the selection of the presidential and vice presidential nominees. In addition, they recommend that each party establish an advisory committee to assist in vice presidential selection. This committee would request that each presidential candidate supply it with a list of his or her vice presidential possibilities no later than the last leg of the primary season. The committee would then conduct its own independent evaluation of the prospective running mates and would be available to offer its advice to the presidential nominee at the convention.[14] This plan has much to recommend it. For one thing, the presidential nominee would continue to play the dominant role in choosing a running mate, thereby ensuring at least a minimum level of compatibility. At the same time, however, there would be a greater opportunity for the public and media to assess possible running mates—assessments that the nominee could not afford to ignore. Finally, the plan would make available to the nominee an additional group of individuals with whom to consult on selecting a running mate.

But this plan has its drawbacks as well. We have no guarantee that nominees will make use of the advisory group or, for that matter, that they will provide the group with a list of possible running mates. Even if the nominee agrees to provide such a list, it may well identify people he has no intention of choosing but who are included solely to assist in gaining the nomination. Moreover, under this plan, nominees would be locked into a list of possibilities well before the events of the convention—events that could well influence the nominee's choice of a running mate.

One final proposal recommends that the choice of a vice presidential candidate be deferred until three weeks after the national convention, at which time each party's national committee would convene to ratify the nominee's choice for the second spot on the ticket. On balance, this "mini" convention plan would appear to be most worthy of serious consideration. To the extent that it requires only a change in party rules, it could be implemented with little difficulty. It also maintains the nominee's prerogative to choose a running mate, subject to final ratification by the party's national committee. And, unlike the proposal outlined above, it does not restrict the nominee to a specific list and allows the decision to be informed by what transpired at the national convention. Finally, the three-week interim period would allow the candidate adequate time to consult on a running mate and give the media and interested publics the opportunity to assess and react to those under consideration. Of course, one might object to the plan on the grounds that a decision by a party's national committee would carry with it less legitimacy than the stamp of approval given by a national convention. In 1972, however, the Democrats used this procedure to pick Sargent Shriver as a replacement for Thomas Eagleton, and the former's candidacy suffered no apparent ill effects as a result. It might also be argued that the vice presidential nomination can be used to heal intraparty frictions and that by delaying the selection for three weeks those frictions would be allowed to fester. While this is certainly a possibility, this reason alone is not sufficiently compelling to outweigh the benefits associated with this proposal.

THE PROBLEM OF VICE PRESIDENTIAL RESPONSIBILITIES

That most vice presidents have faded into obscurity after taking office may be explained by the fact that there has typically been so little for them to do. Several occupants of this office have provided vivid testimony to this reality.

> My country has in its wisdom contrived for me the most insignificant office that ever the invention of man contrived or his imagination conceived.
>
> John Adams

> The Vice President is like a man in a cataleptic state. He cannot speak; he cannot move; he suffers no pain; and yet he is perfectly conscious of everything going on about him.
>
> Thomas Marshall

> It is not a stepping stone to anything except oblivion.
>
> Theodore Roosevelt

> The vice-presidency isn't worth a pitcher of warm spit.
>
> John Garner

> Look at all the Vice Presidents in history. Where are they? They were about as useful as a cow's fifth teat.
>
> Harry Truman

> It's like being naked in the middle of a blizzard with no one to even offer you a match to keep you warm—that's the Vice Presidency.
>
> Lyndon Johnson

> You are trapped, vulnerable and alone. And it does not matter who happens to be President.
>
> Hubert Humphrey

> A little over a week ago, I took a rather unusual step for a Vice President. I said something.
>
> Spiro Agnew

> I am not in a leadership position. . . . The president has the responsibility and the power. . . . The Vice President has no responsibility and no power.
>
> Nelson Rockefeller

> The job is just awkward, an awkward job.
>
> Dan Quayle

The Vice President does exercise certain limited responsibilities, which fall into three general areas: constitutional, statutory, and, finally, any additional assignments a president might choose to give him. We will now examine each of these in greater detail.

Constitutional and Statutory Responsibilities

The major constitutional obligations of the vice president are to assume the presidency in the event of the death or resignation of the president and to function as acting president if the president should become temporarily incapacitated. In accordance with provisions of the Twenty-Fifth Amendment (1967), presidential incapacity may be determined in one of two ways: The president himself may inform the Speaker of the House and president pro tempore of the Senate that he is unable to carry out his powers and duties, or the vice president and a majority of the cabinet officers may inform the Speaker and Senate president pro tempore that the president is not able to carry out his responsibilities. The president resumes his powers and duties when he so informs Congress that he is able to do so, unless the vice president and a majority of the cabinet reach a contrary judgment. In the latter event, the vice president continues to function as acting president only if two-thirds of both houses of Congress concur in the judgment that the president is still incapacitated. In actuality, neither before nor subsequent to the Twenty-Fifth Amendment have vice presidents claimed the powers of the presidency during a period of presidential disability. This is altogether understandable, for no vice president would want to appear eager to seize the reins of power. Thus, during the illnesses of presidents Garfield, Wilson, and Eisenhower, authority, in fact, resided with their key aides.[15] Similarly, in the brief period of Reagan's incapacity following the attempt on his life, the locus of command remained with key advisers who were with him at the hospital. Although Reagan did in fact sign over authority to the vice president during his operation for colon cancer in 1985, George Bush was not immediately informed that such action had in fact been taken.[16]

The only other constitutional responsibility of the vice president is to be president of the Senate, with the right to cast the deciding vote in the event of a tie. This right rarely amounts to much, because the opportunity to break a tie in the Senate occurs, on the average, less than once a year.[17] As for presiding over the Senate, few vice presidents have approached this task with great enthusiasm. Although a vice president skilled in parliamentary tactics and determined to assert himself as presiding officer could become a force to be reckoned with, the Senate membership would surely resent such behavior.

Congress has also given the vice president certain statutory responsibilities, but these hardly constitute the stuff upon which great reputations can be built. Indeed, the only responsibility of some consequence was authorized in a 1949 statute making the vice president an ex officio member of the National Security Council. His other statutory responsibilities are to appoint five midshipmen to the U.S. Naval Academy; appoint four senators to its Board of Visitors; recommend to the president two candidates for the U.S. Military Academy; affix his signature to enrolled bills and joint resolutions before they are forwarded to the president; and, finally, sit on the Board of Regents of the Smithsonian Institution.[18] Observing Vice President Johnson performing this last responsibility, a former associate expressed his shock at the heights from which he had fallen: "I remember one day I was coming off the Senate floor, and I passed him coming out of an elevator wearing a hat. He had a briefcase and looked very businesslike. And I asked him where he had been. He said he had been in a meeting of the Smithsonian Board of Regents talking about the zoo. I thought, 'my God, I don't believe it. Lyndon Johnson and the zoo.'"[19]

Presidential Assignments

Having outlined the constitutional and statutory responsibilities of the vice president, it should be clear that whether he plays a significant role in government will depend upon how much a president is willing to use him. Unfortunately, our presidents have rarely seen fit to involve vice presidents significantly in policymaking. Why has this been so? Lyndon Johnson claimed that the vice president is a constant reminder to the president of his own mortality, and for this reason there is a built-in strain in the relationship: "Every time I came into John Kennedy's presence I felt like a goddamn raven hovering over his shoulders."[20] Although there may be an element of truth in this, one suspects that President Eisenhower put his finger on the more fundamental reason: "If you happen to have a Vice-President who disagrees with you, then you have an impossible situation."[21] Under such circumstances, the president would be in the embarrassing position of having to take back the duties he conferred on the vice president. Moreover, whereas the president has the authority to remove recalcitrant aides and cabinet members from his administration, he has no such authority over his vice president. Thus, granting substantive responsibilities to a vice president is perceived as risky. The risk is all the more palpable since the haste associated with choosing a vice presidential candidate, along with the political considerations factored into that choice, by no means guarantee that a presidential nominee will choose a running mate with whom he has had a close personal relationship. Some presidential candidates, Kennedy and Reagan for example, have chosen running mates who were their political rivals. Others, such as Eisenhower and Nixon, selected individuals they scarcely knew. Nor, incidentally, did the relations between these two presidents and their vice presidents become any closer with the passage of time. On the contrary, Eisenhower hoped to entice Nixon off the ticket in 1956 by offering him a cabinet position instead.[22] And although Nixon was not disposed to drop Agnew in 1972, it was clear to all White House insiders that the president wanted John Connally, not Spiro Agnew, to head the Republican ticket in the 1976 presidential election.[23]

As we shall see later in this chapter, even if a president is of the mind to involve his vice president significantly in policymaking, other problems may arise that render such involvement difficult to sustain. The two people may ultimately disagree on policy issues; or cabinet members may view vice presidential assignments as an incursion into their own departmental jurisdiction; or the vice president and his staff may find their efforts undercut by presidential staff aides who are highly protective of the president's influence—and their own as well.

How, then, have presidents attempted to occupy the time of those serving in the nation's second-highest office?

Cabinet Meetings. For much of our political history, vice presidents did virtually nothing beyond carrying out their constitutionally prescribed responsibilities. The vice president was considered to be a member of the legislative branch and consequently could not rightly perform any executive functions. As Vice President Thomas Jefferson put it, "I consider my office as constitutionally confined to legislative functions, and that I could not take any part whatever in executive consultations, even were it proposed."[24] Acting on this belief, he declined President Adams's invitation to attend cabinet meetings. Not until the presidency of Woodrow Wilson could one detect a slight movement away from this strictly held view. Prior to Wilson's departure for Paris, where he was to participate in drafting the Versailles Treaty, he asked Vice President Marshall to preside over cabinet meetings in his absence. Out of respect for Wilson, Marshall agreed to do so but informed department heads that he questioned the appropriateness of having a member of the legislative branch preside over such a meeting. Vice President Calvin Coolidge accepted Warren Harding's invitation to attend cabinet meetings on a regular basis, and Coolidge in turn invited his vice president, Charles Dawes, to do the same. But Dawes subscribed to the Jeffersonian view of the vice presidency and declined the offer. Presidents from Franklin Roosevelt on, however, have routinely invited their vice presidents to attend cabinet meetings, and no vice presidents have seen fit to raise any objections. Eisenhower went one step further and established the precedent of letting his vice president preside over cabinet meetings on all occasions when he was absent—a task Richard Nixon performed some nineteen times. One should not attach great importance to the presence of vice presidents at cabinet meetings, however, for such gatherings have rarely been used as forums for substantive decision making.

Legislative Liaison.   Since the Constitution places the vice president with one foot in the executive and the other in the legislative branch, he would appear to be uniquely situated to serve as the president's liaison with Congress. But in order for a vice president to perform such a role successfully, he must command the respect of members of Congress, and they must also be convinced that he enjoys the confidence of the president. Usually, one or both of these conditions have been absent. Indeed, aside from Walter Mondale, the only vice president to serve effectively in this role was John Nance Garner, Franklin Roosevelt's first vice president. As early as 1920, FDR had written an article in which he argued that the vice president should be used for precisely this purpose.[25] Moreover, Garner appeared all the more qualified for such a role because he had served as Speaker of the House prior to being tapped for the vice presidency. Once in office, Garner not only succeeded in persuading the president to hold weekly meetings with Congress, but also played a key role in generating congressional support for much of the New Deal legislation passed during Roosevelt's first term. Unfortunately, the relationship between the two men deteriorated quickly following their reelection in 1936. Garner thought the president's court-packing plan was ill conceived and freely said so in the halls of Congress. He also voiced his displeasure with growing budget deficits, as well as Roosevelt's failure to take a harder line on labor strikes. Nor was this all, for when Roosevelt announced his intention to seek a third term, Garner publicly voiced his strong opposition to the decision. Needless to say, an embarrassed and chagrined president was forced to dump Garner from the ticket in 1940 and replace him with Henry Wallace.[26]

Trips and Committees.   Presidents have also tried to occupy their vice presidents by sending them on goodwill missions abroad and appointing them to chair various government committees here at home. Eisenhower, for example, dispatched Nixon on some fifty-four trips around the world and asked him to chair the President's Committee on Government Contracts and the Cabinet Committee on Price Stability. While some claimed that the influence of the vice president had been significantly enhanced in the Eisenhower administration, it became abundantly clear that the president did not really share this view. During an August 1960 press conference, Ike was asked if he could name a single major idea of the vice president's that had been adopted by his administration. The president replied, "If you give me a week I might think of one. I don't remember."[27] No doubt such a response did little to substantiate Nixon's claim that his experience as vice president rendered him more qualified to assume the presidency than his Democratic opponent, John Kennedy.

Following the lead of his predecessor, Kennedy sent Lyndon Johnson on more than thirty goodwill missions around the world and asked him to chair the Peace Corps Advisory Committee, the National Aeronautics and Space Council, and the President's Committee on Equal Employment. In addition, Kennedy was the first chief executive to give the vice president an office in the Executive Office Building across the street from the White House. Prior to this time the vice president's only office was the one located on Capitol Hill, reserved for him by virtue of his constitutional role as president of the Senate. Johnson quickly learned, however, that office space in the executive branch did not portend a more significant role for the vice president in the Kennedy administration. Not long after both men took office, Johnson drafted an executive order and sent it to Kennedy for his signature. The order specified certain policy areas over which the vice president was to have supervision and directed all departments and agencies to forward to Johnson copies of all reports, information, and plans that were being sent to the president. A surprised President Kennedy read the proposed executive order and promptly set it aside—permanently.[28]

Having experienced the frustrations of the vice presidency firsthand, one might have expected that Johnson and Nixon would make a greater effort to increase the responsibilities of their own vice presidents. Neither was disposed to do so, however. A man of considerable ego, President Johnson was not about to share the spotlight with anyone else. Thus, when Vice President Humphrey began speaking out on aid to education shortly after the 1964 election, Johnson immediately summoned him to the Oval Office and told him that education was his issue, not the vice president's. On a future occasion, Johnson would also humiliate Humphrey by instructing him that henceforth he could not use the White House yachts or planes unless he first received permission from presidential staff aide Marvin Watson.[29] The few assignments that were sent Humphrey's way included functioning as a liaison with state and local officials and serving as an ambassador of goodwill abroad. Spiro Agnew did not fare much better as Nixon's vice president. Aside from chairing the Intergovernmental Relations Council until it was abolished in 1972, Agnew was used primarily for the purpose of doing the administration's dirty work, most notably leveling attacks against the eastern media establishment.

Gerald Ford had a cordial relationship with Vice President Nelson Rockefeller, recognized his talents, and thus decided to give him overall responsibility for coordinating the administration's domestic policy process. This assignment represented a departure from the more innocuous committee chores usually meted out to vice presidents. Rockefeller, however, did not hold this responsibility for very long; top presidential aides perceived the dynamic vice president as a threat to their own influence and declined to extend the hand of cooperation to Rockefeller and his staff.[30] Quickly realizing that he could not function effectively under such circumstances, Rockefeller asked to be relieved of this supervisory responsibility.

Up to the time of the Carter presidency, Franklin Roosevelt was the only president who ever accorded his vice president a genuinely significant role in his administration, and, ironically, this single instance also highlights the problems a president faces when he does so. Roosevelt appointed Vice President Wallace as chairman of the Economic Defense Board, renamed the Board of Economic Defense (BED) following the attack on Pearl Harbor. With a supporting staff of some three thousand employees, the BED's responsibilities were concerned with the importing, exporting, and stockpiling of strategic raw materials. In carrying out his mandate, however, Wallace soon found himself locked in conflict with other cabinet members. Secretary of State Cordell Hull charged that BED was making decisions that had definite foreign policy implications and that the vice president had made no effort to engage in any prior consultation with the State Department. Commerce Secretary Jesse Jones, who had been designated by Roosevelt as chairman of the Reconstruction Finance Corporation (RFC), bitterly complained that Wallace had arrogated to himself powers that Congress had placed in the hands of the RFC. Not one to compromise, Wallace made no effort to iron out his differences with Jones. Both men ultimately went public with their dispute, and, after several rounds of mutual recrimination, Roosevelt was compelled to step into the fray. He abolished the BED and replaced it with a new Office of Economic Warfare headed by Leo Crowley. Thus, Wallace's service in a truly significant position came to an abrupt end. The president retained Jones as head of the RFC, but designated someone else to oversee the corporation's responsibilities in the area of international economics.[31]

The Carter-Mondale Precedent

Having noted that vice presidents have rarely been given responsibilities of any significance, we now consider one of the most startling exceptions to this historical pattern. Indeed, the vice presidency of Walter Mondale is wholly distinct from its predecessors, not only because he played a substantive role across a *broad range of issues* but also because he was able to *sustain this role over the course of his four years in office.* Before seeking to explain why this was so, let us first examine the nature of his relationship with Jimmy Carter.

After winning the election, President-elect Carter immediately included Mondale in personnel decisions related to staffing the executive branch and asked him to put together an agenda of key issues that would confront the incoming administration.[32] Once in office, Carter took several unprecedented steps to ensure that his vice president would have direct access to him and other key figures in his administration. He gave Mondale an office close to his in the West Wing of the White House, instituted the practice of having lunch every Monday with him alone, and instructed his vice president that he had the right to invite himself to any meeting on the president's schedule, as well as to meetings of the White House Staff.[33] In addition, Carter specifically requested Mondale's presence in certain critical policymaking forums. In the foreign policy area, for example, the vice president was included in the small group of presidential advisers (Vance, Jordan, and Brzezinski) who met with Carter each Friday to review foreign policy issues, and he was invited to the twice-weekly discussions of intelligence matters with national security adviser Zbigniew Brzezinski and CIA Director Stansfield Turner. The president also sought the vice president's active participation in domestic policy forums and legislative strategy sessions. Finally, to ensure that his vice president would be privy to the written as well as the spoken word, Carter instructed his aides to provide Mondale with copies of all presidential briefing papers.

Of course, it is one thing to be included in administration deliberations and quite another to have an impact upon them. In Mondale's case, however, the evidence suggests that he did in fact significantly influence administration decisions on such matters as SALT, the Middle East, South Africa, the *Bakke* case, and legislative strategy.[34]

If the Carter-Mondale relationship runs contrary to the flow of history, it is important to know why. Certainly, the most fundamental reason lies in the personal chemistry between the two men. Quite simply, they liked and respected one another. That this proved to be the case was no doubt a function of the great care taken by Carter in selecting his running mate. The development of a cordial personal relationship was enhanced as well by the fact that the two men were not political rivals—that is, they had never campaigned against each other. Consequently, they were not faced with the problem of having to overcome a past history of mutual recrimination. Second, through deed as well as word, Carter conveyed his determination to make the vice presidency something more than it had been in the past. Previous presidents had routinely made the same promise, but their backswing invariably exceeded their follow-through. Third, the rivalries that have often developed between presidential and vice presidential staffs did not materialize in the Carter presidency. Immediately after Mondale was chosen for the number-two spot, his staff moved to Georgia and began working closely with Carter aides on the fall election campaign. Consequently, the staffs of both men moved into the White House having already established a cordial working relationship with each other. As one top Mondale aide put it, joining both campaign staffs in Atlanta was "the best thing we ever did."[35] Furthermore, once in office the president sought to reinforce this relationship by including Mondale's aides in presidential staff meetings. Fourth, Mondale recognized only too well that presidential staff aides are highly protective of the president's powers and prerogatives. Accordingly, he assiduously avoided any behavior that might be interpreted as an attempt to upstage his boss. Fifth, in order to avoid the problems faced by Vice President Wallace in the Roosevelt administration, Carter and Mondale agreed that the vice president should not be given assignments that would encroach upon the jurisdiction of department and agency heads. Instead, he would function as a confidential adviser to the president on a whole range of issues.[36] Finally, at the time the Carter administration took over the reins of power, Walter Mondale was virtually the only one in the White House with previous Washington experience. Thus, assuming the precondition of personal compatibility, there was every reason to believe that the president would want to take advantage of his vice president's knowledge of Washington politics.

Reagan and Bush

Reagan saw fit to continue many of the important changes instituted under Carter. He provided Bush with a White House office, lunched privately with him once a week, accorded him access to all presidential briefing papers, and invited vice presidential aides to participate in presidential staff meetings. Beyond this, Bush was also made an ex officio member of each cabinet council. Several specific responsibilities were delegated to Bush as well. He chaired the president's "crisis management team"; headed the high-profile task forces on regulatory relief, terrorism, and drugs; oversaw preparations for Reagan's first economic summit in Ottawa; coordinated federal efforts to assist the city of Atlanta in solving a string of child murders; and chaired a "Special Situation Group" created by Reagan and charged with considering possible administration responses to developments in Poland.[37] Bush was also instrumental in persuading our European allies to accept the deployment of U.S. intermediate-range missiles on their soil—an undertaking that Reagan would point to in the 1988 election campaign as a major Bush accomplishment.

That Bush and Reagan got off to such an auspicious start is, in one sense, a considerable surprise. Not only did both men come from very different backgrounds, but they were also political rivals—and not very friendly ones at that. In the words of George Bush's campaign manager, "Everyone knows that the President did not want to pick George Bush."[38] On the other hand, also at work were several countervailing forces that, taken together, worked to the benefit of the vice president. Reagan's genial nature and lack of vindictiveness enhanced the possibility that past personal animosities could be overcome. Add to this the fact that both men now had a successful vice presidential model (Mondale) to which they could turn for guidance in establishing a workable relationship between the president and vice president. Moreover, Reagan may also have felt a special obligation to forge such a relationship, partly because the Carter-Mondale model was celebrated as a highly constructive development in presidential politics and partly because his advanced age rendered him more vulnerable to death or incapacitation in office. Finally, and of considerable importance, Bush had a valuable ally in the person of James Baker, his one-time campaign manager, who was subsequently tapped by Reagan to be White House chief of staff.[39]

In comparing Bush's impact to Mondale's, it appears that Mondale exerted more influence earlier. Given the circumstances, this is not altogether surprising. In contrast to Carter's policy agenda, Reagan's was not only much more restricted in scope, thereby presenting fewer opportunities for influence, but was also formulated very early, when Bush was still attempting to convince the Reagan White House of his loyalty.[40] Whether Bush over time emerged as a major player on critical issues is less clear. In the 1988 election campaign, Reagan readily attested to Bush's importance but rarely provided much in the way of specifics. Nor do insider accounts of the Reagan administration thus far point to the former vice president as an active participant in White House meetings. But these indications could be deceiving, for Bush quite rightly concluded that his potential for influence was enhanced by keeping a very low profile: "You know, in the Vice President's role, sometimes it is better to quietly express your differences to the President rather than to command attention at the Cabinet meeting or an NSC meeting. It is a question of style, because you don't want to be putting the President on the spot or make him choose between the Vice President and two Cabinet officers."[41] Thus, it may well be that Bush had his greatest impact in those private weekly luncheons with the president. And although neither of them has been inclined to discuss what transpired in these meetings, one close Reagan associate has noted that the president valued them and that Bush took full advantage of them to convey confidential advice to his boss.[42]

Bush and Quayle

That Quayle failed to achieve the influence of Mondale is not surprising, for he was viewed as a liability during the presidential campaign and thus entered the White House carrying a good deal of baggage. Moreover, in contrast to Mondale whose boss was new to the ways of Washington, Quayle's boss had a wealth of Washington experience before being elected president. Aside from the usual committees, foreign trips, and party fund-raising functions that are delegated to vice presidents, Quayle's most significant responsibility appears to have been chairing the White House Council on Competitiveness—a group that did exercise some influence in overseeing the writing of rules and regulations related to implementing legislation. Bush also continued the Carter practice of lunching with his vice president alone once a week, and he also decided to include him in the president's daily national security briefings and the subsequent morning meetings with his chief of staff. However, according to two Washington columnists (David Broder and Bob Woodward) who observed the Quayle vice presidency at close range over a period of many months, there is little evidence to suggest that he was a major player in the Bush administration.[43]

The Clinton-Gore Precedent

If Walter Mondale demonstrated that a vice president can become a significant player over the course of an entire presidency, Al Gore proved that the vice president can achieve influence in the White House second only to that of the president himself.

From the outset, Clinton and Gore were joined at the hip, campaigning together across the length and breadth of the country. As Clinton turned his attention to the transition, Gore was not only a visible presence, standing with the president as he announced major cabinet and staff appointments, but the vice president and his aides also played a major role in the transition process. Gore's longtime adviser (Jack Quinn) was tapped to serve as legal counsel to the Clinton transition staff; his foreign policy adviser (Leon Fueth) was given the position of senior deputy with the national security policy group; and Gore aide Bruce Reed was placed in the number-two spot on the domestic policy team.[44]

That Gore was a key adviser to Clinton on virtually all the major issues of his presidency, is attested to by several Clinton aides. Mark Gearan, for example, who was Clinton's White House director of communications, observed that "you can search but you won't find one major policy decision in this administration that President Clinton made without discussing it with the vice president. Just doesn't happen."[45] Clinton pollster, Dick Morris, echoed this assessment: "As I saw the byplay between Clinton and Gore I began to understand how important the vice president was to the president. Gore is the single person in the world whose advice the president most values. He sees Gore as a junior president. . . ."[46]

Although Gore's influence was indeed wide-ranging, Clinton also gave him the lead role in certain specific policy areas. The president asked him to coordinate U.S. policy on technology transfers to the Russians, the dismantling of nuclear weapons in Ukraine, and the sanctions imposed on Bosnia. In addition, he was responsible for overseeing our relations with Egypt and South Africa, as well as for cultivating a close working relationship with Russian Prime Minister Viktor Chernomyrdin. On the domestic front, Gore was the point man on environmental issues, communications and technology policy, empowerment zones in the inner cities, and the "Reinventing Government" initiative. Nor is this all. He also became intimately involved in the revamping of Clinton's White House staff operation midway into the first term, following persistent charges that it lacked discipline and experience.[47]

In seeking to account for this unique relationship, a number of factors appear relevant. As with Carter and Mondale, the two men had never been political rivals, and consequently, there was no past history to overcome. In addition, the decision to campaign together in the general election campaign provided an early opportunity for both the candidates and their staffs to bond. Third, in a White House populated by individuals short on national political experience, Gore's knowledge of the Washington power structure could not help but be of considerable value to President Clinton. Finally, and most important, the personal chemistry was good, and both men were in basic agreement on a broad range of policy issues. Absent this final consideration, the other factors noted above would have counted for much less.

Before he even took the oath of office for his second term, Bill Clinton made it quite clear that his choice for president in the year 2000 was Albert Gore. No president in over 150 years had ever signaled his choice so soon, nor done so much to make it a reality.[48] These gestures, as much as anything else, testified to Clinton's confidence in and respect for his vice president.

 REFORMING THE VICE PRESIDENCY

Although the vice president appears to have been a significant force in the Carter and Clinton presidencies, the fact remains that for most of our history vice presidents have been an appendix on the executive branch. Not surprisingly, therefore, some political observers have called for changes that are designed to enhance the status of the office.

One such proposal recommends that the president appoint his vice president to a cabinet position in his administration. There are two serious drawbacks associated with this recommendation, however. Let us suppose that a president confers such responsibility upon his vice president and subsequently important policy differences develop between them. Removing a cabinet member is always an unpleasant task, but it would be even more so if he happened to be the vice president. Moreover, whereas the firing of a cabinet member automatically results in his removal from government, a vice president would still remain a member of the president's administration. Most presidents, then, would be highly reluctant to risk a cabinet appointment unless they had great confidence in their vice president—a condition that has frequently been lacking in the past. We may also question whether a cabinet post would provide a vice president with the most appropriate training for the presidency. Heading a department, after all, would be a full-time job, and consequently a vice president's familiarity with policy issues would be narrowly confined to those falling primarily within the purview of that department. The Carter and Clinton approach—relying upon the vice president as a confidential adviser across a broad range of foreign and domestic policy issues—would seem to be far more desirable.

It has also been proposed that the vice president assume the ceremonial obligations now performed by the president in his role as chief of state. The president would then be free to devote all his energies to the task of governing the nation. Unfortunately, this recommendation is neither realistic nor desirable. No president will voluntarily turn over all ceremonial functions to his vice president, for time-consuming though they may be, many of these functions have a political payoff. Therefore, this change could be realized only by a constitutional amendment that formally invested the vice president with the role of chief of state. Presidents would no doubt strongly oppose such an amendment, since the pomp and circumstance accorded them as chief of state lend added stature to the office. Nor is there any evidence to suggest that the American people would wish to see the president treated with any less fanfare than he is now. Finally, although this proposal would somewhat reduce the burdens of the presidency, the performance of ceremonial functions would do very little in the way of preparing the vice president to assume the reins of power.

One final and more drastic proposal also deserves mention here. Unlike the others, it does not seek to enhance the role of the vice president, but rather calls for abolishing the office altogether.[49] Under this plan, if a president died in office, a cabinet member (secretary of state or defense) would be designated to function as acting president until a new election was held some three months later. The newly elected president would then serve out the unexpired term of his predecessor. The abolitionists argue that the haphazard process by which vice presidents are selected may yield individuals who are not qualified to succeed to the presidency; that service in the vice presidency provides no significant training for the presidency, because presidents rarely accord their vice presidents any meaningful involvement in their administrations; and, finally, that vice presidents are not now elected by the people in any genuine sense, but rather are "part of a package deal."[50]

Although these arguments are not lacking in merit, they do not outweigh the problems we would face in the absence of a vice president. For one thing, under current arrangements, the vice president succeeds to the presidency with the full authority of that office behind him, thereby ensuring an element of stability and continuity in government. This advantage would be seriously compromised under a three-month caretaker president, for his brief tenure would in effect restrict him to marking time until his successor was elected. Moreover, the loss of continuity could be even more unsettling if a caretaker president assumed office during a time of national crisis—for example, a war or a presidential assassination. There is also reason to question whether the nomination and general election campaigns could be completed effectively in three months, which is one-third the amount of time we normally allow. Certainly, the brevity of the process would put an even greater premium on media use and provide a distinct advantage to the candidate who is already well known or well-heeled. Finally, under this plan the nation could well be forced to endure two presidential nomination and election campaigns in a relatively brief span of time. James Garfield, for example, died after only seven months in office, and William Henry Harrison just one month following his inauguration. Similarly, had the attempts on the lives of President Reagan and President-elect Roosevelt succeeded, the interval between elections would have been about three months and one month, respectively. Quite obviously, one would encounter the same problem if a president died late in his term. Indeed, if he succumbed in a presidential election year, we would be faced with the nightmare of conducting the interim and quadrennial presidential election campaigns simultaneously.

If the vice presidency is worth preserving, how then can it be made into a more significant entity of our national government? The Carter-Mondale relationship is instructive in this regard. Through a series of initiatives, Jimmy Carter succeeded in structuring an environment that encouraged interaction between president and vice president and at the same time reduced potential sources of friction between the vice president and other administration officials. To the extent that these initiatives have been emulated by each succeeding president, they have now achieved a momentum of their own, thereby greatly increasing the likelihood that future vice presidents will play a much more significant role than those predating the Carter presidency. This is not to say, however, that all will achieve the influence of Mondale or Gore.

The relationship that these vice presidents had with their boss was conditioned by an underlying personal compatibility. And it is this very fact that returns us to the subject that began this chapter, vice presidential selection. Allowing a presidential nominee more time to choose his or her running mate will not, to be sure, guarantee a compatible combination. It could, however, increase the likelihood of such an outcome.

⭐ NOTES

1. Louis Hatch and Earl Shoup, *A History of the Vice Presidency of the United States* (New York: American Historical Society, 1943), p. 415.
2. Allan Sindler, *Unchosen Presidents* (Berkeley: University of California Press, 1976), p. 28.
3. Donald Young, *American Roulette: The History and Dilemma of the Vice Presidency* (New York: Viking, 1974), pp. 181–82.
4. Kenneth O'Donnell and David Powers, with Joe McCarthy, *Johnny, We Hardly Knew Ye* (New York: Pocket Books, 1973), pp. 221–22.
5. James G. O'Hara, Testimony before the Vice Presidential Selection Commission of the Democratic National Committee, Insert-G, p. 14. These documents were supplied to the author by Charles S. Hyneman, a member of the commission.
6. See Carl B. Tubbesing, "Vice-Presidential Candidates and the Home State Advantage: Or 'Tom Who?' Was Tom Eagleton in Missouri," *Western Political Quarterly* 26 (December 1973), 702–16.
7. Herbert Eaton, *Presidential Timber: A History of Nominating Conventions, 1868–1960* (London: The Free Press of Glencoe, 1964), pp. 451, 453.
8. Theodore White, *The Making of the President 1968* (New York: Atheneum, 1969), pp. 250–53.
9. Theodore White, *The Making of the President 1972* (New York: Atheneum, 1973), pp. 197–98.
10. *Washington Post,* August 28, 1988, p. A14.
11. Ibid.
12. Dan Quayle, "Standing Firm: Personal Reflections on Being Vice President," in Timothy Walch, ed., *At the President's Side* (Columbia: University of Missouri Press, 1997), p. 171.
13. See Sindler, *Unchosen Presidents,* chaps. 4, 5.
14. *Report of the Study Group on Vice-Presidential Selection* (Boston: Institute of Politics, Kennedy School of Government, 1976), pp. 10–13.
15. The Research and Policy Committee of the Committee for Economic Development, *Presidential Succession and Inability* (New York: The Committee for Economic Development, 1965), pp. 21, 22.
16. *New York Times,* December 4, 1996, p. A20.
17. Thomas Cronin, *The State of the Presidency* (Boston: Little, Brown, 1975), p. 213.
18. Clinton Rossiter, *The American Presidency* (New York: New American Library, 1960), p. 130.
19. Cited in Merle Miller, *Lyndon: An Oral Biography* (New York: Putnam, 1980), p. 305.
20. Cited in Doris Kearns, *Lyndon Johnson and the American Dream* (New York: Harper & Row, 1976), p. 164.
21. Cited in Young, *American Roulette,* p. 259.
22. Richard Nixon, *Memoirs* (New York: Grosset & Dunlap, 1978), p. 167.
23. William Safire, *Before the Fall: An Inside View of the Pre-Watergate White House* (Garden City, N.Y.: Doubleday, 1975), p. 506.
24. Cited in Arthur Schlesinger, Jr., "On Presidential Succession," *Political Science Quarterly* 89 (Fall 1974), 480.
25. Franklin Roosevelt, "Can the Vice President Be Useful?," *Saturday Evening Post,* October 16, 1920, pp. 8, 81, 82.
26. Young, *American Roulette,* pp. 169–72.
27. Cited in Cronin, *State of the Presidency,* p. 226.
28. Kearns, *Lyndon Johnson and the American Dream,* p. 165.
29. David Halberstam, *The Best and the Brightest* (Greenwich, Conn.: Fawcett, 1969), pp. 647–49.
30. *Washington Post,* January 3, 1978, p. C1.
31. Young, *American Roulette,* pp. 190–93.
32. *New York Times,* December 28, 1976, p. 1; *New York Times,* December 31, 1976, p. A7.
33. Brock Brower, "The Remaking of the Vice President," *New York Times Magazine,* June 5, 1977, pp. 38, 39, 42, 43.

34. *Washington Post,* December 3, 1978, p. C1; Brower, "Remaking the Vice President," p. 39.

35. Brower, "Remaking the Vice President," p. 44.

36. *U.S. News and World Report,* March 28, 1977, p. 62

37. *National Journal,* June 20, 1981, pp. 1096–2100.

38. *Washington Post,* March 30, 1981, p. A8; *Washington Post,* December 17, 1981, p. A21.

39. James Conaway, "The Texas Connection," *Washington Post Magazine,* December 13, 1981, pp. 19–24.

40. Paul C. Light, *Vice-Presidential Power* (Baltimore: Johns Hopkins University Press, 1984), p. 267.

41. Cited in ibid., p. 268.

42. Hedrick Smith, *The Power Game* (New York: Random House, 1988), p. 72.

43. *Washington Post,* January 8, 1992, pp. A1, A14.

44. *Washington Post,* December 13, 1992, p. A23.

45. Cited in *Washington Post,* February 18, 1995, p. A8.

46. Dick Morris, *Behind the Oval Office* (New York: Random House, 1997), p. 119. For other testimony to Gore's influence see *New York Times,* February 19, 1995, pp. A1, A8.

47. *New York Times,* February 19, 1995, p. A1; *Washington Post,* February, 18, 1995, p. A9; *New York Times,* August 28, 1996, p. A10; *Washington Post,* August 26, 1996, pp. A1, A18.

48. *International Herald Tribune,* July 15, 1997, p. 4.

49. See, for example, Schlesinger, "On Presidential Succession," p. 500.

50. Ibid., p. 484.

 Index